CAMBRIDGE Advanced Level Mathematics

D0102037

Pure Mathematics 5 & 6

Hugh Neill and
Douglas Quadling

Series editor Hugh Neill

CAMBRIDGE
UNIVERSITY PRESS

PUBLISHED BY THE PRESS SYNDICATE OF THE UNIVERSITY OF CAMBRIDGE
The Pitt Building, Trumpington Street, Cambridge, United Kingdom

CAMBRIDGE UNIVERSITY PRESS
The Edinburgh Building, Cambridge CB2 2RU, UK
40 West 20th Street, New York, NY 10011-4211, USA
477 Williamstown Road, Port Melbourne, VIC 3207, Australia
Ruiz de Alarcón 13, 28014 Madrid, Spain
Dock House, The Waterfront, Cape Town 8001, South Africa

http://www.cambridge.org

© Cambridge University Press 2001

This book is in copyright. Subject to statutory exception and to the provisions of relevant collective licensing agreements, no reproduction of any part may take place without the written permission of Cambridge University Press.

First published 2001
Fourth printing 2002

Printed in the United Kingdom at the University Press, Cambridge

Typefaces Times, Helvetica *Systems* Microsoft® Word, MathType™

A catalogue record for this book is available from the British Library

ISBN 0 521 78372 0 paperback

Cover image: Images Colour Library

Contents

Introduction

Cambridge Advanced Level Mathematics has been written especially for the OCR modular examination. It consists of one book or half-book corresponding to each module. This book combines the last two Pure Mathematics modules, P5 and P6. The OCR specification does not require that P5 is taken before P6. In this book, the modules are almost independent, and large parts of P6 can be tackled before P5.

The books are divided into chapters roughly corresponding to syllabus headings. Some sections include work which goes beyond the examination specification. These sections are marked with an asterisk (*) in the section heading.

Occasionally within the text paragraphs appear in *this type style*. These paragraphs are usually outside the main stream of the mathematical argument, but may help to give insight, or suggest extra work or different approaches.

References are made throughout the text to previous work in modules P1 to P4. It is expected that students still have access to these books in the classroom, even if they do not have a copy for their personal use.

Numerical work is presented in a form intended to discourage premature approximation. In ongoing calculations inexact numbers appear in decimal form like 3.456..., signifying that the number is held in a calculator to more places than are given. Numbers are not rounded at this stage; the full display could be either 3.456 123 or 3.456 789. Final answers are then stated with some indication that they are approximate, for example '1.23 correct to 3 significant figures'.

There are plenty of exercises, and each chapter contains a Miscellaneous exercise which includes some questions of examination standard. Some of these are longer, but not necessarily harder, than the questions likely to appear in a module examination. A few questions are included which go beyond the requirements of the specification or which, in the authors' judgment, are more demanding than those likely to be set for A level; they are indicated repectively by an asterisk (*) and a dagger (†). In the middle and at the end of both modules there is a set of Revision exercises and there are two practice examination papers for each module.

The authors thank Dr John Smith and Peter Thomas, both of whom read the book carefully and made many extremely useful and constructive comments.

The authors thank OCR and Cambridge University Press for their help in producing this book. However, the responsibility for the text, and for any errors, remains with the authors.

Module P5

Pure Mathematics 5

1 Roots of polynomial equations

This chapter is about the connection between the roots and the coefficients of polynomial equations. When you have completed it you should

- be able to construct a polynomial equation given its roots
- know how to find simple symmetric functions of the roots from the coefficients of an equation
- be able to find an equation whose roots are related in a simple way to the roots of a given equation.

1.1 Quadratic polynomials and quadratic equations

Suppose that you have a quadratic polynomial whose factors you know to be $x-1$ and $x-2$. You might be tempted to write it immediately as $(x-1)(x-2)$ or x^2-3x+2.

The quadratic polynomial x^2-3x+2 certainly does have factors $x-1$ and $x-2$, and it is the simplest quadratic polynomial with these factors. But other quadratic polynomials, such as $2x^2-6x+4$, have the same factors. So also does the quadratic polynomial $a(x^2-3x+2)$ where a is any number except 0.

More generally, if the quadratic ax^2+bx+c has factors $x-\alpha$ and $x-\beta$, then

$$ax^2+bx+c \equiv k(x-\alpha)(x-\beta).$$

You can see at once, by equating coefficients of x^2, that $k=a$.

Then, putting $k=a$ and expanding the polynomial on the right,

$$ax^2+bx+c \equiv a\left(x^2-(\alpha+\beta)x+\alpha\beta\right).$$

By equating coefficients of x and the constant terms, you can see that

$$b=-a(\alpha+\beta) \quad \text{and} \quad c=a\alpha\beta.$$

Summarising:

> If the quadratic ax^2+bx+c has factors $x-\alpha$ and $x-\beta$, then
>
> $$\alpha+\beta=-\frac{b}{a} \quad \text{and} \quad \alpha\beta=\frac{c}{a}.$$

Some quadratic polynomials, such as $3x^2-6x+3=0$, factorise as $k(x-\alpha)^2$, rather than as $k(x-\alpha)(x-\beta)$ with $\alpha \neq \beta$. Such a polynomial is said to have a **repeated factor** $x-\alpha$ with **multiplicity** 2.

If you equate coefficients in

$$ax^2+bx+c \equiv a(x-\alpha)^2 \equiv a\left(x^2-2\alpha x+\alpha^2\right),$$

you get $b=-2a\alpha$ and $c=a\alpha^2$, so

$$2\alpha=-\frac{b}{a} \quad \text{and} \quad \alpha^2=\frac{c}{a}.$$

These are just the equations in the shaded box with $\beta=\alpha$. So the statement in the box remains true for repeated factors, provided that you interpret a repeated factor $x-\alpha$ as two factors $x-\alpha$ and $x-\beta$ with $\beta=\alpha$.

You can also express these results in terms of the roots of quadratic equations. If the quadratic polynomial ax^2+bx+c has factors $x-\alpha$ and $x-\beta$, then the equation $ax^2+bx+c=0$ has roots α and β. The converse of this statement is also true: if the equation $ax^2+bx+c=0$ has roots α and β, then the quadratic polynomial ax^2+bx+c has factors $x-\alpha$ and $x-\beta$.

The repeated factor case corresponds to quadratic equations which have only one root (for which the discriminant $b^2-4ac=0$). Again, the converse is also true: if the quadratic equation has only one root α, then the quadratic polynomial factorises as $a(x-\alpha)^2$.

It follows that:

If the quadratic equation $ax^2+bx+c=0$ has distinct roots α and β, then

$$\alpha+\beta=-\frac{b}{a} \quad \text{and} \quad \alpha\beta=\frac{c}{a}.$$

If the equation has only one root α, these relations are modified by replacing β by α.

Because the equation with one root can be included in the general case by writing $\beta=\alpha$, it is sometimes said that to have 'two equal roots', or 'coincident roots'. You can regard this as a convenient fiction; there is in fact only one root, but you will come to no harm by treating it as a pair of roots which happen to have the same value.

Notice that this is true whether the roots are real or complex. For example, the equation $x^2+2x+5=0$ has roots $\alpha=-1+2\text{i}$ and $\beta=-1-2\text{i}$. You can easily check that

$$\alpha+\beta=(-1+2\text{i})+(-1-2\text{i})=-2, \text{ which is } -\frac{2}{1}, \text{ and that}$$

$$\alpha\beta=(-1+2\text{i})(-1-2\text{i})=(-1)^2+(-2)^2=1+4=5, \text{ which is } \frac{5}{1}.$$

Example 1.1.1
The quadratic equation $x^2-6x+20=0$ has roots α and β. Find $\alpha+\beta$ and $\alpha\beta$, and the value of $\alpha^2+\beta^2$. What can you deduce from the value of $\alpha^2+\beta^2$?

From the relations $\alpha+\beta=-\frac{b}{a}$ and $\alpha\beta=\frac{c}{a}$, you get $\alpha+\beta=6$ and $\alpha\beta=20$.

Since $\alpha^2+\beta^2=(\alpha+\beta)^2-2\alpha\beta$, this gives $\alpha^2+\beta^2=6^2-2\times 20=-4$.

If α and β were real, $\alpha^2+\beta^2$ could not be negative. So α and β must be (conjugate) complex. You can check this for yourself by solving the quadratic equation directly.

Expressions such as $\alpha+\beta$, $\alpha\beta$, $\alpha^2+\beta^2$ and $\frac{1}{\alpha}+\frac{1}{\beta}$ are called **symmetric functions** of α and β. The characteristic of a symmetric function is that if you interchange α and β, the expression is unchanged, apart from the order of the terms and factors. Thus $\alpha^2-\alpha\beta+\beta^2$ is a symmetric function since changing α and β gives $\beta^2-\beta\alpha+\alpha^2$, which is the same as $\alpha^2-\alpha\beta+\beta^2$. However, $\alpha+2\beta$ is not symmetric, as changing α and β gives $2\alpha+\beta$ which is not the same as $\alpha+2\beta$.

Example 1.1.2
For the quadratic equation $ax^2+bx+c=0$, one root is twice the other. Prove that $2b^2=9ac$.

Suppose that the roots of $ax^2+bx+c=0$ are α and 2α. Then $\alpha+2\alpha=-\frac{b}{a}$ and $\alpha\times 2\alpha=\frac{c}{a}$, so $3\alpha=-\frac{b}{a}$ and $2\alpha^2=\frac{c}{a}$.

Therefore $\alpha=-\frac{b}{3a}$ and $\alpha^2=\frac{c}{2a}$, so $\left(-\frac{b}{3a}\right)^2=\frac{c}{2a}$. Thus $\frac{b^2}{9a^2}=\frac{c}{2a}$, so $2b^2=9ac$.

Example 1.1.3
The quadratic equation $x^2+5x+7=0$ has roots α and β. Find an equation with roots 2α and 2β.

Two methods are given. The first uses 'brute force'; the second is more subtle.

Method 1 From the equation $\alpha+\beta=-5$ and $\alpha\beta=7$. Therefore

$$2\alpha+2\beta=2(\alpha+\beta)=-10 \quad \text{and} \quad (2\alpha)(2\beta)=4\alpha\beta=28.$$

An equation which has -10 as the sum of its roots and 28 as the product is

$$x^2-(-10)x+28=0, \quad \text{or} \quad x^2+10x+28=0.$$

Method 2 If $u=2\alpha$ or $u=2\beta$, then $\alpha=\frac{1}{2}u$ or $\beta=\frac{1}{2}u$. Either way, $\frac{1}{2}u$ satisfies the equation $x^2+5x+7=0$. Therefore $\left(\frac{1}{2}u\right)^2+5\left(\frac{1}{2}u\right)+7=0$, or $\frac{1}{4}u^2+\frac{5}{2}u+7=0$. Multiplying through by 4 gives $u^2+10u+28=0$.

Note that the equations $x^2+10x+28=0$ and $u^2+10u+28=0$ have the same roots. It does not matter what letter is given to the 'variable' in the polynomial.

In more complicated situations, Method 2 of Example 1.1.3 is usually more effective than Method 1, and you should use it in preference to Method 1 whenever you can.

Exercise 1A

1 Use the sum and product of the roots to find the simplest quadratic with the following roots.

(a) $2, 3$ (b) $-3, 1$ (c) $2, -2$ (d) $1, -\frac{1}{2}$

2 Write down the sum and product of the roots for each of the following equations.

(a) $x^2 - 2x - 1 = 0$ (b) $2x^2 + 4x - 3 = 0$ (c) $3x^2 - x + 1 = 0$

3 Let the roots of the equation $x^2 - 4x + 2 = 0$ be α and β. Find the values of each of the following symmetric functions.

(a) $3\alpha + 3\beta$ (b) $\alpha^2 + 2\alpha\beta + \beta^2$ (c) $\alpha^2 - \alpha\beta + \beta^2$

(d) $(\alpha - \beta)^2$ (e) $\dfrac{1}{\alpha} + \dfrac{1}{\beta}$ (f) $\dfrac{1}{\alpha^2} + \dfrac{1}{\beta^2}$

4 The equation $x^2 + 2x + 5 = 0$ has roots α and β. Use Method 1 of Example 1.1.3 to find the equations which have the following roots:

(a) $3\alpha, 3\beta$ (b) $1+\alpha, 1+\beta$ (c) $\alpha + 2\beta, 2\alpha + \beta$

(d) α^2, β^2 (e) $\dfrac{1}{\alpha}, \dfrac{1}{\beta}$ (f) $\dfrac{1}{\alpha^2}, \dfrac{1}{\beta^2}$

5 The equation $x^2 + 4x + 7 = 0$ has roots α and β. Use Method 2 of Example 1.1.3 to find the equations which have the following roots:

(a) $3\alpha, 3\beta$ (b) $1+\alpha, 1+\beta$ (c) $\alpha + 2\beta, 2\alpha + \beta$

(d) α^2, β^2 (e) $\dfrac{1}{\alpha}, \dfrac{1}{\beta}$ (f) $\dfrac{1}{\alpha^2}, \dfrac{1}{\beta^2}$

6 One root of the equation $ax^2 + bx + c = 0$ is the reciprocal of the other. Prove that $c = a$.

7 One root of the equation $ax^2 + bx + c = 0$ is three times the other. Prove that $3b^2 = 16ac$.

8 The roots of the equation $ax^2 + bx + c = 0$ differ by 1. Prove that $b^2 - a^2 - 4ac = 0$.

1.2 Roots of cubic and quartic equations

The ideas of Section 1.1 can be extended to polynomials and equations of degree higher than 2.

A general cubic can be written as $ax^3 + bx^2 + cx + d = 0$, where $a \neq 0$. If this has factors $x - \alpha$, $x - \beta$ and $x - \gamma$, then

$$ax^3 + bx^2 + cx + d \equiv k(x-\alpha)(x-\beta)(x-\gamma).$$

Equating coefficients of x^3 shows that $k = a$.

Expanding the product of the factors on the right gives

$$\begin{aligned}(x-\alpha)(x-\beta)(x-\gamma) &= \left(x^2-(\alpha+\beta)x+\alpha\beta\right)(x-\gamma)\\ &= \left(x^2-(\alpha+\beta)x+\alpha\beta\right)x-\left(x^2-(\alpha+\beta)x+\alpha\beta\right)\gamma\\ &= x^3-(\alpha+\beta)x^2+\alpha\beta x-\gamma x^2+(\alpha+\beta)\gamma x-\alpha\beta\gamma\\ &= x^3-(\alpha+\beta+\gamma)x^2+(\beta\gamma+\gamma\alpha+\alpha\beta)x-\alpha\beta\gamma.\end{aligned}$$

This gives the identity

$$ax^3+bx^2+cx+d \equiv a\left(x^3-(\alpha+\beta+\gamma)x^2+(\beta\gamma+\gamma\alpha+\alpha\beta)x-\alpha\beta\gamma\right).$$

Equating coefficients of x^2, x and the constant terms shows that

$$b=-a(\alpha+\beta+\gamma),\quad c=a(\beta\gamma+\gamma\alpha+\alpha\beta)\quad\text{and}\quad d=-a\alpha\beta\gamma.$$

These results can also be stated in terms of the roots of a cubic equation.

If the cubic ax^3+bx^2+cx+d has factors $x-\alpha$, $x-\beta$ and $x-\gamma$, or the cubic equation $ax^3+bx^2+cx+d=0$ has roots α, β and γ, then

$$\alpha+\beta+\gamma=-\frac{b}{a},\quad \beta\gamma+\gamma\alpha+\alpha\beta=\frac{c}{a}\quad\text{and}\quad \alpha\beta\gamma=-\frac{d}{a}.$$

These relations are often written in the form $\sum\alpha=-\frac{b}{a}$, $\sum\alpha\beta=\frac{c}{a}$, $\sum\alpha\beta\gamma=-\frac{d}{a}$, where $\sum\alpha$ denotes $\alpha+\beta+\gamma$, $\sum\alpha\beta$ denotes $\beta\gamma+\gamma\alpha+\alpha\beta$ and so on. This notation is easily used for similar relations in quadratic and higher degree equations.

When the idea of a symmetric function is extended to roots of a cubic equation, the expression has to be unchanged if *any* of the pairs β and γ, γ and α, or α and β are swapped. You can check that $\alpha+\beta+\gamma$, $\beta\gamma+\gamma\alpha+\alpha\beta$ and $\alpha\beta\gamma$ all have this property. For example, swapping α and γ in $\beta\gamma+\gamma\alpha+\alpha\beta$ changes the expression to $\beta\alpha+\alpha\gamma+\gamma\beta$, which is just another way of writing $\beta\gamma+\gamma\alpha+\alpha\beta$.

You may find it surprising that the expression $\beta\gamma+\gamma\alpha+\alpha\beta$ is written this way in preference to $\alpha\beta+\alpha\gamma+\beta\gamma$. The reason is that the first part, $\beta\gamma$, is missing the term in α, $\gamma\alpha$ is missing the term in β and $\alpha\beta$ is missing the term in γ.

A cubic may have repeated factors in two ways:

- It may have a repeated factor of multiplicity 2 and a distinct linear factor, so that it factorises as $a(x-\alpha)^2(x-\gamma)$. The results in the shaded box are then modified by replacing β by α.
- It may have a repeated factor of multiplicity 3, so that it factorises as $a(x-\alpha)^3$. The results are then modified by replacing both β and γ by α.

Example 1.2.1

Which of (a) $\alpha\beta+\alpha\gamma$, (b) $(\beta+\gamma)(\gamma+\alpha)(\alpha+\beta)$, (c) $\beta^2\gamma+\gamma^2\alpha+\alpha^2\beta$ are symmetric functions of α, β and γ?

(a) If you swap α and β in $\alpha\beta+\alpha\gamma$ you get $\beta\alpha+\beta\gamma$, which is not the same expression as $\alpha\beta+\alpha\gamma$. So $\alpha\beta+\alpha\gamma$ is not a symmetric function.

(b) Swapping α and β in $(\beta+\gamma)(\gamma+\alpha)(\alpha+\beta)$ gives $(\alpha+\gamma)(\gamma+\beta)(\beta+\alpha)$, swapping α and γ gives $(\beta+\alpha)(\alpha+\gamma)(\gamma+\beta)$, and swapping β and γ gives $(\gamma+\beta)(\beta+\alpha)(\alpha+\gamma)$. All these are the same as $(\beta+\gamma)(\gamma+\alpha)(\alpha+\beta)$, so the function is symmetric.

(c) Swapping α and β in $\beta^2\gamma+\gamma^2\alpha+\alpha^2\beta$ gives $\alpha^2\gamma+\gamma^2\beta+\beta^2\alpha$, which is not the same as $\beta^2\gamma+\gamma^2\alpha+\alpha^2\beta$, so $\beta^2\gamma+\gamma^2\alpha+\alpha^2\beta$ is not a symmetric function.

Example 1.2.2

The cubic equation $2x^3+3x^2+4x+5=0$ has roots α, β and γ. Find the values of

(a) $\alpha^2+\beta^2+\gamma^2$, (b) $\dfrac{1}{\alpha}+\dfrac{1}{\beta}+\dfrac{1}{\gamma}$.

Using the result in the shaded box, $\alpha+\beta+\gamma=-\frac{3}{2}$, $\beta\gamma+\gamma\alpha+\alpha\beta=\frac{4}{2}=2$ and $\alpha\beta\gamma=-\frac{5}{2}$.

(a) $\alpha^2+\beta^2+\gamma^2=(\alpha+\beta+\gamma)^2-2(\beta\gamma+\gamma\alpha+\alpha\beta)=\left(-\frac{3}{2}\right)^2-2\times2=-\frac{7}{4}$.

(b) $\dfrac{1}{\alpha}+\dfrac{1}{\beta}+\dfrac{1}{\gamma}=\dfrac{\beta\gamma+\gamma\alpha+\alpha\beta}{\alpha\beta\gamma}=\dfrac{2}{-5/2}=-\frac{4}{5}$.

To find the value of a symmetric function of the roots of an equation, it is not always easiest to use the method of Example 1.2.2. Section 1.4 shows a better way to find sums of powers of the roots.

You can extend the ideas and methods of establishing results for cubic polynomials and cubic equations to quartic polynomials and quartic equations.

If the quartic $ax^4+bx^3+cx^2+dx+e$ has factors $x-\alpha$, $x-\beta$, $x-\gamma$ and $x-\delta$, or the quartic equation $ax^4+bx^3+cx^2+dx+e=0$ has roots α, β, γ and δ, then

$$\alpha+\beta+\gamma+\delta=-\frac{b}{a}, \qquad \alpha\beta+\alpha\gamma+\alpha\delta+\beta\gamma+\beta\delta+\gamma\delta=\frac{c}{a},$$

$$\beta\gamma\delta+\alpha\gamma\delta+\alpha\beta\delta+\alpha\beta\gamma=-\frac{d}{a}, \qquad \alpha\beta\gamma\delta=\frac{e}{a}.$$

Example 1.2.3

Three of the four roots of the quartic equation $ax^4+cx^2+dx+e=0$ are equal. Prove that $8c^3+27ad^2=0$ and $12ae+c^2=0$. Find the solution of the equation in terms of the coefficients a and d.

Saying that three of the roots are equal means that the quartic polynomial has a repeated factor $(x-\alpha)^3$. The expressions for the symmetric functions are therefore modified by replacing β and γ by α, so that $\alpha+\alpha+\alpha+\delta=0$, giving $\delta=-3\alpha$.

Also, $\alpha^2+\alpha^2+\alpha\delta+\alpha^2+\alpha\delta+\alpha\delta=\frac{c}{a}$, so $3\alpha^2+3\alpha\delta=\frac{c}{a}$.

Similarly, $\alpha^3+3\alpha^2\delta=-\frac{d}{a}$ and $\alpha^3\delta=\frac{e}{a}$.

Substituting $\delta=-3\alpha$ gives $-6\alpha^2=\frac{c}{a}$, $\quad -8\alpha^3=-\frac{d}{a}$ and $\quad -3\alpha^4=\frac{e}{a}$.

So $\left(-\frac{c}{6a}\right)^3=\left(\frac{d}{8a}\right)^2$ and $-\frac{e}{3a}=\left(-\frac{c}{6a}\right)^2$. These reduce to $8c^3+27ad^2=0$ and $12ae+c^2=0$. The roots are $\frac{1}{2}\left(\frac{d}{a}\right)^{\frac{1}{3}}$ (multiplicity 3) and $-\frac{3}{2}\left(\frac{d}{a}\right)^{\frac{1}{3}}$.

1.3 Finding equations with given roots

Suppose that a given quartic equation $ax^4+bx^3+cx^2+dx+e=0$, where $e\neq 0$, has roots α, β, γ and δ. How can you find the equation with roots $\alpha^{-1}, \beta^{-1}, \gamma^{-1}$ and δ^{-1}?

The best way is to use a substitution method, such as that in Method 2 of Example 1.1.3.

Let u be any one of the new roots, say $u=\alpha^{-1}$. Then $\alpha=u^{-1}$. But since α satisfies the original equation, $a\alpha^4+b\alpha^3+c\alpha^2+d\alpha+e=0$, so

$$a\left(u^{-1}\right)^4+b\left(u^{-1}\right)^3+c\left(u^{-1}\right)^2+d\left(u^{-1}\right)+e=0.$$

Multiplying by u^4 gives

$$a+bu+cu^2+du^3+eu^4=0, \quad \text{or} \quad eu^4+du^3+cu^2+bu+a=0.$$

Since this is true if u is any one of α^{-1}, β^{-1}, γ^{-1} and δ^{-1}, it is the equation required.

Example 1.3.1
The cubic equation $ax^3+bx^2+cx+d=0$ has roots α, β and γ. Find the equation which has roots α^2, β^2 and γ^2.

Let $u=\alpha^2$. Then $\alpha=\pm\sqrt{u}$, so $\pm\sqrt{u}$ satisfies $ax^3+bx^2+cx+d=0$. Therefore

$$a\left(\pm\sqrt{u}\right)^3+b\left(\pm\sqrt{u}\right)^2+c\left(\pm\sqrt{u}\right)+d=0, \qquad \text{or} \qquad \pm au\sqrt{u}+bu\pm c\sqrt{u}+d=0.$$

So $\pm\sqrt{u}(au+c)=-(bu+d)$. Then, squaring both sides,

$au^3+2acu^2+c^2u=b^2u^2+2bdu+d^2$, that is

$$au^3+\left(2ac-b^2\right)u^2+\left(c^2-2bd\right)u-d^2=0.$$

If you let $u=\beta^2$ or $u=\gamma^2$ you get the same result, so

$$au^3+\left(2ac-b^2\right)u^2+\left(c^2-2bd\right)u-d^2=0$$

is the required equation.

Example 1.3.2
The cubic equation $ax^3+bx^2+cx+d=0$ has roots α, β and γ. Find an equation which has roots $\beta+\gamma, \gamma+\alpha$ and $\alpha+\beta$.

Let $u=\beta+\gamma$. Then $u+\alpha=\alpha+\beta+\gamma=-\frac{b}{a}$, so $\alpha=-u-\frac{b}{a}$. But α satisfies the equation $ax^3+bx^2+cx+d=0$, so

$a\left(-u-\frac{b}{a}\right)^3+b\left(-u-\frac{b}{a}\right)^2+c\left(-u-\frac{b}{a}\right)+d=0$, which simplifies to
$a^2u^3+2abu^2+z\left(b^2+ac\right)+bc-ad=0$.

If you let $u=\gamma+\alpha$ or $u=\alpha+\beta$ you get the same result, so

$a^2u^3+2abu^2+\left(b^2+ac\right)u+bc-ad=0$ is the required equation.

1.4 Sums of powers of the roots

You know how to find the sum of the roots of an equation, and you can find the sum of their squares by using the formula

$$\alpha^2+\beta^2+\gamma^2=(\alpha+\beta+\gamma)^2-2(\beta\gamma+\gamma\alpha+\alpha\beta).$$

However, the sums of cubes and of higher powers of roots get progressively harder to find.

For example, to find the sum of cubes you need to find $(\alpha+\beta+\gamma)^3$, which has $3^3=27$ terms; although some of them are the same, the expansion still has 10 terms.

This method will be explained for cubic equations, but a similar method works for equations of any degree.

Consider the equation $ax^3+bx^2+cx+d=0$. As α is a root, $a\alpha^3+b\alpha^2+c\alpha+d=0$. Similarly $a\beta^3+b\beta^2+c\beta+d=0$ and $a\gamma^3+b\gamma^2+c\gamma+d=0$.

Adding these three equations gives

$$a\left(\alpha^3+\beta^3+\gamma^3\right)+b\left(\alpha^2+\beta^2+\gamma^2\right)+c(\alpha+\beta+\gamma)+3d=0.$$

Introducing the notation $S_n=\alpha^n+\beta^n+\gamma^n$, you can write this equation as

$$aS_3+bS_2+cS_1+dS_0=0.$$

Remember that $S_0=\alpha^0+\beta^0+\gamma^0=3$.

The notation $\sum\alpha^2$, $\sum\alpha^3$, and so on, is also used, in which case the relation $aS_3+bS_2+cS_1+dS_0=0$ becomes $a\sum\alpha^3+b\sum\alpha^2+c\sum\alpha+3d=0$. In this book the 'S notation' will be used, but you should recognise the other notation, which could be used in examination questions.

You can take this further by multiplying the three equations $a\alpha^3+b\alpha^2+c\alpha+d=0$, $a\beta^3+b\beta^2+c\beta+d=0$ and $a\gamma^3+b\gamma^2+c\gamma+d=0$ by α^r, β^r and γ^r, where $r\in\mathbb{Z}$, and then adding to get

$$aS_{3+r}+bS_{2+r}+cS_{1+r}+dS_r=0.$$

If α, β and γ are the roots of the cubic equation $ax^3 + bx^2 + cx + d = 0$, and $S_n = \alpha^n + \beta^n + \gamma^n$, where n is a positive integer, then

$$aS_{3+r} + bS_{2+r} + cS_{1+r} + dS_r = 0$$

where $r \in \mathbb{Z}$.

You should recognise that, in the shaded box, there is an equation for each value of r.

Example 1.4.1
The cubic equation $2x^3 + 3x^2 + 4x + 5 = 0$ has roots α, β and γ. Find the values of
(a) $\alpha^3 + \beta^3 + \gamma^3$, (b) $\alpha^4 + \beta^4 + \gamma^4$, (c) $\alpha^{-1} + \beta^{-1} + \gamma^{-1}$.

(a) Since $a = 2$, $b = 3$, $c = 4$ and $d = 5$, using the equation in the shaded box with $r = 0$ gives

$$2S_3 + 3S_2 + 4S_1 + 5S_0 = 0.$$

Since $S_0 = \alpha^0 + \beta^0 + \gamma^0 = 1 + 1 + 1 = 3$, $S_1 = -\frac{3}{2}$, and you know from Example 1.2.2 that $S_2 = -\frac{7}{4}$, you can find S_3.

Therefore $S_3 = -\frac{1}{2}(3S_2 + 4S_1 + 5S_0) = -\frac{1}{2}\left(3 \times \left(-\frac{7}{4}\right) + 4 \times \left(-\frac{3}{2}\right) + 5 \times 3\right) = -\frac{15}{8}$.

(b) Putting $r = 1$ in the equation in the shaded box,

$$2S_4 + 3S_3 + 4S_2 + 5S_1 = 0.$$

So $S_4 = -\frac{1}{2}(3S_3 + 4S_2 + 5S_1) = -\frac{1}{2}\left(3 \times \left(-\frac{15}{8}\right) + 4 \times \left(-\frac{7}{4}\right) + 5 \times \left(-\frac{3}{2}\right)\right) = \frac{161}{16}$.

(c) Putting $r = -1$ in the equation in the shaded box, $2S_2 + 3S_1 + 4S_0 + 5S_{-1} = 0$.

So $S_{-1} = -\frac{1}{5}(2S_2 + 3S_1 + 4S_0) = -\frac{1}{5}\left(2 \times \left(-\frac{7}{4}\right) + 3 \times \left(-\frac{3}{2}\right) + 4 \times 3\right) = -\frac{4}{5}$.

Exercise 1B

1 Find the simplest cubic equations with the following roots.
(a) 2, 3, 4 (b) $-1, 0, 2$ (c) $0, 2, -2$

2 Find the simplest quartic equations with the following roots.
(a) 1, 2, 3, 4 (b) $-1, 0, 1, 2$ (c) $0, 2, -2, 3$

3 Let the roots of the equation $x^3 - 6x + 2 = 0$ be α, β and γ. Find the values of each of the following symmetric functions.
(a) $4\alpha + 4\beta + 4\gamma$ (b) $\alpha^2 + \beta^2 + \gamma^2$
(c) $(\beta - \gamma)^2 + (\gamma - \alpha)^2 + (\alpha - \beta)^2$ (d) $\frac{1}{\alpha} + \frac{1}{\beta} + \frac{1}{\gamma}$

4 Let the roots of the equation $x^4-8x+3=0$ be α, β, γ and δ. Find the values of each of the following symmetric functions.

(a) $2\alpha+2\beta+2\gamma+2\delta$

(b) $\alpha^2+\beta^2+\gamma^2+\delta^2$

(c) $\frac{1}{\alpha}+\frac{1}{\beta}+\frac{1}{\gamma}+\frac{1}{\delta}$

(d) $\alpha^4+\beta^4+\gamma^4+\delta^4$

(e) $(\alpha-\beta)^2+(\alpha-\gamma)^2+(\alpha-\delta)^2+(\beta-\gamma)^2+(\beta-\delta)^2+(\gamma-\delta)^2$

5 The equation $x^3+2x^2+3x+4=0$ has roots α, β and γ. Use Method 2 of Example 1.1.3 to find the equations which have the following roots.

(a) $2\alpha, 2\beta, 2\gamma$

(b) $2+\alpha, 2+\beta, 2+\gamma$

(c) $\alpha^2, \beta^2, \gamma^2$

(d) $\frac{1}{\alpha}, \frac{1}{\beta}, \frac{1}{\gamma}$

6 The equation $x^4-2x^3+2x^2+3x+4=0$ has roots α, β, γ and δ. Use Method 2 of Example 1.1.3 to find the equations which have the following roots.

(a) $2\alpha, 2\beta, 2\gamma, 2\delta$

(b) $2+\alpha, 2+\beta, 2+\gamma, 2+\delta$

(c) $\alpha^2, \beta^2, \gamma^2, \delta^2$

(d) $\frac{1}{\alpha}, \frac{1}{\beta}, \frac{1}{\gamma}, \frac{1}{\delta}$

7 The equation $x^4-3x^3+6x^2-9x+13=0$ has roots α, β, γ and δ. Find the values of each of the following expressions.

(a) $\alpha^2+\beta^2+\gamma^2+\delta^2$

(b) $\frac{1}{\alpha}+\frac{1}{\beta}+\frac{1}{\gamma}+\frac{1}{\delta}$

(c) $\alpha^3+\beta^3+\gamma^3+\delta^3$

(d) $\frac{1}{\alpha^2}+\frac{1}{\beta^2}+\frac{1}{\gamma^2}+\frac{1}{\delta^2}$

8 The roots of the equation $x^3-3bx^2+3cx-d=0$ are in arithmetic progression. Prove that one of the roots is b, and find a condition for the roots to be in arithmetic progression. Find the possible values of the common difference in terms of b and d.

9 Find a condition for the roots of the equation $x^3-bx^2+cx-d=0$ to be in geometric progression. Find in terms of b and d a quadratic equation satisfied by the possible common ratios of the progression.

10 Write down the equation whose roots are p, q and r, where $p+q+r=6$, $qr+rp+pq=11$ and $pqr=6$. Hence solve the equations.

11 Solve the simultaneous equations $p+q+r=6$, $p^2+q^2+r^2=26$ and $pqr=-12$.

12 The product of two of the roots of the equation $ax^4+bx^3+cx^2+dx+e=0$ is equal to the product of the other two roots. Prove that $ad^2=b^2e$.

13 Find the equation whose roots are the reciprocals of the roots of the equation $ax^n+bx^{n-1}+\ldots+cx^2+dx+e=0$. What condition must you impose to obtain your result?

Miscellaneous exercise 1

1 The roots of $x^2-10x+3=0$. Find the values of $\alpha^2+\beta^2$ and $\alpha^4+\beta^4$.

2 You are given that the roots of the equation $x^3+3x^2+7x+5=0$ are in arithmetic progression. Solve the equation.

3 Solve the simultaneous equations $\alpha+\beta=2$, $\alpha\beta=2$.

4 Solve the simultaneous equations $p+q+r=2$, $p^2+q^2+r^2=6$ and $p^3+q^3+r^3=8$.

5 Find the sum of the fourth powers of the roots of the equation $x^4+x+1=0$.

6 The quadratic equation $x^2+5x+13=0$ has roots α and β.

(a) Show that $\alpha^2+\beta^2=-1$, and hence describe the nature of the roots α and β.

(b) Find an equation with integer coefficients whose roots are $\dfrac{\alpha}{\beta}-1$ and $\dfrac{\beta}{\alpha}-1$.

7 The equation $x^2+6x+10=0$ has roots α and β. Find the values of $\alpha^2+\beta^2$ and $\alpha^3+\beta^3$. Find a quadratic equation with integer coefficients having roots $\alpha^3\beta$ and $\alpha\beta^3$.

8 The equation $x^2+3x+1=0$ has roots α and β. Find the values of $\alpha^2+\beta^2$ and $\dfrac{\alpha}{\beta}+\dfrac{\beta}{\alpha}$.

Find an equation with integer coefficients having roots $\dfrac{\alpha+2\beta}{\beta}$ and $\dfrac{\beta+2\alpha}{\alpha}$.

9 The equation $x^3-5x^2+8x-6=0$ has roots α, β and γ. Find the equation whose roots are $\alpha-3$, $\beta-3$ and $\gamma-3$, and solve the original equation.

10 The roots of the equation $x^3-ax^2+bx-c=0$ are α, β and γ. Prove that if $\alpha\beta=\alpha+\beta$ then $\gamma=a+c-b$.

11 Without attempting to solve the equation $3x^3-2x^2+x-1=0$ find the sum of the squares of its roots. Hence show that the equation has one real and two complex roots.

12 The roots of the quartic equation $x^4+9x^3+27x^2+36x+18=0$ are α, β, γ and δ. Find a quartic equation in u whose roots are $\alpha+1$, $\beta+1$, $\gamma+1$ and $\delta+1$. Then substitute $v=u+u^{-1}$ to obtain a quadratic equation in v. Hence solve the original equation.

13 The cubic equation $ax^3+bx^2+cx+d=0$ has the property that two of its roots are the reciprocals of each other. Prove that $a^2-d^2=ac-bd$.

Verify that this condition holds for the equation $9x^3+24x^2-11x-6=0$, and solve it.

14 The roots of the equation $x^3+ax+b=0$ are α, β and γ. Find the equation with roots $\dfrac{\beta}{\gamma}+\dfrac{\gamma}{\beta}$, $\dfrac{\gamma}{\alpha}+\dfrac{\alpha}{\gamma}$ and $\dfrac{\alpha}{\beta}+\dfrac{\beta}{\alpha}$.

15 Show that, by making a substitution of the form $x=y+k$, where k is a suitably chosen constant, the equation $x^3+ax^2+bx+c=0$ can be reduced to the form $y^3+py+q=0$. Find the value of k which achieves this.
(In P6 Section 8.3 and in Exercise 8A, you will see how to solve cubics of this form.)

16 In days before computers, a method based on 'root-squaring' was used to find approximate solutions to polynomial equations. The process was to find successive terms of the sequence S_1, $S_2^{\frac{1}{2}}$, $S_4^{\frac{1}{4}}$ etc. If these converge, they will converge to $\pm\alpha$, where α is the root of largest modulus. Try it, using your computer!

2 Hyperbolic functions

Hyperbolic functions are a link between the exponential function e^x and trigonometric functions. When you have completed the chapter, you should

- know how to express a function as the sum of an even and an odd function
- know the definitions of $\cosh x$, $\sinh x$ and other hyperbolic functions
- know and be able to apply properties of hyperbolic functions and their inverses analogous to those of trigonometric functions
- understand the relation of hyperbolic functions to the rectangular hyperbola
- understand how hyperbolic and circular functions are connected when the independent variable may be complex.

2.1 Even and odd functions

In P1 Sections 3.3 and 8.7, you met the idea of even and odd functions. An **even function** is one such that, for all real numbers x in its domain, $f(x) = f(-x)$. An **odd function** has $f(x) = -f(-x)$. Notice that, for these definitions to be valid, the domain D of f has to be symmetrical about 0: if $x \in D$, then $-x \in D$. A real domain with this property will be called a **symmetrical domain**.

Not all functions are even or odd. For example, $f(x) = x(x+1)$ is not. But you can write $f(x)$ as $x^2 + x$, which is the sum of the even function $g(x) = x^2$ and the odd function $h(x) = x$. In fact, every function with a symmetrical domain can be split up in this way.

Theorem Any function f with a symmetrical domain can be written as the sum of an even function g and an odd function h.

Proof The proof is in two parts. First, suppose that the theorem is true and find the forms that g and h must take; then show that these functions g and h do have the required properties.

If $f(x)$ is written as $g(x) + h(x)$, where g is even and h is odd, then $f(-x)$ must be equal to $g(-x) + h(-x)$, where $g(-x) = g(x)$ and $h(-x) = -h(x)$. So $g(x)$ and $h(x)$ must be chosen to satisfy the two equations

$$g(x) + h(x) = f(x) \quad \text{and} \quad g(x) - h(x) = f(-x).$$

Adding and subtracting these equations gives

$$2g(x) = f(x) + f(-x) \quad \text{and} \quad 2h(x) = f(x) - f(-x).$$

To complete the proof, you have to show that

$$g(x) = \tfrac{1}{2}(f(x) + f(-x)) \quad \text{and} \quad h(x) = \tfrac{1}{2}(f(x) - f(-x)),$$

whose sum is $f(x)$, are respectively even and odd. That is,

$$g(-x) = \tfrac{1}{2}(f(-x) + f(x)) = \tfrac{1}{2}(f(x) + f(-x)) = g(x),$$

and $h(-x) = \tfrac{1}{2}(f(-x) - f(x)) = -\tfrac{1}{2}(f(x) - f(-x)) = -h(x).$

Example 2.1.1

Express $f(x)=\dfrac{1}{1+x}$ as the sum of an even and an odd function.

Since the natural domain of f does not include -1, and the domain of f has to be symmetrical, it must exclude both -1 and 1.

The theorem shows that the even function is

$$g(x)=\tfrac{1}{2}\left(\frac{1}{1+x}+\frac{1}{1-x}\right)=\tfrac{1}{2}\left(\frac{1-x+1+x}{(1+x)(1-x)}\right)=\frac{1}{1-x^2},$$

and the odd function is

$$h(x)=\tfrac{1}{2}\left(\frac{1}{1+x}-\frac{1}{1-x}\right)=\tfrac{1}{2}\left(\frac{1-x-(1+x)}{(1+x)(1-x)}\right)=\frac{-x}{1-x^2}.$$

You can see that, although 1 is not excluded from the natural domain of f, the natural domains of g and h both exclude 1 and -1.

It is interesting to illustrate this result by displaying the graphs of $f(x)$, $g(x)$ and $h(x)$ together using the same axes.

Much the most important application of the theorem is when f is taken to be the exponential function e^x. The functions g and h are then called **hyperbolic functions**, and denoted by the symbols cosh and sinh (pronounced 'shine'). Thus:

$$\cosh x=\tfrac{1}{2}\left(e^x+e^{-x}\right) \quad \text{and} \quad \sinh x=\tfrac{1}{2}\left(e^x-e^{-x}\right)$$

The reasons for using a notation formed by adding 'h' (for 'hyperbolic') to the symbols cos and sin will become clear in Section 2.2. The connection with the hyperbola is explained in Section 2.3.

You can almost certainly get values of $\cosh x$ and $\sinh x$ directly with your calculator, and you should find out how to do this. Since e^x has domain $\mathbb{R}$, $\cosh x$ and $\sinh x$ are defined for all real x. Their graphs are drawn in Figs. 2.1 and 2.2 on the next page. Other points which you should notice are:

- When x is a large positive number, e^{-x} is very small, so that $\cosh x \approx \frac{1}{2}e^x$ and $\sinh x \approx \frac{1}{2}e^x$. When x is negative and $|x|$ is large, $\cosh x \approx \frac{1}{2}e^{-x}$ and $\sinh x \approx -\frac{1}{2}e^{-x}$. These approximations are illustrated by the graphs shown dotted in Fig. 2.1 and Fig. 2.2.
- The range of the sinh function is $\mathbb{R}$. However, the graph of $\cosh x$ has a minimum of 1 when $x=0$, so that the range of cosh is $y\in\mathbb{R}$, $y \geqslant 1$.

2.2 Hyperbolic and trigonometric functions

Many properties of the functions cosh and sinh closely resemble corresponding properties of the trigonometric functions cos and sin. This makes them easy to remember, but you have to be careful to notice where there are differences in the signs.

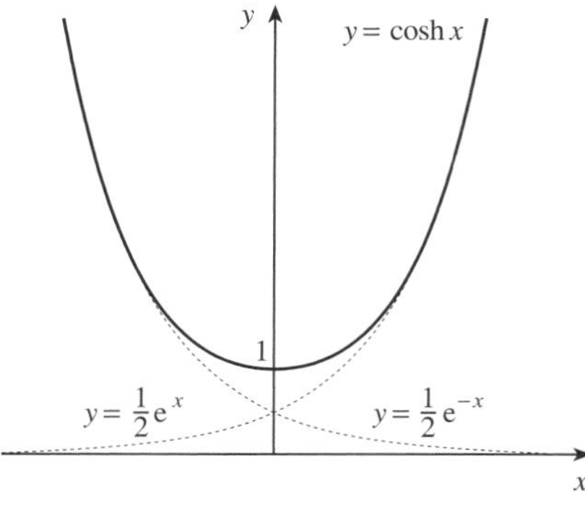

Fig. 2.1

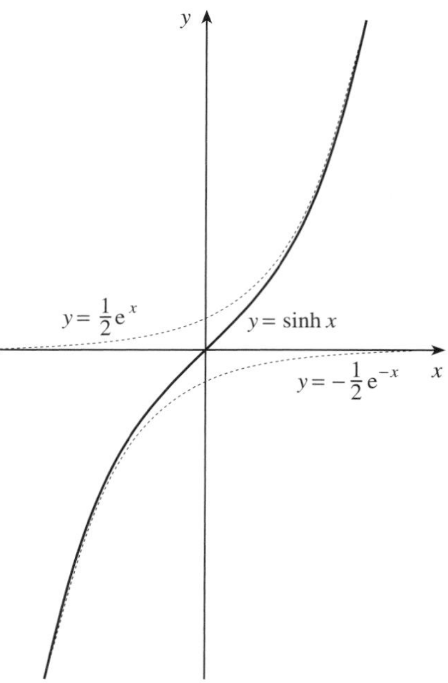

Fig. 2.2

(i) The basic identity

Since $\cosh x + \sinh x \equiv e^x$ and $\cosh x - \sinh x \equiv e^{-x}$,

$$(\cosh x + \sinh x)(\cosh x - \sinh x) \equiv e^x e^{-x} = e^0 = 1.$$

This gives the basic identity for hyperbolic functions:

$$\cosh^2 x - \sinh^2 x \equiv 1$$

Compare this with the Pythagoras identity $\cos^2 x + \sin^2 x \equiv 1$, and note that, while $\cos^2 x$ is replaced by $\cosh^2 x$, $\sin^2 x$ is replaced by $-\sinh^2 x$.

You will often want to use this identity in one of the alternative forms

$$\cosh^2 x \equiv 1 + \sinh^2 x \quad \text{or} \quad \sinh^2 x \equiv \cosh^2 x - 1.$$

(ii) Addition formulae

Expressions for $\cosh(A+B)$ and $\sinh(A+B)$ can be obtained from

$$e^{A+B} \equiv e^A e^B \equiv (\cosh A + \sinh A)(\cosh B + \sinh B) \text{ and}$$

$$e^{-(A+B)} \equiv e^{-A} e^{-B} \equiv (\cosh A - \sinh A)(\cosh B - \sinh B).$$

So $\cosh(A+B) \equiv \frac{1}{2}\left(e^{A+B} + e^{-(A+B)}\right)$

$$\equiv \frac{1}{2}\left(\begin{array}{l}(\cosh A + \sinh A)(\cosh B + \sinh B) \\ \qquad\qquad + (\cosh A - \sinh A)(\cosh B - \sinh B)\end{array}\right)$$

$$\equiv \frac{1}{2}(2\cosh A\cosh B + 2\sinh A\sinh B),$$

and $\sinh(A+B) \equiv \frac{1}{2}\left(e^{A+B} - e^{-(A+B)}\right)$

$$\equiv \frac{1}{2}\left(\begin{array}{l}(\cosh A + \sinh A)(\cosh B + \sinh B) \\ \qquad\qquad - (\cosh A - \sinh A)(\cosh B - \sinh B)\end{array}\right)$$

$$\equiv \frac{1}{2}(2\sinh A\cosh B + 2\cosh A\sinh B),$$

giving the addition formulae:

$$\cosh(A+B) \equiv \cosh A\cosh B + \sinh A\sinh B,$$
$$\sinh(A+B) \equiv \sinh A\cosh B + \cosh A\sinh B.$$

Notice that the formula for $\sinh(A+B)$ carries over directly from that for $\sin(A+B)$, but that in comparing $\cosh(A+B)$ with $\cos(A+B)$ there is a change of sign, $-\sin A\sin B$ being replaced by $+\sinh A\sinh B$.

The easiest way to find formulae for $\cosh(A-B)$ and $\sinh(A-B)$ is to write $A-B$ as $A+(-B)$ and use the even and odd properties $\cosh(-B) = \cosh B$ and $\sinh(-B) = -\sinh B$. This gives:

$$\cosh(A-B) \equiv \cosh A\cosh B - \sinh A\sinh B,$$
$$\sinh(A-B) \equiv \sinh A\cosh B - \cosh A\sinh B.$$

If you put $B = A$ in the formulae for $\cosh(A+B)$ and $\sinh(A+B)$ you get

$$\cosh(A+A) \equiv \cosh A\cosh A + \sinh A\sinh A \equiv \cosh^2 A + \sinh^2 A,$$

and $\sinh(A+A) \equiv \sinh A\cosh A + \cosh A\sinh A \equiv 2\sinh A\cosh A.$

You can write the expression $\cosh^2 A + \sinh^2 A$ in terms of $\cosh A$ or $\sinh A$ alone, using the basic identity in one of the alternative forms given at the end of (i) above.

In this way you get hyperbolic analogues of the double angle formulae:

$$\cosh 2A \equiv \cosh^2 A + \sinh^2 A \equiv 1 + 2\sinh^2 A \equiv 2\cosh^2 A - 1,$$
$$\sinh 2A \equiv 2\sinh A\cosh A.$$

You often, especially in integration, need these in their backwards forms:

$$2\cosh^2 A \equiv 1 + \cosh 2A, \qquad 2\sinh^2 A \equiv \cosh 2A - 1,$$
$$2\sinh A\cosh A \equiv \sinh 2A.$$

(iii) Derivatives

Since $\frac{\mathrm{d}}{\mathrm{d}x}\mathrm{e}^x = \mathrm{e}^x$ and $\frac{\mathrm{d}}{\mathrm{d}x}\mathrm{e}^{-x} = -\mathrm{e}^{-x}$,

$$\frac{\mathrm{d}}{\mathrm{d}x}(\cosh x) = \frac{\mathrm{d}}{\mathrm{d}x}\left(\tfrac{1}{2}\left(\mathrm{e}^x + \mathrm{e}^{-x}\right)\right) = \tfrac{1}{2}\left(\mathrm{e}^x - \mathrm{e}^{-x}\right),$$

and $$\frac{\mathrm{d}}{\mathrm{d}x}(\sinh x) = \frac{\mathrm{d}}{\mathrm{d}x}\left(\tfrac{1}{2}\left(\mathrm{e}^x - \mathrm{e}^{-x}\right)\right) = \tfrac{1}{2}\left(\mathrm{e}^x + \mathrm{e}^{-x}\right).$$

That is:

$$\frac{\mathrm{d}}{\mathrm{d}x}(\cosh x) = \sinh x, \quad \frac{\mathrm{d}}{\mathrm{d}x}(\sinh x) = \cosh x.$$

Note that the similarity with the results for trigonometric functions is close but not exact.

(iv) Integration by substitution

In P4 Section 6.5, it was suggested that the trigonometric substitutions $x = \tan u$, $\sin u$ and $\sec u$ are often useful in finding integrals involving $1 + x^2$, $\sqrt{1-x^2}$ and $\sqrt{x^2-1}$ respectively, using Pythagoras' identities. The basic identity for hyperbolic functions makes it possible to add two further possibilities:

To find an integral involving $\left\{\begin{matrix} 1+x^2 \\ \\ \sqrt{x^2-1} \end{matrix}\right\}$ try substituting $\left\{\begin{matrix} x = \sinh u \\ \\ x = \cosh u \end{matrix}\right\}$.

You now have two choices for integrals involving $1 + x^2$, either $x = \tan u$ or $x = \sinh u$; and similarly for integrals involving $\sqrt{x^2-1}$, either $x = \sec u$ or $x = \cosh u$. Sometimes one substitution leads to an integral which you still don't know how to find, in which case the other may succeed.

Example 2.2.1

Find $\int \sqrt{4+x^2}\,\mathrm{d}x$.

The substitution $x = 2\sinh u$ converts $4 + x^2$ to $4 + 4\sinh^2 u = 4\cosh^2 u$, so that $\sqrt{4+x^2} = 2\cosh u$ (since $\cosh u > 0$). Also $\frac{\mathrm{d}x}{\mathrm{d}u} = 2\cosh u$. Therefore

$$\int \sqrt{4+x^2}\,\mathrm{d}x = \int 2\cosh u \times 2\cosh u\,\mathrm{d}u = \int 4\cosh^2 u\,\mathrm{d}u.$$

This can be integrated by using the $\cosh 2A$ formula (with u for A) in its backwards form $2\cosh^2 u = \cosh 2u + 1$, so

$$\int 4\cosh^2 u\,\mathrm{d}u = \int 2(\cosh 2u + 1)\,\mathrm{d}u = \sinh 2u + 2u + k.$$

To express this in terms of x, notice first that $\sinh 2u = 2\sinh u \cosh u$. Now $2\sinh u = x$, and $\cosh u = \sqrt{1+\sinh^2 u} = \sqrt{1+\left(\frac{1}{2}x\right)^2} = \frac{1}{2}\sqrt{4+x^2}$.

Therefore $\sinh 2u = \frac{1}{2}x\sqrt{4+x^2}$. Also $\sinh u = \frac{1}{2}x$, so that $u = \sinh^{-1}\left(\frac{1}{2}x\right)$. Putting all this together,

$$\int \sqrt{4+x^2}\,dx = \frac{1}{2}x\sqrt{4+x^2} + 2\sinh^{-1}\left(\frac{1}{2}x\right) + k.$$

(v) Maclaurin expansions

The definitions of $\cosh x$ and $\sinh x$, combined with the Maclaurin expansions

$$e^x = 1 + \frac{x}{1!} + \frac{x^2}{2!} + \frac{x^3}{3!} + \frac{x^4}{4!} + \frac{x^5}{5!} + \frac{x^6}{6!} + \frac{x^7}{7!} + \ldots$$

and $$e^{-x} = 1 - \frac{x}{1!} + \frac{x^2}{2!} - \frac{x^3}{3!} + \frac{x^4}{4!} - \frac{x^5}{5!} + \frac{x^6}{6!} - \frac{x^7}{7!} + \ldots,$$

give $\cosh x = 1 + \dfrac{x^2}{2!} + \dfrac{x^4}{4!} + \dfrac{x^6}{6!} + \ldots$ and $\sinh x = \dfrac{x}{1!} + \dfrac{x^3}{3!} + \dfrac{x^5}{5!} + \dfrac{x^7}{7!} + \ldots.$

The expansions differ from those for $\cos x$ and $\sin x$ only in having all the signs positive.

Exercise 2A

1 Use the definitions of $\sinh x$ and $\cosh x$ to evaluate the following. Check your answers by using the hyperbolic function keys on your calculator.

(a) $\cosh 2$ (b) $\sinh \pi$ (c) $\cosh(-e)$ (d) $\sinh(\ln 3)$

(e) $\sinh\left(-\sqrt{2}\right)$ (f) $\cosh 1 + \sinh 1$ (g) $\cosh 2 - \sinh 2$ (h) $\cosh(-2\ln 2)$

2 Find and prove the property of hyperbolic functions corresponding to each of the following properties of trigonometric functions.

(a) $2\sin A \cos B = \sin(A+B) + \sin(A-B)$

(b) $2\sin x \sin y = \cos(x-y) - \cos(x+y)$

(c) $\sin 3x = 3\sin x - 4\sin^3 x$

(d) $8\sin^4 u = 3 - 4\cos 2u + \cos 4u$

(e) $\dfrac{d}{dx}\left(\cos^2 x\right) = -\sin 2x$

(f) $\dfrac{d}{dt}\left(\sin^3 t\right) = 3\sin^2 t \cos t$

(g) $\displaystyle\int \cos 2x\,dx = \frac{1}{2}\sin 2x + k$

(h) $\displaystyle\int \sin^2 u\,du = \frac{1}{2}(u - \sin u \cos u) + k$

3 Find the roots of the following equations in terms of u.

(a) $x^2 - 2x\cosh u + 1 = 0$

(b) $x^2 + 2x\sinh u - 1 = 0$

(c) $x^2 - 2x\cosh u + \sinh^2 u = 0$

(d) $x^2 \sinh 2u + 2x - \sinh 2u = 0$

4 Prove that $\cosh x - 1 = \frac{1}{2}\left(e^{\frac{1}{2}x} - e^{-\frac{1}{2}x}\right)^2$. Deduce that $\cosh x \geqslant 1$ for all real x.

5 Express the following in terms of hyperbolic functions as simply as possible.

(a) $\dfrac{2}{e^x}$ (b) $\sqrt{\left(e^x + e^{-x}\right)^2 - 4}$ (c) $\dfrac{e^x}{1+e^{2x}}$ (d) $\dfrac{e^x + 1}{e^x - 1}$

6 Differentiate these functions with respect to x.

(a) $\sinh^2 x$ (b) $\sqrt{\cosh x}$ (c) $\ln(\sinh x + \cosh x)$

(d) $\dfrac{1}{\sinh x + 2\cosh x}$ (e) $\dfrac{1+\sinh x}{x+\cosh x}$ (f) $\dfrac{\cosh x + \sin x}{\cos x + \sinh x}$ (g) $e^x \cosh x$

7 Find the following indefinite integrals.

(a) $\int \sinh 3x \, dx$ (b) $\int \sinh x \cosh x \, dx$ (c) $\int \cosh^2 x \, dx$

(d) $\int x \sinh x \, dx$ (e) $\int x^2 \cosh 2x \, dx$ (f) $\int e^x \cosh x \, dx$

8* Express each of the following functions as the sum of an even function and an odd function. State the domain over which the relation holds.

(a) $\dfrac{1}{x(2-x)}$ (b) $\dfrac{1}{(1+x)^2}$ (c) $\dfrac{1}{1+e^x}$ (d) $\dfrac{1}{2+\sinh x}$

(e) $\dfrac{\cos x}{1+\sin x}$ (f) $\dfrac{x+3}{x^2+x-2}$ (g) $\dfrac{x-3}{x^2-x+2}$ (h) $\dfrac{e^x}{1+e^{2x}}$

9 Use hyperbolic substitutions to find the following integrals.

(a) $\int \dfrac{1}{\sqrt{1+x^2}} dx$ (b) $\int \dfrac{1}{\sqrt{x^2-9}} dx$ (c) $\int \dfrac{1}{\sqrt{1+9x^2}} dx$

(d) $\int \sqrt{4x^2-1} \, dx$ (e) $\int \dfrac{x^2}{\sqrt{4x^2+25}} dx$ (f) $\int x^2\sqrt{x^2-9} \, dx$

10 Find $\int \cosh 3x \sinh 2x \, dx$,

(a) by expressing the integrand in an alternative hyperbolic form,

(b) by expressing the integrand in exponential form.

Show that your two expressions for the integral are equivalent.

11 Find the Maclaurin expansions of each of the following functions, giving the terms as far as x^6 and an expression for the general term.

(a) $\cosh 2x$ (b) $\sinh^2 x$ (c) $\cosh^3 x$ (d) $\sinh^4 x$

2.3 The rectangular hyperbola

The functions cos and sin are often called the **circular functions** because of their links with the circle. The circle with centre O and radius a, shown in Fig. 2.3, can be described by parametric equations

$$x = a\cos t, \; y = a\sin t,$$

where $0 \leqslant t < 2\pi$. You obtain the usual cartesian equation from these by noting that

$$x^2 + y^2 = a^2\cos^2 t + a^2\sin^2 t = a^2\left(\cos^2 t + \sin^2 t\right) = a^2 \times 1 = a^2,$$

using one of Pythagoras' identities.

If A is the point on the circle with parameter 0 and Q the point with parameter q, then the angle AOQ is equal to q. As the parameter t increases from 0 to q, the point $(a\cos t, a\sin t)$ moves round the circle from A to Q, and the radius sweeps out the region OAQ shown shaded in Fig. 2.3. You know that the area of this region is $\frac{1}{2}a^2q$.

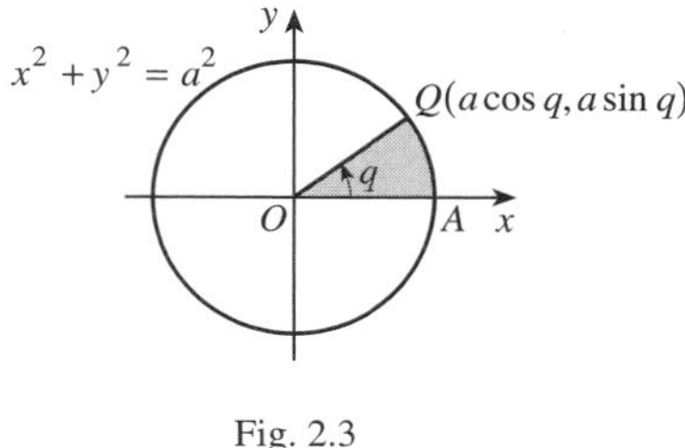

Fig. 2.3

Replacing the circular functions by hyperbolic functions leads to similar results for a rectangular hyperbola, which is the curve shown in Fig. 2.4. Starting with parametric equations $x = a\cosh t$, $y = a\sinh t$, where $t \in \mathbb{R}$, it follows that

$$x^2 - y^2 = a^2\cosh^2 t - a^2\sinh^2 t = a^2\left(\cosh^2 t - \sinh^2 t\right) = a^2 \times 1 = a^2,$$

using the basic identity for hyperbolic functions. The cartesian equation is therefore

$$x^2 - y^2 = a^2.$$

Notice, though, that there is a mismatch between the parametric and cartesian equations. Since y and x appear squared in the cartesian equation, the curve is symmetrical about both the x- and y-axes. It therefore represents a curve in two parts (called 'branches'). But since $\cosh t$ is always positive, the parametric equations give only the branch of the rectangular hyperbola for which $x > 0$, shown in Fig. 2.5. Points for which $t > 0$ lie in the first quadrant, and points for which $t < 0$ lie in the fourth quadrant.

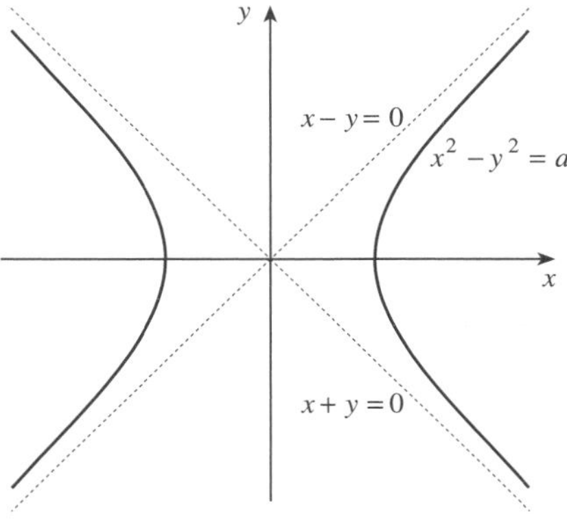

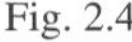
Fig. 2.4

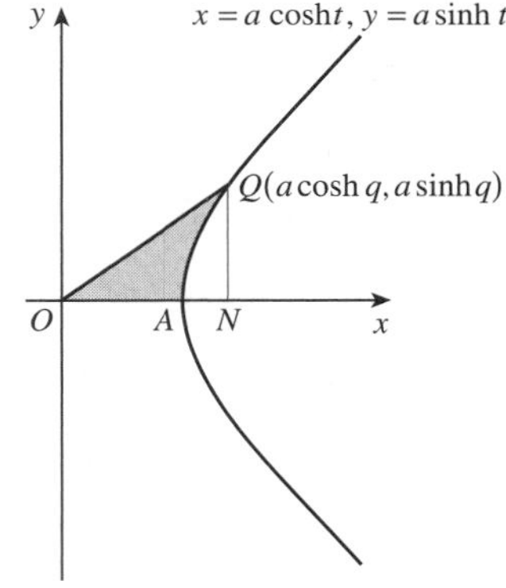

Fig. 2.5

Since $x - y = a\cosh t - a\sinh t = ae^{-t}$, $x - y$ tends to 0 as $t \to \infty$. This shows that the line $x - y = 0$ is an asymptote. By symmetry, $x + y = 0$ is also an asymptote. The reason for describing the hyperbola as 'rectangular' is that these two asymptotes are at right angles to each other.

In Fig. 2.5 the points A and Q have parameters 0 and q respectively, and N is the foot of the perpendicular from Q to the x-axis, with coordinates $(a\cosh q, 0)$. The region ANQ under the curve then has area

$$\int_a^{a\cosh q} y\,\mathrm{d}x.$$

Substituting $x = a\cosh t$, $y = a\sinh t$ transforms this integral into

$$\int_0^q a\sinh t \frac{\mathrm{d}x}{\mathrm{d}t}\,\mathrm{d}t = \int_0^q a\sinh t \times a\sinh t\,\mathrm{d}t,$$

which can be found as

$$\tfrac{1}{2}a^2\int_0^q 2\sinh^2 t\,\mathrm{d}t = \tfrac{1}{2}a^2\int_0^q (\cosh 2t - 1)\,\mathrm{d}t$$
$$= \tfrac{1}{2}a^2\left[\tfrac{1}{2}\sinh 2t - t\right]_0^q = \tfrac{1}{2}a^2(\sinh q\cosh q - q).$$

Also, the area of the triangle ONQ is $\frac{1}{2}a\cosh q \times a\sinh q = \frac{1}{2}a^2\sinh q\cosh q$. It follows that the area of the shaded sector OAQ is

$$\tfrac{1}{2}a^2\sinh q\cosh q - \tfrac{1}{2}a^2(\sinh q\cosh q - q) = \tfrac{1}{2}a^2 q.$$

So the parameter can be given exactly the same interpretation for the circle and the rectangular hyperbola, as $q = \dfrac{2(\text{area of sector } OAQ)}{a^2}$.

2.4 Other hyperbolic functions

The analogy with trigonometric functions can be carried further by defining hyperbolic functions corresponding to tan, sec, cot and cosec. In practice the important ones are

$$\operatorname{sech} x = \frac{1}{\cosh x} \quad \text{and} \quad \tanh x = \frac{\sinh x}{\cosh x} \text{ (pronounced 'tanch' or 'than').}$$

Note that $\operatorname{sech}(-x) = \dfrac{1}{\cosh(-x)} = \dfrac{1}{\cosh x} = \operatorname{sech} x,$

and $\tanh(-x) = \dfrac{\sinh(-x)}{\cosh(-x)} = \dfrac{-\sinh x}{\cosh x} = -\tanh x,$

so that sech is an even function and tanh is an odd function.

Since $\cosh x \geqslant 1$ for all x, values of $\operatorname{sech} x$ always have $0 < \operatorname{sech} x \leqslant 1$, and $\operatorname{sech} x$ tends to 0 as $x \to \pm\infty$. The graph is drawn in Fig. 2.6.

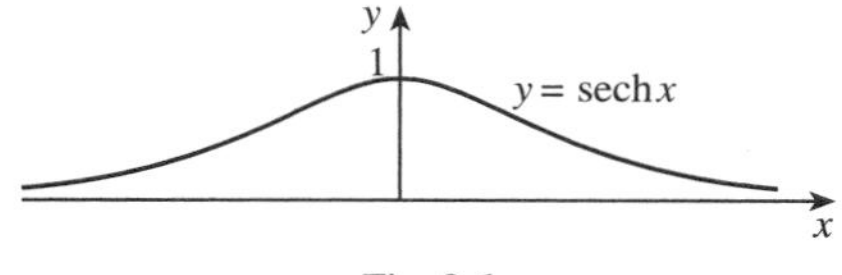

Fig. 2.6

You can express $\tanh x$ in terms of exponentials by noting that $\cosh x$ and $\sinh x$ can be written as

$$\tfrac{1}{2}\mathrm{e}^{-x}\left(\mathrm{e}^{2x} \pm 1\right), \text{ or } \tfrac{1}{2}\mathrm{e}^{x}\left(1 \pm \mathrm{e}^{-2x}\right), \text{ so } \tanh x = \frac{\mathrm{e}^{2x} - 1}{\mathrm{e}^{2x} + 1} = \frac{1 - \mathrm{e}^{-2x}}{1 + \mathrm{e}^{-2x}}.$$

For $x > 0$, $0 < \mathrm{e}^{-2x} < 1$, so that $0 < \tanh x < 1$. Also, since e^{-2x} tends to 0 as $x \to \infty$, $\tanh x$ tends to $\dfrac{1-0}{1+0} = 1$. Corresponding properties for $x < 0$ follow by noting that tanh is an odd function. The graph is drawn in Fig. 2.7.

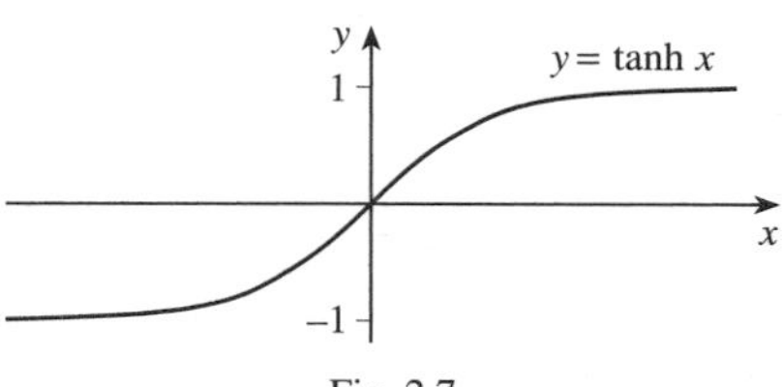

Fig. 2.7

The basic identity $\cosh^2 x - \sinh^2 x \equiv 1$ can be adapted by dividing by $\cosh^2 x$, to give

$$1 - \frac{\sinh^2 x}{\cosh^2 x} = \frac{1}{\cosh^2 x},$$

which is:

$$1 - \tanh^2 x \equiv \operatorname{sech}^2 x.$$

You should also check for yourself that the derivatives are:

$$\frac{d}{dx}\tanh x = \frac{1}{\cosh^2 x} = \operatorname{sech}^2 x, \qquad \frac{d}{dx}\operatorname{sech} x = \frac{-\sinh x}{\cosh^2 x} = -\operatorname{sech} x \tanh x.$$

2.5 Inverse hyperbolic functions

You can see from Fig. 2.2 that sinh is a one–one function with domain and range $\mathbb{R}$, so there is no complication in defining the inverse function $\sinh^{-1}$, also with domain and range $\mathbb{R}$.

However, Fig. 2.1 shows that the function cosh is not one–one. To define $\cosh^{-1}$ you have to begin by restricting the domain of cosh. The obvious way to do this is to define $\cosh^{-1}$ as the inverse of the function $x \mapsto \cosh x$ with domain $\mathbb{R}$, $x \geqslant 0$, and range $\mathbb{R}$, $y \geqslant 1$. The inverse function $x \mapsto \cosh^{-1} x$ then has domain $\mathbb{R}$, $x \geqslant 1$, and range $\mathbb{R}$, $y \geqslant 0$. Fig. 2.8 shows its graph.

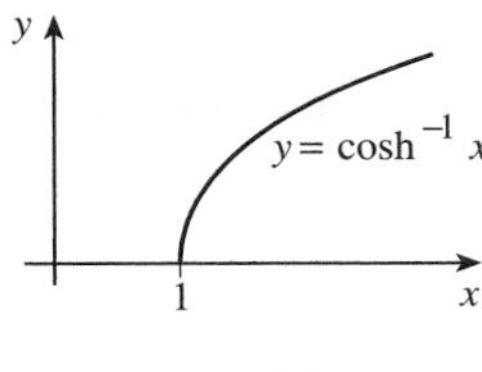

Fig. 2.8

The most important property of these inverse functions is that they can be calculated as logarithms. If $y = \sinh^{-1} x$, then $\sinh y = x$, so

$$\cosh^2 y = 1 + \sinh^2 y = 1 + x^2.$$

Now $\cosh y$ is always positive, so it follows that $\cosh y = \sqrt{1+x^2}$. Therefore

$$e^y = \sinh y + \cosh y = x + \sqrt{1+x^2}, \qquad \text{giving} \qquad y = \ln\left(x + \sqrt{1+x^2}\right).$$

By a similar argument, if $y = \cosh^{-1} x$, then $\cosh y = x$, so

$$\sinh^2 y = \cosh^2 y - 1 = x^2 - 1.$$

Now by definition $\cosh^{-1} x$ is positive or zero, and since $y \geqslant 0$ then $\sinh y \geqslant 0$. Therefore $\sinh y = \sqrt{x^2 - 1}$, so

$$e^y = \cosh y + \sinh y = x + \sqrt{x^2 - 1}, \quad \text{giving} \quad y = \ln\left(x + \sqrt{x^2 - 1}\right).$$

These are important results, which you should remember.

For all x, $\quad \sinh^{-1} x = \ln\left(x + \sqrt{1+x^2}\right).$

For $x \geqslant 1$, $\quad \cosh^{-1} x = \ln\left(x + \sqrt{x^2 - 1}\right).$

Example 2.5.1
Prove that $\cosh^{-1} 3 = 2\sinh^{-1} 1$.

Method 1 The formulae give

$$\cosh^{-1} 3 = \ln\left(3+\sqrt{8}\right) = \ln\left(3+2\sqrt{2}\right) \quad \text{and} \quad \sinh^{-1} 1 = \ln\left(1+\sqrt{2}\right).$$

So
$$\begin{aligned} 2\sinh^{-1} 1 &= 2\ln\left(1+\sqrt{2}\right) = \ln\left(1+\sqrt{2}\right)^2 \\ &= \ln\left(1+2\sqrt{2}+2\right) = \ln\left(3+2\sqrt{2}\right) = \cosh^{-1} 3. \end{aligned}$$

Method 2 If $A = \sinh^{-1} 1$, then $\cosh 2A = 1 + 2\sinh^2 A = 1 + 2\times 1^2 = 3$.

So $\quad \cosh^{-1} 3 = 2A = 2\sinh^{-1} 1$.

Try using your calculator to check this result numerically.

You can also express $\tanh^{-1} x$ as a logarithm, using the exponential form in Section 2.4.

If $y = \tanh^{-1} x$, then $x = \tanh y = \dfrac{e^{2y}-1}{e^{2y}+1}$.

So $\quad xe^{2y} + x = e^{2y} - 1$, giving $1 + x = (1-x)e^{2y}$, and thus $e^{2y} = \dfrac{1+x}{1-x}$.

For the right side to be positive, x must lie between -1 and 1. This you should expect; Fig. 2.7 shows that values of tanh always lie between -1 and 1. Then

$$2y = \ln\frac{1+x}{1-x}.$$

> For $-1 < x < 1$, $\quad \tanh^{-1} x = \frac{1}{2}\ln\dfrac{1+x}{1-x}$.

Example 2.5.2
Find the Maclaurin expansion of $\tanh^{-1} x$, and its interval of validity.

You know the Maclaurin series for $\ln(1+x)$,

$$\ln(1+x) = x - \tfrac{1}{2}x^2 + \tfrac{1}{3}x^3 - \tfrac{1}{4}x^4 + \tfrac{1}{5}x^5 - \ldots \quad \text{for } -1 < x \leqslant 1.$$

Replacing x by $-x$ gives

$$\ln(1-x) = -x - \tfrac{1}{2}x^2 - \tfrac{1}{3}x^3 - \tfrac{1}{4}x^4 - \tfrac{1}{5}x^5 - \ldots \text{ for } -1 < -x \leqslant 1,$$

that is $-1 \leqslant x < 1$.

Since $\tanh^{-1} x = \frac{1}{2}\ln\dfrac{1+x}{1-x}$, you get by subtraction and halving

$$\tanh^{-1} x = x + \tfrac{1}{3}x^3 + \tfrac{1}{5}x^5 + \ldots.$$

The interval of validity is the set of points common to the intervals $-1 < x \leqslant 1$ and $-1 \leqslant x < 1$, that is $-1 < x < 1$.

Compare this with the expansion of $\tan^{-1} x$ *found in P4 Section 7.5.*

You can find the derivatives of the inverse functions in two ways. One is to adapt the method used for $\tan^{-1}$ and $\sin^{-1}$ in P4 Section 6.4. For example, if $y = \sinh^{-1} x$, then $x = \sinh y$, so $\frac{dx}{dy} = \cosh y$, and

$$\frac{dy}{dx} = 1 \Big/ \frac{dx}{dy} = \frac{1}{\cosh y} = \frac{1}{\sqrt{1+\sinh^2 y}} = \frac{1}{\sqrt{1+x^2}}.$$

There is no ambiguity about the sign of the square root, since $\cosh y$ is always positive.

Alternatively, you can find the derivatives from the logarithmic forms above. For example,

$$\frac{d}{dx}\cosh^{-1} x = \frac{d}{dx}\left(\ln\left(x+\sqrt{x^2-1}\right)\right) = \frac{1}{x+\sqrt{x^2-1}} \times \left(1 + \frac{x}{\sqrt{x^2-1}}\right)$$

$$= \frac{1}{x+\sqrt{x^2-1}} \times \left(\frac{\sqrt{x^2-1}+x}{\sqrt{x^2-1}}\right) = \frac{1}{\sqrt{x^2-1}},$$

and $\frac{d}{dx}\tanh^{-1} x = \frac{d}{dx}\left(\tfrac{1}{2}(\ln(1+x) - \ln(1-x))\right) = \tfrac{1}{2}\left(\frac{1}{1+x} + \frac{1}{1-x}\right) = \frac{1}{1-x^2}.$

$$\frac{d}{dx}\cosh^{-1} x = \frac{1}{\sqrt{x^2-1}}, \qquad \frac{d}{dx}\sinh^{-1} x = \frac{1}{\sqrt{1+x^2}}, \qquad \frac{d}{dx}\tanh^{-1} x = \frac{1}{1-x^2}.$$

More generally, if a is a positive constant,

$$\frac{d}{dx}\cosh^{-1}\frac{x}{a} = \frac{1}{\sqrt{\left(\frac{x}{a}\right)^2 - 1}} \times \frac{1}{a} = \frac{1}{\sqrt{x^2-a^2}},$$

and similarly $\frac{d}{dx}\sinh^{-1}\frac{x}{a} = \frac{1}{\sqrt{a^2+x^2}}.$

These results are especially important in their integral forms.

$$\int \frac{1}{\sqrt{x^2-a^2}}\,dx = \cosh^{-1}\frac{x}{a} + k, \qquad \int \frac{1}{\sqrt{a^2+x^2}}\,dx = \sinh^{-1}\frac{x}{a} + k.$$

2.6 Independent methods

Although results for hyperbolic functions are often best obtained by comparison with those for trigonometric functions, this does not always work, or it doesn't pay to use it.

One example is the integral of $\operatorname{sech} x$. You found $\int \sec x \, \mathrm{d}x$ by noticing that

$$\begin{aligned}\frac{\mathrm{d}}{\mathrm{d}x}(\ln(\sec x + \tan x)) &= \frac{1}{\sec x + \tan x} \times \left(\sec x \tan x + \sec^2 x\right) \\ &= \frac{\sec x(\tan x + \sec x)}{\sec x + \tan x} = \sec x.\end{aligned}$$

But if you try differentiating the corresponding hyperbolic function,

$$\begin{aligned}\frac{\mathrm{d}}{\mathrm{d}x}(\ln(\operatorname{sech} x + \tanh x)) &= \frac{1}{\operatorname{sech} x + \tanh x} \times \left(-\operatorname{sech} x \tanh x + \operatorname{sech}^2 x\right) \\ &= \frac{\operatorname{sech} x(-\tanh x + \operatorname{sech} x)}{\operatorname{sech} x + \tanh x},\end{aligned}$$

you do not get a common factor in the numerator and denominator.

However, with hyperbolic functions an alternative method is always available: to go back to the exponential definition. In this example,

$$\int \operatorname{sech} x \, \mathrm{d}x = \int \frac{2}{\mathrm{e}^x + \mathrm{e}^{-x}} \, \mathrm{d}x = \int \frac{2}{\mathrm{e}^{2x} + 1} \mathrm{e}^x \, \mathrm{d}x.$$

The substitution $\mathrm{e}^x = u$ can now be used to express this as

$$\int \frac{2}{u^2 + 1} \frac{\mathrm{d}u}{\mathrm{d}x} \, \mathrm{d}x = \int \frac{2}{u^2 + 1} \, \mathrm{d}u = 2 \tan^{-1} u + k.$$

Therefore

$$\int \operatorname{sech} x \, \mathrm{d}x = 2 \tan^{-1}\left(\mathrm{e}^x\right) + k.$$

Example 2.6.1
(a) Solve $7 \sinh x + 3 \cosh x = 9$. (b) Find $\displaystyle\int \frac{1}{7 \sinh x + 3 \cosh x - 9} \, \mathrm{d}x$.

In exponential form,

$$\begin{aligned}7 \sinh x + 3 \cosh x - 9 &= \tfrac{7}{2}\left(\mathrm{e}^x - \mathrm{e}^{-x}\right) + \tfrac{3}{2}\left(\mathrm{e}^x + \mathrm{e}^{-x}\right) - 9 \\ &= 5\mathrm{e}^x - 2\mathrm{e}^{-x} - 9,\end{aligned}$$

which can be written as

$$\mathrm{e}^{-x}\left(5\mathrm{e}^{2x} - 9\mathrm{e}^x - 2\right) = \mathrm{e}^{-x}\left(5\mathrm{e}^x + 1\right)\left(\mathrm{e}^x - 2\right).$$

(a) It is possible to use a method similar to that for the comparable trigonometric equation, writing $7 \sinh x + 3 \cosh x$ as $R \sinh(x + a)$ with $R \cosh a = 7$ and $R \sinh a = 3$, so that $R^2\left(\cosh^2 a - \sinh^2 a\right) = 49 - 9$, $R = \sqrt{40}$. But it is simpler to put the equation into exponential form

$$\mathrm{e}^{-x}\left(5\mathrm{e}^x + 1\right)\left(\mathrm{e}^x - 2\right) = 0.$$

Since e^{-x} and $5\mathrm{e}^x + 1$ cannot be 0, the only solution is $\mathrm{e}^x = 2$, $x = \ln 2$.

(b) Using the exponential form,

$$\int \frac{1}{7\sinh x + 3\cosh x - 9}\,\mathrm{d}x = \int \frac{\mathrm{e}^x}{\left(5\mathrm{e}^x + 1\right)\left(\mathrm{e}^x - 2\right)}\,\mathrm{d}x.$$

The substitution $\mathrm{e}^x = u$ transforms this to

$$\begin{aligned}\int \frac{1}{(5u+1)(u-2)}\,\mathrm{d}u &= \int \frac{1}{11}\left(\frac{-5}{(5u+1)} + \frac{1}{(u-2)}\right)\mathrm{d}u \\ &= \tfrac{1}{11}\left(-\ln|5u+1| + \ln|u-2|\right) + k \\ &= \tfrac{1}{11}\ln\left|\frac{\mathrm{e}^x - 2}{5\mathrm{e}^x + 1}\right| + k.\end{aligned}$$

Exercise 2B

1 Fill in the missing entries in rows (a) to (d) of the table.

	$\cosh x$	$\sinh x$	$\tanh x$	$\operatorname{sech} x$
(a)	$\frac{13}{5}$			
(b)		$2\sqrt{2}$		
(c)			$\frac{1}{2}$	
(d)				$\frac{4}{5}$

2 Use the logarithmic forms to evaluate the following. Check your answers by using the inverse hyperbolic function keys on your calculator.

(a) $\cosh^{-1} 1.25$ (b) $\sinh^{-1} 2$ (c) $\tanh^{-1}\left(-\frac{1}{4}\right)$ (d) $\sinh^{-1}(-0.7)$

3 Evaluate the following exactly, and check your answers with a calculator.

(a) $\tanh(\ln 3)$ (b) $\mathrm{e}^{\sinh^{-1} 2.4}$ (c) $\tanh\left(\sinh^{-1}\frac{3}{4}\right)$ (d) $\sinh\left(\tanh^{-1}\frac{4}{5}\right)$

4 Solve these equations for x giving your answer in exact form.

(a) $\sinh^{-1} x = 2\cosh^{-1} 2$ (b) $\operatorname{sech}^{-1} x = \cosh^{-1} 2$

(c) $\sinh^{-1} x = \coth^{-1} 3$ (d) $\cosh^{-1}(2x) = \sinh^{-1} x$

(e) $\cosh^{-1} x = \operatorname{sech}^{-1}(x+1)$ (f) $\sinh^{-1}\left(x - \frac{1}{2}\right) = \cosh^{-1} x$

5 Prove that, if $y = \sinh^{-1} x$, then $\left(\mathrm{e}^y\right)^2 - 2x\mathrm{e}^y - 1 = 0$. Solve this quadratic equation for e^y, and hence obtain the expression for $\sinh^{-1}$ in logarithmic form. Investigate the significance of the second root of the quadratic equation.

Find the expression for $\cosh^{-1} x$ in logarithmic form by a similar method.

6 Find the derivatives with respect to x of the following functions.

(a) $\operatorname{sech} x \tanh x$ (b) $\sinh^{-1}\sqrt{x}$ (c) $\sqrt{\operatorname{sech} x + \tanh x}$

(d) $\operatorname{sech}^{-1} x$ (e) $\cosh^{-1}\sqrt{1+x^2}$ (f) $\tanh^{-1}\left(\frac{1-x}{1+x}\right)$

7 (a) Express the functions $\coth x$ and $\operatorname{cosech} x$ in terms of $\cosh x$ and $\sinh x$, and sketch their graphs.

(b) State the domains and ranges of the functions $\coth x$, $\operatorname{cosech} x$, $\coth^{-1} x$, $\operatorname{cosech}^{-1} x$.

(c) Find $\frac{d}{dx}\coth x$, $\frac{d}{dx}\operatorname{cosech} x$, $\frac{d}{dx}\coth^{-1} x$, $\frac{d}{dx}\operatorname{cosech}^{-1} x$.

(d) Express $\coth^{-1} x$ and $\operatorname{cosech}^{-1} x$ in logarithmic form.

8 Evaluate the following integrals, giving your answers as logarithms.

(a) $\int_0^1 \frac{1}{\sqrt{x^2+1}}\,dx$ (b) $\int_{10}^{17} \frac{1}{\sqrt{x^2-64}}\,dx$

(c) $\int_{-1}^1 \frac{1}{\sqrt{x^2+4x+5}}\,dx$ (d) $\int_3^4 \frac{1}{\sqrt{(x+4)(x-2)}}\,dx$

(e) $\int_1^2 \frac{1}{x\sqrt{1+x^2}}\,dx$ $\left(\text{try } x=\frac{1}{u}\right)$ (f) $\int_{\frac{1}{2}}^1 \frac{1}{x\sqrt{(3+4x)(3-2x)}}\,dx$

9 Find the indefinite integrals

(a) $\int \frac{1}{25\cosh x+7\sinh x}\,dx$, (b) $\int \frac{1}{25\sinh x+7\cosh x}\,dx$.

10 Use integration by parts to find the following integrals.

(a) $\int x\tanh^{-1} x\,dx$ (b) $\int \tanh^{-1} x\,dx$ (c) $\int \sinh^{-1} x\,dx$

11 Find $\int \tanh^n x\,dx$, for (a) $n=1$, (b) $n=2$, (c) $n=3$, (d) $n=4$.

12 Prove that, if $0<x<\frac{1}{2}\pi$, $\cosh^{-1}(\sec x)=\ln(\sec x+\tan x)$. Find similar expressions for

(a) $\ln(\sec x-\tan x)$ if $0<x<\frac{1}{2}\pi$, (b) $\ln(\sec x+\tan x)$ if $-\frac{1}{2}\pi<x<0$.

13 Solve the equations $f(x)=a$ for the following functions $f(x)$ and constants a, using the method in Example 2.6.1. Illustrate your solutions with sketch graphs of the functions.

(a) $f(x)=5\cosh x-4\sinh x$, $a=3$ (b) $f(x)=6\cosh x-\sinh x$, $a=6$

(c) $f(x)=5\sinh x-8\cosh x$, $a=8$ (d) $f(x)=3\sinh x+11\cosh x$, $a=16$

14 For the functions and constants in Question 13, find expressions for $\int \frac{1}{f(x)-a}\,dx$.

15† Express each of the functions in Question 13 in one or other of the forms $R\sinh(x+\alpha)$, $R\cosh(x+\alpha)$ (where R may be positive or negative), and hence solve the equations by another method.

16 Find the expansion of $\sinh^{-1} x$ as the sum of powers of x, giving the first three terms and an expression for the general term.

17† Find $\int \frac{1}{\sqrt{x^2-1}}\,dx$ when $x<-1$. Hence evaluate $\int_{-2}^{-1} \frac{1}{\sqrt{x^2-1}}\,dx$. Illustrate your answers graphically.

18[†] Show that, for the rectangular hyperbola $x^2 - y^2 = a^2$ in Section 2.3, alternative parametric equations to $x = a\cosh t$, $y = a\sinh t$ are $x = a\sec u$, $y = a\tan u$. What interval of values of u gives the positive branch of the hyperbola shown in Fig. 2.5?

If $\sinh t = \tan u$, express $\cosh t$ and $\tanh t$ in terms of u. Find expressions for $\frac{dt}{du}$ in terms of u, and for $\frac{du}{dt}$ in terms of t. Use your answers to find (a) $\int \sec u \, du$, (b) $\int \operatorname{sech} t \, dt$.

Match your answer to part (b) with the expression for the integral given in Section 2.6.

2.7* Completing the link

Before reading this section you should jump ahead to Section 7.1 and read about the exponential function e^z when z is complex.

You probably suspect that the analogy between circular and hyperbolic functions is more than a curious accident. The link can be explained by extending the domain of the exponential function to the complex numbers.

Once you have a meaning for e^z, where z is complex, the definitions of $\cosh z$ and $\sinh z$ can be extended in the same way. The proofs of the addition formulae in Section 2.2(ii) then depend only on the rules for indices, which are extended to complex indices in Section 7.1.

Now you know from P4 Section 11.5, that $e^{yi} = \cos y + i\sin y$ and (replacing y by $-y$) $e^{-yi} = \cos y - i\sin y$. Adding and subtracting these equations gives

$$e^{yi} + e^{-yi} = 2\cos y \quad \text{and} \quad e^{yi} - e^{-yi} = 2i\sin y.$$

That is:

$$\cos y = \cosh(yi), \quad i\sin y = \sinh(yi).$$

You can use these equations to show that the addition formulae for circular and hyperbolic functions are the same. For example,

$$\begin{aligned}\cos(A+B) &= \cosh(Ai + Bi) \\ &= \cosh(Ai)\cosh(Bi) + \sinh(Ai)\sinh(Bi) \\ &= \cos A\cos B + i\sin A \times i\sin B \\ &= \cos A\cos B - \sin A\sin B.\end{aligned}$$

Notice that the change of sign arises from the product $i^2 = -1$.

You can link the rules for differentiation in a similar way. Since, from Section 7.1, $\frac{d}{dx}\left(e^{cx}\right) = c\,e^{cx}$, it follows that $\frac{d}{dx}\left(e^{xi}\right) = i\,e^{xi}$ and $\frac{d}{dx}\left(e^{-xi}\right) = -i\,e^{-xi}$, so that $\frac{d}{dx}\cosh(xi) = i\sinh(xi)$. So

$$\frac{d}{dx}\cos x = \frac{d}{dx}\cosh(xi) = i\sinh(xi) = i(i\sin x) = -\sin x.$$

You should appreciate that these are not *proofs* of the addition formulae and the rules for differentiation, since these rules are obtained from the properties of the exponential function summarised at the end of Section 7.1; and these are themselves found using the addition formulae and the rules for differentiating trigonometric functions! What has been shown is that there are not two separate sets of rules, but one set of rules which can be interpreted in terms of either circular or hyperbolic functions.

One further extension is possible. So far the circular functions have only been defined with $\mathbb{R}$ as domain, but it now seems reasonable to complete the link with hyperbolic functions by defining $\cos z$ and $\sin z$, where $z \in \mathbb{C}$, by the equations:

$$\cos z = \cosh(z\mathrm{i}), \quad \sin z = \frac{1}{\mathrm{i}}\sinh(z\mathrm{i})$$

Exercise 2C*

1 Find expressions for $\cos(z\mathrm{i})$ and $\sin(z\mathrm{i})$ in terms of $\cosh z$ and $\sinh z$.

2 Establish the link between

(a) the expressions for $\sin(A+B)$ and $\sinh(A+B)$,

(b) the derivatives $\dfrac{\mathrm{d}}{\mathrm{d}x}(\sin x) = \cos x$ and $\dfrac{\mathrm{d}}{\mathrm{d}x}(\sinh x) = \cosh x$.

3 Express $\cosh(x + y\mathrm{i})$ in the form $a + b\mathrm{i}$. Hence find the general solution of the equation $\cosh z = \frac{1}{2}$.

4 Express $\sin(x + y\mathrm{i})$ in the form $a + b\mathrm{i}$. Hence find the general solution of the equation $\sin z = 2$.

5 Investigate whether the identity $\cos^2 z + \sin^2 z \equiv 1$ is true when z is a complex number.

6 Investigate whether the result $\dfrac{\mathrm{d}}{\mathrm{d}t}(\sin ct) = c\cos ct$ is true when c is a complex number.

7 It has been suggested that, in any formula involving trigonometric functions, each trigonometric function may be replaced by the corresponding hyperbolic function provided that the sign of any product of two sines is changed. (This is known as *Osborn's rule*.) Find some examples which illustrate this rule. Can you find any exceptions? Explain how the rule can be justified by extending the domain of these functions to the complex numbers.

Miscellaneous exercise 2

1 Find the coordinates of the points of inflexion on the graph of $y = \operatorname{sech} x$.

2 Find the area of the region bounded by the graphs of $y = \tanh x$, $y = \operatorname{sech} x$ and $x = 0$.

3 Find the coordinates of the maximum point on the graph of $y = \operatorname{sech} x + \lambda \tanh x$, where λ is constant. Illustrate your answer with sketches of the graph when

(a) $\lambda > 0$, (b) $\lambda < 0$.

4 Show that $\dfrac{\mathrm{d}}{\mathrm{d}x}\left(\sin^{-1}(\tanh x)\right) = \operatorname{sech} x$. (MEI)

5 A curve has equation $y = x\sinh^{-1} x$. Show that $\dfrac{\mathrm{d}^2 y}{\mathrm{d}x^2} = \dfrac{2+x^2}{\left(1+x^2\right)^{\frac{3}{2}}}$. Deduce that the curve has no point of inflexion. (OCR)

6 Show that $\displaystyle\int_5^6 \frac{1}{\sqrt{25x^2-576}}\,\mathrm{d}x = \tfrac{1}{5}\ln\tfrac{3}{2}$. (MEI)

7 Evaluate $\displaystyle\int_0^4 \frac{1}{\sqrt{9x^2+4}}\,\mathrm{d}x$ giving your answer in terms of a natural logarithm. (OCR)

8 Show that $\displaystyle\int_0^{\frac{1}{2}} \tanh^{-1} x\,\mathrm{d}x = \tfrac{1}{4}\ln\tfrac{27}{16}$. (MEI)

9 Find $\displaystyle\int \frac{1}{a^2-x^2}\,\mathrm{d}x$, where $0 < x < a$,

(a) by substituting $x = a\tanh t$, (b) by using partial fractions.

Show algebraically that your solutions are equivalent. (OCR)

10 Draw sketches with the same axes of the graphs of $y = \operatorname{sech} x$ and $y = \dfrac{1}{1+x^2}$. Show that the areas of the regions under the two graphs are equal.
The graphs are rotated through a complete revolution about the x-axis to form surfaces of revolution. Which encloses the larger volume?

11 The function $\mathrm{f}(x)$ is defined to be $\mathrm{f}(x) = 13\cosh x + 5\sinh x$.

(a) For the curve with equation $y = \mathrm{f}(x)$, show that the area under the curve between $x = -a$ and $x = a$ (where $a > 0$) is $\frac{13}{5}(\mathrm{f}(a) - \mathrm{f}(-a))$.

(b) By first expressing $\mathrm{f}(x)$ in terms of e^x and e^{-x}, find the minimum value of $\mathrm{f}(x)$.

(c) Solve the equation $\mathrm{f}(x) = 20$, giving the answers as natural logarithms.

(d) Differentiate $\tan^{-1}\left(\frac{3}{2}\mathrm{e}^x\right)$ with respect to x. Hence find $\displaystyle\int \frac{1}{\mathrm{f}(x)}\,\mathrm{d}x$. (MEI)

12† Find expressions for the indefinite integral $\displaystyle\int \frac{1}{\cosh x + a\sinh x}\,\mathrm{d}x$ distinguishing various possibilities for the value of the constant a.

13 If $\mathrm{f}(x) = \cosh x \cos x$, prove that $\mathrm{f}^{(4)}(x) = -4\mathrm{f}(x)$. Hence expand $\mathrm{f}(x)$ as a Maclaurin series, giving the first three non-zero terms and an expression for the general term.

14* Obtain the results in Question 13 by expressing $\mathrm{f}(x)$ as the real part of $\cosh(1+\mathrm{i})x$.

15* If $z = x + y\mathrm{i}$, show that

(a) $\sinh z = \sinh x \cos y + \mathrm{i} \cosh x \sin y$;

(b) $\sinh z$ is real if and only if $y = n\pi$, where n is an integer;

(c) $|\sinh z|^2 = \cosh^2 x - \cos^2 y$.

Deduce that, if $\sinh z = \mathrm{e}^{\theta \mathrm{i}}$, where θ is real, then

(d) $\cos^2 y = \sinh^2 x$;

(e) $\cos^2 y = \pm\cos\theta$. (OCR)

16† The equations of an ellipse and a hyperbola are $\dfrac{x^2}{\cosh^2 t} + \dfrac{y^2}{\sinh^2 t} = 1$ and $\dfrac{x^2}{\cos^2 s} - \dfrac{y^2}{\sin^2 s} = 1$ respectively, where $t > 0$ and $0 < s < \frac{1}{2}\pi$. Find, in as simple a form as possible, the coordinates of the point in the first quadrant at which they intersect.

Show that the tangents to the curves at their point of intersection are at right angles. Show also that, at the point of intersection, $x + y\mathrm{i} = \cosh(t + s\mathrm{i})$.

17* Find the expansions, as series of powers of x, of

(a) $\cosh\sqrt{x}$, where $x \geqslant 0$, (b) $\cos\sqrt{-x}$, where $x \leqslant 0$.

Use complex numbers to explain the relation between these two functions.

Sketch the graph of the function defined by $\mathrm{f}(x) = \displaystyle\sum_{r=0}^{\infty} \frac{x^r}{(2r)!}$ over the interval $-100 < x < 10$.

Show that the function in part (a) satisfies the differential equation $2\dfrac{\mathrm{d}y}{\mathrm{d}x} = \sqrt{\dfrac{y^2 - 1}{x}}$.

Find a similar differential equation satisfied by the function in part (b).

3 Arc length and surface area

You already know how to use integration to calculate areas and volumes. This chapter extends the technique to other measurements, and shows how the various applications can be combined in a common summation principle. When you have completed it, you should

- be able to find the length of a curve
- be able to find the surface area of a solid of revolution
- be able to apply the summation principle to other mathematical models.

3.1 Arc length in cartesian coordinates

The distance between two points A, B on a curve measured along the curve is called the **arc length** AB. The word 'arc' is used to distinguish it from the length of the straight line segment AB, called the 'chord length'.

The method of calculating arc length is similar to that already used in finding areas under curves and volumes of solids of revolution. Fig. 3.1 shows a curve with equation $y = \mathrm{f}(x)$. Suppose it is required to find the arc length AB joining points with coordinates $(a, \mathrm{f}(a))$ and $(b, \mathrm{f}(b))$. The technique is to introduce a variable into the problem, denoting by s the arc length from A to any point P, with coordinates $(x, \mathrm{f}(x))$. Then s is a function of x, and the arc length AB is the value of this function when $x = b$.

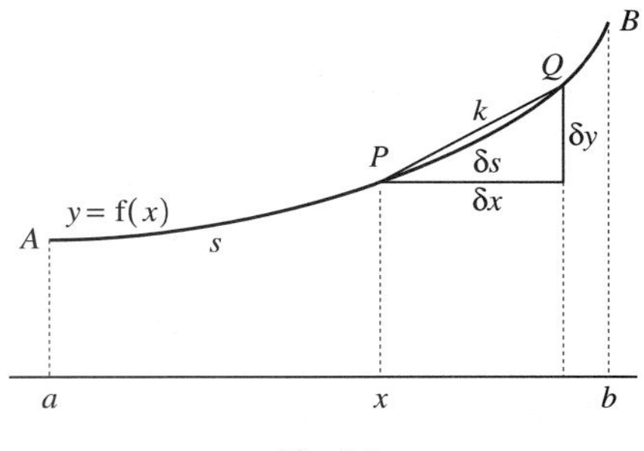

Fig. 3.1

Now take another point Q on the curve close to P, with coordinates $(x + \delta x, y + \delta y)$. (For simplicity, suppose that $\delta x > 0$.) The arc length AQ is then $s + \delta s$, where δs denotes the arc length PQ. The calculation of arc length is based on the property that, as δx tends to 0, the ratio of the arc length to the chord length tends to 1. This can be used to find an expression for $\dfrac{\mathrm{d}s}{\mathrm{d}x}$.

You have already met this property for a circle in P3 Section 2.1. Curves which have this property are called 'rectifiable'. Some very odd curves, including some 'fractal' curves, are not rectifiable, but they will not feature in this chapter.

Denote the chord length PQ by k. Then $k^2 = (\delta x)^2 + (\delta y)^2$, so that $\dfrac{\delta s}{\delta x}$ can be written as

$$\frac{\delta s}{\delta x} = \frac{\delta s}{k} \times \frac{k}{\delta x} = \frac{\delta s}{k} \times \sqrt{1 + \left(\frac{\delta y}{\delta x}\right)^2}.$$

Now let $\delta x \to 0$. Then $\dfrac{\delta s}{k} \to 1$ and $\dfrac{\delta y}{\delta x} \to \dfrac{\mathrm{d}y}{\mathrm{d}x}$, so that in the limit (making the usual assumptions about the properties of limits)

$$\frac{ds}{dx} = \sqrt{1+\left(\frac{dy}{dx}\right)^2} = \sqrt{1+(f'(x))^2}.$$

You can now complete the argument exactly as for area and volume. The corresponding conclusion is:

The arc length of the curve with equation $y = f(x)$ from $x = a$ to $x = b$ is

$$\int_a^b \sqrt{1+\left(\frac{dy}{dx}\right)^2}\,dx = \int_a^b \sqrt{1+(f'(x))^2}\,dx.$$

Example 3.1.1

Fig. 3.2 shows the graph of $y = \frac{1}{2}x\sqrt{x}$ between $(0,0)$ and $\left(1,\frac{1}{2}\right)$. Find the arc length.

The equation is $y = \frac{1}{2}x^{\frac{3}{2}}$, so that $\frac{dy}{dx} = \frac{3}{4}x^{\frac{1}{2}}$. The arc length is therefore

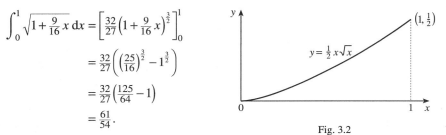

$$\begin{aligned}\int_0^1 \sqrt{1+\tfrac{9}{16}x}\,dx &= \left[\tfrac{32}{27}\left(1+\tfrac{9}{16}x\right)^{\frac{3}{2}}\right]_0^1 \\ &= \tfrac{32}{27}\left(\left(\tfrac{25}{16}\right)^{\frac{3}{2}} - 1^{\frac{3}{2}}\right) \\ &= \tfrac{32}{27}\left(\tfrac{125}{64} - 1\right) \\ &= \tfrac{61}{54}.\end{aligned}$$

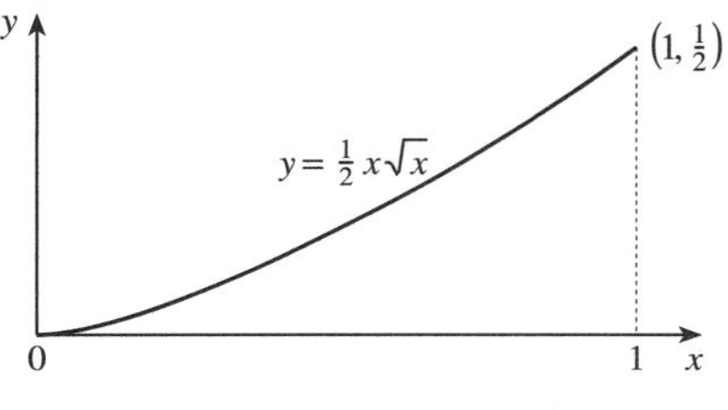

Fig. 3.2

As a check, compare the arc length $\frac{61}{54} = 1.129\ldots$ with the chord length $\sqrt{1^2 + \left(\frac{1}{2}\right)^2} = 1.118\ldots$.

3.2 Arc length for parametric and polar equations

If a curve is described by parametric equations $x = f(t)$, $y = g(t)$, then the arc length can be calculated as an integral with respect to t. If the changes δx and δy result from a change of δt in t, then

$$\frac{\delta s}{\delta t} = \frac{\delta s}{k} \times \frac{k}{\delta t} = \frac{\delta s}{k}\sqrt{\left(\frac{\delta x}{\delta t}\right)^2 + \left(\frac{\delta y}{\delta t}\right)^2}.$$

In the limit, as $\delta t \to 0$, this becomes $\frac{ds}{dt} = 1 \times \sqrt{\left(\frac{dx}{dt}\right)^2 + \left(\frac{dy}{dt}\right)^2}$, so:

The arc length of the curve with equations $x = f(t)$, $y = g(t)$ from $t = t_A$ to $t = t_B$ is

$$\int_{t_A}^{t_B} \sqrt{\left(\frac{dx}{dt}\right)^2 + \left(\frac{dy}{dt}\right)^2}\,dt = \int_{t_A}^{t_B} \sqrt{(f'(t))^2 + (g'(t))^2}\,dt.$$

This formula can be used to find an expression for arc length if the curve is given by an equation in polar coordinates. The angle θ can then be treated as the parameter, and x and y are defined in terms of θ by

$$x = r\cos\theta,\ y = r\sin\theta,$$

where r is a function of θ. These can be differentiated to give

$$\frac{dx}{d\theta} = \frac{dr}{d\theta}\cos\theta - r\sin\theta,\quad \frac{dy}{d\theta} = \frac{dr}{d\theta}\sin\theta + r\cos\theta,$$

so
$$\begin{aligned}\left(\frac{dx}{d\theta}\right)^2 + \left(\frac{dy}{d\theta}\right)^2 &= \left(\frac{dr}{d\theta}\cos\theta - r\sin\theta\right)^2 + \left(\frac{dr}{d\theta}\sin\theta + r\cos\theta\right)^2 \\ &= \left(\frac{dr}{d\theta}\right)^2\left(\cos^2\theta + \sin^2\theta\right) + 2r\frac{dr}{d\theta}(-\cos\theta\sin\theta + \sin\theta\cos\theta) \\ &\qquad + r^2\left(\sin^2\theta + \cos^2\theta\right) \\ &= \left(\frac{dr}{d\theta}\right)^2 + r^2.\end{aligned}$$

The formula for the arc length in polar coordinates is therefore:

The arc length of the curve with equation $r = f(\theta)$ from $\theta = \alpha$ to $\theta = \beta$ is

$$\int_\alpha^\beta \sqrt{r^2 + \left(\frac{dr}{d\theta}\right)^2}\, d\theta = \int_\alpha^\beta \sqrt{(f(\theta))^2 + (f'(\theta))^2}\, d\theta.$$

Example 3.2.1

Find the total length of the cardioid $r = 1 + \cos\theta$.

The complete curve, shown in Fig. 3.3, is obtained by taking values of θ in the interval $-\pi < \theta \leqslant \pi$.

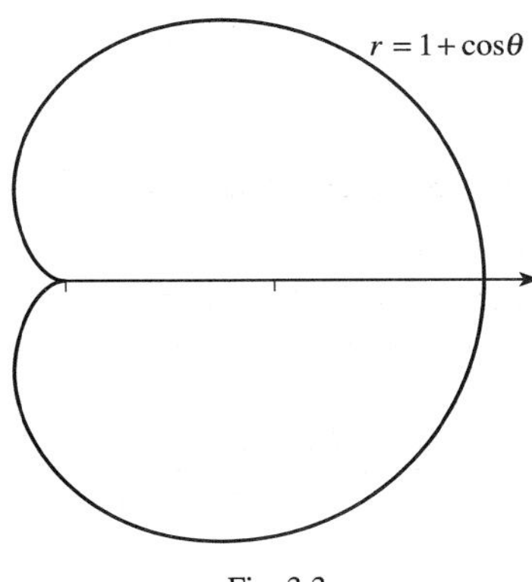

Fig. 3.3

Begin by calculating

$$\begin{aligned} r^2 + \left(\frac{dr}{d\theta}\right)^2 &= (1+\cos\theta)^2 + (-\sin\theta)^2 \\ &= 1 + 2\cos\theta + \cos^2\theta + \sin^2\theta \\ &= 1 + 2\cos\theta + 1 = 2(1+\cos\theta) \\ &= 2\times\left(2\cos^2\tfrac{1}{2}\theta\right) = 4\cos^2\tfrac{1}{2}\theta.\end{aligned}$$

The total arc length is therefore

$$\begin{aligned}\int_{-\pi}^{\pi} \sqrt{4\cos^2\tfrac{1}{2}\theta}\, d\theta &= \int_{-\pi}^{\pi} 2\cos\tfrac{1}{2}\theta\, d\theta \\ &= \left[4\sin\tfrac{1}{2}\theta\right]_{-\pi}^{\pi} = 4 - (-4) = 8.\end{aligned}$$

Example 3.2.2
Find the total length of the astroid, with parametric equations $x = a\cos^3 t$, $y = a\sin^3 t$, where $a > 0$ and $0 \leqslant t < 2\pi$. (See P3 Example 4.4.2.)

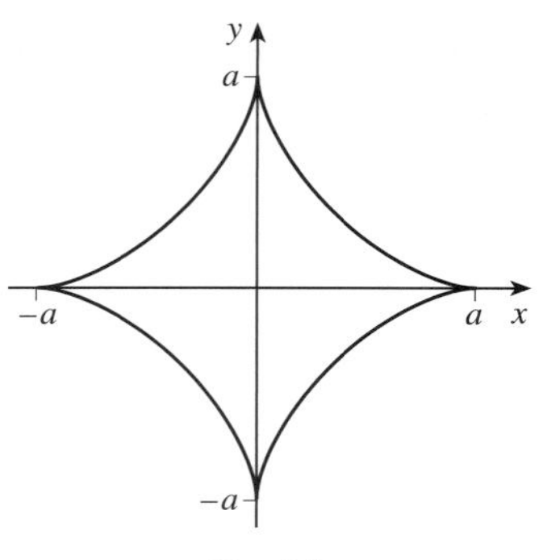

Fig. 3.4

The curve is shown in Fig. 3.4. Begin by calculating $\left(\frac{dx}{dt}\right)^2 + \left(\frac{dy}{dt}\right)^2$, which is

$$\left(-3a\cos^2 t\sin t\right)^2 + \left(3a\sin^2 t\cos t\right)^2.$$

This simplifies to

$$(3a\sin t\cos t)^2\left(\cos^2 t + \sin^2 t\right) = (3a\sin t\cos t)^2 = \left(\tfrac{3}{2}a\sin 2t\right)^2.$$

It is tempting to write $\sqrt{\left(\frac{dx}{dt}\right)^2 + \left(\frac{dy}{dt}\right)^2} = \frac{3}{2}a\sin 2t$, and to try to find the arc length as

$$\int_0^{2\pi} \tfrac{3}{2}a\sin 2t\,dt = \left[-\tfrac{3}{4}a\cos 2t\right]_0^{2\pi} = -\tfrac{3}{4}a(1-1) = 0.$$

The error is that the square root should be $\frac{3}{2}a|\sin 2t|$, and $|\sin 2t|$ is equal to $\sin 2t$ in the first and third quadrants, but $-\sin 2t$ in the second and fourth quadrants. But in this case it is simpler to use the symmetry of the curve about the axes, and to calculate the total arc length as 4 times the arc length in the first quadrant. This gives

$$4\int_0^{\frac{1}{2}\pi} \tfrac{3}{2}a\sin 2t\,dt = -3a[\cos 2t]_0^{\frac{1}{2}\pi} = -3a(-1-1) = 6a.$$

Exercise 3A

In Questions 1 to 3 you should begin by plotting the graph, using a calculator or a computer, before calculating the length of arc required.

1 Find the length of arc of the following curves between the specified points. As a check on your answers, compare the length of arc with the length of the chord joining the end-points.

(a) $y = \frac{1}{3}\sqrt{x}(3-x)$; $(0,0)$, $(3,0)$
(b) $y = \cosh x$; $(-2, \cosh 2)$, $(2, \cosh 2)$
(c) $y = \frac{1}{4}x^2 - \frac{1}{2}\ln x$; $\left(1, \frac{1}{4}\right)$, $\left(e, \frac{1}{4}e^2 - \frac{1}{2}\right)$
(d) $y = \ln\sec x$; $(0,0)$, $\left(\frac{1}{3}\pi, \ln 2\right)$
(e) $y = \frac{1}{4}x^2$; $(0,0)$, $(4,4)$
(f) $y = 2\sqrt{x}$; $(0,0)$, $(4,4)$
(g) $y = \frac{1}{2}x + \frac{1}{2}\sin x\cos x - \frac{1}{4}\tan x$; $(0,0)$, $\left(\frac{1}{4}\pi, \frac{1}{8}\pi\right)$
(h) $y = \ln\sin x$; $\left(\frac{1}{3}\pi, \frac{1}{2}\ln\frac{3}{4}\right)$, $\left(\frac{1}{2}\pi, 0\right)$

2 Find the length of arc of the following curves between the given values of the parameters.

(a) $x = t - \sin t\cos t$, $y = \cos^2 t$; $t = 0$, π
(b) $x = e^t\cos t$, $y = e^t\sin t$; $t = -\pi$, π
(c) $x = 3t^2$, $y = 2t^3$; $t = -1$, 1
(d) $x = t - \tanh t$, $y = \operatorname{sech} t$; $t = 0$, $\ln 2$
(e) $x = \dfrac{t^2+1}{t}$, $y = 2\ln t$; $t = 1, 2$

3 Find the length of arc of the following spiral curves between points with the given polar coordinates.

(a) $r=\theta^2$; $(0,0)$, $\left(4\pi^2,2\pi\right)$

(b) $r=\dfrac{\pi}{\theta}$; $(1,\pi)$, $\left(\frac{1}{5},5\pi\right)$

(c) $r=\mathrm{e}^{\frac{3}{4}\theta}$; $(1,0)$, $\left(\mathrm{e}^{\frac{3}{4}\pi},\pi\right)$

(d) $r=\dfrac{\theta}{\pi}$; $(0,0)$, $(4,4\pi)$

(e) $r=\mathrm{e}^{-\theta}$; $(1,0)$, $\left(\mathrm{e}^{-N},N\right)$ as $N\to\infty$

4 The diagram shows a power cable suspended between points A and B on two pylons at the same horizontal level, 0.2 km apart. Taking the origin at the lowest point of the cable, the equation of the cable is $y=\frac{1}{2}(\cosh 2x-1)$, the units being kilometres. Calculate by how much the length of the cable exceeds the distance between its ends.

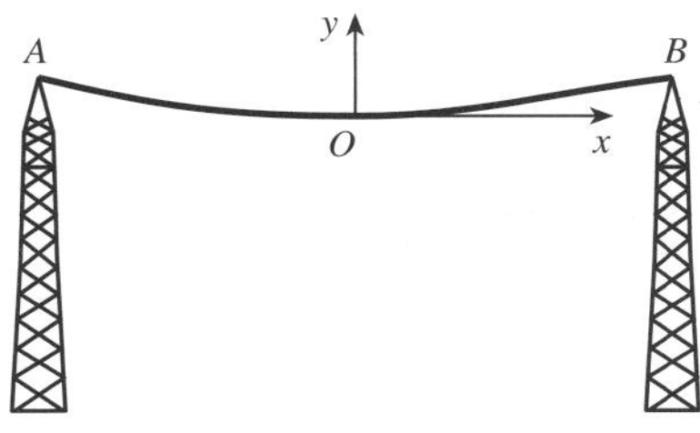

Find also by how much the cable sags below the level of the line AB.

5† Curves called *epicycloids* are formed as the locus of a point on a circle of radius 1 unit which rolls round the circumference of a fixed circle of radius n units, where n is an integer. Their equations are given by

$$x=(n+1)\cos t-\cos(n+1)t,\ y=(n+1)\sin t-\sin(n+1)t.$$

(a) Show that the complete epicycloid is described by taking values of t between 0 and 2π. Use a calculator or computer to plot the epicycloids for $n=1, 2, 3$ and 4.

(b) Show that the point of the rolling circle is at the point of contact with the fixed circle when $t=\dfrac{2r\pi}{n}$, where r is an integer. Hence show that there are n points on the epicycloid which also lie on the fixed circle. Describe the shape of the curve at these points.

(c) Find the length of arc of the epicycloid between two successive points which lie on the fixed circle. Deduce the ratio of the total length of the epicycloid to the circumference of the fixed circle, and find the limit of this ratio as $n\to\infty$.

6† The ellipse with cartesian equation $\dfrac{x^2}{a^2}+\dfrac{y^2}{b^2}=1$ is given by parametric equations $x=a\cos t,\ y=b\sin t$ for $0\leqslant t<2\pi$.

(a) Show that the length of the circumference of the ellipse $\frac{1}{2}x^2+y^2=1$ is equal to the length of arc of one complete oscillation of the graph of $y=\cos x$.

(b) Show that the total length of the curve $r=\cos 2\theta$ is equal to the length of the circumference of the ellipse $\frac{1}{4}x^2+y^2=1$.

(c) Find ellipses whose circumference is equal to the total length of the curves $r=\cos 3\theta$ and $r=\cos 4\theta$.

3.3 Surface area of a solid of revolution

Suppose now that the curve in Fig. 3.1 is rotated about the x-axis, so that it traces out the surface of a solid of revolution. Integration can also be used to calculate the area of this surface.

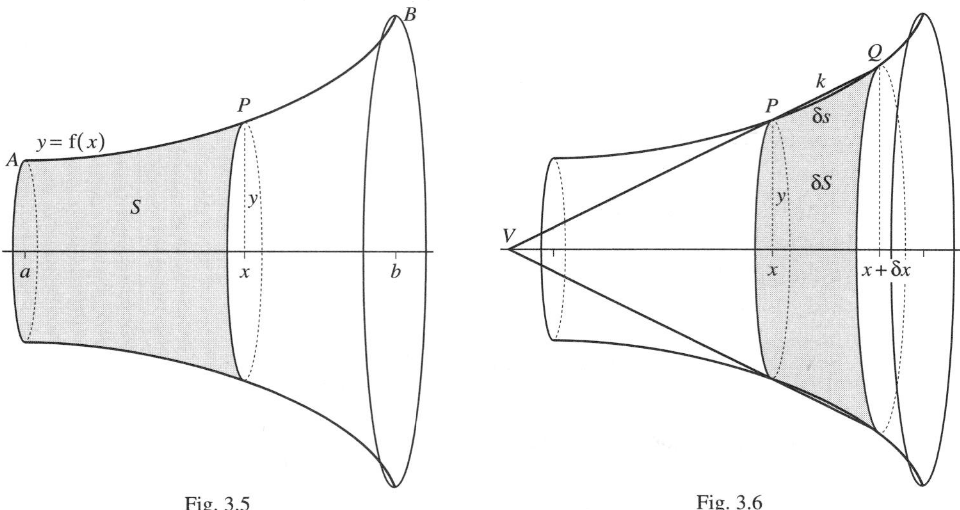

Fig. 3.5

Fig. 3.6

A plane perpendicular to the x-axis through the point P cuts this surface in a circle whose radius is the y-coordinate of P. In the usual way, let S denote the surface area (shown shaded in Fig. 3.5) from the plane through $x = a$ as far as this variable plane.

Fig. 3.6 shows δS as the part of the surface between the planes through P and Q, whose coordinates are (x, y) and $(x + \delta x, y + \delta y)$. Suppose now that the chord QP is produced to meet the x-axis at V. If the line VPQ is also rotated about the x-axis, it traces out the surface of a cone.

This cone has been drawn in Fig. 3.7. Let the part of the conical surface between the planes through P and Q, shown shaded, have area K. Then the calculation of the surface area S is based on the principle that, as δx tends to 0, the ratio of δS to K tends to 1.

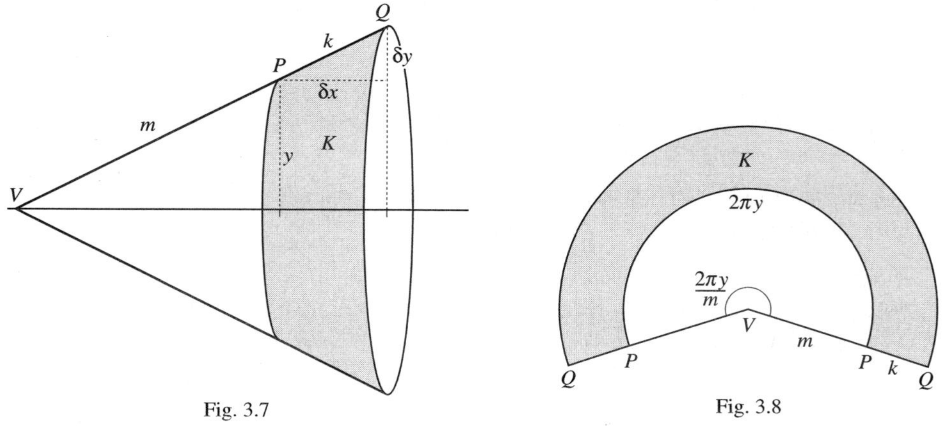

Fig. 3.7

Fig. 3.8

To calculate the area K, slit the conical surface along the line VPQ, and open it out flat. You then get Fig. 3.8 (which is not drawn to the same scale). If $VP = m$, then K is the area of the region between two circular arcs with radii m and $m + k$. The inner arc has length $2\pi y$, which is the circumference of the plane section through P in Fig. 3.6 and 3.7. So the angle of the sector in Fig. 3.8 is $\dfrac{2\pi y}{m}$.

Using the formula $\frac{1}{2}r^2\theta$ for the area of a sector,

$$\begin{aligned} K &= \tfrac{1}{2}(m+k)^2\frac{2\pi y}{m} - \tfrac{1}{2}m^2\frac{2\pi y}{m} \\ &= \frac{\pi y}{m}\left((m+k)^2 - m^2\right) = \frac{\pi y}{m}\left(2mk + k^2\right) \\ &= 2\pi yk\left(1 + \frac{k}{2m}\right). \end{aligned}$$

Everything is now set up to find the limit as $\delta x \to 0$. Write $\dfrac{\delta S}{\delta s}$ as $\dfrac{\delta S}{\delta s} = \dfrac{\delta S}{K} \times \dfrac{K}{k} \times \dfrac{k}{\delta s}$.

The first and last of these factors tend to 1. Also, $\dfrac{K}{k} = 2\pi y\left(1 + \dfrac{k}{2m}\right)$.

Now you can see from Fig. 3.7 that $\dfrac{k}{m} = \dfrac{\delta y}{y}$. As $\delta x \to 0$, $\delta y \to 0$, so $\dfrac{k}{m} \to 0$.

Therefore $\dfrac{K}{k} \to 2\pi y$, so $\dfrac{dS}{ds} = 2\pi y$.

From this you can get formulae for surface area in any system of coordinates. For example, for the cartesian equation $y = f(x)$,

$$\frac{dS}{dx} = \frac{dS}{ds} \times \frac{ds}{dx} = 2\pi y\sqrt{1 + \left(\frac{dy}{dx}\right)^2} = 2\pi f(x)\sqrt{1 + (f'(x))^2}.$$

The area of the surface formed by rotating a curve about the x-axis is found by applying the integral $\int 2\pi y\, ds$ in the appropriate coordinate system. That is, in cartesian, parametric and polar coordinates,

$$\int_a^b 2\pi y\sqrt{1 + \left(\frac{dy}{dx}\right)^2}\, dx,$$

$$\int_{t_A}^{t_B} 2\pi y\sqrt{\left(\frac{dx}{dt}\right)^2 + \left(\frac{dy}{dt}\right)^2}\, dt,$$

$$\int_\alpha^\beta 2\pi r\sin\theta\sqrt{r^2 + \left(\frac{dr}{d\theta}\right)^2}\, d\theta.$$

Example 3.3.1
Find the surface area of the solid formed by rotating the cardioid $r = 1 + \cos\theta$ about the initial line.

Notice that only the upper half of the curve is rotated to obtain the surface, so you must integrate from 0 to π, not from $-\pi$ to π.

Example 3.2.1 showed that $\sqrt{r^2 + \left(\frac{dr}{d\theta}\right)^2}$ is $2\cos\frac{1}{2}\theta$. The surface area is therefore

$$\int_0^{\pi} 2\pi(1+\cos\theta)\sin\theta \times 2\cos\tfrac{1}{2}\theta\,d\theta.$$

Expressing the whole integrand in terms of $\frac{1}{2}\theta$, this is

$$\int_0^{\pi} 2\pi \times 2\cos^2\tfrac{1}{2}\theta \times 2\sin\tfrac{1}{2}\theta\cos\tfrac{1}{2}\theta \times 2\cos\tfrac{1}{2}\theta\,d\theta = \int_0^{\pi} 16\pi\sin\tfrac{1}{2}\theta\cos^4\tfrac{1}{2}\theta\,d\theta.$$

This can be integrated using the substitution $u = \cos\frac{1}{2}\theta$, so that $\frac{du}{d\theta} = -\frac{1}{2}\sin\frac{1}{2}\theta$.

The integral is therefore

$$\int_0^{\pi} 16\pi \times \left(-2\frac{du}{d\theta}\right)u^4\,d\theta = \int_1^0 -32\pi u^4\,du = \int_0^1 32\pi u^4\,du$$
$$= \left[\tfrac{32}{5}\pi u^5\right]_0^1 = \tfrac{32}{5}\pi.$$

If a surface is formed by rotation about the y-axis, the same principles apply but the equation $\frac{dS}{ds} = 2\pi y$ is replaced by $\frac{dS}{ds} = 2\pi x$.

The area formed by rotating a surface about the y-axis is found by applying the integral $\int 2\pi x\,ds$ in the appropriate coordinate system.

Example 3.3.2
The curve $y = x^2$ from $(0,0)$ to $(1,1)$ is rotated about the y-axis. Find the area of the surface formed.

For a cartesian equation the integral takes the form

$$\int 2\pi x\frac{ds}{dx}\,dx = \int 2\pi x\sqrt{1+\left(\frac{dy}{dx}\right)^2}\,dx.$$

For this curve $\frac{dy}{dx} = 2x$, so the surface area is

$$\int_0^1 2\pi x\sqrt{1+4x^2}\,dx = \left[\tfrac{1}{6}\pi\left(1+4x^2\right)^{\frac{3}{2}}\right]_0^1 = \tfrac{1}{6}\pi\left(5\sqrt{5}-1\right).$$

Exercise 3B

1 Find the area of the surface generated by rotating the following curves between the given points about the given axis.

(a) $y = \frac{1}{3}\sqrt{x}(3-x)$ between $(0,0)$ and $(3,0)$ about the x-axis

(b) $y = 2\sqrt{x}$ between $(0,0)$ and $(4,4)$ about the x-axis

(c) $y = \frac{1}{4}x^2$ between $(0,0)$ and $(4,4)$ about the y-axis

(d) $y = \cosh x$ between $(-2, \cosh 2)$ and $(2, \cosh 2)$ about both axes

(e) $y = \dfrac{x^3+5}{5\sqrt{x}}$ between $(1, 1.2)$ and $(4, 6.9)$ about both axes

(f) $y = \sin x$ between $(0,0)$ and $(\pi, 0)$ about the x-axis

2 Find the area of the surface generated by rotating the following curves between the given parameter values about the given axes.

(a) $x = \sin t - t\cos t,\ y = \cos t + t\sin t$ between $t = 0$ and $t = \frac{1}{2}\pi$ about the x-axis

(b) $x = t - \frac{1}{5}t^5,\ y = \frac{2}{3}t^3$ between $t = 0$ and $t = 1$ about both axes

(c) $x = 3t^2,\ y = 2t^3$ between $t = 0$ and $t = 1$ about the y-axis

(d) $x = 5\cos t,\ y = 3\sin t$ between $t = 0$ and $t = \pi$ about the x-axis

(e) $x = \dfrac{t^2+1}{t},\ y = 2\ln t$ between $t = 1$ and $t = 2$ about both axes

3 Find the area of the surface generated by rotating the following curves between the given values of θ about the initial line $\theta = 0$.

(a) $r = a\operatorname{cosec}\theta$ between $\theta = \frac{1}{4}\pi$ and $\frac{1}{2}\pi$

(b) $r = a\sin\theta$ between $\theta = 0$ and π

(c) $r = e^{k\theta}$ between $\theta = 0$ and π

(d) $r = a\sin\alpha\sec(\theta - \alpha)$ between $\theta = 0$ and $\frac{1}{2}\pi$

4 A circle C has radius b and centre $(a, 0)$, where $a > b > 0$. A doughnut is formed by rotating C about the y-axis. By expressing the equation of C in parametric form, find the surface area of the doughnut.

5 An epicycloid with $n = 2$ (see Exercise 3A Question 5) is called a *nephroid*. Its equations are $x = 3\cos t - \cos 3t,\ y = 3\sin t - \sin 3t$.

Draw a sketch of the nephroid, and find the area of the surface formed by rotating it about (a) the x-axis, (b) the y-axis.

3.4 Integrals as limiting sums

You now know a lot of integral formulae for various geometrical measures, and there are many more. It is useful to have a method of writing down such formulae without starting the argument from scratch each time.

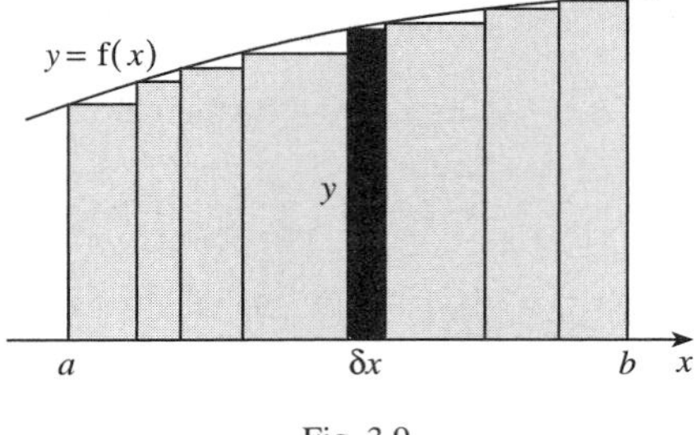

Fig. 3.9

Consider the area under a curve. If you didn't know about the anti-differentiation method, you might try to find such areas as the sum of the areas of a lot of thin rectangles, as illustrated by the shaded regions in Fig. 3.9. A typical rectangle has been blacked in; it has height y (for that particular value of x) and width a small bit of the x-axis, which you can denote by δx. Then the area of this typical rectangle would be $y \times \delta x$, and the total area of all the rectangles can be written as $\sum y\,\delta x$.

This would not of course give you the area exactly, because of the small near-triangular bits that don't fit in. But you could argue that, if the number of rectangles were increased indefinitely, and the width of every rectangle correspondingly decreased, then in the limit the sum would tend to the required area. Symbolically, you could write

$$\lim \sum y\,\delta x = \int_a^b y\,\mathrm{d}x.$$

The essential feature of the argument is that the bits that were left out were very small compared with the whole, and that they can be made as small as you like by making the widths of the rectangles small enough.

This is the basis of the **summation principle**, which can be applied to many calculations other than areas.

> If an interval of the x-axis $a < x < b$ is split into a large number of small pieces, of which a typical one has width δx, and if a quantity can be expressed approximately as a sum $\sum \mathrm{f}(x)\delta x$, where the size of the error tends to zero as the widths of the rectangles tend to 0, then in the limit the sum $\sum \mathrm{f}(x)\delta x$ tends to the integral $\int_a^b \mathrm{f}(x)\,\mathrm{d}x$.

As a second example, take the volume of a solid such as a loaf of bread. If you slice this up and trim the crusts off square, then you get a situation like Fig. 3.9 but in three dimensions. A typical slice has area A (which is a function of x) and thickness δx, so its volume is $A\delta x$. The total volume is then $\sum A\delta x$. The thinner you slice the bread, the less crust would be wasted, and in the limit the total volume of the slices tends to $\int_a^b A\,\mathrm{d}x$. For the special case of a solid of revolution, for which $A = \pi y^2$, you get the familiar formula $\int_a^b \pi y^2\,\mathrm{d}x$ for the volume.

You can also apply this argument to the surface area integral in Section 3.3, though in this case you can't directly identify the bits left over. However, in Fig. 3.6 it is reasonable to conjecture that the area δS of the shaded portion of the surface is approximately equal to the circumference of the cross-section through P multiplied by the arc length δs. The closer Q is to P, the better the approximation is. So the surface area can be written as $\sum 2\pi y\,\delta s$, and in the limit this tends to the integral $\int 2\pi y\,\mathrm{d}s$ over the interval $a < x < b$.

Here are two further examples of applications of the summation principle.

Example 3.4.1
The density of air decreases with increasing height above the earth. If the density ρ kg m^{-3} at a height of h metres is modelled by the equation $\rho = \rho_0 \mathrm{e}^{-kh}$, where ρ_0 kg m^{-3} is the density of air at sea level and k is a constant, calculate the atmospheric pressure at sea level.

Consider a column of air above a patch of earth of area $1\ \mathrm{m}^2$. A small slice of the atmosphere of thickness δh metres at a height h metres would have a volume of $1 \times \delta h\ \mathrm{m}^3$, so its mass would be $\rho\,\delta h$ kg. The total mass of the column of air could then be written as $\sum \rho\,\delta h$ kg approximately. In the limit, taking thinner and thinner slices, this sum would tend to

$$\int_0^\infty \rho\,\mathrm{d}h = \int_0^\infty \rho_0 \mathrm{e}^{-kh}\,\mathrm{d}h = \left[-\frac{\rho_0}{k}\mathrm{e}^{-kh}\right]_0^\infty = \frac{\rho_0}{k}.$$

Atmospheric pressure is due to the weight of the column of air, which is found by multiplying the mass by g, the acceleration of gravity. So this model gives the value of atmospheric pressure as $\frac{g\rho_0}{k}$ N m^{-2}.

The density of air at the top of Everest (8000 m) is often quoted as being about one-third of ρ_0, the sea-level density. This gives $\mathrm{e}^{-8000k} \approx \frac{1}{3}$, or $k \approx \frac{1}{8000}\ln 3 \approx 1.4 \times 10^{-4}$. Approximate values for g and ρ_0 are 9.8 and 1.2 respectively, which gives a value of about 8.4×10^4 N m^{-2} for the atmospheric pressure. This is about 15% below the true value, which suggests that the model is not a bad first approximation.

This calculation does not take account of the curvature of the earth or the variation of the value of g with height, but these have a minor effect.

Example 3.4.2
A new town is being planned. It is to be circular in shape, with a radius of 4 km, and it is proposed that at a distance of r km from the centre the population density should be $50r^2(5-r)$ people per km^2. What is the planned total population of the town?

The town is illustrated by Fig. 3.10. The shaded strip is a region which houses all the people who live between r km and $(r+\delta r)$ km from the centre. The area of this region is approximately equal to the circumference times the width of the strip, which is $2\pi r\,\delta r$ km^2, so the number of people living in this strip should be $50r^2(5-r) \times 2\pi r\,\delta r$. The total population would then be approximately $\sum 100\pi r^3(5-r)\,\delta r$.

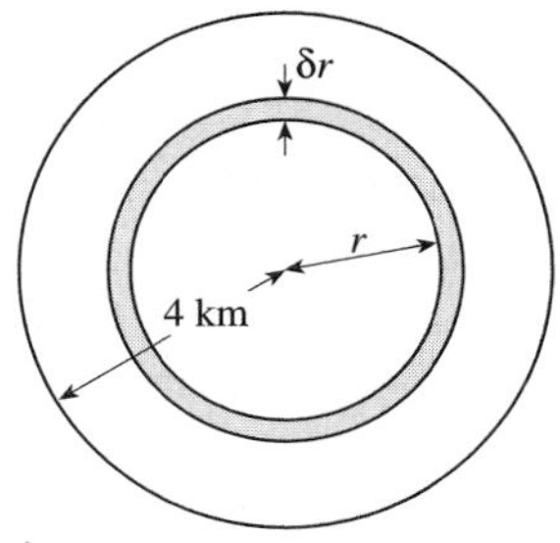

Fig. 3.10

Taking the limit as the widths of the strips tend to 0, this is

$$\int_0^4 \pi\left(500r^3 - 100r^4\right)dr = \left[\pi\left(125r^4 - 20r^5\right)\right]_0^4 = \pi(125\times 256 - 20\times 1024)$$
$$= 11\,520\pi, \quad \text{about 36 000 people.}$$

Exercise 3C

1 A colony of ants occupies a branch AB of length 2 metres. They are most densely concentrated near the end A so that at a distance x metres from A the density of the insects is $1000(5-2x)$ ants per metre. Calculate the total number of ants on the branch, and the average distance of an ant from A.

2 A motorway joins two towns A and B which are 100 km apart. The traffic density at a point P on the motorway is modelled by the formula $\frac{1}{25}\left(x^2 - 120x + 4000\right)$ vehicles per km, where x km is the distance of P from A. What proportion of all the traffic on the motorway is within 10 km of either A or B?

3 A closed curve drawn on a horizontal plane encloses a region of area A, and K is a point at a height h above the plane. A pyramid is formed by joining K to points on the curve by straight line segments. A horizontal plane distance x below K (where $x < h$) cuts the pyramid in a curve X. Explain why X encloses an area of $\dfrac{x^2}{h^2}A$, and deduce a formula involving A and h for the volume enclosed by the pyramid.

A sphere of radius r has surface area S and encloses a volume V. By splitting the interior of the sphere into a large number of small near-pyramids, show that $V = \frac{1}{3}Sr$.

4 On a small island the contour for points at a height h metres above sea level has equation $\left(x - \frac{2}{5}h\right)^2 + y^2 = 100(100-h)$ for $0 \leqslant h \leqslant 100$, the units of coordinates being metres.

Sketch a contour map of the island, and find the volume of the part above sea level.

5 In Example 3.4.2, find the mean distance of an inhabitant of the town from the centre.

6 A predatory animal controls a territory whose shape is a circle of radius a. When hunting it is equally likely to be found anywhere within this territory. Write down the probability that it will be in a ring at a distance between r and $r+\delta r$ from the centre, and deduce the mean distance of the animal from the centre during its hunting trips.

Calculate the probability that it will be found closer to the centre than this mean distance.

7 Taking the earth to be a sphere of radius R metres, and using the model $\rho = \rho_0 e^{-kh}$ given in Example 3.4.1 for the density of air at a height h metres above the earth's surface, write as an integral an expression for the total mass of the earth's atmosphere. Evaluate this, taking $R \approx 6.4\times 10^6$ and using the values for ρ_0 and k given in the example.

8 Two tunnels with a common horizontal floor level have the shape of semicircular cylinders of radius 3 m. The tunnels intersect at right angles. Draw the horizontal cross-section of the two tunnels at a height x m above the floor (where $0 \leqslant x \leqslant 3$), and find the area at this level common to the two tunnels. Hence find the volume of the space at the crossing which is common to both tunnels.

9 A heavy uniform strip of elastic XY has length l and weight W. It is first placed on a horizontal table with the end X nailed to the table. When a force F is applied to the end Y along the line of the elastic, it is found that the elastic stretches by a length kF.

When the elastic is unstretched, two points P and Q on the elastic are at distances x and $x+\delta x$ from Y. The end X of the elastic is now fixed to a point on the ceiling, and it hangs vertically under its own weight with Y below X. Show that the portion PQ is then stretched by an amount $\dfrac{kWx\,\delta x}{l^2}$. Hence find by what length the whole strip stretches.

Miscellaneous exercise 3

1 Show that the length L of the arc of the curve $y^2=4x$ joining the points $(0,0)$ and $(1,2)$ is given by $L=\displaystyle\int_0^1 \sqrt{\frac{1+x}{x}}\,dx$. By using the substitution $x=\sinh^2 u$, show that $L=\sinh^{-1}1+\sqrt{2}$. (OCR)

2 Show that the length of the arc of the parabola $x=at^2$, $y=2at$ from the origin to the point $(a,2a)$ is approximately $2.3a$. (OCR)

3 The parametric equations of a curve are $x=a(t-\sin t)$, $y=a(1-\cos t)$, where a is a positive constant. The arc of this curve between $t=0$ and $t=2\pi$ is rotated completely about the x-axis. Show that the area of the surface of revolution formed is

$$8\pi a^2\int_0^{2\pi}\left(1-\cos^2\left(\tfrac{1}{2}t\right)\right)\sin\left(\tfrac{1}{2}t\right)dt,$$

and hence find this area. (This curve is called a *cycloid*.) (OCR)

4 The 'bell' of a brass instrument is formed by rotating the arc of the parabola $x=at^2, y=2at$ from $t=1$ to $t=3$ about the y-axis. Find the surface area of the bell. (OCR)

5 A curve is defined parametrically by $x=\frac{8}{3}t^{\frac{3}{2}}, y=t^2-2t+4$. The points A and B on the curve are defined by $t=0$ and $t=1$ respectively.

(a) Find the length of the arc AB.

(b) Show that the area of the surface generated by one complete revolution of the arc AB about the y-axis is $\frac{256}{35}\pi$. (OCR)

6 A curve is defined by the parametric equations $x=e^{\theta}\cos\theta$, $y=e^{\theta}\sin\theta$ where $0\leqslant\theta\leqslant\pi$ and θ has its usual meaning in polar coordinates. Show that the gradient at the point P with parameter θ is $\tan\left(\theta+\frac{1}{4}\pi\right)$, and hence that the gradient angle is always $\frac{1}{4}\pi$ greater than θ. Sketch the curve.

The curve is rotated through 2π radians about the x-axis to form a heart-shaped surface. Show that the area of the surface is approximately 950 square units. (OCR)

7 Part of the graph of a curve with equation $y=f(x)$ has length l, and when rotated about the x-axis it generates a surface of area S. Show that, when the part of the graph of $y=f(x)+k$ between the same values of x is rotated about the x-axis, it generates a surface of area $S+2\pi kl$.

8 A glass vessel has the shape of a volume of revolution obtained by rotating the region defined by $y \geqslant x^2$, $0 \leqslant y \leqslant \frac{1}{2}$, about the y-axis through two right angles, where the units are metres. The vessel contains the vapour of a chemical, the density of which at height y metres above the base of the vessel is $2\sqrt{1-2y}$ grams per metre^3. By considering the mass of vapour in a layer between heights y and $y+\delta y$ metres, show that the total mass of vapour in the vessel is $\int_0^{\frac{1}{2}} 2\pi y\sqrt{1-2y}\,\mathrm{d}y$ grams. Evaluate this integral, giving your answer as a rational multiple of π. (OCR)

9† An ellipse has parametric equations $x = a\cos t$, $y = b\sin t$ for $0 \leqslant y \leqslant 2\pi$ where $a > b > 0$.

Show that its perimeter is given by the integral $\int_0^{2\pi} \sqrt{\frac{a^2+b^2}{2} - \frac{a^2-b^2}{2}\cos 2t}\,\mathrm{d}t$.

Hence show that, if the ellipse is close to circular, the perimeter is approximately equal to

$$2\pi\sqrt{\frac{a^2+b^2}{2}}\left(1 - \frac{1}{16}\left(\frac{a^2-b^2}{a^2+b^2}\right)^2 - \frac{15}{1024}\left(\frac{a^2-b^2}{a^2+b^2}\right)^4\right).$$

For approximately what range of values of the ratio $\frac{a}{b}$ is the perimeter given by the formula $2\pi\sqrt{\frac{a^2+b^2}{2}}$ with accuracy within 1%?

10 The points P and Q on the circle $r = a$ have polar coordinates (a, α) and (a, β), with $-\frac{1}{2}\pi \leqslant \alpha \leqslant \beta \leqslant \frac{1}{2}\pi$. The arc PQ is rotated about the line $\theta = \frac{1}{2}\pi$ through a complete revolution. Find an expression for the area of the surface generated.

A globe showing a map of the world is enclosed inside a paper cylinder, touching it at the equator. The planes of the circles of latitude α and β are extended to cut the cylinder in a pair of circles. Show that the area of the surface of the globe between these latitudes is equal to the area cut off on the cylinder. (A figure showing a sphere and a cylinder was carved on the tombstone of Archimedes to commemorate his discovery of this result.)

Explain how this can be used to produce a map of the world on a flat sheet of paper in which areas of different countries are shown in their correct proportions.

11† For many curves the length of arc cannot be calculated exactly because the integral cannot be found as an algebraic formula. But you can find an approximation in one of two ways:

- approximate to the length of arc by the length of a chain of chords;
- express the length of arc as a definite integral, and evaluate this approximately by the trapezium rule.

Investigate the relative merits of these two methods by finding approximations to the length of arc of the following curves. You are given the true values for comparison, correct to 3 significant figures.

(a) $y = x^3$ between $(0,0)$ and $(2,8)$; true value ≈ 8.63

(b) $y = \frac{1}{x}$ between $(1,1)$ and $(5,0.2)$; true value ≈ 4.15

(c) $x = \cos t$, $y = \sin 2t$ between $t = -\frac{1}{2}\pi$ and $t = \frac{1}{2}\pi$; true value ≈ 4.71

(d) $r = 2 + \cos\theta$ from $\theta = -\pi$ to $\theta = \pi$; true value ≈ 13.4

4 Reduction formulae

This chapter deals with a particular type of integral in which an expression in the integrand is raised to a power n. When you have completed it, you should

- be able to find reduction formulae for such integrals
- know various ways in which the integrand can be manipulated so as to get the integral into the form required.

4.1 Straightforward examples

Most of the integrals in this chapter will be found using the rule for integration by parts

$$\int u\frac{dv}{dx}\,dx = uv - \int \frac{du}{dx}v\,dx$$

for either indefinite or definite integrals (see P3 Section 8.2).

Example 4.1.1

Find (a) $\int_1^e x^n \ln x\,dx$, (b) $\int_1^e x(\ln x)^n\,dx$.

It is easier to differentiate $\ln x$ and $(\ln x)^n$ than to integrate them, so in both integrals take the factor involving $\ln x$ as u.

$$\text{(a)}\quad \int_1^e \ln x \times x^n\,dx = \left[\ln x \times \frac{1}{n+1}x^{n+1}\right]_1^e - \int_1^e \frac{1}{x}\times\frac{1}{n+1}x^{n+1}\,dx$$

$$= 1\times\frac{1}{n+1}e^{n+1} - \int_1^e \frac{1}{n+1}x^n\,dx$$

$$= \frac{1}{n+1}e^{n+1} - \left[\left(\frac{1}{n+1}\right)^2 x^{n+1}\right]_1^e$$

$$= \frac{1}{n+1}e^{n+1} - \left(\frac{1}{n+1}\right)^2\left(e^{n+1}-1\right)$$

$$= \frac{1}{(n+1)^2}\left((n+1-1)e^{n+1}+1\right)$$

$$= \frac{1}{(n+1)^2}\left(ne^{n+1}+1\right).$$

$$\text{(b)}\quad \int_1^e (\ln x)^n \times x\,dx = \left[(\ln x)^n \times \tfrac{1}{2}x^2\right]_1^e - \int_1^e n(\ln x)^{n-1}\frac{1}{x}\times\tfrac{1}{2}x^2\,dx$$

$$= 1^n \times \tfrac{1}{2}e^2 - 0^n \times \tfrac{1}{2}1^2 - \int_1^e \tfrac{1}{2}n(\ln x)^{n-1}\times x\,dx$$

$$= \tfrac{1}{2}e^2 - \tfrac{1}{2}n\int_1^e (\ln x)^{n-1}\times x\,dx.$$

You can see that the first integral in this example can be found directly as a formula involving n, but the second has only been found in terms of a similar integral with $n-1$ in place of n. If the integral $\int_1^e (\ln x)^n \times x\,dx$ is denoted by I_n, then it has been shown that

$$I_n = \tfrac{1}{2}e^2 - \tfrac{1}{2}n\,I_{n-1}.$$

A formula like this is called a **reduction formula**. If you can find the integral for some particular value of n, then you can use the formula to find the integral for other values of n.

In this example it is very easy to find

$$I_0 = \int_1^e (\ln x)^0 \times x\,dx = \int_1^e x\,dx = \left[\tfrac{1}{2}x^2\right]_1^e = \tfrac{1}{2}\left(e^2 - 1\right).$$

From this you can use the reduction formula with n equal to 1, 2, 3, ... in turn to find

$$I_1 = \tfrac{1}{2}e^2 - \tfrac{1}{2}I_0 = \tfrac{1}{2}e^2 - \tfrac{1}{4}\left(e^2 - 1\right) = \tfrac{1}{4}\left(e^2 + 1\right),$$
$$I_2 = \tfrac{1}{2}e^2 - \tfrac{2}{2}I_1 = \tfrac{1}{2}e^2 - \tfrac{1}{4}\left(e^2 + 1\right) = \tfrac{1}{4}\left(e^2 - 1\right),$$
$$I_3 = \tfrac{1}{2}e^2 - \tfrac{3}{2}I_2 = \tfrac{1}{2}e^2 - \tfrac{3}{8}\left(e^2 - 1\right) = \tfrac{1}{8}\left(e^2 + 3\right),$$

and so on.

If you go on in this way, you obtain a formula for I_n, as

$$I_n = (-1)^n \frac{n!}{2^{n+1}}\left(e^2\left(1 - \frac{2}{1!} + \frac{2^2}{2!} - \ldots + \frac{(-1)^n 2^n}{n!}\right) - 1\right).$$

You can check for yourself that this gives the right answers for $n = 1, 2, 3,$ and use mathematical induction to prove the general result.

It is also important to ask for which values of n the reduction formula is valid. Since the calculation in (b) involves a term with a factor 0^n, it can only work if $n > 0$. There is nothing in the working to require that n is an integer; but since the only value of n for which you can work out I_n independently is $n = 0$, the reduction formula is only useful if n is a positive integer. (Notice that if $0 < n < 1$ the integrand in I_{n-1} tends to infinity as $x \to 1$; but that does not prevent the integral from having a finite value.)

On the other hand, the integral in (a) is valid for any value of n except -1; it can be positive or negative, and need not be an integer.

For the next example you do not need integration by parts.

Example 4.1.2

Find $\int \tan^n x\,dx$, where n is a positive integer.

You can reduce the index n in this integral by writing $\tan^n x$ as $\tan^{n-2} x \tan^2 x$, and using the identity $\tan^2 x \equiv \sec^2 x - 1$.

$$\int \tan^n x\,dx = \int \tan^{n-2} x\left(\sec^2 x - 1\right)dx = \int \tan^{n-2} x \sec^2 x\,dx - \int \tan^{n-2} x\,dx.$$

Now since $\frac{\mathrm{d}}{\mathrm{d}x}\tan x = \sec^2 x$, the first integral can be written down directly (or if you prefer by using the substitution $t = \tan x$). Writing $\int \tan^n x\,\mathrm{d}x$ as I_n,

$$I_n = \frac{1}{n-1}\tan^{n-1} x - I_{n-2}.$$

In this reduction formula the index n goes down by 2, to $n-2$ rather than $n-1$. If you apply it repeatedly, you will eventually get down to I_0 if n is even, or to I_1 if n is odd. These can both be found:

$$I_0 = \int \tan^0 x\,\mathrm{d}x = \int 1\,\mathrm{d}x = x + k,$$

$$I_1 = \int \tan x\,\mathrm{d}x = \ln|\sec x| + k.$$

From this you can find in succession

$$I_2 = \tan x - I_0 = \tan x - x - k,$$

$$I_3 = \tfrac{1}{2}\tan^2 x - I_1 = \tfrac{1}{2}\tan^2 x - \ln|\sec x| - k,$$

$$I_4 = \tfrac{1}{3}\tan^3 x - I_2 = \tfrac{1}{3}\tan^3 x - \tan x + x + k,$$

$$I_5 = \tfrac{1}{4}\tan^4 x - I_3 = \tfrac{1}{4}\tan^4 x - \tfrac{1}{2}\tan^2 x + \ln|\sec x| + k,$$

and so on.

Exercise 4A

1 If I_n denotes $\int \tanh^n x\,\mathrm{d}x$, prove that $I_n = I_{n-2} - \frac{1}{n-1}\tanh^{n-1} x$ (unless $n=1$). Hence find

(a) $\int \tanh^5 x\,\mathrm{d}x$, (b) $\int \tanh^6 x\,\mathrm{d}x$.

2 If I_n denotes $\int_{\frac{1}{4}\pi}^{\frac{1}{2}\pi} \cot^n \theta\,\mathrm{d}\theta$, find and use a reduction formula to obtain expressions for

(a) I_7, (b) I_8.

Give a reason why $I_8 < I_7$, and verify numerically that your answers to (a) and (b) satisfy this inequality.

3 If I_n denotes $\int_1^{\mathrm{e}} (\ln x)^n\,\mathrm{d}x$, prove that $I_n = \mathrm{e} - nI_{n-1}$. Hence find $\int_1^{\mathrm{e}} (\ln x)^4\,\mathrm{d}x$.

4 Find and use a reduction formula to evaluate $\int_0^1 (1-x)^5 \mathrm{e}^x\,\mathrm{d}x$.

By considering the function $\mathrm{f}(x) = (1-x)^5\mathrm{e}^x$ over the interval $0 < x < 1$, prove that the value of this integral lies between 0 and 1. Hence show that $\mathrm{e} \approx 2.72$.

5 If I_n denotes $\int_0^{\infty} t^n e^{-at}\,dt$, where a is a positive constant, prove that $aI_n = nI_{n-1}$ provided that $n > 0$. Use the method of mathematical induction to deduce that, if n is a positive integer, $I_n = \dfrac{n!}{a^{n+1}}$.

6 Let I_n denote $\int_{-\infty}^{\infty} x^n \phi(x)\,dx$, where $\phi(x)$ is the normal probability function given by $\phi(x) = \dfrac{1}{\sqrt{2\pi}} e^{-\frac{1}{2}x^2}$. By splitting up the integrand as the product of x^{n-1} and $x\phi(x)$, establish the reduction formula $I_n = (n-1)I_{n-2}$ provided that $n > 1$.
Given that $I_0 = 1$, find an expression for I_n for any positive integer n.

7 If C_n denotes $\int_0^{\pi} x^n \cos x\,dx$, and S_n denotes $\int_0^{\pi} x^n \sin x\,dx$, find expressions for C_n and S_n in terms of S_{n-1} and C_{n-1} and state the values of n for which these are valid.

Hence find $\int_0^{\pi} x^5 \sin x\,dx$.

4.2 Algebraic and trigonometric techniques

Often an application of integration by parts is not enough by itself, but a reduction formula can be found by using an algebraic or trigonometric identity.

Example 4.2.1
Use a reduction formula to find (a) $\int \left(1+x^2\right)^{\frac{3}{2}} dx$, (b) $\int \dfrac{1}{\left(1+x^2\right)^3} dx$.

Both of these integrals are of the form $\int \left(1+x^2\right)^n dx$.

Writing the integrand as $\left(1+x^2\right)^n \times 1$ and integrating by parts,

$$\begin{aligned}\int \left(1+x^2\right)^n dx &= \left(1+x^2\right)^n \times x - \int \left(n\left(1+x^2\right)^{n-1} \times 2x\right) \times x\,dx \\ &= x\left(1+x^2\right)^n - 2n\int x^2\left(1+x^2\right)^{n-1} dx.\end{aligned}$$

The integral in the second term is not yet in the required form. But if you replace x^2 by $\left(1+x^2\right)-1$, it can be written as

$$\int \left(\left(1+x^2\right)-1\right)\left(1+x^2\right)^{n-1} dx = \int \left(1+x^2\right)^n dx - \int \left(1+x^2\right)^{n-1} dx.$$

Therefore, denoting $\int \left(1+x^2\right)^n dx$ by I_n, $I_n = x\left(1+x^2\right)^n - 2n(I_n - I_{n-1})$, which can be rearranged as

$$(2n+1)I_n = x\left(1+x^2\right)^n + 2nI_{n-1}.$$

In this reduction formula n can be any number, positive or negative, integer or non-integer.

(a) This is $I_{\frac{3}{2}}$. The reduction formula with $n=\frac{3}{2}$ and $n=\frac{1}{2}$ gives

$$4I_{\frac{3}{2}} = x(1+x^2)^{\frac{3}{2}} + 3I_{\frac{1}{2}} \quad \text{and} \quad 2I_{\frac{1}{2}} = x(1+x^2)^{\frac{1}{2}} + I_{-\frac{1}{2}}.$$

These can be combined to give

$$\begin{aligned} I_{\frac{3}{2}} &= \tfrac{1}{4}x(1+x^2)^{\frac{3}{2}} + \tfrac{3}{4}\left(\tfrac{1}{2}x(1+x^2)^{\frac{1}{2}} + \tfrac{1}{2}I_{-\frac{1}{2}}\right) \\ &= \tfrac{1}{4}x(1+x^2)^{\frac{3}{2}} + \tfrac{3}{8}x(1+x^2)^{\frac{1}{2}} + \tfrac{3}{8}I_{-\frac{1}{2}}. \end{aligned}$$

Now $I_{-\frac{1}{2}}$ is $\displaystyle\int \frac{1}{\sqrt{1+x^2}}\,dx$, which is $\sinh^{-1} x$. Also, the first two terms can be combined by taking out the common factors $\frac{1}{8}x(1+x^2)^{\frac{1}{2}}$. Then

$$\begin{aligned} I_{\frac{3}{2}} &= \tfrac{1}{8}x(1+x^2)^{\frac{1}{2}}\left(2(1+x^2)+3\right) + \tfrac{3}{8}\sinh^{-1} x + k \\ &= \tfrac{1}{8}x(2x^2+5)(1+x^2)^{\frac{1}{2}} + \tfrac{3}{8}\sinh^{-1} x + k. \end{aligned}$$

(b) This is I_{-3}. But if you begin in the usual way by taking n to be -3 in the reduction formula, the integral I_{n-1} on the right is I_{-4}. This goes in the wrong direction, since the aim is to get to I_{-1}, which you know how to integrate. So begin by rearranging the reduction formula as

$$2nI_{n-1} = (2n+1)I_n - x(1+x^2)^n$$

and use this with $n=-2$ and $n=-1$ to obtain

$$-4I_{-3} = -3I_{-2} - x(1+x^2)^{-2} \quad \text{and} \quad -2I_{-2} = -I_{-1} - x(1+x^2)^{-1}.$$

Combining these, you get

$$\begin{aligned} I_{-3} &= \tfrac{3}{4}\left(\tfrac{1}{2}\left(I_{-1} + x(1+x^2)^{-1}\right)\right) + \tfrac{1}{4}x(1+x^2)^{-2} \\ &= \tfrac{3}{8}I_{-1} + \tfrac{3}{8}x(1+x^2)^{-1} + \tfrac{1}{4}x(1+x^2)^{-2}. \end{aligned}$$

Now I_{-1} is $\displaystyle\int \frac{1}{1+x^2}\,dx$, which is $\tan^{-1} x$. So, combining the last two terms,

$$\begin{aligned} I_{-3} &= \tfrac{3}{8}\tan^{-1} x + \tfrac{1}{8}x(1+x^2)^{-2}\left(3(1+x^2)+2\right) + k \\ &= \tfrac{3}{8}\tan^{-1} x + \frac{x(5+3x^2)}{8(1+x^2)^2} + k. \end{aligned}$$

Example 4.2.2

Find $\int_0^{\pi} \sin^n x \, dx$, where n is a positive integer greater than 1.

The trick here is to begin by writing $\sin^n x$ as $\sin^{n-1} x \sin x$. Then $\frac{dv}{dx} = \sin x$, so that $v = -\cos x$.

$$\int_0^{\pi} \sin^n x \, dx = \left[\sin^{n-1} x \times (-\cos x)\right]_0^{\pi} - \int_0^{\pi} (n-1)\sin^{n-2} x \cos x \times (-\cos x)\, dx.$$

Since $n > 1$, $\sin^{n-1} \pi$ and $\sin^{n-1} 0$ are both 0, so that

$$\int_0^{\pi} \sin^n x \, dx = (n-1)\int_0^{\pi} \sin^{n-2} x \cos^2 x \, dx.$$

This is not yet in the form you want, but you can write $\cos^2 x$ as $1 - \sin^2 x$ to get

$$\int_0^{\pi} \sin^n x \, dx = (n-1)\int_0^{\pi} \sin^{n-2} x\left(1 - \sin^2 x\right) dx.$$

Therefore, denoting $\int_0^{\pi} \sin^n x \, dx$ by I_n, $I_n = (n-1)(I_{n-2} - I_n)$,
which you can rearrange to give $nI_n = (n-1)I_{n-2}$.

Using this repeatedly, with $n-2, n-4, \ldots$ in place of n,

$$I_n = \frac{n-1}{n} I_{n-2} = \frac{n-1}{n} \times \frac{n-3}{n-2} I_{n-4} = \frac{n-1}{n} \times \frac{n-3}{n-2} \times \frac{n-5}{n-4} I_{n-6} = \ldots.$$

Since this formula reduces the index by 2 each time, repeated application will reduce it to 0 if n is even and to 1 if n is odd. It is easy to evaluate

$$I_0 = \int_0^{\pi} \sin^0 x \, dx = \int_0^{\pi} 1 \, dx = [x]_0^{\pi} = \pi,$$

and $$I_1 = \int_0^{\pi} \sin^1 x \, dx = \int_0^{\pi} \sin x \, dx = [-\cos x]_0^{\pi} = 1 - (-1) = 2.$$

Therefore, if n is even,

$$\begin{aligned} I_n &= \frac{n-1}{n} \times \frac{n-3}{n-2} \times \frac{n-5}{n-4} \times \ldots \times \frac{1}{2} I_0 \\ &= \frac{(n-1)(n-3)(n-5)\ldots 1}{n(n-2)(n-4)\ldots 2}\pi, \end{aligned}$$

and if n is odd,

$$\begin{aligned} I_n &= \frac{n-1}{n} \times \frac{n-3}{n-2} \times \frac{n-5}{n-4} \times \ldots \times \frac{2}{3} I_1 \\ &= \frac{(n-1)(n-3)(n-5)\ldots 2}{n(n-2)(n-4)\ldots 3} \times 2. \end{aligned}$$

Exercise 4B

1 If I_n denotes $\int_0^1 \frac{x^n}{\sqrt{1+3x}}\,dx$, show that $3(2n+1)I_n = 4 - 2nI_{n-1}$ for $n > 0$. Use this to evaluate $\int_0^1 \frac{x^3}{\sqrt{1+3x}}\,dx$.

2 Find and use reduction formulae to evaluate (a) $\int_0^{\frac{1}{3}\pi} \cos^6 u\,du$, (b) $\int_0^{\ln 2} \sinh^4 u\,du$.

Check your answer to part (b) by expressing $\sinh u$ in exponential form before integrating.

3 Find and use a reduction formula to evaluate (a) $\int_0^1 \frac{1}{(4-x^2)^3}\,dx$, (b) $\int_0^1 \frac{1}{(4-x^2)^{\frac{7}{2}}}\,dx$.

4 If I_n denotes $\int_0^\infty \frac{1}{(1+x^2)^n}\,dx$, prove that $2nI_{n+1} = (2n-1)I_n$, and state the values of n for which this reduction formula is valid. Hence find a formula for I_n if

(a) n is a positive integer, (b) $n = m + \frac{1}{2}$ where m is a positive integer.

5 If I_n denotes $\int_0^{\frac{1}{2}\pi} e^x \cos^n x\,dx$, show that $(n^2+1)I_n = n(n-1)I_{n-2} - 1$, and state the values of n for which the reduction formula is valid. Find I_0 and I_1, and deduce I_2 and I_3.

6 Find $\int_0^5 \frac{x^3}{\sqrt{4+x}}\,dx$, (a) using a reduction formula, (b) using the substitution $4 + x = u$.

7 Let I_n denote the indefinite integral $\int \sec^n x\,dx$. By writing $\sec^n x$ as $\sec^{n-2} x \sec^2 x$ prove that $(n-1)I_n = \sec^{n-2} x \tan x + (n-2)I_{n-2}$. Hence find $\int \sec^3 x\,dx$, $\int \sec^4 x\,dx$ and $\int \sec^5 x\,dx$. Verify your answers by differentiation.

Miscellaneous exercise 4

1 It is given that $I_n = \int_0^1 x^n e^x\,dx$ $(n \geqslant 0)$. Show that $I_n = e - nI_{n-1}$ $(n \geqslant 1)$. Hence show that $I_3 = 6 - 2e$. (OCR)

2 It is given that $I_n = \int_0^{\frac{1}{2}\pi} x^n \sin x\,dx$.

(a) Show that, for $n \geqslant 2$, $I_n = n\left(\frac{1}{2}\pi\right)^{n-1} - n(n-1)I_{n-2}$.

(b) Evaluate I_3, giving your answer in terms of π. (OCR)

3 Given that $I_n = \int_0^{\frac{1}{2}\pi} \sin^n x\,dx$, where n is a non-negative integer, show that $(n+2)I_{n+2} = (n+1)I_n$. Hence find the exact values of I_4 and I_5. (OCR)

4 Let $I_n = \int \cosh^n x \, dx$. Show that $nI_n = \sinh x \cosh^{n-1} x + (n-1)I_{n-2}$. Hence show that $\int_0^{\ln 2} \cosh^4 x \, dx = \frac{3}{8}\left(\frac{245}{128} + \ln 2\right)$. (OCR)

5 Define I_n by $I_n = \int_0^1 \frac{x^n}{\sqrt{1+x^2}} \, dx$, $n \geqslant 0$. Evaluate I_0 and I_1; give your answers to 4 significant figures.

Establish the reduction formula $I_n = \frac{\sqrt{2} - (n-1)I_{n-2}}{n}$ for suitable values of n, which you should state. Hence calculate I_5 and I_6 to 3 significant figures.

Prove, by setting up a suitable inequality for the integrand, that $I_n \to 0$ as $n \to \infty$. (OCR)

6 (a) Show that $\frac{d}{dx}\left(\cos 2x \sin^{n-1} 2x\right) = 2(n-1)\sin^{n-2} 2x - 2n \sin^n 2x$.

(b) It is given that $I_n = \int_{-\frac{1}{2}\pi}^{\frac{1}{2}\pi} \sin^n 2x \, dx \ (n \geqslant 0)$.

Use the result in (a) to show that $I_n = \left(\frac{n-1}{n}\right) I_{n-2}$ $(n \geqslant 2)$. Hence find I_8, leaving your answer in the form $k\pi$, where k is a fraction in its lowest terms. (OCR)

7 If I_n denotes $\int_0^1 \frac{e^x}{(1+x)^n} \, dx$, show that $nI_{n+1} = 1 - \left(\frac{1}{2}\right)^n e + I_n$, and state the values of n for which this is valid. If n is a positive integer, what is the disadvantage of trying to use this reduction formula to find I_n?

8 If $I_{m,n}$ denotes $\int_0^{\frac{1}{2}\pi} \sin^m \theta \cos^n \theta \, d\theta$, prove that $I_{m,n} = \frac{n-1}{m+n} I_{m,n-2}$. By using a suitable substitution, show also that $I_{m,n} = I_{n,m}$, and deduce that $I_{m,n} = \frac{m-1}{m+n} I_{m-2,n}$. Find

(a) $\int_0^{\frac{1}{2}\pi} \sin^8 \theta \cos^9 \theta \, d\theta$, (b) $\int_0^{\frac{1}{2}\pi} \sin^9 \theta \cos^{10} \theta \, d\theta$, (c) $\int_0^{\frac{1}{2}\pi} \sin^8 \theta \cos^{10} \theta \, d\theta$.

9 If $I_{m,n}$ denotes $\int_0^{\infty} \frac{x^m}{\left(x^2 + a^2\right)^n} \, dx$, find a relation between $I_{m,n}$ and $I_{m-2,n-1}$, and state the values of m and n for which this is valid. Hence evaluate

(a) $\int_0^{\infty} \left(\frac{x}{x^2 + a^2}\right)^7 dx$, (b) $\int_0^{\infty} \frac{x^4}{\left(x^2 + a^2\right)^{\frac{7}{2}}} \, dx$.

10 If I_n denotes $\frac{1}{n!}\int_0^x t^n e^{-t} \, dt$, find a relation connecting I_n and I_{n-1}. Deduce that the value of e^x exceeds its Maclaurin polynomial of degree n by $\frac{e^x}{n!}\int_0^x t^n e^{-t} \, dt$.

5 Series and integrals

This chapter shows that there are links between summing series and evaluating integrals. When you have completed it, you should

- be able to find areas under some curves by summing series
- be able to calculate limits of sums of some series as integrals
- be able to use integrals to approximate to sums of series
- understand the link between limiting properties of integrals and sums of series for decreasing functions.

5.1 Finding areas by summing series

It was suggested in Section 3.4 that you can find the area under a curve as the limit of the sum of the areas of a set of rectangles, written symbolically as $\sum y\,\delta x$. Here are two examples which illustrate the method.

Example 5.1.1
Find the area under the curve $y = x + x^3$ from $x = 0$ to $x = a$, where $a > 0$.

Split the interval $0 \leqslant x \leqslant a$ into n equal sub-intervals, each of width h, where $nh = a$. These sub-intervals are $0 \leqslant x \leqslant h$, $h \leqslant x \leqslant 2h$, $2h \leqslant x \leqslant 3h$, ..., $(n-1)h \leqslant x \leqslant nh$. The y-coordinates of the points on the curve $y = x + x^3$ in these intervals satisfy the inequalities $0 \leqslant y \leqslant h + h^3$, $h + h^3 \leqslant y \leqslant (2h) + (2h)^3$ $(2h) + (2h)^3 \leqslant y \leqslant (3h) + (3h)^3$, ..., $((n-1)h) + ((n-1)h)^3 \leqslant y \leqslant (nh) + (nh)^3$.

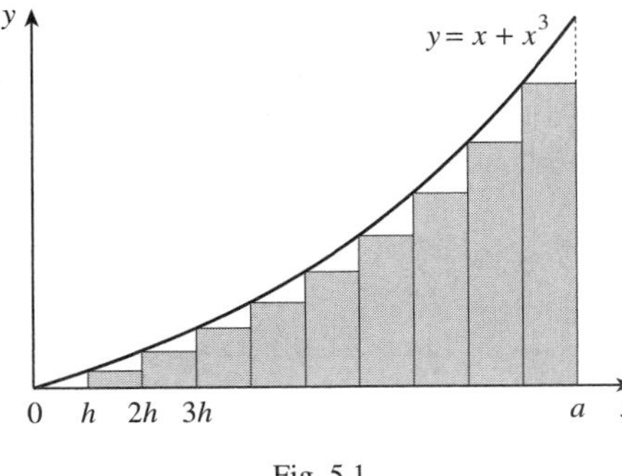

Fig. 5.1

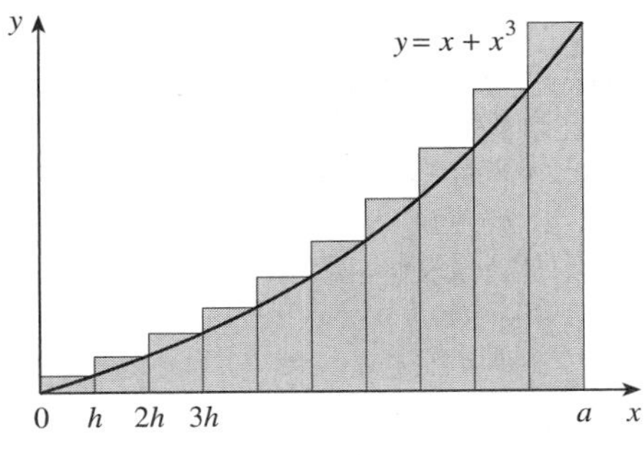

Fig. 5.2

The areas under the curve in each of these sub-intervals lie between the areas of two rectangles, of width h, whose heights are respectively the smallest and largest values of y in the sub-interval. The two sets of rectangles defined in this way are shown in Figs. 5.1 and 5.2 (drawn for the case $n = 10$). It follows that, if A denotes the total area under the curve from 0 to a, then A is bounded below by

$$h\left(0 + 0^3\right) + h\left(h + h^3\right) + h\left(2h + (2h)^3\right) + \ldots + h\left((n-1)h + ((n-1)h)^3\right)$$

and bounded above by

$$h\left(h + h^3\right) + h\left(2h + (2h)^3\right) + h\left(3h + (3h)^3\right) + \ldots + h\left(nh + (nh)^3\right).$$

So A is greater than

$$h^2(0+1+2+\ldots+(n-1))+h^4\left(0^3+1^3+2^3+\ldots+(n-1)^3\right)$$

and less than

$$h^2(1+2+3+\ldots+n)+h^4\left(1^3+2^3+3^3+\ldots+n^3\right).$$

Now in P2 Section 3.3, and P4 Section 2.3, it was shown that the sum of the first n natural numbers is $\frac{1}{2}n(n+1)$ and the sum of their cubes is $\frac{1}{4}n^2(n+1)^2$. So

$$\tfrac{1}{2}(n-1)nh^2+\tfrac{1}{4}(n-1)^2n^2h^4<A<\tfrac{1}{2}n(n+1)h^2+\tfrac{1}{4}n^2(n+1)^2h^4.$$

Since $nh=a$, this can be written as

$$\tfrac{1}{2}\frac{(n-1)}{n}a^2+\tfrac{1}{4}\frac{(n-1)^2}{n^2}a^4<A<\tfrac{1}{2}\frac{(n+1)}{n}a^2+\tfrac{1}{4}\frac{(n+1)^2}{n^2}a^4,$$

or $$\tfrac{1}{2}\left(1-\frac{1}{n}\right)a^2+\tfrac{1}{4}\left(1-\frac{1}{n}\right)^2a^4<A<\tfrac{1}{2}\left(1+\frac{1}{n}\right)a^2+\tfrac{1}{4}\left(1+\frac{1}{n}\right)^2a^4.$$

Now the larger the value of n, the smaller the difference between $1-\dfrac{1}{n}$ and $1+\dfrac{1}{n}$. In the limit, as $n\to\infty$, both $1-\dfrac{1}{n}$ and $1+\dfrac{1}{n}$ tend to 1, so that A is sandwiched between two expressions which both tend to $\frac{1}{2}a^2+\frac{1}{4}a^4$. This can only occur if A is equal to $\frac{1}{2}a^2+\frac{1}{4}a^4$.

Example 5.1.2
Find the area under the curve $y=2^x$ from $x=0$ to $x=1$.

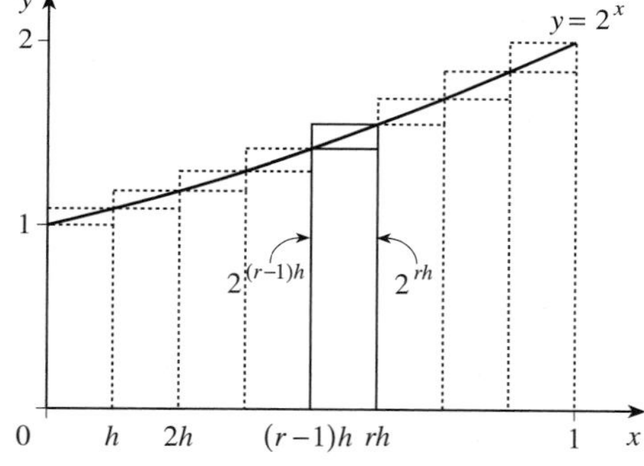

Fig. 5.3

Split the interval from 0 to 1 into n sub-intervals, each of width h, where $nh=1$. Fig. 5.3 shows the rth sub-interval, from $(r-1)h$ to rh. The area under the curve in this sub-interval lies between the areas of rectangles with width h and heights $2^{(r-1)h}$ and 2^{rh}. Therefore the total area, A, lies between

$$\sum_{r=1}^{n}h2^{(r-1)h}=h\left(1+2^h+2^{2h}+\ldots+2^{(n-1)h}\right)$$

and $$\sum_{r=1}^{n}h2^{rh}=h\left(2^h+2^{2h}+\ldots+2^{(n-1)h}+2^{nh}\right).$$

Both of these sums are geometric series with n terms and common ratio 2^h, with first terms h and $h2^h$ respectively. So A satisfies the inequalities

$$h\frac{2^{nh}-1}{2^h-1}<A<h2^h\frac{2^{nh}-1}{2^h-1}.$$

Since $nh = 1$, this simplifies to $\dfrac{h}{2^h - 1} < A < \dfrac{h2^h}{2^h - 1}$.

You want to find the limit of the expressions on the left and right as $n \to \infty$, that is as $h \to 0$. Notice that the expression on the right is just 2^h times that on the left, and 2^h tends to 1 as $h \to 0$. So both expressions have the same limit, and by the same argument as in the previous example

$$A = \lim_{h \to 0} \frac{h}{2^h - 1}.$$

Now in P2 Section 12.1, you found $\lim\limits_{h \to 0} \dfrac{2^h - 1}{h}$. This was shown to be the gradient of $y = 2^x$ at $x = 0$. Later, in Section 12.6, it transpired that this is $\ln 2$. Since $\dfrac{h}{2^h - 1}$ is the reciprocal of $\dfrac{2^h - 1}{h}$, it follows that $A = \dfrac{1}{\ln 2}$.

5.2 Using integrals to find limits

The examples in Section 5.1 are of historical interest. They show how areas were sometimes calculated, from Archimedes until the link between integration and differentiation was discovered. But the argument used can also be reversed and used to calculate limits.

Example 5.2.1
Find the limit, as $n \to \infty$, of $\dfrac{1}{n+1} + \dfrac{1}{n+2} + \dfrac{1}{n+3} + \ldots + \dfrac{1}{2n}$.

The sum has n fractions in all, each of which is between $\dfrac{1}{n}$ and $\dfrac{1}{2n}$, so the sum always lies between 1 and $\frac{1}{2}$. Before going on, use a program to work out the sum for a selection of values of n.

Notice that $\dfrac{1}{n+r}$ can be written as $\dfrac{1}{n} \times \dfrac{1}{1 + r/n}$. If you write $\dfrac{1}{n}$ as h, this is $h \times \dfrac{1}{1 + rh}$, where r takes values from 1 to n. So the sum can be pictured as the sum of the areas of n rectangles of width h and heights $\dfrac{1}{1+h}, \dfrac{1}{1+2h}, \ldots, \dfrac{1}{1+nh} = \dfrac{1}{2}$. These heights are values of $\dfrac{1}{1+x}$ for $x = h, 2h, 3h, \ldots, nh = 1$.

Fig. 5.4 shows these rectangles, which lie under the graph of $y = \dfrac{1}{1+x}$ from $x = 0$ to $x = 1$. As $n \to \infty$, the sum of the areas tends to the area under the curve, that is

$$\int_0^1 \frac{1}{1+x}\,dx = \left[\ln(1+x)\right]_0^1 = \ln 2.$$

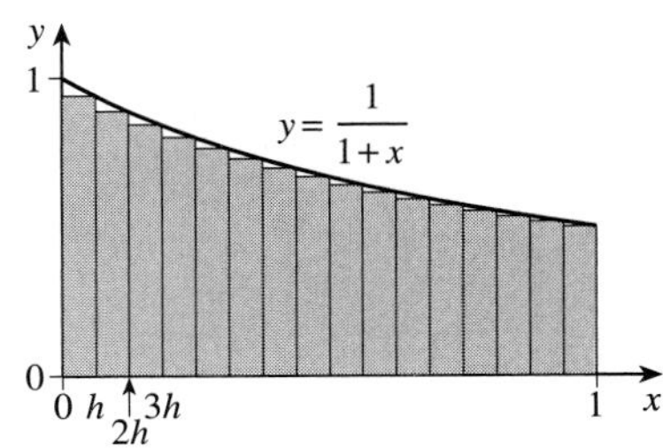

Fig. 5.4

Exercise 5A

1 Find overestimates and underestimates of the areas under the following curves over the given intervals, by using rectangles with the stated widths. Compare your estimates with the exact values of the areas.

(a) $y = 2x + 3$, $0 \leqslant x \leqslant 1$; widths 0.5, 0.1
(b) $y = 3x^2$, $1 \leqslant x \leqslant 2$; widths 0.25, 0.1
(c) $y = \sqrt{x}$, $1 \leqslant x \leqslant 4$; widths 1, 0.5, 0.25
(d) $y = \sin^2 x$, $0 \leqslant x \leqslant \pi$; widths $\frac{1}{4}\pi$, $\frac{1}{6}\pi$
(e) $y = 4x - x^2$, $0 \leqslant x \leqslant 4$; widths 1, 0.1

2 Surfaces of revolution are formed by rotating the following curves over the given intervals about the axes specified. By using discs with the stated thicknesses, find overestimates and underestimates of the volumes enclosed. Compare your estimates with the exact values of the volumes. (Give your answers as multiples of π.)

(a) $y = 3x + 1$ over $0 \leqslant x \leqslant 2$ about the x-axis; thicknesses 0.4, 0.2, 0.1
(b) $y = \sqrt{x}$ over $1 \leqslant x \leqslant 2$ about the x-axis; thicknesses 0.5, 0.2, 0.1
(c) $y = x^2 - 1$ over $1 \leqslant x \leqslant 2$ about the y-axis; thicknesses 1, 0.5, 0.2
(d) $y = 1 + x^2$ over $-1 \leqslant x \leqslant 1$ about the x-axis; thicknesses 0.2, 0.1
(e) $y = x^4$ over $0 \leqslant x \leqslant 1$ about the y-axis; thicknesses 0.2, 0.1

3 Overestimates and underestimates are made of the areas under the following curves over the given intervals, using n rectangles of equal width. Find formulae for these estimates, and the limits of these expressions as $n \to \infty$. Verify that these limits are equal to the values of the areas given by the usual integration method.

(a) $y = 1 + 2x$ over $0 \leqslant x \leqslant 1$
(b) $y = 9a - 4x$ over $0 \leqslant x \leqslant 2a$
(c) $y = 1 + x^2$ over $0 \leqslant x \leqslant 1$
(d) $y = 10 - x^3$ over $0 \leqslant x \leqslant 2$
(e) $y = 4a^2 - x^2$ over $a \leqslant x \leqslant 2a$
(f) $y = x^3$ over $a \leqslant x \leqslant 2a$
(g) $y = 3^x$ over $0 \leqslant x \leqslant 2$
(h) $y = a^x$ over $0 \leqslant x \leqslant b$, where $a > 1$

4 Surfaces of revolution are formed by rotating the following curves over the given intervals about the x-axis. Overestimates and underestimates of the volumes enclosed are made, using n discs of equal thickness. Find formulae for these estimates, and investigate their limits as $n \to \infty$. Verify that these limits are equal to the values of the volumes given by the usual integration method.

(a) $y = \sqrt{ax}$ over $0 \leqslant x \leqslant a$
(b) $y = x + a$ over $0 \leqslant x \leqslant a$
(c) $y = x^{\frac{3}{2}}$ over $2 \leqslant x \leqslant 3$
(d) $y = 2^x$ over $0 \leqslant x \leqslant 1$

5 Use a calculator to find the values of each of the following expressions when $n = 10$, $n = 20$ and $n = 30$. Find their limits as $n \to \infty$.

(a) $\dfrac{1}{n+1} + \dfrac{1}{n+2} + \dfrac{1}{n+3} + \ldots + \dfrac{1}{3n}$
(b) $\dfrac{\sqrt{1} + \sqrt{2} + \sqrt{3} + \ldots + \sqrt{n}}{n\sqrt{n}}$

(c) $n\left(\dfrac{1}{(n+1)^2} + \dfrac{1}{(n+2)^2} + \dfrac{1}{(n+3)^2} + \ldots + \dfrac{1}{(2n)^2}\right)$

(d) $\dfrac{\sqrt[3]{1} + \sqrt[3]{2} + \sqrt[3]{3} + \ldots + \sqrt[3]{n}}{\sqrt[3]{n+1} + \sqrt[3]{n+2} + \sqrt[3]{n+3} + \ldots + \sqrt[3]{2n}}$

6† Suppose that $y=\mathrm{f}(x)$ is increasing over an interval $a \leqslant x \leqslant b$. Let $\frac{b-a}{n}=h$ and, for $0 \leqslant r \leqslant n$, denote $x_r=a+rh$ (so that $x_0=a$ and $x_n=b$) and $y_r=\mathrm{f}(x_r)$. Use this notation to write expressions for the sums of the areas of the rectangles which give underestimates and overestimates of the integral $\int_a^b \mathrm{f}(x)\,\mathrm{d}x$. Show that the average of these estimates is the trapezium rule approximation with n intervals (see P2 Section 5.3). Find an expression for the difference between your two estimates in terms of a, b and n, and draw a diagram to illustrate this quantity. Show that, by taking n large enough, the difference between the overestimate and the underestimate can be made as small as you like.

7† Use the method of Section 5.2 to prove that $\frac{1}{n}\sqrt[n]{\frac{(2n)!}{n!}}$ tends to $\frac{4}{\mathrm{e}}$ as $n \to \infty$.

5.3 Approximating to sums of series

You know many ways of finding integrals, but have only met a few series which you can sum. However, by representing the sum of a series as the area of a set of rectangles, and comparing this with the area under a curve, it is often possible to find approximations to the sum.

Example 5.3.1

Find lower and upper bounds for the sum $\sqrt{1}+\sqrt{2}+\sqrt{3}+\ldots+\sqrt{n}$.

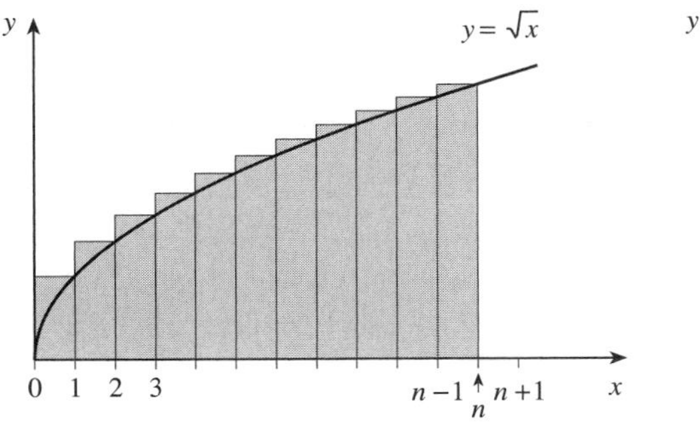

Fig. 5.5

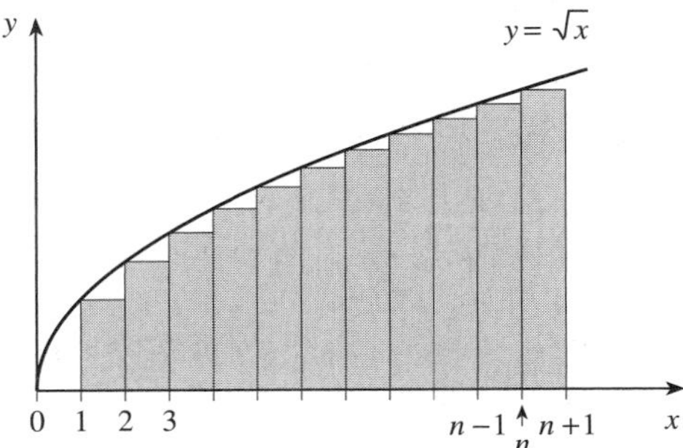

Fig. 5.6

In Fig. 5.5 the sum is represented as the area of a set of n rectangles, each having width 1 and with heights $\sqrt{1}$, $\sqrt{2}$, $\sqrt{3}$, ..., $\sqrt{n}$. These cover the interval $0 \leqslant x \leqslant n$ of the x-axis. The top right corners of these rectangles have coordinates $(1,\sqrt{1})$, $(2,\sqrt{2})$, $(3,\sqrt{3})$, ... $(n,\sqrt{n})$ all of which lie on the curve $y=\sqrt{x}$. Clearly the sum of the areas of the rectangles is greater than the area under the curve, so that

$$\sum_{r=1}^{n}\sqrt{r} > \int_0^n \sqrt{x}\,\mathrm{d}x = \left[\tfrac{2}{3}x^{\frac{3}{2}}\right]_0^n = \tfrac{2}{3}n\sqrt{n}.$$

This gives a lower bound for the sum. To find an upper bound, push all the rectangles to the right by 1 unit, so that they cover the interval $1 \leqslant x \leqslant n+1$. Fig. 5.6 shows that the top left corners of the rectangles now lie on $y = \sqrt{x}$, and it is easy to see that

$$\sum_{r=1}^{n} \sqrt{r} < \int_{1}^{n+1} \sqrt{x}\,dx = \left[\tfrac{2}{3}x^{\frac{3}{2}}\right]_{1}^{n+1} = \tfrac{2}{3}\left((n+1)\sqrt{n+1}-1\right).$$

This method gives remarkably good approximations. For example, if you put $n = 100$ in Example 5.3.1, you find that the sum of the square roots of the first 100 natural numbers lies between $\frac{2}{3} \times 100\sqrt{100} = 666.66\ldots$ and $\frac{2}{3} \times \left(101\sqrt{101}-1\right) = 676.02\ldots$. The correct value of the sum is $671.46\ldots$. Both bounds are within 1% of this.

Example 5.3.2
Find lower and upper bounds for $\sum_{r=m}^{n} \frac{1}{r^2}$, where $n > m$.

Sketch for yourself the graph of $y = \frac{1}{x^2}$, and mark on it points with coordinates

$\left(m, \frac{1}{m^2}\right), \left(m+1, \frac{1}{(m+1)^2}\right), \left(m+2, \frac{1}{(m+2)^2}\right), \ldots, \left(n, \frac{1}{n^2}\right)$. Since $\frac{1}{x^2}$ is a decreasing function, you will get a lower bound by representing the sum by rectangles with these points at the top left corners, so that they cover the interval $m \leqslant x \leqslant n+1$. The curve then lies inside the rectangles, so that

$$\sum_{r=m}^{n} \frac{1}{r^2} > \int_{m}^{n+1} \frac{1}{x^2}\,dx = \left[-\frac{1}{x}\right]_{m}^{n+1} = \frac{1}{m} - \frac{1}{n+1}.$$

To get an upper bound, push all the rectangles to the left by 1 unit. They then cover the interval $m-1 \leqslant x \leqslant n$, and have their top right corners on the curve, so that the curve lies above the rectangles. Therefore

$$\sum_{r=m}^{n} \frac{1}{r^2} < \int_{m-1}^{n} \frac{1}{x^2}\,dx = \left[-\frac{1}{x}\right]_{m-1}^{n} = \frac{1}{m-1} - \frac{1}{n}.$$

Combining these results, $\dfrac{n-m+1}{m(n+1)} < \sum_{r=m}^{n} \dfrac{1}{r^2} < \dfrac{n-m+1}{(m-1)n}$.

5.4 Convergent series and integrals

If a series has infinitely many terms, an important question is whether or not it is convergent. That is, if the terms of the series are $\mathrm{f}(1), \mathrm{f}(2), \mathrm{f}(3), \ldots$ and if S_n denotes the sum sequence

$$S_n = \sum_{r=1}^{n} \mathrm{f}(r),$$

does S_n tend to a limit or to infinity as $n \to \infty$?

It is almost obvious that, if S_n does tend to a limit, then the terms of the series must tend to 0. You can prove this by noting that $S_n = S_{n-1} + \mathrm{f}(n)$, so $\mathrm{f}(n) = S_n - S_{n-1}$.

Now if S_n tends to a limit l, S_{n-1} tends to the same limit l, so $\mathrm{f}(n)$ tends to $l - l = 0$.

You also know that an integral $\int_1^n \mathrm{f}(x)\,\mathrm{d}x$ may or may not converge as $n \to \infty$.

(See P1 Section 10.5.) It turns out that, under certain conditions, there is a close connection between the convergence of the integral and the series.

Suppose that f is a function defined for $x > 0$ which has the two properties

- $\mathrm{f}(x)$ is a decreasing function
- $\mathrm{f}(x)$ tends to 0 as $x \to \infty$.

You know many functions with these properties, such as $\frac{1}{x}, \frac{1}{\sqrt{x}}, \mathrm{e}^{-x}, \frac{1}{x^2+1}$.

Obviously such a function must have $\mathrm{f}(x) > 0$ for all $x > 0$.

Fig. 5.7 shows the graph of such a function, and a set of n rectangles of width 1 whose area represents the sum $\sum_{r=1}^{n} \mathrm{f}(r)$. These rectangles cover the interval $1 \leqslant x \leqslant n+1$ on the x-axis. It is clear from Fig. 5.7 that this sum is greater than the area under the curve from $x = 1$ to $x = n$. The shaded regions have an area which represents the difference

$$d_n = \sum_{r=1}^{n} \mathrm{f}(r) - \int_1^n \mathrm{f}(x)\,\mathrm{d}x, \quad \text{so} \quad d_n > 0.$$

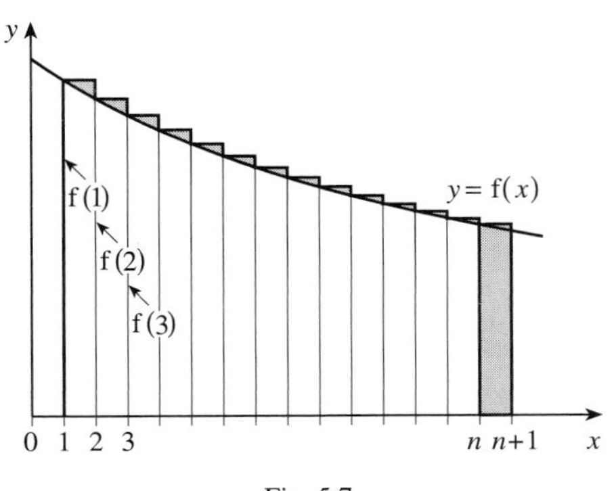

Fig. 5.7

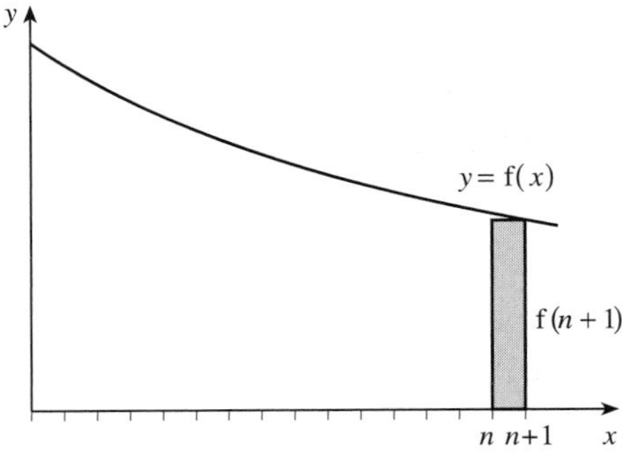

Fig. 5.8

Now d_n is also a sequence. Notice that $d_1 = \mathrm{f}(1) - 0 = \mathrm{f}(1)$.

The term of the sequence after d_n is

$$d_{n+1} = \sum_{r=1}^{n+1} \mathrm{f}(r) - \int_1^{n+1} \mathrm{f}(x)\,\mathrm{d}x, \quad \text{so} \quad d_{n+1} - d_n = \mathrm{f}(n+1) - \int_n^{n+1} \mathrm{f}(x)\,\mathrm{d}x.$$

The quantity on the right side of this equation is the difference between the area of the rectangle and the area under the curve in Fig. 5.8, and this shows that $d_{n+1} - d_n < 0$, that is $d_{n+1} < d_n$.

You now know three things about the sequence d_n: $d_1 = \mathrm{f}(1)$, $d_n > 0$ for all n, and the terms of the sequence decrease as n increases.

Example 5.4.1
Demonstrate these properties of the sequence d_n when $\mathrm{f}(x) = \frac{1}{x}$.

Table 5.9 gives the values of $S_n = \sum_{r=1}^{n} \frac{1}{r}$ and of $\int_1^n \frac{1}{x}\,\mathrm{d}x = \ln n$ for values of $n = 10^k$ for $k = 0, 1, 2, 3, 4, 5$ and 6. The last line gives the difference $d_n = S_n - \ln n$. All entries are rounded correct to 5 decimal places.

n	1	10	10^2	10^3	10^4	10^5	10^6
S_n	1	2.928 97	5.187 38	7.485 47	9.787 61	12.090 15	14.392 73
$\ln n$	0	2.302 59	4.605 17	6.907 76	9.210 34	11.512 93	13.815 51
d_n	1	0.626 38	0.582 21	0.577 72	0.577 27	0.577 22	0.577 22

Table 5.9

You can see from the last line of the table that the values of $d_n = S_n - \ln n$ tend to a limit of about 0.577 22 as $n \to \infty$. This limit is called **Euler's constant**, after the 18th-century Swiss mathematician who first discovered it; mathematicians usually denote it by the Greek letter γ.

The fact that d_n tends to a limit as $n \to \infty$, shown in this example for the function $\mathrm{f}(x) = \frac{1}{x}$, is an inevitable consequence of the properties of d_n listed above. If a sequence is decreasing and positive, it must tend to a limit.

These results can be summed up in the form of a theorem.

Theorem If a function $\mathrm{f}(x)$ is decreasing for $x > 0$ and $\mathrm{f}(x)$ tends to 0 as $x \to \infty$, then $\sum_{r=1}^{n} \mathrm{f}(r) - \int_1^n \mathrm{f}(x)\,\mathrm{d}x$ tends to a limit between 0 and $\mathrm{f}(1)$ as $n \to \infty$.

Now suppose that the infinite integral $\int_1^{\infty} \mathrm{f}(x)\,\mathrm{d}x$ exists. Then, by letting $n \to \infty$ in the equation

$$\sum_{r=1}^{n} \mathrm{f}(r) = d_n + \int_1^n \mathrm{f}(x)\,\mathrm{d}x,$$

it follows that the sum of the series tends to a limit as $n \to \infty$. On the other hand, if $\int_1^n \mathrm{f}(x)\,\mathrm{d}x$ diverges to infinity, then so does the sum of the series. This can be summed up in another theorem.

Theorem If a function $f(x)$ is decreasing for $x > 0$ and $f(x)$ tends to 0 as $x \to \infty$, then the infinite series $\sum_{r=1}^{\infty} f(r)$ converges if and only if $\int_1^{\infty} f(x)\,dx$ exists, and then

$$\int_1^{\infty} f(x)\,dx < \sum_{r=1}^{\infty} f(r) < f(1) + \int_1^{\infty} f(x)\,dx.$$

Example 5.4.2
Investigate whether the infinite series $\frac{1}{\sqrt{1^2+1}} + \frac{1}{\sqrt{2^2+2}} + \frac{1}{\sqrt{3^2+3}} + \ldots$ converges.

The function $f(x) = \frac{1}{\sqrt{x^2+x}}$ is a decreasing function and tends to 0 as $x \to \infty$.

Also $\int_1^n \frac{1}{\sqrt{x^2+x}}\,dx = \int_1^n \frac{1}{\sqrt{\left(x+\frac{1}{2}\right)^2+\frac{3}{4}}}\,dx = \left[\sinh^{-1}\left(\frac{x+\frac{1}{2}}{\frac{\sqrt{3}}{2}}\right)\right]_1^n.$

Since $\sinh^{-1}\left(\frac{2n+1}{\sqrt{3}}\right)$ tends to infinity as $n \to \infty$, the infinite series does not converge.

Exercise 5B

1 Find upper and lower bounds for the following sums. Give your answers in decimal form to 4 significant figures, rounding upper bounds up and lower bounds down.

(a) $\frac{1}{\sqrt{10}} + \frac{1}{\sqrt{11}} + \frac{1}{\sqrt{12}} + \ldots + \frac{1}{\sqrt{99}}$

(b) $\sqrt[3]{100} + \sqrt[3]{101} + \sqrt[3]{102} + \ldots + \sqrt[3]{999}$

(c) $\frac{1}{101} + \frac{2}{102} + \frac{3}{103} + \ldots + \frac{99}{199}$

(d) $\sum_{r=1}^{89} \sin r°$

(e) $\sum_{r=1}^{100} \frac{1}{100^2 + r^2}$

2 If $n > m > 1$, find upper and lower bounds for

(a) $\sum_{r=m}^{n} \frac{1}{r^3}$ (b) $\sum_{r=m}^{n} \frac{r}{1+r^2}$ (c) $\frac{n!}{m!}$

3 For each of the following infinite series $\sum f(r)$ determine whether the series is convergent. If it is, find bounds between which $\sum_{r=1}^{\infty} f(r)$ lies.

(a) $\sum \frac{1}{\sqrt{r}}$ (b) $\sum \frac{1}{r^2}$ (c) $\sum \frac{1}{r \ln r}$ (from $r = 2$) (d) $\sum \frac{1}{r\sqrt{r+1}}$

4 By comparing $\sum_{r=1}^{\infty} a^{-r}$ with $\int_1^{\infty} a^{-x}\,dx$, where $a>1$, obtain the inequalities

$\frac{a-1}{a} < \ln a < a-1.$

5 By writing $f(r)=\frac{1}{r(r+1)}$ in partial fractions, find the sum $\sum_{r=1}^{n} f(r)$ and deduce the value of $\sum_{r=1}^{\infty} f(r)$. By comparing this with the corresponding infinite integral, prove that $\ln 2$ lies between $\frac{1}{2}$ and 1.

Use a similar method with $f(r)=\frac{1}{r(r+1)(r+2)}$ to find bounds for the value of $\ln\frac{4}{3}$.

6 Use the result of Example 5.4.1 to prove that, if k is a positive integer, then $\sum_{r=n+1}^{kn} \frac{1}{r}$ tends to $\ln k$ as $n \to \infty$.

Miscellaneous exercise 5

1 By considering the areas of suitable rectangles, demonstrate that

$$\frac{1}{\sqrt{2}}+\frac{1}{\sqrt{5}}+\frac{1}{\sqrt{10}} < \int_0^3 \frac{1}{\sqrt{1+x^2}}\,dx < 1+\frac{1}{\sqrt{2}}+\frac{1}{\sqrt{5}}.$$ (OCR)

2 Rectangles of equal width h are drawn under the graph of $y=1+x^2$ from $x=0$ to $x=3$. Illustrate this with a sketch. Show that the area of the fourth rectangle is $h+9h^3$, and find (in terms of h) the total area of the first four rectangles.

How many rectangles are there if $h=0.1$? Show that the total area of the rectangles in this case is $3+0.1^3\sum_{i=1}^{29} i^2$. Find the difference between the value of this sum and the exact area under the curve from $x=0$ to $x=3$ found by integration. (OCR)

3 (a) Explain in detail how $\sum_{r=1}^{n} \frac{r}{n^2+r^2}$ is related to the area under the curve $y=\frac{x}{1+x^2}$ between $x=0$ and $x=1$.

(b) Evaluate the limit $L=\lim_{n\to\infty} \sum_{r=1}^{n} \frac{r}{n^2+r^2}$.

(c) Show that $L<\sum_{r=1}^{n} \frac{r}{n^2+r^2} < L+\frac{1}{2n}$. (MEI)

4† The integers s and n satisfy $0 < s < n$.

(a) By considering the area under the curve $y = \frac{1}{x}$, show that $\sum_{r=s+1}^{n} \frac{1}{r} < \int_s^n \frac{1}{x}\,dx < \sum_{r=s}^{n-1} \frac{1}{r}$.

(b) Find the maximum value of $-w \ln w$ for $0 < w < 1$.

Let $P = \frac{s}{n}\left(\frac{1}{s+1} + \frac{1}{s+2} + \frac{1}{s+3} + \ldots + \frac{1}{n}\right)$.

(c) By putting $w = \frac{s}{n}$ and using the results in (a) and (b), show that

$$\frac{s}{n}\ln\left(\frac{n}{s}\right) - \frac{n-s}{n^2} < P < \frac{1}{e}.$$

(d) By taking $w = \frac{1}{e}$ (≈ 0.36788), find a value of n and a value of s for which $P > 0.3675$. Use the result in (c) to justify your choice of values. (MEI)

5† (a) Use the result that $\frac{\ln w}{w} \to 0$ as $w \to \infty$ to show that $\sqrt{x}\ln x \to 0$ as $x \to 0$.

(b) Show that $\frac{\ln x}{\sqrt{x}} \to 0$ as $x \to \infty$.

(c) Explain why $\int_0^1 \frac{\ln x}{\sqrt{x}}\,dx$ is an improper integral, and evaluate this integral.

(d) Given that $x^{-\frac{3}{2}} \ln x$ is a decreasing function for $x > 2$, draw a diagram to show that $\sum_{r=3}^{n} r^{-\frac{3}{2}} \ln r < \int_2^n x^{-\frac{3}{2}} \ln x\,dx$, and write down a similar integral I for which $\sum_{r=3}^{n} r^{-\frac{3}{2}} \ln r > I$.

(e) Deduce that the infinite series $\sum_{r=3}^{\infty} r^{-\frac{3}{2}} \ln r$ is convergent, and show that

$$3.57 < \sum_{r=3}^{\infty} r^{-\frac{3}{2}} \ln r < 3.81.$$

(MEI)

Revision exercise 1

1 Find the exact solutions of the equation $2\cosh x + \sinh x = 2$. (OCR)

2 The roots of the quartic equation $4x^4 + px^3 + qx^2 - x + 3 = 0$ are α, $-\alpha$, $\alpha+\lambda$, $\alpha-\lambda$, where α and λ are real numbers. Express p and q in terms of α and λ. Show that $\alpha = -\frac{1}{2}$, and find the values of p and q. Give the roots of the quartic equation.

Find a quartic equation with integer coefficients which has roots $\dfrac{2}{\alpha}$, $-\dfrac{2}{\alpha}$, $\dfrac{2}{\alpha+\lambda}$, $\dfrac{2}{\alpha-\lambda}$. (MEI)

3 Given that $I_n = \int_0^1 x^n \cos \pi x \, dx$, for $n \geqslant 0$, show that $\pi^2 I_n + n(n-1)I_{n-2} + n = 0$.

Hence show that $\int_0^1 x^4 \cos \pi x \, dx = \dfrac{4(6-\pi^2)}{\pi^4}$. (OCR)

4 The curve C has parametric equations $x = t - \tanh t$, $y = \dfrac{1}{\cosh t}$.

(a) Show that $\left(\dfrac{dx}{dt}\right)^2 + \left(\dfrac{dy}{dt}\right)^2 = \tanh^2 t$.

(b) Show that the length of the arc of the curve C between the points given by $t = 0$ and $t = \ln 2$ is $\ln \frac{5}{4}$. (OCR)

5 Differentiate

(a) $\sin^{-1}\left(\dfrac{x}{2}\right)$, (b) $\cosh^{-1}\left(\dfrac{2}{x}\right)$

with respect to x, where $0 < x < 2$, simplifying your answers as much as possible.

Find $\displaystyle\int \frac{2+3x}{x\sqrt{4-x^2}} \, dx$. (MEI)

6 The equation $16x^3 + kx^2 + 27 = 0$ (where k is a real constant) has roots α, β and γ.

(a) Write down the values of $\beta\gamma + \gamma\alpha + \alpha\beta$ and $\alpha\beta\gamma$, and express k in terms of α, β and γ.

(b) For the case where there is a repeated root, say $\beta = \gamma$, solve the equation, and find the value of k.

(c) For the case $k = 9$, find a cubic equation with integer coefficients which has roots $\dfrac{1}{\alpha}+1$, $\dfrac{1}{\beta}+1$, $\dfrac{1}{\gamma}+1$. (MEI)

7 By considering an appropriate graph, find the limit, as $n \to \infty$, of

$$\frac{1}{n}\left(\frac{1}{1+\left(\frac{1}{n}\right)^2} + \frac{1}{1+\left(\frac{2}{n}\right)^2} + \frac{1}{1+\left(\frac{3}{n}\right)^2} + \ldots + \frac{1}{2}\right).$$

(OCR)

8 (a) Show that $\cosh^4 x = \frac{1}{8}\cosh 4x + \frac{1}{2}\cosh 2x + \frac{3}{8}$. Find the series expansion for $\cosh^4 x$, as far as the term in x^4.

(b) Given that $\sinh\alpha = \frac{3}{4}$, show that $\sinh 2\alpha = \frac{15}{8}$ and find $\sinh 4\alpha$.

(c) Show that $\int_0^3 \left(16+u^2\right)^{\frac{3}{2}} \mathrm{d}u = \frac{735}{4} + 96\ln 2$. (MEI)

9 A curve is defined parametrically for $t \geqslant 0$ by the equations $x = 6t - 3t^2$, $y = 8t^{\frac{3}{2}}$. C is the arc of the curve joining the origin to the point where $t = 1$.

(a) Find the length of C.

(b) Show that the area of the surface generated when C is rotated about the x-axis through one complete revolution is $\frac{2304}{35}\pi$. (OCR)

10 The roots of the quartic equation $x^4 + 8x^3 + 20x^2 + 16x + 4 = 0$ are α, β, γ and δ. Find the values of

(a) $\alpha+\beta+\gamma+\delta$,

(b) $\alpha^2+\beta^2+\gamma^2+\delta^2$,

(c) $\dfrac{1}{\alpha}+\dfrac{1}{\beta}+\dfrac{1}{\gamma}+\dfrac{1}{\delta}$,

(d) $\dfrac{\alpha}{\beta\gamma\delta}+\dfrac{\beta}{\alpha\gamma\delta}+\dfrac{\gamma}{\alpha\beta\delta}+\dfrac{\delta}{\alpha\beta\gamma}$.

By making a suitable substitution, find a quartic equation with roots $\alpha+2$, $\beta+2$, $\gamma+2$ and $\delta+2$. Solve this equation, and hence find the values of α, β, γ and δ. (MEI)

11 The area between the curve $4a^2 y = x^3$ and the x-axis, from $x = 0$ to $x = a$, is rotated about the x-axis to form a solid of revolution. Find the volume and the curved surface area of this solid of revolution. (MEI)

12 Let $I_n = \int_0^1 \cosh^n x \,\mathrm{d}x$. By considering $\frac{\mathrm{d}}{\mathrm{d}x}\left(\sinh x \cosh^{n-1} x\right)$, or otherwise, show that

$nI_n = ab^{n-1} + (n-1)I_{n-2}$, where $a = \sinh 1$ and $b = \cosh 1$.

Show that $I_4 = \frac{1}{8}\left(2ab^3 + 3ab + 3\right)$. (OCR)

13 (a) Show that $\int_3^5 \sqrt{x^2-9}\,\mathrm{d}x = 10 - \frac{9}{2}\ln 3$.

(b) Find the Maclaurin series for $\cosh^{-1}\left(\frac{5}{3}+x\right)$, as far as the term in x^2. (MEI)

14 The parametric equations of a curve are $x = a\cos^3 t$, $y = a\sin^3 t$, where a is a positive constant. Show that $\left(\dfrac{\mathrm{d}x}{\mathrm{d}t}\right)^2 + \left(\dfrac{\mathrm{d}y}{\mathrm{d}t}\right)^2 = 9a^2\sin^2 t\cos^2 t$.

The arc of the curve between $t = 0$ and $t = \frac{1}{2}\pi$ is rotated through 2π radians about the x-axis. Find the area of the surface of revolution so formed, giving your answer in terms of a and π. (OCR)

15 Obtain, using successive differentiation, the first three non-zero terms of the Maclaurin series for $\sinh x$. By considering a suitable value of x, find the sum of the infinite series

$$\frac{1}{2}+\frac{9}{2\times4\times6}+\frac{9^2}{2\times4\times6\times8\times10}+\frac{9^3}{2\times4\times6\times8\times10\times12\times14}+\ldots.$$ (MEI)

16 Show that the arc length of the polar curve $r = \sin^3\frac{1}{3}\theta$, for $0 \leqslant \theta \leqslant 3\pi$, is $\frac{3}{2}\pi$. (MEI)

17 The cubic equation $2x^3 - 3x^2 - 12x - 4 = 0$ has roots α, β and γ.

(a) Write down the values of $\alpha + \beta + \gamma$, $\beta\gamma + \gamma\alpha + \alpha\beta$ and $\alpha\beta\gamma$.

(b) Find $\alpha^2 + \beta^2 + \gamma^2$ and $(\beta\gamma)^2 + (\gamma\alpha)^2 + (\alpha\beta)^2$.

(c) By considering $(\alpha + \beta + \gamma)(\beta\gamma + \gamma\alpha + \alpha\beta)$, show that $\alpha^2\beta + \alpha^2\gamma + \beta^2\gamma + \beta^2\alpha + \gamma^2\alpha + \gamma^2\beta = -15$.

(d) Find a cubic equation with integer coefficients which has roots $\alpha - \beta\gamma$, $\beta - \gamma\alpha$ and $\gamma - \alpha\beta$. (MEI)

18 Show that the length of the arc of the curve $y = \frac{1}{2}x^2$, from the origin to the point where $x = 2$, is $\sqrt{5} + \frac{1}{2}\ln\left(2 + \sqrt{5}\right)$. (OCR)

19 Let $y = x\sinh x$. Show that $\dfrac{\mathrm{d}^2y}{\mathrm{d}x^2} = x\sinh x + 2\cosh x$, and find $\dfrac{\mathrm{d}^4y}{\mathrm{d}x^4}$.

Write down a conjecture for $\dfrac{\mathrm{d}^{2n}y}{\mathrm{d}x^{2n}}$. Use induction to establish a formula for $\dfrac{\mathrm{d}^{2n}y}{\mathrm{d}x^{2n}}$. (OCR)

20 The arc of the curve $y = \mathrm{e}^x$ from the point where $y = \frac{3}{4}$ to the point where $y = \frac{4}{3}$ is rotated through one revolution about the x-axis. Show that the area, S, of the surface generated is given by $S = 2\pi\int_{\frac{3}{4}}^{\frac{4}{3}} \sqrt{1 + y^2}\,\mathrm{d}y$. By using the substitution $y = \sinh u$, show that

$S = \pi\left(\frac{185}{144} + \ln\frac{3}{2}\right)$. (OCR)

21 Show that $\dfrac{\mathrm{d}}{\mathrm{d}x}\left(x^{n-1}\sqrt{16 - x^2}\right) = \dfrac{16(n-1)x^{n-2}}{\sqrt{16 - x^2}} - \dfrac{nx^n}{\sqrt{16 - x^2}}$. Deduce, or prove otherwise,

that if $I_n = \displaystyle\int_0^2 \frac{x^n}{\sqrt{16 - x^2}}\,\mathrm{d}x$, then, for $n \geqslant 2$, $nI_n = 16(n-1)I_{n-2} - 2^n\sqrt{3}$.

Hence find the exact value of I_2. (OCR)

22 A curve has parametric equations $x = 4t - \frac{1}{3}t^3$, $y = 2t^2 - 8$. The arc of the curve given by $0 \leqslant t \leqslant 2\sqrt{3}$ is denoted by C. Find the length of the arc C, and the area of the curved surface generated when the arc C is rotated about the y-axis. (MEI)

23† (a) Draw a diagram to show that $\displaystyle\sum_{r=m+1}^{n} \frac{1}{r^3} < \int_m^n \frac{1}{x^3}\,\mathrm{d}x$, and write down a similar integral I such that $\displaystyle\sum_{r=m+1}^{n} \frac{1}{r^3} > I$.

(b) Prove that the series $\displaystyle\sum_{r=1}^{\infty} \frac{1}{r^3}$ is convergent.

(c) Given that $\displaystyle\sum_{r=1}^{25} \frac{1}{r^3} = 1.20129$, correct to 5 decimal places, show that

$1.2020 < \displaystyle\sum_{r=1}^{\infty} \frac{1}{r^3} < 1.2021$. (MEI)

24† If I_n denotes $\int_0^1 t^{n-1}\sqrt{a^2+b^2t^2}\,\mathrm{d}t$, where $n>2$, prove that

$$(n+1)b^2I_n+(n-2)a^2I_{n-2}=\left(a^2+b^2\right)^{\frac{3}{2}}.$$

A family of curved arcs joining the origin to the point $(1,1)$ is defined by parametric equations $x=t^k$, $y=t^{k+1}$ for $0\leqslant t\leqslant 1$, where the constant k is a positive integer. Show that all the arcs lie below the line segment joining the origin to $(1,1)$, and that the larger the value of k the closer the arc lies to the line segment.

The length of the arc with constant k is denoted by L_k. Find the exact values of L_2, L_4 and L_6, and evaluate these numerically correct to 3 decimal places.

25 The curve $y=c\cosh\frac{x}{c}$ is called a *catenary*, because it is the shape taken by a uniform chain held at its end-points. The point C has coordinates $(0,c)$, and P is a general point of the curve. T is the point on the tangent at P measured backwards such that TP is equal to the arc length CP. If P has coordinates $(cp, c\cosh p)$, with $p>0$, find the coordinates of T in terms of c and p, in as simple a form as possible. You can imagine T as the locus of the end of a taut string as it is unwrapped from the catenary. This locus is called a *tractrix*.

(a) Find the arc length CT along the tractrix in terms of c and p.

(b) The tangent to the tractrix at T cuts the x-axis at U. Show that the distance TU is equal to c. (This is the reason for the name 'tractrix'. Imagine a particle at T being pulled by a string TU, as U moves slowly along the x-axis.)

(c) The tractrix (for $p>0$) is rotated through a complete revolution about the x-axis. Find the area of the surface generated.

26† If I_n denotes $\int_1^\infty \frac{1}{\theta^{n+1}}\sqrt{a^2+\theta^2}\,\mathrm{d}\theta$, and $n>1$, prove that

$$(n+2)a^2I_{n+2}+(n-1)I_n=\left(a^2+1\right)^{\frac{3}{2}}.$$

A family of spiral curves has polar equation $r=\frac{1}{\theta^k}$ for $\theta>0$, where k is a positive integer. All the curves pass through the point with polar coordinates $(1,1)$, go round the origin infinitely many times, and approach the origin as $\theta\to\infty$. Sketch on the same diagram the spirals with $k=1, 2$ and 3.

The spirals with $k\geqslant 2$ have a finite arc length between P and the origin, denoted by L_k. Find the exact values of L_3, L_5 and L_7, and evaluate them correct to 3 decimal places.

6 Linear differential equations

This chapter shows how to solve linear differential equations of first and second order, concentrating on those with constant coefficients. When you have completed it, you should

- recognise linear first and second order differential equations
- know that the solution is of the form particular integral plus complementary function
- know how to find the complementary function for an equation with constant coefficients when the auxiliary equation has real roots, which may be repeated
- know how to find particular integrals by trial with undetermined coefficients.

6.1 Second order differential equations

All the differential equations you have met so far involved only $\frac{\mathrm{d}y}{\mathrm{d}x}$, x and y. But mathematical models for many practical situations are expressed by differential equations which also bring in $\frac{\mathrm{d}^2y}{\mathrm{d}x^2}$. These are called **second order** differential equations.

Example 6.1.1
At the start of the year the population of rabbits on an island is 5000, and is increasing at a rate of 300 per month. The variation in the rate of increase (or decrease) depends on the current population, according to the law $\frac{\mathrm{d}^2P}{\mathrm{d}t^2} = 50 - 0.01P$. Verify that this situation is described by the equation $P = 5000 + 3000\sin(0.1t)$, where t is the time in months after the start of the year.

From the given equation for P,

$$\frac{\mathrm{d}P}{\mathrm{d}t} = 300\cos(0.1t) \quad \text{and} \quad \frac{\mathrm{d}^2P}{\mathrm{d}t^2} = -30\sin(0.1t).$$

There are three things to check.

When $t = 0$, $P = 5000$. That is, the population is 5000 at the start of the year.

When $t = 0$, $\frac{\mathrm{d}P}{\mathrm{d}t} = 300$. That is, the population is increasing at a rate of 300 per month at the start of the year.

For general t, the expression for $\frac{\mathrm{d}^2P}{\mathrm{d}t^2}$ can be written as

$$\frac{\mathrm{d}^2P}{\mathrm{d}t^2} = -0.01 \times 3000\sin(0.1t) = -0.01(P - 5000) = 50 - 0.01P.$$

That is, P satisfies the given second order differential equation.

The equation shows that the population varies from a maximum of 8000 rabbits to a minimum of 2000. The complete cycle takes place over a period of $\frac{2\pi}{0.1}$ months, that is about $5\frac{1}{4}$ years.

Notice that in this example there are two initial conditions to check: the values of P and of $\frac{\mathrm{d}P}{\mathrm{d}t}$ when $t=0$. This is typical of second order differential equations. The general solution usually contains two arbitrary constants, so two conditions are needed to find them.

6.2 Linear differential equations

The first order differential equations described as 'linear' in P4 Chapter 9 are those in which $\frac{\mathrm{d}y}{\mathrm{d}x}$ and y appear only to the first degree. After dividing through by the coefficient of $\frac{\mathrm{d}y}{\mathrm{d}x}$, they can be described by the general form $\frac{\mathrm{d}y}{\mathrm{d}x}+y\,\mathrm{p}(x)=\mathrm{q}(x)$.

The notion of linearity extends to differential equations of second order, and the general form is then $\frac{\mathrm{d}^2y}{\mathrm{d}x^2}+\frac{\mathrm{d}y}{\mathrm{d}x}\mathrm{p}(x)+y\,\mathrm{r}(x)=\mathrm{q}(x)$.

A typical first order linear equation is that in P4 Example 9.2.3, where it was shown that the general solution of

$$\frac{\mathrm{d}y}{\mathrm{d}x}\cos x+y\sin x=\tan x$$

is $\quad y=\frac{1}{2}\sec x+C\cos x$, where C is an arbitrary constant.

It is a common and convenient practice to use capital letters to denote arbitrary constants when solving differential equations, and lower-case letters for other constants.

You will see that the solution is the sum of two parts: one is a specific function and the other contains a multiplicative arbitrary constant. It is interesting to investigate what happens when you substitute each of these parts into the left side of the equation.

If $y=\frac{1}{2}\sec x$, then

$$\begin{aligned}\frac{\mathrm{d}y}{\mathrm{d}x}\cos x+y\sin x&=\left(\tfrac{1}{2}\sec x\tan x\right)\cos x+\left(\tfrac{1}{2}\sec x\right)\sin x\\&=\tfrac{1}{2}\tan x+\tfrac{1}{2}\tan x=\tan x.\end{aligned}$$

If $y=C\cos x$, then

$$\frac{\mathrm{d}y}{\mathrm{d}x}\cos x+y\sin x=(-C\sin x)\cos x+(C\cos x)\sin x=0.$$

Much the same occurs with second order linear equations. Example 6.1.1 is typical. The differential equation can be written as

$$\frac{\mathrm{d}^2P}{\mathrm{d}t^2}+0.01P=50.$$

This is clearly linear, and you can check for yourself that

$$P=5000+A\sin(0.01t)+B\cos(0.01t)$$

is a solution for any values of the constants A and B. If you substitute the separate parts $P = 5000$ and $P = A\sin(0.01t) + B\cos(0.01t)$ in the expression $\frac{d^2P}{dt^2} + 0.01P$ on the left side of the equation, you get the answers 50 for the first and 0 for the second. These are examples of a general rule.

The general solution of a linear differential equation is the sum of two parts: a **particular integral**, which is a solution of the differential equation, and a **complementary function**, which is the general solution of the equation with 0 in place of the terms which are independent of y.

The word 'complementary' means 'completing'. The complementary function is what you have to add to the particular integral to complete the solution of the differential equation.

For the first order equation $\frac{dy}{dx} + y\,p(x) = q(x)$, if $F(x)$ is a particular integral, and $G(x)$ is any solution of the equation with 0 on the right side, then

$$F'(x) + F(x)\,p(x) = q(x) \quad \text{and} \quad G'(x) + G(x)\,p(x) = 0.$$

Since $\frac{d}{dx}(F(x) + G(x)) = F'(x) + G'(x)$ it follows that

$$\begin{aligned} y = F(x) + G(x) \quad \Leftrightarrow \quad \frac{dy}{dx} + p(x)\,y &= (F'(x) + G'(x)) + (F(x) + G(x)\,p(x)) \\ &= (F'(x) + F(x)\,p(x)) + (G'(x) + G(x)\,p(x)) \\ &= q(x) + 0 = q(x). \end{aligned}$$

So a particular integral added to any solution in the complementary function satisfies the original equation. And by a similar argument, if y is any solution of the given equation, then $y - p(x)$ belongs to the complementary function.

Exactly the same argument applies to second order linear equations.

The importance of this result is that, for linear equations, you can split the problem of solution into two parts: finding the complementary function and finding a particular integral. The rest of this chapter deals with these in turn.

Exercise 6A

1 For the following differential equations, state whether they are of first or second order, and whether they are linear or non-linear.

(a) $\frac{dy}{dx} = \frac{1}{x} + \frac{1}{y}$ (b) $\frac{d^2x}{dt^2} + x = \sin 2t$ (c) $x^2\frac{d^2y}{dx^2} - e^x\frac{dy}{dx} = y$

(d) $\frac{du}{dt} = tu + t^2$ (e) $x\frac{d^2x}{dt^2} = t\frac{dx}{dt}$ (f) $xy^2\frac{dy}{dx} = 1 + y$

2 Differentiate the following equations, and find differential equations which they satisfy for all values of the arbitrary constants A and B.

(a) $y = Ax^2 + \mathrm{e}^x$ (b) $Ax + By = 1$ (c) $x = A\sin 2t + B\cos 2t$

(d) $y = Ax + \dfrac{B}{x}$ (e) $\dfrac{x}{A} + \dfrac{y}{1-A} = 1$ (f) $(x+A)(y+B) = 1$

3 For the following equations and differential equations, verify that the equation satisfies the differential equation for all values of the arbitrary constants A and B.

(a) $y = A\sqrt{x}$; $2x\dfrac{\mathrm{d}y}{\mathrm{d}x} = y$ (b) $y = A\sqrt{x} + 2x$; $2x\dfrac{\mathrm{d}y}{\mathrm{d}x} = y + 2x$

(c) $y = A\mathrm{e}^t + B\mathrm{e}^{-t}$; $\dfrac{\mathrm{d}^2y}{\mathrm{d}t^2} - y = 0$ (d) $y = A\mathrm{e}^t + (t+B)\mathrm{e}^{-t}$; $\dfrac{\mathrm{d}^2y}{\mathrm{d}t^2} - y = -2\mathrm{e}^{-t}$

4 Solve the following differential equations, and identify a particular integral and the complementary function.

(a) $\dfrac{\mathrm{d}x}{\mathrm{d}t} = \cos t$ (b) $\dfrac{\mathrm{d}^2y}{\mathrm{d}x^2} = \dfrac{1}{x^2}$ (c) $\dfrac{\mathrm{d}y}{\mathrm{d}x}\sin x + y\cos x = 1$

(d) $\dfrac{\mathrm{d}y}{\mathrm{d}x}\sin x - y\cos x = 1$ (e) $\dfrac{\mathrm{d}}{\mathrm{d}x}\left(x\dfrac{\mathrm{d}y}{\mathrm{d}x}\right) = 1$ (f) $x^2\dfrac{\mathrm{d}^2y}{\mathrm{d}x^2} + 2x\dfrac{\mathrm{d}y}{\mathrm{d}x} = \dfrac{1}{x^2}$

5 A truck is towing a trailer. The coupling connecting them can be modelled as a stiff spring. Both the truck and trailer are initially stationary. The truck starts to move at a constant speed of 4 metres per second, and pulls the trailer along behind it. If the trailer has moved x metres in t seconds, its motion is described by the differential equation

$$\frac{\mathrm{d}^2x}{\mathrm{d}t^2} + 0.04x = 0.16t.$$

Verify that the differential equations and the initial conditions are all satisfied by the equation $x = 4(t - 5\sin 0.2t)$.

6 For these differential equations find the complementary function, guess and verify a particular integral, and hence write down the general solution.

(a) $\dfrac{\mathrm{d}y}{\mathrm{d}x} - 3y = 2\mathrm{e}^x$ (b) $\dfrac{\mathrm{d}y}{\mathrm{d}x} + \dfrac{y}{x} = 4x^2$

(c) $\dfrac{\mathrm{d}^2y}{\mathrm{d}x^2} + \dfrac{\mathrm{d}y}{\mathrm{d}x} = 2\mathrm{e}^{-2x}$ (d) $x\dfrac{\mathrm{d}^2y}{\mathrm{d}x^2} + \dfrac{\mathrm{d}y}{\mathrm{d}x} = \dfrac{3}{x^2}$

7 A stone falls vertically into a lake and sinks to the bottom. It enters the water at a speed of 3 metres per second, and t seconds later its depth is z metres. The fall of the stone is modelled by the differential equation

$$\frac{\mathrm{d}^2z}{\mathrm{d}t^2} + 2\frac{\mathrm{d}z}{\mathrm{d}t} = 10.$$

Show that this differential equation is satisfied by an equation of the form $z = 5t + A + B\mathrm{e}^{-2t}$. Find the values of A and B which give the correct values for the depth z and the speed $\dfrac{\mathrm{d}z}{\mathrm{d}t}$ at time $t = 0$. Draw sketch graphs to show how the depth and speed vary with time as the stone sinks.

8* Find an integrating factor $\mathrm{u}(x)$ such that $\mathrm{u}(x)\left(\frac{\mathrm{d}^2y}{\mathrm{d}x^2}+\frac{2}{x}\frac{\mathrm{d}y}{\mathrm{d}x}\right)$ can be written in the form $\frac{\mathrm{d}}{\mathrm{d}x}\left(\mathrm{u}(x)\frac{\mathrm{d}y}{\mathrm{d}x}\right)$. Hence find the general solution of the differential equation $\frac{\mathrm{d}^2y}{\mathrm{d}x^2}+\frac{2}{x}\frac{\mathrm{d}y}{\mathrm{d}x}=x$.
Identify the complementary function and the particular integral in your solution, and check these by direct substitution in the left side of the differential equation.

6.3 Finding complementary functions: constant coefficients

Many linear differential equations which occur in practice have the form

$$a\frac{\mathrm{d}y}{\mathrm{d}x}+by=\mathrm{q}(x) \quad \text{or} \quad a\frac{\mathrm{d}^2y}{\mathrm{d}x^2}+b\frac{\mathrm{d}y}{\mathrm{d}x}+cy=\mathrm{q}(x)$$

where the coefficients a, b and c are constants. For these, the complementary functions, which satisfy

$$a\frac{\mathrm{d}y}{\mathrm{d}x}+by=0 \quad \text{or} \quad a\frac{\mathrm{d}^2y}{\mathrm{d}x^2}+b\frac{\mathrm{d}y}{\mathrm{d}x}+cy=0,$$

are specially easy to find.

You already know the solution of the first order equation. This is the equation for exponential growth which was solved in P3 Section 9.4. Recasting this in x, y notation, you can obtain the solution of $\frac{\mathrm{d}y}{\mathrm{d}x}=\lambda y$ as $y=C\mathrm{e}^{\lambda x}$, where C is an arbitrary constant. In this case $\lambda=-\frac{b}{a}$, or $a\lambda+b=0$. So the result can be written as:

The complementary function for the differential equation

$$a\frac{\mathrm{d}y}{\mathrm{d}x}+by=\mathrm{q}(x)$$

is $y=C\mathrm{e}^{\lambda x}$, where λ is the root of the equation $a\lambda+b=0$.

Introducing the equation $a\lambda+b=0$, which is called the **auxiliary equation**, may seem an unnecessary complication. It is, however, the key which opens the door to the solution of the second order equation. For this the auxiliary equation is the quadratic equation

$$a\lambda^2+b\lambda+c=0.$$

Before tackling the general theory, it is useful to look at a numerical example.

Example 6.3.1

(a) Investigate whether there are any numbers C and λ such that $y=C\mathrm{e}^{\lambda x}$ satisfies the differential equation $\frac{\mathrm{d}^2y}{\mathrm{d}x^2}-5\frac{\mathrm{d}y}{\mathrm{d}x}+6y=0$.

(b) Find a more general solution of the equation.

(a) If $y = Ce^{\lambda x}$, then $\dfrac{dy}{dx} = C\lambda e^{\lambda x}$ and $\dfrac{d^2y}{dx^2} = C\lambda^2 e^{\lambda x}$. So if y satisfies the differential equation, then

$$C\lambda^2 e^{\lambda x} - 5C\lambda e^{\lambda x} + 6Ce^{\lambda x} = 0 \qquad \text{for all values of } x.$$

This can be written as

$$Ce^{\lambda x}\left(\lambda^2 - 5\lambda + 6\right) = 0, \qquad \text{so} \qquad Ce^{\lambda x}(\lambda - 2)(\lambda - 3) = 0.$$

Now $e^{\lambda x}$ cannot be zero, and $C = 0$ gives you a correct but uninteresting solution. The useful solutions are given by $\lambda = 2$ and $\lambda = 3$. What has been shown so far is that, if $\lambda = 2$ or $\lambda = 3$, then $y = Ce^{\lambda x}$ satisfies the differential equation whatever the value of C.

So two solutions of the differential equation are $y = Ae^{2x}$ and $y = Be^{3x}$, where A and B are arbitrary constants.

(b) To find a more general solution, you want a function of which Ae^{2x} and Be^{3x} are special cases. An obvious possibility is $y = Ae^{2x} + Be^{3x}$. For this function

$$\frac{dy}{dx} = 2Ae^{2x} + 3Be^{3x} \text{ and } \frac{d^2y}{dx^2} = 4Ae^{2x} + 9Be^{3x}.$$

So $$\frac{d^2y}{dx^2} - 5\frac{dy}{dx} + 6y = \left(4Ae^{2x} + 9Be^{3x}\right) - 5\left(2Ae^{2x} + 3Be^{3x}\right) + 6\left(Ae^{2x} + Be^{3x}\right)$$
$$= (4 - 10 + 6)Ae^{2x} + (9 - 15 + 6)Be^{3x} = 0.$$

So a more general solution of the equation is indeed $y = Ae^{2x} + Be^{3x}$.

The example suggests a more general result:

> If the auxiliary equation $a\lambda^2 + b\lambda + c = 0$ for the differential equation
>
> $a\dfrac{d^2y}{dx^2} + b\dfrac{dy}{dx} + cy = q(x)$ has distinct roots α and β,
>
> the complementary function is $y = Ae^{\alpha x} + Be^{\beta x}$.

Notice that this says more than part (b) of Example 6.3.1. There it was shown that $y = Ae^{2x} + Be^{3x}$ is a solution of $\dfrac{d^2y}{dx^2} - 5\dfrac{dy}{dx} + 6y = 0$. What the shaded box asserts is that all the solutions are of this form. The proof which follows establishes the result by deduction rather than verifying an inspired guess.

If the auxiliary equation has two roots α and β, you know from Chapter 1 that $\alpha + \beta = -\dfrac{b}{a}$ and $\alpha\beta = \dfrac{c}{a}$. The complementary function is the most general function satisfying

$$\frac{d^2y}{dx^2} - (\alpha + \beta)\frac{dy}{dx} + \alpha\beta\, y = 0.$$

This can be rearranged as $\frac{d^2y}{dx^2} - \beta\frac{dy}{dx} = \alpha\left(\frac{dy}{dx} - \beta y\right)$, or $\frac{d}{dx}\left(\frac{dy}{dx} - \beta y\right) = \alpha\left(\frac{dy}{dx} - \beta y\right)$.

If you write u in place of $\frac{dy}{dx} - \beta y$, this becomes $\frac{du}{dx} = \alpha u$, which you know how to solve.

So $u = Ce^{\alpha x}$, that is $\frac{dy}{dx} - \beta y = Ce^{\alpha x}$.

This is a first order linear equation, which you know how to solve using an integrating factor $e^{-\beta x}$. But you can use a neat trick to avoid this. Go back to the original equation and swap α and β, writing the equation for the complementary function as

$$\frac{d}{dx}\left(\frac{dy}{dx} - \alpha y\right) = \beta\left(\frac{dy}{dx} - \alpha y\right).$$

Then by exactly the same argument as before, with α and β interchanged,

$$\frac{dy}{dx} - \alpha y = De^{\beta x}.$$

Now subtract this equation from $\frac{dy}{dx} - \beta y = Ce^{\alpha x}$, found above. You then get the solution

$$(\alpha - \beta)y = Ce^{\alpha x} - De^{\beta x}.$$

You can simplify the constants by writing $\frac{C}{\alpha - \beta} = A$ and $\frac{-D}{\alpha - \beta} = B$. This completes the proof, that the most general solution of the equation $\frac{d^2y}{dx^2} + a\frac{dy}{dx} + by = 0$ is $y = Ae^{\alpha x} + Be^{\beta x}$.

The equations in this chapter all have real roots α and β. You will meet equations with complex roots in Chapter 7.

Example 6.3.2
Find the complementary function for the equation $\frac{d^2y}{dx^2} + 6\frac{dy}{dx} + 5y = 2x$.

Begin by writing the auxiliary equation $\lambda^2 + 6\lambda + 5 = 0$, which factorises as $(\lambda + 1)(\lambda + 5) = 0$. The roots α and β are -1 and -5. The complementary function is therefore $Ae^{-x} + Be^{-5x}$.

You can check this by substituting this expression for y in the left side of the differential equation, showing that it boils down to 0.

Example 6.3.3
Find the solution of $\frac{d^2y}{dt^2} + \frac{dy}{dt} - 6y = 0$ for which $y = 7$ when $t = 0$ and y remains finite as $t \to \infty$.

Linear differential equations often have time, represented by t, as the independent variable. You need to be able to solve them using any notation which is appropriate.

The auxiliary equation is $\lambda^2 + \lambda - 6 = 0$, with roots -3 and 2. The solution of the differential equation therefore has the form

$$y = A\mathrm{e}^{-3t} + B\mathrm{e}^{2t}.$$

For y to remain finite as $t \to \infty$, the coefficient B must be 0, so that $y = A\mathrm{e}^{-3t}$. When $t = 0$, $y = A\mathrm{e}^0 = A$, so that $A = 7$. The solution is therefore $y = 7\mathrm{e}^{-3t}$.

This method of finding the complementary function only works if the auxiliary equation has distinct roots α and β. If it has a repeated root α, you can carry the previous argument as far as the solution $u = C\mathrm{e}^{\alpha x}$, which in this case leads to

$$\frac{\mathrm{d}y}{\mathrm{d}x} - \alpha y = C\mathrm{e}^{\alpha x}.$$

But you can't now get a second equation by swapping α and β.

Fortunately this first order linear equation is very easy to solve. Multiplying by the integrating factor, which is $\mathrm{e}^{-\alpha x}$, gives

$$\frac{\mathrm{d}y}{\mathrm{d}x}\mathrm{e}^{-\alpha x} - y\left(\alpha\mathrm{e}^{-\alpha x}\right) = C, \quad \text{or} \quad \frac{\mathrm{d}}{\mathrm{d}x}\left(y\mathrm{e}^{-\alpha x}\right) = C.$$

Integrating this gives $y\mathrm{e}^{-\alpha x} = Cx + D$, that is $y = (Cx + D)\mathrm{e}^{\alpha x}$.

> If the auxiliary equation for the differential equation
>
> $a\frac{\mathrm{d}^2y}{\mathrm{d}x^2} + b\frac{\mathrm{d}y}{\mathrm{d}x} + cy = \mathrm{q}(x)$ has a repeated root α,
>
> the complementary function is $(Cx + D)\mathrm{e}^{\alpha x}$.

Example 6.3.4
Find the complementary function for the equation $\frac{\mathrm{d}^2y}{\mathrm{d}t^2} - 6\frac{\mathrm{d}y}{\mathrm{d}t} + 9y = \mathrm{e}^{3x}$.

The auxiliary equation $\lambda^2 - 6\lambda + 9 = 0$, or $(\lambda - 3)^2 = 0$, has a repeated root $\lambda = 3$. The complementary function is therefore $y = (Cx + D)\mathrm{e}^{3x}$.

You can check this by substitution. If $y = (Cx + D)\mathrm{e}^{3x}$, then

$$\frac{\mathrm{d}y}{\mathrm{d}x} = C\mathrm{e}^{3x} + (Cx + D) \times 3\mathrm{e}^{3x} = (3Cx + C + 3D)\mathrm{e}^{3x},$$

and $$\frac{\mathrm{d}^2y}{\mathrm{d}x^2} = 3C\mathrm{e}^{3x} + (3Cx + C + 3D) \times 3\mathrm{e}^{3x} = (9Cx + 6C + 9D)\mathrm{e}^{3x}.$$

So $$\begin{aligned}\frac{\mathrm{d}^2y}{\mathrm{d}t^2} - 6\frac{\mathrm{d}y}{\mathrm{d}t} + 9y &= ((9Cx + 6C + 9D) - 6(3Cx + C + 3D) + 9(Cx + D))\mathrm{e}^{3x}\\ &= ((9C - 18C + 9C)x + (6C - 6C) + (9D - 18D + 9D))\mathrm{e}^{3x}\\ &= 0, \quad \text{as required.}\end{aligned}$$

6.4 Complementary functions; the general case

The method of solving first order equations using an integrating factor (see P4 Chapter 9) can't be extended to general second order equations $\frac{d^2y}{dx^2}+\frac{dy}{dx}p(x)+yr(x)=q(x)$, in which the coefficients are functions rather than constants.

There is no such simple method of finding the complementary function for a second order equation. But it is still true that:

> The complementary function for a second order linear differential equation has the form $AG_1(x)+BG_2(x)$, where G_1 and G_2 are two independent functions and A and B are arbitrary constants.

The word 'independent' means that one function is not a constant multiple of the other.

Example 6.4.1
Show that $G_1(x)=x$ and $G_2(x)=e^x$ belong to the complementary function of the differential equation $(1-x)\frac{d^2y}{dx^2}+x\frac{dy}{dx}-y=(1-x)^2$. State the complete complementary function.

Substituting $G_1(x)$ and $G_2(x)$ for y in the left side of the equation gives

$$(1-x)0+x\times 1-x \quad \text{and} \quad (1-x)e^x+xe^x-e^x,$$

both of which reduce to 0.

The complementary function is therefore $Ax+Be^x$.

6.5 Finding particular integrals

When you differentiate a polynomial you get another polynomial. When you differentiate an exponential e^{ax} you get a similar exponential. When you differentiate a mixture of sines and cosines you get a mixture of sines and cosines. These facts are often the key to finding a particular integral.

In solving linear equations your aim is to find a function $y=F(x)$ which, when differentiated once or twice and mixed with the coefficients, produces the given function $q(x)$ on the right. It is likely that, if $q(x)$ is a polynomial, the function $F(x)$ will be a polynomial; and similarly for exponentials and mixtures of sines and cosines.

So to find a particular integral, try a function similar to the $q(x)$ you are aiming at, but with undetermined coefficients. When you substitute this in the left side, you will (if you have made a good choice) get some equations to solve for the coefficients.

The method is best understood from some examples.

Example 6.5.1
Solve the differential equation $\frac{dy}{dx}+4y=\sin 2x$.

You might think first of trying $y=a\sin 2x$. But if you differentiate this to find $\frac{dy}{dx}$ you get a term involving $\cos 2x$. So try $y=a\sin 2x+b\cos 2x$, and hope that the cosine terms go out, so that you are left with just a $\sin 2x$ term.

Notice that capital letters have not been used for the coefficients. These are not arbitrary constants, although for the time being they are unknown.

If $y=a\sin 2x+b\cos 2x$, the left side of the differential equation is

$$\begin{aligned}&(2a\cos 2x-2b\sin 2x)+4(a\sin 2x+b\cos 2x)\\&\quad=(4a-2b)\sin 2x+(2a+4b)\cos 2x.\end{aligned}$$

For the cosines to go out, you need $2a+4b=0$, or $a=-2b$. The expression in the line above then reduces to $(4(-2b)-2b)\sin 2x=-10b\sin 2x$. The goal is to get $\sin 2x$ on the right, so choose $b=-0.1$. This gives $a=-2(-0.1)=0.2$.

So a particular integral is $0.2\sin 2x-0.1\cos 2x$.

You have to add to this the complementary function, which is Ce^{-4x}.

The general solution of the differential equation is therefore

$$y=0.2\sin 2x-0.1\cos 2x+Ce^{-4x}.$$

Example 6.5.2
Solve the differential equation $\frac{d^2y}{dx^2}+6\frac{dy}{dx}+5y=2x$, given that $y=0$ and $\frac{dy}{dx}=0$ when $x=0$.

The right side is a polynomial of degree 1, so try to find a solution of the form $y=ax+b$. This gives $\frac{dy}{dx}=a$ and $\frac{d^2y}{dx^2}=0$. The left side of the differential equation is then $0+6a+5(ax+b)$, or $5ax+(6a+5b)$.

The aim is to find a and b so that this is $2x$. Equating coefficients, $5a=2$ and $6a+5b=0$. Therefore $a=0.4$ and $b=-0.48$.

It was shown in Example 6.3.2 that the complementary function is $Ae^{-x}+Be^{-5x}$. The general solution is therefore

$$y=0.4x-0.48+Ae^{-x}+Be^{-5x}.$$

It remains to use the initial conditions to find A and B. Since $\frac{dy}{dx}$ is involved, begin by differentiating to get

$$\frac{dy}{dx}=0.4-Ae^{-x}-5Be^{-5x}.$$

The conditions $y = 0$ and $\frac{dy}{dx} = 0$ when $x = 0$ give two equations for A and B,

$$0 = -0.48 + A + B \quad \text{and} \quad 0 = 0.4 - A - 5B.$$

These have solutions $A = 0.5$ and $B = -0.02$.

The solution satisfying the given initial conditions is therefore

$$y = 0.4x - 0.48 + 0.5\,e^{-x} - 0.02\,e^{-5x}.$$

Example 6.5.3
Find the general solution of the differential equation $\frac{d^2y}{dx^2} - 6\frac{dy}{dx} + 9y = e^{3x}$.

It was shown in Example 6.3.3 that the complementary function is $(Cx + D)e^{3x}$.

The usual procedure suggests trying a particular integral of the form ae^{3x}. But that will not work in this case: since ae^{3x} is part of the complementary function, substituting $y = ae^{3x}$ in the left side produces 0 on the right side.

There is a general rule which often works in such cases:

> If the usual trial integral $y = F(x)$ does not work because it is part of the complementary function, try $y = xF(x)$ instead.

In this example a trial integral $y = axe^{3x}$ will not work either, because that too is part of the complementary function. So try $y = ax^2e^{3x}$. Then

$$\frac{dy}{dx} = a(2x)e^{3x} + ax^2\left(3e^{3x}\right) = a\left(2x + 3x^2\right)e^{3x},$$

$$\frac{d^2y}{dx^2} = a(2 + 6x)e^{3x} + a\left(2x + 3x^2\right)\left(3e^{3x}\right) = a\left(2 + 12x + 9x^2\right)e^{3x}.$$

Substituting these in the left side of the equation gives

$$\frac{d^2y}{dx^2} - 6\frac{dy}{dx} + 9y = a\left(2 + 12x + 9x^2\right)e^{3x} - 6a\left(2x + 3x^2\right)e^{3x} + 9ax^2e^{3x}$$

$$= a\left(2 + (12 - 6\times 2)x + (9 - 6\times 3 + 9)x^2\right)e^{3x} = 2ae^{3x}.$$

To get e^{3x} on the right side you have to make $2a = 1$, so $a = \frac{1}{2}$, and the general solution is $y = \frac{1}{2}x^2e^{3x} + (Cx + D)e^{3x}$, or $y = \left(\frac{1}{2}x^2 + Cx + D\right)e^{3x}$.

Exercise 6B

1 Find general solutions of the following linear differential equations.

(a) $\frac{d^2y}{dx^2} - 4\frac{dy}{dx} + 3y = 0$ (b) $\frac{d^2y}{dx^2} + 3\frac{dy}{dx} - 4y = 0$ (c) $\frac{d^2x}{dt^2} + 7\frac{dx}{dt} + 12x = 0$

(d) $\frac{d^2x}{dt^2} + 12\frac{dx}{dt} + 36x = 0$ (e) $\frac{d^2u}{dx^2} + 6\frac{du}{dx} = 0$ (f) $4\frac{d^2y}{dt^2} - 4\frac{dy}{dt} + y = 0$

2 For each of the following differential equations find the solution which satisfies the given conditions, and sketch its graph.

(a) $\dfrac{d^2y}{dx^2}+3\dfrac{dy}{dx}+2y=0;\quad y=1$ and $\dfrac{dy}{dx}=0$ when $x=0$

(b) $\dfrac{d^2u}{dt^2}+5\dfrac{du}{dt}-6u=0;\quad u=2$ when $t=0$, and u remains finite as $t\to\infty$

(c) $\dfrac{d^2x}{dt^2}-9x=0;\quad x=0$ and $\dfrac{dx}{dt}=3$ when $t=0$

(d) $\dfrac{d^2z}{dy^2}-2\dfrac{dz}{dy}=0;\quad z=1$ when $y=0$, and $z=0$ when $y=1$

(e) $\dfrac{d^2z}{dt^2}+6\dfrac{dz}{dt}+9z=0;\quad z=1$ and $\dfrac{dz}{dt}=-4$ when $t=0$

(f) $\dfrac{d^2y}{dx^2}-6\dfrac{dy}{dx}+8y=0;\quad y=1$ and $\dfrac{dy}{dx}=1$ when $x=0$

3 Find complementary functions for the following differential equations.

(a) $\dfrac{dy}{dx}+2y=10e^{3x}$

(b) $\dfrac{dy}{dx}-3y=6$

(c) $\dfrac{d^2y}{dx^2}+5\dfrac{dy}{dx}+4y=8x-6$

(d) $3\dfrac{d^2u}{dt^2}+4\dfrac{du}{dt}+u=e^{-2t}$

(e) $\dfrac{d^2x}{dt^2}+\dfrac{dx}{dt}=e^{-t}$

(f) $\dfrac{d^2v}{dx^2}-4\dfrac{dv}{dx}+4v=8x+4$

4 Find particular integrals for the differential equations in Question 3.

5 Find the general solution of each of the following differential equations.

(a) $\dfrac{d^2y}{dx^2}-4y=12x$

(b) $2\dfrac{d^2x}{dt^2}+3\dfrac{dx}{dt}+x=6e^{t}$

(c) $2\dfrac{d^2x}{dt^2}+3\dfrac{dx}{dt}+x=6e^{-t}$

(d) $\dfrac{d^2z}{dx^2}+3\dfrac{dz}{dx}=6$

(e) $\dfrac{d^2x}{dt^2}-x=4\cos t$

(f) $\dfrac{d^2y}{dx^2}-2\dfrac{dy}{dx}+y=e^{x}$

6 For the following differential equations find solutions which satisfy the given conditions.

(a) $\dfrac{d^2y}{dx^2}-4\dfrac{dy}{dx}+3y=6;\quad y=2$ and $\dfrac{dy}{dx}=-2$ when $x=0$

(b) $2\dfrac{d^2x}{dt^2}+5\dfrac{dx}{dt}+2x=5\sin t;\quad x=2$ and $\dfrac{dx}{dt}=-3$ when $t=0$

(c) $\dfrac{d^2y}{dx^2}+\dfrac{dy}{dx}=2y-3e^{x};\quad y=2$ when $x=0$, and $y=0$ when $x=2$

(d) $\dfrac{d^2y}{dt^2}+2\dfrac{dy}{dt}-3y=10\sin t;\quad y=0$ when $t=0$, and y remains finite as $t\to\infty$

(e) $\dfrac{d^2u}{dx^2}+2\dfrac{du}{dx}+u=e^{-x};\quad u=1$ when $x=0$, and $\dfrac{du}{dx}=0$ when $x=2$

(f) $\dfrac{d^2y}{dx^2}-y=\cosh x;\quad y=0$ and $\dfrac{dy}{dx}=0$ when $x=0$

7* Verify that $y = x$ and $y = \frac{1}{x}$ satisfy the differential equation $x^2 \frac{d^2y}{dx^2} + x\frac{dy}{dx} - y = 0$.
Write down the general solution of $x^2 \frac{d^2y}{dx^2} + x\frac{dy}{dx} - y = 1$.

8* Show that the differential equation $2x^2 \frac{d^2y}{dx^2} - x\frac{dy}{dx} + y = 0$ has two independent solutions of the form $y = x^k$. Hence find the general solution of $2x^2 \frac{d^2y}{dx^2} - x\frac{dy}{dx} + y = 10x^3$.

Miscellaneous exercise 6

When the independent variable is time, denoted by t, a commonly used convention is to abbreviate the symbols $\frac{dx}{dt}$ to $\dot{x}$ and $\frac{d^2x}{dt^2}$ to $\ddot{x}$ (and similarly with letters other than x).
To give you practice with this convention, it is used in Questions 5 to 8 of this exercise.

1 Find the general solution of the differential equation $\frac{d^2y}{dx^2} - 3\frac{dy}{dx} - 4y = 50\sin 2x$. Given that $y = 0$ when $x = 0$, and that y remains finite as $x \to \infty$, find y in terms of x. (OCR)

2 Find differential equations for which the following are general solutions.

(a) $y = Ae^x + Be^{-2x} + 3\sin x$
(b) $y = x^2 + Ae^x + Be^{3x}$
(c) $y = (x + A)e^{2x} + Be^{-2x}$
(d) $y = 2x + A + Be^{-x}$
(e) $y = (x^2 + Ax + B)e^x$
(f) $y = (x^2 + A)\cosh 3x + B\sinh 3x$

3 (a) Find the general solution of the differential equation $\frac{d^2y}{dx^2} + 3\frac{dy}{dx} + 2y = 2x + 1$.

(b) Find the particular solution for which $y = -1$ and $\frac{dy}{dx} = 0$ when $x = 0$. For this solution, show that $\frac{dy}{dx} = 0$ when $2u^2 - u - 1 = 0$, where $u = e^{-x}$. Deduce that $\frac{dy}{dx} = 0$ only when $x = 0$.

Find the value of x for which $\frac{d^2y}{dx^2} = 0$. Hence show that $\frac{dy}{dx} \leqslant \frac{9}{8}$ for all values of x, and sketch the graph of y against x. (MEI)

4 Find and sketch the curves which satisfy the given differential equations and pass through the given points.

(a) $\frac{d^2y}{dx^2} - \frac{dy}{dx} - 2y = 3e^{-x}$, through $(0, 2)$ and $(2, 0)$

(b) $\frac{d^2y}{dx^2} - 2\frac{dy}{dx} + y = 2e^x$, through $(-1, 0)$ and $(1, 0)$

(c) $\frac{d^2y}{dx^2} - y = 2\sinh x$, through $(-1, 0)$ and $(0, 1)$

5 Solve the following differential equations with the given initial conditions.

(a) $\ddot{x} - x = 5t$; $x = -1$ and $\dot{x} = 0$ when $t = 0$

(b) $\ddot{x} - 4x = 10\cos t$; $x = 0$ and $\dot{x} = 0$ when $t = 0$

(c) $\ddot{x} - 4x = 8e^{2t}$; $x = 0$ and $\dot{x} = 6$ when $t = 0$

6 Investigate the nature of the solutions of the following differential equations for $t > 0$, with the given initial conditions. Give particular attention to the following questions, and illustrate your answers with sketch graphs.

- Does x tend to ∞, $-\infty$ or a finite limit as $t \to \infty$?
- Do x, $\dot{x}$ ever take the value 0?

(a) $\ddot{x} + 6\dot{x} + 5x = 0$; $x = 1$ and $\dot{x} = 1$ when $t = 0$

(b) $\ddot{x} - 6\dot{x} + 8x = 0$; $x = 1$ and $\dot{x} = 3$ when $t = 0$

(c) $\ddot{x} - 4\dot{x} + 4x = 0$; $x = 1$ and $\dot{x} = 1$ when $t = 0$

(d) $\ddot{x} - 3\dot{x} - 4x = 0$; $x = 1$ and $\dot{x} = -2$ when $t = 0$

(e) $\ddot{x} + 10\dot{x} + 25x = 0$; $x = 1$ and $\dot{x} = 2$ when $t = 0$

7† Investigate the solution of the differential equation $\ddot{x} - 2\alpha\dot{x} + \alpha^2 x = 0$ (where $\alpha \neq 0$) for $t \geqslant 0$, if initially $x = 1$ and $\dot{x} = c$ when $t = 0$. Find the conditions for

(a) x to remain finite, to tend to ∞, or to tend to $-\infty$, as $t \to \infty$;

(b) x to be zero for some $t > 0$;

(c) $\dot{x}$ to be zero for some $t > 0$.

Consider the possible orders of the numbers 0, α and c, and illustrate your conclusions with sketch graphs. Check your answers by reference to Question 6 (c) and (e).

8† Investigate the solution of the differential equation $\ddot{x} - (\alpha + \beta)\dot{x} + \alpha\beta x = 0$ (where $\alpha > \beta$) for $t \geqslant 0$, if initially $x = 1$ and $\dot{x} = c$ when $t = 0$. Find the conditions for

(a) x to remain finite, to tend to ∞, or to tend to $-\infty$, as $t \to \infty$;

(b) x to be zero for some $t > 0$;

(c) $\dot{x}$ to be zero for some $t > 0$.

Check your answers by reference to Question 6 (a), (b) and (d).

9 A closed electric circuit is activated by an electromotive force $E = V_0 \sin nt$, where t is time and V_0, n are constants. If the capacitance, inductance and resistance in the circuit (all positive and constant) are denoted by C, L and R respectively, the current I in the circuit at time t satisfies the differential equation

$$L\frac{d^2 I}{dt^2} + R\frac{dI}{dt} + \frac{1}{C}I = \frac{dE}{dt}.$$

Describe the variation of I with t in a circuit for which $CR^2 > 4L$, and show that after some time it settles down to a regular oscillation given by $I = a\sin nt + b\cos nt$, where a and b are constants.

Show that this can be written in the form $I = K\sin(nt + \alpha)$, where K and α are constants. Find an expression for K in terms of V_0, C, L, R and α.

10* Solve the differential equation $x^2\frac{d^2 y}{dx^2} - 3x\frac{dy}{dx} + 3y = -2x^2$, given that the solution for y is a polynomial in x.

7 Calculus with complex numbers

The word 'calculus' covers the techniques of differentiation and integration and their applications. Using complex functions can simplify some of these applications, and bring an unexpected unity to the subject. When you have completed the chapter, you should

- understand the extension of the rules for differentiating e^{cx} and $(ax+b)^n$ when the coefficients are complex numbers
- know how to use complex numbers to integrate functions involving products of exponential and trigonometric functions
- be able to use complex numbers to find particular integrals and complementary functions for linear differential equations
- know how to derive geometrical results using complex parametric equations
- understand that you can find partial fractions using complex linear factors.

The last two sections of the chapter show how complex numbers can be used to throw light on certain topics in real algebra and geometry, including the formulae for arc length that you met in Chapter 3. You may omit these sections if you wish.

7.1 The exponential function

At the end of P4 Chapter 11 it was suggested that, for the complex number $z = x + y\mathrm{i}$, the exponential function should be defined as

$$e^z = e^x(\cos y + \mathrm{i}\sin y).$$

This was justified first from the form of the Maclaurin expansion for $e^{y\mathrm{i}}$, but it can then be shown that other familiar properties of the exponential function follow from this definition. The two most important are rules for indices and differentiation.

Rules for indices If $z = x + y\mathrm{i}$ and $w = u + v\mathrm{i}$ then it follows from the definition that

$$\begin{aligned} e^z e^w &= e^x(\cos y + \mathrm{i}\sin y)e^u(\cos v + \mathrm{i}\sin v) \\ &= e^x e^u(\cos y + \mathrm{i}\sin y)(\cos v + \mathrm{i}\sin v) \\ &= e^{x+u}((\cos y\cos v - \sin y\sin v) + \mathrm{i}(\sin y\cos v + \cos y\sin v)) \\ &= e^{x+u}(\cos(y+v) + \mathrm{i}\sin(y+v)) \\ &= e^{x+u+(y+v)\mathrm{i}} = e^{z+w}. \end{aligned}$$

In a similar way you can prove that $\dfrac{e^z}{e^w} = e^{z-w}$. You can then use mathematical induction to prove that, if n is an integer (positive or negative), then $\left(e^z\right)^n = e^{nz}$.

This is as far as you can go for the time being. Rules for $\left(e^z\right)^w$ where w is not an integer need new definitions. You do not yet have a definition for a^w when both a and w are complex numbers.

Differentiation If x is real, then $\mathrm{e}^{b\mathrm{i}x} = \mathrm{e}^{(bx)\mathrm{i}} = \cos bx + \mathrm{i}\sin bx$.

You can differentiate this to give

$$\frac{\mathrm{d}}{\mathrm{d}x}\mathrm{e}^{b\mathrm{i}x} = -b\sin bx + b\,\mathrm{i}\cos bx = b\,\mathrm{i}(\cos bx + \mathrm{i}\sin bx) = b\,\mathrm{i}\mathrm{e}^{b\mathrm{i}x}.$$

More generally, if $c = a + b\mathrm{i}$, then you can differentiate e^{cx} using the product rule as

$$\begin{aligned}\frac{\mathrm{d}}{\mathrm{d}x}\mathrm{e}^{cx} &= \frac{\mathrm{d}}{\mathrm{d}x}\left(\mathrm{e}^{ax}\times\mathrm{e}^{b\mathrm{i}x}\right) = \frac{\mathrm{d}}{\mathrm{d}x}\left(\mathrm{e}^{ax}\right)\times\mathrm{e}^{b\mathrm{i}x} + \mathrm{e}^{ax}\times\frac{\mathrm{d}}{\mathrm{d}x}\left(\mathrm{e}^{b\mathrm{i}x}\right)\\ &= a\mathrm{e}^{ax}\times\mathrm{e}^{b\mathrm{i}x} + \mathrm{e}^{ax}\times b\,\mathrm{i}\,\mathrm{e}^{b\mathrm{i}x}\\ &= (a + b\,\mathrm{i})\mathrm{e}^{ax+b\mathrm{i}x} = c\,\mathrm{e}^{cx}.\end{aligned}$$

Again, for the time being this rule is restricted to a real variable x. You do not yet have a definition of differentiation with respect to a complex variable z.

If z, w and c are complex, x is real and n is a (positive or negative) integer, then

$$\mathrm{e}^{z}\mathrm{e}^{w} = \mathrm{e}^{z+w}, \quad \frac{\mathrm{e}^{z}}{\mathrm{e}^{w}} = \mathrm{e}^{z-w}, \quad \left(\mathrm{e}^{z}\right)^{n} = \mathrm{e}^{nz} \quad \text{and} \quad \frac{\mathrm{d}}{\mathrm{d}x}\mathrm{e}^{cx} = c\,\mathrm{e}^{cx}.$$

You can use these generalisations as the basis of various applications.

7.2 Integration

Integrals involving expressions such as $\mathrm{e}^{ax}\cos bx$ are tiresome to find by usual methods. Integration by parts must be applied twice to get the answer. The following example shows how such integrals can be found more easily using complex numbers.

Example 7.2.1

Find $\int \mathrm{e}^{x}\cos 3x\,\mathrm{d}x$.

The integrand is the real part of $\mathrm{e}^{x}(\cos 3x + \mathrm{i}\sin 3x)$, which is $\mathrm{e}^{x}\mathrm{e}^{3\mathrm{i}x}$, or $\mathrm{e}^{(1+3\mathrm{i})x}$. Since differentiation of e^{cx} with c complex follows the usual rule, so does the corresponding integration. Thus

$$\int \mathrm{e}^{(1+3\mathrm{i})x}\,\mathrm{d}x = \frac{1}{1+3\mathrm{i}}\mathrm{e}^{(1+3\mathrm{i})x} + k.$$

You can simplify this by writing $\dfrac{1}{1+3\mathrm{i}}$ as $\dfrac{1}{1+3\mathrm{i}}\times\dfrac{1-3\mathrm{i}}{1-3\mathrm{i}} = \dfrac{1-3\mathrm{i}}{10}$. Therefore

$$\frac{1}{1+3\mathrm{i}}\mathrm{e}^{(1+3\mathrm{i})x} = \tfrac{1}{10}\mathrm{e}^{x}(1-3\mathrm{i})(\cos 3x + \mathrm{i}\sin 3x).$$

The required integral is the real part of $\int \mathrm{e}^{(1+3\mathrm{i})x}\,\mathrm{d}x$:

$$\int \mathrm{e}^{x}\cos 3x\,\mathrm{d}x = \tfrac{1}{10}\mathrm{e}^{x}(\cos 3x + 3\sin 3x) + k.$$

7.3 Finding particular integrals

A similar method can be used to find particular integrals for linear differential equations with constant coefficients. The first example shows an alternative way of solving the first order equation in Example 6.5.1.

Example 7.3.1
Find a particular integral for $\frac{\mathrm{d}y}{\mathrm{d}x} + 4y = \sin 2x$.

The right side is the imaginary part of $\mathrm{e}^{2\mathrm{i}x}$. So consider first the differential equation

$$\frac{\mathrm{d}z}{\mathrm{d}x} + 4z = \mathrm{e}^{2\mathrm{i}x}.$$

Since the right side is an exponential, look for a trial solution of the form $z = a\mathrm{e}^{2\mathrm{i}x}$. Since $\frac{\mathrm{d}z}{\mathrm{d}x} = 2a\mathrm{i}\mathrm{e}^{2\mathrm{i}x}$, this will work if $2a\mathrm{i}\mathrm{e}^{2\mathrm{i}x} + 4a\mathrm{e}^{2\mathrm{i}x} \equiv \mathrm{e}^{2\mathrm{i}x}$.

So choose a so that $(2\mathrm{i} + 4)a = 1$, that is

$$a = \frac{1}{2(2+\mathrm{i})} = \frac{2-\mathrm{i}}{2(2+\mathrm{i})(2-\mathrm{i})} = \tfrac{1}{10}(2-\mathrm{i}).$$

This gives a particular integral for z,

$$z = \tfrac{1}{10}(2-\mathrm{i})\mathrm{e}^{2\mathrm{i}x} = \tfrac{1}{10}(2-\mathrm{i})(\cos 2x + \mathrm{i}\sin 2x).$$

A particular integral for y is the imaginary part of z, which is

$$\tfrac{1}{10}(2\sin 2x - \cos 2x).$$

Example 7.3.2
Find a particular integral for $\frac{\mathrm{d}^2x}{\mathrm{d}t^2} + 2\frac{\mathrm{d}x}{\mathrm{d}t} + 5x = \mathrm{e}^{-2t}(2\cos t + \sin t)$.

Expressions like the bracket on the right side arise when you find the real part of a product such as $(a + b\mathrm{i})(\cos t + \mathrm{i}\sin t)$. To get $2\cos t + \sin t$, you need to take $a = 2$ and $-b = 1$. So, writing $\cos t + \mathrm{i}\sin t$ as $\mathrm{e}^{\mathrm{i}t}$, the right side of the differential equation is the real part of $\mathrm{e}^{-2t} \times (2-\mathrm{i})\mathrm{e}^{\mathrm{i}t}$, which can be written as $(2-\mathrm{i})\mathrm{e}^{(-2+\mathrm{i})t}$.

Begin by considering the differential equation

$$\frac{\mathrm{d}^2z}{\mathrm{d}t^2} + 2\frac{\mathrm{d}z}{\mathrm{d}t} + 5z = (2-\mathrm{i})\mathrm{e}^{(-2+\mathrm{i})t},$$

and try a solution $z = a\mathrm{e}^{(-2+\mathrm{i})t}$.

Then $\frac{\mathrm{d}z}{\mathrm{d}t} = a(-2+\mathrm{i})\mathrm{e}^{(-2+\mathrm{i})t}$ and $\frac{\mathrm{d}^2z}{\mathrm{d}t^2} = a(-2+\mathrm{i})^2\mathrm{e}^{(-2+\mathrm{i})t} = a(3-4\mathrm{i})\mathrm{e}^{(-2+\mathrm{i})t}$.

This makes the left side of the equation

$$a\mathrm{e}^{(-2+\mathrm{i})t}((3-4\mathrm{i}) + 2(-2+\mathrm{i}) + 5) = a(4-2\mathrm{i})\mathrm{e}^{(-2+\mathrm{i})t},$$

which has to be identically equal to the right side $(2-\mathrm{i})\mathrm{e}^{(-2+\mathrm{i})t}$.

So the required value of a is $\dfrac{2-\mathrm{i}}{4-2\mathrm{i}}=\dfrac{1}{2}$.

This gives a particular integral $z=\frac{1}{2}\mathrm{e}^{(-2+\mathrm{i})t}=\frac{1}{2}\mathrm{e}^{-2t}(\cos t+\mathrm{i}\sin t)$.

From this you can deduce that a particular integral of the original differential equation is $x=\frac{1}{2}\mathrm{e}^{-2t}\cos t$. The reasoning is as follows.

Write z as $x+y\mathrm{i}$. The differential equation for z becomes

$$\frac{\mathrm{d}^2x}{\mathrm{d}t^2}+\frac{\mathrm{d}^2y}{\mathrm{d}t^2}\mathrm{i}+2\left(\frac{\mathrm{d}x}{\mathrm{d}t}+\frac{\mathrm{d}y}{\mathrm{d}t}\mathrm{i}\right)+5(x+y\mathrm{i})=(2-\mathrm{i})\mathrm{e}^{-2t}(\cos t+\mathrm{i}\sin t).$$

Equating the real parts shows that the equation

$$\frac{\mathrm{d}^2x}{\mathrm{d}t^2}+2\frac{\mathrm{d}x}{\mathrm{d}t}+5x=\mathrm{e}^{-2t}(2\cos t+\sin t)$$

has a particular integral $x=\frac{1}{2}\mathrm{e}^{-2t}\cos t$.

7.4 Complementary functions

Complex numbers also come in when you try to find the complementary function for second order differential equations with constant coefficients. The first step in doing this is to find the roots of the auxiliary equation $a\lambda^2+b\lambda+c=0$. For all the examples in the last chapter these roots were real (distinct or repeated). But in many situations to which these differential equations apply the auxiliary equations have complex roots.

The method of solution is the same, but an extra step is needed at the end to convert the answer into a real form.

Example 7.4.1
Find the complementary function for the equation in Example 7.3.2.

The auxiliary equation $\lambda^2+2\lambda+5=0$ has roots $-1\pm 2\mathrm{i}$, so the complementary function is $A\mathrm{e}^{(-1+2\mathrm{i})t}+B\mathrm{e}^{(-1-2\mathrm{i})t}$.

This can be written as

$$\begin{aligned}
&A\mathrm{e}^{-t}(\cos 2t+\mathrm{i}\sin 2t)+B\mathrm{e}^{-t}(\cos(-2t)+\mathrm{i}\sin(-2t))\\
&\quad=\mathrm{e}^{-t}(A\cos 2t+A\mathrm{i}\sin 2t+B\cos 2t-B\mathrm{i}\sin 2t)\\
&\quad=\mathrm{e}^{-t}((A+B)\cos 2t+(A-B)\mathrm{i}\sin 2t).
\end{aligned}$$

It is simpler to replace the constants $A+B$ and $(A-B)\mathrm{i}$ by single constants C and D, giving the complementary function in the final form

$$\mathrm{e}^{-t}(C\cos 2t+D\sin 2t).$$

Students sometimes think that D must be an imaginary number, but this is not so. In any problem with real initial conditions, C and D will be real. It is the original constants A and B which are complex; since their sum is real and their difference is imaginary, A and B are conjugate complex numbers.

Combining this result with the answer to Example 7.3.2 gives the complete solution of the differential equation:

$$x = \tfrac{1}{2}\mathrm{e}^{-2t}\cos t + \mathrm{e}^{-t}(C\cos 2t + D\sin 2t).$$

Another way of writing the complementary function is $R\mathrm{e}^{-t}\cos(2t-\alpha)$, where $R = \sqrt{c^2+d^2}$ and $\cos\alpha = \dfrac{C}{R}$, $\sin\alpha = \dfrac{D}{R}$.

Example 7.4.2
Solve the differential equation $\dfrac{\mathrm{d}^2x}{\mathrm{d}t^2} + p^2x = 2p\sin pt$.

The auxiliary equation is $\lambda^2 + p^2 = 0$, with roots $\pm p\mathrm{i}$, so the complementary function is $A\mathrm{e}^{p\mathrm{i}t} + B\mathrm{e}^{-p\mathrm{i}t}$, which is $A(\cos pt + \mathrm{i}\sin pt) + B(\cos pt - \mathrm{i}\sin pt)$, or $C\cos pt + D\sin pt$.

The right side is the imaginary part of $2p\mathrm{e}^{p\mathrm{i}t}$. But the particular integral can't be of this form, since $\mathrm{e}^{p\mathrm{i}t}$ is part of the complementary function. So, for the equation $\dfrac{\mathrm{d}^2z}{\mathrm{d}t^2} + p^2z = 2p\mathrm{e}^{p\mathrm{i}t}$, take a trial solution $z = at\mathrm{e}^{p\mathrm{i}t}$. This gives

$$\frac{\mathrm{d}z}{\mathrm{d}t} = a\mathrm{e}^{p\mathrm{i}t} + at\left(p\mathrm{i}\mathrm{e}^{p\mathrm{i}t}\right) = a\mathrm{e}^{p\mathrm{i}t} + atp\mathrm{i}\mathrm{e}^{p\mathrm{i}t},$$
$$\frac{\mathrm{d}^2z}{\mathrm{d}t^2} = ap\mathrm{i}\mathrm{e}^{p\mathrm{i}t} + ap\mathrm{i}\mathrm{e}^{p\mathrm{i}t} + at(p\mathrm{i})^2\mathrm{e}^{p\mathrm{i}t} = 2ap\mathrm{i}\mathrm{e}^{p\mathrm{i}t} - atp^2\mathrm{e}^{p\mathrm{i}t},$$

giving the left side $\dfrac{\mathrm{d}^2z}{\mathrm{d}t^2} + p^2z = 2ap\mathrm{i}\mathrm{e}^{p\mathrm{i}t}$.

This has to equal $2p\mathrm{e}^{p\mathrm{i}t}$, so take $a\mathrm{i} = 1$, giving $a = \dfrac{1}{\mathrm{i}} = -\mathrm{i}$.

The particular integral is then $z = -\mathrm{i}t(\cos pt + \mathrm{i}\sin pt)$. For the given equation the imaginary part is required, which is $x = -t\cos pt$.

The complete solution is therefore

$$x = -t\cos pt + C\cos pt + D\sin pt.$$

Exercise 7A

1 Write out in detail a proof that, if $z = x + y\mathrm{i}$ and $w = u + v\mathrm{i}$, then $\mathrm{e}^z \div \mathrm{e}^w = \mathrm{e}^{z-w}$.

2 Use mathematical induction to prove that, if n is a positive integer, then $\left(\mathrm{e}^z\right)^n = \mathrm{e}^{nz}$. Show that the result also holds if n is a negative integer.

3 Use complex numbers to find the following indefinite integrals.

(a) $\int e^{2x}\cos x\,dx$ (b) $\int e^{x}\sin 4x\,dx$ (c) $\int e^{-x}\cos 2x\,dx$

(d) $\int e^{-4x}\sin 3x\,dx$ (e) $\int xe^{2x}\cos 3x\,dx$ (f) $\int x^2e^{x}\sin x\,dx$

(g) $\int e^{x}\sin^2 x\,dx$ (h) $\int e^{-x}\sin x\sin 3x\,dx$ (i) $\int e^{-x}(2\cos 3x+\sin 3x)\,dx$

4 Find particular integrals for the following differential equations.

(a) $\dfrac{dy}{dt}+2y=5\cos t$ (b) $\dfrac{dy}{dt}-y=e^{t}\cos 2t$

(c) $\dfrac{d^2x}{dt^2}+4\dfrac{dx}{dt}-3x=\sin 2t$ (d) $\dfrac{d^2u}{dt^2}+\dfrac{du}{dt}-2u=\cos t$

(e) $\dfrac{d^2u}{dx^2}-2\dfrac{du}{dx}-3u=\sin x+3\cos x$ (f) $\dfrac{d^2y}{dx^2}-6\dfrac{dy}{dx}+9y=e^{3x}\cos x$

(g) $\dfrac{d^2x}{dt^2}+4x=\sin 2t$ (h) $\dfrac{d^2y}{dx^2}-2\dfrac{dy}{dx}+10y=e^{x}\cos 3x$

5 Find general solutions of the following differential equations.

(a) $\dfrac{d^2y}{dx^2}+4\dfrac{dy}{dx}+5y=0$ (b) $\dfrac{d^2y}{dx^2}-6\dfrac{dy}{dx}+25y=0$ (c) $\dfrac{d^2x}{dt^2}+9x=4e^{-t}$

(d) $\dfrac{d^2u}{dt^2}+2\dfrac{du}{dt}+2u=t$ (e) $\dfrac{d^2x}{dt^2}+x=e^{-t}\cos 2t$ (f) $\dfrac{d^2y}{dx^2}-2\dfrac{dy}{dx}+50y=\sin x$

(g) $\dfrac{d^2x}{dt^2}+2\dfrac{dx}{dt}-15x=\cos 3t$ (h) $\dfrac{d^2y}{dt^2}+6\dfrac{dy}{dt}+10y=e^{-3t}\sin t$

6 For each differential equation find the solution which satisfies the given conditions.

(a) $\dfrac{d^2y}{dx^2}-4\dfrac{dy}{dx}+8y=0$; $y=1$ and $\dfrac{dy}{dx}=2$ when $x=0$

(b) $\dfrac{d^2x}{dt^2}+4\dfrac{dx}{dt}+13x=0$; $x=1$ and $\dfrac{dx}{dt}=4$ when $t=0$

(c) $\dfrac{dy}{dx}+3y=10\cos x$; $y=2$ when $x=0$

(d) $\dfrac{dx}{dt}+x=2e^{-t}\sin 2t$; $x=0$ when $t=0$

(e) $\dfrac{d^2u}{dt^2}+2\dfrac{du}{dt}+2u=2t^2$; $u=0$ and $\dfrac{du}{dt}=0$ when $t=0$

(f) $\dfrac{d^2x}{dt^2}+2\dfrac{dx}{dt}+10x=9e^{-t}$; $x=1$ and $\dfrac{dx}{dt}=2$ when $t=0$

(g) $\dfrac{d^2y}{dx^2}+4\dfrac{dy}{dx}+5y=4(\cos x+\sin x)$; $y=0$ and $\dfrac{dy}{dx}=2$ when $x=0$

(h) $\dfrac{d^2x}{dt^2}-2p\dfrac{dx}{dt}+\left(p^2+q^2\right)x=e^{pt}\cos qt$; $x=a$ and $\dfrac{dx}{dt}=bq$ when $t=0$

7.5* The geometry of curves

You may omit this section if you wish. You will find it specially useful if you are also studying the Mechanics modules.

It was shown in P3 Chapter 4 that a curve can be defined by a pair of equations $x = \mathrm{f}(t)$, $y = \mathrm{g}(t)$, where t is a parameter. Now think of the point (x, y) as representing the complex number $z = x + y\mathrm{i}$ in an Argand diagram.

Then $z = \mathrm{f}(t) + \mathrm{g}(t)\mathrm{i}$ is a complex function of the parameter t, which can be denoted by a single function symbol $\mathrm{h}(t)$.

> The equation $z = \mathrm{h}(t)$, where h is a complex function of a real variable t, is the **complex parametric equation** of a curve in an Argand diagram.

Example 7.5.1
A circle in an Argand diagram has centre $c = a + b\mathrm{i}$ and radius r, where r is a real constant. Find a complex parametric equation for the circle.

In Fig. 7.1, C is the centre and P is a variable point on the circle representing the complex number z. The displacement $\overrightarrow{CP}$ is represented by the complex number $z - c$, which has modulus r. If its argument is t, then $z - c = r\mathrm{e}^{t\mathrm{i}}$.

The equation of the circle is therefore

$$z = c + r\mathrm{e}^{t\mathrm{i}}, \text{ for } -\pi < t \leqslant \pi.$$

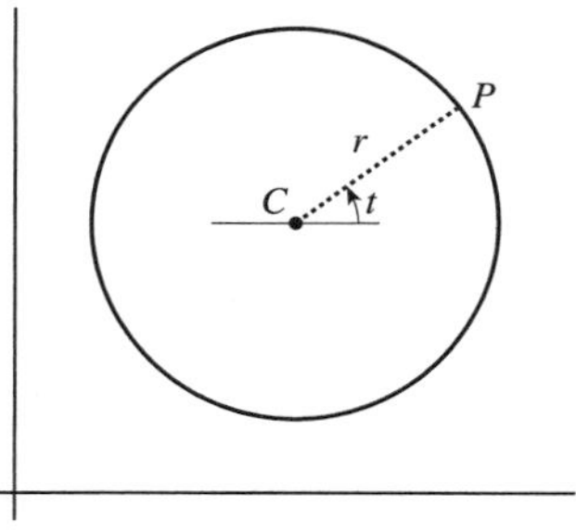

Fig. 7.1

You can recover the cartesian parametric equations by equating the real and imaginary parts in the equation

$$x + y\mathrm{i} = a + b\mathrm{i} + r(\cos t + \mathrm{i}\sin t).$$

This gives $x = a + r\cos t$, $y = b + r\sin t$.

Complex parametric equations provide a neat way of finding expressions for the direction of the tangent and the length of arc at any point of a curve. In Fig. 7.2, P and Q are the points on a curve corresponding to the values t and $t + \delta t$ of the parameter, so that $z = \mathrm{h}(t)$ and $z + \delta z = \mathrm{h}(t + \delta t)$.

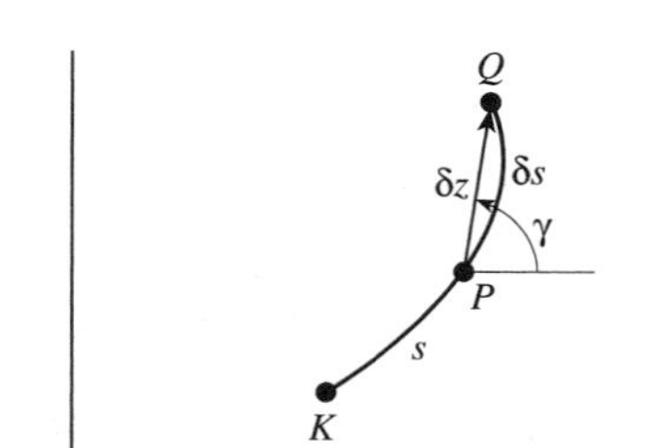

Fig. 7.2

K is a fixed point on the curve from which the arc length is measured; the distances measured along the curve from K to P and to Q are s and $s + \delta s$ respectively.

The next stage of the argument is similar to that used in differentiating trigonometric functions in P3 Section 2.2. The complex number δz, which is $(z + \delta z) - z$, corresponds to the displacement $\overrightarrow{PQ}$. Its modulus is the length PQ and its argument is the angle shown as γ in Fig. 7.2. So $\delta z = PQ\mathrm{e}^{\gamma\mathrm{i}}$.

Dividing by δt, $\dfrac{\delta z}{\delta t} = \dfrac{PQ}{\delta t} e^{\gamma i}$.

Now consider the limiting form of this equation as $\delta t \to 0$. The fraction $\dfrac{PQ}{\delta t}$ can be written as $\dfrac{PQ}{\delta s} \times \dfrac{\delta s}{\delta t}$. The factor $\dfrac{PQ}{\delta s}$ is the ratio of the lengths of the chord to the arc PQ, which tends to 1 as Q tends to P along the curve. So the product tends to $1 \times \dfrac{ds}{dt}$, which is simply $\dfrac{ds}{dt}$.

The angle γ tends to the angle that the tangent at P makes with the x-axis; this angle, shown in Fig. 7.3, is conventionally denoted by the Greek letter ψ. The equation for $\dfrac{\delta z}{\delta t}$ therefore takes the limiting form

$$\frac{dz}{dt} = \frac{ds}{dt} e^{\psi i}.$$

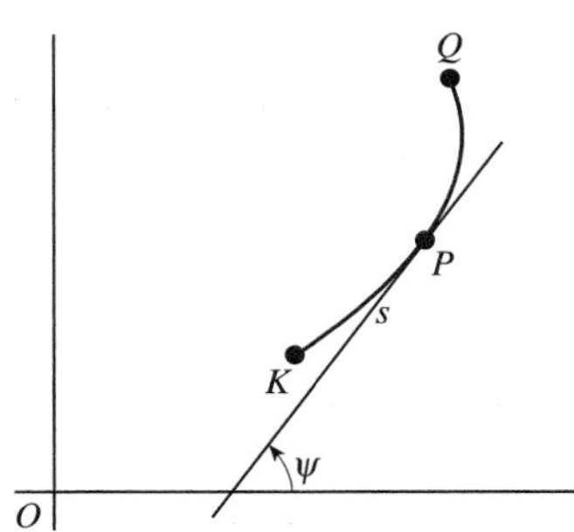

Fig. 7.3

For a curve with complex parametric equation $z = h(t)$, the derivative $\dfrac{dz}{dt}$ has modulus $\dfrac{ds}{dt}$ and argument ψ, where s is the arc length measured (in the direction of increasing t) from a fixed point on the curve, and ψ is the angle from the real axis to the positive tangent.

The requirement that s be measured 'in the direction of increasing t' is included to ensure that $\dfrac{ds}{dt}$ is positive; otherwise it couldn't be the modulus of a complex number. This then defines a positive direction along the tangent.

Example 7.5.2

A thread is wrapped round a cylinder of radius a, with an end P touching the cylinder at K. This end is then unwrapped, keeping the free part of the thread taut. Find an equation for the motion of P, and an expression for the distance from K to P along this path.

In Fig. 7.4, the cylinder is shown in an Argand diagram as a circle with centre O. K is the point $a + 0i$, RP is the free part of the thread and angle KOR is t. The arc length KR is at, which is also the length RP. The displacement $\overrightarrow{RP}$ makes an angle $t - \frac{1}{2}\pi$ with the real axis.

The point P then has complex coordinate

$$z = ae^{ti} + ate^{(t-\frac{1}{2}\pi)i} = ae^{ti} + at\, e^{ti} e^{-\frac{1}{2}\pi i}$$
$$= a(1 - ti)e^{ti},$$

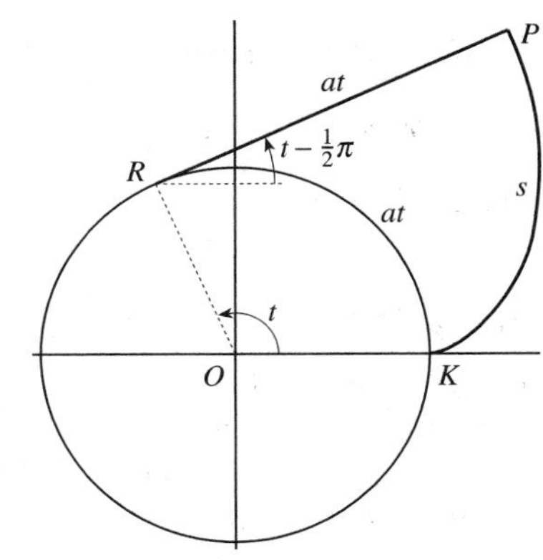

Fig. 7.4

and $\frac{dz}{dt} = a(-i)e^{ti} + a(1-ti)ie^{ti} = a\left(-i + i - ti^2\right)e^{ti} = at\,e^{ti}$.

Since $\frac{dz}{dt} = \frac{ds}{dt}e^{\psi i}$ you can deduce two things from this: that $\frac{ds}{dt} = at$, and that $\psi = t$ (possibly plus some multiple of 2π). The second of these equations confirms that (as you would expect) the tangent to the path of P is parallel to OR, that is at right angles to RP. The first can be integrated to give an expression for the distance s along the path from K to P,

$$s = \tfrac{1}{2}at^2.$$

The equation $\frac{ds}{dt} = \left|\frac{dz}{dt}\right|$ can be used to produce all the formulae for arc length in Chapter 3. Since z can be written in cartesian form $x + y\mathrm{i}$ and in polar form $r\mathrm{e}^{\theta i}$

$$\frac{dz}{dt} = \frac{dx}{dt} + \frac{dy}{dt}i \qquad \text{and} \qquad \frac{dz}{dt} = \frac{dr}{dt}e^{\theta i} + r\frac{d\theta}{dt}ie^{\theta i} = \left(\frac{dr}{dt} + r\frac{d\theta}{dt}i\right)e^{\theta i}.$$

So $$\frac{ds}{dt} = \left|\frac{dx}{dt} + \frac{dy}{dt}i\right| \qquad \text{and} \qquad \frac{ds}{dt} = \left|\frac{dr}{dt} + r\frac{d\theta}{dt}i\right| \qquad (\text{since } \left|e^{\theta i}\right| = 1).$$

Therefore $$\frac{ds}{dt} = \sqrt{\left(\frac{dx}{dt}\right)^2 + \left(\frac{dy}{dt}\right)^2} = \sqrt{\left(\frac{dr}{dt}\right)^2 + r^2\left(\frac{d\theta}{dt}\right)^2}.$$

If y is a function of x, or r is a function of θ, then x or θ themselves can be used as the parameters. The equations then become

$$\frac{ds}{dx} = \sqrt{1 + \left(\frac{dy}{dx}\right)^2} \qquad \text{and} \qquad \frac{ds}{d\theta} = \sqrt{\left(\frac{dr}{d\theta}\right)^2 + r^2}.$$

All of these equations for $\frac{ds}{dt}$, $\frac{ds}{dx}$ and $\frac{ds}{d\theta}$ can be rewritten in the standard integral forms.

You can also obtain results about angles by equating ψ to $\arg\left(\frac{dz}{dt}\right)$. See Exercise 7B Questions 1 to 3.

In applications to mechanics the parameter t is usually time, and z the position of a particle at time t. Then $\frac{dz}{dt}$ represents the velocity, and $\frac{d^2z}{dt^2}$ the acceleration. See Exercise 7B Questions 4 to 7.

7.6* An application to rational functions

This application extends to complex numbers the rules for differentiating $(ax+b)^n$, where a and b are complex numbers and n is a positive or negative integer. These rules can be proved by using the product rule and mathematical induction. You can do this for yourself by following the outline in Exercise 7B Questions 8 and 9.

One advantage of working with complex numbers is that all polynomials can be written as products of linear factors (possibly repeated). In finding partial fractions, for example, you need not distinguish between denominators which split into linear factors and those which don't. A fraction such as $\frac{1}{x^2+1}$ can be written as $\frac{1}{(x+\mathrm{i})(x-\mathrm{i})}$ and then split into partial fractions in the form

$$\frac{1}{(x+\mathrm{i})(x-\mathrm{i})} \equiv \frac{A}{x+\mathrm{i}} + \frac{B}{x-\mathrm{i}}.$$

The usual method extends directly to complex numbers. Multiplying by $x+\mathrm{i}$ gives

$$\frac{1}{x-\mathrm{i}} \equiv A + B\frac{x+\mathrm{i}}{x-\mathrm{i}};$$

then, putting $x=-\mathrm{i}$, $A=\frac{1}{2}\mathrm{i}$. Similarly $B=-\frac{1}{2}\mathrm{i}$. Therefore

$$\frac{1}{x^2+1} = \tfrac{1}{2}\mathrm{i}\left(\frac{1}{x+\mathrm{i}} - \frac{1}{x-\mathrm{i}}\right).$$

The next example makes use of this result.

Example 7.6.1
Find the nth derivative of $\tan^{-1} x$.

If $\mathrm{f}(x)=\tan^{-1} x$, then $\mathrm{f}'(x) = \frac{1}{x^2+1} = \frac{1}{2}\mathrm{i}\left(\frac{1}{x+\mathrm{i}} - \frac{1}{x-\mathrm{i}}\right)$.

To find $\mathrm{f}^{(n)}(x)$ you need the $(n-1)$th derivative of $\frac{1}{x+b}$, where $b=\mathrm{i}$ and $b=-\mathrm{i}$. Generalising from the first few derivatives

$$\frac{-1}{(x+b)^2},\quad \frac{2}{(x+b)^3},\quad \frac{-2\times 3}{(x+b)^4},\quad \ldots$$

suggests the general formula

$$\frac{\mathrm{d}^{(n-1)}}{\mathrm{d}x^{(n-1)}}\left(\frac{1}{x+b}\right) = (-1)^{n-1}\frac{(n-1)!}{(x+b)^n}.$$

You can prove this formally by using mathematical induction.

Putting everything together, with $b=\mathrm{i}$ and $b=-\mathrm{i}$,

$$\begin{aligned}
\mathrm{f}^{(n)}(x) &= \tfrac{1}{2}\mathrm{i}\times(-1)^{n-1}(n-1)!\left(\frac{1}{(x+\mathrm{i})^n} - \frac{1}{(x-\mathrm{i})^n}\right) \\
&= \tfrac{1}{2}(-1)^{n-1}(n-1)!\,\mathrm{i}\times\frac{(x-\mathrm{i})^n-(x+\mathrm{i})^n}{(x+\mathrm{i})^n(x-\mathrm{i})^n} \\
&= \frac{(-1)^{n-1}(n-1)!\,\mathrm{i}}{2\left(x^2+1\right)^n}\left((x-\mathrm{i})^n-(x+\mathrm{i})^n\right).
\end{aligned}$$

The expression in the final bracket can be expanded as

$$(x-\mathrm{i})^n-(x+\mathrm{i})^n=\left(x^n-\binom{n}{1}x^{n-1}\mathrm{i}+\binom{n}{2}x^{n-2}\mathrm{i}^2-\binom{n}{3}x^{n-3}\mathrm{i}^3+\ldots\right)$$

$$-\left(x^n+\binom{n}{1}x^{n-1}\mathrm{i}+\binom{n}{2}x^{n-2}\mathrm{i}^2+\binom{n}{3}x^{n-3}\mathrm{i}^3+\ldots\right)$$

$$=-2\mathrm{i}\left(\binom{n}{1}x^{n-1}+\binom{n}{3}x^{n-3}\mathrm{i}^2+\binom{n}{5}x^{n-5}\mathrm{i}^4+\ldots\right)$$

$$=-2\mathrm{i}\left(\binom{n}{1}x^{n-1}-\binom{n}{3}x^{n-3}+\binom{n}{5}x^{n-5}+\ldots\right).$$

So $$\mathrm{f}^{(n)}(x)=\frac{(-1)^{n-1}(n-1)!}{\left(x^2+1\right)^n}\left(\binom{n}{1}x^{n-1}-\binom{n}{3}x^{n-3}+\binom{n}{5}x^{n-5}+\ldots\right).$$

One final warning. The functions e^z and z^n which have been the subject of this chapter are easily and uniquely defined, but attempts to deal with the inverse functions $\ln z$ and $z^{\frac{1}{n}}$ take you into deep water, which should be entered with great caution.

Exercise 7B*

1 The figure shows a circle of radius a rolling along a horizontal straight line, which is taken as the real axis of an Argand diagram. It starts with the circle touching the line at the origin O. Show that, when the circle has turned through an angle t, the point P which was originally at O is represented by the complex number $z=at+a\mathrm{i}-a\mathrm{i}\mathrm{e}^{-t\mathrm{i}}$.

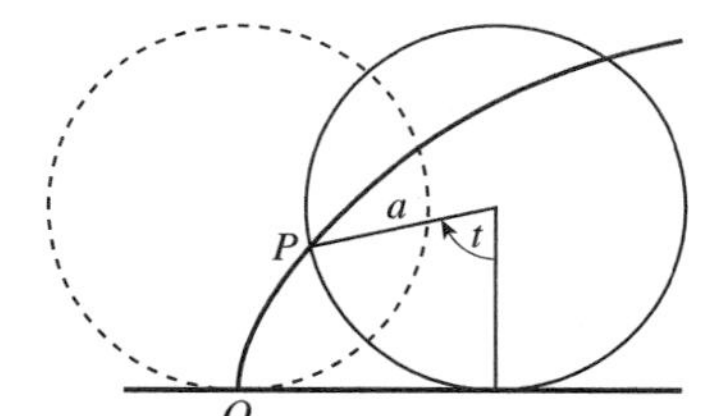

The path described by P is called a *cycloid*. Find the modulus and argument of $\frac{\mathrm{d}z}{\mathrm{d}t}$, and hence find expressions in terms of a and t for

(a) the arc length s of the cycloid from O to P,

(b) the angle ψ which the tangent to the cycloid at P makes with the horizontal.

Hence show that

(c) $s=4a(1-\sin\psi)$, (d) the tangent at P passes through the highest point of the circle.

2 The figure shows a circle of radius a rolling round a fixed circle of radius a and centre A. It starts with the two circles touching each other at the origin O, where AO produced is the positive real axis. When the point of contact has moved through an angle t round the fixed circle, the point of the rolling circle which was originally at O has moved to P. Show that P is represented by the complex number $z=-a+2a\mathrm{e}^{t\mathrm{i}}-a\mathrm{e}^{2t\mathrm{i}}$.

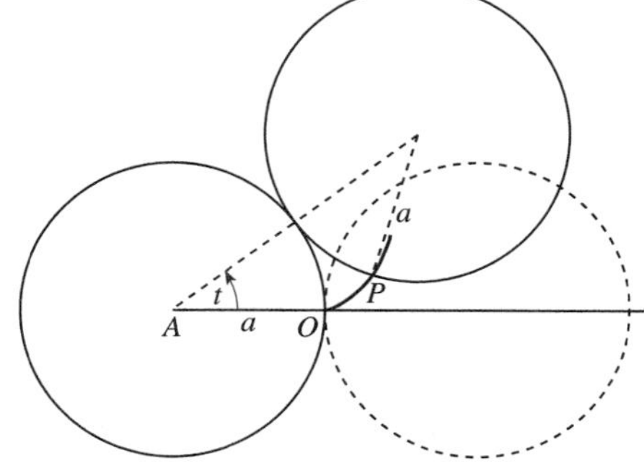

(The question continues on the next page.)

(a) Show that z can be written as $-ae^{ti}\left(e^{\frac{1}{2}ti}-e^{-\frac{1}{2}ti}\right)^2$, and deduce that the polar equation of the curve described by P is $r=2a(1-\cos\theta)$. (This curve is a *cardioid*; compare Fig. 3.3. It is also an *epicycloid* with $n=1$; see Exercise 3A Question 5.)

(b) Find expressions for the arc length s and the tangent angle ψ in terms of t, and show that $s=8a\left(1-\cos\frac{1}{3}\psi\right)$.

3 Show that the equilangular spiral $r=ae^{\theta\cot\alpha}$, where a and α are constants, can be represented by the complex equation $z=ae^{t(\cot\alpha+i)}$. Show that, if the arc length is measured from the point $z=a$, then $s=a\sec\alpha\left(e^{t\cot\alpha}-\alpha\right)$ and $\psi=\arg z+\alpha$.

Interpret the last equation geometrically.

Questions 4 to 7 use the dot notation for differentiation with respect to time; see Miscellaneous exercise 6.

4 A particle P describes a circle of radius a and centre O with complex parametric equation $z=re^{\theta i}$, where $\theta=\omega t$, so that t represents the time in seconds and ω is the constant angular speed in radians per second. Show that that $\dot{z}=a\omega\,i\,e^{\theta i}$, and interpret this equation in terms of the magnitude and direction of the velocity of the particle.

Obtain an expression for $\ddot{z}$, and interpret this in terms of the magnitude and direction of the acceleration.

5 Generalise Question 4 to the situation where the angular speed is not constant, so that θ is some other function of t and $\dot{z}=a\dot{\theta}ie^{\theta i}$.

6 Generalise Question 5 to the situation where the particle describes any plane curve, so that $z=re^{\theta i}$ where r and θ are functions of t. Show that $\dot{z}=\left(\dot{r}+r\dot{\theta}\,i\right)e^{\theta i}$ and obtain an expression for $\ddot{z}$. Interpret these in terms of the velocity and acceleration of the particle.

7 If the parameter t represents time, interpret the equation $\dot{z}=\dot{s}e^{\psi i}$ in Section 7.5 in terms of the velocity of a particle moving along a curve. Differentiate this to obtain an expression for $\ddot{z}$, and interpret this in terms of the acceleration of the particle.

One component of this acceleration has magnitude $\dot{s}\dot{\psi}$. Show that this can be written as $\dfrac{v^2}{\rho}$ where v is the speed of the particle and $\rho=\dfrac{ds}{d\psi}$. (The quantity ρ is called the *radius of curvature*.)

8 Find an expression for the nth derivative of $\dfrac{x}{x^2+1}$.

9 Show that $1+x+x^2$ can be factorised as $(\omega-x)(\omega^2-x)$, where $\omega=e^{\frac{2}{3}\pi i}$. Hence find expressions (with real coefficients) for the first 6 derivatives of $f(x)=\dfrac{1}{1+x+x^2}$.

Expand $f(x)$ as a Maclaurin series as far as the term in x^6. Show that, if the series is continued indefinitely, all the coefficients of x^{3n+2} are zero.

Show that these results can also be obtained by writing $f(x)$ as $\dfrac{1-x}{1-x^3}$.

Miscellaneous exercise 7

1 By expressing $p\cos bt + q\sin bt$ as the real part of $(p - q\mathrm{i})\mathrm{e}^{bt\mathrm{i}}$, find

(a) $\int \mathrm{e}^{at}(p\cos bt + q\sin bt)\,\mathrm{d}t$, (b) $\int t(p\cos bt + q\sin bt)\,\mathrm{d}t$.

2 Sketch the graph of $\mathrm{f}(t) = \mathrm{e}^{-at}\sin t$ for $t \geqslant 0$, where a is a positive constant. If u_n denotes $\int_{n\pi}^{(n+1)\pi} \mathrm{e}^{-at}\sin t\,\mathrm{d}t$, show that u_0, u_1, u_2, ... is a geometric sequence. Find

(a) $\int_0^\infty \mathrm{e}^{-at}\sin t\,\mathrm{d}t$, (b) $\int_0^\infty \mathrm{e}^{-at}|\sin t|\,\mathrm{d}t$.

3 A damped oscillation is modelled, for $t \geqslant 0$, by the differential equation $\frac{\mathrm{d}^2x}{\mathrm{d}t^2} + 2\frac{\mathrm{d}x}{\mathrm{d}t} + 4x = 0$. Find the solution for which $x = 0$ and $\frac{\mathrm{d}x}{\mathrm{d}t} = U$ when $t = 0$.

Find the value of t corresponding to the first stationary value of x. (OCR)

4 A light spring is lying at rest on a smooth horizontal table. One end is fixed and a particle is attached to the other end. The particle is set in motion and subsequently the extension x of the spring satisfies the differential equation $\frac{\mathrm{d}^2x}{\mathrm{d}t^2} + 4k\frac{\mathrm{d}x}{\mathrm{d}t} + 8k^2x = 8kV$, where t is the time from the start of the motion and k and V are positive constants. Find the general solution.

Given that $x = 0$ and $\frac{\mathrm{d}x}{\mathrm{d}t} = 0$ when $t = 0$, find x in terms of t, k and V. Deduce that, as $t \to \infty$, the extension of the spring approaches a constant value. State this value. (OCR)

5 The differential equation governing the current I amps in an electric circuit containing a resistor of R ohms, a capacitor of C farads and an applied electromotive force of E volts, all in series, is $R\frac{\mathrm{d}I}{\mathrm{d}t} + \frac{I}{C} = \frac{\mathrm{d}E}{\mathrm{d}t}$ where R and C are constants and t is time. Initially the current is monitored with $E = E_0$ provided by a battery, and subsequently with $E = E_0 \sin \omega t$, provided by a generator. Find the solution of the differential equation in each of the cases

(a) $E = E_0$, a constant, and initially $I = I_0$;

(b) $E = E_0 \sin \omega t$, where both E_0 and ω are constants, and initially $I = 0$. (MEI)

6 A reservoir supplies a large city. At time t days the level of the water above a fixed mark is x metres, where x and t are related by $\frac{\mathrm{d}^2x}{\mathrm{d}t^2} + 2\frac{\mathrm{d}x}{\mathrm{d}t} + 2x = 30\cos 3t - 35\sin 3t$. When $t = 0$, $x = 2$ and the water level is rising at a rate of 14 metres per day.

(a) Find x in terms of t.

(b) Show that, after a long time, the difference between the highest and lowest water levels is approximately 10 metres. (OCR)

7 Show that the differential equation $\ddot{x}+2\dot{x}+10x=16\cos\omega t$ has a particular integral of the form $A\cos\omega t+B\sin\omega t$, where $A^2+B^2=\dfrac{256}{\left(10-\omega^2\right)^2+4\omega^2}$.

The differential equation models the motion of an oscillating machine part. Explain why the particular integral gives a description of the steady state motion. Deduce that the oscillation is in resonance (that is, has maximum amplitude) when $\omega=2\sqrt{2}$. (OCR)

8 In a simulation, a piece of machinery is subjected to vibrations of the form $a\sin\omega t$ to test the behaviour of one of the components. Different values of ω are used in different tests. The component is not subject to any damping. The displacement, x cm, of the component can be modelled by $\ddot{x}+196x=2\sin\omega t$, where t is the time in seconds.

(a) Find the complementary function.

(b) In the case $\omega\neq 14$, find a particular integral of the form $\lambda\sin\omega t+\mu\cos\omega t$, where λ and μ are to be found in terms of ω. Hence write down the general solution of the differential equation.

(c) In the case $\omega=14$, why will a particular integral of the form given in (b) not satisfy the differential equation? In this case, find the particular integral and hence write down the general solution of the differential equation. Find the solution satisfying $\dot{x}=x=0$ when $t=0$. Describe the nature of the oscillations. (MEI)

9* The situation in Example 7.5.2 is generalised by replacing the circle by any curve given parametrically by $z=\mathrm{h}(t)$. The end of the thread is initially at the point $\mathrm{h}(0)$. Show that, when the part of the thread originally between $\mathrm{h}(0)$ and $\mathrm{h}(t)$ is unwrapped and held taut, the point P is represented by the complex number $z'=z-s\mathrm{e}^{\psi\mathrm{i}}$. Find $\dfrac{\mathrm{d}z'}{\mathrm{d}t}$, and hence show that s' and ψ' (for the curve described by z') are given by $\dfrac{\mathrm{d}s'}{\mathrm{d}t}=\left|s\dfrac{\mathrm{d}\psi}{\mathrm{d}t}\right|$ and $\psi'=\psi\pm\frac{1}{2}\pi$.

Find expressions for s' in terms of t for

(a) the spiral $z=\mathrm{e}^{(1+\mathrm{i})t}$,

(b) the catenary $z=ct+c\mathrm{i}\cosh t$ (see Revision exercise 1 Question 25),

(c) the cycloid $z=at+a\mathrm{i}-a\mathrm{i}\mathrm{e}^{-t\mathrm{i}}$ (see Exercise 7B Question 1).

Draw sketches to illustrate these examples. (The curves are called *involutes*.)

8 Approximations and errors

This chapter revisits the iterative method of solving equations described in P2 Chapter 14, and shows how to estimate the error in an approximate solution. When you have completed it, you should

- know the relation between the errors in successive terms of an iteration, and how it can be demonstrated algebraically and graphically
- be able to estimate how many iterations will be needed to find a root to given accuracy
- know how to use the relation between errors to take a short-cut to the value of the root
- understand the idea and the advantages of quadratic convergence.

8.1 Approximating to roots by iteration

You saw in P2 Chapter 14 that a powerful way of solving an equation $f(x)=0$ is to rewrite it in the form $x=F(x)$, and then to approximate to a root by the terms of a sequence defined by the iteration $x_{r+1}=F(x_r)$ with a starting value close to the root.

Using this method in examples suggested some general results (see P2 Section 14.5).

- The sequence will converge if the gradient of the graph of $y=F(x)$ at and around the root is not too large (roughly between -1 and 1).
- The smaller the modulus of the gradient, the fewer steps will be needed to reach the root to a given accuracy.
- If the gradient is negative the terms will be alternately above and below the root; if it is positive the terms will approach the root from one side.

You now know enough mathematical theory to be able to justify these observations.

The first step is to clarify what is meant by the error associated with an approximation. The aim is to get as close as possible to the root of the equation, which is an exact (but unknown) real number. The **error** is then defined by

$$\text{error} = \text{exact value} - \text{approximate value}.$$

So, if a term x_n of a sequence is used to approximate to the root α of an equation, and the error is denoted by e_n, then

$$e_n = \alpha - x_n.$$

You may find that some books define the error the other way round, as (approximate value – exact value). The definition given here is the more usual one, but it does not matter which you use provided that you are consistent.

Example 8.1.1
Investigate approximations to the root of the equation $\sin x = x - 0.1$.

If you plot the graphs of $\sin x$ and $x-0.1$, it is easy to see that there is only one root, which is about midway between 0.8 and 0.9. So try using the sequence $x_{r+1}=\sin x_r + 0.1$, with $x_0 = 0.85$, to approximate to the root.

If you go on long enough, you will find that the sequence converges on 0.853 75, which is the value of the root α correct to 5 decimal places.

Table 8.1 gives the terms of the sequence as far as $r = 10$, and also the errors $e_r = 0.853\,75 - x_r$.

r	x_r	e_r	r	x_r	e_r
0	0.85	0.003 75	6	0.853 45	0.000 30
1	0.851 28	0.002 47	7	0.853 55	0.000 20
2	0.852 12	0.001 63	8	0.853 62	0.000 13
3	0.852 68	0.001 07	9	0.853 66	0.000 09
4	0.853 05	0.000 70	10	0.853 69	0.000 06
5	0.853 29	0.000 46			

Table 8.1

You can see that the errors are getting smaller all the time. If you examine them more closely, you will notice that they are reduced in about the same proportion at each step. This can be shown by working out $\frac{e_{r+1}}{e_r}$ for each pair of successive terms, as in Table 8.2.

r	0	1	2	3	4
$\frac{e_{r+1}}{e_r}$	0.659	0.660	0.656	0.654	0.657
r	5	6	7	8	9
$\frac{e_{r+1}}{e_r}$	0.652	0.667	0.650	0.692	0.667

Table 8.2

This table shows that at each step the error is reduced to about 0.66 of its previous value. To a good approximation, successive errors form a geometric sequence with common ratio 0.66.

Later values in Table 8.2 seem to vary more erratically because the numbers in Table 8.1 are given to only 5 *decimal places. You can investigate this for yourself, using the value* 0.853 750 16 *for the root and keeping* 8 *decimal places in the table.*

Example 8.1.2

Investigate the errors when the sequence $x_{r+1} = \sqrt[3]{1 - x_r}$ is used to find approximations to the root of $x^3 + x = 1$.

By trial you can find that $x^3 + x - 1$ has values -0.184 when $x = 0.6$ and 0.043 when $x = 0.7$. So, by the sign-change rule, the root of $x^3 + x = 1$ is between 0.6 and 0.7, but closer to 0.7. A suitable choice of starting value is $x_0 = 0.68$.

If you go on long enough, you find that the sequence converges on the value 0.682 33, to 5 decimal places. Table 8.3 gives the approximations produced by the sequence, the errors calculated as $e_r = 0.682\,33 - x_r$, and the ratios of successive errors $\frac{e_{r+1}}{e_r}$.

r	x_r	e_r	$\frac{e_{r+1}}{e_r}$	r	x_r	e_r	$\frac{e_{r+1}}{e_r}$
0	0.680 00	0.002 33	−0.712	6	0.682 01	0.000 32	−0.687
1	0.683 99	−0.001 66	−0.717	7	0.682 55	−0.000 22	−0.727
2	0.681 14	0.001 19	−0.714	8	0.682 17	0.000 16	−0.687
3	0.683 18	−0.000 85	−0.714	9	0.682 44	−0.000 11	−0.727
4	0.681 72	0.000 61	−0.718	10	0.682 24	0.000 09	
5	0.682 77	−0.000 44	−0.727				

Table 8.3

The approximations are alternately too small and too large, so that the errors are alternately positive and negative. You can see from the final column that the ratio of successive errors is more or less constant, with a value of about -0.72.

8.2 Theoretical analysis

To understand the property of errors illustrated by Examples 8.1.1 and 8.1.2, you can choose either an algebraic approach (as in this section) or a graphical equivalent (see Section 8.3).

The algebraic method uses a generalisation of the Maclaurin expansion

$$\mathrm{f}(0) + \frac{\mathrm{f}'(0)}{1!}x + \frac{\mathrm{f}''(0)}{2!}x^2 + \ldots$$

given in P4 Chapter 7. This involves introducing a new function g such that

$$\mathrm{f}(x) \equiv \mathrm{g}(a + x)$$

where a is a constant. (For example, a could be $\frac{1}{2}\pi$, with $\mathrm{f}(x) = \cos x$ and $\mathrm{g}(x) = \sin x$.) This identity can be differentiated, using the chain rule on the right side, to give

$$\mathrm{f}'(x) \equiv \mathrm{g}'(a + x) \times 1 = \mathrm{g}'(a + x),$$
$$\mathrm{f}''(x) \equiv \mathrm{g}''(a + x) \times 1 = \mathrm{g}''(a + x), \quad \text{and so on.}$$

It follows, by putting $x = 0$, that $\mathrm{f}(0) = \mathrm{g}(a)$, $\mathrm{f}'(0) = \mathrm{g}'(a)$, $\mathrm{f}''(0) = \mathrm{g}''(a)$, and so on.

Now substitute these values in the Maclaurin expansion above. The result is the **Taylor expansion** for $\mathrm{g}(a + x)$,

$$\mathrm{g}(a) + \frac{\mathrm{g}'(a)}{1!}x + \frac{\mathrm{g}''(a)}{2!}x^2 + \ldots.$$

You can see that the Maclaurin expansion is just the Taylor expansion with $a = 0$. (It is now known that this result was known by James Gregory, who died in 1675, before either Brook Taylor, 1685–1731, or Colin Maclaurin, 1698–1746, was born.)

Taylor expansions are used in just the same way as Maclaurin expansions. An important application is to produce a sequence of polynomials

$$\mathrm{p}_1(x) = \mathrm{g}(a) + \frac{\mathrm{g}'(a)}{1!}x, \qquad \mathrm{p}_2(x) = \mathrm{g}(a) + \frac{\mathrm{g}'(a)}{1!}x + \frac{\mathrm{g}''(a)}{2!}x^2, \qquad \text{and so on,}$$

which are approximately equal to $\mathrm{g}(a+x)$ when x is small.

Example 8.2.1
Find a quadratic polynomial approximation to $\dfrac{1}{(2+x)^3}$ when x is small.

You can already do this by writing the expression as $\frac{1}{8}\left(1+\frac{1}{2}x\right)^{-3}$ and using the binomial expansion. Alternatively, think of it as $\mathrm{g}(a+x)$, with $\mathrm{g}(x) = x^{-3}$ and $a = 2$. Then $\mathrm{g}'(x) = -3x^{-4}$ and $\mathrm{g}''(x) = 12x^{-5}$, so that $\mathrm{g}(2) = \frac{1}{8}$, $\mathrm{g}'(2) = -\frac{3}{16}$ and $\mathrm{g}''(2) = \frac{12}{32} = \frac{3}{8}$. This gives the Taylor quadratic polynomial approximation

$$\frac{1}{(2+x)^3} \approx \tfrac{1}{8} + \left(-\tfrac{3}{16}\right)x + \tfrac{3}{16}x^2.$$

To apply Taylor expansions to the equation $x = \mathrm{F}(x)$, notice that since $e_r = \alpha - x_r$ and $e_{r+1} = \alpha - x_{r+1}$, the iteration $x_{r+1} = \mathrm{F}(x_r)$ can be written as

$$\alpha - e_{r+1} = \mathrm{F}(\alpha - e_r).$$

Now the right side of this equation has the form $\mathrm{g}(a+x)$, with F in place of g, α for a and $-e_r$ for x. Hopefully the error e_r is small, so the right side of this equation is approximately equal to

$$\mathrm{p}_1(-e_r) = \mathrm{F}(\alpha) + \frac{\mathrm{F}'(\alpha)}{1!}(-e_r) = \mathrm{F}(\alpha) - \mathrm{F}'(\alpha)e_r.$$

The equation then becomes $\alpha - e_{r+1} \approx \mathrm{F}(\alpha) - \mathrm{F}'(\alpha)e_r$.

But α is the exact root of $x = \mathrm{F}(x)$, so that $\alpha = \mathrm{F}(\alpha)$. The final form of the equation is then

$$e_{r+1} \approx \mathrm{F}'(\alpha)e_r.$$

This is the key to understanding all the results about the iterative method in Section 8.1.

First, you can check the numerical values for $\dfrac{e_{r+1}}{e_r}$ found in the examples.

Example 8.1.1 $\mathrm{F}(x) = \sin x + 0.1$ and $\alpha \approx 0.853\,75$, so that $\mathrm{F}'(x) = \cos x$, $\mathrm{F}'(\alpha) = \cos 0.853\,75 \approx 0.657$.

Example 8.1.2 $\mathrm{F}(x) = \sqrt[3]{1-x} = (1-x)^{\frac{1}{3}}$ and $\alpha \approx 0.682\,33$, so that $\mathrm{F}'(x) = \left(-\frac{1}{3}\right)(1-x)^{-\frac{2}{3}}$, $\mathrm{F}'(\alpha) = \left(-\frac{1}{3}\right)(1-0.682\,33)^{-\frac{2}{3}} \approx -0.716$.

The agreement with the ratios found experimentally is very close.

The iterative method converges to the root α if the sequence of errors converges to zero. The error sequence is approximately geometric with common ratio $F'(\alpha)$, and this converges to zero if $F'(\alpha)$ lies between -1 and 1. The smaller the modulus of the gradient, $|F'(\alpha)|$, the more rapidly the error sequence converges to zero. Finally, if $F'(\alpha)$ is negative the signs of the errors are alternately $+$ and $-$, so that terms of the sequence x_r are alternately above and below α; if $F'(\alpha)$ is positive, all the errors have the same sign.

> If the iteration $x_{r+1} = F(x_r)$ is used to find approximations to a root α of the equation $x = F(x)$, the sequence of errors $e_r = \alpha - x_r$ is approximately geometric with common ratio $F'(\alpha)$, provided that $F'(\alpha) \neq 0$.

Example 8.2.2
The iteration $x_{r+1} = \cos x_r$, with $x_0 = 0.7$, is used to find approximations to the root of the equation $x = \cos x$. How many repetitions are needed to obtain an approximation within 10^{-6} of the root?

The starting value $x_0 = 0.7$ was obtained from the sign-change rule, by noting that $0.7 - \cos 0.7 = -0.064\ldots$ and $0.8 - \cos 0.8 = 0.103\ldots$. This shows that the root is between 0.7 and 0.8, and suggests that it is probably closer to 0.7 than to 0.8 so that $|e_0| < 0.05$. (You can check this by working out $0.75 - \cos 0.75$.)

Taking $F(x) = \cos x$, $F'(x) = -\sin x$. Since α is between 0.7 and 0.8, and $\sin 0.7 = 0.64\ldots$ and $\sin 0.8 = 0.71\ldots$, almost certainly $|F'(\alpha)| < 0.7$. In that case, $|e_r| < 0.05 \times (0.7)^r$. So to get within 10^{-6} of the root, choose r so that $0.05 \times (0.7)^r < 10^{-6}$, that is $(0.7)^r < 2 \times 10^{-5}$.

You can solve this by taking logarithms (either to base e or base 10):

$$r \log 0.7 < \log\left(2 \times 10^{-5}\right), \text{ so that } r > \frac{\log\left(2 \times 10^{-5}\right)}{\log 0.7} = 30.3\ldots$$

(with the inequality reversed because $\log 0.7$ is negative).

So 31 iterations should be enough to obtain the root to the required accuracy.

In fact, this calculation has been rather cautious in estimating the error e_0 and the value of $F'(\alpha)$. The iteration actually needs only 27 repetitions to get within 10^{-6} of the root 0.739 085 13. Since you do not know α before you start, you can only make rough estimates of e_0 and $F'(\alpha)$. But the method gives a good idea of how long it will take to achieve the desired accuracy.

8.3 Graphical representations

The results proved in the last section can also be demonstrated by graphical methods.

Fig. 8.4 shows the graphs of $y = F(x)$ and $y = x$, intersecting at a point S at which $x = \alpha$, where $F(\alpha) = \alpha$. P is the point on $y = F(x)$ for which $x = x_r$, so that $y = F(x_r) = x_{r+1}$. This relates an x-coordinate x_r to a y-coordinate x_{r+1}.

But to continue the sequence further you need to show x_{r+1} as an x-coordinate. The clue is to use the line $y = x$. Since Q lies on $y = x$ and has y-coordinate x_{r+1}, its x-coordinate is also x_{r+1}.

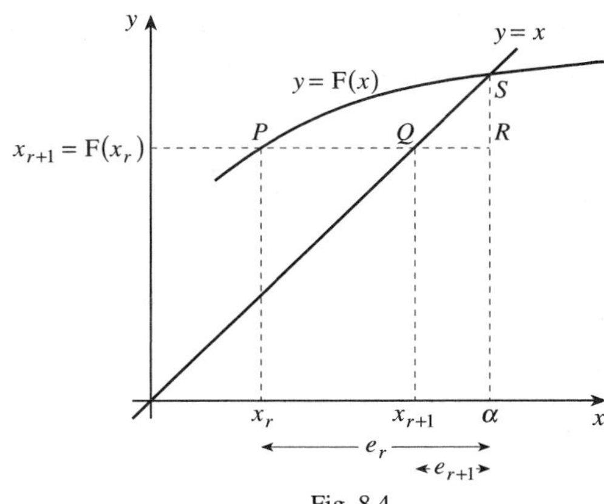

Fig. 8.4

This construction now makes it possible to display the whole sequence as a set of points on the x-axis. This is shown in Fig. 8.5 for the case $0 < F'(\alpha) < 1$, and in Fig. 8.6 for the case $-1 < F'(\alpha) < 0$. These are called, for obvious reasons, a **staircase diagram** and a **cobweb diagram** respectively.

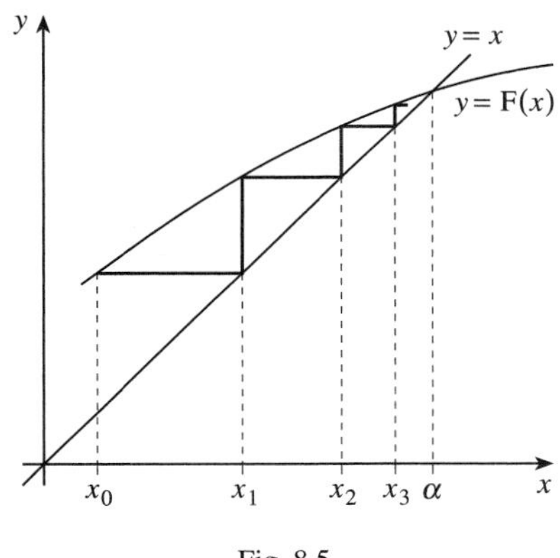

Fig. 8.5

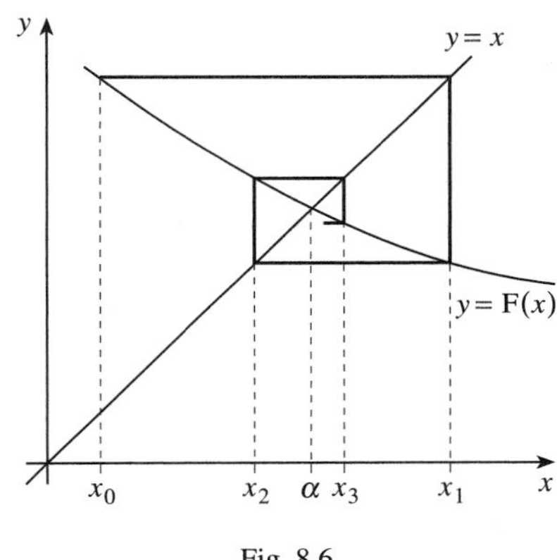

Fig. 8.6

You can see that, if $F'(\alpha)$ is positive, all the terms lie on the same side of the root; but that, if $F'(\alpha)$ is negative, they lie alternately above and below it.

Fig. 8.4 also shows the relation between the errors e_r and e_{r+1}. The length PR is equal to $\alpha - x_r$, which is the error e_r. Similarly QR is equal to e_{r+1}. But since the line QS has gradient 1, RS is also e_{r+1}. It follows that

$$\frac{e_{r+1}}{e_r} = \frac{RS}{PR},$$

which is the gradient of the chord PS. If the error e_r is small, this gradient is approximately equal to the gradient of the tangent to $F(x)$ at S. That is,

$$\frac{e_{r+1}}{e_r} \approx F'(\alpha).$$

8.4* Jumping to a conclusion

The approximation $\frac{e_{r+1}}{e_r} \approx F'(\alpha)$ can be written as $\alpha - x_{r+1} \approx F'(\alpha)(\alpha - x_r)$.

When you do an iteration you find the values of x_r and x_{r+1}. If you could estimate the value of $F'(\alpha)$, you could use this approximation to find an estimate for α.

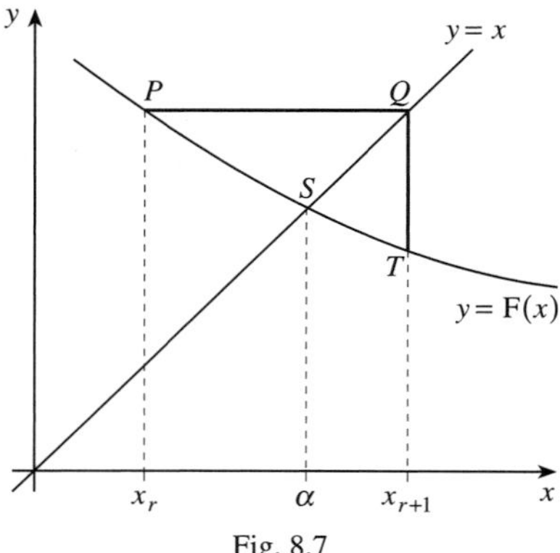

Fig. 8.7

There are two possible ways of estimating $F'(\alpha)$. These work especially well if $F'(\alpha)$ is negative, as in Fig. 8.7. One method is to note that the point P has coordinates $(x_r, F(x_r))$, that is (x_r, x_{r+1}), and similarly T has coordinates (x_{r+1}, x_{r+2}). You can see from the figure that the chord PT is very nearly parallel to the tangent to the curve at S. That is,

$$F'(\alpha) \approx \frac{F(x_{r+1}) - F(x_r)}{x_{r+1} - x_r} = \frac{x_{r+2} - x_{r+1}}{x_{r+1} - x_r}.$$

Alternatively, you can find $F'(x)$ and guess the value of x at which to evaluate it. If $F'(x)$ is not changing very quickly, it makes little much difference if your guess is some distance away from α.

Example 8.4.1
Find an approximation to the root of $x(x+2)^2 = 1$.

A decimal search shows that the root is about 0.2. Take this as x_0.

Table 8.8 lists the first three terms of the iteration $x_{r+1} = \dfrac{1}{(2+x_r)^2}$.

r	0	1	2
x_r	0.2	0.206 61	0.205 38

Table 8.8

Since $F(x) = \dfrac{1}{(2+x)^2}$, $F'(x) = \dfrac{-2}{(2+x)^3}$. So $F'(\alpha) < 0$.

Taking $r = 0$, the approximation $\dfrac{x_{r+2} - x_{r+1}}{x_{r+1} - x_r}$ for $F'(\alpha)$ is

$$\frac{x_2 - x_1}{x_1 - x_0} = \frac{-0.001\,23}{0.006\,61} \approx -0.186.$$

Alternatively, since the approximations are in turn below and above the root, α lies between $0.205\,38$ and $0.206\,61$. Make a guess that α is about 0.206. Then

$$F'(\alpha) \approx F'(0.206) = \frac{-2}{2.206^3} \approx -0.186.$$

So the approximation $e_{r+1} \approx F'(\alpha)e_r$ with $r = 1$ gives

$$\alpha - 0.205\,38 \approx -0.186(\alpha - 0.206\,61),$$

$$\alpha \approx \frac{0.205\,38 + 0.186 \times 0.206\,61}{1 + 0.186} \approx 0.205\,57.$$

You cannot be sure that this is correct to 5 decimal places. But you can now use this number as a new starting value for the iteration. In fact, the root of this equation is $0.205\,569\,4\ldots$, so the method takes you straight to the root to this degree of accuracy.

Exercise 8A

1 Show that the quadratic equation $x^2 - 6x + 7 = 0$ has roots between 1.5 and 1.6, and between 4.4 and 4.5. The equation can be rearranged as $x = \mathrm{F}(x)$, where $\mathrm{F}(x)$ can take any of the forms $\mathrm{F}_1(x) = \dfrac{x^2+7}{6}$, $\mathrm{F}_2(x) = 6 - \dfrac{7}{x}$, $\mathrm{F}_3(x) = \dfrac{7}{6-x}$, $\mathrm{F}_4(x) = \sqrt{6x-7}$.

(a) Use graphs of $y = x$ and $y = \mathrm{F}(x)$ to illustrate each of these.

(b) Explain why, for each $\mathrm{F}(x)$, the sequence defined by $x_{r+1} = \mathrm{F}(x_r)$ can be used to find approximations to one of the roots but not to the other. Identify in each case the root for which the process is effective.

(c) Use the derivative to decide which method gives the most rapid convergence to each of the roots.

(d) Starting with $x_0 = 1.6$ or $x_0 = 4.4$ as appropriate, evaluate and record enough terms of each sequence to give the corresponding root correct to 5 decimal places.

(e) Use the fact that the exact roots are $3 \pm \sqrt{2}$ to evaluate the errors e_r for each iteration. Verify that these are approximately geometric sequences with common ratio approximately equal to the derivatives you calculated in part (c).

(f) For each sequence, estimate how many terms you must take in order to reduce the error to less than 10^{-8}.

2 Apply the methods of Question 1 to the equation $x^2 + 4x - 13 = 0$ with roots close to -6.1 and 2.1, using $\mathrm{F}_1(x) = \dfrac{13-x^2}{4}$, $\mathrm{F}_2(x) = \dfrac{13}{x} - 4$, $\mathrm{F}_3(x) = \dfrac{13}{x+4}$, $\mathrm{F}_4(x) = \sqrt{13-4x}$ or $-\sqrt{13-4x}$.

Compare your conclusions with those in Question 1; identify any important differences.

3 The equation $x^3 - 9x - 2 = 0$ has roots close to -2.9, -0.2 and 3.1. Which of the arrangements $x = \mathrm{F}(x)$, with $\mathrm{F}_1(x) = \sqrt[3]{9x+2}$, $\mathrm{F}_2(x) = \dfrac{x^3-2}{9}$, $\mathrm{F}_3(x) = \sqrt{9 + \dfrac{2}{x}}$ or $-\sqrt{9 + \dfrac{2}{x}}$, $\mathrm{F}_4(x) = \dfrac{2}{x^2 - 9}$ gives the fastest convergence for the sequence $x_{r+1} = \mathrm{F}(x_r)$ to each of the roots? Find approximations to these roots to 4 decimal places. Check your calculations by finding the sum and the product of your answers.

4 Repeat Question 3 for the equation $x^3 + 4x^2 - 4 = 0$ with roots close to -3.7, -1.2 and 0.9, using $\mathrm{F}_1(x) = \sqrt[3]{4 - 4x^2}$, $\mathrm{F}_2(x) = \dfrac{4}{x^2} - 4$, $\mathrm{F}_3(x) = \dfrac{2}{\sqrt{x+4}}$ or $-\dfrac{2}{\sqrt{x+4}}$, $\mathrm{F}_4(x) = \sqrt{1 - \frac{1}{4}x^3}$ or $-\sqrt{1 - \frac{1}{4}x^3}$.

5 Use the iteration method to find a root of each of the following equations with an error less than 10^{-5}. Before starting your calculation, estimate the number of terms you must take in order to achieve the required accuracy.

(a) $x^3 - 12x = 20$ (b) $x^3 - 3x^2 = 4$ (c) $x = \cos 2x$

(d) $x \cosh x = 1$ (e) $\cos x = \sinh x$ (f) $(x+1)(x^2+1) = 10$

6 Draw diagrams similar to Figs. 8.5 and 8.6 to illustrate successive terms of the sequence defined by $x_{r+1} = \mathrm{F}(x_r)$ if $x_0 > \alpha$ and

(a) $\mathrm{F}'(\alpha) < -1$, (b) $-1 < \mathrm{F}'(\alpha) < 0$, (c) $0 < \mathrm{F}'(\alpha) < 1$, (d) $\mathrm{F}'(\alpha) > 1$.

7 Show that the equation $\cos x = \sinh x$ (see Question 5(e)) can be written in the form $x = \mathrm{F}(x)$, where $\mathrm{F}(x) = x + k(\cos x - \sinh x)$. Taking $x_0 = 0.7$, find a value of k for which $\mathrm{F}'(x_0)$ is very small. Use this to solve the equation correct to 8 decimal places.

8 Use the method of Question 7 to find solutions to these equations to 8 decimal places.

(a) $x^2 + \mathrm{e}^{-x} = 1$ (b) $x^2 = \sin x$

(c) $x = \frac{1}{10}\mathrm{e}^x$ (two roots), taking $x_0 = 0.1$ and $x_0 = 3.6$

9* Use Taylor expansions to find cubic polynomials which approximate to the following functions when x is small.

(a) $\tan\left(\frac{1}{4}\pi + x\right)$ (b) $\sqrt{9+x}$ (c) $\sec\left(\frac{1}{3}\pi + x\right)$ (d) $\sin^{-1}\left(\frac{1}{2} + x\right)$

10* For the following sequences $x_{r+1} = \mathrm{F}(x_r)$ and initial values x_0, calculate x_1 and x_2, and then use the method of Section 8.4 to obtain a more accurate approximation to the root of the equation $x = \mathrm{F}(x)$. Find to how many significant figures your answer is correct; if this is less than 5, repeat the process taking your approximation as the new value of x_0.

(a) $x_{r+1} = \mathrm{e}^{-x_r^2}$, $x_0 = 0.65$ (b) $x_{r+1} = \cos x_r$, $x_0 = 0.74$

(c) $x_{r+1} = \sqrt{x_r + 3}$, $x_0 = 2.3$ (d) $x_{r+1} = \ln(x_r + 2)$, $x_0 = 1.2$

11* Show that the process described in Section 8.4 gives an improved approximation to α of $\dfrac{x_{r+2}x_r - x_{r+1}^2}{x_{r+2} + x_r - 2x_{r+1}}$. (This is known as *Aitken's* δ^2 *process*.)

8.5 The case $\mathrm{F}'(\alpha) = 0$

The approximation $e_{r+1} \approx \mathrm{F}'(\alpha)e_r$ is no use if $\mathrm{F}'(\alpha) = 0$ since it then reduces to $e_{r+1} \approx 0$. This tells you that the error is small, but gives you no idea how small.

To see what happens in this case, go back to Section 8.2, where a first degree Taylor polynomial $\mathrm{p}_1(x)$ was used as an approximation to $\mathrm{F}(\alpha - e_r)$.

Using a second degree Taylor polynomial instead gives

$$\mathrm{F}(\alpha - e_r) \approx \mathrm{p}_2(-e_r) = \mathrm{F}(\alpha) + \frac{\mathrm{F}'(\alpha)}{1!}(-e_r) + \frac{\mathrm{F}''(\alpha)}{2!}(-e_r)^2$$

$$= \alpha + \tfrac{1}{2}\mathrm{F}''(\alpha)e_r^2, \text{ since } \mathrm{F}(\alpha) = \alpha \text{ and } \mathrm{F}'(\alpha) = 0.$$

Therefore $\alpha - e_{r+1} \approx \mathrm{F}(\alpha - e_r) \approx \alpha + \frac{1}{2}\mathrm{F}''(\alpha)e_r^2$, so $e_{r+1} \approx -\frac{1}{2}\mathrm{F}''(\alpha)e_r^2$.

There are two things to notice about this result.

- Since the square of a small number is very small, the iterative sequence gets close to the limit α very quickly. A sequence for which the error at each stage is roughly proportional to the square of the error at the previous stage is said to have **quadratic convergence**.
- If $\mathrm{F}''(\alpha)$ is positive, all the errors (except perhaps e_0) are negative; that is, all the terms of the iterative sequence (except perhaps the starting value) are greater than α. This is illustrated in Fig. 8.9, which starts like a cobweb but then becomes a staircase. If $\mathrm{F}''(\alpha)$ is negative, all the errors (except perhaps e_0) are positive.

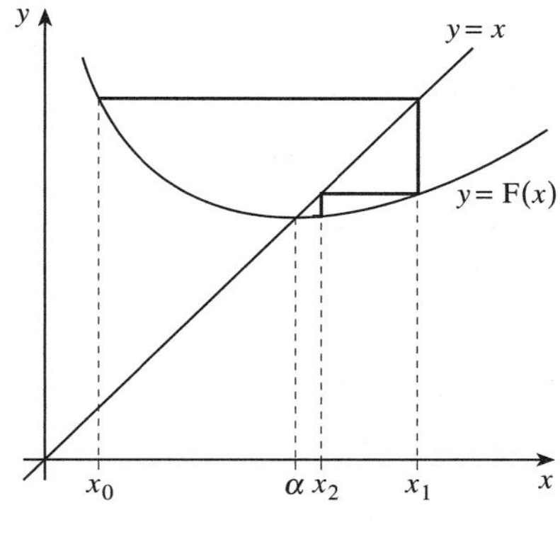

Fig. 8.9

If the iteration $x_{r+1} = \mathrm{F}(x_r)$ is used to find approximations to a root α of the equation $x = \mathrm{F}(x)$, and if $\mathrm{F}'(\alpha) = 0$, the sequence has quadratic convergence to the root.

An iteration for calculating square roots provides an interesting example of quadratic convergence. To solve the equation $x^2 = N$, where $N > 0$, you might try writing it as $x = \frac{N}{x}$ and using the iteration $x_{r+1} = \frac{N}{x_r}$ with a suitable starting value. But this gets you nowhere.

Find out how this iteration behaves if you take, say, $N = 5$ *and* $x_0 = 2$. *If* $\mathrm{F}(x) = \frac{N}{x}$, *what is* $\mathrm{F}'(\sqrt{N})$?

Suppose that you try adding kx to both sides of the equation, as described in P2 Example 14.5.2. Write $kx + x = kx + \frac{N}{x}$, that is $x = \mathrm{F}(x)$ with $\mathrm{F}(x) = \frac{kx + N/x}{k+1}$, and choose k so that $\left|\mathrm{F}'(\sqrt{N})\right|$ is small. Since $\mathrm{F}'(x) = \frac{k - N/x^2}{k+1}$, taking $k = 1$ makes $\mathrm{F}'(\sqrt{N}) = 0$; you can't do better than that! This means that the iteration $x_{r+1} = \mathrm{F}(x_r)$, with $\mathrm{F}(x) = \frac{1}{2}\left(x + \frac{N}{x}\right)$, has quadratic convergence to $\sqrt{N}$.

The relation between successive errors is

$$e_{r+1} = \sqrt{N} - x_{r+1} = \sqrt{N} - \tfrac{1}{2}\left(x_r + \frac{N}{x_r}\right)$$

$$= -\frac{1}{2x_r}\left(x_r^{\,2} - 2\sqrt{N} \times x_r + N\right) = -\frac{1}{2x_r}\left(x_r - \sqrt{N}\right)^2 = -\frac{1}{2x_r}e_r^{\,2}.$$

Example 8.5.1
Find a fraction which approximates to $\sqrt{5}$ with an error of less than 10^{-6}.

Clearly $2 < \sqrt{5} < 2.5$. If you take a starting value greater than $\sqrt{5}$, all the terms of the iterative sequence will be greater than $\sqrt{5}$. So take $x_0 = 2.5$. Then $2.5 > x_1 > x_2 > x_3 > \ldots > 2$ (see Fig. 8.9).

It follows that $\dfrac{1}{2x_r} < \dfrac{1}{4}$, so that $|e_{r+1}| < \frac{1}{4}|e_r|^2$. Since $|e_0| < \frac{1}{2}$,

$$|e_1| < \tfrac{1}{4} \times \left(\tfrac{1}{2}\right)^2 = \frac{1}{2^4}, \qquad |e_2| < \frac{1}{4} \times \left(\frac{1}{2^4}\right)^2 = \frac{1}{2^{10}},$$

$$|e_3| < \tfrac{1}{4} \times \left(\frac{1}{2^{10}}\right)^2 = \frac{1}{2^{22}}, \qquad \text{and so on.}$$

Since $2^{10} = 1024 > 10^3$, it follows that $2^{20} > 10^6$, and so $|e_3| < 10^{-6}$.

Now $x_0 = \dfrac{5}{2}$, $\quad x_1 = \dfrac{1}{2}\left(\dfrac{5}{2} + \dfrac{5}{\frac{5}{2}}\right) = \dfrac{9}{4}$, $\quad x_2 = \dfrac{1}{2}\left(\dfrac{9}{4} + \dfrac{5}{\frac{9}{4}}\right) = \dfrac{161}{72}$,

$$x_3 = \frac{1}{2}\left(\frac{161}{72} + \frac{5}{\frac{161}{72}}\right) = \frac{51\,841}{23\,184}.$$

You can check with your calculator that $\dfrac{51\,841}{23\,184} \approx 2.236\,067\,978$ and $\sqrt{5} \approx 2.236\,067\,977$, so that the agreement is much better than the 10^{-6} required.

Exercise 8B

1 Show that the cubic equation $x^3 - 3x + 1 = 0$ can be written in the form $x = \mathrm{F}(x)$, where $\mathrm{F}(x) = \dfrac{2x^3 - 1}{3(x^2 - 1)}$. Differentiate $\mathrm{F}(x)$, and show that $\mathrm{F}'(x) = 0$ when $x^3 - 3x + 1 = 0$.

Illustrate these properties by plotting the graphs of $y = x$, $y = \mathrm{F}(x)$ and $y = x^3 - 3x + 1$ on a calculator.

Demonstrate quadratic convergence to the roots of this cubic equation by calculating successive terms of the sequence defined by $x_{r+1} = \mathrm{F}(x_r)$, using initial values $x_0 = 0.35$, 1.5 and -1.9, and then calculating the errors in successive terms of the sequence.

2 Repeat Question 1 for

(a) the equation $xe^{2x} = 1$, taking $\mathrm{F}(x) = \dfrac{2x^2 + \mathrm{e}^{-2x}}{2x + 1}$ and $x_0 = 0.4$;

(b) the equation $x = \cos x$, taking $\mathrm{F}(x) = \dfrac{x \sin x + \cos x}{1 + \sin x}$ and $x_0 = 0.75$.

3 Show that, if $\mathrm{F}(x) = \dfrac{1}{3}\left(2x + \dfrac{N}{x^2}\right)$, where $N > 0$, then $x = \mathrm{F}(x)$ when $x = \sqrt[3]{N}$. Show also that $\mathrm{F}'(x) = 0$ for this value of x. Use these results to find a sequence which has quadratic convergence to $\sqrt[3]{N}$, and apply this to calculate $\sqrt[3]{10}$ as accurately as you can.

4 Generalise Question 3 to find a sequence which has quadratic convergence to $\sqrt[m]{N}$, where m is a positive integer. Apply the process to the calculation of $x = \sqrt[5]{30}$.

Miscellaneous exercise 8

1 Explain the advantage of using an iteration $x_{r+1} = \mathrm{F}(x_r)$ for which $\mathrm{F}'(x)$ is small and negative over the interval between x_0 and x_1.

Show that the equation $\mathrm{e}^x = \cot x$ has a root between 0.5 and 0.55. Rewrite this equation as $x = \mathrm{F}(x)$, where $\mathrm{F}(x) = x + k(\mathrm{e}^x - \cot x)$, and find a value of k for which $\mathrm{F}'(x)$ is small and negative over the interval $0.5 < x < 0.55$. Use this to find the root correct to 5 decimal places.

2 Illustrate the iterative method by using it to solve the equations

(a) $x = 3 + \frac{1}{4}x$, (b) $x = 6 - \frac{1}{2}x$,

taking an initial value $x_0 = 0$. For each iteration, calculate the errors e_0, e_1, e_2 and e_3, and suggest an expression for e_r.

What happens if you try to apply the method to the equations

(c) $x = \frac{5}{4}x - 1$, (d) $x = 10 - \frac{3}{2}x$, (e) $x = 8 - x$?

3 By making suitable rearrangements and using an iterative method, find the roots of the following equations correct to 6 decimal places.

(a) $x^2 - 3x - 7 = 0$ (b) $x^3 - 20x + 5 = 0$ (c) $x^4 - 4x^3 + 10 = 0$

(d) $x^4 = \mathrm{e}^x$ (e) $x^3 + 100\cos x = 0$ (f) $\sin x = \ln x$

4 (a) Show that the equation $4x = \mathrm{e}^x$ has a solution, α, near to $x = 2$.

(b) Show numerically that the iteration $x_{r+1} = \frac{1}{4}\mathrm{e}^{x_r}$ fails to converge to α for starting values on each side of α. Show analytically that this iteration will not converge to α.

(c) Show that, for any non-zero k, $x = k\left(\frac{1}{4}\mathrm{e}^x\right) + (1-k)x$ is a rearrangement of the original equation. Investigate numerically the convergence of the corresponding iterations in the two cases $k = 2$ and $k = -1$.

(d) By considering the derivative of the right side of the equation in (c), show that the value of k which gives fastest convergence is about -0.9. (MEI)

5 (a) Define two iterations by $x_{n+1} = \left(1 + ax_n^3\right)^{\frac{1}{4}}$ and $x_{n+1} = \left(\dfrac{x_n^4 - 1}{a}\right)^{\frac{1}{3}}$. Show that each, *if it converges,* does so to a root of the equation $x^4 - ax^3 - 1 = 0$.

(b)* Now take $a = 2$. Carry out whichever of these iterations you think suitable, starting from $x_0 = 2$, to calculate x_1, x_2, x_3, x_4. Use Aitken's acceleration method (that is, the method described in Section 8.4) on your values to find an improved estimate of the root near $x = 2$.

(c) Explain why, when a is very large, one root of the equation must be approximately a. State which of the above iterations is suitable to find this root, and prove your answer. (OCR, adapted)

9 The Newton–Raphson method

This chapter is about the Newton–Raphson method, which is another way of finding roots of equations numerically. When you have completed it, you should

- know and be able to use the Newton–Raphson method
- understand the theory behind the method, and be able to demonstrate it graphically
- know how to estimate the error in answers obtained by using the method
- appreciate that the Newton–Raphson method can be developed into an iterative process with quadratic convergence to the root
- be able to choose an appropriate method for solving a given equation to a given degree of accuracy, taking into account the computing facilities available.

9.1 First principles

The Newton–Raphson method of solving equations was devised by Newton to tackle a problem about the position of a planet in its orbit at a given time. This required the solution of an equation of the form $x - k\sin x = nt$ (called *Kepler's equation*). Joseph Raphson (1648–1715), who was one of the first people to publicise Newton's work, included an example in his textbook applying the method to the solution of a polynomial equation.

Before describing the method in general, here are two examples.

Example 9.1.1
Find an approximation to the root of $x^3 + x = 1$.

This is the equation solved by the iterative method in Example 8.1.2. It was shown there that a suitable choice of starting value is $x = 0.68$.

If the exact root is α, the error in this first approximation is $\alpha - 0.68$. Denote this by e, so that $\alpha = 0.68 + e$.

Now since α is the exact root, $\alpha^3 + \alpha = 1$. Substituting $0.68 + e$ for α gives $(0.68 + e)^3 + (0.68 + e) = 1$, which can be expanded as

$$\left(0.68^3 + 3\times 0.68^2 e + 3\times 0.68e^2 + e^3\right) + (0.68 + e) = 1.$$

This can be simplified to

$$2.3872e + 2.04e^2 + e^3 = 0.005\,568.$$

This looks unpromising. The original equation was a cubic with simple coefficients. The new equation is still cubic, but with more unpleasant coefficients.

But the clue is to notice that e is a small number, so that the powers e^2 and e^3 are very small compared with e. This means that the second and third terms on the left are much smaller than the first, and little accuracy is lost by dropping them. It follows that, with reasonable accuracy,

$$2.3872e \approx 0.005\,568, \quad \text{which gives} \quad e \approx \frac{0.005\,568}{2.3872} \approx 0.002\,33.$$

You can see how good this approximation is by substituting this value for e in the cubic equation above. The three terms on the left are

$$2.3872 \times 0.002\,33 \approx 5.6 \times 10^{-3}, \qquad 2.04 \times 0.002\,33^2 \approx 1.1 \times 10^{-5},$$
$$0.002\,33^3 \approx 1.3 \times 10^{-8}.$$

Clearly the first of these is so much greater than the others that the decision to drop the second and third terms is fully justified.

The error in the approximation 0.68 is about $0.002\,33$, so $\alpha \approx 0.682\,33$. This is correct to 5 decimal places, which shows how powerful the method can be.

Example 9.1.2
Find an approximation to the root of $\sin x = x - 0.1$.

This is the equation solved by the iterative method in Example 8.1.1. A suitable starting value was found to be 0.85, so write $\alpha = 0.85 + e$ where e is the error in this first approximation.

Since $\sin \alpha = \alpha - 0.1$, $\sin(0.85 + e) = (0.85 + e) - 0.1$, so

$$\sin 0.85 \cos e + \cos 0.85 \sin e = 0.75 + e.$$

This cannot be solved exactly for e. But since e is small, $\cos e$ and $\sin e$ can be replaced by the first degree polynomial approximations derived from the Maclaurin expansions

$$\sin e = e - \frac{e^3}{3!} + \ldots \quad \text{and} \quad \cos e = 1 - \frac{e^2}{2!} + \ldots.$$

These approximations are $\sin e \approx e$ and $\cos e \approx 1$; substituting in the above equation, and giving numerical values for $\sin 0.85$ and $\cos 0.85$, yields

$$0.751\,280\,405 \times 1 + 0.659\,983\,145e \approx 0.75 + e,$$

$$\text{so } e \approx \frac{0.001\,280\,405}{0.340\,016\,855} \approx 0.003\,77.$$

The resulting approximation for α, $0.85 + 0.003\,77 = 0.853\,77$, is not quite as close as in Example 9.1.1; the correct value for α to 5 decimal places is $0.853\,75$. But the accuracy is still impressive, considering the small amount of work involved.

9.2 The general result

To apply the Newton–Raphson method, it is best to write the equation in the form $\mathrm{f}(x) = 0$, where f is a known function. Suppose that, for a root α of the equation, a first approximation x_0 has been found (perhaps using a graph or the sign-change rule). The aim is to find a better approximation.

If the error in the first approximation is e, then $e = \alpha - x_0$. So substitute $x_0 + e$ for α in the equation $\mathrm{f}(\alpha) = 0$ to obtain an equation for e,

$$\mathrm{f}(x_0 + e) = 0.$$

The next step is suggested by Example 9.1.2, where $\sin e$ and $\cos e$ were replaced by their first degree Taylor (or Maclaurin) polynomial approximations. In the general case, replace $f(x_0 + e)$ by its first degree Taylor approximation (see Section 8.2) to get

$$f(x_0) + \frac{f'(x_0)}{1!}e \approx 0, \quad \text{or more simply} \quad f(x_0) + f'(x_0)e \approx 0.$$

From this it follows that $e \approx -\dfrac{f(x_0)}{f'(x_0)}$, so $\alpha = x_0 + e \approx x_0 - \dfrac{f(x_0)}{f'(x_0)}$.

This is the basis of the **Newton–Raphson method**:

> If x_0 is an approximation to a root α of the equation $f(x) = 0$,
>
> then usually $x_0 - \dfrac{f(x_0)}{f'(x_0)}$ is a better approximation to α.

Example 9.2.1
Find an approximation to the positive root of the equation $x^2 = e^{-x}$.

Fig. 9.1 shows the graphs of $y = x^2$ and $y = e^{-x}$. The x-coordinate of their point of intersection is about 0.7, so take $x_0 = 0.7$.

Write the equation in the form $f(x) \equiv x^2 - e^{-x} = 0$, and differentiate to obtain $f'(x) = 2x + e^{-x}$. Then a better approximation to the root is

$$0.7 - \frac{f(0.7)}{f'(0.7)} \approx 0.7 - \frac{0.7^2 - e^{-0.7}}{2 \times 0.7 + e^{-0.7}}$$
$$\approx 0.7 - \left(\frac{-0.006\,585\,3}{1.8966}\right)$$
$$\approx 0.703\,47.$$

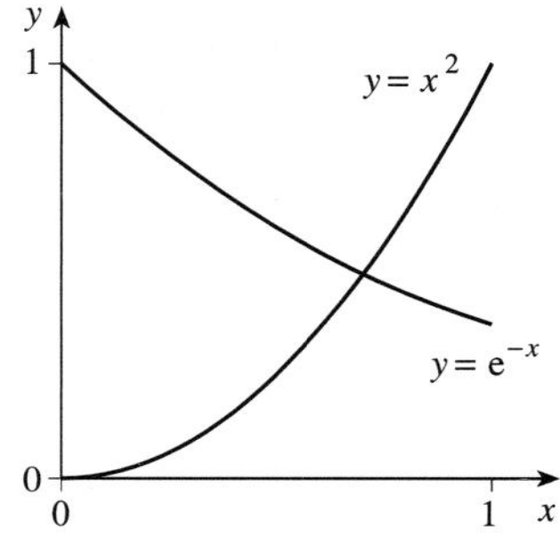

Fig. 9.1

As a test for accuracy, you can calculate $f(0.703\,465) \approx -4.61 \times 10^{-6}$ and $f(0.703\,475) \approx 1.44 \times 10^{-5}$. So, by the sign-change rule, the approximation 0.703 47 gives the root correct to 5 decimal places.

Example 9.2.2
For the earth's motion round the sun the eccentricity is about $\frac{1}{60}$. One month after the time of closest approach, Kepler's equation is $x - \frac{1}{60}\sin x = \frac{1}{6}\pi$ (that is, $\frac{1}{12}$ of a revolution). Find x.

The term $\frac{1}{60}\sin x$ cannot be greater than $\frac{1}{60}$, so for a first approximation choose $x_0 = \frac{1}{6}\pi$. Taking $f(x) = x - \frac{1}{60}\sin x - \frac{1}{6}\pi$, $f'(x) = 1 - \frac{1}{60}\cos x$, so

$$f\left(\tfrac{1}{6}\pi\right) = \tfrac{1}{6}\pi - \tfrac{1}{60}\sin\left(\tfrac{1}{6}\pi\right) - \tfrac{1}{6}\pi = -\tfrac{1}{120}, \quad f'\left(\tfrac{1}{6}\pi\right) = 1 - \tfrac{1}{60}\cos\left(\tfrac{1}{6}\pi\right) = 1 - \tfrac{1}{120}\sqrt{3}.$$

A better approximation to the root is therefore

$$\tfrac{1}{6}\pi - \left(-\tfrac{1}{120} \Big/ \left(1 - \tfrac{1}{120}\sqrt{3}\right) \right) = \tfrac{1}{6}\pi + 0.008\,455.$$

In this application what is of most interest is the difference between x and $\frac{1}{6}\pi$, which measures the angular adjustment needed to allow for the earth's elliptic orbit. This difference is $0.008\,455$ radians, which corresponds in time to $\dfrac{0.008\,455}{2\pi}$ of a year, or about 0.49 days.

Example 9.2.3

Show that, for large values of x, the equation $x \tan x = 1$ has roots close to $x = n\pi$, where n is a positive integer. When n is large, find a better approximation to the root.

The equation $x \tan x = 1$ can be written as $\tan x = \dfrac{1}{x}$. Fig. 9.2 shows that, when x is large, the graphs of $y = \tan x$ and $y = \dfrac{1}{x}$ intersect close to the points where $y = \tan x$ cuts the x-axis, that is $x = n\pi$.

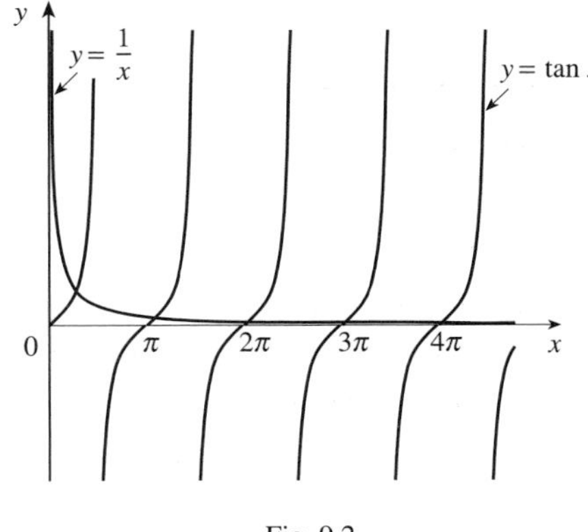

Fig. 9.2

There are a number of different ways of writing the equation to apply the Newton–Raphson method, for example

$$\mathrm{f}(x) \equiv x \tan x - 1 = 0,$$
$$\mathrm{g}(x) \equiv x \sin x - \cos x = 0,$$
$$\mathrm{h}(x) \equiv \tan x - \frac{1}{x} = 0.$$

In this case, the first two give the same improved approximation, but the third gives a different answer. (There is no reason why the answers should always be the same; there are many approximations to an exact root.)

The product rule gives $\mathrm{f}'(x) \equiv 1 \times \tan x + x \sec^2 x$, so that

$$\mathrm{f}(n\pi) = n\pi \times 0 - 1 = -1, \quad \mathrm{f}'(n\pi) = 0 + n\pi \times (\pm 1)^2 = n\pi.$$

The Newton–Raphson method gives a better approximation

$$x \approx n\pi - \frac{-1}{n\pi} = n\pi + \frac{1}{n\pi}.$$

9.3 A graphical representation

The Newton–Raphson method has a simple graphical interpretation. Fig. 9.3 shows the graph of a function $\mathrm{f}(x)$ in the neighbourhood of a root α of the equation $\mathrm{f}(x) = 0$. The graph cuts the x-axis at R, and a point P on the graph close to R has x-coordinate x_0; N is the point $(x_0, 0)$. The tangent to the graph at P cuts the x-axis at T.

The expressions $f(x_0)$ and $f'(x_0)$ which appear in the Newton–Raphson formula are represented by NP and $\frac{NP}{TN}$ respectively, so

$$\frac{f(x_0)}{f'(x_0)} = NP \Big/ \frac{NP}{TN} = NP \times \frac{TN}{NP} = TN.$$

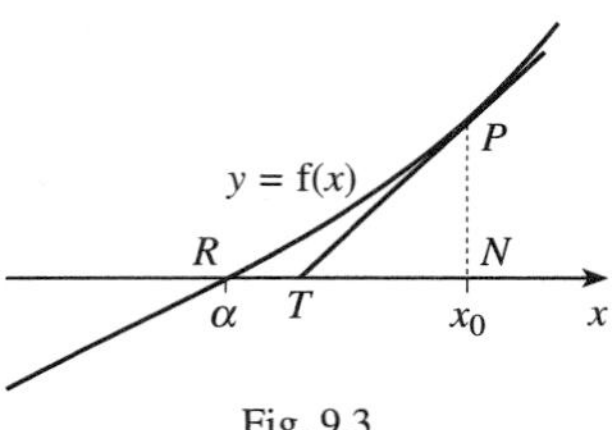

Fig. 9.3

The x-coordinate of T is then $x_0 - TN = x_0 - \frac{f(x_0)}{f'(x_0)}$.

So the Newton–Raphson approximation states that T is closer to R than N is. This is obvious from Fig. 9.3, which shows the simplest case, in which $f(x_0)$ and $f'(x_0)$ are both positive, and the curve bends upwards so that $f''(x)$ is positive between α and x_0.

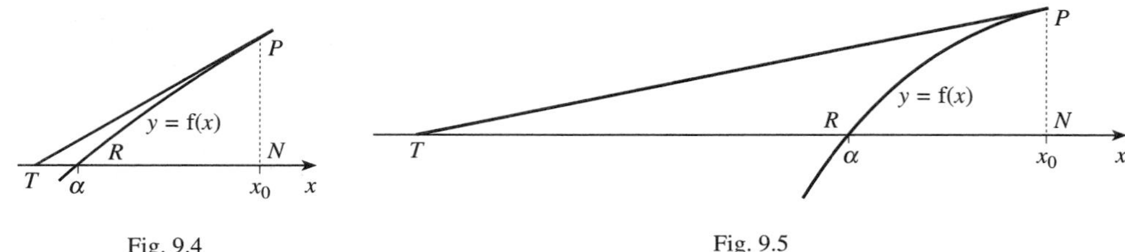

Fig. 9.4 Fig. 9.5

However, Figs. 9.4 and 9.5 show that you need to be cautious in using the method. In these figures $f(x_0)$ and $f'(x_0)$ are still positive, but the graph bends downwards, so that $f''(x)$ is negative between α and x_0. The points T and N then lie on opposite sides of R.

In Fig. 9.4 $f'(x_0)$ is fairly large and the curve bends quite gently, so that $f''(x)$ is small. It is still true that T is closer to R than N, so that $x_0 - \frac{f(x_0)}{f'(x_0)}$ is a better approximation to the root than x_0.

But in Fig. 9.5 $f'(x_0)$ is small and $f''(x)$ is large. You can see that in this case T is further from R than N, so that the method does not give a better approximation to the root. This is why the word 'usually' had to be used in the statement of the method in the last section.

Exercise 9A

1 Use the method in Section 9.1 to approximate to the roots of the following equations. Verify in each case that applying the general Newton–Raphson method in Section 9.2 leads to the same answer.

(a) $x^4 + 3x^2 + 2x - 4 = 0$ close to 0.8

(b) $x^3 + e^x - 2 = 0$ close to 0.6

(c) $\cos x + x - 3 = 0$ close to 3.8

2 For the following functions $f(x)$ and initial values x_0 find the values of $f(x_0)$, $f'(x_0)$ and $f''(x_0)$. Use these to sketch the graph of $y = f(x)$ in the neighbourhood of $x = x_0$. Use the Newton–Raphson method to find a better approximation to a root of $f(x) = 0$ than x_0. Find whether your improved approximation is accurate to 4 decimal places.

(a) $2x\sin x - 3,\ x_0 = 2.5$ (b) $\ln x + e^{-x} - 1,\ x_0 = 2.5$

(c) $\sqrt{x} - \cos x,\ x_0 = 0.65$ (d) $(x^2+2)(x^3+3) - (x^4+4),\ x_0 = -1.1$

3 Show that, for large values of x, the equation $x\sin x = 1$ has roots close to $x = n\pi$, where n is a positive integer. Find a better approximation to the root.

4 Show that each of the following equations has a root in the given interval. By choosing a suitable value of x_0 and using the Newton–Raphson method, find an approximation to the root, and determine to how many decimal places it is accurate. Then use the Newton–Raphson method again, taking the approximation you have found as the new value of x_0, to obtain a better approximation. Determine to how many decimal places this is accurate.

(a) $x^7 - 500 = 0,\ 2.4 < x < 2.5$ (b) $x^2 - \cosh x = 0,\ 1.6 < x < 1.7$

(c) $\sqrt{x} + \sqrt[3]{x} + \sqrt[4]{x} = 4,\ 2.1 < x < 2.2$

5 Draw diagrams similar to Figs. 9.3 and 9.4 for all eight possible combinations of sign of $f(x_0)$, $f'(x_0)$ and $f''(x_0)$. For which of these combinations does T lie between R and N? (You will need these in Exercise 9B Question 6.)

9.4 Estimating accuracy

When you use any approximate method, an important question is always 'how accurate is the answer'? Of course, you can never answer this precisely; if you could, you could find the root exactly, so there would be no need to use an approximate method. But an approximate answer is of little use unless you have some idea of the order of magnitude of its accuracy.

A hint of how this question can be answered for the Newton–Raphson method was given in the paragraph in italics in Example 9.1.1, where the magnitudes of the dropped terms were compared with that of the term which was kept. A similar argument can be used in the general case.

The Newton–Raphson approximation was derived in Section 9.2 by using the first degree Taylor polynomial approximation for $f(x_0 + e)$, that is by dropping the terms involving e^2 and higher powers of e. When e is small, the term in e^2 will be the most significant of these; and this term can be retained by using the second degree Taylor polynomial. That is, the exact equation $f(x_0 + e) = 0$ is replaced by the approximation

$$f(x_0) + \frac{f'(x_0)}{1!}e + \frac{f''(x_0)}{2!}e^2 \approx 0;$$

or, more simply, $f(x_0) + f'(x_0)e + \frac{1}{2}f''(x_0)e^2 \approx 0$.

Now, as before, take all the terms except the second to the other side of the equation, and divide by $f'(x_0)$:

$$e \approx -\frac{f(x_0)}{f'(x_0)} - \frac{f''(x_0)}{2f'(x_0)}e^2.$$

The first term on the right is the Newton–Raphson improvement, as before; the second term is small, since it has e^2 as a factor. So although you can't find it exactly, you can estimate it by replacing e in this term by its approximate value $-\frac{f(x_0)}{f'(x_0)}$. This gives

$$e \approx -\frac{f(x_0)}{f'(x_0)} - \frac{f''(x_0)}{2f'(x_0)}\left(-\frac{f(x_0)}{f'(x_0)}\right)^2 = -\frac{f(x_0)}{f'(x_0)} - \frac{(f(x_0))^2 f''(x_0)}{2(f'(x_0))^3}.$$

When, in the Newton–Raphson method, the first approximation x_0 is replaced by the improved approximation $x_0 - \frac{f(x_0)}{f'(x_0)}$, the error is given approximately by $-\frac{(f(x_0))^2 f''(x_0)}{2(f'(x_0))^3}$.

Example 9.4.1
Estimate the error in the approximation to the root of $x^2 = e^{-x}$ found in Example 9.2.1.

The example used $f(x) = x^2 - e^{-x}$ with $x_0 = 0.7$, so that

$$f(x_0) = 0.7^2 - e^{-0.7} \approx -0.006\,585\,303\,8,$$
$$f'(x_0) = 2 \times 0.7 + e^{-0.7} \approx 1.896\,585\,304,$$
$$f''(x_0) = 2 - e^{-0.7} \approx 1.503\,414\,696.$$

Only the order of magnitude of the error is needed, so it is sufficient to retain 2 significant figures and to estimate the error as

$$-\frac{(-0.0066)^2 \times 1.5}{2 \times 1.9^3} \approx -4.8 \times 10^{-6}.$$

You might therefore expect the answer to be about 5 too large in the 6th decimal place. In fact, if the calculation in Example 9.2.1 had been carried to the 6th decimal place the answer would have been 0.703 472. The correct root to 6 decimal places is 0.703 467, which confirms this error estimate. The decision to give an answer to 5 decimal places in Example 9.2.1 was therefore well founded; the figure in the 5th place could be out by 1 at most, but the figure in the 6th place is unreliable.

You can see that the error estimate $-\frac{(f(x_0))^2 f''(x_0)}{2(f'(x_0))^3}$ confirms the impression given by Figs. 9.4 and 9.5. For the method to work well the error has to be small. This happens if $|f(x_0)|$ and $|f''(x_0)|$ are both small and $|f'(x_0)|$ is large. But in Fig. 9.5 $|f''(x_0)|$ is large and $|f'(x_0)|$ is small, and this combination produces an unacceptably large error.

Notice also the contrast between Fig. 9.3 and Fig. 9.4, which differ in the sign of $f''(x_0)$. The error in Fig. 9.3 is negative, so that T is to the right of R; but in Fig. 9.4 the error is positive, with T to the left of R.

9.5 Newton–Raphson as an iteration

It can well happen that one application of the Newton–Raphson method is not good enough to produce the root of $f(x)=0$ to the accuracy you want. In that case, you can use the first answer as a starting value for a second application.

Example 9.5.1
Find the smallest positive root of $x+\tan x=2$ correct to 8 decimal places.

Writing $f(x)=x+\tan x-2$, you find that $f(0.8)=-0.17\ldots$ and $f(0.9)=0.16\ldots$, which suggests a root about 0.85.

So begin by taking $x_0=0.85$. Then a better approximation is $0.85-\dfrac{f(0.85)}{f'(0.85)}$ where $f(x)=x+\tan x-2$ and $f'(x)=1+\sec^2 x$. So calculate

$$x_0=0.85-\frac{0.85+\tan 0.85-2}{1+\sec^2 0.85}=0.853\,540\,045.$$

You have 9 decimal places here, but this answer may not give the root correct to 8 decimal places. So apply the method again, using $0.853\,540\,045$ in place of 0.85. This gives a second approximation $0.853\,530\,114$, which should be even closer to the root.

Is this close enough? To answer this, calculate a third approximation using $0.853\,530\,114$ as the input value. You will find that this gives you $0.853\,530\,114$ again, which suggests you are as close to the root as you are going to get.

With a suitable calculator, you can carry out these calculations very quickly. The method relies on the fact that the calculator uses ANS as a temporary memory.

Step 1 Enter the first approximation, in this case 0.85, into your calculator, and press ENTER. (On some calculators, this key is called EXE.)

Step 2 Enter $\text{ANS}-\dfrac{\text{ANS}+\tan \text{ANS}-2}{1+\sec^2 \text{ANS}}$.

Step 3 Press ENTER (EXE) for successive approximations to the solution.

The results suggest that, correct to 8 decimal places, the root is $0.853\,530\,11$.

To be quite sure, you can work out $f(x)$ with $x=0.853\,530\,105$ and $x=0.853\,530\,115$, and show that there is a change of sign in the interval. It turns out that the values are -2.95×10^{-8} and $+3.6\times10^{-9}$ respectively. From this you can say with certainty that the root is $0.853\,530\,11$ correct to 8 decimal places.

You will recognise this repeated application of the Newton–Raphson method as another example of iteration, defining a sequence by

$$x_{r+1} = x_r - \frac{f(x_r)}{f'(x_r)}$$

with a suitable value of x_0. Thus in Example 9.5.1,

$$x_0 = 0.85, \quad x_1 = 0.853\,540\,045, \quad x_2 = 0.853\,530\,114, \quad x_3 = 0.853\,530\,114$$

to 9 decimal places.

These calculations are represented graphically (though not to scale) in Fig. 9.6. The graph of $f(x)$ has positive gradient and is bending upwards. Since $f(0.85) < 0$, the starting value is to the left of the root. However, the tangent at $(0.85, f(0.85))$ cuts the x-axis to the right of the root, so that subsequent approximations come in to the root from the right.

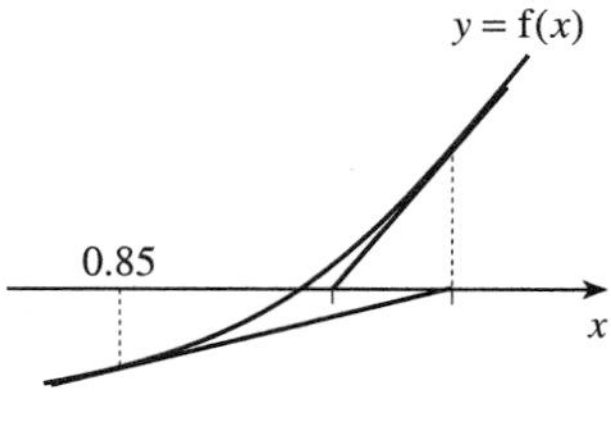

Fig. 9.6

To see what is happening in closer detail, you can break down the calculation into its separate stages and set out the results as in Table 9.7. The first line gives the successive values of x_r calculated in Example 9.5.1. From the values of $f(x_r)$, $f'(x_r)$ and $f''(x_r)$ calculated in the next three lines, you can calculate the 'correction' $-\dfrac{f(x_r)}{f'(x_r)}$ which takes you from x_r to x_{r+1}, and also the error estimate $-\dfrac{(f(x_r))^2 f''(x_r)}{2(f'(x_r))^3}$ which gives you an idea how good an approximation x_{r+1} will be.

x	0.85	0.853 540 045	0.853 530 114
$f(x)$	−0.011 667 286	0.000 032 916	0
$f'(x)$	3.295 801 366	3.314 445 903	
$f''(x)$	5.226 771 596	5.306 991 455	
$-\dfrac{f(x)}{f'(x)}$	0.003 540 045	−0.000 009 931	
Error estimate	-9.9×10^{-6}	-7.9×10^{-11}	

Table 9.7

Although the first approximation was quite close to the root, you can see that the error after the first application of the Newton–Raphson formula was about 1 in the 5th decimal place. This is because the root is in a region where the curve is bending quite fast, as is shown by the large value of $f''(x)$. To get accuracy to 8 decimal places, a second round of the Newton–Raphson method is used, starting at 0.853 540 045, the answer from the first application.

Table 9.7 shows that the error after the second round is about 8 in the 11th decimal place, so you can be confident that the root is 0.853 530 11 correct to 8 decimal places.

9.6 Why Newton–Raphson converges so quickly

What is impressive about the Newton–Raphson method is that it gives a very accurate approximation very quickly. Whereas the iterations in Chapter 8 might require 20 or 30 steps to get to an accuracy of 5 decimal places, a Newton–Raphson iteration will often get there after one or two steps. The reason for this is that Newton–Raphson iteration is an example of quadratic convergence, described in Section 8.5. This is proved in the following theorem.

Theorem The Newton–Raphson iteration

$$x_{r+1} = \mathrm{F}(x_r), \quad \text{where} \quad \mathrm{F}(x) \equiv x - \frac{\mathrm{f}(x)}{\mathrm{f}'(x)},$$

converging to a root α of $\mathrm{f}(x) = 0$, has quadratic convergence.

Proof Notice first that $\mathrm{F}(\alpha) = \alpha - \dfrac{\mathrm{f}(\alpha)}{\mathrm{f}'(\alpha)} = \alpha$, since $\mathrm{f}(\alpha) = 0$. That is,

$$x = x - \frac{\mathrm{f}(x)}{\mathrm{f}'(x)}$$

can be thought of as a rearrangement of $\mathrm{f}(x) = 0$ in the form $x = \mathrm{F}(x)$.

Also, writing $\mathrm{F}(x)$ in the form $x - \mathrm{f}(x) \times \dfrac{1}{\mathrm{f}'(x)}$ and using the product rule of differentiation gives

$$\mathrm{F}'(x) = 1 - \mathrm{f}'(x) \times \frac{1}{\mathrm{f}'(x)} - \mathrm{f}(x) \times \left(-\frac{1}{(\mathrm{f}'(x))^2} \right) \mathrm{f}''(x)$$

$$= \frac{\mathrm{f}(x)\mathrm{f}''(x)}{(\mathrm{f}'(x))^2}.$$

Therefore $\mathrm{F}'(\alpha) = \dfrac{\mathrm{f}(\alpha)\mathrm{f}''(\alpha)}{(\mathrm{f}'(\alpha))^2} = 0$, since $\mathrm{f}(\alpha) = 0$. This is the condition given in Section 8.5 for the iteration $x_{r+1} = \mathrm{F}(x_r)$ to converge quadratically to α.

This is illustrated well by Example 9.5.1. The error in the original starting value was about 3.5×10^{-3}. The errors after the next two steps are about -10^{-5} and -8×10^{-11}. So $e_1 \approx -0.8 e_0{}^2$, and $e_2 \approx -0.8 e_1{}^2$.

Exercise 9B

1 Use the Newton–Raphson method for each of the following equations, with the given initial value x_0, to find a better approximation, and estimate the error. Hence give the root to as many decimal places as the method justifies.

(a) $x^3 - 3x^2 - 2 = 0, \ x_0 = 3.2$

(b) $\sqrt{x-1} - \dfrac{5}{x^2} = 0, \ x_0 = 2.1$

(c) $x + \mathrm{e}^x - 6 = 0, \ x_0 = 1.5$

(d) $x \ln x = 5, \ x_0 = 3.8$

2 Iterate the Newton–Raphson method for each of the following equations, with the given initial value x_0, to find the root as accurately as your calculator permits.

(a) $x^2 - \cos x = 0, x_0 = 0.8$ (b) $\sinh x - \sqrt{4 - x^2} = 0, x_0 = 1.2$ (c) $e^{-x} = \sin x, x_0 = 0.6$

3 Analyse the iterative solutions to the equations in Question 2 by means of a table similar to Table 9.7.

4 Choose an initial value and use the Newton–Raphson method for as many iterations as you need to find approximations to the roots of the following equations correct to 8 decimal places.

(a) $2x^5 + x - 1 = 0$ (b) $x^3 e^x = 1$ (c) $x + \sin x = 1$ (d) $x \sinh x = \cosh x$

5 If a chain of length $2l$ is stretched between two points at the same level a distance $2a$ apart, then it will sag by an amount $\dfrac{\cosh \lambda a - 1}{\lambda}$, where λ is a solution of $\lambda l = \sinh a\lambda$.

Find the sag, correct to 3 significant figures, if a chain of length 21 metres is stretched between two points 20 metres apart.

6† With the notation of the Theorem in Section 9.6, show that $F''(\alpha) = \dfrac{f''(\alpha)}{f'(\alpha)}$. Hence use the result in Section 8.5 to show that successive errors in a Newton–Raphson iteration are related by the approximation $e_{r+1} \approx -\dfrac{f''(\alpha)}{2f'(\alpha)} e_r^2$. Demonstrate this numerically by evaluating successive error estimates in a Newton–Raphson iteration to the root of the equation $\tan x - x - 1 = 0$ with $x_0 = 1.1$.

What is the significance of the minus sign in this relation, and in the formula for the Newton–Raphson error estimate? Use the graphs which you drew in Exercise 9A Question 5 to demonstrate the necessity for these minus signs.

7† Use the Newton–Raphson method to obtain an iteration which converges to $\sqrt[m]{N}$, where N is a positive number and m is a positive integer. (See Exercise 8B Question 4.) Show that successive errors in the iteration are related approximately by $e_{r+1} \approx -\dfrac{m-1}{2\sqrt[m]{N}} e_r^2$. (Use the result in Question 6.)

If x_0 is taken as the integer next above $\sqrt[m]{N}$, and if this is appreciably larger than $\frac{1}{2}(m-1)$, then show that the error should be less than 10^{-D} after k iterations, where k is the integer next above $\dfrac{1}{\log 2} \log\left(1 + \dfrac{D}{\log(2x_0/(m-1))}\right)$ and log denotes the logarithm to base 10.

9.6 Which is the best method?

You now know several methods of finding roots of equations: the sign-change rule and a variety of forms of iterative sequence $x_{r+1} = F(x_r)$, including the Newton–Raphson method. How do you decide which to use for any particular equation?

A lot depends on the accuracy to which you want the answer, and on the computing facilities you are using. For example, the sign-change rule is a very useful way of deciding where to start an iteration, but if you are working with a simple calculator it becomes very laborious if you want an accurate answer (see P2 Section 14.2). However, if you are using a graphic calculator, then being able to zoom in to a root by using smaller and smaller windows makes it possible to get an answer to several decimal places very quickly.

With simple iteration you often need 20 or 30 steps to reach the accuracy you need, but for some equations each step is very easy. For example, to find the root of $x = \cos x$ (see Example 8.2.2) you simply keep pressing the COS key until the number in the display settles down to a constant value. Even more complicated iterations can often be made into simple programs which you can set up with a computer (perhaps on a spreadsheet) or a programmable calculator.

The question then arises whether it is worthwhile doing a calculation like that in Example 8.2.2 to estimate how many steps will be needed, or whether it is better just to run the program (say 10 steps at a time) and stop when it appears to have converged sufficiently.

Other possibilities are to use the trick of modifying an iteration to speed up convergence (as in P2 Example 14.5.2), or to use Newton–Raphson. Each step of the iteration will then be more complicated, but you need far fewer steps. You also have the possibility of doing the first few steps of a simple iteration and then jumping to a more accurate answer by the method described in Section 8.4. You have to balance the reduction in computing time against the time it takes to do the extra algebra.

There is no one answer to the question in the heading of this section. Which method is best varies according to circumstances.

Exercise 9C

The equations in Exercise 9C allow you to investigate for yourself the relative merits of different methods. For each equation restrict yourself to a particular calculator or computer facility, and then try a variety of methods to decide which is best at getting the answer to a given degree of accuracy.

1 (a) $x^4 + 2x^3 + 3x^2 + 4x = 5$ (b) $(x+1)(x^3+3) = x^2 + 2$

(c) $\sqrt{x+1} + \sqrt{x+2} + \sqrt{x+3} = 10$ (d) $e^x + x^2 = 100$

(e) $x \cosh x = 2$ (f) $\sin x = \ln x$

Make up some more for yourself!

Miscellaneous exercise 9

1 Let $f(x) = (x-3)(x^2+1) - 10$. Show that the equation $f(x) = 0$ has a root between $x = 3$ and $x = 4$. Find an approximate solution of $f(x) = 0$ by applying the Newton–Raphson process twice, starting with $x = 4$. (OCR)

2 Use the Newton–Raphson method with an initial value $x = 0.75$ to find, correct to 3 decimal places, the positive root of the equation $x = \cos x$. (OCR)

3 Use the Newton–Raphson method to find, correct to 3 decimal places, the root of $x^5 - 5x = 21$ which is nearly equal to 2. (OCR)

4 Use the Newton–Raphson approximation, with initial approximation 3, to find, correct to 3 decimal places, the only real root of the equation $x \ln x = 4$. (OCR)

5 Use the Newton–Raphson method to find, correct to 3 decimal places, the root of the equation $x^3 - 10x = 25$ which is close to 4. (OCR)

6 Find, correct to 5 decimal places, the coordinates of the points of intersection of

(a) $y = \operatorname{sech} x$ and $y = \dfrac{1}{1+x^2}$, (b) $y = \cos x$ and $y = 1 - \frac{1}{2}x$,

(c) $y = x^3$ and the circle with centre $(1,1)$ and radius 2.

7 Sketch the graph of $y = x \operatorname{sech} x$. Find the coordinates of the stationary points.

8† (a) Show on a sketch graph that, when $|a|$ is small, the equation $\sin x = ax$ has a root near to π. Use one step of the Newton–Raphson method to obtain an approximation to the root. Show that your answer is approximately $\pi(1-a)$.

(b) Find similar approximations to the roots nearest $2n\pi$ and $(2n+1)\pi$ of the equation $\sin x = \dfrac{b}{x}$ when $|b|$ is small. Give your solutions in the form $2n\pi(1+pb)$ and $(2n+1)\pi(1-qb)$, where p and q are constants to be determined. (OCR)

9 (a) Sketch the curve with equation $y = \tan x - 2x$ for $0 < x < \frac{1}{2}\pi$ to show that the equation $\tan x - 2x = 0$ has a solution, α, in that interval.

(b) Obtain the Newton–Raphson iterative formula for the equation $\tan x - 2x = 0$.

(c) Consider the Newton–Raphson iteration with the two starting values $x_0 = 0.9$ and $x_0 = 1.1$. Show that the iteration converges with one of these starting values but not with the other.

(d) There is a value k such that if $k < x_0 < \frac{1}{2}\pi$ the Newton–Raphson iteration with starting value x_0 will converge to α. Show the value k on your sketch; show also the tangent to the curve at $x = k$.

(e) If the starting value x_0 is less than k, the Newton–Raphson iteration may not converge to α. Describe two of the distinct cases which can arise. (MEI)

10* Sketch the graph of $y = \dfrac{\cos x}{\cosh x}$ and find the least number k such that $\cos x + k \cosh x \geqslant 0$ for all real values of x.

11† The quadratic equation $3z^2 - 2z + 1 = 0$ has a root close to $0.3 + 0.5\mathrm{i}$. Assuming that the Newton–Raphson method can be extended to equations with complex unknowns, and that the rules for differentiation are the same as for real functions, find a closer approximation to the root. Illustrate with an Argand diagram the relation between the initial approximation, the closer approximation and the exact root $\frac{1}{3}\left(1 + \sqrt{2}\mathrm{i}\right)$.

12* Use the Newton–Raphson method to find, to 3 decimal places, closer approximations to

(a) the root of $z^3 - 4z + 5 = 0$ close to $1.2 + 0.7\mathrm{i}$,

(b) the root of $\mathrm{e}^z = z$ close to $0.3 + 1.3\mathrm{i}$.

10 Step-by-step approximations

This chapter develops techniques for numerical solution of differential equations. When you have completed it, you should

- be able to use Euler's method and the modified Euler method to find numerical approximations to the solutions of differential equations
- understand that the errors can be reduced by shortening the step length, the amount of reduction that can be expected, and why
- be able to use approximate laws for the reduction of errors to achieve further improvements in accuracy.

10.1 Euler's method

You now know how to solve many differential equations, but there are some whose solutions can't be written as exact algebraic equations. However, it is still possible to solve particular equations as accurately as you want by numerical methods.

Example 10.1.1

A rocket is launched vertically into space. Table 10.1 gives the speed at 10-second intervals after lift-off for 50 seconds. Estimate the height of the rocket at these times.

Time, t (seconds)	0	10	20	30	40	50
Speed, v (km s^{-1})	0	0.63	1.42	2.47	3.99	6.67

Table 10.1

The speed is the rate at which the height of the rocket is increasing. So if the rocket is at height z km after t seconds, the speed is given by $v = \frac{dz}{dt}$. But as only numerical values of $\frac{dz}{dt}$ are available, you can't solve this algebraically to find z in terms of t. As a first approximation you can split the period into 5 time-steps of 10 seconds each, and suppose that over each step the rocket travels with the speed given in the table for the beginning of the step. The calculation can then be set out as in Table 10.2.

Time, t	0	10	20	30	40	50
Height, z	0	0	6.3	20.5		85.1
Speed, $v = \frac{dz}{dt}$	0	0.63	1.42	2.47		
Time interval, δt	10	10	10			
Increase in height, δz	0	6.3	14.2			

Table 10.2

You construct this table one column at a time. In column 1 the initial time (0 seconds) and height (0 km) are entered in rows 1 and 2. Copy the third entry from Table 10.1, and enter the time-step 10 seconds in row 4. Then find the number in row 5 by multiplying the entries in rows 3 and 4; this is only approximately the increase in height, based on the assumption of constant speed over the time-step.

When column 1 is complete, start column 2 by adding the increases in time and height from column 1 to the previous entries for time and height. Then repeat the procedure.

Some spaces in columns 4 and 5 have been left blank for you to fill in for yourself. You should arrive at a value of 85.1 km for the estimated height after 50 seconds.

You can use this step-by-step method to approximate to the solution of a differential equation. The only difference is that the third row is not determined by numerical data, but is calculated from the differential equation.

Starting from a given initial point (x_0, y_0) on the solution curve, you find a sequence of points (x_1, y_1), (x_2, y_2), ... whose x-coordinates form an arithmetic sequence with a suitable common difference δx. The y-coordinates are then calculated so that the points lie as close as possible to the solution curve.

Example 10.1.2
Use the step-by-step method to find an approximation to the solution of $\frac{dy}{dx} = \sqrt{x + y}$, with an initial value $y = 0.2$ when $x = 0$. Use 5 x-steps, each of size 0.2, to estimate values of y from $x = 0$ to $x = 1$.

The calculations are set out in Table 10.3, and illustrated by Fig. 10.4.

x_r	0	0.2	0.4	0.6	0.8	1.0
y_r	0.2	0.289 44	0.429 36	0.611 50		1.087 11
Gradient at (x_r, y_r)	0.447 21	0.699 60	0.910 69			
x-step	0.2	0.2	0.2			
Estimated y-step	0.089 44	0.139 92	0.182 14			

Table 10.3

In Table 10.3 x_r and y_r are the entries in rows 1 and 2 of any column. You then calculate the gradient g as $\sqrt{x_r + y_r}$ and enter it in row 3. Row 4 shows the chosen x-step, h (0.2 in this example), and you then calculate the y-step, $k = gh$. This completes the column. You then start the next column by calculating $x_{r+1} = x_r + h$, $y_{r+1} = y_r + k$.

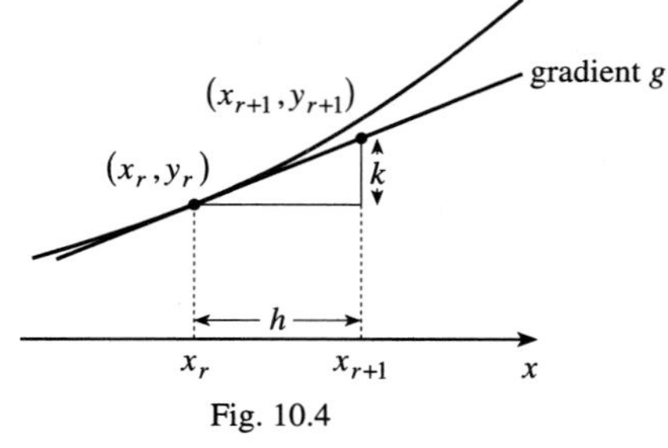

Fig. 10.4

Some spaces have been left in columns 4 and 5 for you to fill in yourself. You should arrive at 1.087 11 as the estimated value of y when $x = 1$.

Example 10.1.2 is typical of **Euler's step-by-step algorithm**:

To find an approximate numerical solution of a first order differential equation:

Step 1 Choose an x-step.

Step 2 In column 1, enter the given initial values of x and y in rows 1 and 2. Denote these by x_0, y_0.

Step 3 In row 3 enter the gradient g, calculated from the differential equation for the values of x_r and y_r in rows 1 and 2.

Step 4 Enter the chosen x-step in row 4. Denote it by h.

Step 5 Calculate the y-step $k = gh$, and enter it in row 5.

Step 6 Calculate $x_{r+1} = x_r + h$, $y_{r+1} = y_r + k$ and enter these in rows 1 and 2 of the next column.

Step 7 If you want to go further, return to Step 3.

With a computer (possibly using a spreadsheet) it is easy to write a program to work through this algorithm.

Exercise 10A

All these questions refer to differential equations which will recur in later exercises in this chapter. You should keep your solutions until you have finished the chapter.

1 A racing car accelerates from 0 to 80 m s^{-1} (about 180 m.p.h.) in 12 seconds. Its speed after successive intervals of 2 seconds is given in the table. Estimate how far the car travels while accelerating.

Time (seconds)	0	2	4	6	8	10	12
Speed (m s^{-1})	0	8	20	40	58	74	80

2 The driver of a train travelling at 100 m s^{-1} applies the brakes and brings the train to rest in 25 seconds. The speed of the train after successive intervals of 5 seconds is given in the table. Approximately how far does the train travel in coming to rest?

Time (seconds)	0	5	10	15	20	25
Speed (m s^{-1})	100	88	60	30	12	0

3 For the differential equation and initial value in Example 10.1.2, carry out similar step-by-step calculations with

(a) 10 x-steps, each of 0.1, (b) 20 x-steps, each of 0.05.

4 Use Euler's step-by-step method to find points on the solution curves of the following differential equations.

(a) $\frac{dy}{dx} = \cos\frac{1}{2}(x+y)$; solution curve through $(0,0)$ over the interval $0 \leqslant x \leqslant 1$, taking x-steps of (i) $h=0.5$, (ii) $h=0.25$;

(b) $\frac{dy}{dx} = \frac{1}{x+2y}$; solution curve through $(1,2)$ over the interval $1 \leqslant x \leqslant 5$, taking x-steps of (i) $h=1$, (ii) $h=0.5$;

(c) $\frac{dy}{dx} = \sqrt{y} + e^{-x}$; solution curve through $(0,1)$ over the interval $0 \leqslant x \leqslant 2$, taking x-steps of (i) $h=1$, (ii) $h=0.5$, (iii) $h=0.25$;

(d) $\frac{dy}{dx} = \frac{\sqrt{x}+\sqrt{y}}{2}$; solution curve through $(1,2)$ over the interval $0 \leqslant x \leqslant 2$, taking x-steps of (i) $h=\pm 0.5$, (ii) $h=\pm 0.25$.

5 The speed v of an object falling from a height satisfies the equation $\frac{dv}{dt} = 10 - 0.01v^{\frac{3}{2}}$, and $v=0$ when $t=0$. Use a step-by-step method to estimate v when $t=20$.

6 The level, h metres, of water in a reservoir satisfies the differential equation $\frac{dh}{dt} = 0.5t - 0.1h$, where t is the time in weeks. When $t=0$, the level is 10 metres.

Find the level when $t=10$,

(a) by using Euler's step-by-step method with step lengths of 2 weeks and 1 week,

(b) by solving the differential equation exactly.

Calculate the errors in using the step-by-step method.

10.2 Errors in Euler's method

The differential equation in Example 10.1.2 can in fact be solved algebraically, but the solution

$$\sqrt{y+x} - \ln\left(1+\sqrt{y+x}\right) - \tfrac{1}{2}x = \sqrt{0.2} - \ln\left(1+\sqrt{0.2}\right)$$

is too complicated to be of much use. You cannot find from it an equation for y in terms of x, or for x in terms of y. The values described as 'exact' (correct to 5 decimal places) in row 2 of Table 10.5 on the next page have not been calculated from this equation, but by using a more advanced modification of Euler's method. However, if you like you can check for yourself that these values do satisfy the above equation.

When you use Euler's method you begin by choosing an x-step. Rows 3 to 5 of Table 10.5 show the results you get if you use x-steps of 0.2, 0.1 and 0.05 respectively. Of course, the shorter the x-step, the more steps you must take to get to a particular value of x. The entries in row 3 are the same as those found in Example 10.1.2, with 5 steps of 0.2.

The numbers of steps in rows 4 and 5 are 10 and 20, but only the values of y for $x = 0.2, 0.4, \ldots, 1$ are shown in the table. You calculated these in Exercise 10A Question 3.

Rows 6 to 8 of Table 10.5 are the errors in the values calculated in rows 3 to 5, found by subtraction from the exact entries in row 2.

		0	0.2	0.4	0.6	0.8	1.0
x		0	0.2	0.4	0.6	0.8	1.0
y (exact)		0.2	0.318 05	0.484 61	0.692 67	0.938 41	1.219 38
y (approx.) with $h =$	0.2	0.2	0.289 44	0.429 36	0.611 50	0.831 64	1.087 11
	0.1	0.2	0.303 43	0.456 51	0.651 48	0.884 32	1.152 45
	0.05	0.2	0.310 68	0.470 46	0.671 95	0.911 22	1.185 75
error with $h =$	0.2	0	0.028 61	0.055 25	0.081 17	0.106 77	0.132 27
	0.1	0	0.014 62	0.028 10	0.041 19	0.054 09	0.066 93
	0.05	0	0.007 37	0.014 15	0.020 72	0.027 19	0.033 63

Table 10.5

Look first along rows 6 to 8 of the table. You can see that the error gets larger with each step taken, but according to a regular pattern. For example, the bottom row shows that after 4 steps of 0.05 the error is about 0.007; after 8 and 12 steps it is about 0.014 and 0.021, roughly twice and three times as much. You will find a similar pattern in rows 6 and 7.

Look down the columns in rows 6 to 8. Each time the x-step is halved, the error is roughly halved. So you can achieve greater accuracy by using a larger number of smaller steps.

Table 10.5 is typical of the results obtained when you use Euler's step-by-step method. They can be summarised as the following error rules:

> For a given x-step, the error is approximately proportional to the number of steps taken.
>
> For a given value of x, the error is approximately proportional to the size of the x-steps used.

10.3 Graphical explanations

Drawing solution curves will help you to see why the error rules hold.

It is useful first to introduce some new notation. An expression like $\sqrt{x+y}$ is an example of a **function of two variables** x and y. Such a function is defined for a **domain** which is a set of number pairs (x, y). For $\sqrt{x+y}$ the natural domain is the set such that $x+y \geqslant 0$, represented in a coordinate plane by the points to the 'north-east' of the line $x+y=0$, shown by the shaded part of Fig. 10.6. For each point of the domain the function defines a unique value, denoted in general by $\mathrm{f}(x, y)$. The set of values taken by the function is its **range**; for $\sqrt{x+y}$ the range is the set of non-negative real numbers.

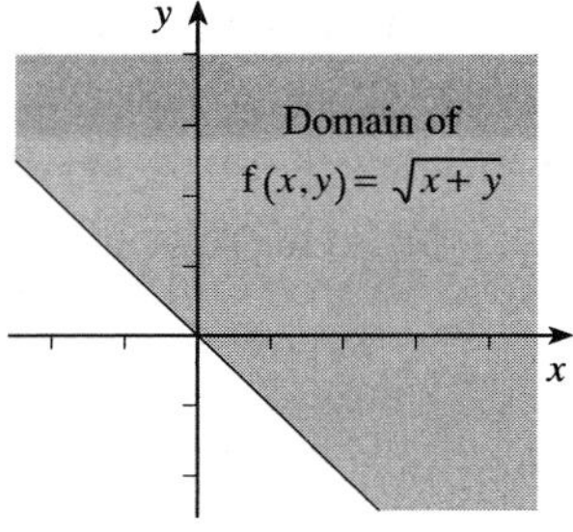

Fig. 10.6

A general first order differential equation can be written as

$$\frac{dy}{dx} = f(x, y)$$

for some function f. This defines, at each point of the domain of f, the gradient of the solution curve through that point. These gradients constitute the **tangent field** for the differential equation. It is illustrated in Fig. 10.7, for the differential equation $\frac{dy}{dx} = \sqrt{x+y}$, by the 'needles' drawn at the corners of the grid. (You can't, of course, show it at more than a few typical points. In Fig. 10.7 these are restricted to the square $0 \leqslant x \leqslant 1$, $0 \leqslant y \leqslant 1$, but the tangent field extends throughout the domain of f.)

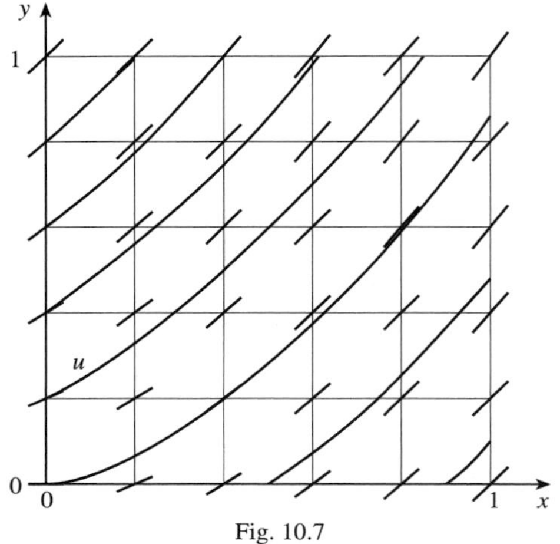

Fig. 10.7

There is a solution curve of the differential equation through each point of the domain of f. Fig. 10.7 shows a few such solution curves, and the needles help you to imagine how others could be drawn. The curve labelled u is the one with initial condition $y = 0.2$ when $x = 0$.

Fig. 10.8 illustrates the step-by-step process in Example 10.1.2. You begin at the point $A(0, 0.2)$. The basis of the Euler method is to suppose that, for the first x-step, the solution can be approximated by a line with gradient equal to the gradient at A. This takes you from A to P, which has coordinates $(0.2, 0.28944)$.

Now you would like P to be on the solution curve u, but in fact it is on a different solution curve, labelled v. The next step therefore takes you from P to Q, where the gradient of PQ is equal to that of the tangent to v at P. The coordinates of Q were calculated in Table 10.3 as $(0.4, 0.429\,36)$, and this lies on the curve labelled w. A further step takes you from Q to R, where R has coordinates $(0.6, 0.611\,50)$ and the gradient of QR is equal to that of the tangent to w at Q.

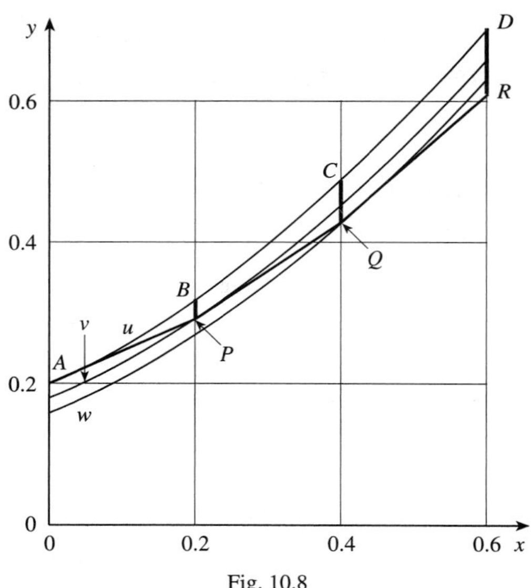

Fig. 10.8

The exact values of y in row 2 of Table 10.5 correspond in the figure to the points $A, B, C, D, \ldots$ on u, and the step-by-step approximations correspond to $A, P, Q, R, \ldots$, so the errors are represented by the lengths PB, QC, RD, ... You can see that the error increases by about the same amount at each step, so the total error is roughly proportional to the number of steps.

The effect of halving the x-step is shown on a larger scale in Fig. 10.9. The points A, P, B and the curves u, v are the same as in Fig. 10.8, so that with $h = 0.2$ Euler's method takes you from A to P. But with an x-step of $h = 0.1$, the first step will go only as far as the mid-point S of AP, and the next step will take you to T, where ST is the tangent to the solution curve through S. The error at $x = 0.2$ is therefore reduced from PB to TB. You can see that the effect of halving the step length is roughly to halve the error.

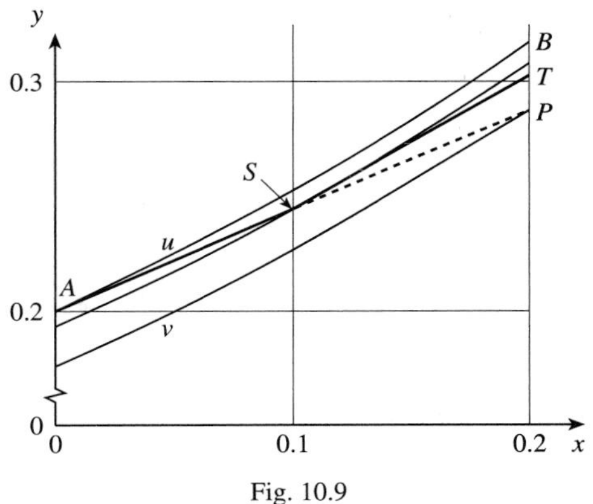

Fig. 10.9

Exercise 10B

1 For the differential equations in Exercise 10A Question 4, draw the tangent fields and use these to make freehand sketches of the solution curves through the given points. On the same diagrams plot the points which you found from the step-by-step method, and compare these with the curves you have sketched.

2 The actual solution curves for the differential equations in Exercise 10A Question 4 pass through the given points. For each curve, find the errors in using the step-by-step method, and see whether these conform with the results summarised at the end of Section 10.2.

(a)	$(0.5, 0.479\,91)$	$(1, 0.854\,59)$		
(b)	$(2, 2.176\,78)$	$(3, 2.320\,01)$	$(4, 2.441\,24)$	$(5, 2.546\,76)$
(c)	$(0.5, 2.003\,07)$	$(1, 3.033\,18)$	$(1.5, 4.121\,94)$	$(2, 5.292\,99)$
(d)	$(0, 1.060\,83)$	$(0.5, 1.457\,16)$	$(1.5, 2.659\,55)$	$(2, 3.425\,15)$

3* This question is designed to establish the error properties stated at the end of Section 10.2 for simple differential equations of the form $\frac{dy}{dx} = f(x)$. The notation for points and curves corresponds to that used in Fig. 10.8.

Let the solution curve have equation $y = F(x)$ passing through the point A with coordinates $(a, F(a))$. This satisfies the differential equation, $F'(x) = f(x)$.

(a) Referring to Fig. 10.8, let the x-coordinate of B be $a + h$. Express the y-coordinates of B and P in terms of a, h and F. Use a Taylor expansion (see Section 8.2) to show that the error in using Euler's method when $x = a + h$ is approximately $\frac{1}{2}h^2 f'(a)$.

(b) If the solution curve v through P has equation $y = F_1(x)$, explain why $F_1(x) = F(x) + k$, and show that $k = hf(a) + F(a) - F(a + h)$. Hence find the y-coordinate of Q, and deduce that the error when $x = a + 2h$ is approximately double that when $x = a + h$.

(c) Suppose now that Euler's method is used with a single step of $2h$. State what the error would be when $x = a + 2h$, and show that doubling the step length has the effect of approximately doubling the error.

4† (a) Use Euler's method starting from $x = 0$ to find an approximation to the solution of the differential equation $\frac{dy}{dx} = y$ which passes through the point $(0,1)$. Take steps of length (i) 0.1 and (ii) 0.05 to find approximations to the value of y when $x = 1$. Compare your approximations with the exact value of y when $x = 1$.

(b) For the same equation, take a step length of $\frac{1}{n}$, giving n steps between $x = 0$ and $x = 1$. Denoting the value of y after the rth step by y_r, show that $y_{r+1} = \left(1 + \frac{1}{n}\right) y_r$, and deduce that the value of y when $x = 1$ is given by $\left(1 + \frac{1}{n}\right)^n$.

(c) Try calculating $\left(1 + \frac{1}{n}\right)^n$ for large values of n.

10.4 Modifying Euler's method

The errors in Euler's method are quite large. They can be reduced by taking shorter x-steps, but this is a lot more work and may introduce rounding errors. It is natural to ask whether the method itself can be improved.

The method's main weakness is that it uses only the gradient at the left end of each step. But the gradient of a solution curve may change considerably in the course of a step. It would be better if the gradients at the left and right ends could be averaged to give a closer estimate for the gradient over the step.

Example 10.4.1
Improve the estimate for the height of the rocket in Example 10.1.1.

Row 3 of Table 10.2 has been replaced by three rows, giving the speeds at the start and end of each time-step (taken from Table 10.1), and the mean of these speeds.

Time	0	10	20	30	40	50
Height	0	3.15	13.40	32.85	65.15	118.45
Speed at start	0	0.63	1.42	2.47	3.99	
Speed at end	0.63	1.42	2.47	3.99	6.67	
Mean of speeds	0.315	1.025	1.945	3.230	5.330	
Time interval	10	10	10	10	10	
Increase in height	3.15	10.25	19.45	32.30	53.30	

Table 10.10

The effect of the modification is to change the estimate of the height from 85.1 m to 118.45 m.

To apply this procedure to a differential equation $\frac{dy}{dx} = f(x, y)$, you would like, as in Fig. 10.8, to find the gradients to curve u at A and B, and then to use the mean of these as an estimate of the gradient over the first step. Unfortunately you can't do this, since you don't know the coordinates of B. But you do know the coordinates of P, and the gradient of curve v at P is likely to be very close to the gradient of u at B. This is the basis of the **modified Euler method**. Referring to Fig. 10.11, the algorithm can be described as follows.

To find an approximate numerical solution of $\frac{dy}{dx} = f(x, y)$:

Step 1 Choose an x-step.

Step 2 In column 1, enter the given initial values of x and y in rows 1 and 2. Denote these by x_0, y_0.

Step 3 In row 3 enter the 'left gradient' $g_1 = f(x_r, y_r)$

Step 4 Enter the chosen x-step in row 4. Denote it by h.

Step 5 Calculate and enter a 'temporary' y-step $k_1 = g_1 h$ in row 5.

Step 6 Calculate the coordinates of P as $x_{r+1} = x_r + h$, $y_{temp} = y_r + k_1$ and enter these in rows 6 and 7.

Step 7 In row 8 enter the estimated 'right gradient' $g_2 = f(x_{r+1}, y_{temp})$.

Step 8 Calculate and enter the mean $g = \frac{1}{2}(g_1 + g_2)$ in row 9.

Step 9 Calculate and enter the y-step $k = gh$ in row 10.

Step 10 Calculate $x_{r+1} = x_r + h$, $y_{r+1} = y_r + k$ and enter these in rows 1 and 2 of the next column.

Step 11 If you want to go further, return to Step 3.

Notice that Steps 1 and 2 are the same as Euler's method, as are the last two steps.

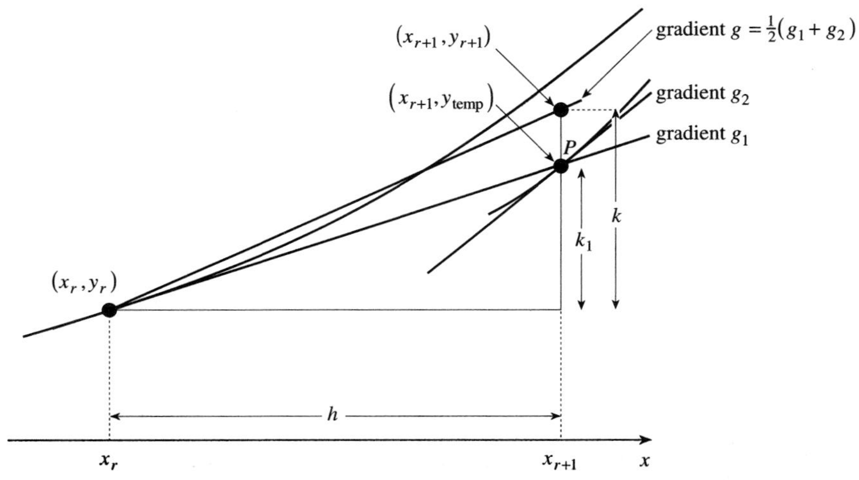

Fig. 10.11

Example 10.4.2
Use the modified Euler method to approximate to the solution of the differential equation in Example 10.1.2.

The calculations are set out in Table 10.12. Some spaces have been left in columns 4 and 5 for you to fill in for yourself. You should arrive finally at 1.209 17 as the estimated value of y when $x = 1.0$.

x_r	0	0.2	0.4	0.6	0.8	1.0
y_r	0.2	0.314 68	0.479 06	0.685 36		1.209 17
$g_1 = \sqrt{x_r + y_r}$	0.447 21	0.717 41	0.937 58			
h	0.2	0.2	0.2			
$k_1 = g_1 h$	0.089 44	0.143 48	0.187 52			
$x_{r+1} = x_r + h$	0.2	0.4	0.6			
$y_{\text{temp}} = y_r + k_1$	0.289 44	0.458 16	0.666 58			
$g_2 = \sqrt{x_{r+1} + y_{\text{temp}}}$	0.699 60	0.926 37	1.125 42			
$g = \frac{1}{2}(g_1 + g_2)$	0.573 41	0.821 89	1.031 50			
$k = gh$	0.114 68	0.164 38	0.206 30			

Table 10.12

Notice that the entries in rows 1 to 5 of column 1 are the same as those in Table 10.3 in Example 10.1.2, but that rows 6 to 10 then refine the approximation before you proceed to column 2.

10.5 Errors in the modified Euler method

Table 10.13, for the modified Euler method with different values of h, corresponds to Table 10.5, calculated in Section 10.2 for the simple Euler method. The entries in rows 1 and 2 are the same as in Table 10.5, and the entries in row 3 are taken from Table 10.12.

	x	0	0.2	0.4	0.6	0.8	1.0
	y (exact)	0.2	0.318 05	0.484 61	0.692 67	0.938 41	1.219 38
y (approx.) with $h =$	0.2	0.2	0.314 68	0.479 06	0.685 36	0.929 58	1.209 17
	0.1	0.2	0.317 11	0.483 09	0.690 68	0.936 02	1.216 62
	0.05	0.2	0.317 80	0.484 22	0.692 15	0.937 79	1.218 67
errors with $h =$	0.2	0	0.003 37	0.005 55	0.007 31	0.008 83	0.010 21
	0.1	0	0.000 94	0.001 52	0.001 99	0.002 39	0.002 76
	0.05	0	0.000 25	0.000 39	0.000 52	0.000 62	0.000 71

Table 10.13

The first thing to notice is how much more accurate the values of y are compared with those produced by the simple Euler method. For example, with $h = 0.2$, the error here when $x = 1.0$ is about 0.01, compared with 0.13 in Table 10.5. To achieve comparable accuracy with Euler's method you would need to reduce the x-step by at least a factor of 10, which would require 50 or more steps rather than 5. So the modified method, though more complicated, involves far less calculation.

Looking along rows 6 to 8 you can see that the error increases with each step, though for this particular differential equation the proportional relation noticed in Table 10.5 is less marked than with the simple method.

You will see a more important difference when you look down the columns. The errors in row 7 are roughly $\frac{1}{4}$ of those in row 6, and those in row 8 roughly $\frac{1}{4}$ of those in row 7. This suggests a rule:

> With the modified Euler method, for a particular value of x, the error is approximately proportional to the square of the size of the x-step used.

So by using the modified method with a small value of h you can get approximations that are very close to the exact solution.

For example, at $x = 1.0$ the error with an x-step of 0.05 is about $0.000\,71$. With an x-step of 0.01 you would expect to reduce this by a factor of $\left(\frac{1}{5}\right)^2 = \frac{1}{25}$, so that the error would then be only about $0.000\,03$.

Exercise 10C

1 For the racing car in Exercise 10A Question 1, find a better estimate for the distance travelled whilst accelerating based on the mean speed over each interval.

2 For the train in Exercise 10A Question 2, find a better estimate for the distance travelled in coming to rest based on the mean speed over each interval.

3 For the differential equation in Example 10.1.2, verify the values of y given in row 4 of Table 10.13, using the modified Euler method with $h = 0.1$.

4 Apply the modified Euler method to the differential equations in Exercise 10A Question 4, with the given intervals and step lengths. Comparing your results with the correct values given in Exercise 10B Question 2, investigate whether the errors using the modified Euler method conform with the result summarised at the end of Section 10.5. *Keep your solutions for use in Exercise 10D Question 1.*

5 Apply the modified Euler method to the differential equation for a falling object in Exercise 10A Question 5. Assuming that the correct value for v when $t = 20$ given by the differential equation is 93.16, compare the errors in the estimates produced by the simple Euler method and the modified method.

6 For the differential equation for the water level in a reservoir in Exercise 10A Question 6, use the modified Euler method with step lengths of 2 weeks and 1 week to estimate the level when $t = 10$. Compare the errors with those obtained when the simple Euler method was used. *Keep your solutions for use in Exercise 10D Question 2.*

10.6* Using error properties to improve accuracy

In Section 8.4, when solving equations, knowing the ratio of successive errors in an iteration enabled you to locate roots more accurately. A similar method can be used here.

The calculations in Section 10.2 suggested that, in Euler's method, the error is approximately proportional to the size of the x-step. This means that if, for a particular differential equation, you use Euler's method twice, once with x-step h and once with x-step $2h$, then the error will be roughly twice as large in the second calculation. For a particular value of x, denote the exact y-value by $y[\text{exact}]$ and the values found by Euler's method by $y[h]$ and $y[2h]$ respectively. Then

$$y[\text{exact}] - y[2h] \approx 2(y[\text{exact}] - y[h]), \quad \text{so} \quad y[\text{exact}] \approx 2y[h] - y[2h].$$

Table 10.14 shows this for Example 10.1.2. Taking h as 0.05 and using the entries in rows 1, 2, 4, 5, 7 and 8 of Table 10.5, values of $2y[0.05] - y[0.1]$ have been calculated.

	x	0	0.2	0.4	0.6	0.8	1.0
	$y[\text{exact}]$	0.2	0.318 05	0.484 61	0.692 67	0.938 41	1.219 38
value of	$y[0.1]$	0.2	0.303 43	0.456 51	0.651 48	0.884 32	1.152 45
	$y[0.05]$	0.2	0.310 68	0.470 46	0.671 95	0.911 22	1.185 75
	$2y[0.05] - y[0.1]$	0.2	0.317 93	0.484 41	0.692 42	0.938 12	1.219 05
error in	$y[0.1]$	0	0.014 62	0.028 10	0.041 19	0.054 09	0.066 93
	$y[0.05]$	0	0.007 37	0.014 15	0.020 72	0.027 19	0.033 63
	$2y[0.05] - y[0.1]$	0	0.000 12	0.000 20	0.000 25	0.000 29	0.000 33

Table 10.14

The last line of the table shows that using this device improves the accuracy dramatically.

Even greater accuracy can be achieved with the modified Euler method. The calculations in Section 10.5 suggested that in this case the error is approximately proportional to the square of the size of the x-step. Thus doubling the x-step will roughly quadruple the error, so

$$y[\text{exact}] - y[2h] \approx 4(y[\text{exact}] - y[h]), \quad \text{giving} \quad y[\text{exact}] \approx \tfrac{1}{3}(4y[h] - y[2h]).$$

For Example 10.4.2, with $h = 0.05$ and using values from Table 10.13, you get Table 10.15.

	x	0	0.2	0.4	0.6	0.8	1.0
	$y[\text{exact}]$	0.2	0.318 05	0.484 61	0.692 67	0.938 41	1.219 38
value of	$y[0.1]$	0.2	0.317 11	0.483 09	0.690 68	0.936 02	1.216 62
	$y[0.05]$	0.2	0.317 80	0.484 22	0.692 15	0.937 79	1.218 67
	$\frac{1}{3}(4y[0.05] - y[0.1])$	0.2	0.318 03	0.484 60	0.692 64	0.938 38	1.219 35
error in	$y[0.1]$	0	0.000 94	0.001 52	0.001 99	0.002 39	0.002 76
	$y[0.05]$	0	0.000 25	0.000 39	0.000 52	0.000 62	0.000 71
	$\frac{1}{3}(4y[0.05] - y[0.1])$	0	0.000 02	0.000 01	0.000 03	0.000 03	0.000 03

Table 10.15

Of course, a lot of work is concealed in this table, since the modified Euler method has been used twice, once with 10 steps of 0.1 and once with 20 steps of 0.05. But this is a good deal less work than other ways of achieving comparable accuracy, such as using the modified Euler method with 100 steps of 0.01.

The accuracy of step-by-step methods can generally be improved by carrying out the calculations with step lengths of h and $2h$ for a suitable value of h, and then using the approximations

$2y[h]-y[2h]$ for Euler's method, and

$\frac{1}{3}(4y[h]-y[2h])$ for the modified Euler method.

Exercise 10D*

1 Apply the procedures for improved accuracy described in Section 10.6 to your results in Exercise 10A Question 4 and Exercise 10C Question 4. Compare your answers with the correct values given in Exercise 10B Question 2.

2 Apply the method of Section 10.6 to your answers to Exercise 10A Question 6(a) and Exercise 10C Question 6, to make improved estimates of the level of water when $t=10$.

How do these compare with the value obtained by solving the differential equation exactly?

3 For the differential equation $\frac{dy}{dx}+y^2=x$ with $y=1$ when $x=0$, use the modified Euler method and the procedure described in Section 10.6 to estimate the values of y when $x=0.2, 0.4, 0.6$ and 0.8.

Explain why there is a minimum point on the solution curve where it cuts the curve $x=y^2$. Draw graphs to illustrate this, and estimate the coordinates of the minimum point. Are there any other stationary points on the solution curve?

4 (a) Use the trapezium rule to estimate the values of $\int_0^1 e^x\,dx$, $\int_0^1 \sin x\,dx$ and $\int_1^2 \frac{1}{x}\,dx$,

(i) with one interval of width $h=1$, (ii) with two intervals of width $h=0.5$,

(iii) with four intervals of width $h=0.25$.

What do your results suggest about the errors in using the trapezium rule?

(b) Draw sketches to show that trapezium rule approximations to $\int_a^b f(x)\,dx$

(i) with n intervals of width $\frac{b-a}{n}$, (ii) with $2n$ intervals of width $\frac{b-a}{2n}$

can be written as (i) $h(y_0+2y_2+2y_4+\ldots+2y_{2n-2}+y_{2n})$,

(ii) $\frac{1}{2}h(y_0+2y_1+2y_2+2y_3+\ldots+2y_{2n-1}+y_{2n})$, where $h=\frac{b-a}{2n}$ and $y_r=f(a+rh)$.

Use the result of part (a), and the method of Section 10.6, to show that the integral can be estimated more accurately as $\frac{1}{3}h(y_0+4y_1+2y_2+4y_3+\ldots+2y_{2n-2}+4y_{2n-1}+y_{2n})$.

Use this expression to find new estimates for the three integrals in part (a), taking $h=0.25$. (This is known as *Simpson's rule.*)

Miscellaneous exercise 10

1 A surveyor measures the gradient of a hill on a straight road at points at intervals of 100 metres, measured along the road surface. The foot of the hill is taken as the origin, and at a distance s up the hill the gradient $g = \frac{dy}{dx}$. Values of g for different values of s are as follows, where x, y and s are in metres.

s	0	100	200	300	400	500	600
g	0	0.05	0.25	0.20	0.12	0.04	0

Prove that $\frac{dx}{ds} = \frac{1}{\sqrt{1+g^2}}$ and $\frac{dy}{ds} = \frac{g}{\sqrt{1+g^2}}$. Use Euler's step-by-step method to find approximate (x, y) coordinates for a number of points on the hill.

An alternative step-by-step method based on the average gradient over each step is more accurate. Use this to find another approximate set of coordinates of points on the hill.

Use graphs to demonstrate the difference between the profiles of the hill given by the two approximate methods.

2 The equation $x\frac{dy}{dx} + y^2 = x^2$ is given to have a solution which has $y = 0$ at $x = 0$.

(a) Explain why this solution cannot be found numerically by a direct application of the Euler method.

(b) Find an approximate solution near $x = 0$ in the form $y = ax + bx^2 + cx^3$. Use this to find an approximate value for y when $x = 0.01$ and give an estimate of the accuracy of your value of y.

(c) Carry out two steps of length 0.01 using the Euler method to estimate y at $x = 0.03$.

(d) Carry out two steps of the modified Euler method starting from 0.01 to estimate y at $x = 0.03$.

Comment on the two values you have found, and on the value from your result in (b) at $x = 0.03$. (OCR)

3 The differential equation $\frac{dy}{dx} = \sqrt{10x + y}$, where $y = 1$ when $x = 1$, is to be solved using the modified Euler method. Use a step length of $h = 0.2$ to obtain an estimate of y when $x = 1.2$, giving your answer to 6 decimal places. Obtain a second estimate taking $h = 0.1$.

* You are now given that the estimate obtained by taking h to be 0.05 is 1.702 283. By considering the differences between successive estimates, obtain the most accurate value possible for y when $x = 1.2$. (MEI)

4 The differential equation $\frac{dy}{dx} = x + \frac{1}{y}$ with initial conditions $x = 0$, $y = 1$ is to be used to estimate y when $x = 0.2$.

(a) Perform a single step of Euler's method with $h = 0.2$ to obtain an initial estimate, α_1, of the value of y when $x = 0.2$.

(b) Obtain, correct to 6 decimal places, a second estimate, α_2, using Euler's method with $h = 0.1$.

(c)* You are now given that the estimates obtained by taking $h = 0.05$, $h = 0.025$ and $h = 0.0125$ are $\alpha_3 = 1.201\,525$, $\alpha_4 = 1.201\,869$ and $\alpha_5 = 1.202\,050$. Obtain the best estimate you can of y when $x = 0.2$. Give your answer to an appropriate number of significant figures.

(d) Obtain the estimate of y when $x = 0.2$ using a single step of the modified Euler method, taking $h = 0.2$. Comment on the accuracy of this estimate and the estimate obtained in (c). (MEI)

5† Consider the differential equation problem $\frac{dy}{dx} = e^x (1 - y)^2$ with $y = 0.9$ at $x = 5$.

(a) Make two Euler steps of length 0.1 to estimate y at $x = 5.2$.

(b) Make two modified Euler steps of length 0.1 to estimate y at $x = 5.2$.

(c) The exact solution of the problem is, for $x \geqslant 5$, $y = 1 - \left(e^x - \left(e^5 - 10\right)\right)^{-1}$. Show that $y < 1$ for all $x \geqslant 5$ and that $y = 1$ is an asymptote to the graph of y.

(d) Calculations using both methods and different step lengths give the values in the table for y at $x = 5.25$, to 6 decimal places.

	$h = 0.01$	$h = 0.05$
Euler method	0.981 760	0.987 336
Modified Euler method	0.980 785	0.979 740

Find the errors in these figures.

Explain why the error in a single step of length h in the Euler method is usually proportional to h^2. How do the errors usually vary with h and the number n of steps (assuming exact computation) for

(i) a single step of the modified Euler method,

(ii) n steps of the Euler method,

(iii) n steps of the modified Euler method?

Comment on the errors in the figures in the table in the light of your answers. (OCR)

Revision exercise 2

1 Find the value of the constant k for which $y = kxe^{4x}$ is a particular integral of the differential equation $\frac{d^2y}{dx^2} - 3\frac{dy}{dx} - 4y = 10e^{4x}$.

Find the general solution of this differential equation. (OCR)

2 The equation $x^3 + 3x^2 - 1 = 0$ has a root between 0 and 1. Use the Newton–Raphson method, with initial approximation 0.5, to find this root correct to 2 decimal places.

Give a clear reason why it would be impossible to use the Newton–Raphson method with initial approximation 0. (OCR)

3 (a) Show that the equation $9e^{-x} = x^2$, $x > 0$, has a solution, α, near to $x = 1.5$.

(b) Show that two possible rearrangements of the equation are $x = 3e^{-\frac{1}{2}x}$ and $x = \ln\left(\frac{9}{x^2}\right)$.

(c) Each of these rearrangements is used iteratively with starting value $x = 1.5$ in order to find the solution, α. Show, numerically or otherwise, that one iteration converges and the other diverges.

(d) An iteration which diverges can sometimes be used to obtain a solution as follows.

Use x_0 to find x_1 from the iterative formula.
Let $x_2 = \frac{1}{2}(x_0 + x_1)$.
Use x_2 to find x_3 from the iterative formula.
Let $x_4 = \frac{1}{2}(x_2 + x_3)$, etc.

Use this method on the diverging iteration in part (c) to discover whether it produces the required solution, α, in this case. (MEI)

4 Find the general solution of the differential equation $\frac{d^2x}{dt^2} + 5\frac{dx}{dt} + 4x = 15\cos 3t - 5\sin 3t$. (OCR)

5 For the differential equation $\frac{dy}{dx} = \frac{1}{\sqrt{x^2 + y^2}}$, points on the solution curve through $(0,1)$ are to be found numerically using Euler's method. Use a step length of $h = 0.25$ to calculate an approximation for $y(1)$, the value of y when $x = 1$.

The table shows values calculated for $y(1)$ for a succession of smaller step lengths.

Step length, h	0.05	0.02	0.01
Approximation for $y(1)$	1.7066	1.7006	1.6986

Assuming that the error in the approximation for $y(1)$ is proportional to h, use the last two entries to find a better estimate for $y(1)$. (MEI)

6 (a) Given that $\mathrm{p}(x)$ is a particular integral of the differential equation $\frac{\mathrm{d}^2y}{\mathrm{d}x^2}+b\frac{\mathrm{d}y}{\mathrm{d}x}+cy=\mathrm{f}(x)$, and $\mathrm{q}(x)$ is a particular integral of the differential equation $\frac{\mathrm{d}^2y}{\mathrm{d}x^2}+b\frac{\mathrm{d}y}{\mathrm{d}x}+cy=\mathrm{g}(x)$, show that a particular integral of the differential equation $\frac{\mathrm{d}^2y}{\mathrm{d}x^2}+b\frac{\mathrm{d}y}{\mathrm{d}x}+cy=\mathrm{f}(x)+\mathrm{g}(x)$ is $\mathrm{p}(x)+\mathrm{q}(x)$.

(b) The voltage V in a circuit at time t is modelled by the differential equation

$$\frac{\mathrm{d}^2V}{\mathrm{d}t^2}+2\frac{\mathrm{d}V}{\mathrm{d}t}+5V=t+\mathrm{e}^{-t}.$$

(i) Find a complementary function as the sum of two linearly independent functions.

(ii) Using the results of part (a) find a particular integral of the differential equation.

(iii) Write down a general solution containing two arbitrary constants. (MEI)

7 The application of Euler's method to solve the differential equation $\frac{\mathrm{d}y}{\mathrm{d}x}=y^2-x+1$, with the initial condition $y=0$ when $x=0$, results in the following incomplete table, where the values shown have been rounded to 4 decimal places and y' denotes $\frac{\mathrm{d}y}{\mathrm{d}x}$.

n	x_n	y_n	y'_n	y_{n+1}	n	x_n	y_n	y'_n	y_{n+1}
0	0	0	1	0.1	6	0.6			
1	0.1	0.1	0.91	0.191	7	0.7			
2	0.2	0.191	0.8365	0.2746	8	0.8		0.5818	0.6761
3	0.3	0.2746	0.7754	0.3522	9	0.9	0.6761	0.5571	0.7318
4	0.4	0.3522	0.7240	0.4246	10	1.0	0.7318	0.5355	0.7853
5	0.5	0.4246	0.6803						

(a) Complete the table, giving your answers to 4 decimal places. Sketch the graph of y against x, for $0 \leqslant x \leqslant 1$.

(b) Why does your graph suggest that $\frac{\mathrm{d}^2y}{\mathrm{d}x^2}<0$ in the range $0<x<1$? If the solution is continued beyond $x=1$, do you think that $\frac{\mathrm{d}^2y}{\mathrm{d}x^2}<0$ will continue to be true? Give reasons for your answer.

(c) If a step length of 0.2 were used throughout instead, would the solution be more accurate or less accurate, and why?

(d) Is the true value of y at $x=1.0$ greater or less than the value 0.7318 given in the table? Would your conclusion remain the same if a step length of 0.001 were used instead in a new calculation? Explain your answers. (MEI)

8 Find linear second order differential equations for which the following are general solutions.

(a) $y=Ax+B\mathrm{e}^{-x}$ (b) $y=Ax^2+\frac{B}{x}+2x$ (c) $y=A\sin x+B\cos x+\tan x$

9† Find values of the constants p and q for which $y = px\sin 2x + qx\cos 2x$ is a particular integral of $\frac{d^2y}{dx^2} + 4y = \sin 2x$. Find the general solution of this differential equation.

Show that, when $x = n\pi$, where n is a large positive integer, $y \approx -\frac{1}{4}n\pi$, whatever the initial conditions, and find a corresponding approximation when $x = \left(n + \frac{1}{2}\right)\pi$. (OCR)

10 (a) One step of the Newton–Raphson method for solving the equation $f(x) = 0$ can be expressed as $x_2 = x_1 - \frac{f(x_1)}{f'(x_1)}$. Draw a sketch to illustrate the method.

(b) Suppose that x_0 is near to x_1. Write down an approximation to $f'(x_1)$ based on x_0 and x_1. Substitute this approximation into the equation in part (a) to obtain the result $x_2 \approx \frac{f(x_0)x_1 - f(x_1)x_0}{f(x_0) - f(x_1)}$.

(c) Let $f(x) = x - \cos x$. Show that the equation has a root in the interval $(0.5, 1)$. Use the iteration $x_{n+2} = \frac{f(x_n)x_{n+1} - f(x_{n+1})x_n}{f(x_n) - f(x_{n+1})}$ to solve the equation, correct to 6 significant figures, taking $x_0 = 0.5$ and $x_1 = 1.0$.

(d) By considering the errors in x_2, x_3 and x_4 show that the convergence of this iteration appears to be better than first order.

(e) Give one advantage and one disadvantage of using the iteration in part (c) rather than the Newton–Raphson method. (MEI)

11 The current in an electrical circuit consisting of an inductor, resistor and capacitor in series with an alternating power source is described by the equation $\frac{d^2I}{dt^2} + 25\frac{dI}{dt} + 100I = -170\sin 20t$, where I is the current in amperes and t is the time in seconds after the power source is switched on.

(a) Find the general solution.

(b) Find the solution such that, when $t = 0$, $\frac{dI}{dt} = I = 0$.

(c) The exponentially decaying terms in the solution describe what is known as the transient current. The non-decaying terms describe the steady state current. Write down an expression for the steady state current for the solution in part (b). Why would this expression remain unchanged if the initial conditions were different?

(d) Express the steady state current in the form $R\sin(20t + \alpha)$, where R and α are to be determined. Verify that, after only 1 second, the magnitude of the transient current is close to 1% of the steady state amplitude, R. (MEI)

12 (a) A solution is sought to the differential equation $\frac{d^2y}{dx^2} + 2\frac{dy}{dx} + 10y = 18e^{-x}$.

(i) Find the general solution.

(ii) Find the solution such that, when $x = 0$, $y = 0$ and $\frac{dy}{dx} = 0$. For this solution, calculate the smallest two positive values of x for which $y = 0$. Sketch the solution, clearly marking these values.

(b) Find the general solution of the differential equation $\frac{d^3y}{dx^3} + 2\frac{d^2y}{dx^2} + 10\frac{dy}{dx} = 0$. (MEI)

13 The equation $x^2 + x = e^{-x}$ is given to have only one root, X, with $0.44 < X < 0.45$.

(a) Show that the iteration $x_{n+1} = \dfrac{e^{-x_n}}{x_n + 1}$ (when started in the given interval) converges to X. Use the value of $F'(x)$ for a suitable function F to estimate the number of steps needed to reduce the initial error by a factor of 10^{-2}.

(b)* Calculate x_1, x_2, x_3 from the iteration in (a) when $x_0 = 0.45$. Use the method of Section 8.4 on x_1, x_2, x_3 to find an approximation to X.

(c) Show that both the iterations $x_{n+1} = e^{-x_n} - x_n^2$ and $x_{n+1} = -1 + \dfrac{e^{-x_n}}{x_n}$ can be derived from the original equation, and that both diverge.

(d) A combined iteration is $x_{n+1} = \frac{3}{2}\left(e^{-x_n} - x_n^2\right) - \frac{1}{2}\left(-1 + \dfrac{e^{-x_n}}{x_n}\right)$. Show that this iteration converges rapidly (near $x_0 = 0.45$) to X. Calculate two steps of this iteration with $x_0 = 0.45$. (OCR)

14† The purpose of this question is to investigate various ways of approximating to the non-zero root of the equation $x^2 = \sin x$.

(a) Calculate the first three steps of the iteration $x_0 = 0.9$, $x_{n+1} = \sqrt{\sin x_n}$ to find approximations to the root. Illustrate the iterative process by means of appropriate sketch graphs.

(b) Use Aitken's δ^2 process (the method described in Section 8.4) to obtain a closer approximation to the root than those calculated in part (a).

(c) You are given that the Aitken method gives the root correct to 4 significant figures. How many steps of the iterative process in part (a) would you expect to be needed to reduce the error in the approximation to less than (i) 10^{-4}, (ii) 10^{-7}?

(d) Approximations to the root can also be found by applying the Newton–Raphson process to the equation $f(x) = 0$, where $f(x) = x^2 - \sin x$. Starting again from an initial value $x_0 = 0.9$, calculate a sequence of approximations x_1, x_2, ..., continuing until the error is less than 10^{-7}. At each step use the approximate error formula $-\dfrac{(f(x_n))^2 f''(x_n)}{2(f'(x_n))^3}$ to estimate the size of the error. (OCR)

Mock examination 1 for P5

Time 1 hour 20 minutes

Answer all the questions.
You are permitted to use a graphic calculator in this paper.

1 The equation $x = \ln(x+2)$ has a positive root α which is a little greater than 1. Draw a diagram to illustrate the convergence to α of the iteration $x_{n+1} = \ln(x_n + 2)$, taking $x_1 = 1$. [3]

The approximations $x_1, x_2, x_3, \ldots$ to α have errors $e_1, e_2, e_3, \ldots$ respectively. Successive (small) errors are such that $e_{n+1} \approx ke_n$, where $k = 0.3$ correct to 1 significant figure. Show how this value of k is obtained from the form of the equation and the approximate value of α. [2]

2 The differential equation $\dfrac{dy}{dx} = \sqrt{x^2 + y^2}$, with $y = 0$ when $x = 0$, is to be solved numerically by a step-by-step method. Use two steps of the modified Euler method, with step length 0.25, to estimate the value of y when $x = 0.5$. [6]

3 (i) Show that $\tanh\left(\frac{1}{2}\ln 3\right) = \frac{1}{2}$. [2]

(ii) Let $I_n = \displaystyle\int_0^{\frac{1}{2}\ln 3} \tanh^n \theta \, d\theta$. By writing $\tanh^n \theta$ as $\tanh^{n-2}\theta \left(1 - \operatorname{sech}^2 \theta\right)$, show that, for $n \geqslant 2$, $I_n = I_{n-2} - \dfrac{1}{(n-1)\,2^{n-1}}$. [3]

(iii) Deduce that $I_{2N} = \frac{1}{2}\ln 3 - \displaystyle\sum_{r=1}^{N} \frac{1}{(2r-1)\,2^{2r-1}}$. [3]

4 Starting from the definition of sinh in terms of exponentials, prove that

$$\sinh^{-1} x = \ln\left(x + \sqrt{x^2 + 1}\right).$$ [3]

Hence prove that $\dfrac{d}{dx}\left(\sinh^{-1} x\right) = \dfrac{1}{\sqrt{x^2 + 1}}$. [2]

By using a binomial expansion and then integrating, deduce that, for small values of x,

$$\sinh^{-1} x \approx x - \tfrac{1}{6}x^3 + \tfrac{3}{40}x^5.$$ [4]

5 (i) Find the values of the constants a and b for which $at + be^{-t}$ is a particular integral for the differential equation $\frac{d^2x}{dt^2} + 2\frac{dx}{dt} = 1 - e^{-t}$. [3]

(ii) Find the solution of the differential equation, given that x and $\frac{dx}{dt}$ are both zero when $t = 0$. [5]

(iii) Show that, for the solution in part (ii), when t is large and positive, $\frac{dx}{dt} \approx \frac{1}{2}$. [2]

6 (i) By means of the substitution $x + \frac{1}{2} = \frac{1}{2}\cosh\theta$, or otherwise, find

$$\int \sqrt{x^2 + x}\,dx.$$ [6]

(ii) The arc of the curve $y = 2\sqrt{x}$ between $x = 0$ and $x = 1$ is rotated completely about the **y-axis**. Find the area of the surface of revolution generated. [4]

7 (i) The equation $x^4 + ax^3 + bx^2 + cx + d = 0$ has roots $\alpha, \beta, \gamma, \delta$ such that $\alpha\beta = 1$ and $\gamma\delta = 1$.

(a) Show that $d = 1$ and that $a = c$. [3]

(b) Show that the equation with roots $\alpha + \beta$ and $\gamma + \delta$ is $x^2 + ax + b - 2 = 0$. [3]

(ii) By using the substitution $y = \frac{1}{x}$, or otherwise, show that any equation of the form $x^4 + px^3 + qx^2 + px + 1 = 0$ has roots which occur in reciprocal pairs. [2]

(iii) Solve the equation $x^4 + 2x^3 - x^2 + 2x + 1 = 0$. [4]

Mock examination 2 for P5

Time 1 hour 20 minutes

Answer all the questions.
You are permitted to use a graphic calculator in this paper.

1 The equation $x^3 + px + q = 0$, where p and q are constants, has roots α, β and γ. Use the substitution $y = x^2$ to find a cubic equation whose roots are α^2, β^2 and γ^2. [3]

Hence, or otherwise, show that $\alpha^4 + \beta^4 + \gamma^4 = 2(\alpha^2\beta^2 + \beta^2\gamma^2 + \gamma^2\alpha^2)$. [3]

2 Find the solution of the differential equation $\frac{d^2y}{dx^2} + 4\frac{dy}{dx} + 4y = 1$ for which $y = 0$ and $\frac{dy}{dx} = 1$ when $x = 0$. [7]

3

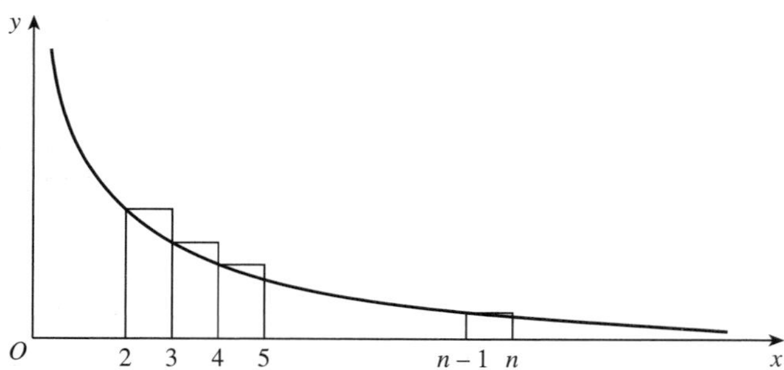

The diagram shows the curve $y = \frac{1}{x^2}$ together with rectangles of unit width above the curve. By considering appropriate areas, show that $\sum_{r=2}^{n-1} \frac{1}{r^2} > \frac{1}{2} - \frac{1}{n}$. [3]

By considering rectangles under the curve, show that $\sum_{r=3}^{n} \frac{1}{r^2} < \frac{1}{2} - \frac{1}{n}$. [1]

Deduce that $\sum_{r=1}^{\infty} \frac{1}{r^2}$ lies between $\frac{3}{2}$ and $\frac{7}{4}$. [3]

4 The diagram shows a sketch of part of the solution curve of the differential equation $\frac{dy}{dx} = \sqrt{\cos y}$, with $y = 0$ when $x = 0$.

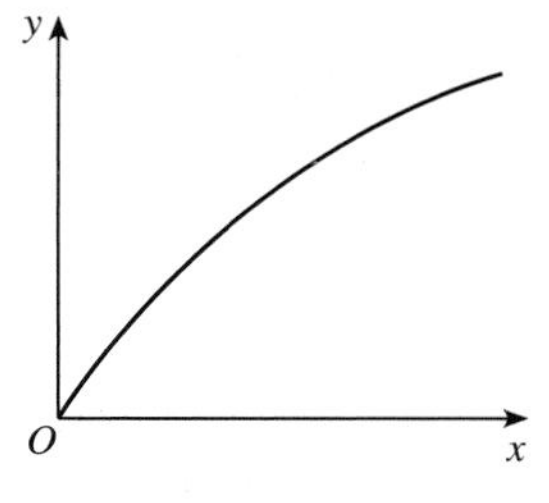

(i) One step of the Euler method, starting at the origin, is used to estimate the value of y when $x = h$, where h is small and positive. Show by means of a sketch why the resulting value of y is an overestimate. [2]

(ii) Show also on your sketch why the value of y resulting from use of the Euler method with two steps of length $\frac{1}{2}h$ gives a better approximation. [2]

(iii) Taking $h = 0.4$, show that the one-step and two-step estimates of y when $x = 0.4$ are very close to each other. [4]

5 Write down expressions for $\sinh 2x$ and $\cosh 2x$ in terms of $\sinh x$ and $\cosh x$, and hence show that $\tanh 2x = \frac{2\tanh x}{1+\tanh^2 x}$. [4]

The equation $\tanh 2x = k \tanh x$, where k is a positive constant, is satisfied by a non-zero value of x. Show that $1 < k < 2$. [4]

6 (i) By writing $\frac{u^2}{1+u^2}$ as $1 - \frac{1}{1+u^2}$, show that the value of x for which $\int_0^x \frac{u^2}{1+u^2}\,du = 1$ satisfies the equation $x = 1 + \tan^{-1} x$. [2]

(ii) The root α of the equation $x = 1 + \tan^{-1} x$ is approximately equal to 2. Find an approximate relationship between small errors in successive approximations to α when the iteration $x_{n+1} = 1 + \tan^{-1} x_n$ is used. [2]

(iii) Use the Newton–Raphson method, applied to the equation $x - \tan^{-1} x - 1 = 0$, with 2 as the first approximation, to find the next two approximations. [4]

(iv) For the application of the Newton–Raphson method in part (iii), the first approximation, 2, is less than α, but the next two approximations (and all further approximations) are greater than α. Illustrate this behaviour by means of a sketch of the graph of $y = x - \tan^{-1} x - 1$ in the neighbourhood of α, showing how the first three approximations are related geometrically. [4]

7 (i) You are **given** that the integral $I_n = \int_0^{\sqrt{3}} \left(1+x^2\right)^n dx$ satisfies the reduction formula $(2n+1)I_n = 4^n\sqrt{3} + 2nI_{n-1}$. Use this formula, with $n = \frac{1}{2}$, to show that

$$\int_0^{\sqrt{3}} \sqrt{1+x^2}\,dx = \tfrac{1}{2}\left(2\sqrt{3} + \ln\left(2+\sqrt{3}\right)\right).$$ [4]

(ii) The curve C has polar equation $r = a\sin^2\theta$, where a is a positive constant. Show that the arc length of C between the points where $\theta = 0$ and $\theta = \frac{1}{2}\pi$ is given by

$$a\int_0^{\frac{1}{2}\pi} \sin\theta\sqrt{1+3\cos^2\theta}\,d\theta.$$ [4]

(iii) Use the substitution $x = \sqrt{3}\cos\theta$, together with the result of part (i), to evaluate this arc length. [4]

Module P6

Pure Mathematics 6

1 Simultaneous linear equations

This chapter is about solving simultaneous equations systematically. When you have completed it you should know

- how to find the unique solution of a set of simultaneous equations if there is one
- the meaning of the terms 'consistent' and 'inconsistent' as applied to simultaneous linear equations
- how to find all the solutions of a set of simultaneous equations when the solution is not unique.

1.1 A simple case

The simplest case of a linear equation is an equation of the type $ax = p$, where $a, p \in \mathbb{R}$ and you have to solve the equation to find x. Even in this simple case, there are three possibilities that you must consider.

> **Case 1** Suppose that $a \neq 0$. Then you can multiply by the reciprocal of a to find the unique solution
>
> $$x = a^{-1}p.$$

An example of this type of equation is $2x = 3$, so $x = 2^{-1} \times 3 = 1\frac{1}{2}$. This equation, which has a solution, is said to be **consistent**.

> **Case 2a** Suppose that $a = 0$. If $p \neq 0$, the equation reduces to $0x = p$, or $0 = p$. This is a contradiction, since, by hypothesis, $p \neq 0$. There is no value of x such that $0x = p$ when $p \neq 0$, so the equation has no solution. In this case, the equation is said to be **inconsistent**.

An example of this type of equation is $0x = 1$.

> **Case 2b** Suppose that $a = 0$. If $p = 0$, the equation reduces to $0x = 0$, which is true for every value of $x \in \mathbb{R}$. The equation has infinitely many solutions, and is **consistent**.

An example (the only one!) of this type of equation is $0x = 0$.

This shows that equations of the form $ax = p$ are always one of three types. In fact you can extend this classification if you regard the equation $ax = p$ as a set of simultaneous equations where there is just one equation and one unknown.

Example 1.1.1
Solve the equation $a(a-1)x = a$ for all values of a.

> If $a \neq 0$ and $a \neq 1$ the coefficient of x is not 0, so you can divide by $a(a-1)$ to obtain $x = \dfrac{a}{a(a-1)} = \dfrac{1}{a-1}$. (Note that you can cancel the factor of a since $a \neq 0$.)

If $a=0$ the equation reduces to $0x=0$, so every value of x is a solution.

If $a=1$ the equation reduces to $0x=1$, so there is no solution.

In the rest of this chapter you will see that simultaneous linear equations in any number of unknowns have solutions which conform to one of these three types.

- They are consistent and have a unique solution.
- They are inconsistent and have no solution.
- They are consistent and have infinitely many solutions.

1.2 One equation and two unknowns

How do you find all the solutions of an equation such as $2x+3y=6$?

You might find it helpful to think geometrically and say that this equation represents a line in two-dimensional space, and as there are infinitely many points on the line, there are infinitely many solutions, two of which are $x=3,\ y=0$ and $x=0,\ y=2$.

But if, going back to the equation $2x+3y=6$, you put $y=2t$, where t is any number, you find $2x=6-6t$, that is $x=3-3t$, thus giving $x=3-3t$, $y=2t$ as the solution.

The solution $y=2t$ was adopted to avoid unnecessary fractions appearing in the final solution of the set of equations. If you can, you should always do this.

You can write this solution in vector notation as

$$\begin{pmatrix}x\\y\end{pmatrix}=\begin{pmatrix}3-3t\\2t\end{pmatrix}=\begin{pmatrix}3\\0\end{pmatrix}+\begin{pmatrix}-3t\\2t\end{pmatrix}=\begin{pmatrix}3\\0\end{pmatrix}+t\begin{pmatrix}-3\\2\end{pmatrix},$$

which you will recognise as the parametric form of the equation of a straight line (see P3 Section 5.6).

In the general case of $ax+by=p$, where a and b are both non-zero, the solution is

$$\begin{pmatrix}x\\y\end{pmatrix}=\begin{pmatrix}\frac{p}{a}\\0\end{pmatrix}+t\begin{pmatrix}-b\\a\end{pmatrix}.$$

If either a or b is zero, then the original equation reduces to one of Case 1, Case 2a and Case 2b in Section 1.1.

1.3 Two equations and two unknowns

The same ideas apply to pairs of simultaneous linear equations of the form

$$\left.\begin{aligned}ax+by&=p\\cx+dy&=q\end{aligned}\right\}$$

where the coefficients are all real numbers. (In this chapter, all the coefficients will be real, so, for brevity, this condition will not be repeated.)

You are familiar with solving simultaneous equations like this when they have a unique solution, although you may not be familiar with the language or technique which will be used to solve them. The technique involves replacing the given set of equations with a simpler but equivalent set, and repeating this process until you have a set of the form

$$\left.\begin{aligned} Kx + Ly &= R \\ My &= S \end{aligned}\right\}.$$

At this stage, provided that neither M nor K is zero, you can solve the final equation and then substitute the value into the first equation to obtain a unique solution. However, if either M or K is zero, there is no solution, or there are an infinite number of solutions.

This technique will generalise to sets of equations with more than two unknowns.

Example 1.3.1
Solve the equations $\left.\begin{aligned} 2x + 3y &= 1 \\ 4x - y &= 9 \end{aligned}\right\}.$

There are three allowable operations that you can perform on these equations and obtain a set of equations which is equivalent. You may:

- multiply an equation by a non-zero number
- subtract a multiple of one equation from another
- exchange two equations.

The resulting set of equations will have precisely the same solutions as the original set.

Here is one way to solve the given equations. The reasons for the individual steps are not given, and you may well, in practice, want to short-cut some of the steps.

$$\left.\begin{aligned} 2x + 3y &= 1 \\ 4x - y &= 9 \end{aligned}\right\} \Leftrightarrow \left.\begin{aligned} 2x + 3y &= 1 \\ 0x - 7y &= 7 \end{aligned}\right\} \Leftrightarrow \left.\begin{aligned} 2x + 3y &= 1 \\ y &= -1 \end{aligned}\right\}.$$

When you get to the last stage, you can tell that the equations have a unique solution with $y = -1$ and then, by substituting in the other equation, that $x = 2$.

The equations have the unique solution $x = 2$, $y = -1$.

Example 1.3.2
Solve the equations $\left.\begin{aligned} -2x + 4y &= 1 \\ 4x - 8y &= 3 \end{aligned}\right\}.$

When you add twice the top equation to the bottom equation you find that

$$\left.\begin{aligned} -2x + 4y &= 1 \\ 4x - 8y &= 3 \end{aligned}\right\} \Leftrightarrow \left.\begin{aligned} -2x + 4y &= 1 \\ 0x + 0y &= 5 \end{aligned}\right\}.$$

The second equation, which is simply $0 = 5$, tells you that the equations are inconsistent and that there is no solution.

Example 1.3.3
Solve the equations $\left.\begin{aligned} -2x + 4y &= 1 \\ 4x - 8y &= -2 \end{aligned}\right\}.$

When you add twice the top equation to the bottom equation you find that

$$\left.\begin{aligned} -2x + 4y &= 1 \\ 4x - 8y &= -2 \end{aligned}\right\} \Leftrightarrow \left.\begin{aligned} -2x + 4y &= 1 \\ 0x + 0y &= 0 \end{aligned}\right\} \Leftrightarrow \left.\begin{aligned} -2x + 4y &= 1 \\ 0 &= 0 \end{aligned}\right\}.$$

These equations are consistent, with infinitely many solutions. They reduce to the type of equation in Section 1.2. If you put $y = t$, where t is any number, then $x = 2t - \frac{1}{2}$. So $x = 2t - \frac{1}{2}$, $y = t$ is a solution for any value of t. You can write this in vector notation as

$$\begin{pmatrix} x \\ y \end{pmatrix} = \begin{pmatrix} 2t - \frac{1}{2} \\ t \end{pmatrix} = \begin{pmatrix} -\frac{1}{2} \\ 0 \end{pmatrix} + t\begin{pmatrix} 2 \\ 1 \end{pmatrix}, \quad \text{or} \quad \begin{pmatrix} x \\ y \end{pmatrix} = \begin{pmatrix} -\frac{1}{2} \\ 0 \end{pmatrix} + t\begin{pmatrix} 2 \\ 1 \end{pmatrix}.$$

You can interpret the situations in Examples 1.3.1 to 1.3.3 geometrically. In Example 1.3.1, the two equations represent two straight lines which are not parallel and so meet in a point. In Example 1.3.2, the two straight lines are parallel and do not meet, so there is no solution. In Example 1.3.3, the two parallel lines are coincident, so there are infinitely many solutions.

Notice that the form of the solution to the equations in Example 1.3.3 is not unique. You could easily have put $x = t$, and then found that $y = \frac{1}{4}(2t + 1)$.

1.4 Three equations and two unknowns

You can think of a set of equations such as $\left.\begin{array}{r} x + 3y = 4 \\ 2x - y = 1 \\ x + y = 3 \end{array}\right\}$ as representing a set of three straight lines in the plane. You would expect these straight lines to form a triangle and to have no points in common. However, the lines may all pass through a point, and then the equations have a unique solution. Or all three equations may represent the same straight line and have infinitely many solutions.

Example 1.4.1

Solve the equations $\left.\begin{array}{r} x + 3y = 4 \\ 2x - y = 1 \\ x + y = 0 \end{array}\right\}$.

$$\left.\begin{array}{r} x + 3y = 4 \\ 2x - y = 1 \\ x + y = 0 \end{array}\right\} \Leftrightarrow \left.\begin{array}{r} x + 3y = 4 \\ 0x - 7y = -7 \\ x + y = 0 \end{array}\right\} \Leftrightarrow \left.\begin{array}{r} x + 3y = 4 \\ -7y = -7 \\ 0x - 2y = -4 \end{array}\right\} \Leftrightarrow \left.\begin{array}{r} x + 3y = 4 \\ y = 1 \\ y = 2 \end{array}\right\} \Leftrightarrow \left.\begin{array}{r} x + 3y = 4 \\ y = 1 \\ 0 = 1 \end{array}\right\}.$$

Looking at the last equation tells you that the equations are inconsistent and that there is no solution.

Example 1.4.2

Solve the equations $\left.\begin{array}{r} x + 3y = 4 \\ 2x - y = 1 \\ x + y = 2 \end{array}\right\}$.

$$\left.\begin{array}{r} x + 3y = 4 \\ 2x - y = 1 \\ x + y = 2 \end{array}\right\} \Leftrightarrow \left.\begin{array}{r} x + 3y = 4 \\ 0x - 7y = -7 \\ x + y = 2 \end{array}\right\} \Leftrightarrow \left.\begin{array}{r} x + 3y = 4 \\ -7y = -7 \\ 0x - 2y = -2 \end{array}\right\} \Leftrightarrow \left.\begin{array}{r} x + 3y = 4 \\ y = 1 \\ y = 1 \end{array}\right\} \Leftrightarrow \left.\begin{array}{r} x + 3y = 4 \\ y = 1 \end{array}\right\}.$$

If you substitute the value $y = 1$ in the first equation, you obtain $x = 1$.

The equations have a unique solution $x = 1$, $y = 1$.

Exercise 1A

1 Find the complete solution of each of the following equations.

(a) $ax = 2$ (b) $ax = a + 1$ (c) $bx = b^2$

(d) $ax = bx + c$ (e) $a(a+1)x = a^2 - 1$ (f) $a^2 + ax = b^2 + bx$

2 Find the solution, if it exists, of each of the following sets of equations.

(a) $\left.\begin{aligned} x - y &= 2 \\ -x + y &= -2 \end{aligned}\right\}$ (b) $\left.\begin{aligned} 2x - y &= 1 \\ 4x - 2y &= 3 \end{aligned}\right\}$ (c) $\left.\begin{aligned} 3x - y &= 0 \\ -6x + 2y &= 0 \end{aligned}\right\}$

3 Find the solution, if it exists, in vector form for each of the following sets of equations.

(a) $\left.\begin{aligned} 2x - 4y &= 6 \\ -4x + 8y &= -12 \end{aligned}\right\}$ (b) $\left.\begin{aligned} x + 3y &= 6 \\ 6x + 18y &= 12 \end{aligned}\right\}$ (c) $\left.\begin{aligned} 5x - 3y &= 10 \\ -10x + 6y &= -20 \end{aligned}\right\}$

4 Find the solutions for each of the following equations for all possible values of the coefficients.

(a) $x + 2y = 2$ (b) $2x + y = p$ (c) $ax + y = p$

(d) $x + ay = a$ (e) $ax + by = ab$ (f) $ax + by = p$

5 Solve the following pairs of simultaneous equations.

(a) $\left.\begin{aligned} x + y &= 2 \\ ax + y &= a^2 - 3 \end{aligned}\right\}$ (b) $\left.\begin{aligned} x + y &= 2 \\ ax + y &= a^2 + 1 \end{aligned}\right\}$ (c) $\left.\begin{aligned} x + y &= 2 \\ ax + y &= 2a^2 \end{aligned}\right\}$

6 Solve, where possible, each of the following sets of equations.

(a) $\left.\begin{aligned} x + y &= 3 \\ 2x - y &= 3 \\ x + 2y &= 4 \end{aligned}\right\}$ (b) $\left.\begin{aligned} 2x - y &= 3 \\ x - y &= 4 \\ 4x + y &= 1 \end{aligned}\right\}$ (c) $\left.\begin{aligned} x + y &= 2 \\ 2x - y &= 7 \\ 3x - ay &= 2 \end{aligned}\right\}$

1.5 One or two equations and three unknowns

The method for solving the equation $x + 2y + 3z = 6$ is similar to that for solving an equation with two unknowns.

Example 1.5.1
Solve the equation $x + 2y + 3z = 6$.

You can let y and z have any values and then find a solution for x. Putting $y = s$ and $z = t$ you get $x = 6 - 2s - 3t$. The solution is therefore

$$\begin{pmatrix} x \\ y \\ z \end{pmatrix} = \begin{pmatrix} 6 - 2s - 3t \\ s \\ t \end{pmatrix} = \begin{pmatrix} 6 \\ 0 \\ 0 \end{pmatrix} + s\begin{pmatrix} -2 \\ 1 \\ 0 \end{pmatrix} + t\begin{pmatrix} -3 \\ 0 \\ 1 \end{pmatrix}.$$

Example 1.5.2

Solve the equations $\left.\begin{aligned} x+2y+3z&=6 \\ 2x+3y+\ z&=7 \end{aligned}\right\}.$

$$\left.\begin{aligned} x+2y+3z&=6 \\ 2x+3y+\ z&=7 \end{aligned}\right\} \Leftrightarrow \left.\begin{aligned} x+2y+3z&=\ \ 6 \\ 0x-\ \ y-5z&=-5 \end{aligned}\right\} \Leftrightarrow \left.\begin{aligned} x+2y+3z&=\ \ 6 \\ -\ \ y-5z&=-5 \end{aligned}\right\}.$$

You can let z have any value and find solutions for x and y. Putting $z=t$ you get $y=5-5t$ and $x=6-2(5-5t)-3t=-4+7t$. The solution is therefore

$$\begin{pmatrix} x \\ y \\ z \end{pmatrix} = \begin{pmatrix} -4+7t \\ 5-5t \\ t \end{pmatrix} = \begin{pmatrix} -4 \\ 5 \\ 0 \end{pmatrix} + t\begin{pmatrix} 7 \\ -5 \\ 1 \end{pmatrix}.$$

1.6 Three equations and three unknowns

When solving three equations in three unknowns, it is even more important to be systematic than in previous cases. Here are some examples that show the different situations that can arise.

Example 1.6.1

Solve the equations $\left.\begin{aligned} 2x+\ \ y-\ \ z&=2 \\ x-2y+3z&=7 \\ 3x+5y-\ \ z&=0 \end{aligned}\right\}.$

The first step is to exchange the first two equations, since it is easier to make the x-coefficients in the second and third equations 0 if the coefficient of x in the first equation is 1. Thus

$$\left.\begin{aligned} 2x+\ \ y-\ \ z&=2 \\ x-2y+3z&=7 \\ 3x+5y-\ \ z&=0 \end{aligned}\right\} \Leftrightarrow \left.\begin{aligned} x-2y+3z&=7 \\ 2x+\ \ y-\ \ z&=2 \\ 3x+5y-\ \ z&=0 \end{aligned}\right\} \Leftrightarrow \left.\begin{aligned} x-2y+3z&=\ \ 7 \\ 0x+5y-7z&=-12 \\ 3x+5y-\ \ z&=\ \ 0 \end{aligned}\right\}$$

$$\Leftrightarrow \left.\begin{aligned} x-\ 2y+\ 3z&=\ \ 7 \\ 5y-\ 7z&=-12 \\ 0x+11y-10z&=-21 \end{aligned}\right\} \Leftrightarrow \left.\begin{aligned} x-\ 2y+\ 3z&=\ \ 7 \\ 5y-\ 7z&=-\ 12 \\ 55y-50z&=-105 \end{aligned}\right\} \Leftrightarrow \left.\begin{aligned} x-2y+\ 3z&=\ \ 7 \\ 5y-\ 7z&=-12 \\ 0y+27z&=\ \ 27 \end{aligned}\right\}$$

$$\Leftrightarrow \left.\begin{aligned} x-2y+3z&=\ \ 7 \\ 5y-7z&=-12 \\ z&=\ \ 1 \end{aligned}\right\}.$$

From the third equation $z=1$; substitute this value in the second equation to find $y=-1$, and then substitute both these values in the first equation to find $x=2$.

These equations have the unique solution $x=2, y=-1, z=1$.

Notice how the solution proceeds systematically. The x-coefficient in the first equation is used to eliminate the x terms in the second and third equations; then the y-coefficient in the second equation is used to eliminate the y term in the third equation. You should aim to do this each time, but you may have to interchange a pair of equations first. For example, the first equation may not contain a term in x.

Example 1.6.2
Solve the equations $\left.\begin{aligned} x - y + z &= 2 \\ 2x + 3y - z &= 4 \\ 3x + 7y - 3z &= 5 \end{aligned}\right\}.$

$$\left.\begin{aligned} x - y + z &= 2 \\ 2x + 3y - z &= 4 \\ 3x + 7y - 3z &= 5 \end{aligned}\right\} \Leftrightarrow \left.\begin{aligned} x - y + z &= 2 \\ 0x + 5y - 3z &= 0 \\ 3x + 7y - 3z &= 5 \end{aligned}\right\} \Leftrightarrow \left.\begin{aligned} x - y + z &= 2 \\ 0x + 5y - 3z &= 0 \\ 0x + 10y - 6z &= -1 \end{aligned}\right\}$$

$$\left.\begin{aligned} x - y + z &= 2 \\ 5y - 3z &= 0 \\ 0y + 0z &= -1 \end{aligned}\right\} \Leftrightarrow \left.\begin{aligned} x - y + z &= 2 \\ 5y - 3z &= 0 \\ 0 &= -1 \end{aligned}\right\}.$$

The last equation shows that these equations are inconsistent and have no solution.

Example 1.6.3
Solve the equations $\left.\begin{aligned} x - y + z &= 2 \\ 2x + 3y - z &= 4 \\ 3x + 7y - 3z &= 6 \end{aligned}\right\}.$

$$\left.\begin{aligned} x - y + z &= 2 \\ 2x + 3y - z &= 4 \\ 3x + 7y - 3z &= 6 \end{aligned}\right\} \Leftrightarrow \left.\begin{aligned} x - y + z &= 2 \\ 0x + 5y - 3z &= 0 \\ 3x + 7y - 3z &= 6 \end{aligned}\right\} \Leftrightarrow \left.\begin{aligned} x - y + z &= 2 \\ 5y - 3z &= 0 \\ 0x + 10y - 6z &= 0 \end{aligned}\right\}$$

$$\Leftrightarrow \left.\begin{aligned} x - y + z &= 2 \\ 5y - 3z &= 0 \\ 0y + 0z &= 0 \end{aligned}\right\} \Leftrightarrow \left.\begin{aligned} x - y + z &= 2 \\ 5y - 3z &= 0 \\ 0 &= 0 \end{aligned}\right\}.$$

These equations are consistent. To solve them, and to avoid fractions, put $z = 5t$ where t is a parameter. In the second equation, $y = 3t$, and then, substituting in the first equation, $x = -2t + 2$. The solution in vector form is

$$\begin{pmatrix} x \\ y \\ z \end{pmatrix} = \begin{pmatrix} -2t + 2 \\ 3t \\ 5t \end{pmatrix} = \begin{pmatrix} 2 \\ 0 \\ 0 \end{pmatrix} + t\begin{pmatrix} -2 \\ 3 \\ 5 \end{pmatrix}.$$

Example 1.6.4
Solve the equations $\left.\begin{aligned} x - y + z &= 2 \\ 2x - 2y + 2z &= 4 \\ 3x - 3y + 3z &= 6 \end{aligned}\right\}.$

Using the same methods as previously, you quickly see that

$$\left.\begin{aligned} x - y + z &= 2 \\ 2x - 2y + 2z &= 4 \\ 3x - 3y + 3z &= 6 \end{aligned}\right\} \Leftrightarrow \left.\begin{aligned} x - y + z &= 2 \\ 0x - 0y + 0z &= 0 \\ 0x - 0y + 0z &= 0 \end{aligned}\right\} \Leftrightarrow \left.\begin{aligned} x - y + z &= 2 \\ 0 &= 0 \\ 0 &= 0 \end{aligned}\right\}.$$

These equations can be solved by the method used in Example 1.5.1. Put $y = s$ and $z = t$, giving $x = 2 + s - t$. In vector form this is

$$\begin{pmatrix} x \\ y \\ z \end{pmatrix} = \begin{pmatrix} 2 + s - t \\ s \\ t \end{pmatrix} = \begin{pmatrix} 2 \\ 0 \\ 0 \end{pmatrix} + s\begin{pmatrix} 1 \\ 1 \\ 0 \end{pmatrix} + t\begin{pmatrix} -1 \\ 0 \\ 1 \end{pmatrix}.$$

Example 1.6.5

Find the value of k for which the set of equations $\left.\begin{aligned} x+2y+3z&=7 \\ 2x+y+4z&=4k^2-3 \\ 2x-2y+kz&=6k \end{aligned}\right\}$ does not have a unique solution. Find the solution in this case.

$$\left.\begin{aligned} x+2y+3z&=7 \\ 2x+y+4z&=4k^2-3 \\ 2x-2y+kz&=6k \end{aligned}\right\} \Leftrightarrow \left.\begin{aligned} x+2y \quad +3z&=7 \\ -3y \quad -2z&=4k^2-17 \\ -6y+(k-6)z&=6k-14 \end{aligned}\right\}$$

$$\Leftrightarrow \left.\begin{aligned} x+2y \quad +3z&=7 \\ -3y \quad -2z&=4k^2-17 \\ (k-2)z&=6k-14-8k^2+34 \end{aligned}\right\} \Leftrightarrow \left.\begin{aligned} x+2y \quad +3z&=7 \\ -3y \quad -2z&=4k^2-17 \\ (k-2)z&=-2\left(4k^2-3k-10\right) \end{aligned}\right\}.$$

The right side of the last equation can be factorised, giving

$$(k-2)z=-2(4k+5)(k-2).$$

If $k \neq 2$, you can divide by $(k-2)$ to get a unique solution.

If $k=2$, this equation reduces to $0=0$, so the equations are consistent. The second equation is now $-3y-2z=-1$. To get a solution with as few fractions as possible, put $z=3t+2$. Then $y=\frac{1}{3}(1-2(3t+2))=-2t-1$ and $x=7-2(-2t-1)-3(3t+2)=3-5t$, which gives, in vector notation,

$$\begin{pmatrix} x \\ y \\ z \end{pmatrix}=\begin{pmatrix} 3 \\ -1 \\ 2 \end{pmatrix}+t\begin{pmatrix} -5 \\ -2 \\ 3 \end{pmatrix}.$$

Exercise 1B

1 Solve, where possible, each of the following sets of equations.

(a) $\left.\begin{aligned} x-y+z&=3 \\ 2x+y-2z&=5 \end{aligned}\right\}$ (b) $\left.\begin{aligned} 2x-y-z&=5 \\ x+y-z&=-1 \end{aligned}\right\}$ (c) $\left.\begin{aligned} 2x+y-3z&=2 \\ -4x-2y+6z&=-1 \end{aligned}\right\}$

(d) $\left.\begin{aligned} 2x+y-3z&=2 \\ -4x-2y+6z&=-4 \end{aligned}\right\}$ (e) $x+y-z=3$ (f) $\left.\begin{aligned} x-2y+z&=0 \\ x+y-2z&=3 \end{aligned}\right\}$

(g) $3x-4y+5z=0$ (h) $\left.\begin{aligned} 3x+y-2z&=4 \\ -9x-3y+6z&=12 \end{aligned}\right\}$ (i) $\left.\begin{aligned} 3x+y-2z&=4 \\ -9x-3y+6z&=-12 \end{aligned}\right\}$

2 Solve, where possible, each of the following sets of equations.

(a) $\left.\begin{aligned} x+y-z&=4 \\ 2x-y-6z&=6 \\ x-2y+3z&=-6 \end{aligned}\right\}$ (b) $\left.\begin{aligned} 2x-y+3z&=5 \\ x+3y-2z&=4 \\ y-z&=2 \end{aligned}\right\}$ (c) $\left.\begin{aligned} x+y+2z&=5 \\ 2x-y+z&=1 \\ x-2y-z&=-4 \end{aligned}\right\}$

(d) $\left.\begin{aligned} y-z&=2 \\ x+2y&=3 \\ x+2z&=-1 \end{aligned}\right\}$ (e) $\left.\begin{aligned} y+z&=2 \\ x+y&=3 \\ x+2y+z&=5 \end{aligned}\right\}$ (f) $\left.\begin{aligned} 2x-y-z&=3 \\ x+2y-3z&=4 \\ 2x+y+z&=-11 \end{aligned}\right\}$

3 Find a vector which is perpendicular to both the vectors $\begin{pmatrix}2\\3\\4\end{pmatrix}$ and $\begin{pmatrix}-1\\2\\1\end{pmatrix}$.

4 The set of equations $\left.\begin{array}{r} x+2y=\lambda x \\ 2x-2y=\lambda y \end{array}\right\}$ has the solution $x=0,\ y=0$. For what value of λ are there other solutions?

5 For a particular value of the constant k, the equations

$$\left.\begin{array}{r} x+\ \ y+\ \ z=3 \\ 2x-\ \ y+\ \ z=8 \\ 7x-5y+kz=l \end{array}\right\}$$

do not have a unique solution. For this value of k, find the value of l for which the equations do have solutions, and give these solutions in vector form.

6 Find the two values of k such that the set of equations

$$\left.\begin{array}{r} x+\ \ y+\qquad\quad z=3 \\ x+2y+\qquad kz=6 \\ x+ky+(k+2)z=9 \end{array}\right\}$$

does not have a unique solution. Solve the equations in each of these two cases.

Miscellaneous exercise 1

1 Solve completely for x the equation $ax^2=b$.

2 Solve the equations $\left.\begin{array}{r} 3x-y-2z=14 \\ 2x+y-\ \ z=\ \ 7 \\ 4x-y+3z=\ \ 7 \end{array}\right\}$.

3 Solve completely the equations $\left.\begin{array}{r} x+ky=k+1 \\ kx+\ \ y=k+1 \end{array}\right\}$.

4 Find a non-zero vector perpendicular to $\begin{pmatrix}1\\3\\5\end{pmatrix}$ and $\begin{pmatrix}-1\\2\\4\end{pmatrix}$.

5 Solve the equations $\left.\begin{array}{r} 2x+3y-z=8 \\ 3x+\ \ y-z=8 \\ 4x-\ \ y-z=8 \end{array}\right\}$.

6 Find the values of k such that the set of equations

$$\left.\begin{array}{r} x+ky+kz=0 \\ kx+\ \ y+kz=0 \\ kx+ky+\ \ z=0 \end{array}\right\}$$

does not have a unique solution. Solve the equations in each of these cases.

7 Solve completely the set of equations $\left.\begin{aligned} ax + by &= a \\ bx + ay &= b \end{aligned}\right\}.$

8 Find the values of k such that the set of equations

$$\left.\begin{aligned} -y + z &= kx \\ y + z &= ky \\ 2z &= kz \end{aligned}\right\}$$

has an infinite number of solutions for x, y and z, and solve these equations for each of these values of k.

9 Solve the following equations for x in terms of the constants a and b.

(a) $(a-1)(b-1)x = a + b - 2$ (b) $(a + b - 2)x = (a-1)(b-1)$

10† Multiply out $(a+b+c)\left(a^2+b^2+c^2-bc-ca-ab\right)$ and $(b-c)^2+(c-a)^2+(a-b)^2$.

The numbers a, b, c, p, q and r are all real and non-zero. Find the condition on a, b and c such that the equations

$$\left.\begin{aligned} ax + by + cz &= p \\ bx + cy + az &= q \\ cx + ay + bz &= r \end{aligned}\right\}$$

should not have a unique solution for x, y and z.

Separate the condition into two cases, and in each case find the condition(s) on p, q and r that there should be infinitely many solutions. (OCR, adapted)

11† Verify that $bc^2 - b^2c + ca^2 - c^2a + ab^2 - a^2b = (b-c)(c-a)(a-b)$.

Show that, if no two of a, b and c are equal, the equations

$$\left.\begin{aligned} x + y + z &= a \\ ax + by + cz &= ab \\ a^2x + b^2y + c^2z &= abc \end{aligned}\right\}$$

have unique solutions for x, y and z, and find them.

Investigate the special cases

(a) $a = b \neq c$, (b) $b = c \neq a$, (c) $a = b = c$.

2 Lines and planes

This chapter is about using vectors to work with lines and planes in three-dimensional space. When you have completed it you should

- understand the significance of all the symbols in the equation of a line in the form $\frac{x-a}{p}=\frac{y-b}{q}=\frac{z-c}{r}$
- be able to use the equation of a plane in any of the forms $\mathbf{r}=\mathbf{a}+s\mathbf{b}+t\mathbf{c}$, $(\mathbf{r}-\mathbf{a})\cdot\mathbf{n}=0$ or $ax+by+cz=d$
- be able to solve problems involving lines and planes in three dimensions.

2.1 Straight lines

You know that the cartesian equation of a straight line in two dimensions has the form $ax+by=c$. In P3 Sections 5.6 and 5.7, you saw that if O is the origin, and if a line is drawn through the point A with position vector $\mathbf{a}$ in the direction of the vector $\mathbf{p}$, the position vector of any point R on the line is given by

$$\mathbf{r}=\mathbf{a}+t\mathbf{p}$$

where t is a parameter.

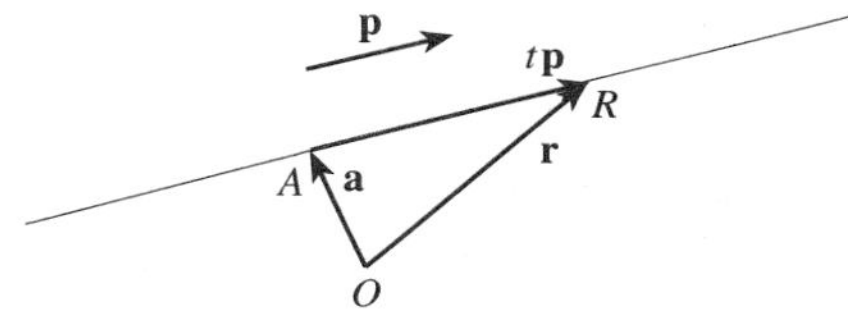

Fig. 2.1

This is shown in Fig. 2.1. You can think of the equation as saying 'To carry out the translation from O to R, start at O, get onto the line at A and then go in the direction of the vector $\mathbf{p}$ until you reach R' (having travelled t times the length of $\mathbf{p}$).

In the next section you will meet the cartesian equation of the line in three dimensions, but the vector form is more concise and is the one you should use if you have a choice.

> Points of a line through A in the direction of $\mathbf{p}$ have position vectors $\mathbf{r}=\mathbf{a}+t\mathbf{p}$, where t is a variable scalar. This is called the **vector equation** of the line.

To find the equation of the line joining two points A and B with position vectors $\mathbf{a}$ and $\mathbf{b}$, shown in Fig. 2.2, first find the direction of the line, which is given by the vector

$$\mathbf{p}=\overrightarrow{AB}=\mathbf{b}-\mathbf{a}.$$

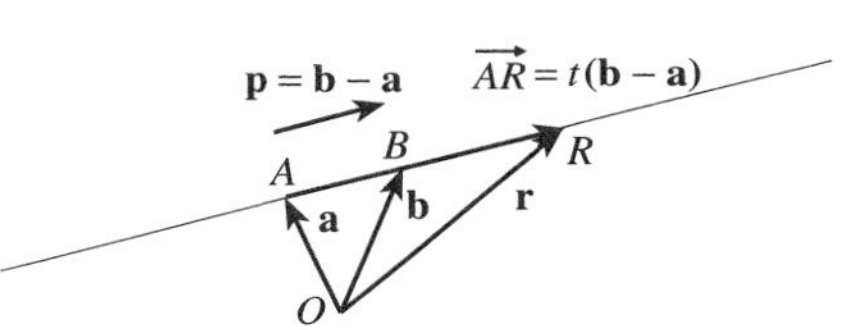

Fig. 2.2

You can then use this vector $\mathbf{p}$ in the equation $\mathbf{r}=\mathbf{a}+t\mathbf{p}$.

Example 2.1.1
Determine whether the points with coordinates $(5,1,-6)$ and $(-7,5,9)$ lie on the line joining $A(1,2,-1)$ to $B(-3,3,4)$.

Using the alphabet convention, P3 Section 5.4, in which O is the origin, $\mathbf{a}$ is the position vector of A, and so on, a vector in the direction of the line is

$$\overrightarrow{AB} = \mathbf{b} - \mathbf{a} = \begin{pmatrix} -3 \\ 3 \\ 4 \end{pmatrix} - \begin{pmatrix} 1 \\ 2 \\ -1 \end{pmatrix} = \begin{pmatrix} -4 \\ 1 \\ 5 \end{pmatrix}.$$

The equation of the line is $\mathbf{r} = \begin{pmatrix} 1 \\ 2 \\ -1 \end{pmatrix} + t\begin{pmatrix} -4 \\ 1 \\ 5 \end{pmatrix}$, or $\begin{pmatrix} x \\ y \\ z \end{pmatrix} = \begin{pmatrix} 1 \\ 2 \\ -1 \end{pmatrix} + t\begin{pmatrix} -4 \\ 1 \\ 5 \end{pmatrix}$.

To find whether $(5,1,-6)$ lies on this line, substitute $x = 5$, $y = 1$ and $z = -6$ to get the vector equation

$$\begin{pmatrix} 5 \\ 1 \\ -6 \end{pmatrix} = \begin{pmatrix} 1 \\ 2 \\ -1 \end{pmatrix} + t\begin{pmatrix} -4 \\ 1 \\ 5 \end{pmatrix}, \quad \text{or} \quad \begin{aligned} 5 &= 1 - 4t \\ 1 &= 2 + t \\ -6 &= -1 + 5t \end{aligned}.$$

These equations are consistent with solution $t = -1$, so $(5,1,-6)$ lies on AB.

To find whether $(-7,5,9)$ lies on AB, try to solve the vector equation

$$\begin{pmatrix} -7 \\ 5 \\ 9 \end{pmatrix} = \begin{pmatrix} 1 \\ 2 \\ -1 \end{pmatrix} + t\begin{pmatrix} -4 \\ 1 \\ 5 \end{pmatrix}, \quad \text{or} \quad \left.\begin{aligned} -7 &= 1 - 4t \\ 5 &= 2 + t \\ 9 &= -1 + 5t \end{aligned}\right\}.$$

You can see quickly that these equations are inconsistent. There is no value of t which satisfies the equations, so $(-7,5,9)$ does not lie on AB.

Example 2.1.2
Prove that the straight line with equation $\mathbf{r} = \begin{pmatrix} 1 \\ 2 \\ -3 \end{pmatrix} + t\begin{pmatrix} 2 \\ -1 \\ 4 \end{pmatrix}$ meets the line joining $(2,4,4)$ to $(3,3,5)$, and find the cosine of the angle between the lines.

The line joining $(2,4,4)$ and $(3,3,5)$ has direction $\begin{pmatrix} 3 \\ 3 \\ 5 \end{pmatrix} - \begin{pmatrix} 2 \\ 4 \\ 4 \end{pmatrix} = \begin{pmatrix} 1 \\ -1 \\ 1 \end{pmatrix}$ and so has equation $\mathbf{r} = \begin{pmatrix} 2 \\ 4 \\ 4 \end{pmatrix} + s\begin{pmatrix} 1 \\ -1 \\ 1 \end{pmatrix}$.

To prove that the lines intersect, you have to show that there is a point on one line which is the same as a point on the other. Suppose that the lines meet when the parameter of the first line is t and the parameter of the second line is s. Then

$$\begin{pmatrix} 1 \\ 2 \\ -3 \end{pmatrix} + t\begin{pmatrix} 2 \\ -1 \\ 4 \end{pmatrix} = \begin{pmatrix} 2 \\ 4 \\ 4 \end{pmatrix} + s\begin{pmatrix} 1 \\ -1 \\ 1 \end{pmatrix}; \quad \text{that is,} \quad \left.\begin{aligned} 2t - s &= 1 \\ -t + s &= 2 \\ 4t - s &= 7 \end{aligned}\right\}.$$

These equations are consistent, with solution $t = 3$ and $s = 5$. Hence the lines intersect. (The point of intersection is $(7, -1, 9)$.)

The angle between the lines is the angle between their direction vectors. Calling this angle θ and using the dot product (see P3 Section 12.4),

$$\begin{pmatrix} 2 \\ -1 \\ 4 \end{pmatrix} \cdot \begin{pmatrix} 1 \\ -1 \\ 1 \end{pmatrix} = \left| \begin{pmatrix} 2 \\ -1 \\ 4 \end{pmatrix} \right| \left| \begin{pmatrix} 1 \\ -1 \\ 1 \end{pmatrix} \right| \cos\theta, \quad \text{giving} \quad \cos\theta = \frac{7}{\sqrt{21}\sqrt{3}} = \frac{\sqrt{7}}{3}.$$

2.2 Cartesian equations of a straight line

You can find the cartesian equations of a straight line by eliminating the parameter t.

For example, for the equation $\mathbf{r} = \begin{pmatrix} 1 \\ 2 \\ -3 \end{pmatrix} + t\begin{pmatrix} 2 \\ -1 \\ 4 \end{pmatrix}$ in Example 2.1.2, writing $\mathbf{r} = \begin{pmatrix} x \\ y \\ z \end{pmatrix}$ puts the equation in the form

$$\begin{pmatrix} x \\ y \\ z \end{pmatrix} = \begin{pmatrix} 1 \\ 2 \\ -3 \end{pmatrix} + t\begin{pmatrix} 2 \\ -1 \\ 4 \end{pmatrix}, \text{ which you can rewrite as } \begin{pmatrix} x-1 \\ y-2 \\ z+3 \end{pmatrix} = t\begin{pmatrix} 2 \\ -1 \\ 4 \end{pmatrix}.$$

You can now split this vector equation into three simultaneous equations

$$x - 1 = 2t, \quad y - 2 = -t, \quad z + 3 = 4t,$$

which give $\dfrac{x-1}{2} = \dfrac{y-2}{-1} = \dfrac{z+3}{4} = t$.

The equations $\dfrac{x-1}{2} = \dfrac{y-2}{-1} = \dfrac{z+3}{4}$, which do not involve t, are the **cartesian equations** for the line.

In general:

> Cartesian equations of the line through (a, b, c) with direction $\begin{pmatrix} l \\ m \\ n \end{pmatrix}$ are
>
> $$\frac{x-a}{l} = \frac{y-b}{m} = \frac{z-c}{n}.$$

There are two observations to make about these equations.

- There are two equations, not a single equation. You will see later that the equation of the form $ax + by + cz = d$, which you might have expected to be the equation of a line in three dimensions, is actually the equation of a plane.
- The equations of some particularly simple lines, that is those with l or m or $n = 0$, cannot be put in this form. For example, the x-axis is a line through the origin $(0, 0, 0)$

in the direction $\begin{pmatrix}1\\0\\0\end{pmatrix}$. To use the result in the shaded box you would have to write it as $\frac{x}{1}=\frac{y}{0}=\frac{z}{0}$, but you shouldn't because division by zero is impossible. (In this case correct cartesian equations are $y=0, z=0$.) In practical problems you would try to organise your coordinate system so that your lines are parallel to the axes, so this could be quite a common occurrence.

You can avoid the cartesian form by turning it immediately into the vector form. For example, by putting each part of the equation equal to t, the cartesian equations

$$\frac{x-a}{l}=\frac{y-b}{m}=\frac{z-c}{n} \qquad \text{become} \qquad x=a+lt, \quad y=b+mt, \quad z=c+nt,$$

which are equivalent to the vector equation $\mathbf{r}=\begin{pmatrix}a\\b\\c\end{pmatrix}+t\begin{pmatrix}l\\m\\n\end{pmatrix}$.

Example 2.2.1
Find the cartesian equations of the line L joining $(-1,4,1)$ to $(3,6,2)$, and find whether this line intersects the straight line M with vector equation $\mathbf{r}=\mathbf{i}+\mathbf{j}+\mathbf{k}+t(\mathbf{i}+2\mathbf{j}-2\mathbf{k})$.

The direction vector of the line L is $\begin{pmatrix}3\\6\\2\end{pmatrix}-\begin{pmatrix}-1\\4\\1\end{pmatrix}=\begin{pmatrix}4\\2\\1\end{pmatrix}$.

The cartesian equations of L are then $\frac{x+1}{4}=\frac{y-4}{2}=\frac{z-1}{1}$.

To find whether L intersects M, use the vector form and replace the cartesian equations of L by $\mathbf{r}=-\mathbf{i}+4\mathbf{j}+\mathbf{k}+t(4\mathbf{i}+2\mathbf{j}+\mathbf{k})$.

Suppose that L and M meet where their parameters are r and s. Then

$$\mathbf{i}+\mathbf{j}+\mathbf{k}+r(\mathbf{i}+2\mathbf{j}-2\mathbf{k})=-\mathbf{i}+4\mathbf{j}+\mathbf{k}+s(4\mathbf{i}+2\mathbf{j}+\mathbf{k}).$$

Equating the coefficients of $\mathbf{i}$, $\mathbf{j}$ and $\mathbf{k}$ gives the equations

$$\left.\begin{aligned}1+r&=-1+4s\\1+2r&=4+2s\\1-2r&=1+s\end{aligned}\right\} \Leftrightarrow \left.\begin{aligned}r-4s&=-2\\2r-2s&=3\\-2r-s&=0\end{aligned}\right\} \Leftrightarrow \left.\begin{aligned}r-4s&=-2\\6s&=7\\-9s&=-4\end{aligned}\right\}.$$

The equations are inconsistent, so the two lines do not intersect.

Exercise 2A

1 Write down vector equations for the following straight lines which pass through the given points and lie in the given directions.

(a) $(1,2,3)$, $\begin{pmatrix}0\\1\\2\end{pmatrix}$ (b) $(0,0,0)$, $\begin{pmatrix}0\\0\\1\end{pmatrix}$ (c) $(2,-1,1)$, $\begin{pmatrix}3\\-1\\1\end{pmatrix}$ (d) $(3,0,2)$, $\begin{pmatrix}4\\-2\\3\end{pmatrix}$

2 Find vector equations for the lines joining the following pairs of points.

(a) $(2,-1,2)$, $(3,-1,4)$ (b) $(1,2,2)$, $(2,-2,2)$ (c) $(3,1,4)$, $(-1,2,3)$

3 Which of these equations of straight lines represent the same straight line as each other?

(a) $\mathbf{r}=\begin{pmatrix}1\\4\\2\end{pmatrix}+t\begin{pmatrix}2\\-1\\2\end{pmatrix}$ (b) $\mathbf{r}=\begin{pmatrix}3\\3\\4\end{pmatrix}+t\begin{pmatrix}2\\-1\\2\end{pmatrix}$

(c) $\mathbf{r}=5\mathbf{i}+2\mathbf{j}+6\mathbf{k}+t(-2\mathbf{i}+\mathbf{j}-2\mathbf{k})$ (d) $\mathbf{r}=\mathbf{i}+4\mathbf{j}+2\mathbf{k}+t(-2\mathbf{i}+\mathbf{j}-2\mathbf{k})$

(e) $\mathbf{r}=-\mathbf{i}+5\mathbf{j}+t(2\mathbf{i}-\mathbf{j}+2\mathbf{k})$ (f) $\mathbf{r}=-\mathbf{i}+5\mathbf{j}+t(-2\mathbf{i}+\mathbf{j}-2\mathbf{k})$

4 Find whether or not the point $(-3,1,5)$ lies on each of the following lines.

(a) $\mathbf{r}=\begin{pmatrix}1\\3\\1\end{pmatrix}+t\begin{pmatrix}-2\\-1\\2\end{pmatrix}$ (b) $\mathbf{r}=\begin{pmatrix}0\\1\\2\end{pmatrix}+t\begin{pmatrix}1\\0\\3\end{pmatrix}$ (c) $\mathbf{r}=\begin{pmatrix}1\\-2\\4\end{pmatrix}+t\begin{pmatrix}-4\\-3\\-1\end{pmatrix}$

5 Determine whether each of the following sets of points lies on a straight line.

(a) $(1,2,-1)$, $(2,4,-3)$, $(4,8,-7)$ (b) $(5,2,-3)$, $(-1,6,-11)$, $(3,-2,4)$

6 Find the point of intersection, if any, of each of the following pairs of lines.

(a) $\mathbf{r}=\begin{pmatrix}1\\3\\1\end{pmatrix}+s\begin{pmatrix}-2\\-1\\2\end{pmatrix}$, $\mathbf{r}=\begin{pmatrix}0\\-2\\8\end{pmatrix}+t\begin{pmatrix}1\\-1\\1\end{pmatrix}$ (b) $\mathbf{r}=\begin{pmatrix}1\\-1\\2\end{pmatrix}+s\begin{pmatrix}-1\\2\\-1\end{pmatrix}$, $\mathbf{r}=\begin{pmatrix}1\\3\\-1\end{pmatrix}+t\begin{pmatrix}2\\-8\\5\end{pmatrix}$

7 Find, where possible, the cartesian equations of the following lines.

(a) $\mathbf{r}=\begin{pmatrix}2\\-4\\1\end{pmatrix}+t\begin{pmatrix}1\\-1\\2\end{pmatrix}$ (b) $\mathbf{r}=\begin{pmatrix}1\\5\\0\end{pmatrix}+t\begin{pmatrix}0\\1\\-2\end{pmatrix}$ (c) $\mathbf{r}=\begin{pmatrix}0\\0\\1\end{pmatrix}+t\begin{pmatrix}1\\3\\2\end{pmatrix}$

8 Find the point of intersection, if any, of each of the following pairs of lines.

(a) $\dfrac{x-1}{3}=\dfrac{y-2}{-1}=\dfrac{z+1}{2}$ and $\dfrac{x-3}{4}=\dfrac{y-2}{-2}=\dfrac{z}{3}$

(b) $\dfrac{x-2}{4}=y=\dfrac{1-z}{2}$ and $\dfrac{x-1}{3}=\dfrac{y-4}{3}=z-1$

(c) $\dfrac{1-x}{2}=y+1=2-z$ and $\dfrac{x}{3}=y-1=\dfrac{z-2}{3}$

9 Find the cosine of the acute angle between the lines with equations

$$\frac{x+3}{2}=\frac{y-4}{-2}=\frac{z-1}{-1} \quad \text{and} \quad \mathbf{r}=3\mathbf{i}-2\mathbf{j}+4\mathbf{k}+t(-2\mathbf{i}+3\mathbf{j}+6\mathbf{k}).$$

2.3 The vector equation of a plane

Suppose that you wish to replace a tile on a roof, and that you need to have some way of specifying that tile among the other tiles on the roof. You could do it by thinking in terms of the vectors $\mathbf{p}$ and $\mathbf{q}$ along the slanting edge and the horizontal edge of the roof respectively. For instance, the tile shown in Fig. 2.3 might be the tile with vector $\frac{1}{2}\mathbf{p}+\frac{2}{3}\mathbf{q}$ relative to the point A. However, if you wish to take the origin O at the base of the vertical from the ground to A, the position vector of the tile relative to O would be $\mathbf{a}+\frac{1}{2}\mathbf{p}+\frac{2}{3}\mathbf{q}$.

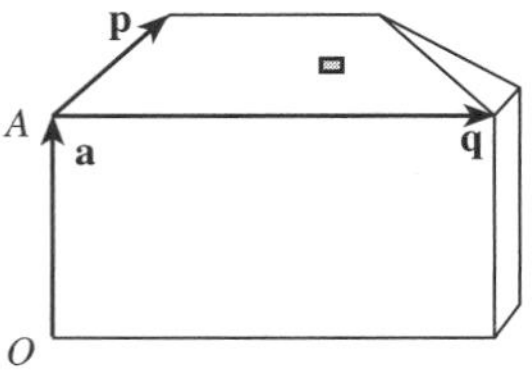

Fig. 2.3

You probably agree that you could specify the position of any tile on the roof by choosing the coefficients of $\mathbf{p}$ and $\mathbf{q}$ suitably.

You can generalise this thinking to define a plane.

Let O be the origin, and let A be a point with position vector $\mathbf{a}$. Let $\mathbf{p}$ and $\mathbf{q}$ be any two non-zero vectors which are not in the same or opposite directions. Then the locus of points R such that $\mathbf{r}=\mathbf{a}+s\mathbf{p}+t\mathbf{q}$ where s and t are parameters which can take any real value is called the **plane** through A defined by $\mathbf{p}$ and $\mathbf{q}$.

Fig. 2.4 shows the plane through A in the direction defined by $\mathbf{p}$ and $\mathbf{q}$, and the point R for which $\mathbf{r}=\mathbf{a}+2\mathbf{p}+\frac{1}{2}\mathbf{q}$, that is with parameters $s=2$ and $t=\frac{1}{2}$.

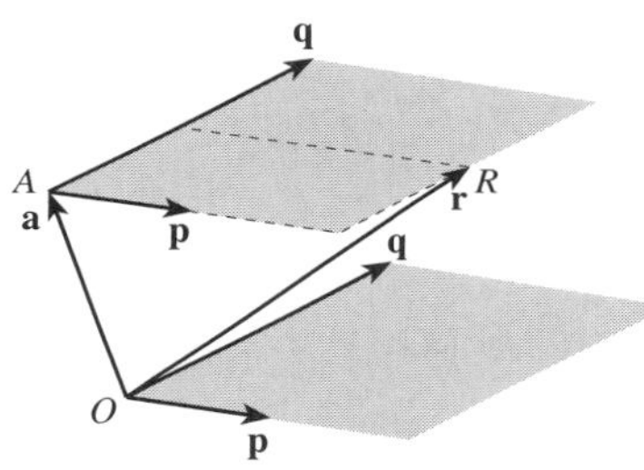

Fig. 2.4

The vector $\mathbf{a}$ plays a very different role in this equation than do the vectors $\mathbf{p}$ and $\mathbf{q}$. The vector $\mathbf{a}$ is the position vector of a point on the plane; $\mathbf{p}$ and $\mathbf{q}$ are vectors which are parallel to two vectors in the plane. Compare this equation with the vector equation $\mathbf{r}=\mathbf{a}+t\mathbf{p}$ of a line, where $\mathbf{a}$ is the position vector of a point on the line, and $\mathbf{p}$ is a vector in the direction of the line.

Notice also the important condition that $\mathbf{p}$ and $\mathbf{q}$ are non-zero vectors which are not in the same or opposite directions. If either of them was the zero vector the plane would degenerate to a line; if they were in the same or opposite directions they would not enable you to reach every point of the plane. Vectors which are in the same or opposite directions are called **parallel**. Thus for the equation $\mathbf{r}=\mathbf{a}+s\mathbf{p}+t\mathbf{q}$ to represent a plane, $\mathbf{p}$ and $\mathbf{q}$ must be non-zero, non-parallel vectors.

> Points of a plane through A defined by the non-zero, non-parallel vectors $\mathbf{p}$ and $\mathbf{q}$ have position vectors $\mathbf{r}=\mathbf{a}+s\mathbf{p}+t\mathbf{q}$, where s and t are variable scalars. This is called the **vector equation of the plane**.

Example 2.3.1

Find the vector equation of the plane through the points $A(1,1,1)$, $B(1,-3,2)$ and $C(1,0,1)$.

Two vectors whose directions are parallel to the plane are

$$\overrightarrow{AB} = \begin{pmatrix}1\\-3\\2\end{pmatrix} - \begin{pmatrix}1\\1\\1\end{pmatrix} = \begin{pmatrix}0\\-4\\1\end{pmatrix} \text{ and } \overrightarrow{AC} = \begin{pmatrix}1\\0\\1\end{pmatrix} - \begin{pmatrix}1\\1\\1\end{pmatrix} = \begin{pmatrix}0\\-1\\0\end{pmatrix}.$$

Thus the vector equation of the plane is $\mathbf{r} = \begin{pmatrix}1\\1\\1\end{pmatrix} + s\begin{pmatrix}0\\-4\\1\end{pmatrix} + t\begin{pmatrix}0\\-1\\0\end{pmatrix}$.

Example 2.3.2

Find the point A where the line $\mathbf{r} = \begin{pmatrix}2\\-1\\2\end{pmatrix} + r\begin{pmatrix}4\\-6\\1\end{pmatrix}$ meets the plane $\mathbf{r} = \begin{pmatrix}1\\0\\-1\end{pmatrix} + s\begin{pmatrix}0\\1\\1\end{pmatrix} + t\begin{pmatrix}1\\-1\\0\end{pmatrix}$.

Let the parameter of A on the line be r, and the parameters of A on the plane be s and t. Then

$$\begin{pmatrix}2\\-1\\2\end{pmatrix} + r\begin{pmatrix}4\\-6\\1\end{pmatrix} = \begin{pmatrix}1\\0\\-1\end{pmatrix} + s\begin{pmatrix}0\\1\\1\end{pmatrix} + t\begin{pmatrix}1\\-1\\0\end{pmatrix}, \text{ that is } \left.\begin{aligned} 4r \quad\;\; - t &= -1 \\ -6r - s + t &= 1 \\ r - s \quad\;\; &= -3 \end{aligned}\right\}.$$

Solving these equations by the usual method gives $r = -1$, $s = 2$ and $t = -3$.

As $r = -1$, the point of intersection has position vector $\begin{pmatrix}2\\-1\\2\end{pmatrix} + (-1)\begin{pmatrix}4\\-6\\1\end{pmatrix} = \begin{pmatrix}-2\\5\\1\end{pmatrix}$.
Its coordinates are therefore $(-2,5,1)$.

Checking by using the values of s and t shows that the point of intersection A has position vector $\begin{pmatrix}1\\0\\-1\end{pmatrix} + 2\begin{pmatrix}0\\1\\1\end{pmatrix} + (-3)\begin{pmatrix}1\\-1\\0\end{pmatrix} = \begin{pmatrix}-2\\5\\1\end{pmatrix}$, as required.

Example 2.3.3

Eliminate the parameters s and t to find a cartesian equation of the plane

$\mathbf{r} = \begin{pmatrix}1\\2\\3\end{pmatrix} + s\begin{pmatrix}1\\-1\\-1\end{pmatrix} + t\begin{pmatrix}2\\-1\\1\end{pmatrix}$.

Writing this equation as $\begin{pmatrix}x\\y\\z\end{pmatrix} = \begin{pmatrix}1\\2\\3\end{pmatrix} + s\begin{pmatrix}1\\-1\\-1\end{pmatrix} + t\begin{pmatrix}2\\-1\\1\end{pmatrix}$ and taking components gives

$$x - 1 = s + 2t, \quad y - 2 = -s - t, \quad z - 3 = -s + t.$$

Adding the first two equations gives $x + y - 3 = t$, and adding the first and third equations gives $x + z - 4 = 3t$, so $3(x + y - 3) = x + z - 4$, giving $2x + 3y - z = 5$.

This suggests that the plane has a linear cartesian equation.

It isn't always as easy as this to eliminate the parameters. You will see in Section 2.5 a method for finding the equation of a plane which is often quicker.

2.4 The cartesian equation of a line in two dimensions

In two dimensions, you can describe the direction of a line by a single number, its gradient. (The only exception is the line parallel to the y-axis.) Things are not so simple for a plane in three dimensions. You can't describe the direction of a plane by a single number. But even in two dimensions it is simpler to describe the direction of a line by a vector rather than a gradient, as the following example shows. The second method suggests an approach which you can extend to three dimensions.

Example 2.4.1
Find the equation of the line through $(1,2)$ perpendicular to the non-zero vector $\begin{pmatrix} l \\ m \end{pmatrix}$.

Method 1 The gradient of the given vector is $\frac{m}{l}$, so the required line has gradient $-\frac{l}{m}$. Its equation is therefore

$$y-2=-\frac{l}{m}(x-1),$$

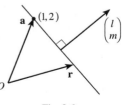

which simplifies directly to $lx+my=l+2m$.

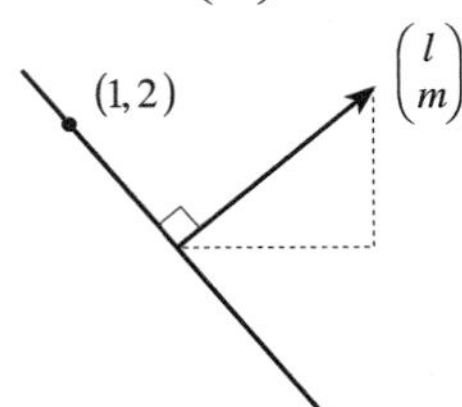

Fig. 2.5

This method breaks down if either l or m is zero. The line in the direction of the vector $\begin{pmatrix} l \\ m \end{pmatrix}$ has gradient $\frac{m}{l}$, provided that $l \neq 0$ as in Fig. 2.5. If $l=0$, then the vector $\begin{pmatrix} l \\ m \end{pmatrix}$ is parallel to the y-axis. (Recall that $\begin{pmatrix} l \\ m \end{pmatrix}$ is not the zero vector.) The line perpendicular to it is parallel to the x-axis, and is therefore $y=2$. This is the same as $lx+my=l+2m$ when $l=0$.

The case when $m=0$ is similar. The equation is still $lx+my=l+2m$, so the required perpendicular is $lx+my=l+2m$ in all cases.

Look at the left side of this equation. The line perpendicular to the vector $\begin{pmatrix} l \\ m \end{pmatrix}$ has an equation of the form $lx+my=k$ where k is a constant. This suggests Method 2.

Method 2 Let $\mathbf{n}=\begin{pmatrix} l \\ m \end{pmatrix}$ be the perpendicular to the line, and $\mathbf{a}$ be the position vector of $(1,2)$. Let $\mathbf{r}$ be the position vector of any other point on the line. See Fig. 2.6.

Then $\mathbf{r}-\mathbf{a}$ is a vector in the direction of the line, and is therefore perpendicular to $\mathbf{n}$. (Recall that in general $\mathbf{p}\cdot\mathbf{q}=|\mathbf{p}||\mathbf{q}|\cos\theta$ where θ is the angle between $\mathbf{p}$ and $\mathbf{q}$. If $\mathbf{p}$ and $\mathbf{q}$ are perpendicular, so that $\cos\theta=0$, then $\mathbf{p}\cdot\mathbf{q}=0$.)

Fig. 2.6

Therefore $(\mathbf{r}-\mathbf{a})\cdot\mathbf{n}=0$, or $\mathbf{r}\cdot\mathbf{n}=\mathbf{a}\cdot\mathbf{n}$.

If $\mathbf{n} = \begin{pmatrix} l \\ m \end{pmatrix}$, $\mathbf{r} = \begin{pmatrix} x \\ y \end{pmatrix}$ and $\mathbf{a} = \begin{pmatrix} 1 \\ 2 \end{pmatrix}$, then the equation $\mathbf{r} \cdot \mathbf{n} = \mathbf{a} \cdot \mathbf{n}$ becomes

$\begin{pmatrix} x \\ y \end{pmatrix} \cdot \begin{pmatrix} l \\ m \end{pmatrix} = \begin{pmatrix} 1 \\ 2 \end{pmatrix} \cdot \begin{pmatrix} l \\ m \end{pmatrix}$, that is $lx + my = l + 2m$.

Method 2 shows what is generally the best way to find the cartesian equation of a plane.

2.5 The cartesian equation of a plane

Let $\mathbf{n}$ be a vector perpendicular to a plane, called the **normal** to the plane, and let $\mathbf{a}$ be the position vector of a point on the plane. Let $\mathbf{r}$ be the position vector of any other point on the plane, as in Fig. 2.7.

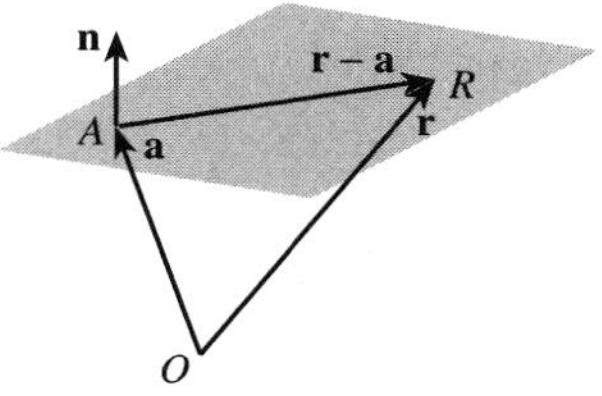

Fig. 2.7

Then $\mathbf{r} - \mathbf{a}$ is a vector parallel to the plane, and is therefore perpendicular to $\mathbf{n}$. Therefore $(\mathbf{r} - \mathbf{a}) \cdot \mathbf{n} = 0$, or $\mathbf{r} \cdot \mathbf{n} = \mathbf{a} \cdot \mathbf{n}$.

This equation, $\mathbf{r} \cdot \mathbf{n} = \mathbf{a} \cdot \mathbf{n}$, is another form of the equation of a plane.

If you write $\mathbf{r} = \begin{pmatrix} x \\ y \\ z \end{pmatrix}$ and $\mathbf{n} = \begin{pmatrix} p \\ q \\ r \end{pmatrix}$, then the equation $\mathbf{r} \cdot \mathbf{n} = \mathbf{a} \cdot \mathbf{n}$ becomes

$$px + qy + rz = \mathbf{a} \cdot \mathbf{n}.$$

This is the cartesian form of the equation of a plane. Notice that the right side is a constant, and the coefficients on the left side are the components of the normal vector. Thus, you can write down the equation of the plane directly if you know a vector normal to it and you know a point on it.

The equation of a plane can take three forms.

Points of a plane through A defined by the non-zero, non-parallel vectors $\mathbf{p}$ and $\mathbf{q}$ have position vectors $\mathbf{r} = \mathbf{a} + s\mathbf{p} + t\mathbf{q}$, where s and t are variable scalars. This is called the **vector equation** of the plane.

Points of a plane through A and perpendicular to the normal vector $\mathbf{n}$ have position vectors $\mathbf{r}$ which satisfy $\mathbf{r} \cdot \mathbf{n} = \mathbf{a} \cdot \mathbf{n}$. This is called the **normal equation** of the plane.

Points of a plane through A and perpendicular to the normal vector $\mathbf{n} = \begin{pmatrix} p \\ q \\ r \end{pmatrix}$ have coordinates (x, y, z) which satisfy $px + qy + rz = k$ where k is a constant determined by the coordinates of A. This is called the **cartesian equation** of the plane.

Example 2.5.1
Find the cartesian equation of the plane through the point $(1,2,3)$ with normal $\begin{pmatrix}4\\5\\6\end{pmatrix}$.

Method 1 The equation is $4x+5y+6z=k$, where k is a constant.

The constant has to be chosen so that the plane passes through $(1,2,3)$.

It is therefore $4x+5y+6z=4\times1+5\times2+6\times3=32$,

so the equation is $4x+5y+6z=32$.

Method 2 Using the equation $\mathbf{r}\cdot\mathbf{n}=\mathbf{a}\cdot\mathbf{n}$ gives $\begin{pmatrix}x\\y\\z\end{pmatrix}\cdot\begin{pmatrix}4\\5\\6\end{pmatrix}=\begin{pmatrix}1\\2\\3\end{pmatrix}\cdot\begin{pmatrix}4\\5\\6\end{pmatrix}$.

This is $4x+5y+6z=4\times1+5\times2+6\times3=32$,
which is $4x+5y+6z=32$.

Example 2.5.2
Find the coordinates of the point of intersection of the line $\mathbf{r}=\begin{pmatrix}1\\0\\1\end{pmatrix}+t\begin{pmatrix}2\\1\\-3\end{pmatrix}$ with the plane $3x+2y+4z=11$.

Rewriting the line in the form $\begin{pmatrix}x\\y\\z\end{pmatrix}=\begin{pmatrix}1\\0\\1\end{pmatrix}+t\begin{pmatrix}2\\1\\-3\end{pmatrix}$ and taking components yields the equations $x=1+2t$, $y=0+t$ and $z=1-3t$. Substituting these into the equation of the plane gives

$$3(1+2t)+2t+4(1-3t)=11, \quad \text{which gives} \quad t=-1.$$

So the line meets the plane at the point with parameter -1, namely $(-1,-1,4)$.

Example 2.5.3
(a) Find the coordinates of the foot of the perpendicular from the point $(1,1,1)$ to the plane $x+2y-2z=9$.
(b) Find the length of this perpendicular.

(a) The normal to the plane $x+2y-2z=9$ has direction $\begin{pmatrix}1\\2\\-2\end{pmatrix}$, and so the line through $(1,1,1)$ perpendicular to the plane has equation $\mathbf{r}=\begin{pmatrix}1\\1\\1\end{pmatrix}+t\begin{pmatrix}1\\2\\-2\end{pmatrix}$.

This meets the plane $x+2y-2z=9$ where $(1+t)+2(1+2t)-2(1-2t)=9$, that is where $9t=8$, or $t=\frac{8}{9}$.

The position vector of the point of intersection is $\begin{pmatrix}1\\1\\1\end{pmatrix}+\frac{8}{9}\begin{pmatrix}1\\2\\-2\end{pmatrix}=\begin{pmatrix}\frac{17}{9}\\\frac{25}{9}\\-\frac{7}{9}\end{pmatrix}$. The coordinates of the foot of the perpendicular are $\left(\frac{17}{9},\frac{25}{9},-\frac{7}{9}\right)$.

(b) You could find the distance of this point from $(1,1,1)$ by using the distance formula, but there is a quicker way.

The length of the vector from $(1,1,1)$ to the plane is $\frac{8}{9}$ of the length of the vector $\begin{pmatrix}1\\2\\-2\end{pmatrix}$, which is $\sqrt{1^2+2^2+(-2)^2}=3$. So the perpendicular distance is $\frac{8}{9}\times 3=\frac{8}{3}$.

Example 2.5.4
Find the acute angle between the line $\dfrac{x-1}{2}=\dfrac{y-3}{4}=\dfrac{z-5}{1}$ and the plane $x-y+z=0$.

As shown in Fig. 2.8, take $\mathbf{n}$ to be a vector normal to the plane, and $\mathbf{p}$ a vector along the line. You can find the angle θ from the dot product $\mathbf{n}\cdot\mathbf{p}$, and the angle between the line and the plane is then $\frac{1}{2}\pi-\theta$.

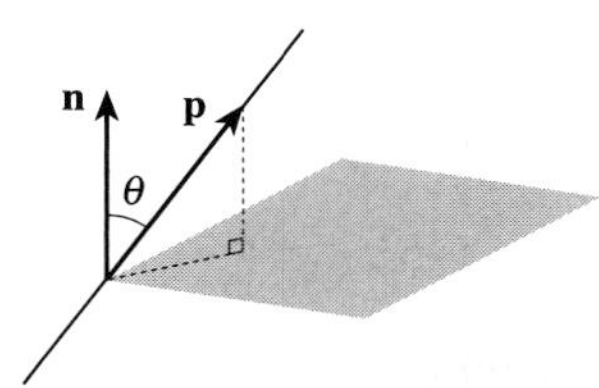

Fig. 2.8

Writing $\dfrac{x-1}{2}=\dfrac{y-3}{4}=\dfrac{z-5}{1}=t$ shows that the line has direction vector $\begin{pmatrix}2\\4\\1\end{pmatrix}$. The normal to the plane is $\begin{pmatrix}1\\-1\\1\end{pmatrix}$.

So the angle θ between them is given by

$$\begin{pmatrix}2\\4\\1\end{pmatrix}\cdot\begin{pmatrix}1\\-1\\1\end{pmatrix}=\left|\begin{pmatrix}2\\4\\1\end{pmatrix}\right|\left|\begin{pmatrix}1\\-1\\1\end{pmatrix}\right|\cos\theta, \text{ that is } \cos\theta=-\frac{1}{\sqrt{21}\sqrt{3}}=-\frac{1}{3\sqrt{7}}.$$

There is a problem. Since $\cos\theta$ is negative, the angle θ is obtuse, so Fig. 2.8 can't be right. The relation between $\mathbf{p}$ and $\mathbf{n}$ is correctly shown in Fig. 2.9. The required angle is $\theta-\frac{1}{2}\pi$, which is

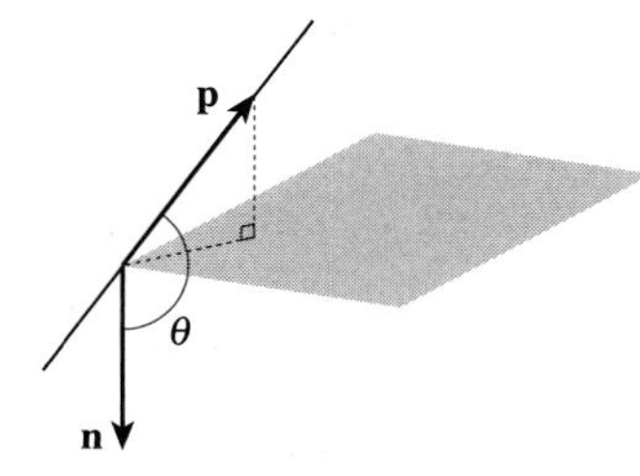

Fig. 2.9

$$\begin{aligned}\cos^{-1}\left(-\frac{1}{3\sqrt{7}}\right)-\tfrac{1}{2}\pi&=\left(\pi-\cos^{-1}\left(\frac{1}{3\sqrt{7}}\right)\right)-\tfrac{1}{2}\pi\\&=\tfrac{1}{2}\pi-\cos^{-1}\left(\frac{1}{3\sqrt{7}}\right)\\&=\sin^{-1}\frac{1}{3\sqrt{7}}\end{aligned}$$

Example 2.5.5
Find the cartesian equation of the plane through $A(1,2,1)$, $B(2,-1,-4)$ and $C(1,0,-1)$.

You can tackle this problem in several ways. You could say that the equation is of the form $ax+by+cz=d$, substitute the coordinates of the points and solve the resulting equations for a, b, c and d.

You could say that $\overrightarrow{AB}=\begin{pmatrix}2\\-1\\-4\end{pmatrix}-\begin{pmatrix}1\\2\\1\end{pmatrix}=\begin{pmatrix}1\\-3\\-5\end{pmatrix}$ and $\overrightarrow{AC}=\begin{pmatrix}1\\0\\-1\end{pmatrix}-\begin{pmatrix}1\\2\\1\end{pmatrix}=\begin{pmatrix}0\\-2\\-2\end{pmatrix}$ lie in the plane, so the vector equation of the plane is $\mathbf{r} = \begin{pmatrix} 1 \\ 2 \\ 1 \end{pmatrix} + s\begin{pmatrix} 1 \\ -3 \\ -5 \end{pmatrix} + t\begin{pmatrix} 0 \\ -2 \\ -2 \end{pmatrix}$. You could then eliminate the parameters s and t to find the cartesian equation.

Here is a third method which involves finding the normal to the plane.

Let $\begin{pmatrix} p \\ q \\ r \end{pmatrix}$ be normal to the plane. As $\begin{pmatrix} 1 \\ -3 \\ -5 \end{pmatrix}$ and $\begin{pmatrix} 0 \\ -2 \\ -2 \end{pmatrix}$ are vectors parallel to the plane, they are perpendicular to the normal, so both products $\begin{pmatrix} 1 \\ -3 \\ -5 \end{pmatrix} \cdot \begin{pmatrix} p \\ q \\ r \end{pmatrix}$ and $\begin{pmatrix} 0 \\ -2 \\ -2 \end{pmatrix} \cdot \begin{pmatrix} p \\ q \\ r \end{pmatrix}$ are zero.

Therefore $\left.\begin{aligned} p-3q-5r&=0 \\ -2q-2r&=0 \end{aligned}\right\}$, or $\left.\begin{aligned} p-3q-5r&=0 \\ q+r&=0 \end{aligned}\right\}$. Using the method of Chapter 1 put $r = t$, then $q = -t$ and, substituting in the first equation, $p = 2t$.

Thus $\begin{pmatrix} p \\ q \\ r \end{pmatrix} = \begin{pmatrix} 2t \\ -t \\ t \end{pmatrix} = t\begin{pmatrix} 2 \\ -1 \\ 1 \end{pmatrix}$ is normal to the plane for all t, except $t = 0$. Since you need only one normal, put $t = 1$, giving $\begin{pmatrix} 2 \\ -1 \\ 1 \end{pmatrix}$ as the normal to the plane.

Therefore the equation is $2x - y + z = k$, and since $(1,2,1)$ lies on the plane, the equation is $2x - y + z = 2\times1 - 1\times2 + 1\times1 = 1$, or $2x - y + z = 1$.

It is good practice to verify that the other points also lie on this plane.

Example 2.5.6
A pyramid of height 3 units stands symmetrically on a rectangular base $ABCD$ with $AB = 2$ units and $BC = 4$ units. Find the acute angle between two adjacent slanting faces.

You could solve this problem by trigonometrical methods, but it is useful to see how you can use vector methods. The strategy is to find the angle between the planes by finding the angle between the normals to the planes.

Let V be the vertex. Take the origin at the centre of the base, and the x- and y-axes parallel to CB and AB, as in Fig. 2.10. Then the coordinates of A, B, C and V are respectively $(2,-1,0)$, $(2,1,0)$, $(-2,1,0)$ and $(0,0,3)$.

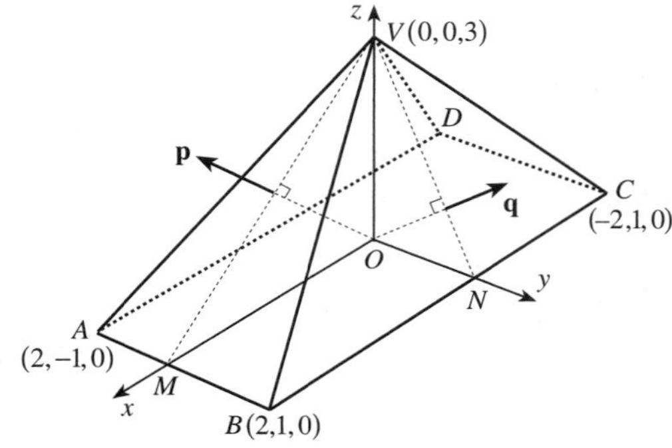

Fig. 2.10

The normal vector $\mathbf{p}$ to the face VAB is in the direction of the perpendicular from O to VM, where M is the mid-point of AB

with coordinates $(2,0,0)$. By symmetry, $\mathbf{p}$ has no y-component, and it is perpendicular to $\overrightarrow{MV} = \begin{pmatrix}0\\0\\3\end{pmatrix} - \begin{pmatrix}2\\0\\0\end{pmatrix} = \begin{pmatrix}-2\\0\\3\end{pmatrix}$, so $\mathbf{p}$ can be taken as $\begin{pmatrix}3\\0\\2\end{pmatrix}$.

Similarly the normal vector $\mathbf{q}$ to the face VBC has no x-component and is perpendicular to $\overrightarrow{NV} = \begin{pmatrix}0\\-1\\3\end{pmatrix}$, so take $\mathbf{q} = \begin{pmatrix}0\\3\\1\end{pmatrix}$.

Let the angle between $\mathbf{p}$ and $\mathbf{q}$ be $\theta°$. Then

$$\left|\begin{pmatrix}3\\0\\2\end{pmatrix}\right|\left|\begin{pmatrix}0\\3\\1\end{pmatrix}\right|\cos\theta° = \begin{pmatrix}3\\0\\2\end{pmatrix}\cdot\begin{pmatrix}0\\3\\1\end{pmatrix}$$

so $\cos\theta° = \dfrac{2}{\sqrt{13}\sqrt{10}} = \dfrac{2}{\sqrt{130}}$ and $\theta \approx 79.9$.

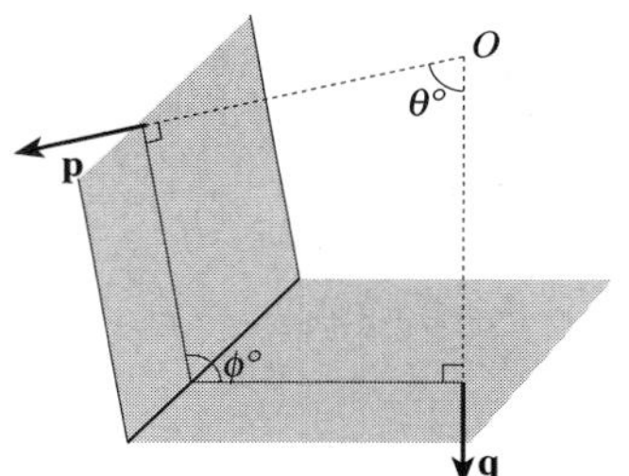

Fig. 2.11

Fig. 2.11 illustrates the relation between the angle $\theta°$ between $\mathbf{p}$ and $\mathbf{q}$, and the angle $\phi°$ between the faces of the pyramid, as viewed from inside the pyramid. This shows that $\phi = 180 - \theta \approx 100.1$.

The faces of the pyramid are therefore at 100.1° to each other.

2.6 Interpreting simultaneous equations geometrically

In Chapter 1 you saw how to solve simultaneous equations with three unknowns. The first case was in Example 1.5.1, where the equation $x + 2y + 3z = 6$ had the solution, expressed in vector form,

$$\begin{pmatrix}x\\y\\z\end{pmatrix} = \begin{pmatrix}6-2s-3t\\s\\t\end{pmatrix} = \begin{pmatrix}6\\0\\0\end{pmatrix} + s\begin{pmatrix}-2\\1\\0\end{pmatrix} + t\begin{pmatrix}-3\\0\\1\end{pmatrix}.$$

You are now in a position to interpret $x + 2y + 3z = 6$ as the cartesian equation of a plane, and the solution of the equation as the vector form of the equation of a plane.

Two planes meet in a line In Example 1.5.2, the vector form of the solution of the equations $\left.\begin{aligned}x+2y+3z&=6\\2x+3y+\ z&=7\end{aligned}\right\}$ was $\begin{pmatrix}x\\y\\z\end{pmatrix} = \begin{pmatrix}-4+7t\\5-5t\\t\end{pmatrix} = \begin{pmatrix}-4\\5\\0\end{pmatrix} + t\begin{pmatrix}-7\\-5\\1\end{pmatrix}$.

Thus two planes whose cartesian equation are given generally meet in the line whose vector equation is the solution to the equations.

Note that the planes could be parallel.

Three planes meet in a point In Example 1.6.1, the equations $\left.\begin{aligned}2x+\ y-\ z&=2\\ x-2y+3z&=7\\ 3x+5y-\ z&=0\end{aligned}\right\}$ had the solution $x=2$, $y=-1$, $z=1$. This corresponds to the general situation where the three planes meet in a point.

Three planes form a prism However, in Example 1.6.2, the equations

$$\left.\begin{aligned}x-\ y+\ z&=2\\ 2x+3y-\ z&=4\\ 3x+7y-3z&=5\end{aligned}\right\}$$

were inconsistent, and there was no solution. This corresponds to the case where the three planes whose cartesian equations are given form a **prism**, as shown in Fig. 2.12.

You can check that the planes corresponding to the first two equations meet in the line

$$\begin{pmatrix}x\\y\\z\end{pmatrix}=\begin{pmatrix}2\\0\\0\end{pmatrix}+t\begin{pmatrix}-2\\3\\5\end{pmatrix}.$$

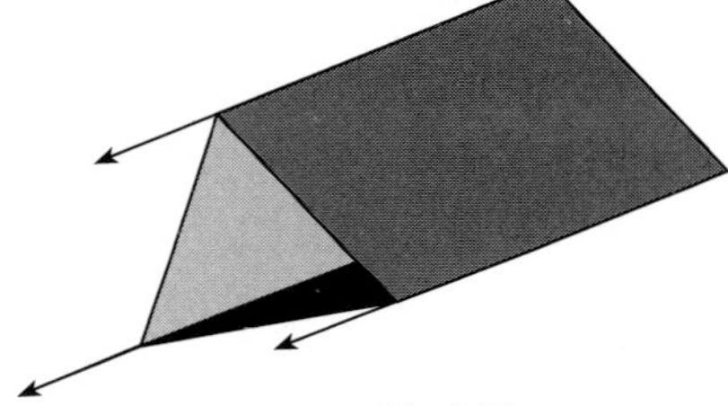

Fig. 2.12

The planes corresponding to the first and third equations and those corresponding to the second and third equations meet in the lines

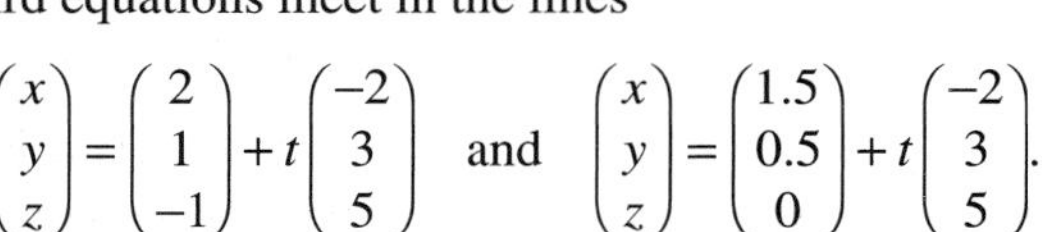

$$\begin{pmatrix}x\\y\\z\end{pmatrix}=\begin{pmatrix}2\\1\\-1\end{pmatrix}+t\begin{pmatrix}-2\\3\\5\end{pmatrix}\quad\text{and}\quad\begin{pmatrix}x\\y\\z\end{pmatrix}=\begin{pmatrix}1.5\\0.5\\0\end{pmatrix}+t\begin{pmatrix}-2\\3\\5\end{pmatrix}.$$

You can see that the three lines are parallel, all having the direction $\begin{pmatrix}-2\\3\\5\end{pmatrix}$.

Three planes form a sheaf The equations in Example 1.6.3,

$$\left.\begin{aligned}x-\ y+\ z&=2\\ 2x+3y-\ z&=4\\ 3x+7y-3z&=6\end{aligned}\right\},$$

had the solution $\begin{pmatrix}x\\y\\z\end{pmatrix}=\begin{pmatrix}2\\0\\0\end{pmatrix}+t\begin{pmatrix}-2\\3\\5\end{pmatrix}$.

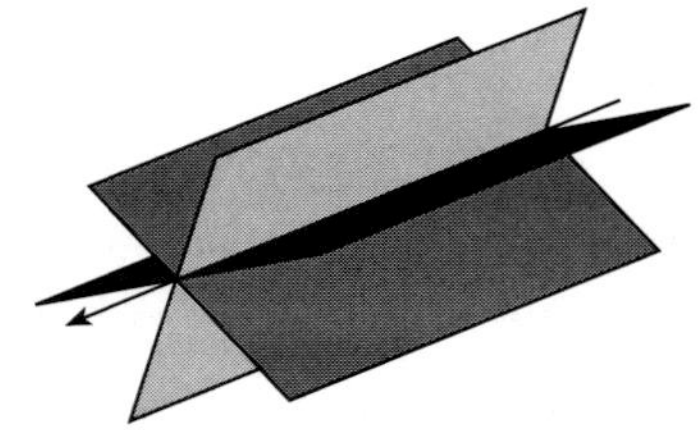

Fig. 2.13

This corresponds to the case where the three planes with the given equations meet in a line, forming a **sheaf**, as in Fig. 2.13.

There are other cases of inconsistency, such as when two of the the planes are parallel and the third is not parallel to them, and also when all three planes are parallel. These cases are left for you to interpret, and to draw your own pictures.

Exercise 2B

1 For each part, find the vector equation of the plane through the given points. Keep your answers for use in Question 8.

(a) $(1,0,0), (0,0,0), (0,1,0)$

(b) $(1,-1,0), (0,1,-1), (-1,0,1)$

(c) $(1,2,3), (2,-1,2), (3,1,-1)$

(d) $(4,-1,2), (0,0,3), (-1,2,0)$

2 For each part, find the coordinates of the point where the given line meets the given plane.

(a) $\mathbf{r} = \begin{pmatrix} -2 \\ 7 \\ 0 \end{pmatrix} + r\begin{pmatrix} -1 \\ 1 \\ 1 \end{pmatrix}$, $\mathbf{r} = \begin{pmatrix} 1 \\ 2 \\ -1 \end{pmatrix} + s\begin{pmatrix} 1 \\ 0 \\ 2 \end{pmatrix} + t\begin{pmatrix} 1 \\ 2 \\ 0 \end{pmatrix}$

(b) $\mathbf{r} = \begin{pmatrix} -1 \\ -7 \\ 8 \end{pmatrix} + r\begin{pmatrix} 4 \\ 2 \\ -2 \end{pmatrix}$, $\mathbf{r} = \begin{pmatrix} 4 \\ 1 \\ -1 \end{pmatrix} + s\begin{pmatrix} 2 \\ -1 \\ 3 \end{pmatrix} + t\begin{pmatrix} -1 \\ 0 \\ 1 \end{pmatrix}$

(c) $\mathbf{r} = \begin{pmatrix} 5 \\ -8 \\ -5 \end{pmatrix} + r\begin{pmatrix} 1 \\ 2 \\ -1 \end{pmatrix}$, $\mathbf{r} = \begin{pmatrix} 1 \\ 0 \\ -3 \end{pmatrix} + s\begin{pmatrix} -1 \\ 1 \\ 0 \end{pmatrix} + t\begin{pmatrix} 0 \\ 1 \\ -1 \end{pmatrix}$

3 Find the coordinates of the point where the line through the origin and $(1,1,1)$ meets the plane through the points $(-1,1,-2)$, $(1,5,-5)$ and $(0,2,-3)$.

4 Find the cartesian equation of the plane through $(1,1,1)$ normal to the vector $\begin{pmatrix} 5 \\ -8 \\ 4 \end{pmatrix}$.

5 Find the cartesian equation of the plane through $(2,-1,1)$ normal to the vector $2\mathbf{i}-\mathbf{j}-\mathbf{k}$.

6 Find a vector perpendicular to both $\mathbf{i}+2\mathbf{j}-\mathbf{k}$ and $3\mathbf{i}-\mathbf{j}+\mathbf{k}$. Hence find the cartesian equation of the plane parallel to both $\mathbf{i}+2\mathbf{j}-\mathbf{k}$ and $3\mathbf{i}-\mathbf{j}+\mathbf{k}$ and which passes through the point $(2,0,-3)$.

7 Find the cartesian equation of the plane with vector equation $\mathbf{r} = \begin{pmatrix} 1 \\ -1 \\ -3 \end{pmatrix} + s\begin{pmatrix} -1 \\ 1 \\ 0 \end{pmatrix} + t\begin{pmatrix} 0 \\ 1 \\ -1 \end{pmatrix}$.

8 Find the cartesian equations of the planes in Question 1.

9 Find the coordinates of two points A and B on the plane $2x+3y+4z=4$. Verify that the vector $\overrightarrow{AB}$ is perpendicular to the normal to the plane.

10 Find the coordinates of the foot of the perpendicular from the point $(2,-3,6)$ to the plane $2x-3y+6z=0$. Hence find the perpendicular distance of the point from the plane.

11 Find the perpendicular distance of the point $(3,1,-2)$ from the plane $2x+y-2z=8$.

12 Verify that the line with equation $\mathbf{r} = 2\mathbf{i}+4\mathbf{j}+\mathbf{k}+t(-4\mathbf{i}+4\mathbf{j}-5\mathbf{k})$ lies wholly in the plane with equation $3x-2y+4z=2$.

13 Find the equation of the plane through $(1,2,-1)$ parallel to the plane $5x+y+7z=20$.

14 Find the equation of the line through $(4,2,-1)$ perpendicular to the plane $3x+4y-z=1$.

15 A cave has a planar roof passing through the points $(0,0,-19)$, $(5,0,-20)$ and $(0,5,-22)$. A tunnel is being bored through the rock from the point $(0,3,4)$ in the direction $-\mathbf{i}+2\mathbf{j}-20\mathbf{k}$. Find in degrees, correct to the nearest degree, the angle between the tunnel and the cave roof.

Miscellaneous exercise 2

1 Prove that the lines with equations $\dfrac{x-2}{3}=\dfrac{-2-y}{3}=z+2$ and $-x=y=-z$ intersect, and find the coordinates of their point of intersection.

2 Find whether the point $(0,3,4)$ lies on the line which passes through $(2,1,-3)$ and $(1,2,6)$.

3 Find the acute angle between the lines with equations $\mathbf{r}=\begin{pmatrix}4\\1\\3\end{pmatrix}+s\begin{pmatrix}1\\1\\1\end{pmatrix}$ and $\mathbf{r}=\begin{pmatrix}2\\2\\7\end{pmatrix}+t\begin{pmatrix}1\\-1\\-2\end{pmatrix}$.

4 Find the cartesian equation of the plane through $(1,3,-7)$, $(2,-5,-3)$ and $(-5,7,2)$.

5 Two planes with equations $\mathbf{r}\cdot\begin{pmatrix}3\\1\\1\end{pmatrix}=2$ and $\mathbf{r}\cdot\begin{pmatrix}2\\5\\-1\end{pmatrix}=15$ intersect in the line L.

(a) Find a direction for the line L.

(b) Show that the point $(1,2,-3)$ lies in both planes, and write down a vector equation for the line L. (OCR)

6 Two planes, Π_1 and Π_2, are defined by the equations $x+2y+z=4$ and $2x-3y=6$ respectively.

(a) Find the acute angle between Π_1 and Π_2.

(b) The planes Π_1 and Π_2 intersect in the line l. Find a vector equation of l.

7 Determine the value of the constant k for which the system of equations

$$\left.\begin{aligned}2x-\ y-\ z&=3\\-4x+7y+3z&=-5\\kx+\ y-\ z&=5\end{aligned}\right\}$$

does not have a unique solution. For this value of k, determine the complete solution to this system. Interpret this solution geometrically. (OCR)

8 The straight line L_1 with vector equation $\mathbf{r}=\mathbf{a}+t\mathbf{b}$ cuts the plane $2x-3y+z=6$ at right angles, at the point $(5,1,-1)$.

(a) Explain why suitable choices for $\mathbf{a}$ and $\mathbf{b}$ would be $\mathbf{a}=5\mathbf{i}+\mathbf{j}-\mathbf{k}$ and $\mathbf{b}=2\mathbf{i}-3\mathbf{j}+\mathbf{k}$.

Another straight line, L_2, has vector equation $\mathbf{r}=s(\mathbf{i}+3\mathbf{j}+2\mathbf{k})$.

(b) (i) Find the angle between the directions of L_1 and L_2, giving your answer to the nearest degree.

(ii) Verify that L_2 cuts the plane $2x-3y+z=6$ at the point $(-1.2,-3.6,-2.4)$.

(iii) Prove that L_1 and L_2 do not meet. (OCR)

9 The line l_1 passes through the point P with position vector $2\mathbf{i}+\mathbf{j}-\mathbf{k}$ and has direction vector $\mathbf{i}-\mathbf{j}$. The line l_2 passes through the point Q with position vector $5\mathbf{i}-2\mathbf{j}-\mathbf{k}$ and has direction vector $\mathbf{j}+2\mathbf{k}$.

(a) Write down equations for l_1 and l_2 in the form $\mathbf{r}=\mathbf{a}+t\mathbf{b}$.

(b) Show that Q lies on l_1.

(c) Find either the acute angle or the obtuse angle between l_1 and l_2.

(d) Show that the vector $\mathbf{n}=2\mathbf{i}+2\mathbf{j}-\mathbf{k}$ is perpendicular to both l_1 and l_2.

(e) Find the cartesian equation for the plane containing l_1 and l_2. (OCR)

10 Find a formula for the perpendicular distance of the point (p,q,r) from the plane with equation $ax+by+cz=d$.

11 Find the value of a for which the simultaneous equations

$$\begin{aligned} 3x+2y-\ \ z&=10,\\ 5x-\ \ y-4z&=17,\\ x+5y+az&=b, \end{aligned}$$

do not have a unique solution for x, y and z.

Show that, for this value of a, the equations are inconsistent unless $b=3$.

For the case where the equations represent three planes having a common line of intersection, L, find equations for L giving your answer in the form

$$\frac{x-p}{l}=\frac{y-q}{m}=\frac{z-r}{n}.$$ (OCR)

3 The vector product

This chapter introduces the vector product of two vectors in three dimensions. When you have completed it, you should be able to

- find the vector product $\mathbf{p}\times\mathbf{q}$ of two vectors $\mathbf{p}$ and $\mathbf{q}$
- solve a variety of problems involving lines and planes in three dimensions.

3.1 The vector product

In P3 Chapter 12, you met the scalar product, or dot product, of two vectors, by which you combine two vectors and get a result which is a scalar. The vector product $\mathbf{p}\times\mathbf{q}$, sometimes for obvious reasons called the cross product, of two vectors $\mathbf{p}$ and $\mathbf{q}$ is a different kind of product. The result $\mathbf{p}\times\mathbf{q}$ is a vector.

The vector $\mathbf{p}\times\mathbf{q}$ has magnitude $|\mathbf{p}||\mathbf{q}|\sin\theta$, where θ is the angle between $\mathbf{p}$ and $\mathbf{q}$ and $0\leqslant\theta\leqslant\pi$. The direction of $\mathbf{p}\times\mathbf{q}$ is perpendicular to both $\mathbf{p}$ and $\mathbf{q}$ such that if you point the first finger of your right hand in the $\mathbf{p}$ direction and the middle finger in the $\mathbf{q}$ direction, your thumb will point in the direction $\mathbf{p}\times\mathbf{q}$.

Fig. 3.1 shows four pairs of vectors $\mathbf{p}$ and $\mathbf{q}$ in the plane of the paper, and indicates the direction of the vector product $\mathbf{p}\times\mathbf{q}$, which is either into or out of the paper, in each case.

It is worth thinking through the actions with your fingers and thumb and making sure you agree with these directions in Fig. 3.1.

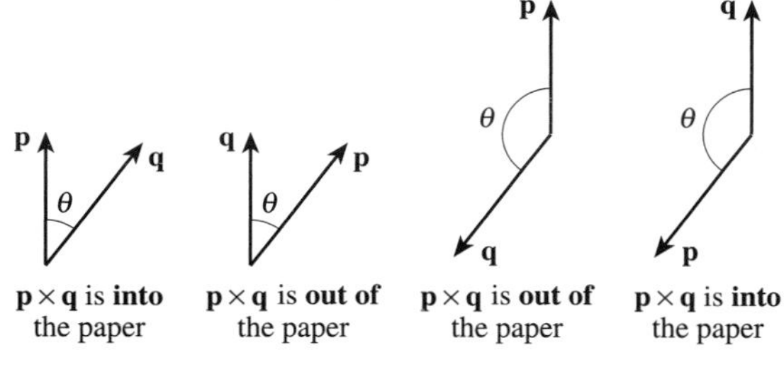

Fig. 3.1

The direction of the resulting vector will be denoted by the unit vector $\hat{\mathbf{n}}$. Thus

$$\mathbf{p}\times\mathbf{q}=|\mathbf{p}||\mathbf{q}|\sin\theta\,\hat{\mathbf{n}}.$$

The method of getting the unit vector $\hat{\mathbf{n}}$ is called the **right-handed rule**.

> The **vector product**, or **cross product**, of two vectors $\mathbf{p}$ and $\mathbf{q}$ is given by
>
> $$\mathbf{p}\times\mathbf{q}=|\mathbf{p}||\mathbf{q}|\sin\theta\,\hat{\mathbf{n}}$$
>
> where $\hat{\mathbf{n}}$ is a unit vector perpendicular to both $\mathbf{p}$ and $\mathbf{q}$ in the right-handed sense.

The definition of the vector product is essentially three-dimensional. The vector product is not defined for vectors which have only two components.

Just as for the dot product, there are a number of rules for manipulating the vector product.

Example 3.1.1
Find the vector products (a) $\mathbf{i}\times\mathbf{j}$, (b) $\mathbf{k}\times\mathbf{k}$, (c) $\mathbf{j}\times\mathbf{i}$.

(a) The magnitude of $\mathbf{i}\times\mathbf{j}$ is $1\times1\times\sin\frac{1}{2}\pi=1$, and its direction is $\mathbf{k}$. A vector of length 1 in the direction of $\mathbf{k}$ is $\mathbf{k}$ itself. Therefore $\mathbf{i}\times\mathbf{j}=\mathbf{k}$.

(b) The magnitude of $\mathbf{k}\times\mathbf{k}$ is $1\times1\times\sin 0=0$, so $\mathbf{k}\times\mathbf{k}=\mathbf{0}$.

(c) The magnitude of $\mathbf{j}\times\mathbf{i}$ is $1\times1\times\sin\frac{1}{2}\pi=1$, and its direction is $-\mathbf{k}$. A vector of length 1 in the direction of $-\mathbf{k}$ is $-\mathbf{k}$ itself. Therefore $\mathbf{j}\times\mathbf{i}=-\mathbf{k}$.

The answers to parts (a) and (c) in the example are a special case of $\mathbf{p}\times\mathbf{q}=-\mathbf{q}\times\mathbf{p}$. If you look again at Fig. 3.1, you will see that using the right-handed rule on $\mathbf{q}$ and $\mathbf{p}$ is the reverse of using it on $\mathbf{p}$ and $\mathbf{q}$. Thus the directions of $\mathbf{q}\times\mathbf{p}$ and $\mathbf{p}\times\mathbf{q}$ are directly opposite each other, but the magnitudes are the same. Therefore $\mathbf{p}\times\mathbf{q}=-\mathbf{q}\times\mathbf{p}$.

If s is a scalar, then $s(\mathbf{p}\times\mathbf{q})=(s\mathbf{p})\times\mathbf{q}$. The proof, like the corresponding proof for dot products, depends on whether s is positive or negative. You are asked to prove this in Exercise 3A Question 5.

Notice that, assuming that $s(\mathbf{p}\times\mathbf{q})=(s\mathbf{p})\times\mathbf{q}$,

$$\mathbf{p}\times(s\mathbf{q})=-((s\mathbf{q})\times\mathbf{p})=-(s(\mathbf{q}\times\mathbf{p}))=-s(\mathbf{q}\times\mathbf{p})=-s(-(\mathbf{p}\times\mathbf{q}))=s(\mathbf{p}\times\mathbf{q}),$$

so $\mathbf{p}\times(s\mathbf{q})=s(\mathbf{p}\times\mathbf{q})$, as you would expect.

Summarising these results:

For vectors $\mathbf{p}$ and $\mathbf{q}$, and a scalar s:

$$\mathbf{p}\times\mathbf{q}=-\mathbf{q}\times\mathbf{p};$$

$$s(\mathbf{p}\times\mathbf{q})=(s\mathbf{p})\times\mathbf{q}=\mathbf{p}\times(s\mathbf{q}).$$

3.2* The distributive rule

The proof of the distributive rule is difficult. You should omit it on a first reading.

The distributive rule, which is essential for manipulating vector products, states that:

For vectors $\mathbf{p}$, $\mathbf{q}$ and $\mathbf{r}$

$$(\mathbf{p}+\mathbf{q})\times\mathbf{r}=\mathbf{p}\times\mathbf{r}+\mathbf{q}\times\mathbf{r}.$$

The proof used is similar to the proof, in P3 Section 12.3, of the distributive rule for dot products. The result will first be proved for the case when $\mathbf{r}$ is a unit vector $\mathbf{u}$, drawn vertically.

In Fig. 3.2, $\mathbf{u}$ is a unit vector in the direction of the vertical line l, and $\mathbf{p} = \overrightarrow{AB}$. The shaded triangles ADM and BEN represent horizontal planes through A and B, cutting the line l at D and E. AN is parallel to l, so AN is perpendicular to NB.

Then the magnitude of $\mathbf{p} \times \mathbf{u}$ is

$$1 \times |\mathbf{p}| \sin\theta = AB \sin\theta = NB.$$

The vector $\mathbf{p} \times \mathbf{u}$, which is perpendicular to both $\mathbf{u}$ and $\mathbf{p}$, is in the horizontal plane and perpendicular to NB.

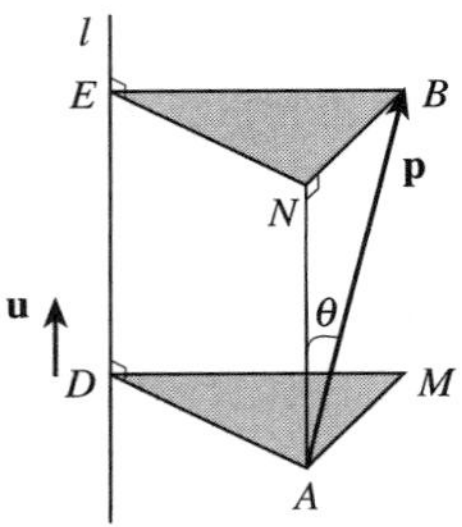

Fig. 3.2

Similarly, in Fig. 3.3, $\mathbf{q} = \overrightarrow{AC}$ and the triangles CFK and CKL lie in the horizontal plane through C which cuts l at F. The vector $\mathbf{q} \times \mathbf{u}$ has magnitude KC and is a horizontal vector perpendicular to KC.

And the vector $\mathbf{p} + \mathbf{q}$ is represented by $\overrightarrow{AC}$, so $(\mathbf{p} + \mathbf{q}) \times \mathbf{u}$ has magnitude LC, and direction perpendicular to LC.

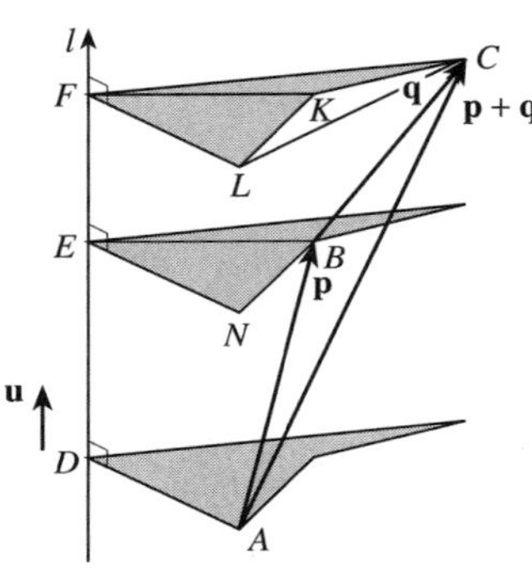

Fig. 3.3

Now notice that, in Fig. 3.3, since the shaded parts of the horizontal planes are congruent, the magnitude and direction of NB are equal to those of LK.

Fig. 3.4 shows a plan view of the triangle LKC, and a copy of triangle LKC rotated through a right angle to get triangle LPQ. Then

$$\mathbf{p} \times \mathbf{u} = \overrightarrow{LP}, \quad \mathbf{q} \times \mathbf{u} = \overrightarrow{PQ}, \quad (\mathbf{p} + \mathbf{q}) \times \mathbf{u} = \overrightarrow{LQ}.$$

Since $\overrightarrow{LP} + \overrightarrow{PQ} = \overrightarrow{LQ}$, it follows that

$$\mathbf{p} \times \mathbf{u} + \mathbf{q} \times \mathbf{u} = (\mathbf{p} + \mathbf{q}) \times \mathbf{u}.$$

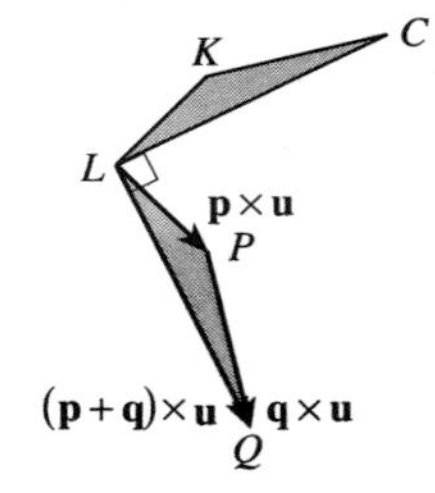

Fig. 3.4

It only remains to show from $\mathbf{p} \times \mathbf{u} + \mathbf{q} \times \mathbf{u} = (\mathbf{p} + \mathbf{q}) \times \mathbf{u}$ that $\mathbf{p} \times \mathbf{r} + \mathbf{q} \times \mathbf{r} = (\mathbf{p} + \mathbf{q}) \times \mathbf{r}$. As $\mathbf{u}$ is a unit vector in the direction of $\mathbf{r}$, $\mathbf{r} = s\mathbf{u}$ where s is a positive constant.

$$\begin{aligned}(\mathbf{p} + \mathbf{q}) \times \mathbf{r} &= (\mathbf{p} + \mathbf{q}) \times (s\mathbf{u}) = s((\mathbf{p} + \mathbf{q}) \times \mathbf{u}) \\ &= s(\mathbf{p} \times \mathbf{u} + \mathbf{q} \times \mathbf{u}) = s(\mathbf{p} \times \mathbf{u}) + s(\mathbf{q} \times \mathbf{u}) \\ &= \mathbf{p} \times (s\mathbf{u}) + \mathbf{q} \times (s\mathbf{u}) = \mathbf{p} \times \mathbf{r} + \mathbf{q} \times \mathbf{r}.\end{aligned}$$

When you have understood the proof for this case, you will then be able to modify the proof for the case when $\mathbf{r}$ is not vertical by re-drawing Fig. 3.3. In the modification of the proof you will need to replace the term 'vertical' by 'in the direction of l', and the term 'horizontal plane' by 'plane perpendicular to l'.

The distributive rule, $(\mathbf{p} + \mathbf{q}) \times \mathbf{r} = \mathbf{p} \times \mathbf{r} + \mathbf{q} \times \mathbf{r}$, enables you to establish results about the vector product in component form.

3.3 Vector products and components

Example 3.1.1 showed the results of some simple calculations involving vector products. Here is a summary of those and similar calculations.

For the basic unit vectors, $\mathbf{i}$, $\mathbf{j}$ and $\mathbf{k}$,

$$\begin{array}{lll} \mathbf{i}\times\mathbf{i}=\mathbf{0} & \mathbf{i}\times\mathbf{j}=\mathbf{k} & \mathbf{i}\times\mathbf{k}=-\mathbf{j} \\ \mathbf{j}\times\mathbf{i}=-\mathbf{k} & \mathbf{j}\times\mathbf{j}=\mathbf{0} & \mathbf{j}\times\mathbf{k}=\mathbf{i} \\ \mathbf{k}\times\mathbf{i}=\mathbf{j} & \mathbf{k}\times\mathbf{j}=-\mathbf{i} & \mathbf{k}\times\mathbf{k}=\mathbf{0} \end{array}$$

It follows that, if vectors $\mathbf{p}$ and $\mathbf{q}$ are written in component form as $\mathbf{p}=p_1\mathbf{i}+p_2\mathbf{j}+p_3\mathbf{k}$ and $\mathbf{q}=q_1\mathbf{i}+q_2\mathbf{j}+q_3\mathbf{k}$, then

$$\begin{aligned} \mathbf{p}\times\mathbf{q} &= (p_1\mathbf{i}+p_2\mathbf{j}+p_3\mathbf{k})\times(q_1\mathbf{i}+q_2\mathbf{j}+q_3\mathbf{k}) \\ &= p_1q_1\mathbf{i}\times\mathbf{i}+p_2q_1\mathbf{j}\times\mathbf{i}+p_3q_1\mathbf{k}\times\mathbf{i}+p_1q_2\mathbf{i}\times\mathbf{j}+p_2q_2\mathbf{j}\times\mathbf{j} \\ &\qquad +p_3q_2\mathbf{k}\times\mathbf{j}+p_1q_3\mathbf{i}\times\mathbf{k}+p_2q_3\mathbf{j}\times\mathbf{k}+p_3q_3\mathbf{k}\times\mathbf{k} \\ &= p_1q_1\mathbf{0}+p_2q_1(-\mathbf{k})+p_3q_1\mathbf{j}+p_1q_2\mathbf{k}+p_2q_2\mathbf{0} \\ &\qquad +p_3q_2(-\mathbf{i})+p_1q_3(-\mathbf{j})+p_2q_3\mathbf{i}+p_3q_3\mathbf{0} \\ &= (p_2q_3-p_3q_2)\mathbf{i}+(p_3q_1-p_1q_3)\mathbf{j}+(p_1q_2-p_2q_1)\mathbf{k}. \end{aligned}$$

In component form:

The vector product of $\mathbf{p}=p_1\mathbf{i}+p_2\mathbf{j}+p_3\mathbf{k}$ and $\mathbf{q}=q_1\mathbf{i}+q_2\mathbf{j}+q_3\mathbf{k}$ is

$$\begin{pmatrix} p_1 \\ p_2 \\ p_3 \end{pmatrix}\times\begin{pmatrix} q_1 \\ q_2 \\ q_3 \end{pmatrix}=\begin{pmatrix} p_2q_3-p_3q_2 \\ p_3q_1-p_1q_3 \\ p_1q_2-p_2q_1 \end{pmatrix}.$$

This result is useful for finding a vector perpendicular to two other vectors, and hence for finding a normal to a plane when you know two vectors which lie in the plane.

Example 3.3.1
Find the vector product $\begin{pmatrix} 1 \\ -3 \\ -5 \end{pmatrix}\times\begin{pmatrix} 0 \\ -1 \\ -2 \end{pmatrix}$.

From the formula $\begin{pmatrix} 1 \\ -3 \\ -5 \end{pmatrix}\times\begin{pmatrix} 0 \\ -1 \\ -2 \end{pmatrix}=\begin{pmatrix} (-3)\times(-2)-(-5)\times(-1) \\ (-5)\times0-1\times(-2) \\ 1\times(-1)-(-3)\times0 \end{pmatrix}=\begin{pmatrix} 1 \\ 2 \\ -1 \end{pmatrix}$.

It is very easy to check whether you have the vector product correct, because you can mentally find the dot product of your answer with each of the original vectors. If both the dot products are zero, your vector product has a good chance of being correct.

The remainder of the chapter shows you the kinds of methods you can use to solve problems about lines and planes. Although the techniques you need to solve these problems are relatively few, they can be applied in many different ways. Use whichever method you like best.

Example 3.3.2
Find the area of the triangle ABC with coordinates $A(1,2,3)$, $B(4,6,2)$ and $C(6,8,10)$.

Since the area of the triangle ABC is given by $\frac{1}{2}AB \times AC \times \sin\theta$, where $\theta =$ angle BAC, the vector product is useful for finding it, as the area is half the magnitude of $\overrightarrow{AB} \times \overrightarrow{AC}$.

$$\overrightarrow{AB} = \begin{pmatrix}4\\6\\2\end{pmatrix} - \begin{pmatrix}1\\2\\3\end{pmatrix} = \begin{pmatrix}3\\4\\-1\end{pmatrix} \quad \text{and} \quad \overrightarrow{AC} = \begin{pmatrix}6\\8\\10\end{pmatrix} - \begin{pmatrix}1\\2\\3\end{pmatrix} = \begin{pmatrix}5\\6\\7\end{pmatrix}, \text{ so}$$

$$\overrightarrow{AB} \times \overrightarrow{AC} = \begin{pmatrix}3\\4\\-1\end{pmatrix} \times \begin{pmatrix}5\\6\\7\end{pmatrix} = \begin{pmatrix}28-(-6)\\-5-21\\18-20\end{pmatrix} = \begin{pmatrix}34\\-26\\-2\end{pmatrix}.$$

The area of the triangle is therefore

$$\tfrac{1}{2}\sqrt{34^2+(-26)^2+(-2)^2} = \tfrac{1}{2}\times 2\sqrt{17^2+13^2+1^2} = \sqrt{459} = 3\sqrt{51}.$$

The area of the triangle is $3\sqrt{51}$.

Exercise 3A

1 Use the definition of vector product to calculate the following.

(a) $\mathbf{i}\times\mathbf{k}$ (b) $\mathbf{j}\times\mathbf{j}$ (c) $\mathbf{i}\times\mathbf{j}$

(d) $\mathbf{i}\times\mathbf{i}$ (e) $\mathbf{k}\times\mathbf{j}$ (f) $\mathbf{j}\times\mathbf{k}$

(g) $\mathbf{i}\times(\mathbf{k}\times\mathbf{j})$ (h) $\mathbf{i}\cdot(\mathbf{k}\times\mathbf{j})$ (i) $\mathbf{i}\times(\mathbf{j}\times\mathbf{i})$

2 Use the component formula to calculate the following vector products. Check your answers by ensuring that the dot product of your answer with each of the given vectors is zero.

(a) $\begin{pmatrix}1\\2\\3\end{pmatrix}\times\begin{pmatrix}-2\\3\\-2\end{pmatrix}$ (b) $\begin{pmatrix}-2\\3\\-1\end{pmatrix}\times\begin{pmatrix}1\\-5\\0\end{pmatrix}$ (c) $\begin{pmatrix}4\\-5\\7\end{pmatrix}\times\begin{pmatrix}2\\-3\\6\end{pmatrix}$

(d) $\begin{pmatrix}5\\-1\\2\end{pmatrix}\times\begin{pmatrix}4\\0\\0\end{pmatrix}$ (e) $\begin{pmatrix}1\\0\\0\end{pmatrix}\times\begin{pmatrix}0\\1\\0\end{pmatrix}$ (f) $\begin{pmatrix}1\\0\\2\end{pmatrix}\times\begin{pmatrix}0\\1\\2\end{pmatrix}$

3 Use the component formula to calculate the following vector products.

(a) $(2\mathbf{i}-\mathbf{j}-\mathbf{k})\times(\mathbf{j}+\mathbf{k})$ (b) $(\mathbf{i}-\mathbf{j})\times(\mathbf{j}-\mathbf{k})$

(c) $(\mathbf{i}+3\mathbf{j}-2\mathbf{k})\times(2\mathbf{i}-3\mathbf{j}+6\mathbf{k})$ (d) $(\mathbf{i}+2\mathbf{j}-2\mathbf{k})\times(-2\mathbf{i}-\mathbf{j}+2\mathbf{k})$

(e) $(3\mathbf{i}+5\mathbf{j}-4\mathbf{k})\times\mathbf{i}$ (f) $(6\mathbf{i}+2\mathbf{j}-3\mathbf{k})\times(2\mathbf{i}-3\mathbf{j}+6\mathbf{k})$

4 Calculate the area of the triangle bounded by the points $(-3,1,3)$, $(2,2,2)$ and $(5,4,3)$.

5 Prove that $s(\mathbf{p}\times\mathbf{q}) = (s\mathbf{p})\times\mathbf{q}$ for any vectors $\mathbf{p}$ and $\mathbf{q}$ and for any scalar s, which could be positive or negative.

3.4 Equations of planes and lines

In this section, the vector product is applied to finding the equations of planes, and to determining the lines of intersection of pairs of planes.

Example 3.4.1 shows a better way of working Example 2.5.5.

Example 3.4.1

Find the cartesian equation of the plane through $A(1,2,1)$, $B(2,-1,-4)$ and $C(1,0,-1)$.

The vectors $\overrightarrow{AB} = \begin{pmatrix} 2 \\ -1 \\ -4 \end{pmatrix} - \begin{pmatrix} 1 \\ 2 \\ 1 \end{pmatrix} = \begin{pmatrix} 1 \\ -3 \\ -5 \end{pmatrix}$ and $\overrightarrow{AC} = \begin{pmatrix} 1 \\ 0 \\ -1 \end{pmatrix} - \begin{pmatrix} 1 \\ 2 \\ 1 \end{pmatrix} = \begin{pmatrix} 0 \\ -2 \\ -2 \end{pmatrix}$ are parallel to the plane, so the normal to the plane is in the direction

$$\begin{pmatrix} 1 \\ -3 \\ -5 \end{pmatrix} \times \begin{pmatrix} 0 \\ -2 \\ -2 \end{pmatrix} = \begin{pmatrix} 6-10 \\ 0-(-2) \\ -2-0 \end{pmatrix} = \begin{pmatrix} -4 \\ 2 \\ -2 \end{pmatrix}.$$

Therefore the equation of the plane is $-4x+2y-2z=k$, and since $(1,2,1)$ lies on the plane, the equation is $-4x+2y-2z=-4\times1+2\times2-2\times1=-2$ or $-4x+2y-2z=-2$, or $2x-y+z=1$.

Example 3.4.2

Find a vector equation of the line of intersection of the planes $x-y+2z=5$ and $3x+2y+z=5$.

To find the line of intersection of the planes you need to find the position vector of a point on the line of intersection, and the direction of the line.

To find a point on the line, put $z=0$ and then solve $x-y=5$ and $3x+2y=5$, to get $y=-2$ and $x=3$. The point $(3,-2,0)$ therefore lies on the line.

To find the direction of the line, note that as it lies in both planes it must be perpendicular to the normals of both planes. Thus its direction is

$$\begin{pmatrix} 1 \\ -1 \\ 2 \end{pmatrix} \times \begin{pmatrix} 3 \\ 2 \\ 1 \end{pmatrix} = \begin{pmatrix} -1-4 \\ 6-1 \\ 2-(-3) \end{pmatrix} = \begin{pmatrix} -5 \\ 5 \\ 5 \end{pmatrix}.$$

Therefore, dividing by the factor 5 for simplicity, the direction of the line is $\begin{pmatrix} -1 \\ 1 \\ 1 \end{pmatrix}$, so the vector equation of the line is $\mathbf{r} = \begin{pmatrix} 3 \\ -2 \\ 0 \end{pmatrix} + t\begin{pmatrix} -1 \\ 1 \\ 1 \end{pmatrix}$.

It does not matter which point on the line you take. If you had put $y=0$, and then found $z=2$ and $x=1$, you would have obtained a different vector equation for the same line. In fact, sometimes there may not be a point for which $z=0$ on the line; in that case put $y=0$, and if this doesn't work put $x=0$. One of them must work!

Example 3.4.3
Find the cartesian equation of the plane containing the point $(2,1,4)$ and the straight line with cartesian equations $\frac{x-1}{3}=\frac{y+2}{5}=z-1$.

You may find it helpful to draw a picture as you work through the solution below.

Writing the straight line in the form $\frac{x-1}{3}=\frac{y+2}{5}=z-1=t$, you find that $\begin{pmatrix}x\\y\\z\end{pmatrix}=\begin{pmatrix}1\\-2\\1\end{pmatrix}+t\begin{pmatrix}3\\5\\1\end{pmatrix}$, so $(1,-2,1)$ lies on the line and the line's direction is $\begin{pmatrix}3\\5\\1\end{pmatrix}$.

To find the normal to the plane, you need two vectors in the plane before you can use the vector product. Two such vectors are the direction vector of the line, $\begin{pmatrix}3\\5\\1\end{pmatrix}$, and the vector from $(2,1,4)$ to $(1,-2,1)$, that is $\begin{pmatrix}1\\-2\\1\end{pmatrix}-\begin{pmatrix}2\\1\\4\end{pmatrix}=\begin{pmatrix}-1\\-3\\-3\end{pmatrix}$.

The normal to the plane is $\begin{pmatrix}3\\5\\1\end{pmatrix}\times\begin{pmatrix}-1\\-3\\-3\end{pmatrix}=\begin{pmatrix}-15-(-3)\\-1-(-9)\\-9-(-5)\end{pmatrix}=\begin{pmatrix}-12\\8\\-4\end{pmatrix}$. Thus, dividing by -4, the vector $\begin{pmatrix}3\\-2\\1\end{pmatrix}$ is normal to the plane. The equation of the plane is $3x-2y+z=k$, and since $(1,-2,1)$ lies in the plane, $3x-2y+z=3+4+1=8$. The equation of the required plane is therefore $3x-2y+z=8$.

Exercise 3B

1 For each part, find the cartesian equation of the plane through the given points.

(a) $(1,0,3), (2,-4,3), (4,-1,2)$

(b) $(2,-1,-1), (-5,3,2), (4,-1,-3)$

(c) $(-3,1,3), (2,2,2), (5,4,3)$

(d) $(1,2,3), (5,6,8), (0,1,2)$

2 Find whether or not the four points $(1,5,4), (2,0,3), (3,-5,0)$ and $(0,10,6)$ lie in a plane.

3 Find cartesian equations of the line of intersection of the planes $x+3y-6z=2$ and $2x+7y-3z=7$.

4 Find the vector equation of the line through $(4,2,-3)$ and parallel to the line of intersection of the planes $3x-2y=6$ and $4x+2z=7$.

5 Find the equation of the plane through $(3,-2,4)$ and $(2,-1,3)$ which is parallel to the line joining $(1,1,1)$ to $(2,3,5)$.

6 Show that the lines $\mathbf{r}=3\mathbf{i}+2\mathbf{j}+\mathbf{k}+t(-\mathbf{i}+2\mathbf{j}+\mathbf{k})$ and $\mathbf{r}=3\mathbf{i}+9\mathbf{j}+2\mathbf{k}+t(2\mathbf{i}+3\mathbf{j}+\mathbf{k})$ are **coplanar**, and find the equation of the plane which contains them. (Lines that are coplanar lie in the same plane.)

7 Find the equation of the plane which passes through the point $(1,2,3)$ and contains the line of intersection of the planes $2x-y+z=4$ and $x+y+z=4$.

3.5 Other techniques

Example 3.51
Find the perpendicular distance from the point $P(2,1,4)$ to the straight line with cartesian equations $\frac{x-1}{3}=\frac{y+2}{5}=z-1$.

Fig. 3.5 shows the situation. The line can be written in vector form $\begin{pmatrix}x\\y\\z\end{pmatrix}=\begin{pmatrix}1\\-2\\1\end{pmatrix}+t\begin{pmatrix}3\\5\\1\end{pmatrix}$, so its direction is $\begin{pmatrix}3\\5\\1\end{pmatrix}$ and $(1,-2,1)$ is a point on the line. Call this point A, and let N be the point where the perpendicular from P meets the line.

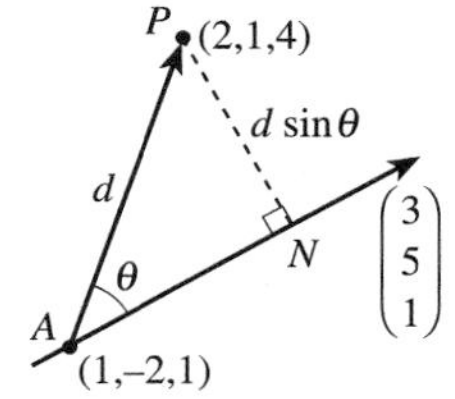

Fig. 3.5

If AP has length d, and the angle between AP and the given line is θ, the perpendicular distance AN is $d\sin\theta$.

The factor $\sin\theta$ suggests a vector product. In fact, $d\sin\theta$ is the magnitude of the vector product $\overrightarrow{AP}\times\mathbf{n}$, where $\mathbf{n}$ is a unit vector in the direction of the line.

$$\overrightarrow{AP}=\begin{pmatrix}2\\1\\4\end{pmatrix}-\begin{pmatrix}1\\-2\\1\end{pmatrix}=\begin{pmatrix}1\\3\\3\end{pmatrix} \quad\text{and}\quad \mathbf{n}=\frac{1}{\sqrt{3^2+5^2+1^2}}\begin{pmatrix}3\\5\\1\end{pmatrix}=\frac{1}{\sqrt{35}}\begin{pmatrix}3\\5\\1\end{pmatrix},$$

so $$\overrightarrow{AP}\times\mathbf{n}=\begin{pmatrix}1\\3\\3\end{pmatrix}\times\frac{1}{\sqrt{35}}\begin{pmatrix}3\\5\\1\end{pmatrix}=\frac{1}{\sqrt{35}}\begin{pmatrix}-12\\8\\-4\end{pmatrix}=\frac{4}{\sqrt{35}}\begin{pmatrix}-3\\2\\-1\end{pmatrix},$$

and $$\left|\frac{4}{\sqrt{35}}\begin{pmatrix}-3\\2\\-1\end{pmatrix}\right|=\frac{4}{\sqrt{35}}\times\sqrt{9+4+1}=\frac{4\sqrt{14}}{\sqrt{35}}=\frac{4\sqrt{2}}{\sqrt{5}}.$$

The perpendicular distance from P to the line is $\frac{4\sqrt{2}}{\sqrt{5}}$.

Example 3.5.2
Find the shortest distance between the two lines $\mathbf{r}=\mathbf{i}+2\mathbf{j}+3\mathbf{k}+t(-2\mathbf{i}+\mathbf{j}-5\mathbf{k})$ and $\mathbf{r}=3\mathbf{i}-4\mathbf{j}-\mathbf{k}+t(\mathbf{i}+\mathbf{j}+\mathbf{k})$.

The shortest distance between the lines is along the line PQ where PQ is perpendicular to both lines. See Fig. 3.6.
Therefore PQ is in the direction of the cross product of the direction vectors $\begin{pmatrix}-2\\1\\-5\end{pmatrix}$ and $\begin{pmatrix}1\\1\\1\end{pmatrix}$.

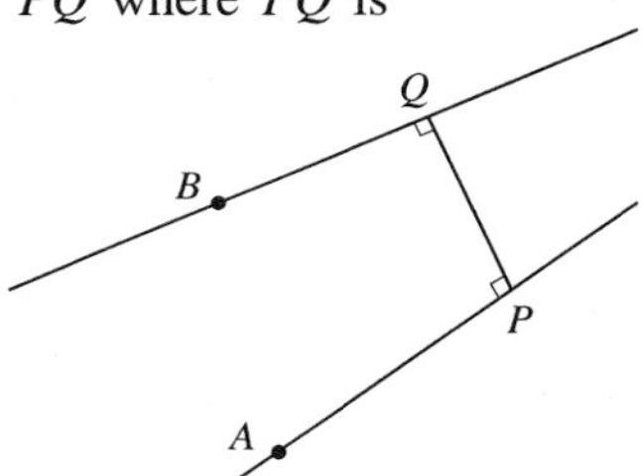

Fig. 3.6

This cross product is

$$\begin{pmatrix}-2\\1\\-5\end{pmatrix}\times\begin{pmatrix}1\\1\\1\end{pmatrix}=\begin{pmatrix}1-(-5)\\(-5)-(-2)\\-2-1\end{pmatrix}=\begin{pmatrix}6\\-3\\-3\end{pmatrix},$$

so $\overrightarrow{PQ}$ is in the direction $\begin{pmatrix} 2 \\ -1 \\ -1 \end{pmatrix}$. A unit vector $\mathbf{u}$ in the direction $\overrightarrow{PQ}$ is

$$\mathbf{u} = \frac{1}{\sqrt{2^2 + (-1)^2 + (-1)^2}} \begin{pmatrix} 2 \\ -1 \\ -1 \end{pmatrix} = \frac{1}{\sqrt{6}} \begin{pmatrix} 2 \\ -1 \\ -1 \end{pmatrix}.$$

Now let A and B be any points on the two lines. The most obvious choice is to take A as $(1,2,3)$ and B as $(3,-4,-1)$, from the vector equations of the lines, but any other points would do equally well.

Then the vector $\overrightarrow{AB} = \begin{pmatrix} 3 \\ -4 \\ -1 \end{pmatrix} - \begin{pmatrix} 1 \\ 2 \\ 3 \end{pmatrix} = \begin{pmatrix} 2 \\ -6 \\ -4 \end{pmatrix}$. The shortest distance will be the magnitude of the projection of $\overrightarrow{AB}$ on the direction PQ, which was shown in P3 Section 12.4 to be $\overrightarrow{AB} \cdot \mathbf{u}$, where $\mathbf{u}$ is the unit vector in the direction $\overrightarrow{PQ}$.

Hence the shortest distance is $\left| \begin{pmatrix} 2 \\ -6 \\ -4 \end{pmatrix} \cdot \frac{1}{\sqrt{6}} \begin{pmatrix} 2 \\ -1 \\ -1 \end{pmatrix} \right| = \frac{1}{\sqrt{6}} |(4+6+4)| = \frac{14}{\sqrt{6}}$.

You may find it interesting to take any other points L and M on the two lines and show that $\overrightarrow{LM}$ leads to the same result.

Exercise 3C

1 Find a vector equation for the perpendicular from the origin to the line of intersection of the planes $3x - 2y - z = 7$ and $x + 2y + 3z = 7$.

2 Find the vector equation of the common perpendicular to the lines with cartesian equations $x = y = z$ and $\frac{x-4}{3} = \frac{y-4}{2} = z - 2$.

3 Find the distance of the point $(1,1,4)$ from the line $\mathbf{r} = \mathbf{i} - 2\mathbf{j} + \mathbf{k} + t(-2\mathbf{i} + \mathbf{j} + 2\mathbf{k})$.

Miscellaneous exercise 3

1 Find the following cross products.

(a) $\begin{pmatrix} 8 \\ -3 \\ 1 \end{pmatrix} \times \begin{pmatrix} 7 \\ -2 \\ 0 \end{pmatrix}$ (b) $\begin{pmatrix} 4 \\ -1 \\ -3 \end{pmatrix} \times \begin{pmatrix} 3 \\ 5 \\ 1 \end{pmatrix}$ (c) $\begin{pmatrix} 2 \\ 0 \\ 1 \end{pmatrix} \times \begin{pmatrix} 1 \\ 0 \\ 2 \end{pmatrix}$

2 Find the following cross products.

(a) $(3\mathbf{i} - 2\mathbf{k}) \times 2\mathbf{k}$ (b) $5\mathbf{k} \times (\mathbf{i} + 2\mathbf{j} - 3\mathbf{k})$ (c) $(2\mathbf{i} + \mathbf{j}) \times (2\mathbf{i} + \mathbf{j})$

3 Find the equation of the plane through $(1,2,-4)$ perpendicular to the line joining $(3,1,-1)$ to $(1,4,7)$.

4 Prove that the planes $2x-3y+z=4$, $x+4y-z=7$ and $3x-10y+3z=1$ meet in a line.

5 Find the equation of the plane which passes through the point $(3,-4,1)$ and which is parallel to the plane containing the point $(1,2,-1)$ and the line $x=y=z$.

6 Find the length of the common perpendicular between the lines $x=y-1=2z-1$ and $2x=-y=3z$.

7 The position vectors $\mathbf{a}$, $\mathbf{b}$ and $\mathbf{c}$ of A, B and C relative to an origin O are $\begin{pmatrix}4\\3\\-3\end{pmatrix}$, $\begin{pmatrix}2\\0\\2\end{pmatrix}$ and $\begin{pmatrix}5\\1\\-1\end{pmatrix}$ respectively.

(a) Write down the vectors $\mathbf{c}-\mathbf{a}$ and $\mathbf{b}-\mathbf{a}$.

(b) Use a vector method to calculate the area of the triangle ABC. (OCR)

8 Let l_1 denote the line passing through the points $A(2,-1,1)$ and $B(0,5,-7)$, and l_2 denote the line passing through the points $C(1,-1,1)$ and $D(1,-4,5)$.

(a) Write down a vector equation of the line l_1 and a vector equation of the line l_2.

(b) Show that the lines l_1 and l_2 intersect, and determine the point of intersection.

(c) Calculate the acute angle between the lines l_1 and l_2.

(d) Determine a vector perpendicular to both lines l_1 and l_2 and hence show that the cartesian equation of the plane containing l_1 and l_2 is $4y+3z=-1$.

9 The position vectors $\mathbf{a}$, $\mathbf{b}$ and $\mathbf{c}$ of three points A, B and C are $\begin{pmatrix}2\\-1\\4\end{pmatrix}$, $\begin{pmatrix}1\\1\\3\end{pmatrix}$ and $\begin{pmatrix}3\\-2\\1\end{pmatrix}$ respectively.

(a) Determine $(\mathbf{a}-\mathbf{b})\times(\mathbf{c}-\mathbf{b})$.

(b) Hence, or otherwise,

(i) find a vector equation for the plane through A, B and C giving your answer in the form $\mathbf{r}\cdot\mathbf{n}=d$;

(ii) find, in surd form, an expression for the area of the triangle ABC. (OCR)

10 Two lines have vector equations $\mathbf{r}=\begin{pmatrix}12\\0\\2\end{pmatrix}+\lambda\begin{pmatrix}14\\4\\-5\end{pmatrix}$ and $\mathbf{r}=\begin{pmatrix}-1\\1\\6\end{pmatrix}+\mu\begin{pmatrix}-1\\1\\1\end{pmatrix}$.

(a) Determine a unit vector, $\mathbf{u}$, which is perpendicular to both lines.

(b) Find the shortest distance between the two lines. (OCR)

11 The line l_1 passes through the point A, whose position vector is $\mathbf{i}-\mathbf{j}-5\mathbf{k}$, and is parallel to the vector $\mathbf{i}-\mathbf{j}-4\mathbf{k}$. The line l_2 passes through the point B, whose position vector is $2\mathbf{i}-9\mathbf{j}-14\mathbf{k}$, and is parallel to the vector $2\mathbf{i}+5\mathbf{j}+6\mathbf{k}$. The point P on l_1 and the point Q on l_2 are such that PQ is perpendicular to both l_1 and l_2.

(a) Find the length of PQ.

(b) Find a vector perpendicular to the plane Π which contains PQ and l_2.

(c) Find the perpendicular distance from A to Π. (OCR)

12 The points A and B have position vectors $\mathbf{a} = \begin{pmatrix} -1 \\ 4 \\ 7 \end{pmatrix}$ and $\mathbf{b} = \begin{pmatrix} 8 \\ -7 \\ 4 \end{pmatrix}$ respectively. The line l_1 has vector equation $\mathbf{r} = \begin{pmatrix} -1 \\ 4 \\ 7 \end{pmatrix} + \lambda \begin{pmatrix} -1 \\ 4 \\ 3 \end{pmatrix}$ where λ is a scalar parameter, while the line l_2 passes through B and is parallel to the vector $\begin{pmatrix} 1 \\ 4 \\ -1 \end{pmatrix}$.

(a) Write down the vector $\mathbf{b} - \mathbf{a}$.

(b) Write down a vector equation for the line l_2.

(c) Determine the unit vector $\hat{\mathbf{n}}$, where $\hat{\mathbf{n}}$ is perpendicular to both the lines l_1 and l_2.

(d) Find the shortest distance between l_1 and l_2. (OCR)

13 The coordinates of four points are $A(2,-9,-5)$, $B(5,-4,-4)$, $C(8,15,4)$ and $D(7,18,6)$.

(a) Calculate the vector product $\overrightarrow{AB} \times \overrightarrow{CD}$.

(b) Show that the lines AB and CD intersect, and find the coordinates of the point of intersection.

(c) Find, in the form $ax + by + cz + d = 0$, the equation of the plane Π which contains the four points A, B, C and D.

(d) Find the equation of the plane which contains the line AB and is perpendicular to the plane Π. (MEI)

14† Find a formula in terms of the vectors $\mathbf{a}$, $\mathbf{b}$, $\mathbf{c}$ and $\mathbf{d}$ for the shortest distance between the lines $\mathbf{r} = \mathbf{a} + t\mathbf{b}$ and $\mathbf{r} = \mathbf{c} + t\mathbf{d}$.

4 Matrices

This chapter explains why and how matrices are defined, and how to add, subtract and multiply them. When you have completed it, you should

- be able to carry out operations of matrix addition, subtraction and multiplication
- know the terms zero (or null) matrix, and identity (or unit) matrix
- know the meaning of the terms 'singular' and 'non-singular'
- know that under certain circumstances matrices have inverses.

4.1 What is a matrix?

Suppose that you wanted to program a computer to solve a pair of simultaneous linear equations such as

$$\left.\begin{aligned} x+2y&=3 \\ 2x+3y&=4 \end{aligned}\right\}.$$

What are the essential ingredients of this pair of equations? What information do you need to give to the computer?

Notice that the equations $\left.\begin{aligned} x+2y&=3 \\ 2x+3y&=4 \end{aligned}\right\}$ are essentially the same as $\left.\begin{aligned} p+2q&=3 \\ 2p+3q&=4 \end{aligned}\right\}.$

You would not change the way that you solve the equations just because the unknowns are labelled p and q instead of x and y. This suggests that all the necessary information is held by the array of coefficients and symbols

$$\begin{matrix} 1 & 2 & = & 3 \\ 2 & 3 & = & 4 \end{matrix}$$

You don't even need the equals signs, provided that you remember what the array means and what the symbols in it stand for. Thus all the information is held by the array

$$\begin{matrix} 1 & 2 & 3 \\ 2 & 3 & 4 \end{matrix}$$

It turns out to be useful to think of a rectangular array of numbers like this as a single object, called a **matrix**. It is usual to write a matrix in brackets, and to denote it by a single letter written in bold-faced type. Thus $\mathbf{A}=\begin{pmatrix} 1 & 2 & 3 \\ 2 & 3 & 4 \end{pmatrix}$.

A matrix has **rows** and **columns**. In this example, $\mathbf{A}$ has 2 rows and 3 columns and is called a '2 by 3' matrix. The matrix $\mathbf{A}$ is said to have **size** 2×3. If the number of rows is equal to the number of columns, the matrix is **square**. The individual numbers in the matrix are called **elements**. Notice that a matrix with just one column, such as $\begin{pmatrix} 2 \\ 4 \end{pmatrix}$, looks just like a vector in component form. Such a matrix is sometimes called a **column vector.** An extension of this idea is that a matrix with just one row, such as $(1 \quad 2 \quad 3)$, is called a **row vector**.

A matrix $\mathbf{A}$ is a rectangular array of numbers, called **elements**.

A matrix $\mathbf{A}$ with m rows and n columns is called an $m \times n$ matrix. If $m = n$, $\mathbf{A}$ is said to be a **square** matrix.

A matrix with n rows and 1 column is called a **column matrix**, or a **column vector**.

A matrix with 1 row and n columns is called a **row matrix**, or a **row vector**.

Matrices can arise from many sources other than simultaneous equations. For example, suppose that Amy and Bob go to a baker's shop to buy cakes, doughnuts and eclairs. The numbers of each that they buy is given by the array of numbers in Table 4.1.

	Cakes	Doughnuts	Eclairs
Amy	2	1	1
Bob	4	0	2

Table 4.1

The array of numbers in Table 4.1 is another example of a matrix. If you wanted to work out the cost, you would strip it of its headings and simply use the numbers in a 'purchase matrix'

$$\mathbf{P} = \begin{pmatrix} 2 & 1 & 1 \\ 4 & 0 & 2 \end{pmatrix}.$$

Suppose that on the next day they make purchases represented by the matrix

$$\mathbf{Q} = \begin{pmatrix} 3 & 0 & 1 \\ 1 & 3 & 1 \end{pmatrix}.$$

Then on the two days together they will have bought $\begin{pmatrix} 5 & 1 & 2 \\ 5 & 3 & 3 \end{pmatrix}$, and it is natural to denote this by $\mathbf{P}+\mathbf{Q}$. Thus

$$\mathbf{P}+\mathbf{Q} = \begin{pmatrix} 2 & 1 & 1 \\ 4 & 0 & 2 \end{pmatrix} + \begin{pmatrix} 3 & 0 & 1 \\ 1 & 3 & 1 \end{pmatrix} = \begin{pmatrix} 5 & 1 & 2 \\ 5 & 3 & 3 \end{pmatrix}.$$

If they make the same purchase $\mathbf{P}$ on five days the total bought will be

$$5\mathbf{P} = \begin{pmatrix} 10 & 5 & 5 \\ 20 & 0 & 10 \end{pmatrix}.$$

These examples suggest the general definitions of sums and multiples of matrices given in the next section.

4.2 Addition and multiplication by a scalar

Two $m \times n$ matrices $\mathbf{A}$ and $\mathbf{B}$ are defined to be **equal** if all the elements in corresponding positions are equal. Two matrices of different sizes cannot be equal.

Thus if you are given that $\begin{pmatrix} a & b \\ c & d \end{pmatrix} = \begin{pmatrix} 0 & 1 \\ 2 & -1 \end{pmatrix}$ you can deduce that $a = 0$, $b = 1$, $c = 2$ and $d = -1$. But $\begin{pmatrix} 1 & 2 \\ 3 & 4 \end{pmatrix} \neq \begin{pmatrix} 1 & 3 \\ 2 & 4 \end{pmatrix}$ and $\begin{pmatrix} 1 & 2 \\ 3 & 4 \end{pmatrix} \neq \begin{pmatrix} 1 & 2 & 0 \\ 3 & 4 & 0 \end{pmatrix}$.

Addition of two $m \times n$ matrices $\mathbf{A}$ and $\mathbf{B}$ is performed by adding the corresponding elements. Thus, if $\mathbf{A} = \begin{pmatrix} 1 & 2 \\ 3 & 4 \end{pmatrix}$ and $\mathbf{B} = \begin{pmatrix} 1 & 3 \\ 2 & 4 \end{pmatrix}$, then their sum

$$\mathbf{A} + \mathbf{B} = \begin{pmatrix} 1 & 2 \\ 3 & 4 \end{pmatrix} + \begin{pmatrix} 1 & 3 \\ 2 & 4 \end{pmatrix} = \begin{pmatrix} 1+1 & 2+3 \\ 3+2 & 4+4 \end{pmatrix} = \begin{pmatrix} 2 & 5 \\ 5 & 8 \end{pmatrix}.$$

You cannot add matrices if they have different sizes.

You can easily check by using numerical examples that:

For any matrices $\mathbf{A}$, $\mathbf{B}$ and $\mathbf{C}$ of equal sizes,

$$\mathbf{A} + \mathbf{B} = \mathbf{B} + \mathbf{A} \quad \text{and} \quad (\mathbf{A} + \mathbf{B}) + \mathbf{C} = \mathbf{A} + (\mathbf{B} + \mathbf{C}).$$

To prove that $\mathbf{A} + \mathbf{B} = \mathbf{B} + \mathbf{A}$ and similar properties is straightforward, and left to you.

Notice that the $m \times n$ matrix $\mathbf{O}$ which has all its elements 0 behaves like the number 0 in that, for any $m \times n$ matrix $\mathbf{A}$,

$$\mathbf{A} + \mathbf{O} = \mathbf{O} + \mathbf{A} = \mathbf{A}.$$

The matrix $\mathbf{O}$ is called the $m \times n$ zero matrix or null matrix, or, if it is clear what size is meant, just the **zero matrix** or **null matrix**. Notice that the 2×2 matrix $\mathbf{O}$, that is $\begin{pmatrix} 0 & 0 \\ 0 & 0 \end{pmatrix}$, is different from the 2×3 matrix $\mathbf{O}$, that is $\begin{pmatrix} 0 & 0 & 0 \\ 0 & 0 & 0 \end{pmatrix}$. In practice, there is no confusion about the fact that they are both called $\mathbf{O}$.

In some books the matrix $\mathbf{O}$ is denoted by $\mathbf{Z}$ (for zero) or by $\mathbf{0}$.

If s is any number and $\mathbf{A}$ any $m \times n$ matrix, the product $s\mathbf{A}$ is the $m \times n$ matrix formed by multiplying every element of $\mathbf{A}$ by s. The process is called **multiplying by a scalar**.

It is easy to check the following rules, which you can prove for yourself.

$1\mathbf{A} = \mathbf{A}$,	$s(t\mathbf{A}) = (st)\mathbf{A}$,	$0\mathbf{A} = \mathbf{O}$,
$(s+t)\mathbf{A} = s\mathbf{A} + t\mathbf{A}$,	$s(\mathbf{A} + \mathbf{B}) = s\mathbf{A} + s\mathbf{B}$,	$s\mathbf{O} = \mathbf{O}$.

Subtraction of two matrices $\mathbf{A}$ and $\mathbf{B}$ is defined by

$$\mathbf{X} = \mathbf{A} - \mathbf{B} \quad \Leftrightarrow \quad \mathbf{B} + \mathbf{X} = \mathbf{A}.$$

You can easily show that $\mathbf{A} - \mathbf{B} = \mathbf{A} + (-1)\mathbf{B}$.

These definitions of equality, addition, multiplication by a scalar, and subtraction enable you to carry out matrix arithmetic in the way that you would expect.

Example 4.2.1
Let $\mathbf{A}=\begin{pmatrix}-1 & -2\\ 3 & 1\end{pmatrix}$ and $\mathbf{B}=\begin{pmatrix}2 & 6\\ -3 & 4\end{pmatrix}$. Calculate (a) $\mathbf{A}+\mathbf{B}$, (b) $2\mathbf{A}+3\mathbf{B}$, (c) $\mathbf{A}-\mathbf{B}$.

(a) $$\mathbf{A}+\mathbf{B}=\begin{pmatrix}-1 & -2\\ 3 & 1\end{pmatrix}+\begin{pmatrix}2 & 6\\ -3 & 4\end{pmatrix}=\begin{pmatrix}-1+2 & -2+6\\ 3+(-3) & 1+4\end{pmatrix}=\begin{pmatrix}1 & 4\\ 0 & 5\end{pmatrix}.$$

(b) $$2\mathbf{A}+3\mathbf{B}=2\begin{pmatrix}-1 & -2\\ 3 & 1\end{pmatrix}+3\begin{pmatrix}2 & 6\\ -3 & 4\end{pmatrix}=\begin{pmatrix}-2 & -4\\ 6 & 2\end{pmatrix}+\begin{pmatrix}6 & 18\\ -9 & 12\end{pmatrix}$$
$$=\begin{pmatrix}-2+6 & -4+18\\ 6+(-9) & 2+12\end{pmatrix}=\begin{pmatrix}4 & 14\\ -3 & 14\end{pmatrix}.$$

(c) $$\mathbf{A}-\mathbf{B}=\begin{pmatrix}-1 & -2\\ 3 & 1\end{pmatrix}+(-1)\begin{pmatrix}2 & 6\\ -3 & 4\end{pmatrix}=\begin{pmatrix}-1 & -2\\ 3 & 1\end{pmatrix}+\begin{pmatrix}-2 & -6\\ 3 & -4\end{pmatrix}$$
$$=\begin{pmatrix}-1-2 & -2-6\\ 3+3 & 1+(-4)\end{pmatrix}=\begin{pmatrix}-3 & -8\\ 6 & -3\end{pmatrix}.$$

In practice you will usually shorten such calculations by omitting some of the steps.

Example 4.2.2
Solve for $\mathbf{X}$ the matrix equation $\mathbf{A}+3\mathbf{X}=4\mathbf{B}$.

In this example, you must assume that all the matrices are the same size, say $m\times n$, otherwise addition would not be defined. You naturally want to write down immediately that $\mathbf{X}=\frac{1}{3}(4\mathbf{B}-\mathbf{A})$. Fortunately you can, but you should be able to justify the steps using the various rules given in this section.

$$\begin{aligned}\mathbf{A}+3\mathbf{X}=4\mathbf{B} \quad &\Leftrightarrow \quad 3\mathbf{X}=4\mathbf{B}-\mathbf{A}\\ &\Leftrightarrow \quad \tfrac{1}{3}(3\mathbf{X})=\tfrac{1}{3}(4\mathbf{B}-\mathbf{A})\\ &\Leftrightarrow \quad \left(\tfrac{1}{3}\times 3\right)\mathbf{X}=\tfrac{1}{3}(4\mathbf{B}-\mathbf{A})\\ &\Leftrightarrow \quad 1\mathbf{X}=\tfrac{1}{3}(4\mathbf{B}-\mathbf{A})\\ &\Leftrightarrow \quad \mathbf{X}=\tfrac{1}{3}(4\mathbf{B}-\mathbf{A}).\end{aligned}$$

You may wonder whether all of that was necessary. The answer is that as the rules for addition, multiplication by a scalar and subtraction are precisely those for real numbers, matrices behave in the way that you expect, and you *could* have written the answer straight down. It may surprise you, however, that you are used to doing quite so many steps in your head!

4.3 Multiplying two matrices

The rules for adding two matrices and multiplying a matrix by a scalar were rather obvious. The rule for multiplying two matrices is not at all obvious.

Return to Amy and Bob at the baker's shop. Recall that what they bought was given by the matrix $\mathbf{P}=\begin{pmatrix}2 & 1 & 1\\ 4 & 0 & 2\end{pmatrix}$. Suppose now that there are actually two shops, X and Y, that they could buy at, and that these shops charge prices in pence given by Table 4.2.

	Shop X	Shop Y
Cakes	40	45
Doughnuts	30	25
Eclairs	50	40

Table 4.2

Stripping out the headings gives a cost matrix $\mathbf{C}=\begin{pmatrix}40 & 45\\30 & 25\\50 & 40\end{pmatrix}$.

Now suppose that Amy and Bob want to compare how much they would spend in each shop.

Amy would spend $2\times40+1\times30+1\times50=160$ pence in shop X.

Amy would spend $2\times45+1\times25+1\times40=155$ pence in shop Y.

Bob would spend $4\times40+0\times30+2\times50=260$ pence in shop X.

Bob would spend $4\times45+0\times25+2\times40=260$ pence in shop Y.

You could now put these results in a table, as in Table 4.3.

	Shop X	Shop Y
Amy	160	155
Bob	260	260

Table 4.3

The corresponding matrix, $\begin{pmatrix}160 & 155\\260 & 260\end{pmatrix}$, obtained by multiplying purchases by costs, is called the product matrix $\mathbf{PC}$. Thus

$$\begin{aligned}\mathbf{PC}&=\begin{pmatrix}2 & 1 & 1\\4 & 0 & 2\end{pmatrix}\begin{pmatrix}40 & 45\\30 & 25\\50 & 40\end{pmatrix}\\&=\begin{pmatrix}2\times40+1\times30+1\times50 & 2\times45+1\times25+1\times40\\4\times40+0\times30+2\times50 & 4\times45+0\times25+2\times40\end{pmatrix}\\&=\begin{pmatrix}160 & 155\\260 & 260\end{pmatrix}.\end{aligned}$$

Notice how the individual elements of $\mathbf{PC}$ are calculated. The process of calculating

$$2\times40+1\times30+1\times50=160$$

gives the same result as the scalar product $\begin{pmatrix}2\\1\\1\end{pmatrix}\cdot\begin{pmatrix}40\\30\\50\end{pmatrix}$ of the vectors $\begin{pmatrix}2\\1\\1\end{pmatrix}$ and $\begin{pmatrix}40\\30\\50\end{pmatrix}$. It is useful to think of the element in the first row and first column of $\mathbf{PC}$ as the 'scalar product' of the first row of $\mathbf{P}$ and the first column of $\mathbf{C}$.

More generally, the element in the ith row and jth column of **PC** is the scalar product of the ith row of **P** and the jth column of **C**. Check this for yourself.

This idea of taking the scalar product of rows from the left matrix with columns from the right matrix is central to the multiplication of two matrices. Here are some examples.

Example 4.3.1
Find **AB** and **BA** when $\mathbf{A}=\begin{pmatrix}1 & 2\\ 3 & 4\end{pmatrix}$ and $\mathbf{B}=\begin{pmatrix}5 & 6\\ 7 & 8\end{pmatrix}$.

$$\mathbf{AB}=\begin{pmatrix}1 & 2\\ 3 & 4\end{pmatrix}\begin{pmatrix}5 & 6\\ 7 & 8\end{pmatrix}=\begin{pmatrix}1\times5+2\times7 & 1\times6+2\times8\\ 3\times5+4\times7 & 3\times6+4\times8\end{pmatrix}=\begin{pmatrix}19 & 22\\ 43 & 50\end{pmatrix};$$

$$\mathbf{BA}=\begin{pmatrix}5 & 6\\ 7 & 8\end{pmatrix}\begin{pmatrix}1 & 2\\ 3 & 4\end{pmatrix}=\begin{pmatrix}5\times1+6\times3 & 5\times2+6\times4\\ 7\times1+8\times3 & 7\times2+8\times4\end{pmatrix}=\begin{pmatrix}23 & 34\\ 31 & 46\end{pmatrix}.$$

An important fact emerges from this example. You cannot assume that **AB** and **BA** are equal. In fact, for matrices in general, $\mathbf{AB}\neq\mathbf{BA}$.

Matrices are not commutative under multiplication.

In general, the product of the matrices $\begin{pmatrix}a & b\\ c & d\end{pmatrix}$ and $\begin{pmatrix}e & f\\ g & h\end{pmatrix}$ is

$$\begin{pmatrix}a & b\\ c & d\end{pmatrix}\begin{pmatrix}e & f\\ g & h\end{pmatrix}=\begin{pmatrix}ae+bg & af+bh\\ ce+dg & cf+dh\end{pmatrix}.$$

Example 4.3.2
Find the products **AB** and **BA** when $\mathbf{A}=\begin{pmatrix}2 & -3 & 1\\ -5 & 2 & -2\end{pmatrix}$ and $\mathbf{B}=\begin{pmatrix}1 & 3\\ 2 & 4\\ 3 & 6\end{pmatrix}$.

Although **A** and **B** are not square matrices, you can still use the principle that the element in the ith row and jth column of the product matrix is the scalar product of the ith row of the left matrix with the jth column of the right matrix.

$$\mathbf{AB}=\begin{pmatrix}2 & -3 & 1\\ -5 & 2 & -2\end{pmatrix}\begin{pmatrix}1 & 3\\ 2 & 4\\ 3 & 6\end{pmatrix}$$

$$=\begin{pmatrix}2\times1+(-3)\times2+1\times3 & 2\times3+(-3)\times4+1\times6\\ (-5)\times1+2\times2+(-2)\times3 & (-5)\times3+2\times4+(-2)\times6\end{pmatrix}=\begin{pmatrix}-1 & 0\\ -7 & -19\end{pmatrix},$$

and $$\mathbf{BA}=\begin{pmatrix}1 & 3\\ 2 & 4\\ 3 & 6\end{pmatrix}\begin{pmatrix}2 & -3 & 1\\ -5 & 2 & -2\end{pmatrix}$$

$$=\begin{pmatrix}1\times2+3\times(-5) & 1\times(-3)+3\times2 & 1\times1+3\times(-2)\\ 2\times2+4\times(-5) & 2\times(-3)+4\times2 & 2\times1+4\times(-2)\\ 3\times2+6\times(-5) & 3\times(-3)+6\times2 & 3\times1+6\times(-2)\end{pmatrix}=\begin{pmatrix}-13 & 3 & -5\\ -16 & 2 & -6\\ -24 & 3 & -9\end{pmatrix}.$$

You can see from this example that **AB** and **BA** are not always the same size. The next example shows that sometimes it is not even possible to multiply two matrices.

Example 4.3.3

Let $\mathbf{A}=\begin{pmatrix}-1 & 2\\ -3 & -7\end{pmatrix}$, $\mathbf{B}=\begin{pmatrix}3\\ -1\end{pmatrix}$ and $\mathbf{C}=\begin{pmatrix}2 & 5\end{pmatrix}$. Determine which of the products $\mathbf{A}^2$, $\mathbf{AB}$, $\mathbf{AC}$, $\mathbf{BA}$, $\mathbf{B}^2$, $\mathbf{BC}$, $\mathbf{CA}$, $\mathbf{CB}$ and $\mathbf{C}^2$ exist and calculate those which do.

Why might a matrix product not exist? The scalar product rule for rows and columns relies on the length of the rows of the left matrix matching the length of the columns of the right matrix, otherwise you cannot carry out the scalar product.

$$\mathbf{A}^2=\begin{pmatrix}-1 & 2\\ -3 & -7\end{pmatrix}\begin{pmatrix}-1 & 2\\ -3 & -7\end{pmatrix}=\begin{pmatrix}-5 & -16\\ 24 & 43\end{pmatrix}; \qquad \mathbf{AB}=\begin{pmatrix}-1 & 2\\ -3 & -7\end{pmatrix}\begin{pmatrix}3\\ -1\end{pmatrix}=\begin{pmatrix}-5\\ -2\end{pmatrix};$$

$$\mathbf{AC}=\begin{pmatrix}-1 & 2\\ -3 & -7\end{pmatrix}(2 \quad 5) \text{ does not exist;} \qquad \mathbf{BA}=\begin{pmatrix}3\\ -1\end{pmatrix}\begin{pmatrix}-1 & 2\\ -3 & -7\end{pmatrix} \text{ does not exist;}$$

$$\mathbf{B}^2=\begin{pmatrix}3\\ -1\end{pmatrix}\begin{pmatrix}3\\ -1\end{pmatrix} \text{ does not exist;} \qquad \mathbf{BC}=\begin{pmatrix}3\\ -1\end{pmatrix}(2 \quad 5)=\begin{pmatrix}6 & 15\\ -2 & -5\end{pmatrix};$$

$$\mathbf{CA}=(2 \quad 5)\begin{pmatrix}-1 & 2\\ -3 & -7\end{pmatrix}=(-17 \quad -31); \qquad \mathbf{CB}=(2 \quad 5)\begin{pmatrix}3\\ -1\end{pmatrix}=(1);$$

$$\mathbf{C}^2=(2 \quad 5)(2 \quad 5) \text{ does not exist.}$$

The scalar product rule for multiplying matrices implies that you can only multiply two matrices if they are **conformable** for multiplication. That is, if $\mathbf{A}$ is an $m\times n$ matrix and $\mathbf{B}$ is a $p\times q$ matrix, then the product $\mathbf{AB}$ exists if, and only if, $n=p$. The size of the product is then $m\times q$.

Thus multiplying matrices of sizes $m\times n$ and $n\times q$ results in a $m\times q$ matrix.

Exercise 4A

1 Let $\mathbf{A}=\begin{pmatrix}1 & 2\\ 3 & 4\end{pmatrix}$ and $\mathbf{B}=\begin{pmatrix}2 & 3\\ 4 & -1\end{pmatrix}$. Calculate the matrices

(a) $\mathbf{A}+\mathbf{B}$, (b) $\mathbf{A}-\mathbf{B}$, (c) $3\mathbf{A}+2\mathbf{B}$, (d) $4\mathbf{A}-3\mathbf{B}$.

2 Solve for $\mathbf{X}$ the matrix equation $2\mathbf{X}+3\mathbf{A}=4\mathbf{X}-3\mathbf{B}$. What do you need to assume about the sizes of $\mathbf{A}$, $\mathbf{B}$ and $\mathbf{X}$?

3 Prove that, for matrices $\mathbf{A}$, $\mathbf{B}$ and $\mathbf{C}$ of the same size, $\mathbf{A}+(\mathbf{B}+\mathbf{C})=(\mathbf{A}+\mathbf{B})+\mathbf{C}$.

4 Find the products $\mathbf{AB}$ and $\mathbf{BA}$ where $\mathbf{A}=\begin{pmatrix}1 & 2\\ 3 & 4\end{pmatrix}$ and $\mathbf{B}=\begin{pmatrix}2 & 3\\ 4 & -1\end{pmatrix}$.

5 Let $\mathbf{A}=\begin{pmatrix}2 & 3 & -1\\ 1 & 3 & 5\\ -3 & -2 & 2\end{pmatrix}$ and $\mathbf{B}=\begin{pmatrix}4 & -2 & -3\\ 5 & 1 & 2\\ 2 & -4 & 1\end{pmatrix}$. Calculate $\mathbf{AB}$ and $\mathbf{BA}$.

6 Let $\mathbf{A}=\begin{pmatrix}-3 & 2 & 6\\ 2 & -1 & 2\end{pmatrix}$ and $\mathbf{B}=\begin{pmatrix}6 & 2\\ 3 & 2\\ 2 & -1\end{pmatrix}$. Calculate $\mathbf{AB}$ and $\mathbf{BA}$.

7 Although in general, it is true that $\mathbf{AB} \neq \mathbf{BA}$, there are matrices $\mathbf{A}$ and $\mathbf{B}$ such that $\mathbf{AB} = \mathbf{BA}$. Find such a pair $\mathbf{A}$ and $\mathbf{B}$ in which none of the elements is 0.

8 Let $\mathbf{A} = \begin{pmatrix} 1 \\ -1 \\ 1 \end{pmatrix}$, $\mathbf{B} = \begin{pmatrix} -4 & 2 & 3 \\ -2 & 3 & -3 \end{pmatrix}$ and $\mathbf{C} = (2 \quad 3 \quad 1)$. Calculate those of the following matrix products which exist.

(a) $\mathbf{AB}$ (b) $\mathbf{BA}$ (c) $\mathbf{AC}$ (d) $\mathbf{CA}$
(e) $\mathbf{BC}$ (f) $\mathbf{CB}$ (g) $(\mathbf{CA})\mathbf{B}$ (h) $\mathbf{C}(\mathbf{AB})$

9 Find a matrix $\mathbf{X}$ such that $\mathbf{X}\begin{pmatrix} 1 & 2 \\ 3 & 7 \end{pmatrix} = \begin{pmatrix} 1 & 0 \\ 0 & 1 \end{pmatrix}$. Calculate the product $\begin{pmatrix} 1 & 2 \\ 3 & 7 \end{pmatrix}\mathbf{X}$.

Try to do the same calculations for $\begin{pmatrix} 1 & 2 \\ 3 & 6 \end{pmatrix}$.

10 Let $\mathbf{A} = \begin{pmatrix} a & b \\ c & d \end{pmatrix}$, $\mathbf{X} = \begin{pmatrix} x \\ y \end{pmatrix}$ and $\mathbf{P} = \begin{pmatrix} p \\ q \end{pmatrix}$. Show that solving the matrix equation $\mathbf{AX} = \mathbf{P}$ is equivalent to solving the simultaneous equations $\left.\begin{matrix} ax + by = p \\ cx + dy = q \end{matrix}\right\}$ and that this is equivalent to solving the vector equation $x\begin{pmatrix} a \\ c \end{pmatrix} + y\begin{pmatrix} b \\ d \end{pmatrix} = \begin{pmatrix} p \\ q \end{pmatrix}$.

11 Find the matrix $\mathbf{X}$ such that $\begin{pmatrix} 1 & 2 & 2 \\ 1 & 3 & -1 \\ 2 & 4 & 5 \end{pmatrix}\mathbf{X} = \begin{pmatrix} 1 & 0 & 0 \\ 0 & 1 & 0 \\ 0 & 0 & 1 \end{pmatrix}$. Calculate $\mathbf{X}\begin{pmatrix} 1 & 2 & 2 \\ 1 & 3 & -1 \\ 2 & 4 & 5 \end{pmatrix}$.

12 Verify that $\mathbf{A}(\mathbf{B}+\mathbf{C}) = \mathbf{AB}+\mathbf{AC}$, $(\mathbf{B}+\mathbf{C})\mathbf{A} = \mathbf{BA}+\mathbf{CA}$ and $(\mathbf{AB})\mathbf{C} = \mathbf{A}(\mathbf{BC})$ for the following matrices:

$$\mathbf{A} = \begin{pmatrix} 3 & 2 \\ 6 & -2 \end{pmatrix}, \quad \mathbf{B} = \begin{pmatrix} 1 & -1 \\ 2 & 0 \end{pmatrix} \quad \text{and} \quad \mathbf{C} = \begin{pmatrix} 2 & -1 \\ 1 & 3 \end{pmatrix}.$$

13 Let $\mathbf{A} = (2 \quad -3)$, $\mathbf{B} = \begin{pmatrix} 3 & 2 \\ -4 & 1 \end{pmatrix}$ and $\mathbf{C} = \begin{pmatrix} 4 \\ -1 \end{pmatrix}$. Verify that $(\mathbf{AB})\mathbf{C} = \mathbf{A}(\mathbf{BC})$.

14 Establish results for the products $\mathbf{AO}$ and $\mathbf{OA}$.

15 Prove for 2×2 matrices $\mathbf{A}$ and $\mathbf{B}$ and a scalar s that $(s\mathbf{A})\mathbf{B} = s(\mathbf{AB})$.

16 Prove that $\mathbf{A}(\mathbf{B}+\mathbf{C}) = \mathbf{AB}+\mathbf{AC}$ when $\mathbf{A}$, $\mathbf{B}$ and $\mathbf{C}$ are 2×2 matrices.

4.4 Rules for multiplication

To state the rule for multiplying two matrices, you need more notation.

The element in the ith row and jth column of a matrix $\mathbf{A}$ is denoted by a_{ij} using two suffixes i and j, the first for the row number and the second for the column number. This is called **double suffix notation**. To say that $\mathbf{A}$ is the matrix having the element a_{ij} in the ith row and jth column, you would write

$$\mathbf{A} = \{a_{ij}\}$$

if there was no ambiguity about the size of $\mathbf{A}$. If you need also to indicate that $\mathbf{A}$ has m rows and n columns, you would write

$$\mathbf{A} = \{a_{ij}, i = 1, 2, \ldots, m, j = 1, 2, \ldots, n\}.$$

Let $\mathbf{A} = \{a_{ij}\}$ be an $m \times n$ matrix, and $\mathbf{B} = \{b_{jk}\}$ be an $n \times p$ matrix.

Then the product matrix $\mathbf{AB}$ exists, and the element in the ith row and kth column is given by the sum

$$a_{i1}b_{1k} + a_{i2}b_{2k} + \ldots + a_{in}b_{nk}.$$

$\mathbf{AB}$ is an $m \times p$ matrix.

From this it is possible to prove a number of rules, but it is not easy. However, Questions 12 to 16 in Exercise 4A suggest (correctly) that the following are true.

For matrices $\mathbf{A}$, $\mathbf{B}$ and $\mathbf{C}$, and for scalars s:

$$\mathbf{A}(\mathbf{B}+\mathbf{C}) = \mathbf{AB} + \mathbf{AC}, \qquad (\mathbf{B}+\mathbf{C})\mathbf{A} = \mathbf{BA} + \mathbf{CA},$$
$$\mathbf{A}(\mathbf{BC}) = (\mathbf{AB})\mathbf{C}, \qquad s(\mathbf{AB}) = (s\mathbf{A})\mathbf{B} = \mathbf{A}(s\mathbf{B}),$$
$$\mathbf{AO} = \mathbf{O}, \qquad \mathbf{OA} = \mathbf{O}.$$

In general, $\mathbf{AB} \neq \mathbf{BA}$.

4.5 Division of matrices

Now that you can multiply matrices, what about division? That is, given two matrices $\mathbf{A}$ and $\mathbf{B}$, can you find a matrix $\mathbf{X}$ such that $\mathbf{AX} = \mathbf{B}$ or $\mathbf{XA} = \mathbf{B}$?

This question is more complicated for matrices than for numbers; amongst other reasons, because the answer depends on the sizes of $\mathbf{A}$ and $\mathbf{B}$, and because multiplication is not commutative. So it is best to approach the problem in stages.

With numbers, one way of approaching the division $b \div a$, that is the solution of $ax = b$, is to begin by finding the reciprocal (or inverse) $\frac{1}{a}$, and then to notice that, if $x = \frac{1}{a} \times b$, then $ax = a \times \left(\frac{1}{a} \times b\right) = \left(a \times \frac{1}{a}\right) \times b = 1 \times b = b$.
The same method can be used for matrices. The first step is to find the matrix equivalent of the number 1, with the property that $1 \times b = b$.

Example 4.5.1
Find the matrix $\begin{pmatrix} p & q \\ r & s \end{pmatrix}$ such that $\begin{pmatrix} p & q \\ r & s \end{pmatrix}\begin{pmatrix} a & b \\ c & d \end{pmatrix} = \begin{pmatrix} a & b \\ c & d \end{pmatrix}$ for any matrix $\begin{pmatrix} a & b \\ c & d \end{pmatrix}$.

If $\begin{pmatrix} p & q \\ r & s \end{pmatrix}\begin{pmatrix} a & b \\ c & d \end{pmatrix} = \begin{pmatrix} a & b \\ c & d \end{pmatrix}$, then $\begin{pmatrix} pa+qc & pb+qd \\ ra+sc & rb+sd \end{pmatrix} = \begin{pmatrix} a & b \\ c & d \end{pmatrix}$, so

$pa + qc = a$ for all a and c; $ra + sc = c$ for all a and c;
$pb + qd = b$ for all b and d; $rb + sd = d$ for all b and d.

If the first equation is satisfied for all a and c, it is satisfied when $a=1$ and $c=0$; so $p=1$. It is also satisfied when $a=0$ and $c=1$, so $q=0$. These values also satisfy the second equation.

If the third equation is satisfied for all a and c, it is satisfied when $a=1$ and $c=0$; so $r=0$. It is also satisfied when $a=0$ and $c=1$, so $s=1$. These values also satisfy the last equation.

Therefore the matrix $\begin{pmatrix} p & q \\ r & s \end{pmatrix} = \begin{pmatrix} 1 & 0 \\ 0 & 1 \end{pmatrix}$.

As a check, you can verify that $\begin{pmatrix} 1 & 0 \\ 0 & 1 \end{pmatrix}\begin{pmatrix} a & b \\ c & d \end{pmatrix} = \begin{pmatrix} a & b \\ c & d \end{pmatrix}$.

The matrix $\begin{pmatrix} 1 & 0 \\ 0 & 1 \end{pmatrix}$, which also has the property that $\begin{pmatrix} a & b \\ c & d \end{pmatrix}\begin{pmatrix} 1 & 0 \\ 0 & 1 \end{pmatrix} = \begin{pmatrix} a & b \\ c & d \end{pmatrix}$, is called the **$2 \times 2$ identity matrix**, and is denoted by $\mathbf{I}$. Similarly the **3×3 identity matrix** is $\begin{pmatrix} 1 & 0 & 0 \\ 0 & 1 & 0 \\ 0 & 0 & 1 \end{pmatrix}$, and is also denoted by $\mathbf{I}$. When you write a matrix statement such as

$$\mathbf{IX} = \mathbf{XI} = \mathbf{X}$$

then the size of the identity matrix $\mathbf{I}$ has to be the correct size for multiplication by $\mathbf{X}$. This means that if $\mathbf{X}$ is 2×2 then $\mathbf{I}$ will be 2×2, and if $\mathbf{X}$ is 3×3 then $\mathbf{I}$ is 3×3. However, if $\mathbf{X}$ is not square, and is, say, $m \times n$, then the two $\mathbf{I}$s in the equation $\mathbf{IX} = \mathbf{XI} = \mathbf{X}$ have different sizes. The left $\mathbf{I}$ will be $m \times m$ and the right $\mathbf{I}$ $n \times n$. This sounds horrendous, but it is never a problem in practice. If you wish to specify the size, then it is usual to write $\mathbf{I}_n$ for the $n \times n$ identity matrix.

A useful way of describing where the 1s occur in the identity matrix is to say that they appear on the **leading diagonal**, which, for a square matrix, runs from the top left corner to the bottom right. In a matrix which is not square, the leading diagonal consists of those elements which have the same row and column number.

> An **identity matrix** is a square matrix consisting of 1s on the leading diagonal and 0s everywhere else. The identity matrix with n rows and n columns is denoted by $\mathbf{I}_n$.
>
> If $\mathbf{X}$ is any matrix with m rows and n columns, then $\mathbf{I}_m\mathbf{X} = \mathbf{XI}_n = \mathbf{X}$.
>
> There is no such thing as a non-square identity matrix.

The next step in the division problem is to find the equivalent of the reciprocal $\dfrac{1}{a}$. The question is:

Given a matrix $\mathbf{A}$ is there a matrix $\mathbf{C}$ such that $\mathbf{AC} = \mathbf{CA} = \mathbf{I}$?

The answer to this question is ‘sometimes’ if $\mathbf{A}$ is a square matrix, and ‘never’ if $\mathbf{A}$ is not square. It is easy to give reasons for the answer ‘never’.

Suppose $\mathbf{A}$ is an $m \times n$ matrix, where $m \neq n$. If the product $\mathbf{AC}$ is square and $\mathbf{A}$ is $m \times n$, then $\mathbf{C}$ must be $n \times m$, and the product $\mathbf{AC}$ is $m \times m$. However, similar reasoning shows that $\mathbf{CA}$ must be an $n \times n$ matrix. You supposed at the outset that $m \neq n$, so $\mathbf{AC} \neq \mathbf{CA}$.

It is also easy to show that if $\mathbf{A}$ is square, the answer to the question is only 'sometimes'. If $\mathbf{A} = \mathbf{I}$, then take $\mathbf{C} = \mathbf{I}$, and the answer is 'yes'; and if $\mathbf{A} = \mathbf{O}$, then $\mathbf{AC} = \mathbf{CA} = \mathbf{O}$ for all matrices $\mathbf{C}$, and the answer is 'no'.

However, if for a given matrix $\mathbf{A}$ there is a matrix $\mathbf{C}$ such that $\mathbf{AC} = \mathbf{CA} = \mathbf{I}$, then division becomes possible. For if $\mathbf{AX} = \mathbf{B}$, then multiplying by $\mathbf{C}$ on the left is, in effect, dividing by $\mathbf{A}$.

$$\mathbf{AX} = \mathbf{B} \quad \Rightarrow \quad \mathbf{C}(\mathbf{AX}) = \mathbf{CB} \quad \Rightarrow \quad (\mathbf{CA})\mathbf{X} = \mathbf{CB} \quad \Rightarrow \quad \mathbf{IX} = \mathbf{CB} \quad \Rightarrow \quad \mathbf{X} = \mathbf{CB}.$$

Notice also that the last line is reversible. If $\mathbf{C}$ exists, then

$$\mathbf{X} = \mathbf{CB} \quad \Rightarrow \quad \mathbf{AX} = \mathbf{A}(\mathbf{CB}) \quad \Rightarrow \quad \mathbf{AX} = (\mathbf{AC})\mathbf{B} \quad \Rightarrow \quad \mathbf{AX} = \mathbf{IB} \quad \Rightarrow \quad \mathbf{AX} = \mathbf{B}.$$

So $\quad \mathbf{AX} = \mathbf{B} \quad \Leftrightarrow \quad \mathbf{X} = \mathbf{CB}.$

A similar argument can be used if the order of multiplication is reversed, to obtain

$$\mathbf{XA} = \mathbf{B} \quad \Leftrightarrow \quad \mathbf{X} = \mathbf{BC}.$$

Try writing out the proof for yourself.

Given a square matrix $\mathbf{A}$, a matrix $\mathbf{C}$ such that $\mathbf{AC} = \mathbf{CA} = \mathbf{I}$ is called the **inverse** of $\mathbf{A}$, and written as $\mathbf{A}^{-1}$. If $\mathbf{A}^{-1}$ exists, the matrix $\mathbf{A}$ is said to be **non-singular**. If no such matrix exists, then the matrix $\mathbf{A}$ is said to be **singular**. Thus:

A square matrix $\mathbf{A}$ has an inverse $\mathbf{A}^{-1}$ if and only if $\mathbf{A}$ is non-singular.

Notice also that if $\mathbf{AC} = \mathbf{CA} = \mathbf{I}$, then $\mathbf{CA} = \mathbf{AC} = \mathbf{I}$; so if $\mathbf{C}$ is the inverse of $\mathbf{A}$, $\mathbf{A}$ is also the inverse of $\mathbf{C}$. That is, $\mathbf{C} = \mathbf{A}^{-1}$ if and only if $\mathbf{A} = \mathbf{C}^{-1}$.

In Chapter 6, two important facts will be shown. You should assume them for now.

- If $\mathbf{A}$ is square and $\mathbf{CA} = \mathbf{I}$, then $\mathbf{AC} = \mathbf{I}$.
- Given $\mathbf{A}$, the matrix $\mathbf{C}$ such that $\mathbf{CA} = \mathbf{I}$, if it exists, is unique.

Example 4.5.2
Multiply the matrices $\mathbf{A} = \begin{pmatrix} -1 & 2 & -3 \\ 2 & -7 & 1 \\ -1 & 3 & 2 \end{pmatrix}$ and $\mathbf{B} = \begin{pmatrix} -17 & -13 & -19 \\ -5 & -5 & -5 \\ -1 & 1 & 3 \end{pmatrix}$. Deduce that $\mathbf{A}$ is non-singular and find its inverse. Solve for $\mathbf{X}$ the matrix equation $\mathbf{AX} = \mathbf{B}$.

$$\mathbf{AB} = \begin{pmatrix} -1 & 2 & -3 \\ 2 & -7 & 1 \\ -1 & 3 & 2 \end{pmatrix}\begin{pmatrix} -17 & -13 & -19 \\ -5 & -5 & -5 \\ -1 & 1 & 3 \end{pmatrix} = \begin{pmatrix} 10 & 0 & 0 \\ 0 & 10 & 0 \\ 0 & 0 & 10 \end{pmatrix} = 10\mathbf{I}.$$

Therefore $\frac{1}{10}(\mathbf{AB}) = \mathbf{A}\left(\frac{1}{10}\mathbf{B}\right) = \mathbf{I}$, so the inverse of $\mathbf{A}$ is

$$\mathbf{A}^{-1} = \frac{1}{10}\mathbf{B} = \begin{pmatrix} -1.7 & -1.3 & -1.9 \\ -0.5 & -0.5 & -0.5 \\ -0.1 & 0.1 & 0.3 \end{pmatrix}$$; since $\mathbf{A}^{-1}$ exists, $\mathbf{A}$ is non-singular.

If $\mathbf{AX} = \mathbf{B}$, then $\mathbf{X} = \mathbf{A}^{-1}\mathbf{B} = \frac{1}{10}\mathbf{BB} = \frac{1}{10}\mathbf{B}^2$, so

$$\mathbf{X} = \frac{1}{10}\begin{pmatrix} -17 & -13 & -19 \\ -5 & -5 & -5 \\ -1 & 1 & 3 \end{pmatrix}^2 = \frac{1}{10}\begin{pmatrix} 373 & 267 & 331 \\ 115 & 85 & 105 \\ 9 & 11 & 23 \end{pmatrix} = \begin{pmatrix} 37.3 & 26.7 & 33.1 \\ 11.5 & 8.5 & 10.5 \\ 0.9 & 1.1 & 2.3 \end{pmatrix}.$$

Exercise 4B

1 Find a matrix $\mathbf{X}$ such that $\mathbf{X}\begin{pmatrix} 5 & 3 \\ 3 & 2 \end{pmatrix} = \begin{pmatrix} 1 & 0 \\ 0 & 1 \end{pmatrix}$.

2 Find a matrix $\mathbf{X}$ such that $\mathbf{X}\begin{pmatrix} 5 & 2 \\ 7 & 3 \end{pmatrix} = \begin{pmatrix} 1 & 0 \\ 0 & 1 \end{pmatrix}$.

3 Find the inverse of the following 2×2 matrices.

(a) $\begin{pmatrix} 2 & 2 \\ 3 & 4 \end{pmatrix}$ (b) $\begin{pmatrix} -2 & -5 \\ 3 & 7 \end{pmatrix}$ (c) $\begin{pmatrix} a & b \\ c & d \end{pmatrix}$

4 Find the inverse of the matrix $\begin{pmatrix} -3 & -5 \\ 5 & 9 \end{pmatrix}$ and use it to find matrices $\mathbf{X}$ which satisfy the following equations:

(a) $\begin{pmatrix} -3 & -5 \\ 5 & 9 \end{pmatrix}\mathbf{X} = \begin{pmatrix} 4 \\ 8 \end{pmatrix}$, (b) $\begin{pmatrix} -3 & -5 \\ 5 & 9 \end{pmatrix}\mathbf{X} = \begin{pmatrix} 4 & -4 \\ 8 & 12 \end{pmatrix}$.

5 Let $\mathbf{M} = \begin{pmatrix} 1 & 2 & -1 \\ 2 & 1 & 2 \\ 1 & 0 & 1 \end{pmatrix}$. Show that $\mathbf{M}^3 - 3\mathbf{M}^2 = 2\mathbf{I}$ and hence show that $\mathbf{M}^{-1} = \frac{1}{2}\left(\mathbf{M}^2 - 3\mathbf{M}\right)$.

6 Find the inverse of $\begin{pmatrix} 2 & 3 \\ 4 & 5 \end{pmatrix}$ and use it to solve the equation $\begin{pmatrix} 2 & 3 \\ 4 & 5 \end{pmatrix}\begin{pmatrix} x \\ y \end{pmatrix} = \begin{pmatrix} 1 \\ 3 \end{pmatrix}$.

7 Find the matrix product $\begin{pmatrix} 1 & 4 & -5 \\ 1 & 5 & k \\ 1 & 3 & -7 \end{pmatrix}\begin{pmatrix} -29 & 13 & 17 \\ 5 & -2 & -3 \\ -2 & 1 & 1 \end{pmatrix}$, giving your answer in terms of k.

Hence find the inverse of the matrix $\begin{pmatrix} -29 & 13 & 17 \\ 5 & -2 & -3 \\ -2 & 1 & 1 \end{pmatrix}$.

8 Verify that $\mathbf{A}(\mathbf{BC}) = (\mathbf{AB})\mathbf{C}$ for the matrices $\mathbf{A} = (x \quad y)$, $\mathbf{B} = \begin{pmatrix} a & h \\ h & b \end{pmatrix}$ and $\mathbf{C} = \begin{pmatrix} x \\ y \end{pmatrix}$.

9 Verify that $\begin{pmatrix} 1 & -2 \\ -2 & 4 \end{pmatrix}\begin{pmatrix} 6 & 4 \\ 2 & 5 \end{pmatrix} = \begin{pmatrix} 1 & -2 \\ -2 & 4 \end{pmatrix}\begin{pmatrix} 2 & 2 \\ 0 & 4 \end{pmatrix}$. Note that in matrix algebra $\mathbf{AB} = \mathbf{AC}$ does not imply that $\mathbf{B} = \mathbf{C}$ without extra information about the matrix $\mathbf{A}$.

Show that, if $\mathbf{A}^{-1}$ exists, then $\mathbf{AB} = \mathbf{AC} \Rightarrow \mathbf{B} = \mathbf{C}$.

Miscellaneous exercise 4

1 The matrix $\mathbf{M}$ is given by $\mathbf{M} = \begin{pmatrix} 2 & 3 \\ 1 & 4 \end{pmatrix}$. Show that $\mathbf{M}^2 = 6\mathbf{M} - 5\mathbf{I}$, and verify that $\mathbf{M}^{-1} = \frac{6}{5}\mathbf{I} - \frac{1}{5}\mathbf{M}$.

2 Let $\mathbf{A} = \begin{pmatrix} 13 & -7 & 2 \\ 4 & -3 & 2 \\ 3 & -2 & 1 \end{pmatrix}$. Calculate the matrix $\mathbf{A}^3 - 11\mathbf{A}^2 - 3\mathbf{A}$.

3 Let $\mathbf{M}$ be the 2×2 matrix $\begin{pmatrix} a & b \\ c & d \end{pmatrix}$.

(a) Show that, for all values of a, b, c and d,

$$\mathbf{M}^2 - (a+d)\mathbf{M} + (ad - bc)\mathbf{I} = \mathbf{O}$$

where $\mathbf{I} = \begin{pmatrix} 1 & 0 \\ 0 & 1 \end{pmatrix}$ and $\mathbf{O} = \begin{pmatrix} 0 & 0 \\ 0 & 0 \end{pmatrix}$.

(b) In the case when $a = 3$, $b = -5$, $c = 4$ and $d = -1$:

(i) write down a quadratic equation satisfied by $\mathbf{M}$;

(ii) hence find the values of the constants p and q such that $\mathbf{M}^{-1} = p\mathbf{M} + q\mathbf{I}$.

4 If $\mathbf{M} = \begin{pmatrix} 5 & 2 \\ 3 & 1 \end{pmatrix}$, find a matrix $\mathbf{P}$ of the form $\begin{pmatrix} a & b \\ 0 & d \end{pmatrix}$ such that $\mathbf{PM} = \begin{pmatrix} 1 & 0 \\ k & 1 \end{pmatrix}$, giving the values of a, b and d. Then find a matrix $\mathbf{Q}$ such that $\mathbf{QPM} = \begin{pmatrix} 1 & 0 \\ 0 & 1 \end{pmatrix}$. (OCR)

5 $\mathbf{M} = \begin{pmatrix} a & 1 \\ c & d \end{pmatrix}$ and $\mathbf{M}\begin{pmatrix} 5 \\ 2 \end{pmatrix} = \begin{pmatrix} -3 \\ 11 \end{pmatrix}$.

(a) Find the value of a.

(b) Given that $\mathbf{M}\left\{\begin{pmatrix} 5 \\ 2 \end{pmatrix} + \begin{pmatrix} 0 \\ 1 \end{pmatrix}\right\} = \begin{pmatrix} -2 \\ 14 \end{pmatrix}$, find $\mathbf{M}$.

6 The matrix $\mathbf{A}$ is given by $\mathbf{A} = \begin{pmatrix} \cos x & -\sin x \\ \sin x & \cos x \end{pmatrix}$.

(a) Prove by mathematical induction that $\mathbf{A}^n = \begin{pmatrix} \cos(nx) & -\sin(nx) \\ \sin(nx) & \cos(nx) \end{pmatrix}$ for integers $n \geqslant 1$.

(b) Determine whether the result is also true for $n = -1$. (OCR)

7 Let $\mathbf{A}$ be the matrix $\mathbf{A} = \begin{pmatrix} 1 & 2 & 3 \\ 4 & -1 & 2 \\ 2 & 3 & -2 \end{pmatrix}$.

(a) For some real constant p, the matrix $\mathbf{B}$ is given by $\mathbf{B} = \begin{pmatrix} -4 & 13 & 7 \\ 12 & -8 & 10 \\ p & 1 & -9 \end{pmatrix}$. Find the product $\mathbf{AB}$, giving the elements (where appropriate) in terms of p.

(b) (i) Given that $\mathbf{AB} = k\mathbf{I}$, where k is a scalar constant and $\mathbf{I}$ is the 3×3 identity matrix, determine the value of p, and state the value of k.

(ii) Deduce the inverse matrix, $\mathbf{A}^{-1}$, of $\mathbf{A}$. (OCR)

8† Let $\mathbf{A}$, $\mathbf{B}$ and $\mathbf{C}$ be real 2×2 matrices and denote $\mathbf{AB} - \mathbf{BA}$ by $[\mathbf{A}, \mathbf{B}]$.

Prove that

(a) $[\mathbf{A}, \mathbf{A}] = \mathbf{O}$;

(b) $[[\mathbf{A}, \mathbf{B}], \mathbf{C}] + [[\mathbf{B}, \mathbf{C}], \mathbf{A}] + [[\mathbf{C}, \mathbf{A}], \mathbf{B}] = \mathbf{O}$;

(c) $[\mathbf{A}, \mathbf{B}] = \mathbf{I} \quad \Rightarrow \quad [\mathbf{A}, \mathbf{B}^m] = m\mathbf{B}^{m-1}$ for all positive integers m.

The trace $\operatorname{Tr}(\mathbf{A})$ of a matrix $\mathbf{A} = \begin{pmatrix} a_{11} & a_{12} \\ a_{21} & a_{22} \end{pmatrix}$ is defined by $\operatorname{Tr}(\mathbf{A}) = a_{11} + a_{22}$.

Prove that

(d) $\operatorname{Tr}(\mathbf{A} + \mathbf{B}) = \operatorname{Tr}(\mathbf{A}) + \operatorname{Tr}(\mathbf{B})$;

(e) $\operatorname{Tr}(\mathbf{AB}) = \operatorname{Tr}(\mathbf{BA})$;

(f) $\operatorname{Tr}(\mathbf{I}) = 2$.

Deduce that there are no matrices satisfying $[\mathbf{A}, \mathbf{B}] = \mathbf{I}$. Does this in any way invalidate the statement in part (c)? (MEI)

5 Matrices and transformations

This chapter looks at matrices in a different way, as transformations of the plane. You will think of multiplication by a matrix in terms of functions, and use your knowledge of functions to gain more insights. When you have completed it, you should

- understand how to use 2×2 matrices to represent geometrical transformations, including rotations, reflections, enlargements, stretches and shears
- know how to find the matrix which carries out a given transformation
- know that the matrix product $\mathbf{AB}$ represents the result of the matrix transformation carried out by $\mathbf{B}$ followed by the transformation carried out by $\mathbf{A}$.

5.1 Matrices and transformations

Suppose that you multiply the matrix $\mathbf{M} = \begin{pmatrix} 2 & -1 \\ 1 & 1 \end{pmatrix}$ by the matrix, or column vector, $\begin{pmatrix} 2 \\ -1 \end{pmatrix}$ to get the product $\begin{pmatrix} 2 & -1 \\ 1 & 1 \end{pmatrix}\begin{pmatrix} 2 \\ -1 \end{pmatrix} = \begin{pmatrix} 5 \\ 1 \end{pmatrix}$. You can think of this as the matrix $\mathbf{M}$ operating on the vector $\mathbf{v} = \begin{pmatrix} 2 \\ -1 \end{pmatrix}$ to give another vector $\mathbf{v}' = \begin{pmatrix} 5 \\ 1 \end{pmatrix}$. The matrix $\mathbf{M}$ can operate in the same way on any vector with two components to give another vector with two components. For example, $\mathbf{M}$ operates on $\mathbf{w} = \begin{pmatrix} -1 \\ 1 \end{pmatrix}$ to give $\mathbf{w}' = \begin{pmatrix} 2 & -1 \\ 1 & 1 \end{pmatrix}\begin{pmatrix} -1 \\ 1 \end{pmatrix} = \begin{pmatrix} -3 \\ 0 \end{pmatrix}$.

The matrix $\mathbf{M}$ is said to carry out a **transformation**, or a **mapping**, of each vector into its **image**. In this book, the term 'transformation' will be used.

If you interpret the vectors which are being transformed as position vectors, you can illustrate matrix transformations geometrically by drawing a diagram of some of the position vectors before and after transforming them. This is shown in Fig. 5.1, where the vectors $\mathbf{v}$ and $\mathbf{w}$, shown by broken lines, are transformed into $\mathbf{v}'$ and $\mathbf{w}'$.

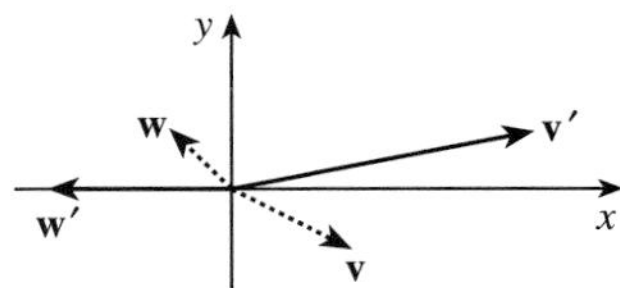

Fig. 5.1

The key to understanding matrix transformations is to consider their effect on the **unit square** $OABC$ formed by the origin and the points $A(1,0)$, $B(1,1)$ and $C(0,1)$. The images of $\begin{pmatrix} 0 \\ 0 \end{pmatrix}$ and of the position vectors $\mathbf{a} = \begin{pmatrix} 1 \\ 0 \end{pmatrix}$, $\mathbf{b} = \begin{pmatrix} 1 \\ 1 \end{pmatrix}$, and $\mathbf{c} = \begin{pmatrix} 0 \\ 1 \end{pmatrix}$ under the matrix $\mathbf{M} = \begin{pmatrix} 2 & -1 \\ 1 & 1 \end{pmatrix}$ are

$$\begin{pmatrix} 2 & -1 \\ 1 & 1 \end{pmatrix}\begin{pmatrix} 0 \\ 0 \end{pmatrix} = \begin{pmatrix} 0 \\ 0 \end{pmatrix}, \qquad \mathbf{a}' = \begin{pmatrix} 2 & -1 \\ 1 & 1 \end{pmatrix}\begin{pmatrix} 1 \\ 0 \end{pmatrix} = \begin{pmatrix} 2 \\ 1 \end{pmatrix},$$

$$\mathbf{b}' = \begin{pmatrix} 2 & -1 \\ 1 & 1 \end{pmatrix}\begin{pmatrix} 1 \\ 1 \end{pmatrix} = \begin{pmatrix} 1 \\ 2 \end{pmatrix}, \qquad \mathbf{c}' = \begin{pmatrix} 2 & -1 \\ 1 & 1 \end{pmatrix}\begin{pmatrix} 0 \\ 1 \end{pmatrix} = \begin{pmatrix} -1 \\ 1 \end{pmatrix}.$$

The points A', B' and C', shown in Fig. 5.2, have coordinates $(2,1)$, $(1,2)$ and $(-1,1)$, and you will notice that $OA'B'C'$ is a parallelogram. This is said to be the image of the unit square under the transformation.

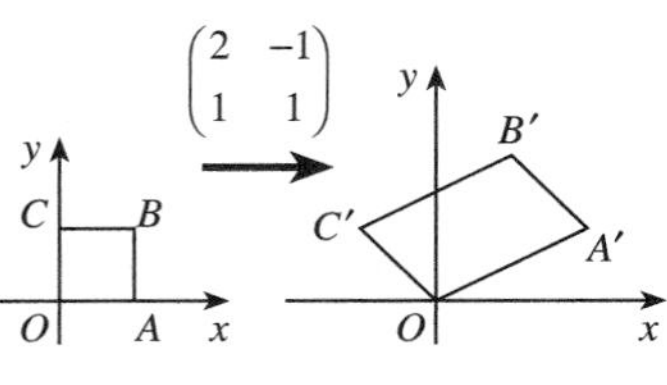

Fig. 5.2

In Fig. 5.2 the unit square and its image have been separated to make it easier to distinguish them. But to understand what is happening geometrically, you should imagine the two figures superimposed, as in Fig. 5.1.

In describing the image of the unit square as a parallelogram, a shift has taken place from the idea of transforming position vectors to the idea of transforming points. This is fine, but you need to understand that when you transform a shape, you are really transforming the position vectors of points of that shape.

The fact that the image of the unit square is a parallelogram is no coincidence, but a consequence of the distributive rule $\mathbf{X}(\mathbf{Y}+\mathbf{Z}) = \mathbf{XY}+\mathbf{XZ}$ for matrices. In fact it follows from a much more general result.

Theorem If $OUVW$ is a parallelogram, then the image $OU'V'W'$ is also a parallelogram.

Proof Using the conventional notation for position vectors,

$$OUVW \text{ is a parallelogram} \quad \Leftrightarrow \quad \mathbf{v} = \mathbf{u} + \mathbf{w}.$$

Therefore $\mathbf{Mv} = \mathbf{M}(\mathbf{u}+\mathbf{w}) = \mathbf{Mu}+\mathbf{Mw}$; that is, $\mathbf{v}' = \mathbf{u}' + \mathbf{w}'$.

So $OU'V'W'$ is a parallelogram.

Since the unit square is a parallelogram, it follows from the theorem that its image is a parallelogram.

What happens if you enlarge a vector by a scalar factor? For example, you have seen that the image of $\mathbf{v} = \begin{pmatrix} 2 \\ 1 \end{pmatrix}$ under $\begin{pmatrix} 2 & -1 \\ 1 & 1 \end{pmatrix}$ is $\mathbf{v}' = \begin{pmatrix} 5 \\ 1 \end{pmatrix}$. The image of $3\mathbf{v} = \begin{pmatrix} 6 \\ 3 \end{pmatrix}$ is $\begin{pmatrix} 2 & -1 \\ 1 & 1 \end{pmatrix}\begin{pmatrix} 6 \\ 3 \end{pmatrix} = \begin{pmatrix} 15 \\ 3 \end{pmatrix}$, which is $3\mathbf{v}'$. It seems that if a vector is multiplied by a scalar, then its image is multiplied by the same scalar.

The general result is a consequence of the matrix rule $\mathbf{X}(s\mathbf{Y}) = s(\mathbf{XY})$. Taking $\mathbf{X}$ to be a transformation matrix $\mathbf{M}$ and $\mathbf{Y}$ a position vector $\mathbf{u}$ shows that, if $\mathbf{w} = s\mathbf{v}$, then its image

$$\mathbf{w}' = \mathbf{M}(s\mathbf{v}) = s(\mathbf{Mv}) = s\mathbf{v}'.$$

You can now combine this result with the parallelogram theorem to find the effect of transforming a complete coordinate grid of squares.

Let $\mathbf{M}$ be any 2×2 matrix $\mathbf{M} = \begin{pmatrix} p & q \\ r & s \end{pmatrix}$. Then $\mathbf{M}\begin{pmatrix} 1 \\ 0 \end{pmatrix} = \begin{pmatrix} p \\ r \end{pmatrix}$ and $\mathbf{M}\begin{pmatrix} 0 \\ 1 \end{pmatrix} = \begin{pmatrix} q \\ s \end{pmatrix}$, and the unit square is transformed into the parallelogram whose adjacent sides are formed by the position vectors $\begin{pmatrix} p \\ r \end{pmatrix}$ and $\begin{pmatrix} q \\ s \end{pmatrix}$.

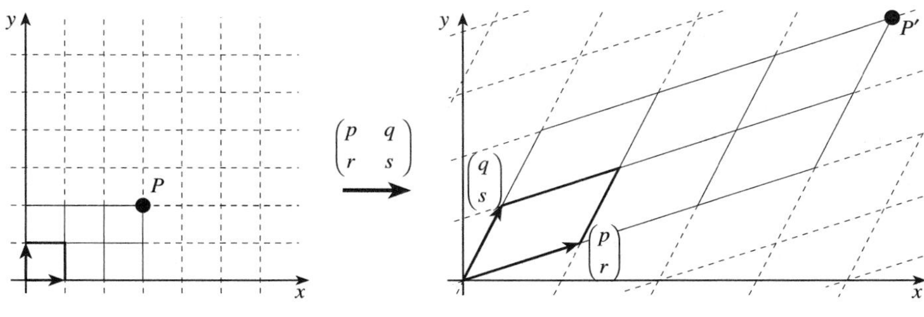

Fig. 5.3

Fig. 5.3 shows this parallelogram, and the images of some squares on the original grid.

As $\mathbf{M}\begin{pmatrix} 3 \\ 2 \end{pmatrix} = \mathbf{M}\left(3\begin{pmatrix} 1 \\ 0 \end{pmatrix} + 2\begin{pmatrix} 0 \\ 1 \end{pmatrix}\right) = \mathbf{M}\left(3\begin{pmatrix} 1 \\ 0 \end{pmatrix}\right) + \mathbf{M}\left(2\begin{pmatrix} 0 \\ 1 \end{pmatrix}\right)$

$$= 3\mathbf{M}\begin{pmatrix} 1 \\ 0 \end{pmatrix} + 2\mathbf{M}\begin{pmatrix} 0 \\ 1 \end{pmatrix} = 3\begin{pmatrix} p \\ r \end{pmatrix} + 2\begin{pmatrix} q \\ s \end{pmatrix},$$

you can deduce that, relative to a grid of parallelograms based on the image of the unit square, P' is 'three parallelograms along and two up'.

In general, writing $\begin{pmatrix} 1 \\ 0 \end{pmatrix}$ as $\mathbf{i}$, $\begin{pmatrix} 0 \\ 1 \end{pmatrix}$ as $\mathbf{j}$, and $\mathbf{Mi} = \mathbf{u}$, $\mathbf{Mj} = \mathbf{v}$ and using the matrix rules,

$$\mathbf{M}(x\mathbf{i} + y\mathbf{j}) = \mathbf{M}(x\mathbf{i}) + \mathbf{M}(y\mathbf{j}) = x\mathbf{M}(\mathbf{i}) + y\mathbf{M}(\mathbf{j}) = x\mathbf{u} + y\mathbf{v}.$$

Thus, the grid of squares on the original set of axes has been transformed to a grid of parallelograms. This means that you can get all the information you require about a matrix transformation by looking at the image of the unit square.

A 2×2 matrix $\mathbf{M}$ transforms parallelograms into parallelograms.

In particular, $\mathbf{M}$ transforms a grid of squares into a grid of parallelograms, and the image of any point relative to the grid of squares is the corresponding point relative to the grid of parallelograms.

Example 5.1.1
Illustrate the matrix $\mathbf{R} = \begin{pmatrix} 0 & -1 \\ 1 & 0 \end{pmatrix}$ geometrically. Identify the geometric transformation carried out by $\mathbf{R}$.

The images of $\begin{pmatrix} 1 \\ 0 \end{pmatrix}$ and $\begin{pmatrix} 0 \\ 1 \end{pmatrix}$ are $\begin{pmatrix} 0 & -1 \\ 1 & 0 \end{pmatrix}\begin{pmatrix} 1 \\ 0 \end{pmatrix} = \begin{pmatrix} 0 \\ 1 \end{pmatrix}$ and $\begin{pmatrix} 0 & -1 \\ 1 & 0 \end{pmatrix}\begin{pmatrix} 0 \\ 1 \end{pmatrix} = \begin{pmatrix} -1 \\ 0 \end{pmatrix}$ respectively. The image of the unit square $OABC$ (see Fig. 5.4) is the congruent square $OA'B'C'$. If you now superimpose the two figures, you will see that the matrix $\mathbf{R}$ has carried out a rotation about the origin through $\frac{1}{2}\pi$ anticlockwise.

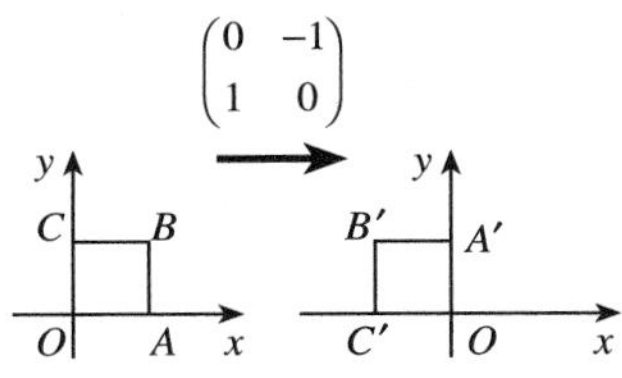

Fig. 5.4

Example 5.1.2
Illustrate the matrix $\mathbf{M}=\begin{pmatrix}-1 & 0\\ 0 & 1\end{pmatrix}$ geometrically. Identify the geometric transformation carried out by $\mathbf{M}$.

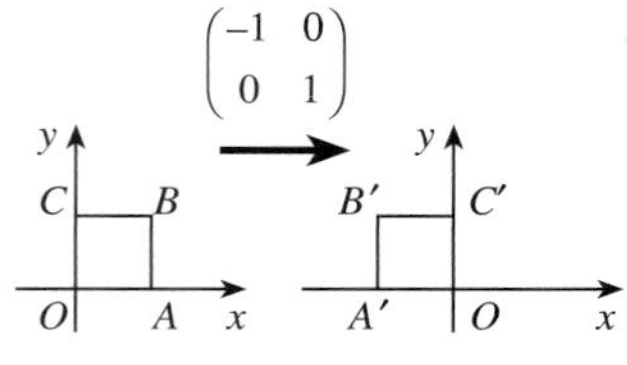

Fig. 5.5

The images of $\begin{pmatrix}1\\0\end{pmatrix}$ and $\begin{pmatrix}0\\1\end{pmatrix}$ are $\begin{pmatrix}-1 & 0\\ 0 & 1\end{pmatrix}\begin{pmatrix}1\\0\end{pmatrix}=\begin{pmatrix}-1\\0\end{pmatrix}$ and $\begin{pmatrix}-1 & 0\\ 0 & 1\end{pmatrix}\begin{pmatrix}0\\1\end{pmatrix}=\begin{pmatrix}0\\1\end{pmatrix}$ respectively. The image of the unit square $OABC$, shown in Fig. 5.5, is the congruent square $OA'B'C'$. Superimposing the figures shows that the matrix $\mathbf{M}$ has carried out a reflection in the y-axis.

Notice that the matrices in Examples 5.1.1 and 5.1.2 transform the unit square into squares with the same vertices, but that the vertices are lettered in different orders. This shows that you need to take care about the orientation of the image of the unit square to find whether or not the square has been 'flipped over'.

Example 5.1.3
Illustrate the matrix $\mathbf{M}=\begin{pmatrix}0.8 & 0.4\\ 0.4 & 0.2\end{pmatrix}$ geometrically.

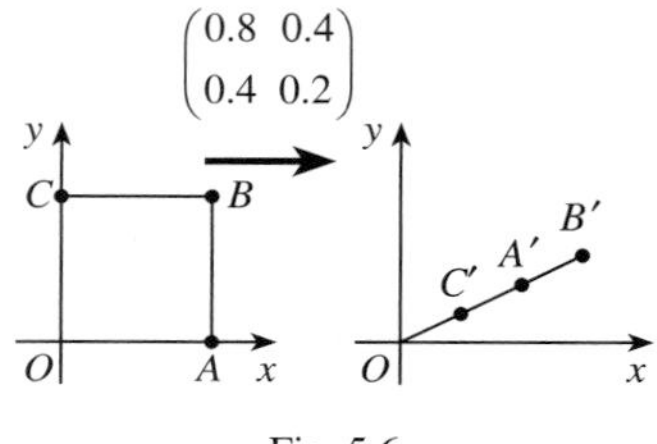

Fig. 5.6

Fig. 5.6 shows the image of the unit square. The 'parallelogram' with adjacent sides formed by the columns $\begin{pmatrix}0.8\\0.4\end{pmatrix}$ and $\begin{pmatrix}0.4\\0.2\end{pmatrix}$ of the matrix $\mathbf{M}$ has collapsed to a straight line because $\begin{pmatrix}0.8\\0.4\end{pmatrix}$ and $\begin{pmatrix}0.4\\0.2\end{pmatrix}$ lie in the same direction.

Although strictly speaking the shape $OA'B'C'$ in Fig. 5.6 is not a parallelogram, it is useful to think of it as a degenerate parallelogram. The opposite 'sides' OA' and $C'B'$ are equal and parallel, and so are the opposite sides OC' and $A'B'$; so in this sense it satisfies the rules for a parallelogram. It will be convenient not to regard this as an exception to the rule that matrices transform parallelograms to parallelograms, but to recognise that sometimes parallelograms may degenerate to straight lines.

Exercise 5A

1 Identify the geometric transformation carried out by each of the following matrices.

(a) $\begin{pmatrix}1 & 0\\ 0 & -1\end{pmatrix}$ (b) $\begin{pmatrix}0 & 1\\ 1 & 0\end{pmatrix}$ (c) $\begin{pmatrix}0 & 1\\ -1 & 0\end{pmatrix}$ (d) $\begin{pmatrix}1 & 1\\ 0 & 1\end{pmatrix}$

(e) $\begin{pmatrix}-1 & 0\\ 0 & -1\end{pmatrix}$ (f) $\begin{pmatrix}2 & 0\\ 0 & 1\end{pmatrix}$ (g) $\begin{pmatrix}-2 & 0\\ 0 & -2\end{pmatrix}$ (h) $\begin{pmatrix}1 & 1\\ 1 & 1\end{pmatrix}$

2 Draw a diagram to show the position vectors $\begin{pmatrix}0\\0\end{pmatrix}, \begin{pmatrix}5\\0\end{pmatrix}, \begin{pmatrix}5\\5\end{pmatrix}$ and $\begin{pmatrix}0\\5\end{pmatrix}$ before and after they have been transformed by the matrix $\mathbf{M}=\begin{pmatrix}0.8 & -0.6\\ 0.6 & 0.8\end{pmatrix}$. Identify the geometric transformation carried out by $\mathbf{M}$.

3 Interpret geometrically the transformation carried out by $\begin{pmatrix} 3 & -4 \\ 4 & 3 \end{pmatrix}$.

4 Describe the geometric transformation carried out by $\begin{pmatrix} 0 & 0 \\ 0 & 0 \end{pmatrix}$.

5 Prove that the transformation carried out by the matrix $\mathbf{M} = \begin{pmatrix} l^2 & lm \\ lm & m^2 \end{pmatrix}$, where $l^2 + m^2 = 1$, transforms every vector $\mathbf{a}$ onto a line, and find the angle between the vectors $\mathbf{Ma}$ and $\mathbf{Ma} - \mathbf{a}$.

6 Show that the matrix $\begin{pmatrix} 0 & 1 & 0 \\ 0 & 0 & 1 \\ 1 & 0 & 0 \end{pmatrix}$ represents a rotation about the line with equations $x = y = z$. Through what angle is this rotation, looking from the origin in the direction positive x, y and z?

5.2 Finding the matrix of a given transformation

Suppose that you know that a transformation can be carried out by a matrix. How can you find the matrix which carries out that transformation?

The simplest method is based on the fact that, if the unknown matrix is $\begin{pmatrix} p & q \\ r & s \end{pmatrix}$, then the image of $\begin{pmatrix} 1 \\ 0 \end{pmatrix}$ is $\begin{pmatrix} p \\ r \end{pmatrix}$ and the image of $\begin{pmatrix} 0 \\ 1 \end{pmatrix}$ is $\begin{pmatrix} q \\ s \end{pmatrix}$. Therefore, if you can find the images of the vectors $\begin{pmatrix} 1 \\ 0 \end{pmatrix}$ and $\begin{pmatrix} 0 \\ 1 \end{pmatrix}$, you can find the matrix $\begin{pmatrix} p & q \\ r & s \end{pmatrix}$.

It is not necessary to learn the matrices for each of the transformations which follow. If you understand the general method, you can write them down very quickly.

Rotation through an angle θ

Let $\mathbf{R}_\theta = \begin{pmatrix} a & b \\ c & d \end{pmatrix}$ represent a rotation through θ anticlockwise about the origin.

In Fig. 5.7, the unit square, shown dashed, has been rotated about the origin through an angle θ anticlockwise. Since the side of the square is 1 unit, the coordinates of A' and C' are $(\cos\theta, \sin\theta)$ and $(-\sin\theta, \cos\theta)$ respectively.

So the images of $\begin{pmatrix} 1 \\ 0 \end{pmatrix}$ and $\begin{pmatrix} 0 \\ 1 \end{pmatrix}$ are $\begin{pmatrix} \cos\theta \\ \sin\theta \end{pmatrix}$ and $\begin{pmatrix} -\sin\theta \\ \cos\theta \end{pmatrix}$. The matrix which carries out the transformation is $\mathbf{R}_\theta = \begin{pmatrix} \cos\theta & -\sin\theta \\ \sin\theta & \cos\theta \end{pmatrix}$.

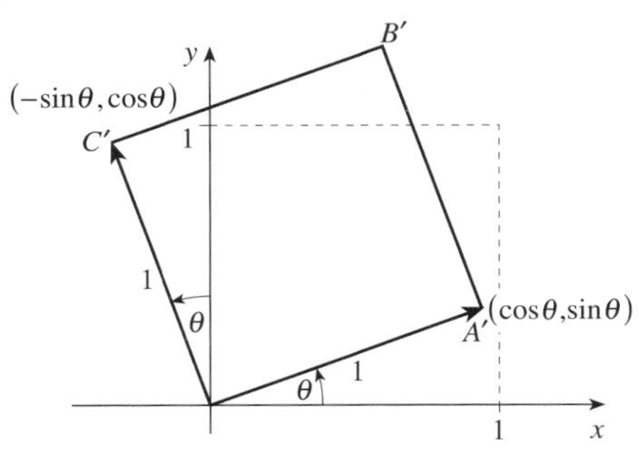

Fig. 5.7

In Example 5.1.1, you saw that the matrix $\begin{pmatrix} 0 & -1 \\ 1 & 0 \end{pmatrix}$ represents a rotation of $\frac{1}{2}\pi$. This is a special case of $\mathbf{R}_\theta = \begin{pmatrix} \cos\theta & -\sin\theta \\ \sin\theta & \cos\theta \end{pmatrix}$ with $\theta = \frac{1}{2}\pi$.

Reflection in the line at θ to the x-axis

In Fig. 5.8, the mirror makes an angle θ with the x-axis. The image, A', of $\begin{pmatrix} 1 \\ 0 \end{pmatrix}$ has position vector $\begin{pmatrix} \cos 2\theta \\ \sin 2\theta \end{pmatrix}$. The line OC' makes an angle of $\theta - \left(\frac{1}{2}\pi - \theta\right) = \frac{1}{2}\pi - \theta$ with the x-axis, so the image, C', of $\begin{pmatrix} 0 \\ 1 \end{pmatrix}$ is $\begin{pmatrix} \cos\left(\frac{1}{2}\pi - 2\theta\right) \\ -\sin\left(\frac{1}{2}\pi - 2\theta\right) \end{pmatrix}$, or $\begin{pmatrix} \sin 2\theta \\ -\cos 2\theta \end{pmatrix}$. Putting this information together, the matrix $\mathbf{M}_\theta$ which represents this transformation is given by

$$\mathbf{M}_\theta = \begin{pmatrix} \cos 2\theta & \sin 2\theta \\ \sin 2\theta & -\cos 2\theta \end{pmatrix}.$$

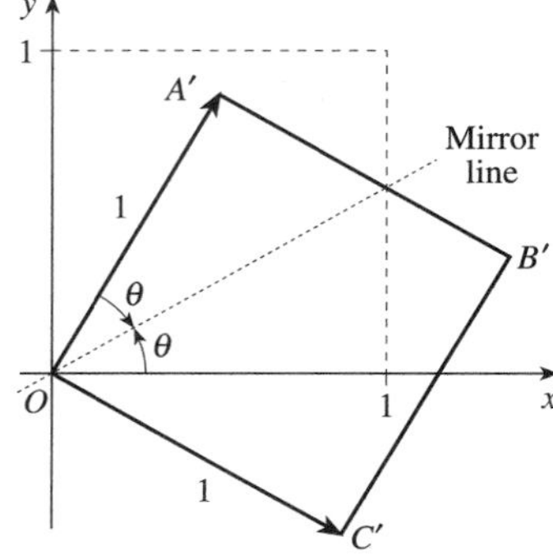

Fig. 5.8

In Example 5.1.2, you saw that the matrix $\begin{pmatrix} -1 & 0 \\ 0 & 1 \end{pmatrix}$ represents a reflection in the y-axis. This is a special case of $\mathbf{M}_\theta = \begin{pmatrix} \cos 2\theta & \sin 2\theta \\ \sin 2\theta & -\cos 2\theta \end{pmatrix}$ with $\theta = \frac{1}{2}\pi$.

Enlargement with centre the origin

If the scale factor of the enlargement is k, the image of $\begin{pmatrix} 1 \\ 0 \end{pmatrix}$ has position vector $\begin{pmatrix} k \\ 0 \end{pmatrix}$, and the image of $\begin{pmatrix} 0 \\ 1 \end{pmatrix}$ is $\begin{pmatrix} 0 \\ k \end{pmatrix}$. The matrix of the enlargement is $\begin{pmatrix} k & 0 \\ 0 & k \end{pmatrix}$.

Stretches parallel to the axes

Under a stretch in the x-direction with scale factor k, the image of $\begin{pmatrix} 1 \\ 0 \end{pmatrix}$ is $\begin{pmatrix} k \\ 0 \end{pmatrix}$ and the image of $\begin{pmatrix} 0 \\ 1 \end{pmatrix}$ is $\begin{pmatrix} 0 \\ 1 \end{pmatrix}$ (see Fig. 5.9).

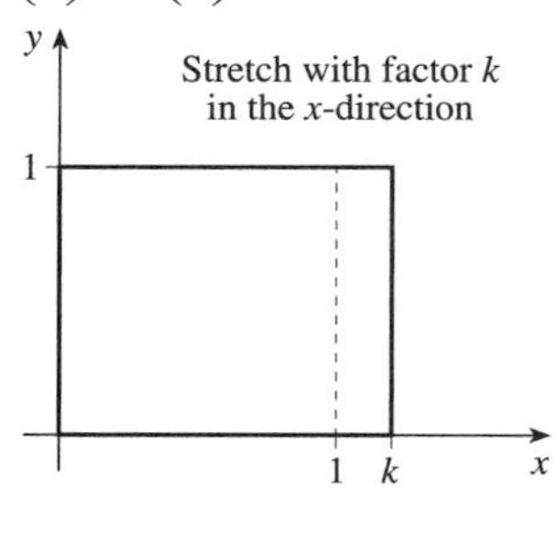

Fig. 5.9

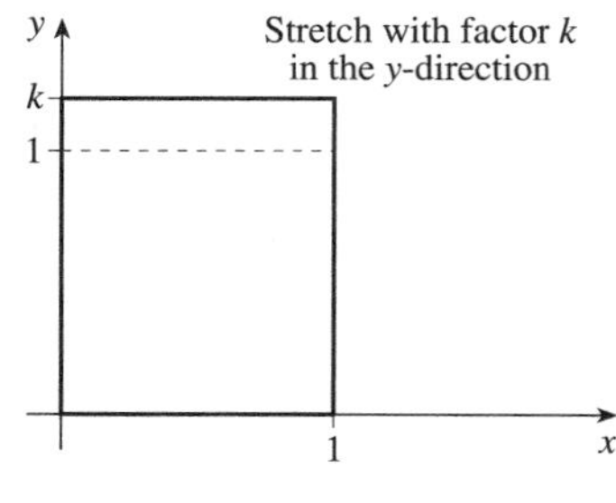

Fig. 5.10

The matrix of a stretch in the x-direction with scale factor k is $\begin{pmatrix} k & 0 \\ 0 & 1 \end{pmatrix}$. Similarly, from Fig. 5.10, the matrix of a stretch in the y-direction with scale factor k is $\begin{pmatrix} 1 & 0 \\ 0 & k \end{pmatrix}$.

Shears parallel to the axes

In a shear parallel to the x-axis, points on the x-axis remain fixed. Points not on the x-axis move parallel to the x-axis in proportion to their distances from the x-axis (see Fig. 5.10).

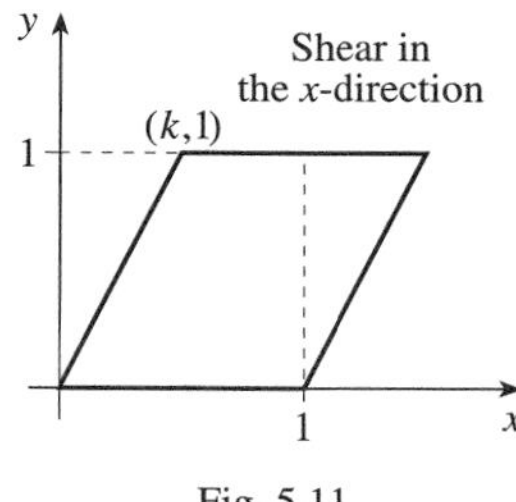

Fig. 5.11

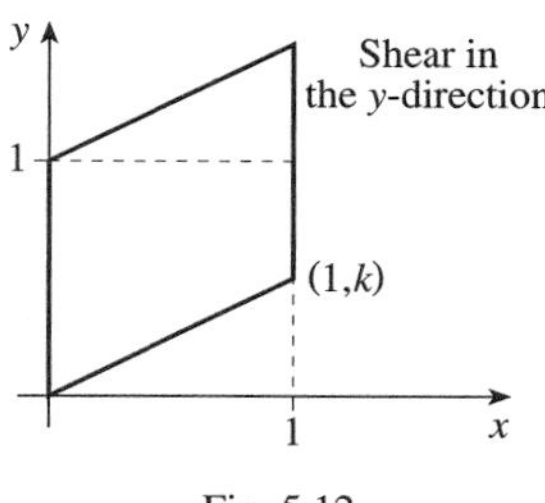

Fig. 5.12

From the images of $\begin{pmatrix}1\\0\end{pmatrix}$ and $\begin{pmatrix}0\\1\end{pmatrix}$ in Fig. 5.10, the matrix of a shear parallel to the x-axis is $\begin{pmatrix}1 & k\\0 & 1\end{pmatrix}$. And from the images of $\begin{pmatrix}1\\0\end{pmatrix}$ and $\begin{pmatrix}0\\1\end{pmatrix}$ in Fig. 5.11, $\begin{pmatrix}1 & 0\\k & 1\end{pmatrix}$ is the matrix of a shear parallel to the y-axis.

Note that you can describe a shear by the constant k, or by the angle $\cot^{-1} k$ through which lines parallel to the axis turn.

Example 5.2.1

Show that a reflection in the line $y = x\tan\theta$ followed by a reflection in the line $y = x\tan\phi$ is equivalent to a rotation about the origin, and find the angle of rotation.

The matrices which represent reflections in the lines $y = x\tan\theta$ and $y = x\tan\phi$ are $\begin{pmatrix}\cos 2\theta & \sin 2\theta\\ \sin 2\theta & -\cos 2\theta\end{pmatrix}$ and $\begin{pmatrix}\cos 2\phi & \sin 2\phi\\ \sin 2\phi & -\cos 2\phi\end{pmatrix}$. The vector $\begin{pmatrix}1\\0\end{pmatrix}$ is first transformed to $\begin{pmatrix}\cos 2\theta\\ \sin 2\theta\end{pmatrix}$, and subsequently to

$$\begin{pmatrix}\cos 2\phi & \sin 2\phi\\ \sin 2\phi & -\cos 2\phi\end{pmatrix}\begin{pmatrix}\cos 2\theta\\ \sin 2\theta\end{pmatrix} = \begin{pmatrix}\cos 2\phi\cos 2\theta + \sin 2\phi\sin 2\theta\\ \sin 2\phi\cos 2\theta + (-\cos 2\phi)\sin 2\theta\end{pmatrix}$$
$$= \begin{pmatrix}\cos 2(\phi-\theta)\\ \sin 2(\phi-\theta)\end{pmatrix}.$$

Similarly $\begin{pmatrix}0\\1\end{pmatrix}$ is first transformed to $\begin{pmatrix}\sin 2\theta\\ -\cos 2\theta\end{pmatrix}$, and subsequently to

$$\begin{pmatrix}\cos 2\phi & \sin 2\phi\\ \sin 2\phi & -\cos 2\phi\end{pmatrix}\begin{pmatrix}\sin 2\theta\\ -\cos 2\theta\end{pmatrix} = \begin{pmatrix}\cos 2\phi\sin 2\theta + \sin 2\phi(-\cos 2\theta)\\ \sin 2\phi\sin 2\theta + (-\cos 2\phi)(-\cos 2\theta)\end{pmatrix}$$
$$= \begin{pmatrix}-\sin 2(\phi-\theta)\\ \cos 2(\phi-\theta)\end{pmatrix}.$$

The matrix which represents the combined transformation is therefore

$$\begin{pmatrix}\cos 2(\phi-\theta) & -\sin 2(\phi-\theta)\\ \sin 2(\phi-\theta) & \cos 2(\phi-\theta)\end{pmatrix},$$

which represents a rotation through an angle of $2(\phi-\theta)$ anticlockwise.

Example 5.2.2
Given that a matrix $\mathbf{M}$ transforms $\begin{pmatrix}2\\1\end{pmatrix}$ to $\begin{pmatrix}1\\3\end{pmatrix}$ and $\begin{pmatrix}1\\1\end{pmatrix}$ to $\begin{pmatrix}3\\2\end{pmatrix}$, find $\mathbf{M}$.

Method 1 This is the 'brute force' method. Let $\mathbf{M}=\begin{pmatrix}a & b\\c & d\end{pmatrix}$.

Then, since $\mathbf{M}\begin{pmatrix}2\\1\end{pmatrix}=\begin{pmatrix}1\\3\end{pmatrix}$, $\begin{pmatrix}a & b\\c & d\end{pmatrix}\begin{pmatrix}2\\1\end{pmatrix}=\begin{pmatrix}1\\3\end{pmatrix}$ so $2a+b=1$ and $2c+d=3$.

Similarly, since $\begin{pmatrix}a & b\\c & d\end{pmatrix}\begin{pmatrix}1\\1\end{pmatrix}=\begin{pmatrix}3\\2\end{pmatrix}$, $a+b=3$ and $c+d=2$. Solving these equations gives $a=-2$, $b=5$, $c=1$ and $d=1$. Therefore $\mathbf{M}=\begin{pmatrix}-2 & 5\\1 & 1\end{pmatrix}$.

Method 2 This method is subtler.

As $\begin{pmatrix}2\\1\end{pmatrix}-\begin{pmatrix}1\\1\end{pmatrix}=\begin{pmatrix}1\\0\end{pmatrix}$, $\mathbf{M}\begin{pmatrix}1\\0\end{pmatrix}=\mathbf{M}\begin{pmatrix}2\\1\end{pmatrix}-\mathbf{M}\begin{pmatrix}1\\1\end{pmatrix}=\begin{pmatrix}1\\3\end{pmatrix}-\begin{pmatrix}3\\2\end{pmatrix}=\begin{pmatrix}-2\\1\end{pmatrix}$.

And since $\begin{pmatrix}0\\1\end{pmatrix}=2\begin{pmatrix}1\\1\end{pmatrix}-\begin{pmatrix}2\\1\end{pmatrix}$, $\mathbf{M}\begin{pmatrix}0\\1\end{pmatrix}=2\mathbf{M}\begin{pmatrix}1\\1\end{pmatrix}-\mathbf{M}\begin{pmatrix}2\\1\end{pmatrix}=2\begin{pmatrix}3\\2\end{pmatrix}-\begin{pmatrix}1\\3\end{pmatrix}=\begin{pmatrix}5\\1\end{pmatrix}$.

Finally, since the left column of $\mathbf{M}$ is the image of $\begin{pmatrix}1\\0\end{pmatrix}$ and the right column is the image of $\begin{pmatrix}0\\1\end{pmatrix}$, $\mathbf{M}=\begin{pmatrix}-2 & 5\\1 & 1\end{pmatrix}$.

To find the matrix $\mathbf{M}$ which carries out a given transformation:

find the image of $\begin{pmatrix}1\\0\end{pmatrix}$, which gives the first column of $\mathbf{M}$;

and the image of $\begin{pmatrix}0\\1\end{pmatrix}$, which gives the second column of $\mathbf{M}$.

Exercise 5B

1 Find the matrices corresponding to each of the following transformations:
(a) a reflection in the y-axis,
(b) a reflection in the line $y=-x$,
(c) a shear in which the position vector of the point $\begin{pmatrix}4\\3\end{pmatrix}$ is transformed to $\begin{pmatrix}7\\3\end{pmatrix}$ and the x-axis remains fixed.

2 Find the matrix which carries out an anticlockwise rotation about the origin of
(a) $\frac{1}{3}\pi$,
(b) $\tan^{-1}\dfrac{b}{a}$.

3 Find the matrix which carries out an **orthogonal projection** onto the line $5y=12x$. (The image of each point is the foot of the perpendicular from the point to the line.)

4 (a) Find the orthogonal projection of the position vector of the point (x, y, z) onto the line $\mathbf{r} = t\begin{pmatrix}1\\2\\2\end{pmatrix}$, and find the 3×3 matrix $\mathbf{M}$ which carries out this transformation.

(b) Show that all the vectors which are transformed to the position vector $s\begin{pmatrix}1\\2\\2\end{pmatrix}$ for a fixed $s \in \mathbb{R}$ lie in a plane, and find the equation of the plane.

(c) Show that $\mathbf{M}^2 = \mathbf{M}$ and that $(\mathbf{I}-\mathbf{M})^2 = \mathbf{I}-\mathbf{M}$ and interpret $\mathbf{I}-\mathbf{M}$ geometrically.

5.3 Successive transformations

Suppose one matrix transformation $\mathbf{M}$ is followed by another matrix transformation $\mathbf{N}$. Let $\mathbf{r}$ be any vector. Then, using the associative rule for multiplying matrices,

$$\mathbf{N}(\mathbf{M}\mathbf{r}) = (\mathbf{N}\mathbf{M})\mathbf{r},$$

so the matrix of the combined transformation is the product matrix $\mathbf{NM}$.

> The matrix product $\mathbf{NM}$ represents the matrix transformation $\mathbf{M}$ followed by the matrix transformation $\mathbf{N}$.

This reversal of order is the same as what happens when you compose functions, which you met in P2 Section 2.2.

Example 5.3.1
Use the matrix $\mathbf{R}_\theta$ to prove that $\cos 2\theta = \cos^2\theta - \sin^2\theta$ and $\sin 2\theta = 2\sin\theta\cos\theta$.

It was shown in Section 5.2 that $\mathbf{R}_\theta = \begin{pmatrix}\cos\theta & -\sin\theta\\ \sin\theta & \cos\theta\end{pmatrix}$.

To carry out a rotation of 2θ, you can rotate through an angle 2θ directly, in which case the matrix is $\mathbf{R}_{2\theta} = \begin{pmatrix}\cos 2\theta & -\sin 2\theta\\ \sin 2\theta & \cos 2\theta\end{pmatrix}$. Or alternatively, you could rotate first through θ, and then another θ, which you can do by multiplying the matrix $\mathbf{R}_\theta = \begin{pmatrix}\cos\theta & -\sin\theta\\ \sin\theta & \cos\theta\end{pmatrix}$ by itself.

Thus, $\mathbf{R}_{2\theta} = \mathbf{R}_\theta\mathbf{R}_\theta$; that is,

$$\begin{pmatrix}\cos 2\theta & -\sin 2\theta\\ \sin 2\theta & \cos 2\theta\end{pmatrix} = \begin{pmatrix}\cos\theta & -\sin\theta\\ \sin\theta & \cos\theta\end{pmatrix}\begin{pmatrix}\cos\theta & -\sin\theta\\ \sin\theta & \cos\theta\end{pmatrix}$$

$$= \begin{pmatrix}\cos\theta\cos\theta - \sin\theta\sin\theta & -\cos\theta\sin\theta - \sin\theta\cos\theta\\ \sin\theta\cos\theta + \cos\theta\sin\theta & -\sin\theta\sin\theta + \cos\theta\cos\theta\end{pmatrix}$$

$$= \begin{pmatrix}\cos^2\theta - \sin^2\theta & -2\sin\theta\cos\theta\\ 2\sin\theta\cos\theta & \cos^2\theta - \sin^2\theta\end{pmatrix}.$$

As these two matrices are equal, their elements are equal. So, looking at the first column, $\cos 2\theta = \cos^2\theta - \sin^2\theta$ and $\sin 2\theta = 2\sin\theta\cos\theta$.

Example 5.3.2
Use the matrices $\mathbf{M}_\theta$ and $\mathbf{M}_{\theta+\frac{1}{2}\pi}$ to prove that successive reflections in mirrors which are at right angles to each other are equivalent to a half-turn.

From Section 5.2, $\mathbf{M}_\theta = \begin{pmatrix} \cos 2\theta & \sin 2\theta \\ \sin 2\theta & -\cos 2\theta \end{pmatrix}$. Replacing θ by $\theta + \frac{1}{2}\pi$ gives

$$\mathbf{M}_{\theta+\frac{1}{2}\pi} = \begin{pmatrix} \cos(2\theta+\pi) & \sin(2\theta+\pi) \\ \sin(2\theta+\pi) & -\cos(2\theta+\pi) \end{pmatrix} = \begin{pmatrix} -\cos 2\theta & -\sin 2\theta \\ -\sin 2\theta & \cos 2\theta \end{pmatrix}.$$

Then
$$\mathbf{M}_{\theta+\frac{1}{2}\pi}\mathbf{M}_\theta = \begin{pmatrix} -\cos 2\theta & -\sin 2\theta \\ -\sin 2\theta & \cos 2\theta \end{pmatrix}\begin{pmatrix} \cos 2\theta & \sin 2\theta \\ \sin 2\theta & -\cos 2\theta \end{pmatrix}$$
$$= \begin{pmatrix} -\cos^2 2\theta - \sin^2 2\theta & -\cos 2\theta \sin 2\theta + \sin 2\theta \cos 2\theta \\ -\sin 2\theta \cos 2\theta + \cos 2\theta \sin 2\theta & -\sin^2 2\theta - \cos^2 2\theta \end{pmatrix}$$
$$= \begin{pmatrix} -1 & 0 \\ 0 & -1 \end{pmatrix}.$$

Since the last matrix represents a rotation of π, that is a half-turn, the product of successive reflections in mirrors that are at right angles to each other is equivalent to a half-turn.

Exercise 5C

1 Write down the matrices $\mathbf{A}$ and $\mathbf{B}$ which represent rotations of $\frac{1}{6}\pi$ and $\frac{1}{3}\pi$ anticlockwise about the origin. Verify that $\mathbf{B} = \mathbf{A}^2$, and that $\mathbf{AB} = \mathbf{BA}$, and interpret these geometrically.

2 A, B and C are the three points whose position vectors are $\begin{pmatrix} 1 \\ 0 \end{pmatrix}$, $\begin{pmatrix} 1 \\ 3 \end{pmatrix}$ and $\begin{pmatrix} 2 \\ 0 \end{pmatrix}$ respectively. Two matrices $\mathbf{P}$ and $\mathbf{Q}$ are given by $\mathbf{P} = \begin{pmatrix} 0 & -1 \\ 1 & 0 \end{pmatrix}$ and $\mathbf{Q} = \begin{pmatrix} 1 & 0 \\ 0 & -1 \end{pmatrix}$. When the position vectors of A, B and C are pre-multiplied by $\mathbf{P}$ (multiplied on the left by $\mathbf{P}$) they become the position vectors of A_1, B_1 and C_1, which in turn become the position vectors of A_2, B_2 and C_2 when they are pre-multiplied by $\mathbf{Q}$. What single matrix transforms ABC to $A_2B_2C_2$?

If $\mathbf{M} = \begin{pmatrix} 0 & 1 \\ -1 & 1 \end{pmatrix}$, verify that $\mathbf{M}^3 = \mathbf{P}^2$. State with a reason how many successive multiplications by $\mathbf{M}$ will restore ABC to its original position.

3 Let $\mathbf{M}$ be the matrix which represents a reflection in the line $y = x\tan\alpha$. Calculate the matrix $\mathbf{N} = \frac{1}{2}(\mathbf{I}+\mathbf{M})$, and verify that $\mathbf{N}^2 = \mathbf{N}$. Show that if $\mathbf{r}$ is any vector, then the vector $\mathbf{Nr}$ is parallel to $y = x\tan\alpha$, and that $\mathbf{r} - \mathbf{Nr}$ is perpendicular to $y = x\tan\alpha$. Identify the transformation carried out by $\mathbf{N}$ and interpret the equation $\mathbf{N}^2 = \mathbf{N}$ geometrically.

4 Let $\mathbf{M}$ be a matrix of the form $\mathbf{M} = \begin{pmatrix} a & -b \\ b & a \end{pmatrix}$ where $a, b \in \mathbb{R}$. Show that the product of two matrices of this type is another matrix of this type. Find the geometric transformation carried out by this matrix, and interpret your result in terms of complex numbers.

5 Use the matrices $\mathbf{R}_\theta$ and $\mathbf{R}_\phi$ to derive the formulae for $\sin(\theta+\phi)$ and $\cos(\theta+\phi)$.

Miscellaneous exercise 5

1 By thinking geometrically, find a matrix $\mathbf{M}$ other than the identity matrix such that $\mathbf{M}^3 = \mathbf{I}$.

2 Let $\mathbf{A}(\theta)$ and $\mathbf{B}(\theta)$ be the matrices $\begin{pmatrix} \cos\theta & \sin\theta \\ \sin\theta & -\cos\theta \end{pmatrix}$ and $\begin{pmatrix} \cos\theta & -\sin\theta \\ \sin\theta & \cos\theta \end{pmatrix}$ respectively.

(a) Interpret $\mathbf{A}(\theta)$ geometrically.

(b) Prove that $\mathbf{A}(\alpha)\mathbf{A}(\beta) = \mathbf{B}(\phi)$ where ϕ is to be determined in terms of α and β, and interpret the result geometrically.

(c) Prove that $\mathbf{A}(\alpha)\mathbf{A}(\beta)\mathbf{A}(\gamma) = \mathbf{A}(\gamma)\mathbf{A}(\beta)\mathbf{A}(\alpha)$ and interpret the result geometrically.

3 $\mathbf{S}$ is the matrix $\begin{pmatrix} 1 & 0 \\ 2 & 1 \end{pmatrix}$. Draw a sketch showing the unit square $OABC$, where O is the origin, A is $(1,0)$, B is $(1,1)$ and C is $(0,1)$, and its image $OA'B'C'$ when the column vectors representing the points are multiplied by $\mathbf{S}$. Describe the geometrical transformation involved. If a point P is known to lie on the line $y = -x$, what can you say about its image under the transformation represented by $\mathbf{S}$?

$\mathbf{R}$ is the matrix $\begin{pmatrix} 0 & -1 \\ -1 & 0 \end{pmatrix}$. State the geometrical transformation represented by $\mathbf{R}$.

Calculate the matrix $\mathbf{X}$ given by $\mathbf{X} = \mathbf{RSR}$, and state what geometrical transformation $\mathbf{X}$ represents.

4 The matrix $\mathbf{A}$ is $\begin{pmatrix} \frac{1}{\sqrt{2}} & -\frac{1}{\sqrt{2}} \\ \frac{1}{\sqrt{2}} & \frac{1}{\sqrt{2}} \end{pmatrix}$. By considering the effect on the unit square, or otherwise, describe the geometrical transformation represented by $\mathbf{A}$.

The matrix $\mathbf{C}$ is $\begin{pmatrix} 1 & -1 \\ \frac{1}{\sqrt{2}} & \frac{1}{\sqrt{2}} \end{pmatrix}$ and represents the combined effect of the transformation represented by $\mathbf{A}$ followed by the transformation represented by a matrix $\mathbf{B}$.

(a) Find $\mathbf{B}$.

(b) Describe fully the transformation represented by $\mathbf{B}$. (OCR)

5 The matrix $\begin{pmatrix} 5 & 10 \\ -3 & -8 \end{pmatrix}$ transforms the point (x, y) to the point (x', y'), where $\begin{pmatrix} x' \\ y' \end{pmatrix} = \begin{pmatrix} 5 & 10 \\ -3 & -8 \end{pmatrix}\begin{pmatrix} x \\ y \end{pmatrix}$. Find the values of m such that all points on the line $y = mx$ transform to points which are also on the line $y = mx$. (MEI, adapted)

6 A geometric transformation in the xy-plane is represented by the 2×2 matrix $\mathbf{R}$. The transformation may be considered as an anticlockwise rotation about the origin through 60° followed by a stretch in the x-direction with scale factor 2.

(a) Write down the matrix $\mathbf{P}$ which represents the rotation.

(b) Write down the matrix $\mathbf{Q}$ which represents the stretch.

(c) Hence find $\mathbf{R}$. (OCR)

7 The matrix **C** is $\begin{pmatrix} -1 & 0 \\ 0 & 2 \end{pmatrix}$. The geometrical transformation represented by **C** may be considered as the result of a reflection followed by a stretch. By considering the effect on the unit square, or otherwise, describe fully the reflection and the stretch.

Find matrices **A** and **B** which represent the reflection and the stretch respectively. (OCR)

8 The matrix **M** is given by $\mathbf{M} = \begin{pmatrix} 1 & -1 \\ 0 & 1 \end{pmatrix}$.

Describe fully the geometrical transformation represented by **M**.

The matrix **C** is given by $\mathbf{C} = \begin{pmatrix} \frac{1}{2} & \frac{1}{2}\left(\sqrt{3}-1\right) \\ -\frac{1}{2}\sqrt{3} & \frac{1}{2}\left(\sqrt{3}+1\right) \end{pmatrix}$.

C represents the combined effect of the transformation represented by **M** followed by the transformation represented by the matrix **B**.

(a) Find the matrix **B**.

(b) Describe fully the geometrical transformation represented by **B**. (OCR)

9* Interpret geometrically the transformation carried out by the matrix

$$\mathbf{L} = \begin{pmatrix} l^2 & lm & ln \\ ml & m^2 & mn \\ nl & nm & n^2 \end{pmatrix}$$

where $l^2 + m^2 + n^2 = 1$.

6 Determinants and inverses

This chapter takes a new look at simultaneous equations in terms of matrices and vectors. When you have completed it, you should know

- that a square matrix has an inverse if and only if its determinant is non-zero
- how to evaluate determinants of 2×2 and 3×3 matrices
- how the area scale factor of a transformation is related to the determinant of the corresponding matrix
- ways of finding the inverse of 2×2 and 3×3 matrices
- how to use inverse matrices to solve simultaneous equations.

6.1 A new interpretation for simultaneous equations

The key question to be investigated in this section and the next is, 'Under what conditions do the simultaneous equations $\left.\begin{aligned} ax+by=p \\ cx+dy=q \end{aligned}\right\}$ have a unique solution, no solution, or an infinite number of solutions?'

You can write the simultaneous equations $\left.\begin{aligned} ax+by=p \\ cx+dy=q \end{aligned}\right\}$ in at least two alternative forms: the matrix form $\begin{pmatrix} a & b \\ c & d \end{pmatrix}\begin{pmatrix} x \\ y \end{pmatrix}=\begin{pmatrix} p \\ q \end{pmatrix}$, and the vector form $x\begin{pmatrix} a \\ c \end{pmatrix}+y\begin{pmatrix} b \\ d \end{pmatrix}=\begin{pmatrix} p \\ q \end{pmatrix}$. It turns out to be easier to think about the equations in these forms when deriving a condition for them to have a unique solution.

In the vector form $x\begin{pmatrix} a \\ c \end{pmatrix}+y\begin{pmatrix} b \\ d \end{pmatrix}=\begin{pmatrix} p \\ q \end{pmatrix}$, solving the equations is equivalent to finding a combination of the vectors $\begin{pmatrix} a \\ c \end{pmatrix}$ and $\begin{pmatrix} b \\ d \end{pmatrix}$ which gives the vector $\begin{pmatrix} p \\ q \end{pmatrix}$.

Case 1 The vectors $\begin{pmatrix} a \\ c \end{pmatrix}$ and $\begin{pmatrix} b \\ d \end{pmatrix}$ are not in the same direction. The situation is shown in Fig. 6.1.

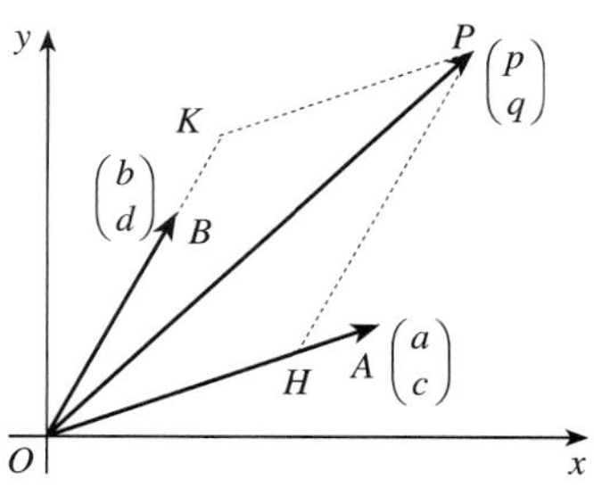

Fig. 6.1

Let $\overrightarrow{OA}=\begin{pmatrix} a \\ c \end{pmatrix}$, $\overrightarrow{OB}=\begin{pmatrix} b \\ d \end{pmatrix}$ and $\overrightarrow{OP}=\begin{pmatrix} p \\ q \end{pmatrix}$.

Now draw a line through P parallel to OB to meet OA (produced if necessary) in H, and another line through P parallel to OA to meet OB (produced if necessary) in K. Then $\overrightarrow{OH}+\overrightarrow{OK}=\overrightarrow{OP}$. But $\overrightarrow{OH}=r\overrightarrow{OA}$ and $\overrightarrow{OK}=s\overrightarrow{OB}$, where r and s are scalars, so $r\overrightarrow{OA}+s\overrightarrow{OB}=\overrightarrow{OP}$; that is,

$$r\begin{pmatrix} a \\ c \end{pmatrix}+s\begin{pmatrix} b \\ d \end{pmatrix}=\begin{pmatrix} p \\ q \end{pmatrix}.$$

Then $x = r$ and $y = s$ is the solution of the equations, and from the nature of the method of solution this solution is unique. Moreover, the fact that there is a solution does not depend on the values of p and q.

Case 2 The non-zero vectors $\begin{pmatrix} a \\ c \end{pmatrix}$ and $\begin{pmatrix} b \\ d \end{pmatrix}$ are in the same direction.

If $\begin{pmatrix} p \\ q \end{pmatrix}$ is not in the same direction as $\begin{pmatrix} a \\ c \end{pmatrix}$ and $\begin{pmatrix} b \\ d \end{pmatrix}$, as in Fig. 6.2, there is no solution to the equation $x\begin{pmatrix} a \\ c \end{pmatrix} + y\begin{pmatrix} b \\ d \end{pmatrix} = \begin{pmatrix} p \\ q \end{pmatrix}$ because every vector of the form $x\begin{pmatrix} a \\ c \end{pmatrix} + y\begin{pmatrix} b \\ d \end{pmatrix}$ has the same direction as $\begin{pmatrix} a \\ c \end{pmatrix}$ and $\begin{pmatrix} b \\ d \end{pmatrix}$.

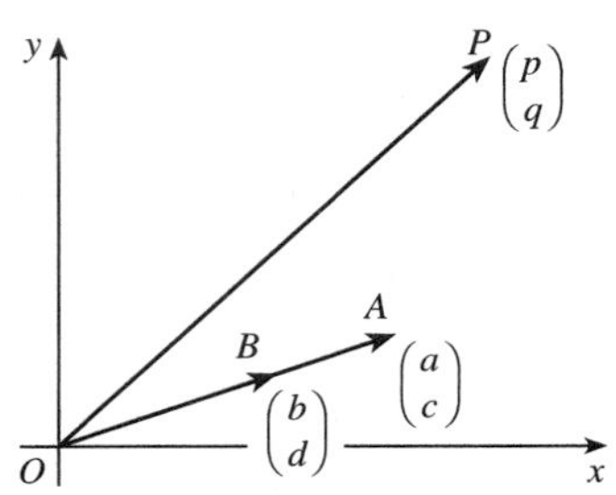

Fig. 6.2

If $\begin{pmatrix} p \\ q \end{pmatrix}$ is in the same direction as $\begin{pmatrix} a \\ c \end{pmatrix}$ and $\begin{pmatrix} b \\ d \end{pmatrix}$, shown in Fig. 6.3, you can find combinations of $\begin{pmatrix} a \\ c \end{pmatrix}$ and $\begin{pmatrix} b \\ d \end{pmatrix}$ which build up to give $\begin{pmatrix} p \\ q \end{pmatrix}$. You can express $\begin{pmatrix} p \\ q \end{pmatrix}$ in the form $k\begin{pmatrix} a \\ c \end{pmatrix}$ or as $l\begin{pmatrix} b \\ d \end{pmatrix}$.

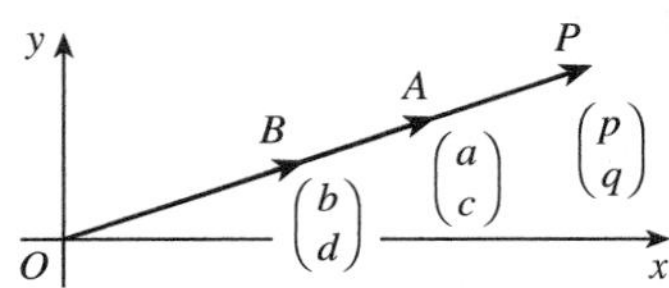

Fig. 6.3

Thus there are two solutions, $x = k$, $y = 0$, and $x = 0$, $y = l$, and actually many more that you can find.

The case when one or both of the vectors $\begin{pmatrix} a \\ c \end{pmatrix}$ and $\begin{pmatrix} b \\ d \end{pmatrix}$ is the zero vector is left for you to tackle, but you will see that, depending on the vector $\begin{pmatrix} p \\ q \end{pmatrix}$, there is either no solution or an infinite number of solutions to the equation $x\begin{pmatrix} a \\ c \end{pmatrix} + y\begin{pmatrix} b \\ d \end{pmatrix} = \begin{pmatrix} p \\ q \end{pmatrix}$.

Recall that the vectors $\begin{pmatrix} a \\ c \end{pmatrix}$ and $\begin{pmatrix} b \\ d \end{pmatrix}$ are the images of $\begin{pmatrix} 1 \\ 0 \end{pmatrix}$ and $\begin{pmatrix} 0 \\ 1 \end{pmatrix}$ under the matrix transformation $\begin{pmatrix} a & b \\ c & d \end{pmatrix}$, and that the image of the unit square under the transformation is the parallelogram whose adjacent sides are formed by the position vectors $\begin{pmatrix} a \\ c \end{pmatrix}$ and $\begin{pmatrix} b \\ d \end{pmatrix}$. Then in Case 1 you see that, if the vectors $\begin{pmatrix} a \\ c \end{pmatrix}$ and $\begin{pmatrix} b \\ d \end{pmatrix}$ form a parallelogram, the equations $x\begin{pmatrix} a \\ c \end{pmatrix} + y\begin{pmatrix} b \\ d \end{pmatrix} = \begin{pmatrix} p \\ q \end{pmatrix}$ have a unique solution; but if the parallelogram collapses, there is either no solution or an infinite number of solutions.

You can summarise the result of the discussion as follows:

The simultaneous equations $\left.\begin{aligned} ax+by=p \\ cx+dy=q \end{aligned}\right\}$,

matrix equation $\begin{pmatrix} a & b \\ c & d \end{pmatrix}\begin{pmatrix} x \\ y \end{pmatrix}=\begin{pmatrix} p \\ q \end{pmatrix}$ and

vector equation $x\begin{pmatrix} a \\ c \end{pmatrix}+y\begin{pmatrix} b \\ d \end{pmatrix}=\begin{pmatrix} p \\ q \end{pmatrix}$, which are equivalent,

have a unique solution for x and y if, and only if, the parallelogram whose adjacent sides are formed by the position vectors $\begin{pmatrix} a \\ c \end{pmatrix}$ and $\begin{pmatrix} b \\ d \end{pmatrix}$ does not collapse.

The previous analysis was essentially geometric in character. In the next section, the geometric result in the shaded box above is used to derive an algebraic condition for the equations to have a unique solution.

6.2 Determinants of 2×2 matrices

One way to determine whether or not the parallelogram described in the shaded box collapses is to find an expression for its area. The parallelogram collapses if the area is zero.

Let $\mathbf{M}=\begin{pmatrix} a & b \\ c & d \end{pmatrix}$. The matrix $\mathbf{M}$ transforms the unit position vectors $\begin{pmatrix} 1 \\ 0 \end{pmatrix}$ and $\begin{pmatrix} 0 \\ 1 \end{pmatrix}$ into $\begin{pmatrix} a \\ c \end{pmatrix}$ and $\begin{pmatrix} b \\ d \end{pmatrix}$, so it transforms the unit square $OABC$ into the parallelogram $OA'B'C'$ shown in Fig. 6.4, with coordinates $(0,0)$, (a,c), $(a+b,c+d)$ and (b,d).

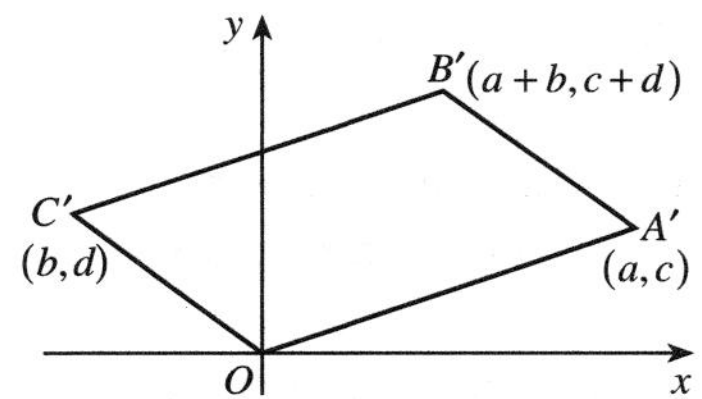

Fig. 6.4

Now think in three dimensions with a z-axis coming out of the paper towards you. The vectors $\begin{pmatrix} a \\ c \end{pmatrix}$ and $\begin{pmatrix} b \\ d \end{pmatrix}$ become $\begin{pmatrix} a \\ c \\ 0 \end{pmatrix}$ and $\begin{pmatrix} b \\ d \\ 0 \end{pmatrix}$. Recalling that $\mathbf{p}\times\mathbf{q}=|\mathbf{p}||\mathbf{q}|\sin\theta\,\hat{\mathbf{n}}$, the area of the parallelogram is

$$\left|\begin{pmatrix} a \\ c \\ 0 \end{pmatrix}\times\begin{pmatrix} b \\ d \\ 0 \end{pmatrix}\right|=\left|\begin{pmatrix} 0 \\ 0 \\ ad-bc \end{pmatrix}\right|=|ad-bc|.$$

The quantity $ad-bc$ is called the **determinant** of the matrix $\mathbf{M}=\begin{pmatrix} a & b \\ c & d \end{pmatrix}$. It is denoted by $\det\mathbf{M}$.

For the 2×2 matrix $\mathbf{M}=\begin{pmatrix} a & b \\ c & d \end{pmatrix}$, $\det\mathbf{M}=\det\begin{pmatrix} a & b \\ c & d \end{pmatrix}=ad-bc$.

An alternative notation for the determinant is $\begin{vmatrix} a & b \\ c & d \end{vmatrix}$, *but this has the disadvantage that the vertical lines can be confused with the notation for modulus.*

The area of $OA'B'C'$ is actually $|ad-bc|$, not $ad-bc$; but under what circumstances is $ad-bc$ negative? In Fig. 6.5, you would calculate the area as $\left|\begin{pmatrix} b \\ d \\ 0 \end{pmatrix} \times \begin{pmatrix} a \\ c \\ 0 \end{pmatrix}\right| = \left|\begin{pmatrix} 0 \\ 0 \\ bc-ad \end{pmatrix}\right|$.

But what is it that distinguishes Fig. 6.5 from Fig. 6.4? If you go round the perimeter of the parallelogram, taking the vertices in the order O, A', B', C', then in Fig. 6.4 the sense is anticlockwise, which is the same as in the original unit square $OABC$; but in Fig. 6.5 the sense is clockwise.

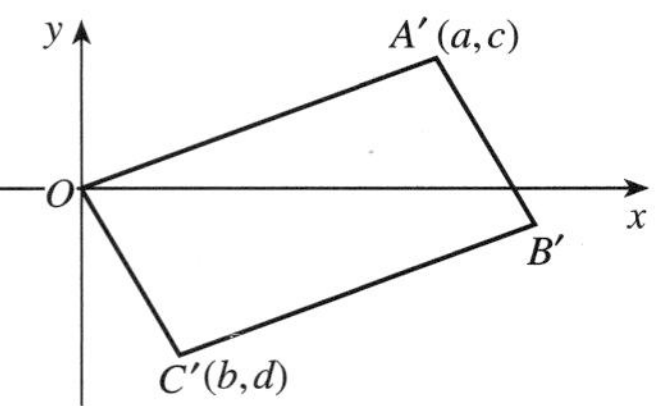

Fig. 6.5

In Fig. 6.5, the right-handed rule for the vector product (Section 3.1) means that the sense of the vector product is into the paper, that is in the opposite direction from the sense in Fig. 6.4. In both cases the following rule holds.

> When the unit square is transformed by the matrix $\mathbf{M} = \begin{pmatrix} a & b \\ c & d \end{pmatrix}$ into a parallelogram, the area of the parallelogram is given by
>
> $$|\det \mathbf{M}| = |ad-bc|.$$
>
> If $ad-bc>0$ the sense in which the perimeter of the parallelogram is traced is unaltered by the transformation; if $ad-bc<0$ the sense is reversed.

You can see the effect of the sign in the determinant by turning back to Chapter 5 and comparing Examples 5.1.1 and 5.1.2. In Example 5.1.1, $\det \mathbf{R} = 0\times 0-(-1)\times 1 = 1$, and the perimeter $OA'B'C'$ in Fig. 5.4 is traced anticlockwise. In Example 5.1.2, $\det \mathbf{M} = (-1)\times 1 - 0\times 0 = -1$, and the perimeter in Fig. 5.5 is traced clockwise. Rotation preserves sense, but reflection reverses it.

If the object which is transformed is a shape other than the unit square, then the area of its image is still found by multiplying the original area by $|\det \mathbf{M}|$. For example, looking back to Fig. 5.3, the ratio of the area of the six parallelograms on the right to the area of the corresponding six squares on the left is the same as the ratio of the area of the parallelogram with the thick border to the area of the unit square, which is $\det \mathbf{M}$. So the rule can be generalised as follows.

> When a region is transformed by the 2×2 matrix $\mathbf{M}$, its area is multiplied by the area scale factor $|\det \mathbf{M}|$. The sense in which the perimeter is described is unaltered if $\det \mathbf{M} > 0$, reversed if $\det \mathbf{M} < 0$.

A special case is that, in Fig. 6.4, the parallelogram collapses if $\det \mathbf{M} = 0$. So the geometric condition of Section 6.1 can now be expressed in terms of the determinant.

The simultaneous equations $\left.\begin{matrix} ax+by=p \\ cx+dy=q \end{matrix}\right\}$,

matrix equation $\begin{pmatrix} a & b \\ c & d \end{pmatrix}\begin{pmatrix} x \\ y \end{pmatrix}=\begin{pmatrix} p \\ q \end{pmatrix}$ and

vector equation $x\begin{pmatrix} a \\ c \end{pmatrix}+y\begin{pmatrix} b \\ d \end{pmatrix}=\begin{pmatrix} p \\ q \end{pmatrix}$, which are all equivalent,

have a unique solution for x and y if, and only if, $\det\begin{pmatrix} a & b \\ c & d \end{pmatrix} \neq 0$.

Compare the 'determinant', which determines whether or not a set of simultaneous equations has a unique solution, with the 'discriminant' of a quadratic. Both are readily computable indicators of whether a more subtle condition holds.

Determinants have the important property that the determinant of the product of two matrices is equal to the product of their determinants.

Theorem If $\mathbf{M}=\begin{pmatrix} a & b \\ c & d \end{pmatrix}$ and $\mathbf{N}=\begin{pmatrix} e & f \\ g & h \end{pmatrix}$, then $\det(\mathbf{NM})=\det\mathbf{N}\det\mathbf{M}$.

Proof You can think of this in either algebraic or geometric terms, so two proofs are given.

Method 1 Since $\mathbf{NM}=\begin{pmatrix} ea+fc & eb+fd \\ ga+hc & gb+hd \end{pmatrix}$,

$$\det(\mathbf{NM})=(ea+fc)(gb+hd)-(eb+fd)(ga+hc).$$

You have to show that this is equal to $\det\mathbf{N}\times\det\mathbf{M}$, which is

$$(eh-fg)(ad-bc).$$

You can check for yourself that the results of multiplying out these two expressions are the same.

Method 2 If you apply the transformations $\mathbf{M}$ and $\mathbf{N}$ in succession to any object, the area is multiplied first by $|\det\mathbf{M}|$ and then by $|\det\mathbf{N}|$, so the combined transformation $\mathbf{NM}$ multiplies the area by $|\det\mathbf{N}|\times|\det\mathbf{M}|$. Therefore $|\det(\mathbf{NM})|=|\det\mathbf{N}|\times|\det\mathbf{M}|$.

Also, the sense is preserved in the combined transformation if, in both transformations, the sense is either preserved or reversed. That is, $\det(\mathbf{NM})>0$ if both $\det\mathbf{M}>0$ and $\det\mathbf{N}>0$, or both $\det\mathbf{M}<0$ and $\det\mathbf{N}<0$; in either case, $\det\mathbf{N}\times\det\mathbf{M}>0$. Otherwise, $\det(\mathbf{NM})<0$ and $\det\mathbf{N}\times\det\mathbf{M}<0$.

Therefore, since the two sides agree both in modulus and in sign,

$$\det(\mathbf{NM})=\det\mathbf{N}\det\mathbf{M}.$$

For 2×2 matrices **N** and **M**,

$$\det(\mathbf{NM}) = \det \mathbf{N} \det \mathbf{M}.$$

Example 6.2.1
Find the determinants of

(a) the rotation matrix $\begin{pmatrix} \cos\theta & -\sin\theta \\ \sin\theta & \cos\theta \end{pmatrix}$, (b) the reflection matrix $\begin{pmatrix} \cos 2\theta & \sin 2\theta \\ \sin 2\theta & -\cos 2\theta \end{pmatrix}$.

Method 1 (a) $\det\begin{pmatrix} \cos\theta & -\sin\theta \\ \sin\theta & \cos\theta \end{pmatrix} = \cos\theta\cos\theta - (-\sin\theta)\sin\theta = \cos^2\theta + \sin^2\theta = 1.$

(b) $\det\begin{pmatrix} \cos 2\theta & \sin 2\theta \\ \sin 2\theta & -\cos 2\theta \end{pmatrix} = \cos 2\theta(-\cos 2\theta) - \sin 2\theta \sin 2\theta$

$$= -\cos^2 2\theta - \sin^2 2\theta = -1.$$

Method 2 (a) Since $\begin{pmatrix} \cos\theta & -\sin\theta \\ \sin\theta & \cos\theta \end{pmatrix}$ is a rotation the area scale factor is 1 and the sense of any vertices is anticlockwise, so $\det\begin{pmatrix} \cos\theta & -\sin\theta \\ \sin\theta & \cos\theta \end{pmatrix} = 1.$

(b) Since $\begin{pmatrix} \cos 2\theta & \sin 2\theta \\ \sin 2\theta & -\cos 2\theta \end{pmatrix}$ is a reflection, the area scale factor is 1, but the sense of any vertices is clockwise. Therefore $\det\begin{pmatrix} \cos 2\theta & \sin 2\theta \\ \sin 2\theta & -\cos 2\theta \end{pmatrix} = -1.$

6.3 Determinants of 3×3 matrices

All of the previous theory applies, with obvious adjustments, to sets of three simultaneous equations with three unknowns. The main difference is the form of the expression for the determinant.

It helps to begin by making a change in notation. If you stick with single letters for coefficients, you use up to 15 different letters in writing the equations. So it pays to economise by using a suffix notation, with a_1, a_2 and a_3 as the coefficients of x in the three equations, b_1, b_2 and b_3 as the coefficients of y, and so on.

In the space of three dimensions a unit cube is transformed by a matrix **M** into a solid called a parallelepiped. The position vectors $\mathbf{i} = \begin{pmatrix} 1 \\ 0 \\ 0 \end{pmatrix}$, $\mathbf{j} = \begin{pmatrix} 0 \\ 1 \\ 0 \end{pmatrix}$ and $\mathbf{k} = \begin{pmatrix} 0 \\ 0 \\ 1 \end{pmatrix}$, which represent the edges of the unit cube through the origin, are transformed into the vectors $\mathbf{a} = \begin{pmatrix} a_1 \\ a_2 \\ a_3 \end{pmatrix}$, $\mathbf{b} = \begin{pmatrix} b_1 \\ b_2 \\ b_3 \end{pmatrix}$ and $\mathbf{c} = \begin{pmatrix} c_1 \\ c_2 \\ c_3 \end{pmatrix}$ by the matrix $\mathbf{M} = \begin{pmatrix} a_1 & b_1 & c_1 \\ a_2 & b_2 & c_2 \\ a_3 & b_3 & c_3 \end{pmatrix}$. Fig. 6.6 shows the cube under the transformation **M**. The determinant of **M** is a number which measures the volume scale factor of the transformation.

The volume of a parallelepiped is calculated as the area of one of the parallelogram faces multiplied by the corresponding 'height', that is the distance between that face and the face parallel to it. The area of the face bounded by $\mathbf{b}$ and $\mathbf{c}$ is $|\mathbf{b}||\mathbf{c}|\sin\theta$, where θ is the angle between $\mathbf{b}$ and $\mathbf{c}$. Its magnitude is the same as that of $\mathbf{b}\times\mathbf{c}$. See Section 3.1.

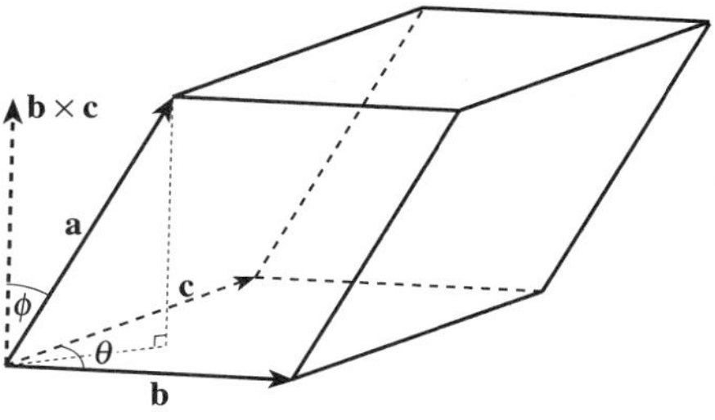

Fig. 6.6

The height of the parallelepiped is $|\mathbf{a}|\cos\phi$, where ϕ is the angle between the vector $\mathbf{a}$ and the vector $\mathbf{b}\times\mathbf{c}$. The magnitude of the volume is therefore the same as the scalar product of $\mathbf{a}$ with $\mathbf{b}\times\mathbf{c}$, that is $\mathbf{a}\cdot(\mathbf{b}\times\mathbf{c})$. Then

$$\begin{aligned}\mathbf{a}\cdot(\mathbf{b}\times\mathbf{c}) &= \begin{pmatrix}a_1\\a_2\\a_3\end{pmatrix}\cdot\begin{pmatrix}b_2c_3-b_3c_2\\b_3c_1-b_1c_3\\b_1c_2-b_2c_1\end{pmatrix}\\&= a_1(b_2c_3-b_3c_2)+a_2(b_3c_1-b_1c_3)+a_3(b_1c_2-b_2c_1)\\&= a_1b_2c_3-a_1b_3c_2+a_2b_3c_1-a_2b_1c_3+a_3b_1c_2-a_3b_2c_1.\end{aligned}$$

This last expression is denoted by $\det\begin{pmatrix}a_1&b_1&c_1\\a_2&b_2&c_2\\a_3&b_3&c_3\end{pmatrix}$ or by $\begin{vmatrix}a_1&b_1&c_1\\a_2&b_2&c_2\\a_3&b_3&c_3\end{vmatrix}$. The best way to calculate the determinant is to use the fact that

$$\det\begin{pmatrix}a_1&b_1&c_1\\a_2&b_2&c_2\\a_3&b_3&c_3\end{pmatrix}=\mathbf{a}\cdot(\mathbf{b}\times\mathbf{c}).$$

It can be shown that, as in the case of equations with two unknowns:

> The equations $\begin{matrix}a_1x+b_1y+c_1z=p\\a_2x+b_2y+c_2z=q\\a_3x+b_3y+c_3z=r\end{matrix}$, $\begin{pmatrix}a_1&b_1&c_1\\a_2&b_2&c_2\\a_3&b_3&c_3\end{pmatrix}\begin{pmatrix}x\\y\\z\end{pmatrix}=\begin{pmatrix}p\\q\\r\end{pmatrix}$ and
>
> $x\begin{pmatrix}a_1\\a_2\\a_3\end{pmatrix}+y\begin{pmatrix}b_1\\b_2\\b_3\end{pmatrix}+z\begin{pmatrix}c_1\\c_2\\c_3\end{pmatrix}=\begin{pmatrix}p\\q\\r\end{pmatrix}$, which are equivalent,
>
> have a unique solution for x, y and z if, and only if, $\det\begin{pmatrix}a_1&b_1&c_1\\a_2&b_2&c_2\\a_3&b_3&c_3\end{pmatrix}\neq 0$.

In the same way as for 2×2 matrices, it is also true that:

> For 3×3 matrices $\mathbf{M}$ and $\mathbf{N}$, $\det(\mathbf{NM})=\det\mathbf{N}\det\mathbf{M}$.

In three dimensions, the sign of the determinant indicates the configuration of the vectors $\mathbf{a}$, $\mathbf{b}$ and $\mathbf{c}$. Fig. 6.6 shows these forming a right-handed set; that is, if you point the first and middle fingers of your right hand in the $\mathbf{a}$ and $\mathbf{b}$ directions, your thumb can be pointed in the $\mathbf{c}$ direction. If $\mathbf{a}$, $\mathbf{b}$ and $\mathbf{c}$ form a right-handed set, $\det \mathbf{M} > 0$; if they form a left-handed set, $\det \mathbf{M} < 0$.

There is an important symmetry in the expression for the determinant of a 3×3 matrix. You can easily check that if $\mathbf{a}$, $\mathbf{b}$ and $\mathbf{c}$ form a right-handed set, then so do $\mathbf{b}$, $\mathbf{c}$ and $\mathbf{a}$ and $\mathbf{c}$, $\mathbf{a}$ and $\mathbf{b}$. So the volume of a parallelepiped can be calculated equally well as $\mathbf{b}\cdot(\mathbf{c}\times\mathbf{a})$ or as $\mathbf{c}\cdot(\mathbf{a}\times\mathbf{b})$. It follows that:

$$\mathbf{a}\cdot(\mathbf{b}\times\mathbf{c}) = \mathbf{b}\cdot(\mathbf{c}\times\mathbf{a}) = \mathbf{c}\cdot(\mathbf{a}\times\mathbf{b}).$$

But if you change the order of any two letters, the sign is reversed. For example, if $\mathbf{a}$, $\mathbf{b}$ and $\mathbf{c}$ form a right-handed set then $\mathbf{a}$, $\mathbf{c}$ and $\mathbf{b}$ form a left-handed set, so that

$$\mathbf{a}\cdot(\mathbf{c}\times\mathbf{b}) = -\det \mathbf{M}.$$

Example 6.3.1
Calculate the determinant of the matrix $\mathbf{M} = \begin{pmatrix} 1 & 2 & 3 \\ 4 & 5 & 6 \\ 7 & 8 & 10 \end{pmatrix}$.

$$\mathbf{b}\times\mathbf{c} = \begin{pmatrix} 2 \\ 5 \\ 8 \end{pmatrix} \times \begin{pmatrix} 3 \\ 6 \\ 10 \end{pmatrix} = \begin{pmatrix} 50-48 \\ 24-20 \\ 12-15 \end{pmatrix} = \begin{pmatrix} 2 \\ 4 \\ -3 \end{pmatrix}, \text{ so } \det \mathbf{M} = \begin{pmatrix} 1 \\ 4 \\ 7 \end{pmatrix} \cdot \begin{pmatrix} 2 \\ 4 \\ -3 \end{pmatrix} = 2 + 16 - 21 = -3.$$

Try for yourself working out the determinant as $\begin{pmatrix} 2 \\ 5 \\ 8 \end{pmatrix} \cdot \begin{pmatrix} 3 \\ 6 \\ 10 \end{pmatrix} \times \begin{pmatrix} 1 \\ 2 \\ 3 \end{pmatrix}$ or $\begin{pmatrix} 3 \\ 6 \\ 10 \end{pmatrix} \cdot \begin{pmatrix} 1 \\ 2 \\ 3 \end{pmatrix} \times \begin{pmatrix} 2 \\ 5 \\ 8 \end{pmatrix}$.

Example 6.3.2
Find the values of k such that $\det \begin{pmatrix} 1 & k & 0 \\ 3 & 0 & k \\ k & 1 & 1 \end{pmatrix} = 0$. Interpret your solution in terms of simultaneous equations.

$$\mathbf{b}\times\mathbf{c} = \begin{pmatrix} k \\ 0 \\ 1 \end{pmatrix} \times \begin{pmatrix} 0 \\ k \\ 1 \end{pmatrix} = \begin{pmatrix} -k \\ -k \\ k^2 \end{pmatrix}, \text{ so } \det \begin{pmatrix} 1 & k & 0 \\ 3 & 0 & k \\ k & 1 & 1 \end{pmatrix} = \begin{pmatrix} 1 \\ 3 \\ k \end{pmatrix} \cdot \begin{pmatrix} -k \\ -k \\ k^2 \end{pmatrix} = -k - 3k + k^3 = k^3 - 4k.$$

Thus the determinant is zero when $k^3 - 4k = 0$, that is when $k = 0, \pm 2$.

This shows that the equations $\left.\begin{aligned} x + ky \quad &= p \\ 3x \quad + kz &= q \\ kx + y + z &= r \end{aligned}\right\}$ do not have a unique solution when $k = 0, \pm 2$.

You can check this for yourself by putting these values of k in the equations and solving them by the methods in Section 1.6.

Example 6.3.3

Let $\mathbf{M} = \begin{pmatrix} a_1 & b_1 & c_1 \\ a_2 & b_2 & c_2 \\ a_3 & b_3 & c_3 \end{pmatrix}$, and consider $\mathbf{N} = \begin{pmatrix} a_1 & b_1 + ka_1 & c_1 \\ a_2 & b_2 + ka_2 & c_2 \\ a_3 & b_3 + ka_3 & c_3 \end{pmatrix}$, where $\mathbf{N}$ is the matrix found by adding k times the first column to the second. Prove that $\det \mathbf{N} = \det \mathbf{M}$.

$$\begin{aligned} \text{Then } \det \mathbf{N} &= \mathbf{a}\cdot((\mathbf{b}+k\mathbf{a})\times\mathbf{c}) = \mathbf{a}\cdot((\mathbf{b}\times\mathbf{c})+(k\mathbf{a}\times\mathbf{c})) \\ &= \mathbf{a}\cdot(\mathbf{b}\times\mathbf{c}) + \mathbf{a}\cdot(k\mathbf{a}\times\mathbf{c}) \\ &= \mathbf{a}\cdot(\mathbf{b}\times\mathbf{c}) + k\mathbf{a}\cdot(\mathbf{a}\times\mathbf{c}) \\ &= \det\mathbf{M} + k\mathbf{a}\cdot(\mathbf{a}\times\mathbf{c}). \end{aligned}$$

From the previous shaded box, with $\mathbf{a}$ written in place of $\mathbf{b}$,

$$\mathbf{a}\cdot(\mathbf{a}\times\mathbf{c}) = \mathbf{a}\cdot(\mathbf{c}\times\mathbf{a}) = \mathbf{c}\cdot(\mathbf{a}\times\mathbf{a}).$$

So, leaving out the middle part of the equation, $\mathbf{a}\cdot(\mathbf{a}\times\mathbf{c}) = \mathbf{c}\cdot(\mathbf{a}\times\mathbf{a})$. But $\mathbf{a}\times\mathbf{a} = 0$, so $\mathbf{c}\cdot(\mathbf{a}\times\mathbf{a}) = 0$ and $\mathbf{a}\cdot(\mathbf{a}\times\mathbf{c}) = 0$. Therefore $\det\mathbf{N} = \det\mathbf{M} + k\times 0 = \det\mathbf{M}$.

Investigate for yourself the corresponding results for other columns.

You can interpret this result geometrically by noticing that the parallelepiped with $\mathbf{a}$, $\mathbf{b}$ and $\mathbf{c}$ as adjacent edges is transformed into the parallelepiped with $\mathbf{a}$, $\mathbf{b}+k\mathbf{a}$ and $\mathbf{c}$ as adjacent edges by a shear. Just as in two dimensions shears do not alter area, in three dimensions shears do not alter volume. Also the sense of the vertices is unchanged, so $\det\mathbf{N} = \det\mathbf{M}$.

Exercise 6A

1 Find the value of each of the following determinants.

(a) $\begin{vmatrix} 1 & -2 \\ -3 & 6 \end{vmatrix}$ (b) $\begin{vmatrix} \cosh\alpha & \sinh\alpha \\ \sinh\alpha & \cosh\alpha \end{vmatrix}$ (c) $\begin{vmatrix} t & 0 \\ 0 & t^{-1} \end{vmatrix}$ $(t \neq 0)$

2 Find the value of the determinant of each of the following matrices.

(a) $\begin{pmatrix} \cos n\theta & \sin n\theta \\ \sin n\theta & \cos n\theta \end{pmatrix}$ (b) $\begin{pmatrix} \cos n\theta & -\sin n\theta \\ \sin n\theta & \cos n\theta \end{pmatrix}$ (c) $\begin{pmatrix} \cosh\alpha & \sinh\alpha \\ \sinh\alpha & -\cosh\alpha \end{pmatrix}$

3 Find the value(s) of α for which the following equations do not have unique solutions.

(a) $\left.\begin{aligned} \alpha x + y &= p \\ x + \alpha y &= q \end{aligned}\right\}$ (b) $\left.\begin{aligned} \alpha x + y &= ky \\ x + \alpha y &= kx \end{aligned}\right\}$ (c) $\left.\begin{aligned} x\cos\alpha + y\sin\alpha &= p \\ x\cos\beta + y\sin\beta &= q \end{aligned}\right\}$

4 Find the value of each of the following determinants.

(a) $\begin{vmatrix} 1 & 2 & 3 \\ 4 & 5 & 6 \\ 7 & 8 & 10 \end{vmatrix}$ (b) $\begin{vmatrix} -1 & 0 & 1 \\ 1 & -1 & 0 \\ 0 & 1 & -1 \end{vmatrix}$ (c) $\begin{vmatrix} 0 & 1 & 1 \\ 1 & 0 & 1 \\ 1 & 1 & 0 \end{vmatrix}$

5 Find the value of the determinant of each of the following matrices.

(a) $\begin{pmatrix} 0 & 1 & 0 \\ 0 & 0 & 1 \\ 1 & 0 & 0 \end{pmatrix}$ (b) $\begin{pmatrix} 1 & 1 & 3 \\ -2 & 5 & 3 \\ -1 & 3 & 2 \end{pmatrix}$ (c) $\begin{pmatrix} a & d & e \\ 0 & b & f \\ 0 & 0 & c \end{pmatrix}$

6 Find the value(s) of k such that these sets of equations do not have unique solutions.

(a) $\left.\begin{array}{r} kx - y = 0 \\ -4x + ky = 0 \end{array}\right\}$ (b) $\left.\begin{array}{r} 2x + 3y = kx \\ 2x + y = ky \end{array}\right\}$ (c) $\left.\begin{array}{r} -2y - 3z = kx \\ 4x + 6y + 6z = ky \\ 7x + 8y + 10z = kz \end{array}\right\}$

7 Here is another way to find the area of the dotted parallelogram in the diagram.

(a) Find the matrix of the shear parallel to the y-axis which transforms the position vector (a,c) to the position vector of $(a,0)$.

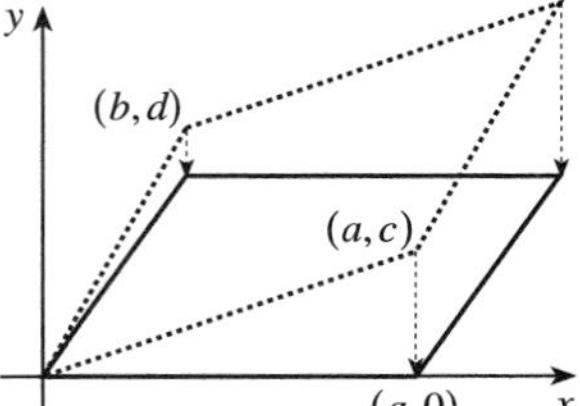

(b) Find the image of the position vector of (b,d) under the same transformation.

(c) Show how you can deduce that the area of the parallelogram is $ad - bc$, provided that $a \neq 0$.

(d) How can you resolve the case when $a = 0$?

8 Let $\mathbf{M} = \begin{pmatrix} a_1 & b_1 & c_1 \\ a_2 & b_2 & c_2 \\ a_3 & b_3 & c_3 \end{pmatrix}$ and $\mathbf{N} = \begin{pmatrix} ka_1 & b_1 & c_1 \\ ka_2 & b_2 & c_2 \\ ka_3 & b_3 & c_3 \end{pmatrix}$. Prove that $\det \mathbf{N} = k \det \mathbf{M}$ and deduce that $\det(k\mathbf{M}) = k^3 \det \mathbf{M}$. Interpret your results geometrically.

6.4 Finding inverse matrices

The method of finding inverses shown in this section is efficient for use on computers. You will see later, in Sections 6.5 and 6.6, that for 2×2 and 3×3 matrices with integer entries there are easier methods if you are using pen and paper. The method about to be described generalises easily to square matrices of any size; however, the methods of Sections 6.5 and 6.6 do not generalise so easily.

Example 6.4.1

If $\mathbf{A}\begin{pmatrix} x \\ y \end{pmatrix} = \begin{pmatrix} p \\ q \end{pmatrix}$, where $\mathbf{A} = \begin{pmatrix} 1 & 2 \\ 3 & 4 \end{pmatrix}$, find a matrix $\mathbf{C}$ such that $\begin{pmatrix} x \\ y \end{pmatrix} = \mathbf{C}\begin{pmatrix} p \\ q \end{pmatrix}$.

Think of $\mathbf{A}\begin{pmatrix} x \\ y \end{pmatrix} = \begin{pmatrix} p \\ q \end{pmatrix}$ as the pair of simultaneous equations

$$\left.\begin{array}{l} 1x + 2y = 1p + 0q \\ 3x + 4y = 0p + 1q \end{array}\right\}$$

where the coefficients on the left side of the equations are those of the matrix $\mathbf{A}$, and coefficients of 0 and 1 are shown rather than suppressed on the right side.

Now solve the equations in the usual way, including substituting back to find x.

Subtract $3 \times$ the top row from the bottom row: $\left.\begin{array}{l} 1x + 2y = 1p + 0q \\ 0x - 2y = -3p + 1q \end{array}\right\}.$

Divide the bottom row by -2: $\left.\begin{array}{l} 1x + 2y = 1p + 0q \\ 0x + 1y = \frac{3}{2}p - \frac{1}{2}q \end{array}\right\}.$

Subtract $2\times$the bottom row from the top row: $\left.\begin{array}{l} 1x+0y=-2p+1q \\ 0x+1y=\ \frac{3}{2}p-\frac{1}{2}q \end{array}\right\}.$

Therefore $\begin{pmatrix} x \\ y \end{pmatrix}=\begin{pmatrix} -2 & 1 \\ \frac{3}{2} & -\frac{1}{2} \end{pmatrix}\begin{pmatrix} p \\ q \end{pmatrix}$, so $\mathbf{C}=\begin{pmatrix} -2 & 1 \\ \frac{3}{2} & -\frac{1}{2} \end{pmatrix}$.

What is going on here? Two things. First, the solution of $\mathbf{A}\begin{pmatrix} x \\ y \end{pmatrix}=\begin{pmatrix} p \\ q \end{pmatrix}$ is $\begin{pmatrix} x \\ y \end{pmatrix}=\mathbf{C}\begin{pmatrix} p \\ q \end{pmatrix}$.

Secondly, if you substitute $\mathbf{C}\begin{pmatrix} p \\ q \end{pmatrix}$ for $\begin{pmatrix} x \\ y \end{pmatrix}$ in the equation $\mathbf{A}\begin{pmatrix} x \\ y \end{pmatrix}=\begin{pmatrix} p \\ q \end{pmatrix}$ you get $\mathbf{AC}\begin{pmatrix} p \\ q \end{pmatrix}=\begin{pmatrix} p \\ q \end{pmatrix}$, which you can write as $(\mathbf{AC})\begin{pmatrix} p \\ q \end{pmatrix}=\begin{pmatrix} p \\ q \end{pmatrix}$. Since this is true for any p and q, $\mathbf{AC}=\mathbf{I}$. And, substituting $\mathbf{A}\begin{pmatrix} x \\ y \end{pmatrix}$ for $\begin{pmatrix} p \\ q \end{pmatrix}$ in $\begin{pmatrix} x \\ y \end{pmatrix}=\mathbf{C}\begin{pmatrix} p \\ q \end{pmatrix}$ gives $\begin{pmatrix} x \\ y \end{pmatrix}=\mathbf{CA}\begin{pmatrix} x \\ y \end{pmatrix}=(\mathbf{CA})\begin{pmatrix} x \\ y \end{pmatrix}$ for any x and y, so $\mathbf{CA}=\mathbf{I}$.

Therefore $\mathbf{AC}=\mathbf{CA}=\mathbf{I}$. From Section 4.5, $\mathbf{C}$ is the inverse of $\mathbf{A}$; that is, $\mathbf{C}=\mathbf{A}^{-1}$.

Therefore the inverse of $\mathbf{A}=\begin{pmatrix} 1 & 2 \\ 3 & 4 \end{pmatrix}$ is $\mathbf{A}^{-1}=\begin{pmatrix} -2 & 1 \\ \frac{3}{2} & -\frac{1}{2} \end{pmatrix}$.

If you now recall Sections 6.1 and 6.2, the solution of the set of equations

$$\left.\begin{array}{l} 1x+2y=1p+0q \\ 3x+4y=0p+1q \end{array}\right\}$$

is unique if the determinant is not zero. In this case, $\det\begin{pmatrix} 1 & 2 \\ 3 & 4 \end{pmatrix}=1\times4-2\times3=-2\neq0$.

Thus the solution $\begin{pmatrix} x \\ y \end{pmatrix}=\mathbf{A}^{-1}\begin{pmatrix} p \\ q \end{pmatrix}$ is unique, so the inverse, $\mathbf{A}^{-1}$, of $\mathbf{A}$ is unique.

Generalising from this example:

> If $\mathbf{A}$ is square and $\det\mathbf{A}\neq0$, there exists a unique matrix $\mathbf{C}$ such that $\mathbf{AC}=\mathbf{CA}=\mathbf{I}$.
>
> If $\mathbf{CA}=\mathbf{I}$, then $\mathbf{AC}=\mathbf{I}$.

Alternatively you can say that the following statements regarding a 2×2 matrix are equivalent. There are corresponding statements for other square matrices.

$\det\mathbf{A}\neq0$.	$\mathbf{A}^{-1}$ exists and is unique.
$\mathbf{A}$ is non-singular.	The equation $\mathbf{A}\begin{pmatrix} x \\ y \end{pmatrix}=\begin{pmatrix} p \\ q \end{pmatrix}$ has a unique solution.

Notice that in the process of solving the equations in Example 6.4.1 the labels x, y, p and q have little importance except to help you realise where the process comes from. You might just as well have dropped the labels, and written

$$\left.\begin{array}{cc|cc} 1 & 2 & 1 & 0 \\ 3 & 4 & 0 & 1 \end{array}\right\} \Leftrightarrow \quad \ldots \quad \ldots \quad \Leftrightarrow \left.\begin{array}{cc|cc} 1 & 0 & -2 & 1 \\ 0 & 1 & \frac{3}{2} & -\frac{1}{2} \end{array}\right\}$$

Example 6.4.2
Find the inverse of $\mathbf{M} = \begin{pmatrix} 1 & 2 & -1 \\ 3 & 7 & -1 \\ 5 & 11 & -1 \end{pmatrix}$.

Use the procedure outlined for 2×2 matrices with the shortened notation: the annotation $r_2{}' = r_2 - 3r_1$ means that the new second row is obtained from the old second row minus 3 times the old first row.

$$\left.\begin{array}{ccc|ccc} 1 & 2 & -1 & 1 & 0 & 0 \\ 3 & 7 & -1 & 0 & 1 & 0 \\ 5 & 11 & -1 & 0 & 0 & 1 \end{array}\right\} \begin{array}{c} r_2{}' = r_2 - 3r_1 \\ \Leftrightarrow \end{array} \left.\begin{array}{ccc|ccc} 1 & 2 & -1 & 1 & 0 & 0 \\ 0 & 1 & 2 & -3 & 1 & 0 \\ 5 & 11 & -1 & 0 & 0 & 1 \end{array}\right\}$$

$$\begin{array}{c} r_3{}' = r_3 - 5r_1 \\ \Leftrightarrow \end{array} \left.\begin{array}{ccc|ccc} 1 & 2 & -1 & 1 & 0 & 0 \\ 0 & 1 & 2 & -3 & 1 & 0 \\ 0 & 1 & 4 & -5 & 0 & 1 \end{array}\right\} \begin{array}{c} r_3{}' = r_3 - r_2 \\ \Leftrightarrow \end{array} \left.\begin{array}{ccc|ccc} 1 & 2 & -1 & 1 & 0 & 0 \\ 0 & 1 & 2 & -3 & 1 & 0 \\ 0 & 0 & 2 & -2 & -1 & 1 \end{array}\right\}$$

$$\begin{array}{c} r_3{}' = \frac{1}{2}r_3 \\ \Leftrightarrow \end{array} \left.\begin{array}{ccc|ccc} 1 & 2 & -1 & 1 & 0 & 0 \\ 0 & 1 & 2 & -3 & 1 & 0 \\ 0 & 0 & 1 & -1 & -\frac{1}{2} & \frac{1}{2} \end{array}\right\} \begin{array}{c} r_2{}' = r_2 - 2r_3 \\ \Leftrightarrow \end{array} \left.\begin{array}{ccc|ccc} 1 & 2 & -1 & 1 & 0 & 0 \\ 0 & 1 & 0 & -1 & 2 & -1 \\ 0 & 0 & 1 & -1 & -\frac{1}{2} & \frac{1}{2} \end{array}\right\}$$

$$\begin{array}{c} r_1{}' = r_1 + r_3 \\ \Leftrightarrow \end{array} \left.\begin{array}{ccc|ccc} 1 & 2 & 0 & 0 & -\frac{1}{2} & \frac{1}{2} \\ 0 & 1 & 0 & -1 & 2 & -1 \\ 0 & 0 & 1 & -1 & -\frac{1}{2} & \frac{1}{2} \end{array}\right\} \begin{array}{c} r_1{}' = r_1 - 2r_2 \\ \Leftrightarrow \end{array} \left.\begin{array}{ccc|ccc} 1 & 0 & 0 & 2 & -\frac{9}{2} & \frac{5}{2} \\ 0 & 1 & 0 & -1 & 2 & -1 \\ 0 & 0 & 1 & -1 & -\frac{1}{2} & \frac{1}{2} \end{array}\right\}.$$

The inverse of $\mathbf{M}$ is $\mathbf{M}^{-1} = \begin{pmatrix} 2 & -\frac{9}{2} & \frac{5}{2} \\ -1 & 2 & -1 \\ -1 & -\frac{1}{2} & \frac{1}{2} \end{pmatrix}$.

There are plenty of opportunities for making mistakes so you should always check by calculating $\mathbf{MM}^{-1}$ or $\mathbf{M}^{-1}\mathbf{M}$ to make sure that the result is $\mathbf{I}$.

Before giving examples of the way in which inverse matrices are used, it is worth looking at other methods of finding an inverse matrix.

6.5 Inverting 2×2 matrices

Exercise 4B Question 3(c) showed that the inverse of $\begin{pmatrix} a & b \\ c & d \end{pmatrix}$ is $\dfrac{1}{ad-bc}\begin{pmatrix} d & -b \\ -c & a \end{pmatrix}$ if $ad - bc \neq 0$. You also saw that if $ad - bc = 0$, $\begin{pmatrix} a & b \\ c & d \end{pmatrix}$ has no inverse.

The inverse of the matrix $\mathbf{A}=\begin{pmatrix} a & b \\ c & d \end{pmatrix}$ is given by

$$\mathbf{A}^{-1}=\frac{1}{ad-bc}\begin{pmatrix} d & -b \\ -c & a \end{pmatrix}$$

provided that $\det\mathbf{A}\equiv ad-bc\neq 0$.

Always check your answer by calculating $\mathbf{AA}^{-1}$ and seeing that it actually is $\mathbf{I}$.

One result that you should expect is that $\det\mathbf{A}^{-1}=\dfrac{1}{\det\mathbf{A}}$. If the matrix $\mathbf{A}$ multiplies area by a factor of $\det\mathbf{A}$, then the inverse matrix should multiply area by the factor $\dfrac{1}{\det\mathbf{A}}$.

Theorem If $\mathbf{A}$ is a 2×2 matrix, and $\det\mathbf{A}\neq 0$, then $\det\mathbf{A}^{-1}=\dfrac{1}{\det\mathbf{A}}$.

Proof $1=\det\mathbf{I}=\det\left(\mathbf{A}^{-1}\mathbf{A}\right)=\left(\det\mathbf{A}^{-1}\right)\times(\det\mathbf{A})$, so $\det\mathbf{A}^{-1}=\dfrac{1}{\det\mathbf{A}}$.

If you write $\det\mathbf{A}$ as Δ, then $\mathbf{A}^{-1}=\begin{pmatrix} \frac{d}{\Delta} & -\frac{b}{\Delta} \\ -\frac{c}{\Delta} & \frac{a}{\Delta} \end{pmatrix}$. You can now find the inverse of $\mathbf{A}^{-1}$ as $\left(\mathbf{A}^{-1}\right)^{-1}=\dfrac{1}{\det\mathbf{A}^{-1}}\begin{pmatrix} \frac{a}{\Delta} & \frac{b}{\Delta} \\ \frac{c}{\Delta} & \frac{d}{\Delta} \end{pmatrix}=\dfrac{1}{1/\Delta}\times\dfrac{1}{\Delta}\begin{pmatrix} a & b \\ c & d \end{pmatrix}=\mathbf{A}$, as you would expect.

You can use the inverse matrix to solve equations involving matrices.

Example 6.5.1
Find the inverse of $\begin{pmatrix} 4 & -5 \\ 3 & 7 \end{pmatrix}$, and use it to solve the equations $\left.\begin{matrix} 4x-5y=3 \\ 3x+7y=13 \end{matrix}\right\}$.

The inverse of $\begin{pmatrix} 4 & -5 \\ 3 & 7 \end{pmatrix}$ is $\frac{1}{43}\begin{pmatrix} 7 & 5 \\ -3 & 4 \end{pmatrix}$.

Writing the equations $\left.\begin{matrix} 4x-5y=3 \\ 3x+7y=13 \end{matrix}\right\}$ as $\begin{pmatrix} 4 & -5 \\ 3 & 7 \end{pmatrix}\begin{pmatrix} x \\ y \end{pmatrix}=\begin{pmatrix} 3 \\ 13 \end{pmatrix}$, the solution is

$$\begin{pmatrix} x \\ y \end{pmatrix}=\begin{pmatrix} 4 & -5 \\ 3 & 7 \end{pmatrix}^{-1}\begin{pmatrix} 3 \\ 13 \end{pmatrix}=\frac{1}{43}\begin{pmatrix} 7 & 5 \\ -3 & 4 \end{pmatrix}\begin{pmatrix} 3 \\ 13 \end{pmatrix}=\frac{1}{43}\begin{pmatrix} 21+65 \\ -9+52 \end{pmatrix}=\begin{pmatrix} 2 \\ 1 \end{pmatrix}.$$

Therefore the unique solution is $x=2$, $y=1$.

Whether this is a more effective way of solving the simultaneous equations than the usual elimination method is a matter of debate. Use whichever method suits you better.

Example 6.5.2
Solve for $\mathbf{M}$ the matrix equation $\mathbf{M}\begin{pmatrix}2 & 1\\1 & 1\end{pmatrix}=\begin{pmatrix}1 & 3\\3 & 2\end{pmatrix}$.

To solve, multiply on the right by $\begin{pmatrix}2 & 1\\1 & 1\end{pmatrix}^{-1}=\frac{1}{1}\begin{pmatrix}1 & -1\\-1 & 2\end{pmatrix}=\begin{pmatrix}1 & -1\\-1 & 2\end{pmatrix}$. Thus

$$\begin{aligned}\mathbf{M}\begin{pmatrix}2 & 1\\1 & 1\end{pmatrix}=\begin{pmatrix}1 & 3\\3 & 2\end{pmatrix} &\Leftrightarrow \mathbf{M}\begin{pmatrix}2 & 1\\1 & 1\end{pmatrix}\begin{pmatrix}2 & 1\\1 & 1\end{pmatrix}^{-1}=\begin{pmatrix}1 & 3\\3 & 2\end{pmatrix}\begin{pmatrix}2 & 1\\1 & 1\end{pmatrix}^{-1}\\ &\Leftrightarrow \mathbf{MI}=\begin{pmatrix}1 & 3\\3 & 2\end{pmatrix}\begin{pmatrix}1 & -1\\-1 & 2\end{pmatrix}\\ &\Leftrightarrow \mathbf{M}=\begin{pmatrix}1 & 3\\3 & 2\end{pmatrix}\begin{pmatrix}1 & -1\\-1 & 2\end{pmatrix}=\begin{pmatrix}-2 & 5\\1 & 1\end{pmatrix}.\end{aligned}$$

Therefore $\mathbf{M}=\begin{pmatrix}-2 & 5\\1 & 1\end{pmatrix}$.

Compare this example with Example 5.2.2. If $\mathbf{M}$ transforms $\begin{pmatrix}2\\1\end{pmatrix}$ to $\begin{pmatrix}1\\3\end{pmatrix}$ and $\begin{pmatrix}1\\1\end{pmatrix}$ to $\begin{pmatrix}3\\2\end{pmatrix}$, then $\mathbf{M}\begin{pmatrix}2\\1\end{pmatrix}=\begin{pmatrix}1\\3\end{pmatrix}$ and $\mathbf{M}\begin{pmatrix}1\\1\end{pmatrix}=\begin{pmatrix}3\\2\end{pmatrix}$, so that $\mathbf{M}\begin{pmatrix}2 & 1\\1 & 1\end{pmatrix}=\begin{pmatrix}1 & 3\\3 & 2\end{pmatrix}$. Then using the method of Example 5.2.2, $\mathbf{M}=\begin{pmatrix}-2 & 5\\1 & 1\end{pmatrix}$.

6.6 Inverting 3×3 matrices

Suppose that you want to find the inverse of the matrix $\mathbf{A}=\begin{pmatrix}a_1 & b_1 & c_1\\a_2 & b_2 & c_2\\a_3 & b_3 & c_3\end{pmatrix}$. Let the inverse be $\begin{pmatrix}p_1 & p_2 & p_3\\q_1 & q_2 & q_3\\r_1 & r_2 & r_3\end{pmatrix}$ (note the way that the letters and subscripts are written)

so that $\begin{pmatrix}p_1 & p_2 & p_3\\q_1 & q_2 & q_3\\r_1 & r_2 & r_3\end{pmatrix}\begin{pmatrix}a_1 & b_1 & c_1\\a_2 & b_2 & c_2\\a_3 & b_3 & c_3\end{pmatrix}=\begin{pmatrix}1 & 0 & 0\\0 & 1 & 0\\0 & 0 & 1\end{pmatrix}$.

Let $\mathbf{p}=\begin{pmatrix}p_1\\p_2\\p_3\end{pmatrix}$, $\mathbf{q}=\begin{pmatrix}q_1\\q_2\\q_3\end{pmatrix}$, $\mathbf{r}=\begin{pmatrix}r_1\\r_2\\r_3\end{pmatrix}$, $\mathbf{a}=\begin{pmatrix}a_1\\a_2\\a_3\end{pmatrix}$, $\mathbf{b}=\begin{pmatrix}b_1\\b_2\\b_3\end{pmatrix}$ and $\mathbf{c}=\begin{pmatrix}c_1\\c_2\\c_3\end{pmatrix}$.

Then $\begin{pmatrix}p_1 & p_2 & p_3\\q_1 & q_2 & q_3\\r_1 & r_2 & r_3\end{pmatrix}\begin{pmatrix}a_1 & b_1 & c_1\\a_2 & b_2 & c_2\\a_3 & b_3 & c_3\end{pmatrix}=\begin{pmatrix}\mathbf{p.a} & \mathbf{p.b} & \mathbf{p.c}\\\mathbf{q.a} & \mathbf{q.b} & \mathbf{q.c}\\\mathbf{r.a} & \mathbf{r.b} & \mathbf{r.c}\end{pmatrix}$.

Comparing the entries of the two product matrices, you can see from the top row that you want $\mathbf{p.b}=\mathbf{p.c}=0$. Therefore $\mathbf{p}$ is perpendicular to both $\mathbf{b}$ and $\mathbf{c}$, and so lies in the direction $\mathbf{b}\times\mathbf{c}$. Similarly $\mathbf{q}$ is perpendicular to $\mathbf{c}$ and $\mathbf{a}$, and $\mathbf{r}$ is perpendicular to $\mathbf{a}$ and $\mathbf{b}$.

So construct a matrix $\mathbf{C}$ whose *rows* are the elements of $\mathbf{b}\times\mathbf{c}$, $\mathbf{c}\times\mathbf{a}$ and $\mathbf{a}\times\mathbf{b}$. Then the elements along the leading diagonal of the product $\mathbf{CA}$ are $(\mathbf{b}\times\mathbf{c}).\mathbf{a}$, $(\mathbf{c}\times\mathbf{a}).\mathbf{b}$ and $(\mathbf{a}\times\mathbf{b}).\mathbf{c}$. But dot products are commutative, so these expressions are $\mathbf{a}.(\mathbf{b}\times\mathbf{c})$, $\mathbf{b}.(\mathbf{c}\times\mathbf{a})$ and $\mathbf{c}.(\mathbf{a}\times\mathbf{b})$. From Section 6.3, each of these expressions is equal to $\det\mathbf{A}$.

Therefore the matrix product $\mathbf{CA} = \begin{pmatrix} \det \mathbf{A} & 0 & 0 \\ 0 & \det \mathbf{A} & 0 \\ 0 & 0 & \det \mathbf{A} \end{pmatrix}$, so $\mathbf{A}^{-1} = \dfrac{1}{\det \mathbf{A}}\mathbf{C}$.

As $\dfrac{1}{\det \mathbf{A}}$ *is a scalar, the right side does not involve division by a matrix. You can also see why the condition that* $\det \mathbf{A} \neq 0$ *appears in calculating the inverse matrix.*

The process is summed up as an algorithm.

To find the inverse of a 3×3 matrix $\mathbf{A}$, with columns $\mathbf{a}$, $\mathbf{b}$ and $\mathbf{c}$.

Step 1 Find the cross products $\mathbf{b} \times \mathbf{c}$, $\mathbf{c} \times \mathbf{a}$ and $\mathbf{a} \times \mathbf{b}$.

Step 2 Construct the matrix $\mathbf{C}$ with these cross products as rows.

Step 3 Calculate $\mathbf{CA}$ (as a check): it should be $(\det \mathbf{A})\mathbf{I}$.

Step 4 Divide $\mathbf{C}$ by $\det \mathbf{A}$ to get $\mathbf{A}^{-1} = \dfrac{1}{\det \mathbf{A}}\mathbf{C}$.

Example 6.6.1
Find the inverse of $\mathbf{A} = \begin{pmatrix} 1 & 2 & 3 \\ 4 & 5 & 6 \\ 7 & 8 & 10 \end{pmatrix}$.

$$\begin{pmatrix} 2 \\ 5 \\ 8 \end{pmatrix} \times \begin{pmatrix} 3 \\ 6 \\ 10 \end{pmatrix} = \begin{pmatrix} 2 \\ 4 \\ -3 \end{pmatrix}, \quad \begin{pmatrix} 3 \\ 6 \\ 10 \end{pmatrix} \times \begin{pmatrix} 1 \\ 4 \\ 7 \end{pmatrix} = \begin{pmatrix} 2 \\ -11 \\ 6 \end{pmatrix}, \quad \begin{pmatrix} 1 \\ 4 \\ 7 \end{pmatrix} \times \begin{pmatrix} 2 \\ 5 \\ 8 \end{pmatrix} = \begin{pmatrix} -3 \\ 6 \\ -3 \end{pmatrix}.$$

$$\mathbf{C} = \begin{pmatrix} 2 & 4 & -3 \\ 2 & -11 & 6 \\ -3 & 6 & -3 \end{pmatrix}.$$

$$\mathbf{CA} = \begin{pmatrix} 2 & 4 & -3 \\ 2 & -11 & 6 \\ -3 & 6 & -3 \end{pmatrix}\begin{pmatrix} 1 & 2 & 3 \\ 4 & 5 & 6 \\ 7 & 8 & 10 \end{pmatrix} = \begin{pmatrix} -3 & 0 & 0 \\ 0 & -3 & 0 \\ 0 & 0 & -3 \end{pmatrix} = -3\mathbf{I}.$$

The inverse of $\mathbf{A} = \begin{pmatrix} 1 & 2 & 3 \\ 4 & 5 & 6 \\ 7 & 8 & 10 \end{pmatrix}$ is $\mathbf{A}^{-1} = -\frac{1}{3}\begin{pmatrix} 2 & 4 & -3 \\ 2 & -11 & 6 \\ -3 & 6 & -3 \end{pmatrix}$.

If you check the cross products as you find them, then all you need to do in the third step is to find the elements on the main diagonal, and check that they are equal. This will give you the determinant which you then use as a divisor to find the inverse.

The statement in Section 4.5, that if an inverse matrix exists it is unique, guarantees that the matrix $\dfrac{1}{\det \mathbf{A}}\mathbf{C}$ has the property that $\mathbf{A}\left(\dfrac{1}{\det \mathbf{A}}\mathbf{C}\right) = \mathbf{I}$, but it is not easy to see geometrically from the construction of $\dfrac{1}{\det \mathbf{A}}\mathbf{C}$ why this is so.

Example 6.6.2

Solve the equations $\left.\begin{aligned} x+2y+\ 3z&=-1 \\ 4x+5y+\ 6z&=-1 \\ 7x+8y+10z&=\ \ 0 \end{aligned}\right\}.$

You can write these equations as $\mathbf{A}\begin{pmatrix} x \\ y \\ z \end{pmatrix} = \begin{pmatrix} -1 \\ -1 \\ 0 \end{pmatrix}$, with $\mathbf{A} = \begin{pmatrix} 1 & 2 & 3 \\ 4 & 5 & 6 \\ 7 & 8 & 10 \end{pmatrix}$.

Then multiplying on the left by $\mathbf{A}^{-1}$ (which exists since $\mathbf{A}$ is the matrix of Example 6.3.1) you find

$$\mathbf{A}^{-1}\mathbf{A}\begin{pmatrix} x \\ y \\ z \end{pmatrix} = \mathbf{A}^{-1}\begin{pmatrix} -1 \\ -1 \\ 0 \end{pmatrix} \quad\Leftrightarrow\quad \mathbf{I}\begin{pmatrix} x \\ y \\ z \end{pmatrix} = \mathbf{A}^{-1}\begin{pmatrix} -1 \\ -1 \\ 0 \end{pmatrix} \quad\Leftrightarrow\quad \begin{pmatrix} x \\ y \\ z \end{pmatrix} = \mathbf{A}^{-1}\begin{pmatrix} -1 \\ -1 \\ 0 \end{pmatrix}.$$

Thus $\begin{pmatrix} x \\ y \\ z \end{pmatrix} = -\frac{1}{3}\begin{pmatrix} 2 & 4 & -3 \\ 2 & -11 & 6 \\ -3 & 6 & -3 \end{pmatrix}\begin{pmatrix} -1 \\ -1 \\ 0 \end{pmatrix} = -\frac{1}{3}\begin{pmatrix} -6 \\ 9 \\ -3 \end{pmatrix} = \begin{pmatrix} 2 \\ -3 \\ 1 \end{pmatrix}$, so $x=2,\ y=-3,\ z=1$.

Using the inverse matrix to solve a set of simultaneous linear equations, as in Example 6.6.2, looks beguilingly simple. But that is only because you had already found $\mathbf{A}^{-1}$ in an earlier example. If you have to begin by calculating the matrix from scratch, the method is hardly worthwhile.

If you can use a calculator or computer to find the inverse matrix, then the method of Example 6.6.2 might be useful.

However, if you don't know that the set of equations has a unique solution when you start, it is certainly better to use the methods of Chapter 1. The decision about the choice of methods might be different if some or all of the coefficients are unknowns rather than numbers. For instance, if you had been given Example 6.3.2 in Chapter 1 rather than Chapter 6 and been asked for which values of k the equations

$$\left.\begin{aligned} x+ky\qquad &= p \\ 3x\qquad +kz &= q \\ kx+\ y+\ z &= r \end{aligned}\right\}$$

have either no solution or solutions which are not unique, the question would have been difficult. Using the determinant to find the critical values of k makes it much easier.

Provided that the entries in the matrix to be inverted consist of fairly small integers, the method using vector products is easier to use with pen and paper than the method of Section 6.4.

If the numbers involved are large or are decimals, then you will wish to use a computer. Large integers and decimals present no problem for a computer which is programmed to find an inverse matrix.

The important issue when using a computer is that the generalisation of the method of this section to inverting $n \times n$ matrices takes a multiple of $n!$ operations while the method based on Section 6.4 takes a multiple of n^3 operations to find an inverse. This difference matters, even for a powerful computer, as n gets large.

6.7 Inverse of a product

If you know that $\mathbf{A}$ and $\mathbf{B}$ are both square matrices, what can you say about the inverse of the matrix product $\mathbf{AB}$?

Suppose that either $\mathbf{A}$ or $\mathbf{B}$ is singular so that either $\det\mathbf{A} = 0$ or $\det\mathbf{B} = 0$. Then

$$\det(\mathbf{AB}) = \det\mathbf{A}\det\mathbf{B} = 0,$$

so $\mathbf{AB}$ is singular and has no inverse.

If $\det\mathbf{A} \neq 0$ and $\det\mathbf{B} \neq 0$, then $\det(\mathbf{AB}) = \det\mathbf{A}\det\mathbf{B} \neq 0$, $\mathbf{AB}$ is non-singular and has an inverse. You can use the fact that

$$(\mathbf{AB})\mathbf{X} = \mathbf{I} \quad\Leftrightarrow\quad \mathbf{A}(\mathbf{BX}) = \mathbf{I} \quad\Leftrightarrow\quad \mathbf{BX} = \mathbf{A}^{-1}\mathbf{I} \quad\Leftrightarrow\quad \mathbf{X} = \mathbf{B}^{-1}\mathbf{A}^{-1}$$

to say that the inverse of $\mathbf{AB}$ is $\mathbf{B}^{-1}\mathbf{A}^{-1}$.

As a check, notice that, with this $\mathbf{X}$, $\mathbf{X}(\mathbf{AB}) = \mathbf{I}$.

> For non-singular matrices $\mathbf{A}$ and $\mathbf{B}$,
>
> $$(\mathbf{AB})^{-1} = \mathbf{B}^{-1}\mathbf{A}^{-1}.$$

This is the same rule that you met with functions in P2 Section 2.6.

Example 6.7.1
You are given that $\mathbf{A}^{-1} = \begin{pmatrix} -1 & 2 & -3 \\ 2 & -7 & 1 \\ -1 & 3 & 2 \end{pmatrix}$ and $\mathbf{B} = \begin{pmatrix} 2 & 1 & -4 \\ -2 & 3 & 5 \\ -1 & -3 & 2 \end{pmatrix}$. Find $\left(\mathbf{AB}^{-1}\right)^{-1}$.

Since $\left(\mathbf{AB}^{-1}\right)^{-1} = \left(\mathbf{B}^{-1}\right)^{-1}\mathbf{A}^{-1} = \mathbf{BA}^{-1}$,

$$\left(\mathbf{AB}^{-1}\right)^{-1} = \mathbf{BA}^{-1} = \begin{pmatrix} 2 & 1 & -4 \\ -2 & 3 & 5 \\ -1 & -3 & 2 \end{pmatrix}\begin{pmatrix} -1 & 2 & -3 \\ 2 & -7 & 1 \\ -1 & 3 & 2 \end{pmatrix} = \begin{pmatrix} 4 & -15 & -13 \\ 3 & -10 & 19 \\ -7 & 25 & 4 \end{pmatrix}.$$

6.8 Simultaneous linear equations

In Section 1.1, the solution of the equation $ax = p$, where $a, p \in \mathbb{R}$, was discussed, and the solution was given as $x = a^{-1}p$ provided that $a \neq 0$.

If $a = 0$, the equation may or may not have a solution, depending on the value of p.

You can now generalise this statement to systems of simultaneous linear equations of the form $\mathbf{Ax} = \mathbf{p}$, where either $\mathbf{A}$ is a 2×2 matrix and $\mathbf{x}$ and $\mathbf{p}$ are column vectors with 2 components, or $\mathbf{A}$ is a 3×3 matrix and $\mathbf{x}$ and $\mathbf{p}$ are column vectors with 3 components.

So, if $\mathbf{A}$ is non-singular, then $\mathbf{x} = \mathbf{A}^{-1}\mathbf{p}$.

If $\mathbf{A}$ is singular, the equation may or may not have a solution, depending on the vector $\mathbf{p}$.

The condition that $a \neq 0$ in the equation $ax = p$ in Section 1.1 has been replaced by the condition that $\mathbf{A}$ is non-singular in the equation $\mathbf{Ax} = \mathbf{p}$.

If you are prepared to think of a as a 1×1 matrix, and to say that a being non-singular means that $a \neq 0$, then all these equations fit into the same pattern.

Exercise 6B

1 Use the method of row operations to find the inverses of the following matrices.

(a) $\begin{pmatrix} 1 & -1 \\ 1 & 1 \end{pmatrix}$ (b) $\begin{pmatrix} 4 & 9 \\ 3 & 7 \end{pmatrix}$ (c) $\begin{pmatrix} 3 & -5 \\ -4 & 7 \end{pmatrix}$

2 Use the method of row operations to find the inverses of the following matrices.

(a) $\begin{pmatrix} 1 & -2 & 3 \\ 1 & -1 & 2 \\ -2 & 4 & -5 \end{pmatrix}$ (b) $\begin{pmatrix} 1 & 1 & 1 \\ -1 & 0 & 1 \\ -2 & -2 & 0 \end{pmatrix}$ (c) $\begin{pmatrix} 1 & -2 & -1 \\ 2 & -1 & -1 \\ 1 & -2 & 1 \end{pmatrix}$

3 Find the inverse, if it exists, of each of the following matrices.

(a) $\begin{pmatrix} 2 & -1 \\ -5 & 4 \end{pmatrix}$ (b) $\begin{pmatrix} 2 & -6 \\ -3 & 9 \end{pmatrix}$ (c) $\begin{pmatrix} 5 & -3 \\ 10 & -5 \end{pmatrix}$

4 Find the inverse, if it exists, of each of the following matrices.

(a) $\begin{pmatrix} 1 & -2 & -3 \\ 2 & -1 & -4 \\ 3 & -3 & -5 \end{pmatrix}$ (b) $\begin{pmatrix} 1 & -2 & -1 \\ 2 & 1 & 5 \\ 3 & -2 & 3 \end{pmatrix}$ (c) $\begin{pmatrix} 2 & -1 & 3 \\ 1 & 2 & 1 \\ 3 & -4 & 5 \end{pmatrix}$

5 By finding the appropriate inverse matrices, find the solutions of the following equations.

(a) $\left.\begin{aligned} 2x + 3y &= -1 \\ 3x - 2y &= 18 \end{aligned}\right\}$ (b) $\left.\begin{aligned} -3x + 2y &= 13 \\ -5x + 4y &= 23 \end{aligned}\right\}$ (c) $\left.\begin{aligned} 2x + 5y &= 9 \\ -5x + 2y &= -8 \end{aligned}\right\}$

6 By finding the appropriate inverse matrices, find the solutions of the following equations.

(a) $\left.\begin{aligned} 2x - y - z &= 4 \\ x + 2y &= 10 \\ y - z &= 2 \end{aligned}\right\}$ (b) $\left.\begin{aligned} x + y - z &= 3 \\ 3x - 2y - z &= 1 \\ 2x + 3y - z &= 9 \end{aligned}\right\}$ (c) $\left.\begin{aligned} 2x - 3y + 4z &= 7 \\ x - 2y + 3z &= 5 \\ 3x - 5y + 2z &= 2 \end{aligned}\right\}$

7 Let $\begin{pmatrix} a \\ b \end{pmatrix}$ stand for the expression $e^x(a\cos x + b\sin x)$, where a and b are constants. Find a 2×2 matrix $\mathbf{D}$ which, when it pre-multiplies the vector $\begin{pmatrix} a \\ b \end{pmatrix}$, gives the derivative of $e^x(a\cos x + b\sin x)$ with respect to x.

Use the matrix $\mathbf{D}$ to find

(a) the second derivative of $e^x(a\cos x + b\sin x)$; (b) $\int e^x(a\cos x + b\sin x)\,dx$.

Generalise the method to find $\int e^{px}(a\cos qx + b\sin qx)\,dx$.

Miscellaneous exercise 6

1 (a) Solve the equation $\begin{vmatrix} x & 10 \\ 2 & x-1 \end{vmatrix} = 0$.

(b) Show that, for each of these values of x, $\begin{vmatrix} 3 & 0 & y \\ 6 & x & 10 \\ 0 & 2 & x-1 \end{vmatrix} = 12y$. (OCR)

2 The matrix $\mathbf{A} = \begin{pmatrix} 3 & 1 & -3 \\ 2 & 4 & 3 \\ -4 & 2 & -1 \end{pmatrix}$.

(a) (i) Show that $\mathbf{A}^2 = \mathbf{A} + 20\mathbf{I}$ where $\mathbf{I}$ is the 3×3 identity matrix.

(ii) Deduce the inverse matrix, $\mathbf{A}^{-1}$, of $\mathbf{A}$.

(b) Determine the unique solution of the system of equations

$$\left.\begin{aligned} 3x + y - 3z &= 9 \\ 2x + 4y + 3z &= 11 \\ -4x + 2y - z &= 23 \end{aligned}\right\}.$$

(OCR)

3 Determine the value of the constant k for which the system of equations

$$\left.\begin{aligned} 2x - y - z &= 3 \\ -4x + 7y + 3z &= -5 \\ kx + y - z &= 5 \end{aligned}\right\}$$

does not have a unique solution.

For this value of k, determine the complete solution to this system.

Interpret this solution geometrically. (OCR)

4 Find a 3×3 matrix $\mathbf{M}$ such that $\mathbf{Mp} = \mathbf{q}$, $\mathbf{Mq} = -2\mathbf{r}$, and $\mathbf{Mr} = 2\mathbf{p} + 4\mathbf{r}$, where

$$\mathbf{p} = \begin{pmatrix} 2 \\ 0 \\ -1 \end{pmatrix}, \quad \mathbf{q} = \begin{pmatrix} -3 \\ -2 \\ 1 \end{pmatrix}, \quad \mathbf{r} = \begin{pmatrix} 1 \\ 3 \\ 0 \end{pmatrix}.$$

Find also the vector $\mathbf{M}^{-1}\mathbf{p}$. (OCR)

5 (a) Given that $\mathbf{M} = \begin{pmatrix} 1 & 5 & a \\ 2 & -4 & 1 \\ 4 & 6 & 7 \end{pmatrix}$, evaluate $\det \mathbf{M}$ in terms of a.

(b) Hence show that, whatever the values of p, q and r, the equations

$$\begin{aligned} x + 5y + az &= p, \\ 2x - 4y + z &= q, \\ 4x + 6y + 7z &= r, \end{aligned}$$

have a unique solution provided $a \neq 3$.

(c) For the case where $\mathbf{M}$ is non-singular, find $\mathbf{M}^{-1}$ and hence find, in terms of a, the solution of the equations when $p = 1$, $q = 0$, $r = -2$.

(d) Interpret the equations geometrically when $a = 3$, $p = -18$, $q = 7$, $r = -29$. (OCR)

6 It is given that the matrix $\mathbf{M} = \begin{pmatrix} 2 & 0 & -1 \\ 0 & 4 & a \\ 9 & -5 & -7 \end{pmatrix}$ is non-singular.

(a) Find the set of possible values of a.

(b) Find the inverse of $\mathbf{M}$.

(c) Solve the equations

$$\begin{aligned} 2x \qquad - z &= 1, \\ 4y + az &= -3, \\ 9x - 5y - 7z &= 2, \end{aligned}$$

for x, y, z in terms of a. (OCR)

7 (a) The square matrices **P** and **Q**, of the same size, have inverses $\mathbf{P}^{-1}$ and $\mathbf{Q}^{-1}$. Simplify $(\mathbf{PQ})(\mathbf{Q}^{-1}\mathbf{P}^{-1})$, and hence write down the inverse of $\mathbf{PQ}$.

(b) Evaluate the matrix product $\begin{pmatrix} a & a^2 & a^2 \\ -1 & a & a \\ 0 & 0 & -a \end{pmatrix}\begin{pmatrix} a & -a^2 & 0 \\ 1 & a & 2a \\ 0 & 0 & -2a \end{pmatrix}$ and hence write down the inverse of the matrix $\begin{pmatrix} a & -a^2 & 0 \\ 1 & a & 2a \\ 0 & 0 & -2a \end{pmatrix}$ (when $a \neq 0$).

(c) Let $\mathbf{A} = \begin{pmatrix} 1 & -1 & 0 \\ 1 & 1 & 2 \\ 0 & 0 & -2 \end{pmatrix}$, $\mathbf{B} = \begin{pmatrix} 2 & 4 & 4 \\ -1 & 2 & 2 \\ 0 & 0 & -2 \end{pmatrix}$ and $\mathbf{C} = \mathbf{AB}$. Use your answers to part (b) to find $\mathbf{A}^{-1}$ and $\mathbf{B}^{-1}$, and hence find $\mathbf{C}^{-1}$. (MEI)

8 The matrix **A** is given by $\mathbf{A} = \begin{pmatrix} 2 & -1 & 1 \\ 0 & 3 & 1 \\ 1 & 1 & a \end{pmatrix}$, where $a \neq 1$. Find the inverse of **A**.

Hence, or otherwise, find the point of intersection of the three planes with equations

$$\begin{aligned} 2x - y + z &= 0, \\ 3y + z &= 1, \\ x + y + az &= 3. \end{aligned}$$

(OCR)

9 The matrix **A** is given by $\mathbf{A} = \begin{pmatrix} 2 & 6 & a \\ 1 & a & 1 \\ 2 & 1 & 3 \end{pmatrix}$. Show that **A** is non-singular, whatever the value of the real constant a.

(a) Find, in terms of a, the inverse of **A**.

(b) Given that $a = 3$, verify that $\mathbf{A}^{-1} = \begin{pmatrix} -\frac{8}{5} & 3 & \frac{3}{5} \\ \frac{1}{5} & 0 & -\frac{1}{5} \\ 1 & -2 & 0 \end{pmatrix}$

(c) Given that $a = 3$, find the point which is mapped onto the point $(4, 3, 2)$ by the transformation represented by the matrix **A**. (OCR)

10 Find the values of k for which the simultaneous equations

$$\begin{aligned} kx + 2y + z &= 0, \\ 3x \qquad - 2z &= 4, \\ 3x - 6ky - 4z &= 14, \end{aligned}$$

do not have a unique solution for x, y and z.

Show that, when $k = -2$, the equations are inconsistent, and give a geometrical interpretation of the situation in this case. (OCR)

Revision exercise 3

1 The matrices $\mathbf{A}$ and $\mathbf{B}$ are given by $\mathbf{A} = \begin{pmatrix} 3 & 1 & 1 \\ a & 1 & 1 \\ 3a+2 & 3 & 2 \end{pmatrix}$, $\mathbf{B} = \begin{pmatrix} -1 & 1 & 0 \\ a+2 & 4-3a & a-3 \\ -2 & 3a-7 & 3-a \end{pmatrix}$.

Evaluate $\mathbf{AB}$, and hence or otherwise find $\mathbf{A}^{-1}$, given that $a \neq 3$.

Show that, if $a \neq 3$, the equations

$$\begin{aligned} 3x + \;\; y + \;\; z &= 1, \\ ax + \;\; y + \;\; z &= 0, \\ (3a+2)x + 3y + 2z &= 2, \end{aligned}$$

have a unique solution, and find this solution, simplifying your results for x, y, z as much as possible.

Determine whether there are any solutions when $a = 3$, and give a geometrical interpretation of your conclusion. (OCR)

2 Three planes have equations

$$\begin{aligned} x + 2y + az &= 1, \\ 2x - \;\; y + 5z &= 11, \\ 3x + \;\; y + 8z &= b. \end{aligned}$$

(a) Show that if $a \neq 3$ then the planes have exactly one common point.

(b) Show that if $a = 3$ and $b \neq 12$ then the planes have no common point.

(c) Give an overall description of the configuration of the planes when $a = 3$ and $b = 12$. (OCR)

3 The lines l_1 and l_2 intersect at the point C with position vector $\mathbf{i} + 5\mathbf{j} + 11\mathbf{k}$. The equations of l_1 and l_2 are $\mathbf{r} = \mathbf{i} + 5\mathbf{j} + 11\mathbf{k} + \lambda(3\mathbf{i} + 2\mathbf{j} - 2\mathbf{k})$ and $\mathbf{r} = \mathbf{i} + 5\mathbf{j} + 11\mathbf{k} + \mu(8\mathbf{i} + 11\mathbf{j} + 6\mathbf{k})$, where λ and μ are real parameters. Find, in the form $ax + by + cz = d$, an equation of the plane Π which contains l_1 and l_2.

The point A has position vector $4\mathbf{i} - \mathbf{j} + 5\mathbf{k}$ and the line through A perpendicular to Π meets Π at B. Find

(a) the length of AB,

(b) the perpendicular distance of B from l_1, giving your answer correct to 3 significant figures.

4 With respect to an origin O, the point A has position vector $30\mathbf{i} - 3\mathbf{j} - 5\mathbf{k}$. The line l passes through O and is parallel to the vector $4\mathbf{i} - 5\mathbf{j} - 3\mathbf{k}$. The point B on l is such that AB is perpendicular to l. In either order,

(a) find the length of AB, (b) find the position vector of B.

The plane Π passes through A and is parallel to both l and the vector $-2\mathbf{i} + 2\mathbf{j} + \mathbf{k}$. The point Q on AB is such that $AQ = \frac{1}{4}QB$. Find, correct to 2 decimal places, the perpendicular distance from Q to Π. (OCR)

5 The matrix $\mathbf{A}$ is given by $\mathbf{A} = \begin{pmatrix} 1 & a & 0 \\ -1 & 1 & 0 \\ a & 5 & 1 \end{pmatrix}$, where $a \neq -1$.

(a) Find $\mathbf{A}^{-1}$.

(b) Given that $a = 2$, find the coordinates of the point which is mapped onto the point with coordinates $(1,2,3)$ by the transformation represented by $\mathbf{A}$. (OCR)

6 The plane π has equation $\mathbf{r}\cdot(2\mathbf{i} - 3\mathbf{j} + 6\mathbf{k}) = 0$, and P and Q are the points with position vectors $7\mathbf{i} + 6\mathbf{j} + 5\mathbf{k}$ and $\mathbf{i} + 3\mathbf{j} - \mathbf{k}$ respectively. Find the position vector of the point in which the line passing through P and Q meets the plane π.

Find, in the form $ax + by + cz = d$, the equation of the plane which contains the line PQ and which is perpendicular to π. (OCR)

7 The matrix $\mathbf{C}$ is given by $\mathbf{C} = \mathbf{AB}$, where $\mathbf{A} = \begin{pmatrix} 0 & 1 \\ 1 & 0 \end{pmatrix}$, $\mathbf{B} = \begin{pmatrix} 3 & -4 \\ 4 & 3 \end{pmatrix}$.

(a) Evaluate $\mathbf{C}$.

(b) Find the point of the xy-plane which, under the transformation represented by $\mathbf{C}$, becomes the point with coordinates $(50,-100)$. (OCR, adapted)

8 The matrices $\mathbf{A}$, $\mathbf{B}$ and $\mathbf{C}$ are defined as follows:

$$\mathbf{A} = \begin{pmatrix} \frac{1}{2}\sqrt{3} & \frac{1}{2} \\ -\frac{1}{2} & \frac{1}{2}\sqrt{3} \end{pmatrix}, \qquad \mathbf{B} = \begin{pmatrix} 1 & 0 \\ 0 & -1 \end{pmatrix}, \qquad \mathbf{C} = \mathbf{A}^{-1}\mathbf{BA}.$$

In either order,

(a) evaluate $\mathbf{C}$,

(b) describe the single geometrical transformation represented by $\mathbf{C}$. (OCR)

9 Matrices $\mathbf{A}$ and $\mathbf{B}$ are given by $\mathbf{A} = \begin{pmatrix} 1 & 0 & 0 \\ 1 & -1 & 0 \\ 1 & 0 & a \end{pmatrix}$ and $\mathbf{B} = \begin{pmatrix} 1 & 1 & 1 \\ 0 & 1 & -1 \\ 0 & 0 & 2 \end{pmatrix}$, where $a \neq 0$.

(a) Find the inverse of $\mathbf{A}$.

(b) Given that $\mathbf{B}^{-1} = \begin{pmatrix} 1 & -1 & -1 \\ 0 & 1 & \frac{1}{2} \\ 0 & 0 & \frac{1}{2} \end{pmatrix}$, find the matrix $\mathbf{C}$ such that $\mathbf{ABC} = \mathbf{I}$, where $\mathbf{I}$ is the identity matrix.

10 The matrices $\mathbf{A}$ and $\mathbf{B}$ are given by $\mathbf{A} = \begin{pmatrix} 3 & -4 \\ 4 & 3 \end{pmatrix}$, $\mathbf{B} = \begin{pmatrix} 1 & 0 \\ 0 & -1 \end{pmatrix}$.

Under the transformation represented by $\mathbf{AB}$, a triangle P transforms to the triangle Q whose vertices are $(0,0)$, $(9,12)$ and $(22,-4)$.

(a) Find the coordinates of the vertices of P.

(b) State the area of P and hence find the area of Q.

(c) Find the area of the image of P under the transformation represented by $\mathbf{ABA}^{-1}$.

(OCR)

7 De Moivre's theorem

This chapter presents a theorem about nth powers of complex numbers, which can also be used to find nth roots. When you have completed it, you should

- know the statement and the proof of de Moivre's theorem
- know the nth roots of unity and their representation in an Argand diagram
- know algebraic properties of the nth roots of unity, and be able to use them in algebraic and geometric applications
- know how to find the nth roots of any complex number.

7.1 Powers of complex numbers

The rules for multiplying and dividing complex numbers are especially simple if the numbers are written in polar form (sometimes called modulus-argument form), as $r(\cos\theta + \mathrm{i}\sin\theta)$; see P4 Chapter 11. This is because of the rule

$$(\cos\alpha + \mathrm{i}\sin\alpha)(\cos\beta + \mathrm{i}\sin\beta) = \cos(\alpha+\beta) + \mathrm{i}\sin(\alpha+\beta).$$

This rule can also be written in its exponential version as

$$\mathrm{e}^{\alpha\mathrm{i}}\mathrm{e}^{\beta\mathrm{i}} = \mathrm{e}^{(\alpha+\beta)\mathrm{i}}.$$

When the indices are more complicated algebraic expressions, it is helpful to use the alternative notation $\exp(z)$ in place of e^z. The rule then takes the form

$$\exp(\alpha\mathrm{i})\exp(\beta\mathrm{i}) = \exp((\alpha+\beta)\mathrm{i}).$$

The advantage of using the exp *notation is mainly felt in printed mathematics. If index notation is used with something like* $\left(\frac{\alpha}{n} + \frac{2r\pi}{n}\right)\mathrm{i}$ *in the index, the expression looks very top-heavy, and the type is so small that it is difficult to read. When you are writing mathematics for yourself, these considerations are not so important. In this chapter* exp *has been used from the start, so that you can get used to it with simple examples.*

Putting both α and β equal to ϕ leads to the double angle formula

$$(\exp(\phi\mathrm{i}))^2 = \exp(\phi\mathrm{i})\exp(\phi\mathrm{i}) = \exp((\phi+\phi)\mathrm{i}) = \exp(2\phi\mathrm{i}).$$

Then putting $\alpha = 2\phi$ and $\beta = \phi$ gives

$$(\exp(\phi\mathrm{i}))^3 = (\exp(\phi\mathrm{i}))^2\exp(\phi\mathrm{i}) = \exp(2\phi\mathrm{i})\exp(\phi\mathrm{i}) = \exp(3\phi\mathrm{i})$$

and so on. These results suggest a general rule.

De Moivre's theorem For $n \in \mathbb{Z}$, $(\exp(\phi\mathrm{i}))^n = \exp(n\phi\mathrm{i})$.

Proof It is convenient to begin by clearing some special cases out of the way.

The result is trivial for $n = 1$, since both sides are $\exp(\phi\mathrm{i})$.

If $n = 0$, the left side is $(\exp(\phi\mathrm{i}))^0 = 1$ and the right side is $\exp(0) = 1$.

If $n=-1$, the left side is $\left(\exp(\phi\mathrm{i})\right)^{-1}=\dfrac{1}{\exp(\phi\mathrm{i})}$ and the right side is $\exp(-\phi\mathrm{i})$.

Since, by the multiplication rule, $\exp(\phi\mathrm{i})\exp(-\phi\mathrm{i})=\exp((\phi-\phi)\mathrm{i})=\exp(0)=1$,

it follows that $\left(\exp(\phi\mathrm{i})\right)^{-1}=\dfrac{1}{\exp(\phi\mathrm{i})}=\exp(-\phi\mathrm{i})$.

For positive values of n, you can use mathematical induction. The basis case, for $n=1$, has already been noted. The inductive step is that, if $\left(\exp(\phi\mathrm{i})\right)^k=\exp(k\phi\mathrm{i})$, then

$$\begin{aligned}\left(\exp(\phi\mathrm{i})\right)^{k+1}&=\left(\exp(\phi\mathrm{i})\right)^k\exp(\phi\mathrm{i})=\exp(k\phi\mathrm{i})\exp(\phi\mathrm{i})\\&=\exp((k\phi+\phi)\mathrm{i})=\exp((k+1)\phi\mathrm{i}).\end{aligned}$$

This establishes the theorem for all positive integers n.

If n is a negative integer, write n as $-m$. Then

$$\begin{aligned}\left(\exp(\phi\mathrm{i})\right)^n=\left(\exp(\phi\mathrm{i})\right)^{-m}&=\frac{1}{\left(\exp(\phi\mathrm{i})\right)^m}\\&=\frac{1}{\exp(m\phi\mathrm{i})}\quad\text{(using the theorem for positive integral index } m)\\&=\exp(-m\phi\mathrm{i})\qquad(\text{since }\exp(m\phi\mathrm{i})\exp(-m\phi\mathrm{i})=\exp(0)=1)\\&=\exp(n\phi\mathrm{i}).\end{aligned}$$

This completes the proof for all $n\in\mathbb{Z}$.

You will need to recognise this result in all three notations.

De Moivre's theorem, for $n\in\mathbb{Z}$.

Trigonometric version: $(\cos\phi+\mathrm{i}\sin\phi)^n=\cos n\phi+\mathrm{i}\sin n\phi$.

Exponential version: $\left(\mathrm{e}^{\phi\mathrm{i}}\right)^n=\mathrm{e}^{n\phi\mathrm{i}}$, or $\left(\exp(\phi\mathrm{i})\right)^n=\exp(n\phi\mathrm{i})$.

De Moivre was born in France, but emigrated to England as a young man in 1688 to escape religious persecution. Although he certainly knew the theorem named after him, it was first published in its trigonometrical form by Euler in 1748.

The theorem has a delightful representation in an Argand diagram. As $z=\cos\phi+\mathrm{i}\sin\phi$ has modulus 1, all the powers of z also have modulus 1. This means that all integral powers of z correspond to points on the unit circle. The theorem shows that these points are equally spaced round the circle, as shown in Fig. 7.1.

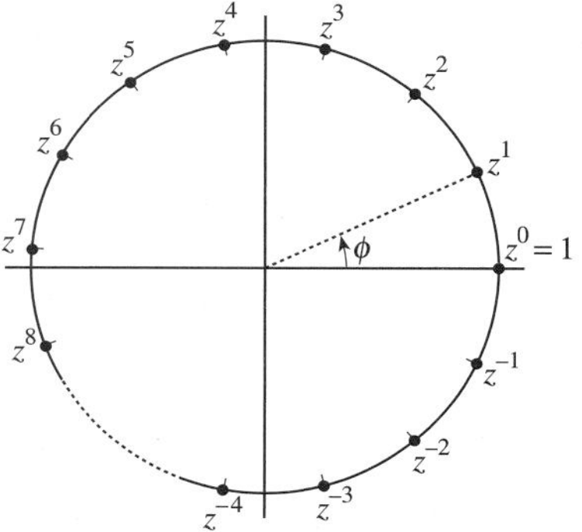

Fig. 7.1

Example 7.1.1
Show in an Argand diagram the points corresponding to z^n, $n \in \mathbb{Z}$, where
(a) $z = 0.9\mathrm{e}^{\mathrm{i}}$, (b) $z = 1 + \mathrm{i}$.
In each case find the polar equation of a curve which passes through all the points.

(a) If $z = 0.9\mathrm{e}^{\mathrm{i}}$, then $z^n = 0.9^n \mathrm{e}^{n\mathrm{i}}$ is represented on an Argand diagram by a point with polar coordinates $r = 0.9^n, \theta = n$. As n increases, values of r decrease in geometric progression, and values of θ increase in arithmetic progression with common difference 1 radian.

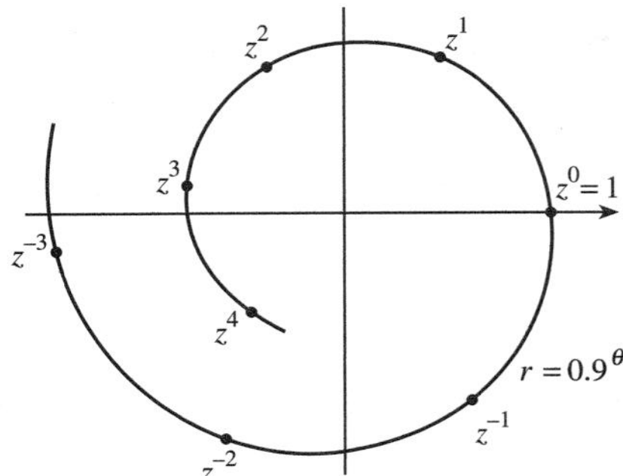

Fig. 7.2

The points all lie on the curve with equation $r = 0.9^\theta$ (see Fig. 7.2). Since $0.9 = \mathrm{e}^{\ln 0.9}$, $r = 0.9^\theta$ can be written as $r = \mathrm{e}^{\theta \ln 0.9} \approx \mathrm{e}^{-0.105\theta}$.

(b) The number $1 + \mathrm{i}$ has modulus $\sqrt{2}$ and argument $\frac{1}{4}\pi$, so $z = 2^{\frac{1}{2}} \exp\left(\frac{1}{4}\pi \mathrm{i}\right)$ and $z^n = 2^{\frac{1}{2}n} \exp\left(n\left(\frac{1}{4}\pi \mathrm{i}\right)\right)$. Thus $r = 2^{\frac{1}{2}n}$ and $\theta = \frac{1}{4}n\pi$. As n increases, values of r increase geometrically with common ratio $\sqrt{2}$ and values of θ increase arithmetically with common difference $\frac{1}{4}\pi$.

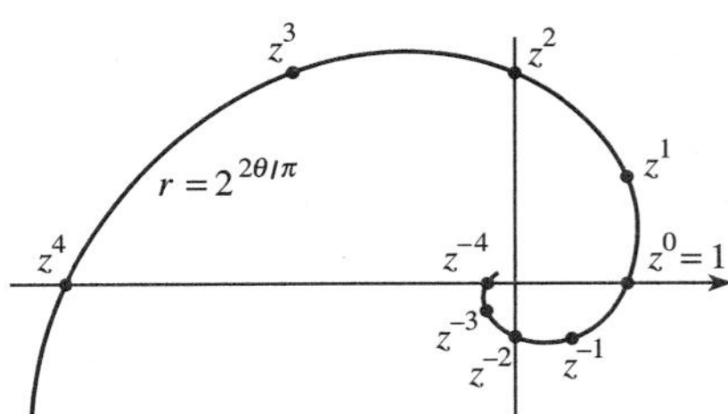

Fig. 7.3

Since $n = \dfrac{4\theta}{\pi}$, the points all lie on the curve with equation $r = 2^{2\theta/\pi}$, or

$$r = \exp\left(\frac{2\theta \ln 2}{\pi}\right) \approx \mathrm{e}^{0.441\theta} \text{ (see Fig. 7.3).}$$

The curves in both parts (a) and (b) are examples of equiangular spirals (see P4 Example 9.4.2).

7.2 The *n*th roots of unity

Fig. 7.1 can only show a small number of points z^n, where $z = \mathrm{e}^{\phi \mathrm{i}}$. If you go on plotting these points on an Argand diagram, there are two possibilities. Either you get a new point each time (so that eventually the points are densely packed round the circumference of the unit circle), or they start to repeat. Since the angle increases by the same amount each time, as soon as you get one repetition all subsequent points will also be repetitions.

One of the points is of course $z^0 = 1$, and in fact the first repetition with a positive index is always $z^n = 1$. To prove this, you need only note that if the first repetition were $z^n = z^m$, with $n > m \geqslant 1$, then you could divide by z to get $z^{n-1} = z^{m-1}$ with $n - 1 > m - 1 \geqslant 0$, which contradicts the claim that $z^n = z^m$ is the first repetition. So m must be 0, which means that $z^n = 1$ is the first repetition.

It then follows that there are just n different values of z^n, and that these are $1, z, z^2, z^3, \ldots, z^{n-1}$. The points representing these on an Argand diagram are vertices of a regular polygon.

The vertex of the polygon nearest to 1 (anticlockwise) has argument $\frac{2\pi}{n}$. If ω denotes $\exp\left(\frac{2\pi}{n}\mathrm{i}\right)$, then the remaining vertices in order round the polygon are $\omega^2, \omega^3, \ldots, \omega^{n-1}$. This is shown in Fig. 7.4.

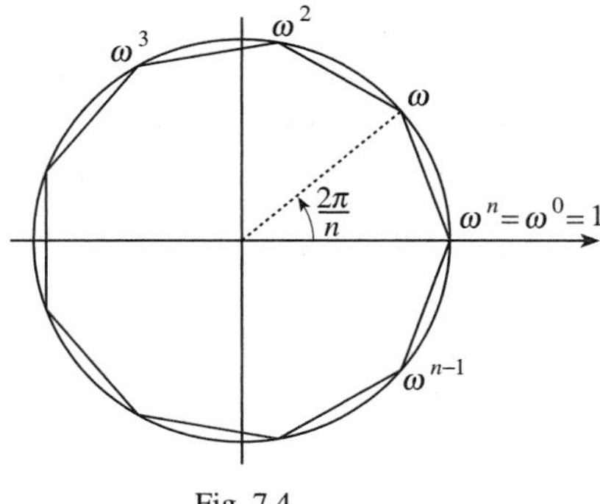

Fig. 7.4

An important result is that each of these numbers raised to the nth power equals 1. This is because, for any $r \in \mathbb{Z}$,

$$\left(\omega^r\right)^n = \omega^{rn} = \left(\omega^n\right)^r = 1^r = 1.$$

You can also see this geometrically. If you go round a regular n-gon jumping r points at each step, then after n steps you will have made r complete revolutions ending up at 1.

The complex numbers $1, \omega, \omega^2, \omega^3, \ldots, \omega^{n-1}$ are therefore all nth roots of 1. They are usually known by the slightly quaint name of **the *n*th roots of unity.**

> The nth roots of unity are $1, \omega, \omega^2, \omega^3, \ldots, \omega^{n-1}$, where
>
> $\omega = \exp\left(\frac{2\pi}{n}\mathrm{i}\right)$; that is, $\exp\left(\frac{2r\pi}{n}\mathrm{i}\right)$ for $0 \leqslant r \leqslant n-1$.

You can also derive the second equation in the shaded box algebraically. If $z = k\mathrm{e}^{\theta\mathrm{i}}$, where $k > 0$, then $z^n = k^n\mathrm{e}^{n\theta\mathrm{i}}$. For this to equal $1 = 1\mathrm{e}^{0\mathrm{i}}$, k^n must equal 1 and $n\theta$ must differ from 0 by a multiple of 2π. That is, $k = 1$ and $\theta = \frac{2r\pi}{n}$, where $r \in \mathbb{Z}$.

Notice that this holds for any integer r. The restriction $0 \leqslant r \leqslant n-1$ in the definition above ensures that the n values of z are all different; but you can achieve this equally well by letting r take any n consecutive integral values. The integers from 0 to $n-1$ are not always the most convenient, as the next example shows.

Example 7.2.1
Pair off the non-real nth roots of unity as conjugate complex numbers
(a) when $n = 5$, (b) when $n = 6$.

The roots are shown in Argand diagrams in Figs. 7.5 and 7.6, on the next page.

(a) The points are at the vertices of a regular pentagon, with radii separated by angles of $\frac{2}{5}\pi$. Apart from 0, the arguments of the roots are $\frac{2}{5}\pi$, $\frac{4}{5}\pi$, $-\frac{4}{5}\pi$, $-\frac{2}{5}\pi$. Thus the non-real roots are $\exp\left(\frac{2}{5}r\pi\mathrm{i}\right)$ for $r = \pm 1$ and ± 2.

(b) The points are at the vertices of a regular hexagon, with radii separated by angles of $\frac{2}{6}\pi = \frac{1}{3}\pi$. There are two real roots, 1 and -1, and the arguments of the other roots are $\frac{1}{3}\pi$, $\frac{2}{3}\pi$, $-\frac{2}{3}\pi$, $-\frac{1}{3}\pi$. Thus the non-real roots are $\exp\left(\frac{1}{3}r\pi\mathrm{i}\right)$ for $r = \pm 1$ and ± 2.

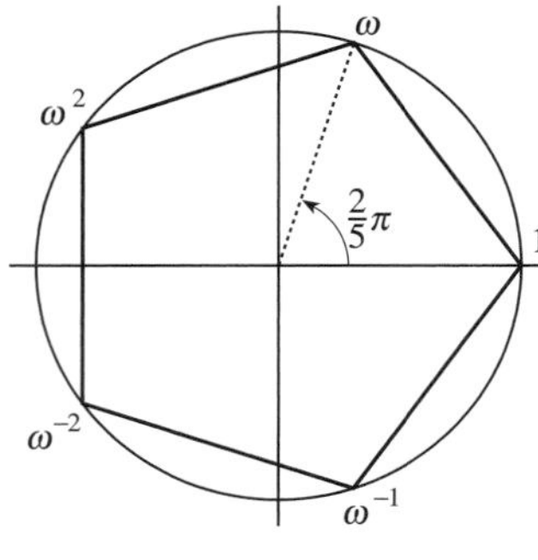

Fig. 7.5

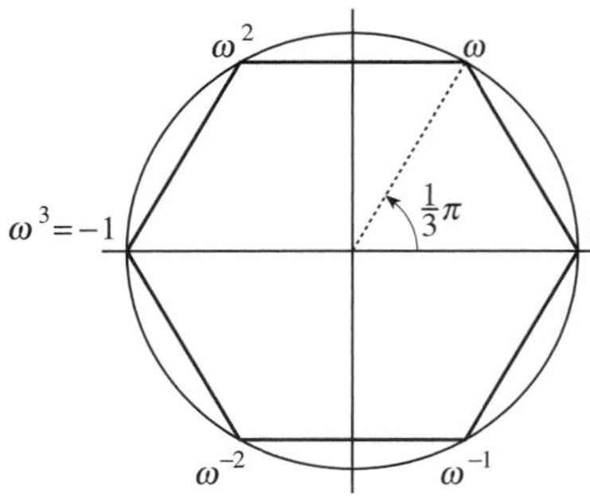

Fig. 7.6

You should check the generalisation of this example for yourself.

For any natural number $n \geqslant 3$, the nth roots of unity are

$$1 \text{ and } \exp\left(\frac{2r\pi}{n}\mathrm{i}\right) \text{ for } r = \pm 1, \pm 2, \ldots, \pm \tfrac{1}{2}(n-1) \text{ if } n \text{ is odd;}$$

$$1, -1 \text{ and } \exp\left(\frac{2r\pi}{n}\mathrm{i}\right) \text{ for } r = \pm 1, \pm 2, \ldots, \pm\left(\tfrac{1}{2}n - 1\right) \text{ if } n \text{ is even.}$$

7.3 Applications in algebra and geometry

The cube roots of unity, 1, ω and ω^2 where $\omega = \exp\left(\frac{2}{3}\pi\mathrm{i}\right)$, are the roots of the equation

$$z^3 - 1 = 0.$$

Now you know from P5 Chapter 1 that the sum of the roots of the cubic equation $az^3 + bz^2 + cz + d = 0$ is $-\dfrac{b}{a}$. In this case $a = 1$ and $b = 0$, so

$$1 + \omega + \omega^2 = 0.$$

This important relation has many applications.

Example 7.3.1
Multiply out the product $\left(a + b\omega + c\omega^2\right)\left(a + b\omega^2 + c\omega\right)$, where $\omega = \exp\left(\frac{2}{3}\pi\mathrm{i}\right)$.

The product has nine terms. Those involving a^2, b^2 and c^2 are $aa = a^2$, $(b\omega)\left(b\omega^2\right) = b^2\omega^3 = b^2$ and $\left(c\omega^2\right)(c\omega) = c^2\omega^3 = c^2$, since $\omega^3 = 1$. The terms involving bc are

$$(b\omega)(c\omega) + \left(c\omega^2\right)\left(b\omega^2\right) = bc\left(\omega^2 + \omega^4\right) = bc\left(\omega^2 + \omega\right) = bc(-1) = -bc.$$

This simplification uses $\omega^4 = \left(\omega^3\right)\omega = \omega$ and $1 + \omega + \omega^2 = 0$.

Similarly, the terms involving ca and ab are

$$a(c\omega)+(c\omega^2)a = ca(\omega+\omega^2) = ca(-1) = -ca,$$

and $$a(b\omega^2)+(b\omega)a = ab(\omega^2+\omega) = ab(-1) = -ab.$$

This gives for the complete product

$$(a+b\omega+c\omega^2)(a+b\omega^2+c\omega) = a^2+b^2+c^2-bc-ca-ab.$$

Example 7.3.2

A triangle is formed by points representing complex numbers a, b and c in an Argand diagram. Find the condition for the triangle to be equilateral.

There are two cases. Going round the triangle anticlockwise, the points A, B, C corresponding to a, b, c may occur in the order ABC (Fig. 7.7) or ACB (Fig. 7.8). In Fig. 7.7 the displacement $\overrightarrow{BC}$ is transformed into $\overrightarrow{CA}$ by a rotation through $+\frac{2}{3}\pi$. In complex number arithmetic this is equivalent to obtaining $a-c$ by multiplying $c-b$ by a number with modulus 1 and argument $\frac{2}{3}\pi$, that is by the cube root of unity ω.

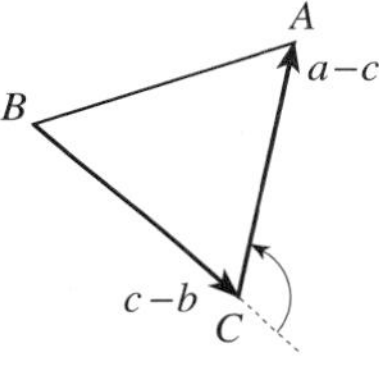

Fig. 7.7

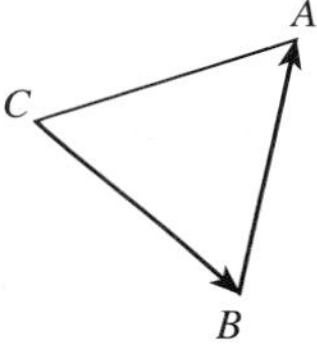

Fig. 7.8

So $\quad a-c=(c-b)\omega, \quad$ that is $\quad a+b\omega-c(1+\omega)=0,$

or $\quad a+b\omega+c\omega^2=0 \quad (\text{since } 1+\omega+\omega^2=0).$

You can get the equivalent condition for Fig. 7.8 by interchanging b and c in this condition, which gives

$$a+c\omega+b\omega^2=0, \quad \text{that is} \quad a+b\omega^2+c\omega=0.$$

For one or the other of these conditions to be true, it is necessary and sufficient that

$$(a+b\omega+c\omega^2)(a+b\omega^2+c\omega)=0.$$

Using the result of Example 7.3.1, you can write this rule as

$$a^2+b^2+c^2-bc-ca-ab=0.$$

Example 7.3.3

Find the condition for the roots of the equation $z^3+pz^2+qz+r=0$ to represent the vertices of an equilateral triangle in an Argand diagram.

Since $(a+b+c)^2=a^2+b^2+c^2+2bc+2ca+2ab$, the condition at the end of Example 7.3.2 can be written as

$$(a+b+c)^2=3bc+3ca+3ab.$$

You know from P5 Chapter 1 that $a+b+c=-p$ and $bc+ca+ab=q$. The condition is therefore

$$(-p)^2=3q, \quad \text{that is} \quad p^2=3q.$$

The equation $1+\omega+\omega^2=0$ connecting the cube roots of unity can be generalised to give a similar equation for the nth roots. You can prove this either by extending the condition for the sum of the roots to be zero to the nth degree equation $z^n-1=0$, or by using the formula for the sum of a geometric progression. If $\omega=\exp\left(\frac{2\pi}{n}\mathrm{i}\right)$, then

$$1+\omega+\omega^2+\ldots+\omega^{n-1}=\frac{1-\omega^n}{1-\omega}=0, \quad \text{since } \omega^n=1.$$

For $n\in\mathbb{N}$, $n>1$, the sum of the nth roots of unity, $1+\omega+\omega^2+\ldots+\omega^{n-1}$, is equal to zero.

Exercise 7A

1 Use de Moivre's theorem to express the following in the form $a+b\mathrm{i}$. Give the answers exactly where possible, otherwise give them to 3 significant figures.

(a) $(1-\mathrm{i})^8$ (b) $\left(1-\sqrt{3}\mathrm{i}\right)^{-9}$ (c) $\left(\exp\frac{1}{4}\pi\mathrm{i}\right)^9$

(d) $\left(\cos\frac{3}{5}\pi+\mathrm{i}\sin\frac{3}{5}\pi\right)^{15}$ (e) $\left(\sin\frac{1}{7}\pi+\mathrm{i}\cos\frac{1}{7}\pi\right)^{-35}$ (f) $(8-6\mathrm{i})^{30}$

(g) $(0.6+0.7\mathrm{i})^{-8}$ (h) $\left(\frac{7+4\mathrm{i}}{8+\mathrm{i}}\right)^{10}$

2 Show in an Argand diagram the points corresponding to z^n, $n\in\mathbb{Z}$, for the following values of z. State for each the smallest positive value of n (if any) for which z^n is real, and whether z^n is positive or negative for this value of n.

(a) i (b) e^{i} (c) $\exp\frac{4}{5}\pi\mathrm{i}$

(d) $\cos\frac{1}{3}\pi+\mathrm{i}\sin\frac{1}{3}\pi$ (e) $\sqrt{3}+\mathrm{i}$ (f) $2-\mathrm{i}$

(g) $\frac{1}{1+\mathrm{i}}$ (h) $\frac{3+4\mathrm{i}}{5}$

3 (a) Write down, in an exact form, all the 8th roots of 1 in the form $a+b\mathrm{i}$.

(b) Write down in the form $a+b\mathrm{i}$, to 3 decimal places, all the 7th roots of 1.

4 Multiply out the products

(a) $(a+b\omega)(a+b\omega^2)$ where $\omega=\exp\frac{2}{3}\pi\mathrm{i}$,

(b) $(a+b\omega)(a+b\omega^2)(a+b\omega^3)(a+b\omega^4)$ where $\omega=\exp\frac{2}{5}\pi\mathrm{i}$.

5† If $\alpha=\exp\frac{2}{5}\pi\mathrm{i}$, $\beta=\exp\frac{4}{5}\pi\mathrm{i}$, $\gamma=\exp\frac{6}{5}\pi\mathrm{i}$ and $\delta=\exp\frac{8}{5}\pi\mathrm{i}$, express β, γ and δ as powers of α.

If $p=a+b\alpha+c\alpha^2+d\alpha^3+e\alpha^4$, $q=a+b\beta+c\beta^2+d\beta^3+e\beta^4$, $r=a+b\gamma+c\gamma^2+d\gamma^3+e\gamma^4$, $s=a+b\delta+c\delta^2+d\delta^3+e\delta^4$ and the product $pqrs$ is multiplied out, find the coefficients of

(a) a^4, (b) a^3b, (c) a^2b^2, (d) a^2bc, (e) $abcd$.

6 Find the nth roots of -1 for

(a) $n=2$, (b) $n=3$, (c) $n=4$, (d) $n=5$, (e) $n=6$,

and arrange the complex roots in conjugate pairs. Suggest and prove a generalisation of your results for any positive integer n.

7 In Example 7.3.3 show that, if $p^2=3q$, the cubic equation can be written in the form $\left(z+\frac{1}{3}p\right)^3=s$. Use this to prove by another method that the points in an Argand diagram representing the roots form an equilateral triangle.

8 If triangles ABC and XYZ are drawn in an Argand diagram, both labelled anticlockwise round the triangle, show that they are similar if and only if $\dfrac{a-c}{b-c}=\dfrac{x-z}{y-z}$. Obtain the condition in Example 7.3.2 by showing that a triangle ABC is similar to BCA if and only if the triangle is equilateral.

9 A triangle ABC is drawn in an Argand diagram, with its vertices labelled anticlockwise round the triangle. Equilateral triangles BCX, CAY, ABZ are drawn outside the triangle. Show that $x=-b\omega^2-c\omega$, where $\exp\frac{2}{3}\pi\mathrm{i}$, and write down similar expressions for y and z. Hence find complex numbers representing the displacements $\overrightarrow{XA}$, $\overrightarrow{YB}$ and $\overrightarrow{ZC}$. Show that these displacements are equal in magnitude, and that they make angles of $\frac{2}{3}\pi$ with each other. (It can also be proved that the lines XA, YB and ZC meet at a single point, but this is not easy to prove using complex numbers.)

10 With the notation of Question 9, let P, Q and R be the centres of the three equilateral triangles. Prove that the triangle PQR is equilateral.

11 A triangle ABC is drawn in an Argand diagram, with its vertices labelled clockwise round the triangle. Starting at any point P in the plane, rotate anticlockwise through angles of $\frac{2}{3}\pi$ about A, B and C in succession to arrive at points Q, R and S. Show that S and P coincide if and only if the triangle ABC is equilateral.

12 ABC is a triangle in an Argand diagram. Starting at any point P in the plane, rotate through angles of $\frac{1}{3}\pi$ about A, B, C, A, B and C in succession to arrive at points Q, R, S, T, U and V. Show that V is the same point as P.

Investigate similar results for

(a) a quadrilateral $ABCD$, (b) a pentagon $ABCDE$.

7.4 An application to factors

Writing the roots as conjugate complex pairs, as in Section 7.2, is useful when you want to combine complex factors in pairs to produce factors with real coefficients. The key identity for this purpose is

$$\left(z-\mathrm{e}^{\theta\mathrm{i}}\right)\left(z-\mathrm{e}^{-\theta\mathrm{i}}\right)\equiv z^2-\left(\mathrm{e}^{\theta\mathrm{i}}+\mathrm{e}^{-\theta\mathrm{i}}\right)z+1\equiv z^2-2z\cos\theta+1,$$

using the fact that

$$\mathrm{e}^{\theta\mathrm{i}}+\mathrm{e}^{-\theta\mathrm{i}}\equiv(\cos\theta+\mathrm{i}\sin\theta)+(\cos\theta-\mathrm{i}\sin\theta)\equiv 2\cos\theta.$$

You know from the factor theorem that, if z_1, z_2, ..., z_n are the nth roots of unity, then

$$z^n - 1 = (z - z_1)(z - z_2)\ldots(z - z_n).$$

So, from the pairing of these roots and the results in the shaded box at the end of Section 7.2:

If n is odd, the factors of $z^n - 1$ are $z - 1$ and $z^2 - 2z\cos\left(\frac{2r\pi}{n}\right) + 1$ for $r = 1, 2, \ldots, \frac{1}{2}(n-1)$.
If n is even, the factors of $z^n - 1$ are $z - 1$, $z + 1$ and $z^2 - 2z\cos\left(\frac{2r\pi}{n}\right) + 1$ for $r = 1, 2, \ldots, \left(\frac{1}{2}n - 1\right)$.

For example, from Example 7.2.1, you can deduce that

$$\begin{aligned} z^5 - 1 &= (z-1)\left(z^2 - 2z\cos\left(\tfrac{2}{5}\pi\right) + 1\right)\left(z^2 - 2z\cos\left(\tfrac{4}{5}\pi\right) + 1\right) \\ &= (z-1)\left(z^2 - 2z\cos\left(\tfrac{2}{5}\pi\right) + 1\right)\left(z^2 + 2z\cos\left(\tfrac{1}{5}\pi\right) + 1\right), \end{aligned}$$

since $\cos\left(\frac{4}{5}\pi\right) = \cos\left(\pi - \frac{4}{5}\pi\right) = -\cos\left(\frac{1}{5}\pi\right)$; and that

$$\begin{aligned} z^6 - 1 &= (z-1)(z+1)\left(z^2 - 2z\cos\left(\tfrac{1}{3}\pi\right) + 1\right)\left(z^2 - 2z\cos\left(\tfrac{2}{3}\pi\right) + 1\right) \\ &= (z-1)(z+1)\left(z^2 - z + 1\right)\left(z^2 + z + 1\right), \end{aligned}$$

since $\cos\left(\frac{1}{3}\pi\right) = \frac{1}{2}$ and $\cos\left(\frac{2}{3}\pi\right) = -\frac{1}{2}$.

7.5 The *n*th roots of a general complex number

Example 7.5.1
Find the fifth roots of i, and illustrate them on an Argand diagram.

Since $i^2 = -1$, $i^4 = (-1)^2 = 1$, so $i^5 = i$. One fifth root of i is therefore i itself.

If z is any fifth root of i, then $z^5 = i$, so $\left(\frac{z}{i}\right)^5 = \frac{z^5}{i^5} = 1$ (since $i^5 = i$). This means that $\frac{z}{i}$ must be one of the fifth roots of unity. If these are denoted by 1, ω, ω^2, ω^3 and ω^4, where $\omega = \exp\left(\frac{2}{5}\pi i\right)$, then z is equal to i, $i\omega$, $i\omega^2$, $i\omega^3$ or $i\omega^4$.

Now i has argument $\frac{1}{2}\pi$, and multiplying by ω rotates this about the origin through $\frac{2}{5}\pi$. So i, $i\omega$, $i\omega^2$, ... have arguments $\frac{1}{2}\pi$, $\frac{1}{2}\pi + \frac{2}{5}\pi$, $\frac{1}{2}\pi + \frac{4}{5}\pi$, ... The fifth roots of i are therefore $\exp\left(\frac{1}{2}\pi\right)$, $\exp\left(\frac{9}{10}\pi\right)$, $\exp\left(\frac{13}{10}\pi\right)$, $\exp\left(\frac{17}{10}\pi\right)$ and $\exp\left(\frac{21}{10}\pi\right)$.

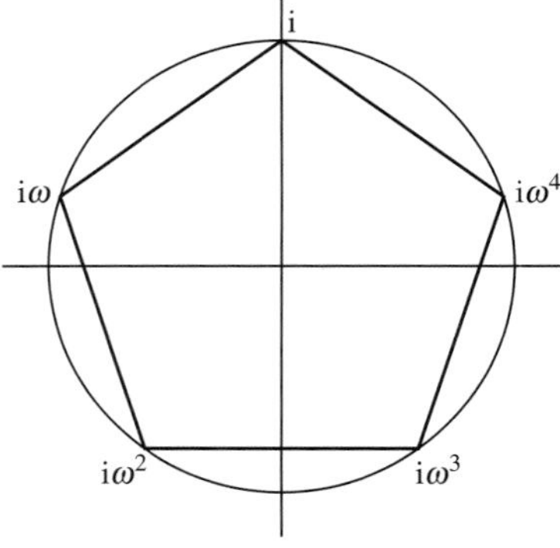

Fig. 7.9

These roots are shown in an Argand diagram in Fig. 7.9 as points on the unit circle at the vertices of a regular pentagon. Notice that, unlike the fifth roots of unity in Example 7.2.1, these roots don't split into conjugate pairs.

The results of Example 7.5.1 can be generalised. Whenever you find the nth roots of any complex number, you always get points in an Argand diagram at the vertices of a regular polygon with its centre at the origin.

The algebraic argument used in Section 7.2 to find the nth roots of unity can be extended to find the nth roots of any complex number, written in modulus-argument form as $a\mathrm{e}^{\alpha \mathrm{i}}$, where $a > 0$. If $z = k\mathrm{e}^{\theta \mathrm{i}}$ is an nth root, with $k > 0$, then you want to determine k and θ so that

$$k^n \mathrm{e}^{n\theta \mathrm{i}} = a\mathrm{e}^{\alpha \mathrm{i}}.$$

For this to be true, k^n must equal a, and $n\theta$ must differ from α by a multiple of 2π. That is, $k = \sqrt[n]{a}$ and $n\theta = \alpha + 2r\pi$, which gives

$$\theta = \frac{\alpha}{n} + \frac{2r\pi}{n}.$$

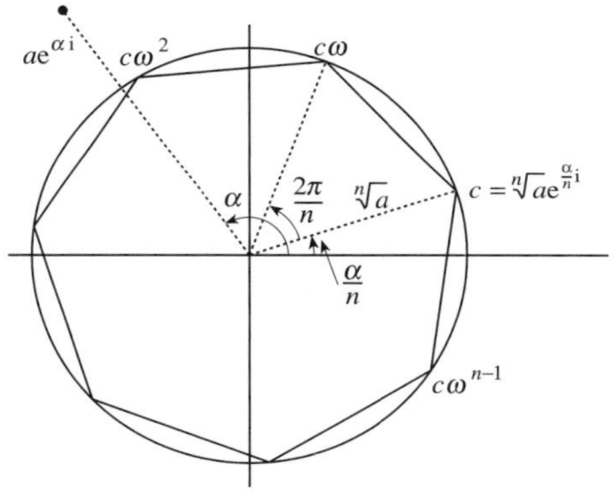

Fig. 7.10

Fig. 7.10 shows these nth roots in an Argand diagram. They all lie on a circle with centre O and radius $\sqrt[n]{a}$, at angles which go up in steps of $\frac{2\pi}{n}$ as r increases through $\mathbb{Z}$. You therefore get different roots for any n consecutive integral values of r, such as $0 \leqslant r \leqslant n-1$, and they then start to repeat. The corresponding points are at the vertices of a regular n-gon, and can be written in the form $c\omega^r$, where c denotes the root $\sqrt[n]{a}\exp\left(\frac{\alpha}{n}\mathrm{i}\right)$.

> The nth roots of the complex number $a\mathrm{e}^{\alpha \mathrm{i}}$ are
>
> $$\sqrt[n]{a}\exp\left(\left(\frac{\alpha}{n} + \frac{2r\pi}{n}\right)\mathrm{i}\right) = \sqrt[n]{a}\exp\left(\frac{\alpha}{n}\mathrm{i}\right)\omega^r$$
>
> for $r \in \mathbb{Z}$, $0 \leqslant r \leqslant n-1$.

Example 7.5.2
Express $z^{2n} - 2z^n \cos n\beta + 1$ as the product of n quadratic factors with real coefficients.

The identity $z^2 - 2z\cos\theta + 1 \equiv \left(z - \mathrm{e}^{\theta \mathrm{i}}\right)\left(z - \mathrm{e}^{-\theta \mathrm{i}}\right)$ used in Section 7.4 can be adapted, replacing z by z^n and θ by $n\beta$, to give

$$z^{2n} - 2z^n \cos n\beta + 1 \equiv \left(z^n - \mathrm{e}^{n\beta \mathrm{i}}\right)\left(z^n - \mathrm{e}^{-n\beta \mathrm{i}}\right).$$

The roots of the equation $z^n = e^{n\beta i}$ are $z = \exp\left(\left(\beta + \dfrac{2r\pi}{n}\right)i\right)$, and the roots of $z^n = e^{-n\beta i}$ are $z = \exp\left(\left(-\beta + \dfrac{2s\pi}{n}\right)i\right)$, for n consecutive integral values of r and s. If you take $r = 0, 1, 2, \ldots, n-1$ in the first instance, and $s = 0, -1, -2, \ldots, -(n-1)$ in the second, then corresponding values of r and s give the roots in conjugate complex pairs. This is illustrated in Fig. 7.11. Writing $s = -r$, the pairs of factors are then

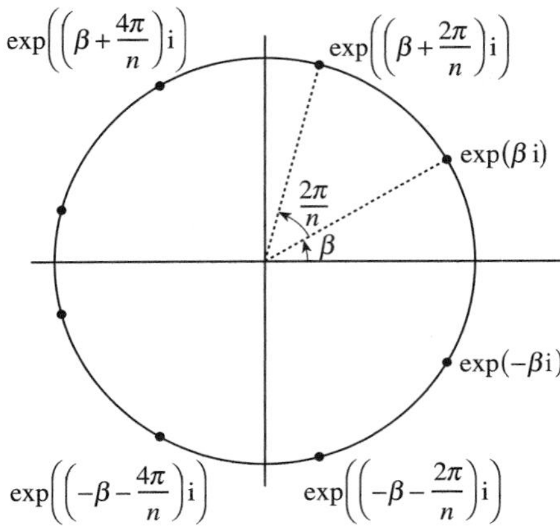

Fig. 7.11

$$z - \exp\left(\left(\beta + \frac{2r\pi}{n}\right)i\right) \quad \text{and} \quad z - \exp\left(\left(-\beta - \frac{2r\pi}{n}\right)i\right),$$

whose product is

$$z^2 - 2z\cos\left(\beta + \frac{2r\pi}{n}\right) + 1 \quad \text{for} \quad r = 0, 1, 2, \ldots, n-1.$$

These are the n quadratic factors required.

Exercise 7B

1 Find exact expressions for the nth roots of z if

(a) $n = 3$ and $z = i$, (b) $n = 4$ and $z = -8(1 + \sqrt{3}i)$, (c) $n = 6$ and $z = -64$.

Use the binomial theorem to check your answers.

2 Find, correct to 3 decimal places, the nth roots of z if

(a) $n = 4$ and $z = -i$, (b) $n = 5$ and $z = 4(1+i)$.

3 Express the following polynomials as the product of real factors. Check your answers by multiplying out the factors.

(a) $z^4 + 1$ (b) $z^8 - 16$ (c) $z^4 + z^2 + 1$ (d) $z^6 - z^3 + 1$

4 For the following values of z, p and q, write down all the values of (i) $\left(z^{\frac{1}{q}}\right)^p$ and (ii) $\left(z^p\right)^{\frac{1}{q}}$. Give your answers in the form $e^{\theta i}$, where $-\pi < \theta < \pi$, and illustrate them on an Argand diagram. What general result is suggested by your answers?

(a) $z = e^{\pi i}, p = 5, q = 3$ (b) $z = e^{\frac{1}{4}\pi i}, p = 4, q = 2$

(c) $z = e^{\frac{1}{2}\pi i}, p = 6, q = 4$ (d) $z = e^{\frac{3}{4}\pi i}, p = 3, q = 6$

5† An equilateral triangle ABC has vertices at the points 1, ω, ω^2 in an Argand diagram, where $\omega = \exp\frac{2}{3}\pi\mathrm{i}$, and P is the point $\frac{1}{2}(1+\mathrm{i})$. Use the identity $z^3 - 1 \equiv (z-1)(z-\omega)(z-\omega^2)$ to show that the product of the distances PA, PB and PC is $\frac{1}{4}\sqrt{26}$.

6† A regular pentagon $ABCDE$ has its vertices on a circle with radius r and centre O. A point P is at a distance d from O, and angle $AOP = \theta$. Prove that the product of the distances PA, PB, PC, PD and PE is $\sqrt{d^{10} - 2d^5r^5\cos 5\theta + r^{10}}$.

7† The vertices of an n-gon $P_0P_1P_2\ldots P_{n-1}$ lie on a circle of unit radius, and Q is the mid-point of the arc P_0P_1. Find the products of the distances

(a) $QP_0, QP_1, QP_2, \ldots, QP_{n-1}$,

(b) $P_0P_1, P_0P_2, P_0P_3, \ldots, P_0P_{n-1}$.

Miscellaneous exercise 7

1 Write $z_1 = 1+\mathrm{i}$ and $z_2 = 2(-1+\mathrm{i})$ in polar form. Show that $z_1{}^3 = z_2$.

Find the two other cube roots of z_2 in polar form, and sketch the three cube roots in an Argand diagram.

Write down the cube roots of $z_3 = 2(-1-\mathrm{i})$ in polar form. (OCR)

2 Write the complex number $8\mathrm{i}$ in the form $r\mathrm{e}^{\theta\mathrm{i}}$ (where $r > 0$ and $-\pi < \theta \leqslant \pi$).

Find the three cube roots of $8\mathrm{i}$, giving your answers in the form $a + b\mathrm{i}$. Illustrate these cube roots on an Argand diagram.

Hence solve the equation $\left(\mathrm{i}z - 2\sqrt{3}\right)^3 = 8\mathrm{i}$, giving your answers in the form $a + b\mathrm{i}$. (MEI)

3 If $\omega = \cos\theta + \mathrm{i}\sin\theta$, show that $\dfrac{1+\omega}{1-\omega} = \mathrm{i}\cot\frac{1}{2}\theta$.

Write down the roots of $z^n = -1$, where n is a positive integer. Hence, by writing z as $\dfrac{x-1}{x+1}$, prove that the roots of $(x-1)^n = -(x+1)^n$ are $\mathrm{i}\cot\dfrac{(2r+1)\pi}{2n}$ for $r = 0, 1, 2, \ldots, n-1$. (OCR)

4 Find all the fourth roots of -4, giving your answers in the form $p + q\mathrm{i}$, where p and q are real. Hence solve the equation $(z-1)^4 = -4(z+1)^4$, giving your answers in the form $x + y\mathrm{i}$ where x and y are real. (OCR)

5 Solve the equation $z^5 + 32 = 0$, giving the roots in the form $r\mathrm{e}^{\alpha\mathrm{i}}$ (where $r > 0$ and $-\pi < \alpha \leqslant \pi$). Illustrate the roots on an Argand diagram.

If $\left(\dfrac{1-2w}{w}\right)^5 + 32 = 0$, show that w has the form $\frac{1}{4}(1 - \mathrm{i}\tan\beta)$, and state the four possible values of β in the interval $-\pi < \beta \leqslant \pi$. On a separate Argand diagram, illustrate the four possible values of w. (MEI)

8 Further trigonometry

This chapter shows how some trigonometric results can be developed by using de Moivre's theorem. When you have completed it, you should

- be able to express trigonometric functions of multiples of an angle in terms of functions of the angle itself
- be able to use these relations to investigate the roots of polynomial equations
- be able to express powers of sines and cosines of an angle in terms of trigonometric functions of multiples of the angle
- know that some power series can be extended to complex variables
- be able to use sums of power series to find sums of trigonometric series.

8.1 Some useful notation

If $z = x + y\text{i}$ is a complex number, then x and y are respectively the real and imaginary parts of z. The notation used is

$$\text{Re}(z) = x \quad \text{and} \quad \text{Im}(z) = y.$$

Applying this to de Moivre's theorem, $(\cos\theta + \text{i}\sin\theta)^n = \cos n\theta + \text{i}\sin n\theta$, gives

$$\text{Re}\left((\cos\theta + \text{i}\sin\theta)^n\right) = \cos n\theta \quad \text{and} \quad \text{Im}\left((\cos\theta + \text{i}\sin\theta)^n\right) = \sin n\theta.$$

To simplify the look of the algebra, it will be convenient in this chapter to abbreviate $\cos\theta$, $\sin\theta$ and $\tan\theta$ to c, s and t. Then

$$\cos n\theta = \text{Re}\left((c + s\text{i})^n\right) \quad \text{and} \quad \sin n\theta = \text{Im}\left((c + s\text{i})^n\right).$$

You can easily verify for yourself the following properties of the functions Re and Im.

> The real and imaginary parts of z are denoted by $\text{Re}(z)$ and $\text{Im}(z)$.
>
> For complex numbers z and w, and a real number a,
>
> $$\text{Re}(az) = a\,\text{Re}(z), \qquad \text{Im}(az) = a\,\text{Im}(z),$$
> $$\text{Re}(z + w) = \text{Re}(z) + \text{Re}(w), \qquad \text{Im}(z + w) = \text{Im}(z) + \text{Im}(w),$$
> $$z + z^* = 2\,\text{Re}(z), \qquad z - z^* = 2\,\text{Im}(z)\,\text{i}.$$

8.2 Multiple angle formulae

When you first met the double angle formulae, they were obtained as a special case of the addition formulae, writing $B = A$ in the formula for $\sin(A + B)$ to get $\sin 2A$. It is easy to extend this to $\sin 3A = \sin(A + 2A)$ and $\sin 4A = \sin 2(2A)$, but the method gets laborious if you try to use it to find $\sin nA$ for a large value of n, where $n \in \mathbb{N}$.

It is much easier to use the expressions in the last section for $\cos n\theta$ and $\sin n\theta$ as the real and imaginary parts of $(c + s\text{i})^n$, which can be expanded by the binomial theorem as

$$\left(\begin{array}{l} (c+s\mathrm{i})^n = c^n + \binom{n}{1}c^{n-1}(s\mathrm{i}) + \binom{n}{2}c^{n-2}(s\mathrm{i})^2 + \binom{n}{3}c^{n-3}(s\mathrm{i})^3 + \ldots \\ \qquad\qquad + \binom{n}{n-1}c(s\mathrm{i})^{n-1} + (s\mathrm{i})^n. \end{array} \right)$$

Since the successive powers of i are $\mathrm{i}^2 = -1$, $\mathrm{i}^3 = -\mathrm{i}$, $\mathrm{i}^4 = 1$, and then repeat indefinitely following the pattern i, -1, $-\mathrm{i}$, 1, the terms of the binomial expansion are real and imaginary in turn. It follows that

$$\cos n\theta = \mathrm{Re}\left((c+s\mathrm{i})^n\right) = c^n - \binom{n}{2}c^{n-2}s^2 + \binom{n}{4}c^{n-4}s^4 + \ldots,$$

and $$\sin n\theta = \mathrm{Im}\left((c+s\mathrm{i})^n\right) = \binom{n}{1}c^{n-1}s - \binom{n}{3}c^{n-3}s^3 + \binom{n}{5}c^{n-5}s^5 - \ldots.$$

The dots at the end of these expansions indicate that they continue for as long as the powers of c are non-negative and the powers of s are less than or equal to n. The precise expression for the last term depends on whether n is odd or even, and its sign depends on the remainder when n is divided by 4.

Example 8.2.1

Find expressions in terms of powers of $\cos\theta$ and/or $\sin\theta$ for
(a) $\cos 5\theta$, (b) $\sin 7\theta$, (c) $\sin 8\theta$.

$$\begin{aligned} \text{(a)}\ \cos 5\theta &= \mathrm{Re}\left((c+s\mathrm{i})^5\right) = c^5 - \binom{5}{2}c^3s^2 + \binom{5}{4}cs^4 \\ &= c^5 - 10c^3s^2 + 5cs^4. \end{aligned}$$

You could leave the answer in this form, but it is often more useful to give it in terms of c alone, using Pythagoras' identity to write s^2 as $1-c^2$. Then $s^4 = \left(1-c^2\right)^2$, so

$$\begin{aligned} \cos 5\theta &= c^5 - 10c^3\left(1-c^2\right) + 5c\left(1-c^2\right)^2 \\ &= c^5 - 10c^3\left(1-c^2\right) + 5c\left(1-2c^2+c^4\right) \\ &= c^5 - 10c^3 + 10c^5 + 5c - 10c^3 + 5c^5 \\ &= (1+10+5)c^5 + (-10-10)c^3 + 5c \\ &= 16\cos^5\theta - 20\cos^3\theta + 5\cos\theta, \end{aligned}$$

replacing the abbreviation c by $\cos\theta$.

$$\begin{aligned} \text{(b)}\ \sin 7\theta &= \mathrm{Im}\left((c+s\mathrm{i})^n\right) = \binom{7}{1}c^6s - \binom{7}{3}c^4s^3 + \binom{7}{5}c^2s^5 - \binom{7}{7}s^7 \\ &= 7c^6s - 35c^4s^3 + 21c^2s^5 - s^7. \end{aligned}$$

Since c appears only to even powers, you can replace c^2 by $1-s^2$ to obtain an expansion involving only s.

That is,

$$\begin{aligned}\sin 7\theta &= 7(1-s^2)^3 s - 35(1-s^2)^2 s^3 + 21(1-s^2)s^5 - s^7 \\ &= 7s - 21s^3 + 21s^5 - 7s^7 \\ &\quad - 35s^3 + 70s^5 - 35s^7 \\ &\quad + 21s^5 - 21s^7 \\ &\quad - s^7 \\ &= 7\sin\theta - 56\sin^3\theta + 112\sin^5\theta - 64\sin^7\theta.\end{aligned}$$

It is easy to make a mistake in working through this algebra, so it is a good idea to check the coefficients by taking a particular value for θ. For example, putting $\theta = \frac{1}{2}\pi$ gives $\sin\frac{7}{2}\pi = -1$ on the left, and $7 - 56 + 112 - 64 = -1$ on the right.

(c) $$\begin{aligned}\sin 8\theta &= \binom{8}{1}c^7 s - \binom{8}{3}c^5 s^3 + \binom{8}{5}c^3 s^5 - \binom{8}{7}cs^7 \\ &= 8c^7 s - 56c^5 s^3 + 56c^3 s^5 - 8cs^7.\end{aligned}$$

You can't write this as a polynomial in either c or s alone, because both c and s appear to odd powers. But it is possible to keep just a single factor of c or s and to express the remaining factor entirely in terms of the other. Thus

$$\begin{aligned}\sin 8\theta &= 8cs\left(c^6 - 7c^4 s^2 + 7c^2 s^4 - s^6\right) \\ &= 8cs\left((1-s^2)^3 - 7(1-s^2)^2 s^2 + 7(1-s^2)s^4 - s^6\right) \\ &= 8cs\big(1 - 3s^2 + 3s^4 - s^6 \\ &\quad - 7s^2 + 14s^4 - 7s^6 \\ &\quad + 7s^4 - 7s^6 \\ &\quad - s^6\big) \\ &= 8\cos\theta\sin\theta\left(1 - 10\sin^2\theta + 24\sin^4\theta - 16\sin^6\theta\right).\end{aligned}$$

In this case values of θ such as 0, $\frac{1}{2}\pi$ or π are of no use as a check on the coefficients, since both sides are obviously zero. But you could use $\frac{1}{4}\pi$, for which $\sin\theta = \cos\theta = \dfrac{1}{\sqrt{2}}$, so that the left side is 0 and the right side is $8 \times \frac{1}{2}\left(1 - \frac{10}{2} + \frac{24}{4} - \frac{16}{8}\right) = 4(1 - 5 + 6 - 2) = 0$.

Example 8.2.2

Find expressions in terms of $\tan\theta$ for (a) $\tan 5\theta$, (b) $\tan 6\theta$.

(a) You can express $\tan 5\theta$ in terms of c and s by using

$$\tan 5\theta = \frac{\sin 5\theta}{\cos 5\theta} = \frac{5c^4 s - 10c^2 s^3 + s^5}{c^5 - 10c^3 s^2 + 5cs^4}.$$

The method is now to divide both the top and bottom lines of this fraction by c^5.

Then $\dfrac{c^4 s}{c^5} = \dfrac{s}{c} = t$, $\dfrac{c^3 s^2}{c^5} = \dfrac{s^2}{c^2} = t^2$, and so on.

So $\quad \tan 5\theta = \dfrac{5t - 10t^3 + t^5}{1 - 10t^2 + 5t^4}$, $\quad$ where $\quad t = \tan\theta$.

(b) The same method gives

$$\begin{aligned}\tan 6\theta &= \frac{\sin 6\theta}{\cos 6\theta} = \frac{6c^5 s - 20c^3 s^3 + 6cs^5}{c^6 - 15c^4 s^2 + 15c^2 s^4 - s^6} \\ &= \frac{6t^5 - 20t^3 + 6t^5}{1 - 15t^2 + 15t^4 - t^6} \qquad \text{(dividing both top and bottom by } c^6\text{).}\end{aligned}$$

It is easy to generalise Example 8.2.2 to give a formula for $\tan n\theta$ for any $n \in \mathbb{N}$, as

$$\tan n\theta = \frac{nt - \binom{n}{3}t^3 + \ldots}{1 - \binom{n}{2}t^2 + \ldots}.$$

Notice that the highest power of $\tan\theta$ is in the numerator when n is odd, and in the denominator when n is even.

8.3 Application to polynomial equations

The expansions found in the last section can be used to express the roots of some polynomial equations in trigonometric form.

Example 8.3.1
Write each of the following equations as polynomial equations in $c = \cos\theta$, and solve them.
(a) $\cos 5\theta = 0$ $\quad$ (b) $\cos 5\theta = 1$
Use your answers to find expressions for $\cos\frac{1}{10}\pi$, $\cos\frac{3}{10}\pi$, $\cos\frac{1}{5}\pi$ and $\cos\frac{2}{5}\pi$.

(a) Using $\cos 5\theta = 16c^5 - 20c^3 + 5c$ from Example 8.2.1(a),

$$\cos 5\theta = 0 \quad\Leftrightarrow\quad 16c^5 - 20c^3 + 5c = 0.$$

Now $\cos 5\theta = 0$ if 5θ is an odd multiple of $\frac{1}{2}\pi$, so that $\theta = \frac{1}{10}\pi$, $\frac{3}{10}\pi$, $\frac{5}{10}\pi$ and so on. Since $\cos\theta$ is a decreasing function over the interval $0 \leqslant \theta \leqslant \pi$, you get different values for $c = \cos\theta$ by taking $\theta = \frac{1}{10}r\pi$ for $r = 1, 3, 5, 7$ and 9. As expected, the quintic polynomial equation $16c^5 - 20c^3 + 5c = 0$ has five roots.

Now the root $c = 0$ corresponds to $r = 5$, since $\cos\frac{5}{10}\pi = \cos\frac{1}{2}\pi = 0$. It follows that $\cos\frac{1}{10}\pi$, $\cos\frac{3}{10}\pi$, $\cos\frac{7}{10}\pi$ and $\cos\frac{9}{10}\pi$ are the roots of $16c^4 - 20c^2 + 5 = 0$.

Notice that

$$\cos\tfrac{7}{10}\pi = \cos\left(\pi - \tfrac{3}{10}\pi\right) = -\cos\tfrac{3}{10}\pi \quad \text{and} \quad \cos\tfrac{9}{10}\pi = \cos\left(\pi - \tfrac{1}{10}\pi\right) = -\cos\tfrac{1}{10}\pi.$$

The roots can therefore be written as $\pm\cos\frac{1}{10}\pi$ and $\pm\cos\frac{3}{10}\pi$.

Now the equation for $16c^4-20c^2+5=0$ is a quadratic in c^2, with roots

$$c^2=\frac{20\pm\sqrt{80}}{32}=\frac{5\pm\sqrt{5}}{8}.$$

Since $\cos\frac{1}{10}\pi>\cos\frac{3}{10}\pi$, it follows that

$$\cos\tfrac{1}{10}\pi=\sqrt{\frac{5+\sqrt{5}}{8}} \quad\text{and}\quad \cos\tfrac{3}{10}\pi=\sqrt{\frac{5-\sqrt{5}}{8}}.$$

(b) Beginning as in part (a),

$$\cos 5\theta=1 \quad\Leftrightarrow\quad 16c^5-20c^3+5c-1=0.$$

For $\cos 5\theta$ to equal 1, 5θ must be a multiple of 2π, so that $\theta=\frac{2}{5}r\pi$ for $r\in\mathbb{Z}$. This gives $c=\cos 0=1$, $c=\cos\frac{2}{5}\pi$, $c=\cos\frac{4}{5}\pi$, but no more, since $\cos\frac{6}{5}\pi=\cos\left(2\pi-\frac{4}{5}\pi\right)=\cos\frac{4}{5}\pi$, and similarly $\cos\frac{8}{5}\pi=\cos\frac{2}{5}\pi$, after which $\frac{10}{5}\pi=2\pi$ begins a repetition of the cycle.

You can easily check that $c=1$ is a root of the polynomial equation, so that a factor $c-1$ can be separated out, giving

$$(c-1)\left(16c^4+16c^3-4c^2-4c+1\right)=0.$$

This leaves the equation

$$16c^4+16c^3-4c^2-4c+1=0$$

with the other two roots, $\cos\frac{2}{5}\pi$ and $\cos\frac{4}{5}\pi$.

Clearly there is something odd here! You would expect a quartic equation to have four roots, not two. So it seems that the two roots might be repeated roots, in which case the quartic polynomial would be the square of a quadratic, Pc^2+Qc+R for some constants P, Q and R.

To investigate this, note that

$$\left(Pc^2+Qc+R\right)^2\equiv P^2c^4+2PQc^3+\left(Q^2+2PR\right)c^2+2QRc+R^2.$$

So if the hunch is correct, it should be possible to find P, Q and R so that

$$P^2=16,\quad 2PQ=16,\quad Q^2+2PR=-4,\quad 2QR=-4\quad\text{and}\quad R^2=1.$$

Working from left to right, you can easily find that the first three equations are satisfied by $P=4$, $Q=2$ and $R=-1$, and that these values also fit the last two equations. So

$$16c^4+16c^3-4c^2-4c+1\equiv\left(4c^2+2c-1\right)^2.$$

It is now easy to complete the analysis. The quadratic equation

$$4c^2+2c-1=0$$

has roots $\frac{-2 \pm \sqrt{20}}{8}$, or $\frac{-1 \pm \sqrt{5}}{4}$, and these are the values of $\cos\frac{2}{5}\pi$ and $\cos\frac{4}{5}\pi$.
By considering the signs, it follows that

$$\cos\tfrac{2}{5}\pi = \frac{\sqrt{5}-1}{4} \quad \text{and} \quad \cos\tfrac{4}{5}\pi = -\frac{\sqrt{5}+1}{4}.$$

Finally, note that $\cos\frac{1}{5}\pi = \cos\left(\pi - \frac{4}{5}\pi\right) = -\cos\frac{4}{5}\pi$, so $\cos\frac{1}{5}\pi = \frac{\sqrt{5}+1}{4}$.

Example 8.3.2
Use the expansion of $\tan n\theta$ for some value of n to find $\tan\frac{1}{12}\pi$.

Since $3 \times \frac{1}{12}\pi = \frac{1}{4}\pi$, and $\tan\frac{1}{4}\pi = 1$, $\frac{1}{12}\pi$ is one of the roots of $\tan 3\theta = 1$.
Writing $\tan 3\theta$ in terms of $t = \tan\theta$, this equation is

$$\frac{3t - t^3}{1 - 3t^2} = 1,$$

which can be rearranged as $t^3 - 3t^2 - 3t + 1 = 0$.

To find all the roots of this cubic equation, you need three roots of $\tan 3\theta = 1$ which give different values of $t = \tan\theta$. These can be taken as $3\theta = \frac{1}{4}\pi$, $\frac{5}{4}\pi$ and $\frac{9}{4}\pi$, so that $\theta = \frac{1}{12}\pi$, $\frac{5}{12}\pi$ and $\frac{9}{12}\pi = \frac{3}{4}\pi$.

Now $\tan\frac{3}{4}\pi = -1$, so one factor of the cubic must be $t + 1$. The equation is then

$$(t+1)\left(t^2 - 4t + 1\right) = 0,$$

so $\tan\frac{1}{12}\pi$ and $\tan\frac{5}{12}\pi$ are the roots of $t^2 - 4t + 1 = 0$.

Since $\tan\frac{1}{12}\pi < \tan\frac{5}{12}\pi$, $\tan\frac{1}{12}\pi$ is the smaller root, $t = 2 - \sqrt{3}$.

The next example uses angles in degrees rather than radians. Obviously the addition formulae are valid whichever unit is used, but you have to be careful to restrict the use of degrees to this part of the discussion. When you refer to the argument of a complex number, or use the exponential notation $e^{\theta i}$, it is essential to use radian notation.

Example 8.3.3
Use a substitution $x = k\cos\theta°$, for some number k, to solve the cubic equation $x^3 - 3x - 1 = 0$.

This equation was solved by numerical methods in P2 Example 14.5.1. With the methods of this chapter you can find exact expressions for the roots.

The expansion of $\cos 3\theta$ is

$$c^3 - 3cs^2 = c^3 - 3c\left(1 - c^2\right) = 4c^3 - 3c,$$

so $\cos 3\theta° = 4\cos^3\theta° - 3\cos\theta°$.

The aim is to find a value of k so that, with the given substitution,

$$x^3 - 3x = (k\cos\theta^\circ)^3 - 3k\cos\theta^\circ = k^3\cos^3\theta^\circ - 3k\cos\theta^\circ$$

is a multiple of $\cos 3\theta^\circ$. This requires $\frac{k^3}{4} = \frac{3k}{3}$, or $k^2 = 4$ (since $k = 0$ is unhelpful).

Take the root $k = 2$. Then substituting $x = 2\cos\theta^\circ$, the equation $x^3 - 3x = 1$ becomes

$$8\cos^3\theta^\circ - 6\cos\theta^\circ = 1, \quad \text{which is} \quad 2\cos 3\theta^\circ = 1, \quad \text{or} \quad \cos 3\theta^\circ = \tfrac{1}{2}.$$

You want three roots of this equation which give different values for $\cos\theta^\circ$. Taking $3\theta = 60$, 420 and 780 gives $\theta = 20$, 140 and 260, so $x = 2\cos 20^\circ \approx 1.879$, $x = 2\cos 140^\circ \approx -1.532$ and $x = 2\cos 260^\circ \approx -0.347$ correct to 3 decimal places.

This example leads to a method of solving any cubic equation of the form $x^3 + ax^2 + bx + c = 0$. First, you can make the substitution $x = y - \frac{1}{3}a$, to get a cubic equation for y for which the coefficient of y^2 is 0. (See P5 Miscellaneous exercise 1 Question 15.) Then you can complete the solution by using the method of Example 8.3.3, or a comparable method using a hyperbolic substitution (see Exercise 8A Questions 13 to 15).

You might wonder whether you can also solve equations of higher degree. The answer is 'yes' for quartic equations, but that is as far as you can go. It was proved by the Norwegian mathematician Niels Abel (1802–1829), using ideas from groups, that there is no general method of solving polynomial equations of degree higher than 4.

However, some special equations of higher degree can be solved by methods like the one in Example 8.3.3. One example of a solvable cubic equation is the subject of Exercise 8A Question 10.

Exercise 8A

1 Find expressions for the following in terms of $c = \cos\theta$ and $s = \sin\theta$. Check your answers by substituting a suitable value for θ in the original expression and in the answer.

(a) $\sin 3\theta$ (b) $\sin 5\theta$ (c) $\cos 6\theta$

(d) $\sin 6\theta$ (e) $\cos 9\theta$ (f) $\sin 9\theta$

2 Find expressions for the following in terms of $t = \tan\theta$.

(a) $\tan 4\theta$ (b) $\tan 7\theta$ (c) $\tan 8\theta$

3 Write the equation $\cos 4\theta = -\frac{1}{2}$ as a polynomial equation in $c = \cos\theta$. Factorise this equation, and match its roots with those of the original equation.

4 Write the equation $\sin 6\theta = 0$ as an equation in $c = \cos\theta$ and $s = \sin\theta$. Factorise this equation, and match its roots with those of the original equation.

5 Use the expansion of $\sin 8\theta$ found in Example 8.2.1(c) to find an equation whose roots are $\pm\sin\frac{1}{8}\pi$, $\pm\sin\frac{3}{8}\pi$. Hence find an expression for $\sin\frac{1}{8}\pi$ in surd form.

6 Show that $\tan\frac{1}{16}\pi$ is a root of the equation $t^4 + 4t^3 - 6t^2 - 4t + 1 = 0$. What are the other roots? Show that the equation can be expressed in the form $u^2 + 4u - 4 = 0$, where $u = t - t^{-1}$. Hence find the value of $\tan\frac{1}{16}\pi$.

7 Show that $\tan 9°$ is the smallest positive root of the equation $t^4 - 4t^3 - 14t^2 - 4t + 1 = 0$. Writing $t + t^{-1} = u$, obtain the equation $u^2 - 4u - 16 = 0$. Hence show that $\tan 9° = 1 + \sqrt{5} - \sqrt{5 + 2\sqrt{5}}$.

8 Prove that three roots of $\cos 5\theta + \cos 4\theta = 0$ are $\frac{1}{9}\pi$, $\frac{5}{9}\pi$ and $\frac{7}{9}\pi$. Hence, if α, β and γ denote $\cos\frac{1}{9}\pi$, $\cos\frac{5}{9}\pi$ and $\cos\frac{7}{9}\pi$, find the values of $\alpha + \beta + \gamma$, $\beta\gamma + \gamma\alpha + \alpha\beta$ and $\alpha\beta\gamma$.

9 Write $\sin 5\theta = \frac{1}{2}$ as a polynomial equation in $s = \sin\theta$. Find five different roots of this equation in trigonometric form, and hence find one simple factor of the polynomial. Deduce that $x^4 + x^3 - 4x^2 - 4x + 1 = 0$ has roots $2\sin\frac{1}{30}r\pi$ for $r = 1$, 13, -7 and -11.

10 Show that if $x = k\cos\theta$, for a suitable value of k, the equation $x^5 - 5x^3 + 5x + 1 = 0$ can be written in the form $\cos 5\theta = a$. Hence find the five roots of the polynomial equation, correct to 3 decimal places.

11 Show that if $c = \cos\theta$ and $s = \sin\theta$, then

$$(c + s\mathrm{i})^n + (c - s\mathrm{i})^n = 2\cos n\theta \quad \text{and} \quad (c + s\mathrm{i})^n - (c - s\mathrm{i})^n = 2\mathrm{i}\sin n\theta.$$

Use these to obtain the expressions for $\cos n\theta$ and $\sin n\theta$ in Section 8.2.

Show similarly that if $C = \cosh u$ and $S = \sinh u$, then

$$(C + S)^n + (C - S)^n = 2\cosh nu \quad \text{and} \quad (C + S)^n - (C - S)^n = 2\sinh nu.$$

Deduce comparable expressions for $\cosh nu$ and $\sinh nu$.

12 Use the result of Question 11 to write the following in terms of $\cosh u$ and/or $\sinh u$.

(a) $\cosh 3u$ (b) $\sinh 3u$ (c) $\cosh 5u$ (d) $\sinh 7u$ (e) $\sinh 8u$

13† Why does the method in Example 8.3.3 break down for the equation $x^3 - 3x - 5 = 0$? (This equation was solved by decimal search in P2 Section 14.2.)

Show that the real root of this equation can be found by using the substitution $x = k\cosh u$ and the answer to Question 12(a).

14† Use the answer to Question 12(b) to solve the equation $x^3 + 3x = 7$.

15† Use the methods in Example 8.3.3 and Questions 13, 14 to solve the following equations.

(a) $x^3 - 6x = 4$ (b) $x^3 - 9x = 15$ (c) $x^3 + 6x = 5$

(d) $x^3 - 12x + 20 = 0$ (e) $x^3 - 12x + 5 = 0$

8.4 The formulae in reverse

The multiple angle formulae give $\cos n\theta$ or $\sin n\theta$ in terms of powers of $\cos\theta$ or $\sin\theta$. But sometimes it is useful to reverse the process to express powers of $\cos\theta$ or $\sin\theta$ in terms of functions of multiple angles.

You can do this by combining binomial expansions and de Moivre's theorem. The key is to notice that, if z denotes $z = \cos\theta + \mathrm{i}\sin\theta$, then $\frac{1}{z}$ is $\cos\theta - \mathrm{i}\sin\theta$, so

$$2\cos\theta = z + \frac{1}{z} \quad \text{and} \quad 2\mathrm{i}\sin z = z - \frac{1}{z}.$$

Also, by de Moivre's theorem, $z^s = \cos s\theta + \mathrm{i}\sin s\theta$ and $\dfrac{1}{z^s} = \cos s\theta - \mathrm{i}\sin s\theta$. Therefore:

If $z = \mathrm{e}^{\theta \mathrm{i}} = \cos\theta + \mathrm{i}\sin\theta$ and $s \in \mathbb{N}$,

$$2\cos s\theta = z^s + \frac{1}{z^s} \quad \text{and} \quad 2\mathrm{i}\sin s\theta = z^s - \frac{1}{z^s}.$$

Example 8.4.1
Find expressions in terms of multiple angles for (a) $\cos^5\theta$, (b) $\sin^6\theta$.

(a) If $z = \cos\theta + \mathrm{i}\sin\theta$,

$$(2\cos\theta)^5 = \left(z + \frac{1}{z}\right)^5 = z^5 + 5z^4 \times \frac{1}{z} + 10z^3 \times \frac{1}{z^2} + 10z^2 \times \frac{1}{z^3} + 5z \times \frac{1}{z^4} + \frac{1}{z^5}$$
$$= z^5 + 5z^3 + 10z + \frac{10}{z} + \frac{5}{z^3} + \frac{1}{z^5},$$

which can be rearranged as $\left(z^5 + \dfrac{1}{z^5}\right) + 5\left(z^3 + \dfrac{1}{z^3}\right) + 10\left(z + \dfrac{1}{z}\right)$.

So, using the result in the shaded box above with $s = 5$, 3 and 1,

$$32\cos^5\theta = 2\cos 5\theta + 5(2\cos 3\theta) + 10(2\cos\theta).$$

That is, $\cos^5\theta = \frac{1}{16}(\cos 5\theta + 5\cos 3\theta + 10\cos\theta)$.

(b) $$(2\mathrm{i}\sin\theta)^6 = \left(z - \frac{1}{z}\right)^6$$
$$= z^6 - 6z^5 \times \frac{1}{z} + 15z^4 \times \frac{1}{z^2} - 20z^3 \times \frac{1}{z^3} + 15z^2 \times \frac{1}{z^4} - 6z \times \frac{1}{z^5} + \frac{1}{z^6}$$
$$= z^6 - 6z^4 + 15z^2 - 20 + \frac{15}{z^2} - \frac{6}{z^4} + \frac{1}{z^6}$$
$$= \left(z^6 + \frac{1}{z^6}\right) - 6\left(z^4 + \frac{1}{z^4}\right) + 15\left(z^2 + \frac{1}{z^2}\right) - 20,$$

so $-64\sin^6\theta = 2\cos 6\theta - 6(2\cos 4\theta) + 15(2\cos 2\theta) - 20$.

That is, $\sin^6\theta = -\frac{1}{32}(\cos 6\theta - 6\cos 4\theta + 15\cos 2\theta - 10)$.

The method is especially useful for finding integrals of powers of sines and cosines.

Example 8.4.2
Find $\displaystyle\int \sin^5\theta \,\mathrm{d}\theta$.

As $$(2\mathrm{i}\sin\theta)^5 = \left(z - \frac{1}{z}\right)^5 = z^5 - 5z^3 + 10z - \frac{10}{z} + \frac{5}{z^3} - \frac{1}{z^5}$$
$$= \left(z^5 - \frac{1}{z^5}\right) - 5\left(z^3 - \frac{1}{z^3}\right) + 10\left(z - \frac{1}{z}\right),$$

$$32\mathrm{i}\sin^5\theta = 2\mathrm{i}\sin 5\theta - 5(2\mathrm{i}\sin 3\theta) + 10(2\mathrm{i}\sin\theta);$$

so $$\sin^5\theta = \tfrac{1}{16}(\sin 5\theta - 5\sin 3\theta + 10\sin\theta).$$

So $$\int \sin^5\theta\,\mathrm{d}\theta = \tfrac{1}{16}\left(-\tfrac{1}{5}\cos 5\theta + \tfrac{5}{3}\cos 3\theta - 10\cos\theta\right) + k$$

$$= -\tfrac{1}{80}\cos 5\theta + \tfrac{5}{48}\cos 3\theta - \tfrac{5}{8}\cos\theta + k.$$

Exercise 8B

1 Express these powers in terms of sines and/or cosines of multiples of θ. Check your answers by substituting a suitable value for θ in the original expression and in the answer.

(a) $\cos^3\theta$ (b) $\sin^4\theta$ (c) $\cos^6\theta$

(d) $\sin^7\theta$ (e) $\sin^3\theta\cos^2\theta$ (f) $\sin^4\theta\cos^3\theta$

2 Express x in terms of u such that $2\cosh su$ can be written as $x^s + \dfrac{1}{x^s}$. Use this to express the following powers in terms of hyperbolic functions of multiples of u.

(a) $\cosh^3 u$ (b) $\sinh^4 u$ (c) $\cosh^6 u$

(d) $\sinh^7 u$ (e) $\sinh^3 u\cosh^2 u$ (f) $\sinh^4 u\cosh^3 u$

3 Find the following indefinite integrals in terms of sines and/or cosines of multiples of θ.

(a) $\displaystyle\int \cos^4\theta\,\mathrm{d}\theta$ (b) $\displaystyle\int \sin^5\theta\,\mathrm{d}\theta$ (c) $\displaystyle\int \sin^2\theta\cos^3\theta\,\mathrm{d}\theta$

4 Find the following indefinite integrals, expressing your answers in terms of hyperbolic functions.

(a) $\displaystyle\int \cosh^4 u\,\mathrm{d}u$ (b) $\displaystyle\int \sinh^5 u\,\mathrm{d}u$ (c) $\displaystyle\int \sinh^2 u\cosh^3 u\,\mathrm{d}u$

5 Evaluate

(a) $\displaystyle\int_0^{\frac{1}{4}\pi} \sin^3\theta\,\mathrm{d}\theta$, (b) $\displaystyle\int_0^{\frac{1}{2}\pi} \cos^8\theta\,\mathrm{d}\theta$, (c) $\displaystyle\int_{-\frac{1}{2}\pi}^{\frac{1}{2}\pi} \sin^4\theta\cos^2\theta\,\mathrm{d}\theta$.

6 If $n \in \mathbb{N}$, prove that $\displaystyle\int_0^{\frac{1}{2}\pi} \cos^{2n}\theta\,\mathrm{d}\theta = \frac{\pi}{2^{2n+1}}\binom{2n}{n}$.

8.5 Power series with a complex variable

You have met many series of the form

$$u_0 + u_1x + u_2x^2 + u_3x^3 + \ldots$$

where the coefficients u_0, u_1, u_2, u_3, ... form a sequence of real numbers and x is a real variable. These are examples of **power series**, because each term contains a power of x.

Some of these power series have a finite number of terms, ending with u_nx^n, so that the series is a polynomial. Examples are binomial expansions for $(1+x)^n$ when $n \in \mathbb{N}$ and finite geometric progressions. Other series continue indefinitely, and for certain values of x (the interval of validity) they converge to a limit. Examples of these are binomial expansions when n is not a positive integer, infinite geometric series and Maclaurin expansions for functions such as e^x, $\sin x$ and $\ln(1+x)$.

What happens if the real variable x is replaced by a complex variable z (the coefficients remaining real)? For finite series it clearly makes no difference, since the laws of complex algebra are the same as those of real algebra (except for inequalities). But infinite series need to be looked at more carefully.

Infinite geometric series

Infinite geometric series are easy to deal with, because you know the formula for

$$a + az + az^2 + \ldots + az^{n-1} = \frac{a(1-z^n)}{1-z} \qquad \text{where } a \neq 0 \text{ and } z \neq 1,$$

which can be proved for complex z in the same way as it was for real r in P2 Section 10.2. The condition for this sum to converge to a limit as $n \to \infty$ is that z^n must tend to 0.

The behaviour of z^n as n varies was described in Section 7.1, and is illustrated in Figs. 7.1, 7.2 and 7.3. When $|z| = 1$ the points representing z^n are equally stepped round the unit circle, and so never converge to a limit. (The value $z = 1$ is excluded, because the formula for the sum of a geometric series then doesn't hold.) When $|z| > 1$ the sequence of points spirals out without limit, but when $|z| < 1$ it spirals inwards, and can be brought as close to 0 as you like by taking n large enough.

So the only difference between the real and the complex case is that the interval of validity (real numbers between -1 and 1) is replaced by a **region of validity** (complex numbers with modulus less than 1).

The infinite geometric series $\sum_{s=0}^{\infty} az^s$ converges to $\frac{a}{1-z}$ if $|z| < 1$.

This result can be shown geometrically by a diagram like Fig. 8.1, which is drawn for the values $a = 1$ and $z = \frac{1}{2}(1+i)$. Starting from the origin, displacements $\overrightarrow{OP_0}$, $\overrightarrow{P_0P_1}$, $\overrightarrow{P_1P_2}$, ... represent the terms a, az, az^2, ... of the series. The displacement $\overrightarrow{OP_n}$ then represents the finite sum $\sum_{s=0}^{n} az^s$. You can see the points P_n getting ever closer to a limiting point L, which represents $\frac{a}{1-z}$ in the Argand diagram.

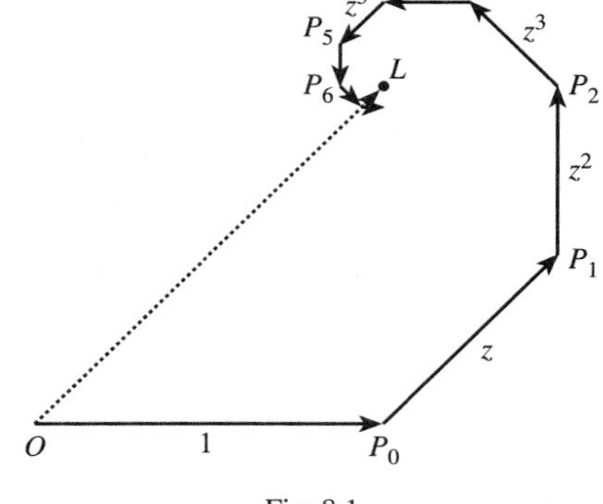

Fig. 8.1

For the particular values used in Fig. 8.1, each displacement is obtained from its predecessor by a scalar multiplication by $|z| = \frac{1}{\sqrt{2}}$ combined with a rotation of $\arg z = \frac{1}{4}\pi$. The limit is

$$\frac{1}{1-\frac{1}{2}(1+\mathrm{i})}=\frac{2}{1-\mathrm{i}}=\frac{2(1+\mathrm{i})}{(1-\mathrm{i})(1+\mathrm{i})}=\frac{2(1+\mathrm{i})}{2}=(1+\mathrm{i}).$$

Binomial expansions

The infinite geometric series is a special case of the binomial expansion $(1-z)^n$ when $n=-1$. Infinite binomial expansions when n is a negative integer can all be used in the complex form $(1+z)^n$, within a region of validity $|z|<1$. The proof is more difficult than for the geometric series, however, and won't be attempted here.

The extension to non-integral values of n is more complicated. For example, if $n=\frac{1}{5}$, the series is still convergent for $|z|<1$, but you have to decide which of the five complex fifth roots of $1+z$ is the limit.

The exponential series

The Maclaurin series for e^x can be generalised directly for a complex variable, as

$$\mathrm{e}^z=1+\frac{z}{1!}+\frac{z^2}{2!}+\frac{z^3}{3!}+\ldots,$$

and this is valid for all values of z. The proof is too difficult to give here, but a geometrical illustration is very convincing. Fig. 8.2 shows the series for $z=\frac{1}{2}(1+\mathrm{i})$, converging to the limit $\mathrm{e}^{\frac{1}{2}}\mathrm{e}^{\frac{1}{2}\mathrm{i}}$ with modulus $\sqrt{\mathrm{e}}$ and argument $\frac{1}{2}$.

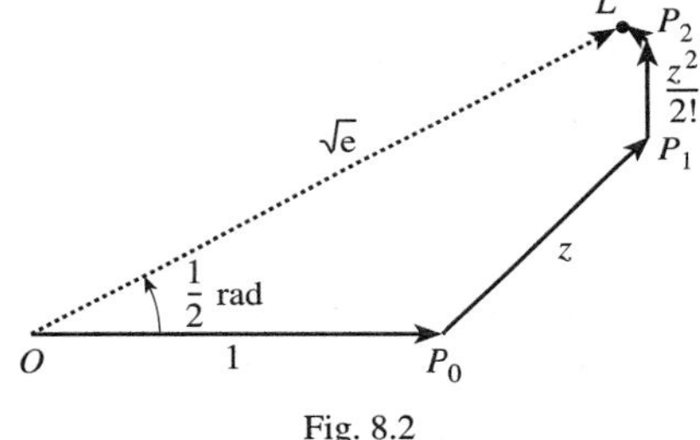

Fig. 8.2

As $\cos z$ and $\sin z$ can be expressed in terms of exponential functions (see P5 Section 2.7), their series expansions can also be extended for use with complex variables.

However, since the exponential function is not one–one (because $\exp z_1=\exp z_2$ if z_1 and z_2 differ by a multiple of $2\pi\mathrm{i}$), there are additional difficulties in extending the definition of natural logarithm, and therefore in generalising the $\ln(1+x)$ series for a complex variable.

8.6 Trigonometric series

If in a power series you put $z=\mathrm{e}^{\theta\mathrm{i}}=\cos\theta+\mathrm{i}\sin\theta$, you get

$$u_0+u_1\mathrm{e}^{\theta\mathrm{i}}+u_2\mathrm{e}^{2\theta\mathrm{i}}+u_3\mathrm{e}^{3\theta\mathrm{i}}+\ldots.$$

If the coefficients are real, each term $u_s\mathrm{e}^{s\theta\mathrm{i}}$ has real part $u_s\cos s\theta$ and imaginary part $u_s\sin s\theta$. So if S denotes the sum of the power series,

$$\mathrm{Re}(S)=u_0+u_1\cos\theta+u_2\cos2\theta+u_3\cos3\theta+\ldots$$

$$\text{and}\quad \mathrm{Im}(S)=\qquad u_1\sin\theta+u_2\sin2\theta+u_3\sin3\theta+\ldots.$$

Series like this are called **trigonometric series**.

You can sometimes reverse this process, and find an expression for the sum of a trigonometric series as the real or imaginary part of the sum of a power series.

Example 8.6.1

Find expressions for the sums of the series

(a) $1+\frac{1}{2}\cos\theta+\frac{1}{4}\cos 2\theta+\frac{1}{8}\cos 3\theta+\ldots,$

(b) $\binom{n}{1}\sin\theta+\binom{n}{2}\sin 2\theta+\binom{n}{3}\sin 3\theta+\ldots+\sin n\theta,$ where $n\in\mathbb{N}$,

(c) $1+\dfrac{\cos\theta}{1!}+\dfrac{\cos 2\theta}{2!}+\dfrac{\cos 3\theta}{3!}+\ldots.$

(a) This is the real part of the infinite geometric series

$$1+\tfrac{1}{2}e^{\theta i}+\tfrac{1}{4}e^{2\theta i}+\tfrac{1}{8}e^{3\theta i}+\ldots$$

with common ratio $z=\frac{1}{2}e^{\theta i}$. Since $|z|=\frac{1}{2}<1$, this series is convergent, with limit $\dfrac{1}{1-\frac{1}{2}e^{\theta i}}$.

To find the real part, you have to convert this fraction into the form $a+bi$. You can do this by multiplying top and bottom by the conjugate of the denominator, which is $1-\frac{1}{2}e^{-\theta i}$. The denominator then becomes

$$\begin{aligned}\left(1-\tfrac{1}{2}e^{\theta i}\right)\left(1-\tfrac{1}{2}e^{-\theta i}\right)&=1-\tfrac{1}{2}\left(e^{\theta i}+e^{-\theta i}\right)+\tfrac{1}{4}\left(e^{\theta i}e^{-\theta i}\right)\\&=1-\tfrac{1}{2}(2\cos\theta)+\tfrac{1}{4}=\tfrac{5}{4}-\cos\theta.\end{aligned}$$

The real part of the numerator $1-\frac{1}{2}e^{-\theta i}$ is $1-\frac{1}{2}\cos\theta$. The sum of the trigonometric series is therefore

$$\frac{1-\frac{1}{2}\cos\theta}{\frac{5}{4}-\cos\theta}=\frac{2(2-\cos\theta)}{5-4\cos\theta}.$$

(b) You can write the series as the imaginary part of the finite binomial expansion

$$1+\binom{n}{1}e^{\theta i}+\binom{n}{2}e^{2\theta i}+\binom{n}{3}e^{3\theta i}+\ldots+e^{n\theta i}=\left(1+e^{\theta i}\right)^n.$$

The simplest way of separating this into real and imaginary parts is to write $1+e^{\theta i}$ as

$$\left(e^{-\frac{1}{2}\theta i}+e^{\frac{1}{2}\theta i}\right)e^{\frac{1}{2}\theta i}=2\cos\tfrac{1}{2}\theta\, e^{\frac{1}{2}\theta i}.$$

So $\left(1+e^{\theta i}\right)^n=2^n\cos^n\frac{1}{2}\theta\, e^{\frac{1}{2}n\theta i}$, whose imaginary part is $2^n\cos^n\frac{1}{2}\theta\sin\frac{1}{2}n\theta$.

(c) The series is the real part of

$$1+\frac{e^{\theta i}}{1!}+\frac{e^{2\theta i}}{2!}+\frac{e^{3\theta i}}{3!}+\ldots=\exp\left(e^{\theta i}\right),\quad\text{or}\quad\exp(\cos\theta+i\sin\theta).$$

Now the real part of $\exp(a+bi)$, or $e^a e^{bi}$, is $e^a\cos b$, so the real part of $\exp(\cos\theta+i\sin\theta)$ is

$$e^{\cos\theta}\cos(\sin\theta).$$

Exercise 8C

1 Show that

(a) $1+4\cos 2\theta+6\cos 4\theta+4\cos 6\theta+\cos 8\theta=16\cos 4\theta\cos^4\theta$,

(b) $1+\cos 2\theta+\cos 4\theta+\cos 6\theta+\cos 8\theta=\dfrac{\cos 4\theta\sin 5\theta}{\sin\theta}$ provided that $\theta\neq n\pi, n\in\mathbb{Z}$.

2 Show that the sum $e^{\theta i}-e^{3\theta i}+e^{5\theta i}-\ldots-e^{19\theta i}$ can be expressed in the form $\dfrac{1-e^{20\theta i}}{2\cos\theta}$ provided that θ is not an odd multiple of $\frac{1}{2}\pi$. Hence find expressions for the sums $\sin\theta-\sin 3\theta+\sin 5\theta-\ldots-\sin 19\theta$ and $\cos\theta-\cos 3\theta+\cos 5\theta-\ldots-\cos 19\theta$.

3 Show that $\dfrac{e^{n\theta i}-1}{e^{\theta i}-1}=\dfrac{\sin\frac{1}{2}n\theta}{\sin\frac{1}{2}\theta}e^{\frac{1}{2}(n-1)\theta i}$, provided that θ is not a multiple of 2π.

Use this to find an expression for the sum

$$\cos\alpha+\cos(\alpha+\theta)+\cos(\alpha+2\theta)+\ldots+\cos(\alpha+(n-1)\theta).$$

Show that this sum is 0 if θ is a multiple of $\dfrac{2\pi}{n}$ but not of 2π. Give a geometrical explanation for this.

4 Sum the following trigonometric series.

(a) $\sin\theta-\frac{1}{3}\sin 2\theta+\frac{1}{9}\sin 3\theta-\frac{1}{27}\sin 4\theta+\ldots$

(b) $1+\dfrac{\cos 2\theta}{2!}+\dfrac{\cos 4\theta}{4!}+\dfrac{\cos 6\theta}{6!}+\ldots$

(c) $1-\binom{n}{1}\cos\theta\cos\theta+\binom{n}{2}\cos^2\theta\cos 2\theta-\binom{n}{3}\cos^3\theta\cos 3\theta+\ldots+(-1)^n\cos^n\theta\cos n\theta$,

distinguishing the cases $n=4k$, $n=4k+1$, $n=4k+2$ and $n=4k+3$, where $k\in\mathbb{N}$.

5 Sum the series $\sinh u-\frac{1}{3}\sinh 2u+\frac{1}{9}\sinh 3u-\frac{1}{27}\sinh 4u+\ldots$, and state the values of u for which your answer is valid.

6 Sum the series

$$1-\binom{n}{1}\cosh u\cosh u+\binom{n}{2}\cosh^2 u\cosh 2u-\ldots+(-1)^n\cosh^n u\cosh nu,$$

distinguishing the cases when n is even and n is odd.

7 Find the sums of the following series when $z=1.2+0.4i$. Give your answers correct to 2 decimal places, and illustrate them with a diagram.

(a) $1+2z+3z^2+4z^3+\ldots$

(b) $1+\dfrac{z}{1!}+\dfrac{z^2}{2!}+\dfrac{z^3}{3!}+\ldots$

(c) $1+5z+10z^2+10z^3+5z^4+z^5$

(d) $1+z+z^2+z^3+z^4+z^5$

8† Overestimates and underestimates are made of the area under the graph $y=\cos x$ over the interval $0\leqslant x\leqslant\beta$, where $\beta\leqslant\frac{1}{2}\pi$, using n rectangles of equal width. By summing suitable trigonometric series, find formulae for these estimates in terms of n and β, and investigate their limits as $n\to\infty$.

Miscellaneous exercise 8

1 Use de Moivre's theorem to show that $\sin 5\theta = 16\sin^5\theta - 20\sin^3\theta + 5\sin\theta$. Hence show that $\sin\frac{1}{30}\pi$ is a root of the equation $32x^5 - 40x^3 + 10x - 1 = 0$. (OCR)

2 Prove that the only real solutions of the equation $\sin 5\theta = 5\sin\theta$ are given by $\theta = n\pi$, where n is an integer. (OCR)

3 By considering the equation $\cos 5\theta = 0$, show that the exact value of $\cos^2\frac{1}{10}\pi$ is $\dfrac{5+\sqrt{5}}{8}$. (OCR)

4 By considering the equation $\tan 5\theta = 0$, show that the exact value of the smaller positive root of the equation $t^4 - 10t^2 + 5 = 0$ is $\tan\frac{1}{5}\pi$. (OCR)

5 Use de Moivre's theorem to show that $\cos 6\theta = 32\cos^6\theta - 48\cos^4\theta + 18\cos^2\theta - 1$. Deduce that, for all θ, $0 \leqslant \cos^6\theta - \frac{3}{2}\cos^4\theta + \frac{9}{16}\cos^2\theta \leqslant \frac{1}{16}$. (OCR)

6 Use the results of Example 8.3.1 to give exact expressions of the coordinates of the vertices of a regular pentagon with its centre at the origin and one vertex at the point $(0,1)$. (See Fig. 7.9 in Example 7.5.1.) Check your answers by showing that all the sides are of equal length.

7 Write the equation $\sin 7\theta = 0$ as an equation in $s = \sin\theta$, and state its roots. Use the substitution $x = s^2$ to find an equation whose roots are $\sin^2\frac{1}{7}\pi$, $\sin^2\frac{2}{7}\pi$ and $\sin^2\frac{3}{7}\pi$.

Hence find the values of

(a) $\sin\frac{1}{7}\pi\sin\frac{2}{7}\pi\sin\frac{3}{7}\pi$,

(b) $\cos\frac{2}{7}\pi + \cos\frac{4}{7}\pi + \cos\frac{6}{7}\pi$,

(c) $\operatorname{cosec}^2\frac{1}{7}\pi + \operatorname{cosec}^2\frac{2}{7}\pi + \operatorname{cosec}^2\frac{3}{7}\pi$.

8† Write the equation $\sin 7\theta = -1$ as an equation in $s = \sin\theta$, and state its roots. Hence show that $\sin\frac{1}{14}\pi - \sin\frac{3}{14}\pi + \sin\frac{5}{14}\pi = \frac{1}{2}$.

9 Show that, if $\cos 4\theta = \cos 3\theta$, then θ is $\frac{2}{7}r\pi$ for some $r \in \mathbb{Z}$. Hence find a cubic equation whose roots are $\cos\frac{2}{7}\pi$, $\cos\frac{4}{7}$ and $\cos\frac{6}{7}\pi$. Use a numerical method to calculate the positive root of this equation correct to 6 decimal places. Then use the sum and the product of the roots to calculate the other two roots to the same degree of accuracy.

10 Expand $\left(z - \dfrac{1}{z}\right)^4\left(z + \dfrac{1}{z}\right)^2$, and hence find the constants p, q, r and s such that

$\sin^4\theta\cos^2\theta = p + q\cos 2\theta + r\cos 4\theta + s\cos 6\theta$.

Using a suitable substitution, show that $\displaystyle\int_1^2 x^4\sqrt{4-x^2}\,\mathrm{d}x = \frac{4}{3}\pi + \sqrt{3}$. (MEI)

11 Sketch the curve whose polar equation is $r = a\cos^3\theta$, and calculate the area of the region enclosed by it.

12 Find the volume of revolution formed by rotating the region under the graph $y = \sin^4 x$ for $0 \leqslant x \leqslant \pi$ about the x-axis.

13 Sum the geometric series $z+z^2+z^3+\ldots+z^8$, $z\neq 1$.

Show that if $z=e^{\theta i}$ then $1-z^8=-2ie^{4\theta i}\sin 4\theta$. Write down a similar expression for $1-z$.

Hence find $\sum_{r=1}^{8}\cos r\theta$. (OCR)

14 Infinite series C and S are defined as follows:

$$C=\frac{\cos\theta}{2}-\frac{\cos 2\theta}{4}+\frac{\cos 3\theta}{8}-\frac{\cos 4\theta}{16}+\ldots,\quad S=\frac{\sin\theta}{2}-\frac{\sin 2\theta}{4}+\frac{\sin 3\theta}{8}-\frac{\sin 4\theta}{16}+\ldots.$$

Show that $C+Si=\dfrac{2e^{\theta i}+1}{5+4\cos\theta}$. Hence find expressions for C and S in terms of $\cos\theta$ and $\sin\theta$. (MEI)

15† Show that the quartic equation $x^4-8x^2+4=0$ may be written in the form $(f(x))^2-(g(x))^2=0$, where $f(x)=x^2-2$ and $g(x)$ is suitably chosen. Use this to find the roots of the quartic equation in the form $\pm\left(c\pm d\sqrt{3}\right)$, where c and d are integers.

Prove that $\cos 4\theta=8\cos^4\theta-8\cos^2\theta+1$, and use this to show that, if x is replaced by $k\cos\theta$ with k suitably chosen, the quartic equation may be expressed in the form $\cos 4\theta=\frac{1}{2}$.

Obtain the roots of the quartic equation in the form $k\cos\theta_i$. Hence express $\cos 15°$ in surd form. (OCR)

16† Write down the expansions of $\exp z$, $\exp\omega z$ and $\exp\omega^2 z$ as power series, where $\omega=\exp\frac{2}{3}\pi i$. Hence find the sum of the series $1+\dfrac{z^3}{3!}+\dfrac{z^6}{6!}+\dfrac{z^9}{9!}+\ldots$, and deduce the sum of the trigonometric series $1+\dfrac{\cos 3\theta}{3!}+\dfrac{\cos 6\theta}{6!}+\dfrac{\cos 9\theta}{9!}+\ldots$.

17† Prove that, if $n\in\mathbb{N}$, $\displaystyle\sum_{s=0}^{\infty}\frac{1}{(sn)!}=\frac{1}{n}\sum_{r=0}^{n-1}\exp\left(\cos\frac{2r\pi}{n}\right)\cos\left(\sin\frac{2r\pi}{n}\right)$.

Verify this numerically in the cases $n=4$, $n=5$ and $n=6$.

18 The triangular numbers t_s, where $s\in\mathbb{N}$, are defined inductively by $t_1=1$ and $t_{s+1}=t_s+(s+1)$. Use the expansion of $(1-z)^{-3}$ to find the value of $\displaystyle\sum_{s=1}^{\infty}\left(\tfrac{1}{2}\right)^s t_s\cos\tfrac{1}{3}s\pi$.

9 Groups

This chapter introduces and develops the idea of a group. When you have completed it you should

- know the axioms for a group
- know how to decide whether a given structure is, or is not, a group
- be able to use algebraic methods to prove simple properties of groups
- know what is meant by the order of a group
- recognise some types of groups.

9.1 Mathematical structure

What are the similarities and differences between the multiplication of matrices and the multiplication of real numbers? How are complex numbers under multiplication equivalent to certain kinds of matrices under multiplication? And what is the connection between the composition of certain functions and the symmetries of a rectangle? The idea of a 'group' gives some answers to questions like these.

The value of the idea is that, if you can show that certain structures, such as those described in the previous paragraph, satisfy the same properties, and you can prove theorems and results using these properties, then all the structures with these properties will obey the theorems and have corresponding results. It is thus time-saving and thought-saving to catalogue structures in this way.

The word 'structure' has now been used several times, but it is not clear precisely what is meant by a structure. It will be helpful to start by introducing some notation and expanding on the idea of a set.

9.2 Set notation

You have met already the abbreviations $\mathbb{N}$, $\mathbb{Z}$ and $\mathbb{R}$ for the natural numbers, integers and real numbers respectively. The symbols $\mathbb{C}$ and $\mathbb{Q}$ will be used for the complex numbers and the rational numbers (fractions, including integers, which are fractions with denominator 1) respectively. It is useful to introduce two other pieces of notation in conjunction with $\mathbb{R}$, $\mathbb{Z}$, $\mathbb{C}$ and $\mathbb{Q}$: the notation $\mathbb{R}-\{0\}$ is used to mean the real numbers except 0; similar notations apply with $\mathbb{Z}$, $\mathbb{C}$ and $\mathbb{Q}$. The superscript $+$ on $\mathbb{R}$, that is $\mathbb{R}^+$, means the positive real numbers; similarly with $\mathbb{Z}^+$ and $\mathbb{Q}^+$. Finally, $\mathbb{R}_0^+$ means the positive real numbers together with 0; similarly for $\mathbb{Z}_0^+$ and $\mathbb{Q}_0^+$.

Recall that positive and negative have no meaning with complex numbers. That is why there is no symbol $\mathbb{C}^+$ or $\mathbb{C}_0^+$.

The members of a set are often called its **elements**.

When you need to consider other sets, the braces notation is used, either with a list or with an explanation. Here are some examples.

The elements of the set $\{0,2,4,6,8\}$ are the numbers 0, 2, 4, 6 and 8.

The set $\{1, x, x^2, \ldots, x^n\}$ consists of the integer powers of x from 0 to n inclusive. If there is any doubt about the nature of n you could write this as $\{x^r : r \in \mathbb{Z},\ 0 \leqslant r \leqslant n\}$, where the quantity before the colon tells you the nature of what is in the set, and what follows the colon makes the description more precise.

The set $\{x \in \mathbb{R} : 0 \leqslant x \leqslant 1\}$ is the set of real numbers lying from 0 to 1. Similarly $\{z \in \mathbb{C} : |z| = 1\}$ means the set of complex numbers with modulus 1.

In some books, $\mathbb{R}^*$ or $\mathbb{R} \setminus \{0\}$ are used instead of $\mathbb{R} - \{0\}$.

9.3 Binary operations

Each of the structures mentioned in Section 9.1 had, in addition to the set of elements, an operation: for example, real numbers and the operation of multiplication.

Multiplication of real numbers is an example of a **binary operation**; another binary operation is the dot product $\mathbf{a} \cdot \mathbf{b}$ of two vectors $\mathbf{a}$ and $\mathbf{b}$.

> A binary operation $\circ$ on a set S is a rule which assigns to each ordered pair of elements x, y in S exactly one element denoted by $x \circ y$.

The binary operation $\circ$ is often pronounced 'blob'!

Notice that multiplication, addition and subtraction are binary operations on $\mathbb{Z}$. On the other hand division is not, since $x \div 0$ has no meaning. Multiplication, addition and subtraction are binary operations on $\mathbb{R}$, $\mathbb{C}$ and $\mathbb{Q}$, and division is a binary operation on $\mathbb{R} - \{0\}$, $\mathbb{C} - \{0\}$ and $\mathbb{Q} - \{0\}$.

In the definition of binary operation, notice that $x \circ y$ does not have to be an element of the set S. For example, the scalar product of two vectors is not a vector. However, in cases where the binary operation on S always gives a result which is in the set S, the operation is said to be **closed**.

In some books, the term 'binary operation' is used to mean a closed binary operation.

Example 9.3.1
Decide which of the following operations on the given sets are binary operations. For those which are binary operations, say whether or not they are closed.

(a) $\mathbb{N}$, where $a \circ b$ means $a - b$
(b) $\mathbb{N}$, where $a \circ b$ means the lowest common multiple (lcm) of a and b
(c) $\mathbb{R}$, where $a \circ b$ means the greater of a and b
(d) $\mathbb{Z}$, where $a \circ b$ means a

(a) A binary operation. Since, for example, $1 - 2$ is not defined in $\mathbb{N}$, the operation is not closed.

(b) A binary operation. The lowest common multiple (lcm) of two positive integers a and b is always defined. As the lcm is a positive integer, the operation is closed.

(c) A binary operation. The greater of a and b is defined, except when $a = b$ when it is understood that $a \circ b$ is equal to either a or b. It is closed since the result is in $\mathbb{R}$.

(d) A binary operation. As a is in $\mathbb{Z}$ the result $a \circ b = a$ is also in $\mathbb{Z}$, so the binary operation is closed.

In Example 9.3.1 operations (b) and (c), the order in which a and b are written does not matter since $a \circ b = b \circ a$, but in operations (a) and (d) the order does matter.

A binary operation $\circ$ on a set S is **commutative**
if $a \circ b = b \circ a$ for all $a, b \in S$;
otherwise it is **not commutative**.

Important examples of non-commutative binary operations are division on $\mathbb{R} - \{0\}$, subtraction on $\mathbb{R}$, and the multiplication of square matrices.

If you have expressions of the form $(a \circ b) \circ c$ and $a \circ (b \circ c)$ where $\circ$ is a binary operation and $a, b, c \in S$, it may or may not be true that $(a \circ b) \circ c = a \circ (b \circ c)$. For example, for the binary operation $+$ on $\mathbb{R}$, you can say that $(a + b) + c = a + (b + c)$, but for the binary operation $-$ on $\mathbb{R}$, $(4 - 2) - 1 = 1$ and $4 - (2 - 1) = 3$; so in general, $(a - b) - c \neq a - (b - c)$.

A binary operation $\circ$ on a set S is **associative**
if $(a \circ b) \circ c = a \circ (b \circ c)$ for all $a, b, c \in S$;
otherwise it is **not associative**.

When a binary operation is associative, you may leave out the brackets and write $a \circ b \circ c$, since both ways of evaluating it give the same answer.

Example 9.3.2
Say whether or not the following closed binary operations are commutative and associative.
(a) $\mathbb{N}$: multiplication
(b) Matrices of the form $\begin{pmatrix} x & x \\ 0 & 0 \end{pmatrix}$, where $x \in \mathbb{R}$: matrix multiplication
(c) Vectors in three dimensions: vector product
(d) $\mathbb{Z}$: the operation $a \circ b$ defined as $a + b - ab$

(a) For natural numbers $ab = ba$ and $(ab)c = a(bc)$, so the operation is commutative and associative.

(b) $\begin{pmatrix} x & x \\ 0 & 0 \end{pmatrix}\begin{pmatrix} y & y \\ 0 & 0 \end{pmatrix} = \begin{pmatrix} xy & xy \\ 0 & 0 \end{pmatrix}$ and $\begin{pmatrix} y & y \\ 0 & 0 \end{pmatrix}\begin{pmatrix} x & x \\ 0 & 0 \end{pmatrix} = \begin{pmatrix} yx & yx \\ 0 & 0 \end{pmatrix}$. As $x, y \in \mathbb{R}$, $xy = yx$, and so $\begin{pmatrix} x & x \\ 0 & 0 \end{pmatrix}\begin{pmatrix} y & y \\ 0 & 0 \end{pmatrix} = \begin{pmatrix} y & y \\ 0 & 0 \end{pmatrix}\begin{pmatrix} x & x \\ 0 & 0 \end{pmatrix}$. Thus the operation is commutative. Since matrix multiplication is associative, this operation is associative.

(c) Since $\mathbf{i} \times \mathbf{j} = \mathbf{k}$ and $\mathbf{j} \times \mathbf{i} = -\mathbf{k}$, the operation is not commutative. Since $(\mathbf{i} \times \mathbf{j}) \times \mathbf{j} = \mathbf{k} \times \mathbf{j} = -\mathbf{i}$ and $\mathbf{i} \times (\mathbf{j} \times \mathbf{j}) = \mathbf{i} \times \mathbf{0} = \mathbf{0}$, the operation is not associative.

(d) $a \circ b = a + b - ab = b + a - ba = b \circ a$ so the operation is commutative.

$$\begin{aligned}(a \circ b) \circ c &= (a + b - ab) \circ c = (a + b - ab) + c - (a + b - ab)c \\ &= a + b - ab + c - ac - bc + abc\end{aligned}$$

and $$\begin{aligned}a \circ (b \circ c) &= a \circ (b + c - bc) = a + (b + c - bc) - a(b + c - bc) \\ &= a + b + c - bc - ab - ac - abc.\end{aligned}$$

As these expressions are equal, the operation is associative.

You can also define binary operations for sets which have only a finite number of elements.

You can use a combination table to show the details of a closed binary operation on a small set. Table 9.1 shows the result of 'last digit arithmetic' on $\{2,4,6,8\}$. For example, $2 \times 8 = 16$ has last digit 6, so $2 \circ 8 = 6$. This is shown in the shaded cell in Table 9.1. Stated formally, the binary operation $\circ$ on the set $\{2,4,6,8\}$ given by $a \circ b$ is the remainder after the product ab is divided by 10.

		Second number			
	$\circ$	2	4	6	8
	2	4	8	2	6
First	4	8	6	4	2
number	6	2	4	6	8
	8	6	2	8	4

Table 9.1

A binary operation can actually be *defined* by a combination table. For example, Table 9.2 defines a binary operation $\circ$ on the set $\{a,b,c\}$.

$\circ$	a	b	c
a	b	a	c
b	a	c	b
c	b	b	a

Table 9.2

You can see immediately that $\circ$ is a binary operation, and also that it is closed, because Table 9.2 shows the result of every possible combination of two members of the set.

You can also tell quickly from a table if a binary operation is commutative by looking for symmetry about the leading diagonal. Table 9.2 is not symmetrical since $c \circ a = b$ and $a \circ c = c$ and therefore the operation is not commutative.

Without detailed checking you can't tell from a table whether or not the binary operation is associative. To find out it is usually easier to exploit some other knowledge about the table.

Exercise 9A

1 Decide which of the following operations are binary operations on the given sets. If an operation is not a binary operation, give one reason. For those which are binary operations, check whether they are closed, commutative and associative.

(a) $-$ on $\mathbb{Z}^+$

(b) matrix multiplication on 2×2 matrices

(c) $\circ$ on $\mathbb{Z}^+$, where $a \circ b = a^b$

(d) $\circ$ on $\mathbb{R}$, where $a \circ b = |a-b|$

(e) $\circ$ on $\mathbb{R}$, where $a \circ b = 0$ for all $a, b \in \mathbb{R}$

(f) $\circ$ on $\mathbb{R}$, where $a \circ b = a + b - ab$

(g) $\circ$ on $\mathbb{R}$, where $a \circ b = b$ for all $a, b \in \mathbb{R}$

(h) $\circ$ on $\mathbb{R}^+$, where $a \circ b = a^b$

(i) $\circ$ on $\{1,3,7,9\}$, where $a \circ b$ is the remainder when $a \times b$ is divided by 10

9.4 Identity elements

The numbers 0 and 1 in $\mathbb{R}$ are very special. When the operation is addition, the number 0 has the property that

$$a + 0 = 0 + a = a$$

for every number a in $\mathbb{R}$.

Similarly, when the operation is multiplication, the number 1 has the property that

$$a \times 1 = 1 \times a = a$$

for every number a in $\mathbb{R} - \{0\}$.

In each of these examples you have a set S that is closed under a binary operation $\circ$ and an element, often denoted by e, with the property that $a \circ e = e \circ a = a$ for all members of the set S. This element e is called an **identity** element for the set S with the operation $\circ$.

A set with a closed binary operation need not have an identity element.

Example 9.4.1
Show that the set $\mathbb{Z}$ with the operation of subtraction does not have an identity element.

The element 0 is the only element with the property that $a - 0 = a$ for every $a \in \mathbb{Z}$, but as $0 - a = -a$, 0 is not an identity element for $\mathbb{Z}$ under subtraction.

Example 9.4.2
Find the identity element in $\mathbb{R} - \{1\}$ with the binary operation $a \circ b = a + b - ab$.

$$a \circ e = a \quad \Leftrightarrow \quad a + e - ea = a \quad \Leftrightarrow \quad e - ea = 0 \quad \Leftrightarrow \quad e(1-a) = 0.$$

For this to be true for all a in $\mathbb{R} - \{1\}$, you need $e = 0$.

As $a \circ b = b \circ a$, there is no need to check separately that $e \circ a = a$.

9.5 Inverse elements

Consider again the two numbers discussed at the beginning of Section 9.4, 0 and 1 in $\mathbb{R}$.

For each number $a \in \mathbb{R}$, there exists a number $(-a) \in \mathbb{R}$ such that

$$(-a)+a=a+(-a)=0.$$

For each number $a \in \mathbb{R}-\{0\}$, there exists a number $a^{-1} \in \mathbb{R}-\{0\}$ such that

$$a^{-1} \times a = a \times a^{-1} = 1.$$

In ordinary algebraic notation these statements look quite different, but $\mathbb{R}$ and $\mathbb{R}-\{0\}$ are both examples of a set S closed under a binary operation $\circ$, with an identity element e. The two statements mean that for each element a in S there exists an element b with the property that $a \circ b = b \circ a = e$. This element b is called an **inverse** of a.

Example 9.5.1
Find an inverse of a in $\mathbb{R}-\{1\}$ with the binary operation $a \circ b = a+b-ab$.

In Example 9.4.2, it was shown that the identity element is 0.

$$b \circ a = e \quad \Leftrightarrow \quad b+a-ba=0 \quad \Leftrightarrow \quad b=\frac{a}{a-1}$$

so, as $a \neq 1$, $\dfrac{a}{a-1}$ is an inverse of a.

As $a \circ b = b \circ a$, there is no need to check separately that $a \circ b = e$.

Summarising the discussion in this and the previous section gives the following:

Let S be a set with a closed binary operation $\circ$.

If there exists an element $e \in G$ such that, for all $a \in G$, $e \circ a = a \circ e = a$, then e is an **identity element** for S with the operation $\circ$.

If for each element $a \in S$, there exists an element $b \in S$ such that $b \circ a = a \circ b = e$, where e is an identity element for S, then b is called an **inverse** of a in S with the operation $\circ$.

Exercise 9B

1 In each part of this question a set with a closed binary operation is given. Find the identity element, if it exists, and if it does exist, find the inverse of a general element a, if it exists.

(a) Vectors with 3 components: vector product

(b) 2×2 matrices: matrix multiplication

(c) $\mathbb{C}$: multiplication

(d) $\mathbb{R}$: $\circ$ where $a \circ b = |a-b|$

(e) $\mathbb{R}$: $\circ$ where $a \circ b = b$ for all $a, b \in \mathbb{R}$

(f) The set of matrices of the form $\begin{pmatrix} x & x \\ 0 & 0 \end{pmatrix}$, where $x \in \mathbb{R}-\{0\}$: matrix multiplication

(g) $\{2,4,6,8\}$: $\circ$ where $a \circ b$ is the remainder when $a \times b$ is divided by 10

(h) $\{2,4,6,8\}$: $\circ$ where $a \circ b$ is the remainder when $a+b$ is divided by 10

(i) $\{1,3,7,9\}$: $\circ$ where $a \circ b$ is the remainder when $a \times b$ is divided by 10

9.6 Groups

You have now seen that mathematical structures can be distinguished by various properties: they may or may not be closed or associative, and they may or may not have identity and inverse elements. Structures with all these properties are especially important.

A set G, with a binary operation $\circ$, is called a **group** if it has four properties.

1. **Closure:** $a \circ b \in G$ for all $a, b \in G$; that is, the operation is closed.
2. **Associativity**: $a \circ (b \circ c) = (a \circ b) \circ c$ for all $a, b, c \in G$; that is, the binary operation is associative.
3. **Identity**: there exists an identity element $e \in G$ such that for all $a \in G$, $e \circ a = a \circ e = a$.
4. **Inverse:** for each element $a \in G$, there exists an inverse element $b \in G$ such that $b \circ a = a \circ b = e$.

The group G with binary operation $\circ$ is denoted by $(G, \circ)$.

Notice that a group operation need not be commutative.

It is an important fact that there is only one element $e \in G$ with the property that for all $a \in G$, $e \circ a = a \circ e = a$. Once you know that there is only one such element, you can call it *the* identity element for $(G, \circ)$. Similarly, given an element $a \in G$, there is only one inverse element $b \in G$ such that $b \circ a = a \circ b = e$, so you can talk about *the* inverse of a. The notation a^{-1} is used for the inverse of a.

These facts about the uniqueness of the identity and the uniqueness of the inverse for each element are proved at end of the section. Assume them for now.

Groups may have a finite or an infinite number of elements. Examples of infinite groups are $(\mathbb{Z}, +)$, $(\mathbb{R} - \{0\}, \times)$ and $(\{z \in \mathbb{C} : |z| = 1\}, \times)$. Example 9.6.1 shows a finite group.

The number of elements in a group is called its **order**.

If a group has an infinite number of elements, it is said to have **infinite order**.

To prove that a set with an infinite number of elements is a group, you cannot use arguments based on tables.

Example 9.6.1
Prove that the set $\{1, \mathrm{i}, -1, -\mathrm{i}\}$ with the operation of multiplication is a group.

For a set as small as this, it is often easiest to show that the binary operation is closed by constructing a table. Table 9.3 shows the results.

$\times$	1	i	−1	−i
1	1	i	−1	−i
i	i	−1	−i	1
−1	−1	−i	1	i
−i	−i	1	i	−1

Table 9.3

There are four properties to establish, namely the four properties of the group.

1 **Closure**: The table shows that the operation of multiplication is closed since every possible product is a member of the set $\{1, \mathrm{i}, -1, -\mathrm{i}\}$.

2 **Associativity**: Multiplication of complex numbers is associative, so multiplication of these elements is associative.

3 **Identity**: The element 1 is the identity element, since $1 \times z = z \times 1 = z$ for every complex number z.

4 **Inverse**: The inverses of 1, -1, i and $-\mathrm{i}$ are 1, -1, $-\mathrm{i}$ and i respectively, so every element has an inverse.

Therefore $\{1, \mathrm{i}, -1, -\mathrm{i}\}$ with the operation of multiplication is a group.

The row corresponding to the identity element is the same as the row of 'column labels' at the top of the table; the column corresponding to the identity element is the same as the column of 'row labels' at the left of the table.

You may have noticed that each element of the group in Table 9.3 appears just once in every row and once in every column. This is necessary for a group.

Theorem In a group table, each element appears just once in every row.

Proof The elements which appear in a row are those of the form $a \circ x$ where a is fixed and x ranges over the elements of the group. Suppose that two elements in a row are the same. Then $a \circ x = a \circ y$ for some x and y, with $x \neq y$. Therefore

$$\begin{aligned} a \circ x = a \circ y \quad &\Rightarrow \quad a^{-1} \circ (a \circ x) = a^{-1} \circ (a \circ y) \\ &\Rightarrow \quad (a^{-1} \circ a) \circ x = (a^{-1} \circ a) \circ y \\ &\Rightarrow \quad e \circ x = e \circ y \\ &\Rightarrow \quad x = y. \end{aligned}$$

This is a contradiction, so no element appears more than once in each row.

If there are n elements in the group, then there are n elements in the row of the group table, which, by the previous argument, must all be different. Therefore each element appears just once in each row.

The proof for columns is left to you in Exercise 9C Question 4.

This theorem has no meaning for infinite groups, because you can't draw a table, but the cancelling argument that

$$a \circ x = a \circ y \quad \Rightarrow \quad x = y$$

is valid for infinite groups.

Suppose that a and b are known and that you want to solve the equation $a \circ x = b$ for x.

$$\begin{aligned} a \circ x = b \quad &\Leftrightarrow \quad a^{-1} \circ (a \circ x) = a^{-1} \circ b \\ &\Leftrightarrow \quad (a^{-1} \circ a) \circ x = a^{-1} \circ b \\ &\Leftrightarrow \quad e \circ x = a^{-1} \circ b \\ &\Leftrightarrow \quad x = a^{-1} \circ b. \end{aligned}$$

There are corresponding results if the order of a and x is reversed:

$$x \circ a = y \circ a \quad \Rightarrow \quad x = y \qquad \text{and} \qquad x \circ a = b \quad \Leftrightarrow \quad x = b \circ a^{-1}.$$

In a finite group, each element appears exactly once in each row and each column of the group table.

For any group, $a \circ x = a \circ y \quad \Rightarrow \quad x = y$ and $x \circ a = y \circ a \quad \Rightarrow \quad x = y$. This is called the **cancellation law**.

For any group, $a \circ x = b \quad \Leftrightarrow x = a^{-1} \circ b$ and $x \circ a = b \quad \Leftrightarrow \quad x = b \circ a^{-1}$.

An $n \times n$ table in which each element occurs just once in each row and each column is called a **Latin square** and is used in the design of statistical experiments. A group table is always a Latin square, but the reverse is not true. See Exercise 9C Question 2.

Example 9.6.2
Prove that the set of non-singular 2×2 matrices with the operation of matrix multiplication is a group.

The matrices must be non-singular so that inverse matrices exist.

1 **Closure**: The product of two non-singular 2×2 matrices $\mathbf{M}$ and $\mathbf{N}$ is a 2×2 matrix $\mathbf{MN}$. Since $\mathbf{M}$ and $\mathbf{N}$ are non-singular, $\det \mathbf{M} \neq 0$ and $\det \mathbf{N} \neq 0$, and since $\det \mathbf{MN} = \det \mathbf{M} \det \mathbf{N}$ (Section 6.2), $\det \mathbf{MN} \neq 0$, so $\mathbf{MN}$ is non-singular. The operation of matrix multiplication is therefore closed.

2 **Associativity**: Since matrix multiplication is associative (Section 4.4) the group operation is associative.

3 **Identity**: The 2×2 identity matrix $\mathbf{I}$ is non-singular and is a member of the set. It has the property that for any matrix $\mathbf{M}$ in the set $\mathbf{IM} = \mathbf{MI} = \mathbf{M}$.

4 **Inverse**: If $\mathbf{M}$ is non-singular, then $\mathbf{M}^{-1}$ exists and is non-singular, so there exists an element in the set such that $\mathbf{M}^{-1}\mathbf{M} = \mathbf{MM}^{-1} = \mathbf{I}$.

Therefore the set of non-singular 2×2 matrices with the operation of matrix multiplication is a group.

There is an important difference between the groups in Examples 9.6.1 and 9.6.2. In Example 9.6.1 the binary operation is commutative, while in the second it is not.

In a group $(G,\circ)$, if $a \circ b = b \circ a$ for all $a, b \in G$, the group $(G,\circ)$ is said to be **commutative** or **abelian**.

The word 'abelian' is in honour of the Norwegian mathematician Niels Abel.

The next example gives you practice in carrying out calculations in a group. Index notation, which is defined in Chapter 10, is used informally, so that $a^2 = a \circ a$, and so on.

Example 9.6.3
Let $(G,\circ)$ be a group in which $a^3 = e$, $b^2 = e$ and $a \circ b = b \circ a^2$. Show that $b \circ (a^2 \circ b) = a$, $b \circ a = a^2 \circ b$, and simplify the product $(a \circ b)^2$.

Note that, as $a^3 = e$, $a^{-1} = a^2$, and as $b^2 = e$, $b^{-1} = b$.

$$b \circ (a^2 \circ b) = b \circ a \circ (a \circ b) = b \circ a \circ (b \circ a^2) = b \circ (a \circ b) \circ a^2$$
$$= b \circ (b \circ a^2) \circ a^2 = b^2 \circ a^4 = a.$$

Since $b \circ (a^2 \circ b) = a$,

$$b \circ a = b \circ (b \circ a^2 \circ b) = b^2 \circ a^2 \circ b = e \circ a^2 \circ b = a^2 \circ b.$$

$$(a \circ b)^2 = (a \circ b) \circ (a \circ b) = a \circ (b \circ a) \circ b = a \circ (a^2 \circ b) \circ b = a^3 \circ b^2 = e \circ e = e.$$

Here are some important algebraic results about groups and inverses. These results will be used continually in the sections which follow.

Theorem A group $(G,\circ)$ has the following properties.
(a) The identity element for a group $(G,\circ)$ is unique.
(b) For any $a \in G$, the inverse of a is unique.
(c) For $a, b \in G$, if $a \circ b = e$, then $a = b^{-1}$ and $b = a^{-1}$ and $b \circ a = e$.
(d) For $a, b \in G$, $(a \circ b)^{-1} = b^{-1} \circ a^{-1}$.
(e) For $a \in G$, $(a^{-1})^{-1} = a$.

One strategy for showing that an element is unique is to suppose that there are two such elements, and then to prove that they must be the same.

Proof (a) Suppose that there are two identity elements, e and f.
Since e is an identity, $e \circ a = a$ for any a. Putting $a = f$, gives, $e \circ f = f$.
Since f is an identity, $a \circ f = a$. Putting $a = e$, gives $e \circ f = e$.
Therefore $f = e$, and the identity element for a group is unique.

(b) Suppose that a has two inverses, b and c.
Then $a \circ b = e$ and $c \circ a = e$.

So $c = c \circ e = c \circ (a \circ b) = (c \circ a) \circ b = e \circ b = b$,
and the inverse of a is unique.

(c) To prove $a = b^{-1}$, multiply $a \circ b = e$ on the right by b^{-1}. Then

$$\begin{aligned} a \circ b = e \quad &\Rightarrow \quad (a \circ b) \circ b^{-1} = e \circ b^{-1} \\ &\Rightarrow \quad a \circ \left(b \circ b^{-1}\right) = b^{-1} \\ &\Rightarrow \quad a \circ e = b^{-1} \\ &\Rightarrow \quad a = b^{-1}. \end{aligned}$$

The proof of the second part is similar. Then

$$b \circ a = b \circ b^{-1} = e.$$

(d) The proof involves showing that $(a \circ b) \circ \left(b^{-1} \circ a^{-1}\right)$ is e, and using part (c).

$$\begin{aligned} (a \circ b) \circ \left(b^{-1} \circ a^{-1}\right) &= a \circ \left(b \circ \left(b^{-1} \circ a^{-1}\right)\right) = a \circ \left(\left(b \circ b^{-1}\right) \circ a^{-1}\right) \\ &= a \circ \left(e \circ a^{-1}\right) = a \circ a^{-1} = e. \end{aligned}$$

Then, using part (c), $(a \circ b)^{-1} = b^{-1} \circ a^{-1}$.

(e) Since $a \circ a^{-1} = e$, using part (c) with $b = a^{-1}$, $\left(a^{-1}\right)^{-1} = a$.

Exercise 9C

1 Which of the following sets with the given operations are not groups? Give what you believe to be the simplest reason why each is not a group.

(a) $\mathbb{N}$, under addition

(b) $\mathbb{Q}^+$, under multiplication

(c) $\{1,2,3,4,5\}$, where $a \circ b$ is the remainder after ab is divided by 6

(d) $\{1,2,3,4,5,6\}$, where $a \circ b$ is the remainder after ab is divided by 7

(e) $\{1,2,3,4,5,6\}$, where $a \circ b$ is the remainder after $a + b$ is divided by 6

(f) $\{0,1,2,3,4,5\}$, where $a \circ b$ is the remainder after $a + b$ is divided by 6

(g) $\{1,3,5,7,9\}$, where $a \circ b$ is the remainder after ab is divided by 10

(h) Rational numbers of the form $\frac{m}{2^n}$, where m, $n \in \mathbb{Z}$, under addition

(i) Rational numbers of the form $\frac{m}{2^n}$, where m, $n \in \mathbb{Z}$, under multiplication

(j) Numbers of the form 2^n, $n \in \mathbb{Z}$, under multiplication

(k) Matrices of the form $\begin{pmatrix} a & -b \\ b & a \end{pmatrix}$, where $a, b \in \mathbb{R}$, $a^2 + b^2 \neq 0$ under matrix multiplication

(l) Even integers under addition

2 Show that this table is not a group table.

	e	a	b	c
e	e	b	c	b
a	a	c	b	e
b	c	b	e	a
c	b	e	a	c

3 Let the following functions be defined for the domain $x \in \mathbb{R} - \{0,1\}$.

$\mathrm{i}: x \mapsto x$ $\quad \mathrm{p}: x \mapsto 1-x$ $\quad \mathrm{q}: x \mapsto \dfrac{1}{x}$ $\quad \mathrm{r}: x \mapsto \dfrac{1}{1-x}$

Show that these functions, together with two more functions which you should find, form a group under composition of functions.

4 Prove that in a finite group table, each element appears just once in every column.

5 Prove that $(\mathbb{Z} - \{0\}, \times)$ is not a group.

6 Prove that the set of nth roots of unity (see Section 7.2) form a group under multiplication.

7 Show that functions of the form $\mathrm{f}(x) = ax + b$, where $a, b \in \mathbb{R}$ and $a \neq 0$, form a group under the operation of composition of functions. What is the inverse of $x \mapsto ax + b$?

8 Let $(G, \circ)$ be a group in which $a^4 = e$, $b^2 = e$ and $a \circ b = b \circ a^3$. Show that $b \circ a = a^3 \circ b$, $b \circ (a^2 \circ b) = a^2$, and simplify the product $(a \circ b) \circ (a^2 \circ b)$.

9† Consider the set of number pairs (a,b) where $a, b \in \mathbb{R}$ and a and b are not both zero. The rule for combining the number pairs is $(a,b) \circ (c,d) = (bc + ad, bd - ac)$. Show that this set with this operation is a group.

10† Let $(G, \circ)$ and $(H, \bullet)$ be groups, and consider the set (g,h) where $g \in G$ and $h \in H$. Let a binary operation $\times$ be defined by $(g_1, h_1) \times (g_2, h_2) = (g_1 \circ g_2, h_1 \bullet h_2)$. Show that this set with this operation is a group.

9.7 Modular arithmetic and addition

Modular arithmetic is a kind of 'arithmetic with remainders'. When you divide a natural number by n, the remainder is one of the numbers $0, 1, 2, \ldots, n-1$. So consider the set $\mathbb{Z}_n = \{0, 1, 2, \ldots, n-1\}$ with the following rule for combining the elements.

$a \oplus b$ is the remainder when $a + b$ is divided by n.

1 **Closure**: As the remainder after division by n belongs to $\mathbb{Z}_n$, the operation is closed.

2 **Associativity**: Suppose that $a + b = nr + x$, where $x \in \mathbb{Z}_n$, and $x + c = ns + y$, where $y \in \mathbb{Z}_n$. Then $x = a \oplus b$, and $y = x \oplus c = (a \oplus b) \oplus c$.

Now $(a+b)+c = (nr+x)+c = nr+(x+c) = nr+(ns+y) = (nr+ns)+y$

$$= n(r+s)+y,$$

so $y=(a\oplus b)\oplus c$ is the remainder when $(a+b)+c$ is divided by n.

Similarly, $a\oplus(b\oplus c)$ is the remainder when $a+(b+c)$ is divided by n.

But $(a+b)+c=a+(b+c)$, so $(a\oplus b)\oplus c=a\oplus(b\oplus c)$.

3 **Identity**: The number 0 acts as the identity since $a\oplus 0=0\oplus a=a$ for all $a\in\mathbb{Z}_n$.

4 **Inverse**: If $a=0$, consider 0. Then $0\oplus 0=0$, so 0 is the inverse of 0. Now consider $a\neq 0$, where $a\in\mathbb{Z}_n$. Consider $n-a$. As $n>n-a>0$, $n-a\in\mathbb{Z}_n$; and $(n-a)\oplus a=((n-a)+a)-n=0$ and $a\oplus(n-a)=(a+(n-a))-n=0$. Therefore $n-a$ is the inverse of a.

Therefore $\mathbb{Z}_n$ with this rule is a group. The group is called $(\mathbb{Z}_n,+)$, the group of **integers modulo *n* (mod *n*) under addition**. Notice that, now that the basic properties of modular arithmetic have been established, there is no need to go on using the 'ringed' addition sign. You can use the ordinary addition sign without ambiguity.

Table 9.4 is a group table for $(\mathbb{Z}_4,+)$

+	0	1	2	3
0	0	1	2	3
1	1	2	3	0
2	2	3	0	1
3	3	0	1	2

Table 9.4

9.8 Modular arithmetic and multiplication

You can also do modular arithmetic with multiplication, making the definition

$a\otimes b$ is the remainder when ab is divided by n.

However, there are two important differences between multiplication and addition.

- The number 0 has the property that $0\times a=a\times 0=0$ for all $a\in\mathbb{Z}_n$. It follows that $(\mathbb{Z}_n,\otimes)$ cannot be a group, since 0 does not have an inverse. So it is best to consider $\mathbb{Z}_n-\{0\}$, that is the set $\{1,2,\ldots,n-1\}$.
- If n is not prime, then $(\mathbb{Z}_n-\{0\},\otimes)$ is not closed. For example, in $\mathbb{Z}_6$, $2\otimes 3=0$ which is not in $\mathbb{Z}_6-\{0\}$. So you can only get a group if n is a prime number.

So consider the set $\mathbb{Z}_p-\{0\}=\{1,2,\ldots,p-1\}$, where p is a prime number.

1 **Closure**: Since the remainder after division by p belongs to $\mathbb{Z}_p-\{0\}$, the operation is closed. Note that the remainder cannot be 0 because that would mean that $ab=xp$ and as the right side is divisible by p, the left side is also divisible by p. But $0<a,b\leqslant p-1$ so this is impossible.

2 **Associativity**: Suppose that $ab=pr+x$, where $x\in\mathbb{Z}_p-\{0\}$, and $xc=ps+y$ where $y\in\mathbb{Z}_p-\{0\}$. Then $x=a\otimes b$, and $y=x\otimes c=(a\otimes b)\otimes c$.

Now $(ab)c = (pr + x)c = (pr)c + (xc) = p(rc) + (ps + y)$
$= (p(rc) + ps) + y = p(rc + s) + y,$

so $y = (a \otimes b) \otimes c$ is the remainder when $(ab)c$ is divided by p.

Similarly, $a \otimes (b \otimes c)$ is the remainder when $a(bc)$ is divided by p.

But $(ab)c = a(bc)$, so $(a \otimes b) \otimes c = a \otimes (b \otimes c)$.

3 **Identity**: The number 1 acts as the identity since $a \otimes 1 = 1 \otimes a = a$ for all $a \in \mathbb{Z}_p - \{0\}$.

4 **Inverse**: For $a \in \mathbb{Z}_n$, consider the elements $\{1 \otimes a, 2 \otimes a, \ldots, (p-1) \otimes a\}$. These elements are all different, since if two of them, say $r \otimes a$ and $s \otimes a$, are equal, then $r \otimes a$ and $s \otimes a$ have the same remainder on division by p. Suppose that $ra = kp + x$ and $sa = lp + x$ where k and l are integers and $x \in \mathbb{Z}_p - \{0\}$. Then

$$ra - kp = sa - lp, \quad \text{so} \quad ra - sa = lp - kp, \quad \text{that is} \quad (r-s)a = (l-k)p.$$

Now p divides the right side; so p divides the left side, and must divide either a or $r - s$. But $a \in \mathbb{Z}_p - \{0\}$, so p does not divide a; and $-(p-1) \leqslant r - s \leqslant p - 1$, so the only possibility is that $r - s = 0$, or $r = s$. So no two of the set $\{1 \otimes a, 2 \otimes a, \ldots, (p-1) \otimes a\}$ are equal. As they are all different, and there are $p - 1$ of them, one of them must be 1. Suppose that $b \otimes a = 1$. Then $a \otimes b = 1$, from the definition of $\otimes$, so b is the inverse of a.

The proof that the inverse exists is interesting because it does not actually produce the inverse of each element. It only shows that each element must have an inverse.

So $\mathbb{Z}_p - \{0\}$ with this rule is a group which is called $(\mathbb{Z}_p - \{0\}, \times)$, the group of **non-zero integers modulo *p* (mod *p*) under multiplication**. Notice that, as for addition, the multiplication sign rather than the 'ringed' multiplication sign is used. Table 9.5 shows $(\mathbb{Z}_5 - \{0\}, \times)$.

$\times$	1	2	3	4
1	1	2	3	4
2	2	4	1	3
3	3	1	4	2
4	4	3	2	1

Table 9.5

From Table 9.5, the inverse of 3 is 2, and vice versa. But if you had to find the inverse of 7 in $(\mathbb{Z}_{59} - \{0\}, \times)$, it would not be so easy.

Example 9.8.1
Find the inverse of 5 in $(\mathbb{Z}_{11} - \{0\}, \times)$.

$2 \times 5 = 10$, $3 \times 5 = 4$, $4 \times 5 = 9$, $5 \times 5 = 3$, $6 \times 5 = 8$, $7 \times 5 = 2$, $8 \times 5 = 7$, $9 \times 5 = 1$.

Therefore the inverse of 5 is 9.

You can often use brute force in this way to find inverses in a small group.

Note that in Example 9.8.1, if you want inverses of other elements, things get progressively easier. You now know that the inverse of 5 is 9, so the inverse of 9 is 5. But since $3 = 5 \times 5$,

$$3^{-1} = (5 \times 5)^{-1} = 5^{-1} \times 5^{-1} = 9 \times 9 = 4,$$

so $4^{-1} = 3$.

If you want 2^{-1}, you need now try only 2, 6, 7, 8 and 10. Once you spot $2^{-1} = 6$, you can deduce from $6 \times 5 = 8$ that

$$8^{-1} = (6 \times 5)^{-1} = 5^{-1} \times 6^{-1} = 9 \times 2 = 7.$$

This leaves 10 as its own inverse.

9.9 A group of symmetries

Let $\mathbf{E}$ be the equilateral triangle ABC shown in Fig. 9.6, and let the lines x, y and z and the points 1, 2 and 3 be fixed in the plane. Define the following transformations of the plane containing $\mathbf{E}$.

- X is 'reflect in the line x'.
- Y is 'reflect in the line y'.
- Z is 'reflect in the line z'.
- R is 'rotate by $\frac{2}{3}\pi$ anticlockwise about O'.
- S is 'rotate by $\frac{4}{3}\pi$ anticlockwise about O'.
- I is 'do nothing'.

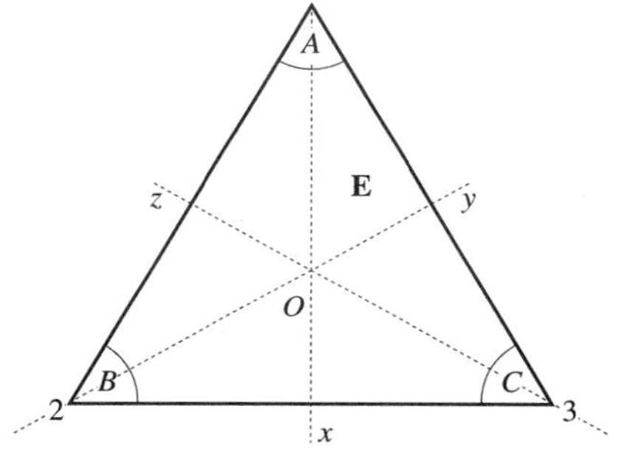

Fig. 9.6

Each of these transformations of the plane leaves the triangle where it is now, although it may change the positions of the vertices which make up the triangle $\mathbf{E}$. This kind of transformation is called a **symmetry** of $\mathbf{E}$.

You can describe the transformation X by writing $\begin{pmatrix} 1 & 2 & 3 \\ A & B & C \end{pmatrix} \xrightarrow{X} \begin{pmatrix} 1 & 2 & 3 \\ A & C & B \end{pmatrix}$

where the notation in the first bracket shows that A started in position 1, B in position 2 and C in position 3, and after the transformation by X, A is still in position 1, B is now in position 3 and C is in position 2.

To combine operations use the rule 'followed by', that is the rule for combining functions (P2 Section 2.2).

The transformation RX (X followed by R) is

$$\begin{pmatrix} 1 & 2 & 3 \\ A & B & C \end{pmatrix} \xrightarrow{X} \begin{pmatrix} 1 & 2 & 3 \\ A & C & B \end{pmatrix} \xrightarrow{R} \begin{pmatrix} 1 & 2 & 3 \\ B & A & C \end{pmatrix}$$

which is the same as transformation Z. Thus $RX = Z$. Similarly $SR = I$.

You can make up Table 9.7, which shows how each of the transformations I, R, S, X, Y and Z combines with the others, using the rule 'followed by'. The result is always one of I, R, S, X, Y and Z, so 'followed by' is a binary operation on the set $\{I, R, S, X, Y, Z\}$.

In Table 9.7, the result $RX = Z$ is shown by going along the row containing R and down the column containing X.

		First operation performed					
		I	R	S	X	Y	Z
	I	I	R	S	X	Y	Z
Second	R	R	S	I	Z	X	Y
operation	S	S	I	R	Y	Z	X
performed	X	X	Y	Z	I	R	S
	Y	Y	Z	X	S	I	R
	Z	Z	X	Y	R	S	I

Table 9.7

As 'followed by' is the rule of combination of functions, it is associative.

The transformation I is the identity element.

Each element has an inverse. The inverses of I, R, S, X, Y and Z are respectively I, S, R, X, Y and Z.

So the set $\{I, R, S, X, Y, Z\}$ and the operation 'followed by' is a group. It is called the **dihedral group of the triangle** and is given the symbol D_3. Similar groups are defined for all regular polygons: the symbol for the dihedral group of the n-sided polygon is D_n.

The word 'dihedral' means having or being contained by two plane faces.

Exercise 9D

1 Write out the group table for $(\mathbb{Z}_5, +)$, and write down the inverse of 2.

2 Write out a group table for $(\mathbb{Z}_7 - \{0\}, \times)$.

3 Write out a table of operations for $(\mathbb{Z}_8 - \{0\}, \times)$. Give one reason why $(\mathbb{Z}_8 - \{0\}, \times)$ is not a group. Give a reason why $(\mathbb{Z}_q - \{0\}, \times)$ is not a group if q is not prime.

4 Write out the group table for the symmetries of a non-square rectangle.

5 Write out the group table for D_4, the dihedral group of the square. (Keep this group table for use with future exercises.)
(Let R be an anticlockwise quarter-turn about the origin, and use the notation R^2 and R^3 for the other rotations. Let H and V be reflections in the x- and y-axes, and L and M be reflections in the lines $y = -x$ and $y = x$. Put the operations in the order, I, R, R^2, R^3, H, L, V, M. Your table should then match the one given in the answers.)

6 Calculate 7×9 and 4×15 in $(\mathbb{Z}_{59} - \{0\}, \times)$. Use your answers to find the inverses of

(a) 4, (b) 7, (c) 28, (d) 49.

7 Try constructing a table for a group of order 4 in which the elements are called e, a, b and c and are written in that order along the top row. Show that there are five such tables.

Miscellaneous exercise 9

1 Write out a group table in which the only elements are e, a, b.

2 Let $(G,\circ)$ be a group with eight elements $\{e, a, a^2, a^3, b, a\circ b, a^2\circ b, a^3\circ b\}$ in which $a^4 = e$, $b^2 = a^2$ and $a^3\circ b = b\circ a$. Show that $(a\circ b)^2 = a^2$, $(a^3\circ b)\circ(a\circ b) = e$. Write out the group table for $(G,\circ)$.

3 The set S consists of the eight elements 9^1, 9^2, …, 9^8 where the operation is addition modulo 64. Determine each of the elements of S as an integer between 0 and 63.

Under multiplication modulo 64, the set S forms a group G with identity 1. Write down the inverses of each of the remaining elements of G.

A group in which each element x can be written as a power of a particular element g of the group is said to be a cyclic group; and such an element g is called a generator of the group. Write down all the possible generators of G.

4 Construct the composition table for $(S,\circ)$, where the binary operation $\circ$ is defined on the set $S = \{0,1,2,3,4,5,6\}$ by $x\circ y = x + y - xy$ modulo 7.

One of the elements of S is removed to form a set S' of order 6, such that $(S',\circ)$ forms a group. State which element is to be deleted, and prove that $(S',\circ)$ is a group.

5 Show that the Latin square shown below is not a group table.

	e	a	b	c	d
e	e	a	b	c	d
a	a	b	c	d	e
b	b	e	d	a	c
c	c	d	e	b	a
d	d	c	a	e	b

6 A binary operation $*$ is defined on the set $\mathbb{Q} - \{0\}$ of non-zero rational numbers as follows:

$$x * y = xy \qquad \text{if } x > 0,$$
$$x * y = \frac{x}{y} \qquad \text{if } x < 0.$$

Prove that $(\mathbb{Q} - \{0\}, *)$ is a non-commutative group. (OCR)

7 The operation $*$ is defined on the set $S = \{x \in \mathbb{R} : x \neq \pm 1\}$ by $a * b = \dfrac{a+b}{1+ab}$ for $a, b \in S$.

(a) Determine the identity element of S under $*$.

(b) For each $a \in S$, describe the inverse element a^{-1} of a.

(c) Prove that $*$ is associative on S.

(d) Prove that S, under the operation $*$, does not form a group. (OCR)

10 Subgroups

This chapter extends the study of groups by investigating groups within other groups. When you have completed it, you should know

- what is meant by the order of an element
- what is meant by a cyclic group, and how to show that a group is, or is not, cyclic
- what a subgroup is, and how to test for a subgroup
- that the order of a subgroup divides the order of the group
- that the order of an element divides the order of the group
- that all groups of prime order are cyclic.

10.1 Notation

It can be tedious to use the notation $(G, \circ)$ for a group, and it is quite usual to leave out the symbol for the operation and to use multiplicative notation. From now on, provided there is no ambiguity, the symbol G will be used for a group and ab will be used instead of $a \circ b$.

However, in some groups, such as $\mathbb{Z}$, the operation is addition, and then it is usual to retain the + sign. It is a convention that, whenever additive notation is used, the group is commutative.

Here is an example of a proof in the new notation.

Example 10.1.1
Let G be a group in which every element is its own inverse. Prove that G is commutative.

Let $a, b \in G$. Then $ab \in G$. As $ab \in G$, it is its own inverse so $(ab)^{-1} = ab$. Therefore $b^{-1}a^{-1} = ab$, and as $a^{-1} = a$ and $b^{-1} = b$, $ba = ab$. So G is commutative.

10.2 Powers of elements

In Example 9.6.3, you saw that when you multiply an element a of a group G by itself, you obtain aa, which is written as a^2. This leads to the following definition.

Let a be an element of a group G. If n is a positive integer, then

$$a^n = \overbrace{aa\ldots a}^{n \text{ times}} \quad \text{and} \quad a^{-n} = \overbrace{a^{-1}a^{-1}\ldots a^{-1}}^{n \text{ times}}.$$

The power a^0 is defined to be e.

Many of the usual index rules are satisfied for all integers $m, n \in \mathbb{Z}$, but they require proof. Here are two examples of such proofs. If you wish, you may omit them, and assume the results of the next shaded box.

Example 10.2.1
Show that $a^m a^n = a^{m+n}$ when m is a positive integer and n is a negative integer.

Let $n = -N$, so that N is positive. Then $a^m a^{-N} = \overbrace{aa\ldots a}^{m \text{ times}}\overbrace{a^{-1}a^{-1}\ldots a^{-1}}^{N \text{ times}}$.

Case 1 Suppose that $m > N$. Then

$$a^m a^{-N} = \overbrace{aa\ldots a}^{m \text{ times}}\overbrace{a^{-1}a^{-1}\ldots a^{-1}}^{N \text{ times}} = \overbrace{aa\ldots a}^{(m-N)\text{ times}} = \overbrace{aa\ldots a}^{(m+n)\text{ times}} = a^{m+n}.$$

Case 2 Suppose that $m = N$. Then

$$a^m a^{-N} = \overbrace{aa\ldots a}^{m \text{ times}}\overbrace{a^{-1}a^{-1}\ldots a^{-1}}^{m \text{ times}} = e = a^0 = a^{m-N} = a^{m+n}.$$

Case 3 Suppose that $m < N$. Then

$$a^m a^{-N} = \overbrace{aa\ldots a}^{m \text{ times}}\overbrace{a^{-1}a^{-1}\ldots a^{-1}}^{N \text{ times}} = \overbrace{a^{-1}a^{-1}\ldots a^{-1}}^{(N-m)\text{ times}} = a^{-(N-m)} = a^{m-N} = a^{m+n}.$$

Therefore, in all cases, $a^m a^n = a^{m+n}$ when m is a positive integer and n is a negative integer.

Example 10.2.2
Show that $a^{-m} = \left(a^m\right)^{-1} = \left(a^{-1}\right)^m$ when m is a positive integer.

From Case 2 above, $a^m a^{-m} = e$, so a^{-m} is the inverse of a^m, that is $a^{-m} = \left(a^m\right)^{-1}$.

By definition, $\overbrace{a^{-1}a^{-1}\ldots a^{-1}}^{m \text{ times}} = a^{-m}$; but $\overbrace{a^{-1}a^{-1}\ldots a^{-1}}^{m \text{ times}} = \left(a^{-1}\right)^m$. So $a^{-m} = \left(a^{-1}\right)^m$.

Therefore $a^{-m} = \left(a^m\right)^{-1} = \left(a^{-1}\right)^m$ when m is a positive integer.

There are a number of possible results like this. They are summarised by:

> In a group G, $a^m a^n = a^{m+n}$, $\left(a^m\right)^n = a^{mn}$, $a^{-m} = \left(a^m\right)^{-1} = \left(a^{-1}\right)^m$, where m and $n \in \mathbb{Z}$.
>
> In general $(ab)^m \neq a^m b^m$, unless the group G is commutative.

It is clear that in a finite group the powers of an element cannot all be different from each other. For example, in $(\mathbb{Z}_7 - \{0\}, \times)$,

$$2^2 = 4, \quad 2^3 = 2 \times 4 = 1, \quad 2^4 = 2 \times 1 = 2, \quad \text{and so on.}$$

In D_3, $R^2 = S$, $R^3 = RS = I$, $R^4 = R$, and so on.

Theorem Let a be an element of a finite group G. Then the powers of a cannot all be different, and there is a smallest positive integer k such that $a^k = e$.

Proof Consider the set of all possible powers of a. There are infinitely many of them. Since G is finite they cannot all be different. Let r and s be two positive integers, with $r < s$, such that $a^r = a^s$. Then

$$a^{s-r} = a^s a^{-r} = a^r a^{-r} = e.$$

Therefore there is at least one positive power, $s - r$, of a which gives the identity element. Let k be the smallest of these powers, so that $a^k = e$.

There is always a smallest power. See P4 Example 3.3.6.

Let a be an element of a group G. Then a is said to have **finite order** if $a^n = e$ for some positive integer n. The least such n is called the **order** of a.

If no such n exists, the element a has **infinite order**.

'Order' is used quite differently here from its use in the context of 'order of a group'. Some books use the word 'period' instead of 'order' in this context.

Note that, from the definition, in any group the order of the identity e is 1.

Example 10.2.3
Find the orders of the elements of (a) $(\mathbb{Z}_7 - \{0\}, \times)$, (b) D_3.

(a) The orders of the elements of $(\mathbb{Z}_7 - \{0\}, \times)$ can be worked out systematically:

The element 1 has order 1.
As $2^1 = 2$, $2^2 = 4$, $2^3 = 1$, the order of 2 is 3.
As $3^1 = 3$, $3^2 = 2$, $3^3 = 6$, $3^4 = 4$, $3^5 = 5$, $3^6 = 1$, the order of 3 is 6.
As $4^1 = 4$, $4^2 = 2$, $4^3 = 1$, the order of 4 is 3.
As $5^1 = 5$, $5^2 = 4$, $5^3 = 6$, $5^4 = 2$, $5^5 = 3$, $5^6 = 1$, the order of 5 is 6.
As $6^1 = 6$, $6^2 = 1$, the order of 6 is 2.

(b) Using Table 9.7, the orders of I, X, Y and Z are respectively 1, 2, 2 and 2. Since $R^2 = S$ and $R^3 = RS = I$, the order of R is 3.
Finally $S^2 = R$ and $S^3 = SR = I$, so the order of S is 3.

Example 10.2.4
In $(\mathbb{R} - \{0\}, \times)$, give an element of (a) finite order greater than 1, (b) infinite order.

(a) As an element a of finite order has to satisfy the equation $a^n = 1$ and belong to $\mathbb{R} - \{0\}$, the only possibilities are 1 and -1. Since 1 has order 1 and -1 has order 2, the only example is -1.

(b) The element 2 has infinite order since $2^n \neq 1$ for any positive integer n.

10.3 Cyclic groups

If G is a group, it is sometimes the case that G consists entirely of the powers of a single element. In this case the group is said to be **generated** by this element.

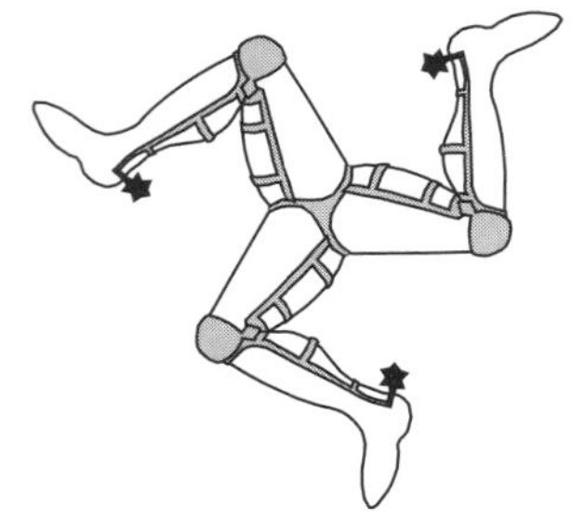

Fig. 10.1

An example of a finite group of this type is the group of symmetries of an object such as the Manx symbol in Fig. 10.1. This group consists of the set $\{I, R, R^2\}$, where R is a rotation of $\frac{2}{3}\pi$, together with the operation 'followed by'. Note that R^2, which is a rotation of $-\frac{2}{3}\pi$, is also a generator.

Groups like this are called **cyclic groups**. In the definition of a cyclic group which follows, recall that from the definition of the powers of an element a, $a^0 = e$.

> Let G be a group. If there is an element $a \in G$ such that every element of G has the form a^n for $n \in \mathbb{Z}$, then G is called a **cyclic** group. The element a is called a **generator** for G. The notation $G = \langle a \rangle$ is used to show that G is generated by a.

If you can find an element of a group whose order is equal to the order of the group, then it follows that the group is cyclic. One way of showing that a group is not cyclic is to find the order of each element and show that none of them is the order of a group. But there may be simpler ways of showing that a group is not cyclic; for example, if a group is not commutative, it can't be cyclic, because all cyclic groups are commutative.

Example 10.3.1
Show that the groups $(\mathbb{Z}_7, +)$ and $(\mathbb{Z}_7 - \{0\}, \times)$ are cyclic groups.

To show that $(\mathbb{Z}_7, +)$ is cyclic, you need to interpret the multiplicative notation of the definition of cyclic groups so that you can apply it to a group which uses additive notation.

In $(\mathbb{Z}_7, +)$, 1 is a generator because $1+1=2$, $1+1+1=3$, $1+1+1+1=4$, $1+1+1+1+1=5$, $1+1+1+1+1+1=6$ and $1+1+1+1+1+1+1=0$.

In $(\mathbb{Z}_7 - \{0\}, \times)$, 3 is a generator. See Example 10.2.3(a).

Example 10.3.2
Show that $(\mathbb{Z}, +)$ is a cyclic group.

If an element a is a generator, the group consists of the set of elements $\{\ldots, a^{-3}, a^{-2}, a^{-1}, e, a, a^2, a^3, \ldots\}$. When $a = 1$, $a^2 = 1+1 = 2$, $a^3 = 1+1+1 = 3$ etc., and $a^{-1} = -1$, $a^{-2} = (-1)+(-1) = -2$ etc. Therefore 1 is a generator for $(\mathbb{Z}, +)$, and so $(\mathbb{Z}, +)$ is a cyclic group.

Note that -1 is also a generator for $(\mathbb{Z}, +)$.

Example 10.3.3
Show that the group $(\mathbb{Q}^+, \times)$ is not a cyclic group.

Notice first that 1 is not a generator, since all its powers are 1, and that -1 is not a generator since all its powers are 1 or -1.

Suppose now that x is a generator, where $x \neq 1$ or -1. Then $x^n = -1$ for some value of n, so $|x^n| = |-1| = 1$, giving $|x|^n = 1$. But $x \neq 1$ or -1, so this is a contradiction. So $(\mathbb{Q}^+, \times)$ is not a cyclic group.

10.4 Subgroups

Look again at Table 9.7 for the group D_3, reprinted as Table 10.2 with the title D_3 in the top left corner. Part of the table is shaded; as $S = R^2$, this is the group $\{I, R, R^2\}$ of Fig. 10.1.

D_3	I	R	S	X	Y	Z
I	I	R	S	X	Y	Z
R	R	S	I	Z	X	Y
S	S	I	R	Y	Z	X
X	X	Y	Z	I	R	S
Y	Y	Z	X	S	I	R
Z	Z	X	Y	R	S	I

Table 10.2

The set $\{I, R, S\}$ with the operation 'followed by' is a smaller group inside the whole group; this is called a subgroup of D_3.

If you re-draw the table with the elements in the order $\{I, X, R, S, Y, Z\}$ you would find that there is also a small group $\{I, X\}$ in the top left corner. So $\{I, X\}$ is another subgroup of D_3. So too are $\{I, Y\}$ and $\{I, Z\}$.

In addition to these subgroups of D_3, the identity group $\{I\}$, and the whole group $\{I, R, S, X, Y, Z\}$ are also regarded as subgroups of D_3. The subgroups $\{I\}$ and D_3 are called trivial subgroups of D_3. The remaining subgroups are called proper subgroups of D_3.

If H is a subset of a group G with operation $\circ$, such that H is a group with operation $\circ$, then H is a **subgroup** of G.

Every group G has two **trivial** subgroups, $\{e\}$ and G itself.

Subgroups of G other than $\{e\}$ and G are called **proper** subgroups.

Example 10.4.1
Explain why $(\mathbb{Q} - \{0\}, \times)$ is not a subgroup of $(\mathbb{Q}, +)$.

Although $\mathbb{Q} - \{0\}$ is a subset of $\mathbb{Q}$, the operations in the two groups are different, so $(\mathbb{Q} - \{0\}, \times)$ is not a subgroup of $(\mathbb{Q}, +)$.

Example 10.4.2
Find all the subgroups of $(\mathbb{Z}_6, +)$, saying which are proper subgroups.

The subgroups are $\{0\}$, $\{0,3\}$, $\{0,2,4,6\}$ and $\mathbb{Z}_6$ itself. Of these the proper subgroups are $\{0,3\}$ and $\{0,2,4,6\}$ with the operation of addition modulo 6.

Example 10.4.3
Find a finite proper subgroup and an infinite proper subgroup of $(\mathbb{C}-\{0\}, \times)$.

A finite proper subgroup is $\{1,-1\}$. An infinite proper subgroup is $\{\mathbb{R}-\{0\}, \times\}$.

Theorem Let G be a group, and let H be a subset of G. Then H is a subgroup of G if

- $a \in H$ and $b \in H \Rightarrow ab \in H$
- $e \in H$ and
- $a \in H \quad \Rightarrow \quad a^{-1} \in H$.

Proof If $a \in H$ and $b \in H \Rightarrow ab \in H$, then the operation of G is closed in H.

Suppose that $a, b, c \in H$. Then, since H is a subset of G, $a, b, c \in G$. But the group operation in G is associative, so $(ab)c = a(bc)$. Therefore the operation is associative in H.

Since $ea = ae = a$ for each $a \in G$, it is true for each $a \in H$.

For $a \in H$, and hence $a^{-1} \in H$, $a^{-1}a = aa^{-1} = e$ because a^{-1} is the inverse of a in G.

Therefore H is a subgroup of G.

Example 10.4.4
Verify that $(\mathbb{Z}_0^+, +)$, which satisfies the first two conditions of the theorem but not the third, is not a subgroup of $(\mathbb{Z}, +)$.

Since $-1 \notin \mathbb{Z}_0^+$, the element 1 in $\mathbb{Z}_0^+$ has no inverse, so $(\mathbb{Z}_0^+, +)$ is not a group and therefore is not a subgroup of $(\mathbb{Z}, +)$.

Example 10.4.5
Prove that $H = \{12x + 21y : x, y \in \mathbb{Z}\}$ is a subgroup of $(\mathbb{Z}, +)$.

As x and y are integers, $12x + 21y$ is an integer, so H is a subset of $\mathbb{Z}$.

If $p, q \in H$, then $p = 12x_1 + 21y_1$ and $q = 12x_2 + 21y_2$ for integers x_1, y_1, x_2 and y_2. So $p + q = (12x_1 + 21y_1) + (12x_2 + 21y_2) = 12(x_1 + x_2) + 21(y_1 + y_2)$ where $x_1 + x_2$ and $y_1 + y_2$ are integers. Therefore $p + q \in H$.

Since $0 = 12 \times 0 + 21 \times 0$, and 0 is an integer, $0 \in H$.

If $p = 12x_1 + 21y_1 \in H$, then $-p = -(12x_1 + 21y_1) = 12(-x_1) + 21(-y_1)$. As $-x_1$ and $-y_1$ are integers, $-p \in H$. Also $(-p) + p = p + (-p) = 0$ so $-p$ is the inverse of p. Therefore the inverse of p is a member of H.

Therefore H is a subgroup of G.

What is this subgroup? Notice first that any factor of both 12 and 21 divides $12x+21y$, so the highest common factor of 12 and 21, namely 3, divides every member of H.

If you take $x=2$ and $y=-1$, you find that $2\times 12+(-1)\times 21=3$ is a member of H, so H consists of all multiples of 3.

This argument can be generalised to show that for positive integers a and b, $H=\{ax+by : x, y\in\mathbb{Z}\}$ is a subgroup of $(\mathbb{Z},+)$, and consists of multiples of the highest common factor of a and b.

Subgroups of a finite group

For a finite group G it is usually easy to check from a table whether a subset H is a subgroup. You need only check that the operation on the subset H is closed. For example, in Table 10.2, once you have seen that $\{I, R, S\}$ is closed, you do not need to check the other group properties. This is summarised in the following theorem.

Theorem Let G be a group, and let H be a finite subset of G. Then H is a subgroup of G if $a\in H$ and $b\in H \Rightarrow ab\in H$.

Proof If $a\in H$ and $b\in H \Rightarrow ab\in H$, the operation of G is closed in H.

The proof of associativity is the same as for the previous theorem.

If, in the statement '$a\in H$ and $b\in H \Rightarrow ab\in H$', you put $a, a^2, a^3, \ldots$ in turn instead of b, you find that $a^2\in H$, $a^3\in H$, $a^4\in H$ for all positive powers of a. Using the theorem in Section 10.2, let the order of a be k, so $a^k=e$, and $e\in H$.

Now consider a^{k-1}. Since $a^{k-1}a=a^k=e$, a^{k-1} is the inverse of a. But $a^{k-1}\in H$, so $a^{-1}\in H$.

By the previous theorem, H is a subgroup of G.

10.5 The subgroup generated by an element

In D_3 the set of powers of R is $\{R, R^2=S, R^3=I\}$, that is $\{R, S, I\}$, and you saw in Section 10.3 that this is a subgroup of D_3.

Similarly, in $(\mathbb{Z}_7-\{0\},\times)$, the powers of 2 are $\{2, 2^2=4, 2^3=1\}$, that is $\{2,4,1\}$, which is a subgroup of $(\mathbb{Z}_7-\{0\},\times)$.

Also, in $(\mathbb{Q},\times)$, the powers of 2, $\{\ldots, 2^{-s}, \ldots, 2^{-1}, 1, 2, \ldots, 2^r, \ldots\}$, form a subgroup.

In fact, the set of powers of an element is always a subgroup.

Theorem Let a be an element of a group G. Then the set of all powers of a, $H=\{a^n : n\in\mathbb{Z}\}$ is a subgroup of G.

Proof If $p, q\in H$, then $p=a^r$ and $q=a^s$ for integers r and s. Then $pq=a^ra^s=a^{r+s}$, and since $r+s$ is an integer, $pq\in H$.

Since 0 is an integer, $a^0\in H$. And since $a^0=e$ by definition, $e\in H$.

If $p\in H$, then $p=a^r$ for an integer r. Therefore $-r$ is an integer, and so $a^{-r}\in H$. But $a^{-r}a^r=a^{r-r}=e$, so a^{-r} is the inverse of p, and belongs to H.

Therefore $H = \{a^n : n \in \mathbb{Z}\}$ is a subgroup of G.

This proof applies to both finite and infinite groups.

The subgroup H of a group G defined by $H = \{a^n : n \in \mathbb{Z}\}$ is said to be the subgroup **generated** by a.

If an element a has infinite order, then the group generated by a is $\{\ldots, a^{-2}, a^{-1}, e, a, a^2, \ldots\}$, and is infinite.

If an element a has finite order n, then the group generated by a is $\{e, a, a^2, \ldots, a^{n-1}\}$. The order of the subgroup generated by a is then the same as the order of a.

Notice that the subgroup generated by an element is a cyclic subgroup, and that the order of the cyclic subgroup is the same as the order of the generating element.

Exercise 10A

1 The tables below show two groups: one of them is cyclic and one is not. Identify which is which, find all the generators of the cyclic group, and prove that the other group is not cyclic.

	e	a	b	c
e	e	a	b	c
a	a	e	c	b
b	b	c	e	a
c	c	b	a	e

	e	a	b	c
e	e	a	b	c
a	a	b	c	e
b	b	c	e	a
c	c	e	a	b

2 Prove that the groups $(\mathbb{Z}_5, +)$ and $(\mathbb{Z}_6, +)$ are cyclic, and find all their generators.

3 Find the orders of the elements of the two groups of Question 1.

4 (a) Find the orders of the elements of the group D_4 (see Exercise 9D Question 5).

(b) Find the cyclic subgroups of D_4.

(c) Find two proper non-cyclic subgroups of D_4.

5 Prove that if G is cyclic it is commutative.

6 Prove that the set $(\{\ldots, -3n, -2n, -n, 0, n, 2n, 3n, \ldots\}, +)$, where $n \in \mathbb{N}$, is a cyclic group.

7 Find a finite subgroup, apart from $\{1\}$, of the group $(\mathbb{R} - \{0\}, \times)$.

8 Find all the subgroups of (a) $(\mathbb{Z}_4, +)$ and (b) $(\mathbb{Z}_5, +)$.

9 Show that the group of functions $\{x \mapsto ax : a \in \mathbb{R}, a \neq 0\}$ is a subgroup of the group $\{x \mapsto ax + b : a, b \in \mathbb{R}, a \neq 0\}$ under the operation of composition of functions.

10 Let G be a group, and let g be a fixed element of G. Prove that the set of elements which commute with g, that is $H = \{x \in G : gx = xg\}$ is a subgroup of G. Identify the subgroup H for the following groups and elements.

(a) G is D_3 and g is R. (b) G is D_3 and g is X.

(c) G is the set of 2×2 matrices under multiplication and g is $\begin{pmatrix} 1 & 1 \\ 0 & 1 \end{pmatrix}$.

(d) G is Q_4 (see Question 11) and g is q. (e) G is A_4 (see Question 12) and g is x.

11 Find all the subgroups of the quaternion group denoted by Q_4, shown in the table. Keep a note of their orders for the next section.

Q_4	e	a	b	c	p	q	r	s
e	e	a	b	c	p	q	r	s
a	a	b	c	e	s	p	q	r
b	b	c	e	a	r	s	p	q
c	c	e	a	b	q	r	s	p
p	p	q	r	s	b	c	e	a
q	q	r	s	p	a	b	c	e
r	r	s	p	q	e	a	b	c
s	s	p	q	r	c	e	a	b

12* The group A_4 of rotational symmetries of the regular tetrahedron has order 12 and is shown in the table below. Find all the subgroups, and make a note of their orders for the next section. Check that A_4 has no subgroup of order 6.

A_4	e	a	b	c	x	y	z	t	p	q	r	s
e	e	a	b	c	x	y	z	t	p	q	r	s
a	a	e	c	b	z	t	x	y	s	r	q	p
b	b	c	e	a	t	z	y	x	q	p	s	r
c	c	b	a	e	y	x	t	z	r	s	p	q
x	x	t	y	z	p	s	q	r	e	c	a	b
y	y	z	x	t	r	q	s	p	c	e	b	a
z	z	y	t	x	s	p	r	q	a	b	e	c
t	t	x	z	y	q	r	p	s	b	a	c	e
p	p	r	s	q	e	b	c	a	x	z	t	y
q	q	s	r	p	b	e	a	c	t	y	x	z
r	r	p	q	s	c	a	e	b	y	t	z	x
s	s	q	p	r	a	c	b	e	z	x	y	t

10.6 Lagrange's theorem

If you look back at some of the results of Exercise 10A in which you found subgroups of finite groups, and the examples before Exercise 10A, you find that

- the subgroups of D_3, which has order 6, have orders 1, 2, 3 and 6;
- the subgroups of $(\mathbb{Z}_4,+)$, which has order 4, have orders 1, 2 and 4;
- the subgroups of $(\mathbb{Z}_5,+)$, which has order 5, have orders 1 and 5;
- the subgroups of D_4, which has order 8, have orders 1, 2, 4 and 8;
- the subgroups of Q_4, which has order 8, have orders 1, 2, 4 and 8;
- the subgroups of A_4, which has order 12, have orders 1, 2, 3, 4 and 12.

You have enough evidence to conjecture that, for finite groups, the order of a subgroup divides the order of the group. This result is called Lagrange's theorem. Joseph-Louis Lagrange lived from 1736 to 1813.

Lagrange's theorem The order of a subgroup of a finite group G divides the order of G.

Lagrange's theorem has a number of immediate consequences, called **corollaries**.

Corollary 1 The order of an element of a finite group G divides the order of G.

The order of an element a is equal to the order of the subgroup generated by a. By Lagrange's theorem, the order of a divides the order of the group.

Corollary 2 A group of prime order has no proper subgroups.

If the order of a group G is a prime number, p, by Lagrange's theorem the only possible subgroups will have orders 1 and p. But these subgroups will be the trivial subgroups consisting of the identity only and the whole group. Therefore there are no proper subgroups.

Corollary 3 Every group G of prime order p is cyclic.

Consider an element $a \in G$ other than the identity. As the order of a divides p, and a is not the identity, the order of a must be p itself. Therefore a is a generator for G, and G is cyclic.

It is tempting to think that the converse of Lagrange's theorem might be true, that if the order of a finite group G has a factor n, then there is a subgroup of G with order n; but this is actually false. A_4, the group with 12 elements in Exercise 10A Question 12, has no subgroup of order 6.

Exercise 10B

1 Use Lagrange's theorem to state the possible orders of subgroups of a group of order 24.

2 Prove that the order of a finite group with at least two elements but no proper subgroups is prime.

10.7* Proof of Lagrange's theorem

You may, if you wish, omit this section.

Let H be a subgroup of a finite group G. The idea of the proof of Lagrange's theorem is to show that the elements of the finite group G can be parcelled up into separate packages, called cosets, one of which is the subgroup H itself. It will turn out that all these packages have the same number of elements as H. Lagrange's theorem then follows easily.

If $a \in G$, then the set $Ha = \{ha : h \in H\}$ is called a **right coset** of H in G.

Example 10.7.1
Find the right cosets of the subgroup $\{I, X\}$ in D_3.

To find the right cosets, write out part of the group table of D_3 with the elements of the subgroup $\{I, X\}$ in the top places in the left column.

	I	R	S	X	Y	Z
I	I	R	S	X	Y	Z
X	X	Y	Z	I	R	S

Each column of the table is a right coset of the subgroup $\{I, X\}$ in D_3. To see that this is true, notice that the first column consists of the subgroup multiplied on the right by I; the second column consists of the elements $IR = R$ and $XR = Y$, that is the elements I and X of the subgroup $\{I, X\}$ multiplied on the right by R; and so on.

Recall that, as the order in which the elements of a set are written is irrelevant, the set $\{I, X\}$ is the same as the set $\{X, I\}$. Similarly $\{R, Y\} = \{Y, R\}$ and $\{S, Z\} = \{Z, S\}$. There are three distinct right cosets: $\{I, X\}$, $\{R, Y\}$ and $\{S, Z\}$.

Notice that the elements of the group are divided equally among three cosets.

Example 10.7.2
The group Q_4, called the quaternion group, is shown in the table below. Find the right cosets of the subgroups $H_1 = \{e, b\}$ and $H_2 = \{e, a, b, c\}$.

Q_4	e	a	b	c	p	q	r	s
e	e	a	b	c	p	q	r	s
a	a	b	c	e	s	p	q	r
b	b	c	e	a	r	s	p	q
c	c	e	a	b	q	r	s	p
p	p	q	r	s	b	c	e	a
q	q	r	s	p	a	b	c	e
r	r	s	p	q	e	a	b	c
s	s	p	q	r	c	e	a	b

Proceed as in Example 10.7.1, and write out just those rows of the group table for Q_4 which contain the elements of the subgroup in the column on the left.

	e	a	b	c	p	q	r	s
e	e	a	b	c	p	q	r	s
b	b	c	e	a	r	s	p	q

The right cosets of H_1 are $\{e,b\}$, $\{a,c\}$, $\{p,r\}$ and $\{q,s\}$.

Working in the same way with the subgroup $H_2 = \{e,a,b,c\}$ gives the following table.

	e	a	b	c	p	q	r	s
e	e	a	b	c	p	q	r	s
a	a	b	c	e	s	p	q	r
b	b	c	e	a	r	s	p	q
c	c	e	a	b	q	r	s	p

The right cosets of H_2 are $\{e,a,b,c\}$ and $\{p,q,r,s\}$.

Notice that, for both H_1 and H_2, the order of the subgroup multiplied by the number of cosets gives the order of the group.

Lagrange's theorem follows from the three parts of the following mini-theorem.

Mini-theorem Let H be a subgroup of a finite group G. Then:

(a) any two right cosets of H in G are either identical or have no elements in common;
(b) all the right cosets of H in G have the same number of elements;
(c) every element of G is in some right coset of H in G.

Proof (a) Let a and b be elements of G. Then there are two cases. Either b belongs to Ha, or it does not.

Case 1 b belongs to Ha. Then $b = ha$ for some $h \in H$. Let x be any element of Hb. Then $x = h_1 b = h_1 ha = h_2 a$, where $h_2 \in H$, since H is a subgroup. But $h_2 a \in Ha$, so $x \in Ha$, and all the elements of Hb are members of Ha.

Case 2 b does not belong to Ha. Then no element of Hb belongs to Ha, since if $h_1 b = h_2 a$, then $b = h_1^{-1} h_2 a = h_3 a$ where $h_3 \in H$, a contradiction.

So either all elements of Hb are in Ha or no elements of Hb are in Ha. Now notice the symmetrical roles of a and b, in the sense that you could also prove that either all elements of Ha are in Hb or no elements of Ha are in Hb. Thus any two right cosets of H in G are either identical or have no elements in common.

(b) G is finite, so H is finite. Let H have n elements, $H = \{h_1, h_2, \ldots, h_n\}$. Then the elements of Ha are $\{h_1 a, h_2 a, \ldots, h_n a\}$. No two of these are the same, since if

$h_r a = h_s a$ then $h_r = h_s$ by the cancellation law; so Ha also has n elements. Therefore every right coset of H has n elements.

(c) Let a be any element of G. Then the coset Ha contains a because $e \in H$ and you can write $a = ea$.

All the bricks are now to hand to prove Lagrange's theorem.

Lagrange's theorem Let H be a subgroup of a finite group G. Then the order of H divides the order of G.

Proof Let G and H have orders m and n respectively. Then by mini-theorem (b), each right coset of H has exactly n elements. By mini-theorem (a), any two of the right cosets either are identical or have no elements in common. Suppose that there are d distinct cosets. These d cosets therefore account for nd elements of the group G. But part (c) of the mini-theorem states that every element of the group is in some coset, so these nd elements account for all the elements of the group. Thus $nd = m$, so n divides m.

Therefore the order of H divides the order of G.

Exercise 10C*

1 Find the right cosets of the subgroups $\{I, R, S\}$, $\{I\}$ and D_3 itself in the group D_3.

2 Find the right cosets of $\{0, 3\}$ in $(\mathbb{Z}_6, +)$. (You will have to use additive notation.)

3 The table in Exercise 10A Question 12 shows the group A_4, the symmetry group of the tetrahedron. Find the right cosets of

(a) $H_1 = \{e, a, b, c\}$, (b) the subgroup H_2 generated by x.

4 Find the right cosets of the subgroup $\{0, \pm 3, \pm 6, \ldots\}$ of the group $(\mathbb{Z}, +)$.

Miscellaneous exercise 10

1 Let G be a commutative group. Prove that the set of elements of order 2, together with the identity element, that is $H = \{a \in G : a^2 = e\}$, is a subgroup of G.

2 G is a commutative group, and $H = \{x \in G : x^3 = e\}$. Prove that H is a subgroup of G.

3 Let G be a commutative group. Prove that the set of elements of finite order, $H = \{a \in G : a^n = e, \text{ some } n\}$, is a subgroup of G.

4 You are given that the set $\{1, 2, 3, \ldots, 12\}$ forms a group G under multiplication modulo 13. A subgroup with n elements is said to have order n. Find, or explain why none exists, a subgroup of G with order

(a) 2, (b) 3, (c) 5. (OCR)

5 The functions $\mathrm{i}(x)$, $\mathrm{a}(x)$, $\mathrm{b}(x)$, $\mathrm{c}(x)$ are defined for all $x \neq 0$, $x \neq 1$ by

$$\mathrm{i}(x) = x, \quad \mathrm{a}(x) = \frac{1}{x}, \quad \mathrm{b}(x) = 1 - x \quad \text{and} \quad \mathrm{c}(x) = \frac{1}{1-x}.$$

The operation $\otimes$ is defined as the composition of functions: that is,

$$(\mathrm{p} \otimes \mathrm{q})(x) = \mathrm{pq}(x) = \mathrm{p}\{\mathrm{q}(x)\}.$$

(a) Show that the set of functions $\{\mathrm{i}, \mathrm{a}, \mathrm{b}, \mathrm{c}\}$ is not closed under $\otimes$, and find two further functions $\mathrm{d}(x)$ and $\mathrm{e}(x)$ such that $\{\mathrm{i}, \mathrm{a}, \mathrm{b}, \mathrm{c}, \mathrm{d}, \mathrm{e}\}$ is closed under $\otimes$.

(b) Copy and complete the composition table for the set $G = \{\mathrm{i}, \mathrm{a}, \mathrm{b}, \mathrm{c}, \mathrm{d}, \mathrm{e}\}$, under $\otimes$.

$\otimes$	i	a	b	c	d	e
i	i	a	b	c	d	e
a	a	i		b		
b	b		i			
c	c		a		i	
d	d			i		a
e	e	c				i

(c) Hence show that $(G, \oplus)$ forms a group. (You may assume that the composition of functions is associative.)

(d) Find whether G is a commutative group, giving reasons.

(e) Find whether G is a cyclic group, giving reasons.

(f) Write down all the subgroups of G. (OCR)

6 Show that the matrices $\begin{pmatrix} a & b \\ c & d \end{pmatrix}$, where $ad \neq bc$, form a group G under matrix multiplication. Show that the following subsets of G form subgroups of G.

(a) $\begin{pmatrix} a & b \\ 0 & 1 \end{pmatrix}$ (b) $\begin{pmatrix} 1 & b \\ 0 & 1 \end{pmatrix}$ (c) $\begin{pmatrix} a & 0 \\ 0 & 1 \end{pmatrix} (a \neq 0)$

(d) Find a proper subgroup of (a) which contains (b) as a proper subgroup.

(e) Find a subgroup of G of order 4.

7 The law of composition $*$ is defined by $a * b = a + b - 2$ where a and b are numbers in arithmetic modulo 6.

(a) Show that the set $\{0, 1, 2, 3, 4, 5\}$ forms a group G under $*$ in arithmetic modulo 6.

(b) Find all the subgroups of G.

8† Let H and K be finite subgroups of a finite group G, and let the orders of H and K be relatively prime; that is, they have no common factors apart from 1. Prove that the only element common to H and K is the identity element.

11 Isomorphisms of groups

This chapter is about groups that are identical to each other as regards their structure. When you have completed it, you should know

- what is meant by isomorphic groups or an isomorphism between groups
- all the different (non-isomorphic) groups with orders up to seven.

11.1 What are isomorphic groups?

The word 'isomorphic' means 'equal in form'. When the word is applied to a pair of groups it means that the groups are structurally the same as each other.

For example, consider the groups $(\mathbb{Z}_4, +)$ and $(\{1, \mathrm{i}, -1, -\mathrm{i}\}, \times)$ in Tables 11.1 and 11.2.

+	0	1	2	3
0	0	1	2	3
1	1	2	3	0
2	2	3	0	1
3	3	0	1	2

Table 11.1

×	1	i	−1	−i
1	1	i	−1	−i
i	i	−1	−i	1
−1	−1	1	1	i
−i	−i	1	i	−1

Table 11.2

You can see that these tables, apart from their labelling, are identical. The symbol 1 appears in Table 11.2 in every place that the symbol 0 appears in Table 11.1. Similarly i appears in place of 1, −1 appears in place of 2 and −i in place of 3.

Groups with tables that are related in this way are said to be **isomorphic** to each other. In applying this statement, however, you need to take care. Table 11.3 shows the group $(\{2, 4, 6, 8\}, \times (\text{mod } 10))$.

×(mod 10)	2	4	6	8
2	4	8	2	6
4	8	6	4	2
6	2	4	6	8
8	6	2	8	4

Table 11.3

×(mod 10)	6	2	4	8
6	6	2	4	8
2	2	4	8	6
4	4	8	6	2
8	8	6	2	4

Table 11.4

You might think that the group defined by this table is not isomorphic to $(\mathbb{Z}_4, +)$, but in fact, it is. The group identity is 6, so try rearranging the elements as in Table 11.4, so that they are in the order 6, 2, 4, 8, with the group identity first. You can now see, by comparing Table 11.4 with Table 11.1, that the group *is* isomorphic to $(\mathbb{Z}_4, +)$.

So tables can be helpful for detecting isomorphisms between small groups, but you must not be misled by the way the elements are arranged in the table. For larger groups, tables are cumbersome to use. For infinite groups, tables cannot be used at all.

However, you can use tables to develop a general definition of isomorphism of groups G and H. The important idea is that to every $a \in G$ in Table 11.5, there corresponds an $A \in H$ in Table 11.6. Moreover, if an element x in G is the product of two elements a and b, that is $x = ab$, an X must appear in the corresponding position in H, as the product of the image of a and the image of b, that is $X = AB$.

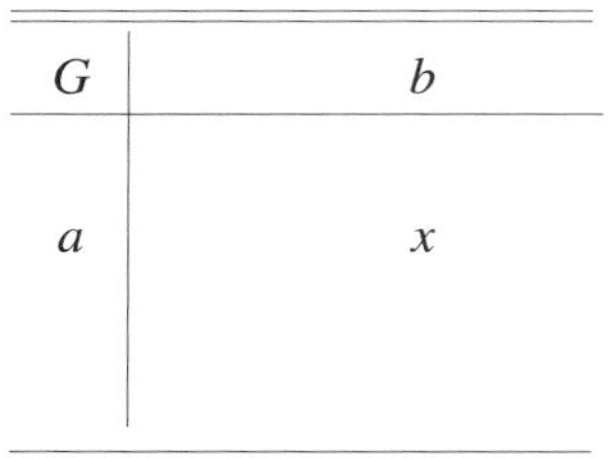

Table 11.5

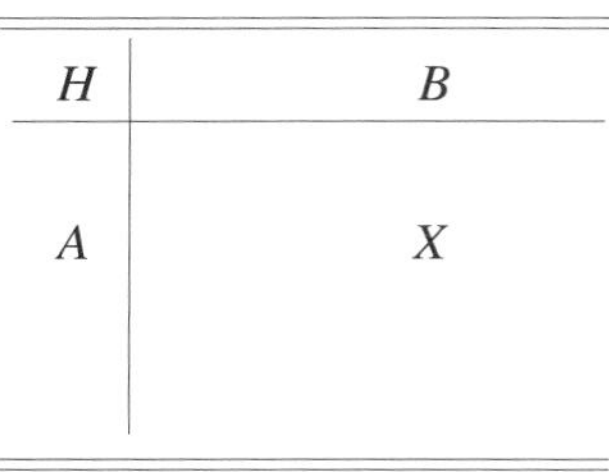

Table 11.6

The language of the previous paragraph should remind you of the language of functions in P2 Chapter 2. To go further it is necessary to widen the definition of function from the one that you met in P2.

11.2 Another look at functions

In P2, all the functions that you met had domain $\mathbb{R}$, or a subset of $\mathbb{R}$, and the result $\mathrm{f}(x)$ of a function f operating on a real number x was always a real number.

It is possible for the domain to be any set. For the purposes of this chapter, the domain will be the elements of a group.

In addition to the domain there is a 'target set', which includes the elements $\mathrm{f}(x)$, where x is an element of the domain. The element $\mathrm{f}(x)$ is called the **image** of x. The set of images $\mathrm{f}(x)$ is called the **range** of the function f.

In general, if a function f has domain A and a target set B, you denote this by $\mathrm{f}: A \to B$.

The meaning of one–one is almost exactly what it was in P2 Section 2.5. That is, a function f defined for some domain D is **one–one** if, for each y in the range of f, there is only one element $x \in D$ such that $y = \mathrm{f}(x)$.

Looking again at Tables 11.5 and 11.6, and the paragraph above them, you can define a function $\mathrm{f}: G \to H$, such that $\mathrm{f}(a) = A$, $\mathrm{f}(b) = B$ and $\mathrm{f}(x) = X$. The condition that $X = AB$, you can now write as $\mathrm{f}(x) = \mathrm{f}(a)\mathrm{f}(b)$, and since $x = ab$, it follows that $\mathrm{f}(ab) = \mathrm{f}(a)\mathrm{f}(b)$.

11.3 A definition of isomorphism

In addition to the condition that $\mathrm{f}(ab) = \mathrm{f}(a)\mathrm{f}(b)$ you would also expect isomorphic finite groups to have the same order. You can make sure that this happens by imposing two conditions: by allowing no spare elements in H which are not the images of elements in G, that is, the range of f is H; and by requiring that different elements of G be sent to different elements of H, that is, f is one–one. Summarising:

Two groups $(G,\circ)$ and $(H,\bullet)$ are **isomorphic** if there exists a function $\mathrm{f}: G \to H$ such that

- the range of f is H
- f is one–one
- $\mathrm{f}(a \circ b) = \mathrm{f}(a) \bullet \mathrm{f}(b)$ for all $a, b \in G$.

The function $\mathrm{f}: G \to H$ is called an **isomorphism**.

The definition looks oddly asymmetrical between the two groups G and H, but it isn't really. If you write $\mathrm{f}^{-1} = \mathrm{F}$, the definition could be reversed in terms of F by writing $\mathrm{F}: H \to G$, with $\mathrm{F}(A \bullet B) = \mathrm{F}(A)\mathrm{F}(B) = a \circ b$.

It is usual to drop the group operation symbols $\circ$ and $\bullet$, and to use multiplicative notation for both groups. Then $\mathrm{f}(a \circ b) = \mathrm{f}(a) \bullet \mathrm{f}(b)$ becomes $\mathrm{f}(ab) = \mathrm{f}(a)\mathrm{f}(b)$.

It is comforting that many of the things that you would expect to be true about isomorphic groups are indeed true. Here are three important examples.

Theorem If $\mathrm{f}: G \to H$ is an isomorphism of G and H, and e is the identity in G, then $\mathrm{f}(e)$ is the identity in H. If $a \in G$, then $\mathrm{f}\left(a^{-1}\right)$ is the inverse of $\mathrm{f}(a)$ in H.

You must expect to use the relation $\mathrm{f}(ab) = \mathrm{f}(a)\mathrm{f}(b)$ *in this proof.*

Proof Let e be the identity in G. If $a \in G$, then $\mathrm{f}(e)\mathrm{f}(a) = \mathrm{f}(ea) = \mathrm{f}(a)$ and $\mathrm{f}(a)\mathrm{f}(e) = \mathrm{f}(ae) = \mathrm{f}(a)$. Therefore $\mathrm{f}(e)$ is the identity in H. Call it e_H.

To prove that $\mathrm{f}\left(a^{-1}\right)$ is the inverse of $\mathrm{f}(a)$, you must prove that $\mathrm{f}\left(a^{-1}\right)\mathrm{f}(a) = \mathrm{f}(a)\mathrm{f}\left(a^{-1}\right) = e_H$. Starting with $\mathrm{f}\left(a^{-1}\right)\mathrm{f}(a)$, you find that $\mathrm{f}\left(a^{-1}\right)\mathrm{f}(a) = \mathrm{f}\left(a^{-1}a\right) = \mathrm{f}(e) = e_H$. Also $\mathrm{f}(a)\mathrm{f}\left(a^{-1}\right) = \mathrm{f}\left(aa^{-1}\right) = \mathrm{f}(e) = e_H$, so the theorem is proved.

Theorem If $\mathrm{f}: G \to H$ is an isomorphism of G and H, the order of the element $a \in G$ is the same as the order of $\mathrm{f}(a) \in H$.

Proof Let n be the order of a. Then n is the smallest positive integer such that $a^n = e$. Consider

$$(\mathrm{f}(a))^n = \overbrace{\mathrm{f}(a)\mathrm{f}(a)\ldots\mathrm{f}(a)}^{n \text{ of these}} = \mathrm{f}(aa\ldots a) = \mathrm{f}\left(a^n\right) = \mathrm{f}(e) = e_H.$$

But is n the *least* positive integer such that $(\mathrm{f}(a))^n = e_H$? Suppose that the order of $\mathrm{f}(a)$ is m where $m < n$. Then $(\mathrm{f}(a))^m = e_H$.

As $\mathrm{f}\left(a^m\right) = (\mathrm{f}(a))^m = e_H$, there are two elements, a^n and a^m, with image e_H. But $a^n \neq a^m$, since $a^n = e$ and n is the smallest positive integer such that $a^n = e$ and $m < n$. This contradicts the fact that the isomorphism $\mathrm{f}: G \to H$ is one–one. Therefore the order of $a \in G$ is the same as the order of $\mathrm{f}(a) \in H$.

This theorem is particularly useful for proving that two groups are not isomorphic. Just look at the elements of each group and find their orders. If they don't match, the groups are not isomorphic.

Example 11.3.1
Prove that $(\mathbb{Z}_6,+)$ is not isomorphic to D_3.

The elements $0, 1, 2, 3, 4, 5 \in \mathbb{Z}_6$ have orders $1, 6, 3, 2, 3, 6$ respectively.
The elements $I, R, R^2, X, Y, Z \in D_3$ have orders $1, 3, 3, 2, 2, 2$ respectively.
Therefore the groups are not isomorphic.

Example 11.3.2
Prove that $(\mathbb{R},+)$ is not isomorphic to $(\mathbb{C}-\{0\},\times)$.

The only element of finite order in $(\mathbb{R},+)$ is 0, which has order 1. In $(\mathbb{C}-\{0\},\times)$ the element -1 has order 2. Therefore the groups are not isomorphic.

Theorem (a) Every infinite cyclic group is isomorphic to $(\mathbb{Z},+)$.
(b) Every finite cyclic group of order n is isomorphic to $(\mathbb{Z}_n,+)$.

To prove that two groups are isomorphic, produce a function from the first group to the second, and show that the function is an isomorphism.

Proof For both parts (a) and (b), the method is to take a generator a of the cyclic group G, and to define a function $\mathrm{f}:\mathbb{Z}\to G$ or $\mathrm{f}:\mathbb{Z}_n\to G$ such that $\mathrm{f}(r)=a^r$. Then every element of G is the image of some element of $\mathbb{Z}$ or $\mathbb{Z}_n$, so that the range of f is G.

(a) **Infinite case** To prove that f is one–one, suppose that $\mathrm{f}(r)=\mathrm{f}(s)$ with $r>s$. Then $a^r=a^s$, so $a^{r-s}=e$ for $r-s\neq 0$. But this contradicts the fact that G is an infinite cyclic group. Therefore f is one–one.

To prove that $\mathrm{f}(r+s)=\mathrm{f}(r)\mathrm{f}(s)$, consider first $\mathrm{f}(r+s)=a^{r+s}$. But $a^{r+s}=a^r a^s=\mathrm{f}(r)\mathrm{f}(s)$, so $\mathrm{f}:\mathbb{Z}\to G$ is an isomorphism.

(b) **Finite case** Let the order of G be n.

Define $\mathrm{f}:\mathbb{Z}_n\to G$ by $\mathrm{f}(r)=a^r$ for $0\leqslant r<n$.

To prove that f is one–one, suppose that $\mathrm{f}(r)=\mathrm{f}(s)$ with $r>s$. Then $a^r=a^s$, so $a^{r-s}=e$. But as $0\leqslant s<r<n$, so $0<r-s<n$, which contradicts the fact that n is the order of G. Therefore f is one–one.

Finally, to prove that $\mathrm{f}(r+s)=\mathrm{f}(r)\mathrm{f}(s)$ there are two cases to consider. Notice first that $0\leqslant r+s<2n$, so that either $0\leqslant r+s<n$ or $n\leqslant r+s<2n$.

If $0\leqslant r+s<n$, then $\mathrm{f}(r+s)=a^{r+s}=a^r a^s=\mathrm{f}(r)\mathrm{f}(s)$.

However, if $n\leqslant r+s<2n$, then the sum of r and s in $\mathbb{Z}_n$ is $r+s-n$, so

$$\mathrm{f}(r+s)=\mathrm{f}(r+s-n)=a^{r+s-n}=a^r a^s e=a^r a^s=\mathrm{f}(r)\mathrm{f}(s).$$

Therefore $\mathrm{f}:\mathbb{Z}\to G$ is an isomorphism.

This theorem says that cyclic groups of a given order are isomorphic. This is sometimes stated as, 'there is only one cyclic group of a given order, up to isomorphism'.

Example 11.3.3

Prove that the following groups are isomorphic to each other.

(a) Rotational symmetries of a Catherine wheel with 10 spokes

(b) $(\mathbb{Z}_{11} - \{0\}, \times)$

(c) $(\mathbb{Z}_{10}, +)$

(d) 10th roots of unity under multiplication

The groups are all cyclic. Possible generators are (a) rotation through $\frac{1}{5}\pi$, (b) 2, (c) 1, (d) $\exp(\frac{1}{5}\pi\mathrm{i})$. The groups all have 10 elements, so they are isomorphic.

Exercise 11

1 Show that the group $(\{1,-1\},\times)$ is isomorphic to $(\mathbb{Z}_2,+)$.

2 Use the function $\mathrm{f}(x) = \mathrm{e}^x$ to show that $(\mathbb{R},+)$ is isomorphic to $(\mathbb{R}^+,\times)$.

3 Show that $(\mathbb{Z}_{13} - \{0\}, \times(\mathrm{mod}\,13))$ is isomorphic to $(\mathbb{Z}_{12},+)$.

4 Prove that the group of even integers under addition is isomorphic to the group of integers under addition.

5 Prove that $(\mathbb{R} - \{0\},\times)$ is not isomorphic to $(\mathbb{C} - \{0\},\times)$.

6 Let g be a fixed element of the group G. Prove that $\mathrm{f}: G \to G$ defined by $\mathrm{f}(a) = g^{-1}ag$ is an isomorphism from G to itself.

11.4 Group generators

You met the idea of a group generator in the context of cyclic groups in Section 10.3. However, you can extend the idea to non-cyclic groups.

Consider the group of symmetries of a rectangle which is not a square (see Exercise 9D Question 4). The individual symmetries are the identity e, the reflections a and b in the axes of symmetry, and the rotation of 180° about the centre, which you can obtain by carrying out either first a then b or first b then a. In fact, you can describe this group by saying that it is generated by a and b given that $a^2 = b^2 = e$ and $ab = ba$. You can then simplify any expression in a and b, such as bab^2aba^2 by moving all the b terms to the left using the relation $ab = ba$ to get b^4a^4. Using $a^2 = b^2 = e$ simplifies this to e.

Similarly, the group D_3, described in Table 9.7, is generated by R and X. Notice first that $S = R^2$, $Y = XR$, $Z = XS = XR^2$ and $R^3 = X^2 = I$, so that every element can be written in terms of R and X. But notice also that the two equations $XR = Y$ and $R^2X = SX = Y$ give the relation $XR = R^2X$ between R and X.

These relations are sufficient to carry out any calculations within the group.

Now consider XR^2.

$$XR^2 = (XR)R = \left(R^2X\right)R = R^2(XR) = R^2\left(R^2X\right) = R^4X = RX.$$

You can construct a table for D_3 using only R and X. The entries shown in Table 11.7 are easy to supply. The other entries come from calculations such as

$$(XR)\left(XR^2\right) = X(RX)R^2 = X\left(XR^2\right)R^2 = X^2R^4 = R,$$

and $\left(R^2\right)(XR) = \left(R^2X\right)R = (XR)R = XR^2,$

in which the terms in X are progressively moved to the left using the given relation $XR = R^2X$ and the relation $RX = XR^2$, which was derived from it. Try filling in the rest of the table for yourself.

	I	R	R^2	X	XR	XR^2
I	I	R	R^2	X	XR	XR^2
R	R	R^2	I			
R^2	R^2	I	R			
X	X	XR	XR^2	I		
XR	XR	XR^2	X		I	
XR^2	XR^2	X	XR			I

Table 11.7

Thus the group D_3 is generated by R and X where $R^3 = X^2 = I$ and $XR = R^2X$.

In the next section, the idea of generators will be used extensively.

11.5 Classifying groups of order up to 7

The only group of order 1 is the group consisting of the identity element only.

As every group of prime order is cyclic (see Section 10.6) the only groups of orders 2, 3, 5 and 7 are cyclic.

This leaves groups of orders 4 and 6. They need a much more detailed treatment.

Groups of order 4

Let G be a group of order 4. As the orders of the elements must divide the order of the group, all the elements of G, other than the identity, have order 4 or 2.

If there is an element of order 4, the group G is cyclic, and is isomorphic to $(\mathbb{Z}_4, +)$.

If there is no element of order 4, all the elements other than the identity have order 2.

Now an element of order 2 is its own inverse; that is, $a^2 = e \Leftrightarrow a = a^{-1}$. Recall from Example 10.1.1 that a group in which every element is its own inverse is commutative.

Let a and b be two distinct non-identity elements of G, and consider the element ba.

As the group is commutative, $ba = ab$.

At this stage the group table shown in Table 11.8 is incomplete.

	e	a	b
e	e	a	b
a	a	e	
b	b		e

Table 11.8

	e	a	b	ba
e	e	a	b	ba
a	a	e	ba	b
b	b	ba	e	a
ba	ba	b	a	e

Table 11.9

The element ba in Table 11.8, shown shaded, cannot be b or e because b and e are already in the same row. And it cannot be a since a is in the same column. So ba is distinct from the other elements, and $G = \{e, a, b, ba\}$.

Complete the table for yourself using similar arguments. You should end up with Table 11.9.

This group is called the four-group. It is denoted by V after the German word *vier* meaning 'four'. It is isomorphic to the group of symmetries of the rectangle. See Exercise 9D Question 4.

There are thus two, and only two, distinct groups of order 4, the cyclic group $(\mathbb{Z}_4, +)$, and V. Every group of order 4 is isomorphic to one of them.

In Exercise 9D Question 7 you showed that there are five possible group tables. In fact, all the groups defined by these tables are isomorphic either to $(\mathbb{Z}_4, +)$ or to V.

Groups of order 6

Let G be a group of order 6. As the orders of the elements must divide the order of the group, all the elements of G, other than the identity, have order 6, 3 or 2.

If there is an element of order 6, the group G is cyclic, and is isomorphic to $(\mathbb{Z}_6, +)$.

If there is no element of order 6, suppose that there is an element a of order 3. Then the group includes the elements e, a and a^2, and there must be another element b such that $b \neq a$, a^2 or a^3. Thus the elements of G are $\{e, a, a^2, b, ba, ba^2\}$. It is easy to check that none of these six elements can be equal to one another. At this stage the incomplete group table appears as in Table 11.10.

	e	a	a^2	b	ba	ba^2
e	e	a	a^2	b	ba	ba^2
a	a	a^2	e			
a^2	a^2	e	a			
b	b	ba	ba^2			
ba	ba	ba^2	b			
ba^2	ba^2	b	ba			

Table 11.10

Now consider b^2. It is in the same row as b, ba and ba^2, so it can't be any of them. This leaves only $b^2 = a$, $b^2 = a^2$ or $b^2 = e$ as possibilities.

Suppose first that $b^2 = a$. Then $b^3 = b(b^2) = ba$, $b^4 = b(b^3) = b(ba) = b^2a = a^2$, $b^5 = b(b^4) = ba^2$ and $b^6 = b(b^5) = b(ba^2) = b^2a^2 = aa^2 = a^3 = e$. As these powers of b are all different, the order of b would be 6, contrary to hypothesis.

A similar argument shows that if $b^2 = a^2$, the order of b would also be 6. Try it!

Therefore $b^2 = e$.

Now consider the product ab. It is in the same row as a, a^2 and e and in the same column as b, so it can't be any of them. That leaves two cases, $ab = ba$ and $ab = ba^2$.

Suppose $ab = ba$ and consider the various powers of ab:

$$(ab)^2 = abab = a(ba)b = aabb = a^2b^2 = a^2e = a^2,$$

$$(ab)^3 = (ab)^2 ab = a^2ab = a^3b = b, \qquad (ab)^4 = (ab)^2(ab)^2 = a^2a^2 = a,$$

$$(ab)^5 = (ab)^3(ab)^2 = ba^2, \qquad (ab)^6 = (ab)^2(ab)^4 = a^2a = a^3 = e.$$

So the order of ab is 6, contrary to hypothesis. Thus $ab \neq ba$.

If $ab = ba^2$, you can construct a table, using computations such as

$$(ba^2)(ba) = ba^2ba = ba(ab)a = baba^2a = bab = bba^2 = a^2;$$

$$(ba)(ba^2) = baba^2 = b(ab)a^2 = bba^2a^2 = b^2a^4 = a.$$

Complete the table for yourself. You should get the result shown in Table 11.11.

	e	a	a^2	b	ba	ba^2
e	e	a	a^2	b	ba	ba^2
a	a	a^2	e	ba^2	b	ba
a^2	a^2	e	a	ba	ba^2	b
b	b	ba	ba^2	e	a	a^2
ba	ba	ba^2	b	a^2	e	a
ba^2	ba^2	b	ba	a	a^2	e

Table 11.11

Comparing Table 11.11 with the completed version of Table 11.7, you can easily see that this group is isomorphic to the group D_3.

Suppose now that G has no elements of order 6 or of order 3. Then all the elements other than the identity have order 2, and the group is commutative (see Example 10.1.1).

Then, if a and b are two distinct, non-identity elements in G, the argument goes precisely as for the non-cyclic group of order 4: G contains e, a, b and ba, but there are no more products of a and b with results distinct from these. But $\{e, a, b, ab\}$ is V, a group of order 4 and, by Lagrange's theorem, a group of order 6 cannot have a subgroup of order 4. So the supposition that all the elements have order 2 leads to a contradiction.

Therefore the only distinct groups of order 6 are $(\mathbb{Z}_6,+)$ and D_3. Every group of order 6 is isomorphic to one or the other of them.

The groups of order up to and including 7 are

$(\mathbb{Z}_2,+)$ of order 2, $(\mathbb{Z}_3,+)$ of order 3, $(\mathbb{Z}_4,+)$ and V of order 4,

$(\mathbb{Z}_5,+)$ of order 5, $(\mathbb{Z}_6,+)$ and D_3 of order 6, $(\mathbb{Z}_7,+)$ of order 7.

Miscellaneous exercise 11

1 (a) The set S consists of the eight elements 9^1, 9^2, …, 9^8 written in arithmetic modulo 64. Determine each of the elements of S as an integer between 0 and 63.

Under multiplication modulo 64, the set S forms a group G, with identity 1. Write down the orders of each of the remaining elements of G.

Write down all the possible generators for G, and list all the subgroups of G.

(b) The group H consists of the set $\{1,9,31,39,41,49,71,79\}$ under multiplication modulo 80. Determine, with justification, whether G and H are isomorphic. (OCR)

2 The set $S=\{1,2,p,q,7,8\}$ with the operation of multiplication modulo 9 forms a group G.

(a) By considering the closure of G, find the integers p and q where $0<p<q<9$.

(b) State the inverse of each element of G, and write down all the subgroups of G.

(c) Given that $\omega=\cos\frac{1}{3}\pi+\mathrm{i}\sin\frac{1}{3}\pi$, and H is the group $\{\omega,\omega^2,\omega^3,\omega^4,\omega^5,\omega^6\}$ under multiplication of complex numbers, find with reasons whether G and H are isomorphic. (OCR)

3 (a) Prove that the set $\{1,3,5,9,11,13\}$ together with the operation of multiplication modulo 14 forms a group G. (You may assume that the operation is associative.)

List all the subgroups of G with fewer than three elements.

(b) The group of symmetry transformations of the equilateral triangle under the operation of composition is H. Describe geometrically the six elements of H.

(c) Determine, with reasons, whether G and H are isomorphic.

Find a subgroup of G with three elements. Is it isomorphic to a subgroup of H? (OCR)

4 Prove that the set $\{1,2,4,7,8,k,13,14\}$ together with the operation multiplication modulo 15 forms a group G, provided k takes one particular value. State this value of k. (You may assume that the operation is associative, but the other axioms for a group must be clearly verified.)

If H is a subgroup of G of order n, use Lagrange's theorem to find all the possible values of n.

Find three subgroups of order 4, each containing the elements 1 and 4, and prove that exactly two of them are isomorphic. (OCR)

5 Given that the multiplication of complex numbers is associative, show that the set $\{1, -1, i, -i\}$ forms a group G under multiplication of complex numbers.

Prove also that the set $\{1, 7, 18, 24\}$ under multiplication modulo 25 forms a group H.

Determine, with reasons, whether G and H are isomorphic. (OCR)

6 (a) The law of composition $*$ is defined by $a * b = a + b - ab$. Given that a, b and c are real numbers, prove that $a * (b * c) = (a * b) * c$.

(b) The law of composition $\circ$ is defined by $a * b = a + b - ab$ evaluated modulo 7 so that $2 \circ 4 = 5$ for example.

Copy and complete the combination table for the set $\{0, 2, 3, 4, 5, 6\}$ with law of composition $\circ$.

$\circ$	0	2	3	4	5	6
0	0	2	3	4	5	6
2	2	0	6	5	4	3

(c) Prove that the set $\{0, 2, 3, 4, 5, 6\}$ forms a group G under $\circ$.

(d) Determine, with reasons, whether G is isomorphic to the group of rotations of the regular hexagon. (OCR)

7 The elements of the group G_n are the number 1 and the integers between 1 and n which have no factor in common with n; for example, the elements of G_4 are 1, 3. The operation of the group is multiplication modulo n. Write out the tables of G_5, G_8, G_{10} and G_{12}.

State which groups are isomorphic, giving your reasons. (OCR)

Revision exercise 4

1 A set $H = \{g, h, i, j, k, m\}$ has a binary operation with composition table

	g	h	i	j	k	m
g	j	m	g	k	h	i
h	m	i	h	g	j	k
i	g	h	i	j	k	m
j	k	g	j	m	i	h
k	h	j	k	i	m	g
m	i	k	m	h	g	j

Explain carefully why H is not a group. (MEI)

2 A non-abelian group G consists of eight 2×2 matrices, and the binary operation is matrix multiplication. The eight distinct elements of G can be written as $G = \{\mathbf{I}, \mathbf{A}, \mathbf{A}^2, \mathbf{A}^3, \mathbf{B}, \mathbf{AB}, \mathbf{A}^2\mathbf{B}, \mathbf{A}^3\mathbf{B}\}$, where $\mathbf{I}$ is the identity matrix and $\mathbf{A}$, $\mathbf{B}$ are 2×2 matrices such that $\mathbf{A}^4 = \mathbf{I}$, $\mathbf{B}^2 = \mathbf{I}$ and $\mathbf{BA} = \mathbf{A}^3\mathbf{B}$.

(a) Show that $(\mathbf{A}^2\mathbf{B})(\mathbf{AB}) = \mathbf{A}$ and $(\mathbf{AB})(\mathbf{A}^2\mathbf{B}) = \mathbf{A}^3$.

(b) Evaluate the products

(i) $(\mathbf{AB})\mathbf{A}$, (ii) $(\mathbf{AB})(\mathbf{AB})$, (iii) $\mathbf{B}(\mathbf{A}^2)$.

(c) Find the order of each element of G.

(d) Show that $\{\mathbf{I}, \mathbf{A}^2, \mathbf{B}, \mathbf{A}^2\mathbf{B}\}$ is a subgroup of G.

(e) Find the other two subgroups of G which have order 4.

(f) For each of the three subgroups of order 4, state whether or not it is a cyclic subgroup. (MEI)

3 (a) Show that the set $\{2, 4, 6, 8\}$ forms a group G_1 under multiplication modulo 10.

(b) The functions $\{e, f, g, h\}$ are defined for real values of x $(x \neq 1)$, and

$$e(x) = x, \quad f(x) = 2 - x, \quad g(x) = \frac{x-2}{x-1}.$$

The set of functions $\{e, f, g, h\}$ forms a group G_2 under composition of functions so that $f * g$ is the function h, where $h(x) = fg(x)$. Show that $g * g = e$ and that $f * g = g * f$.

Copy the table and use the fact that G_2 is a group to complete it.

$*$	e	f	g	h
e	e	f	g	h
f	f		h	
g	g	h	e	
h	h			

(c) Determine, with reasons, whether G_1 and G_2 are isomorphic. (OCR)

4 Use de Moivre's theorem to calculate the value of $(1-2\mathrm{i})^{20}$. (OCR)

5 (a) By writing $2\cos\theta = z + z^{-1}$, where $z = \cos\theta + \mathrm{i}\sin\theta$, prove that

$$32\cos^6\theta = \cos 6\theta + 6\cos 4\theta + 15\cos 2\theta + 10.$$

(b) Evaluate exactly $\int_0^{\frac{1}{4}\pi} \cos^6\theta \, \mathrm{d}\theta$. (OCR)

6 (a) An infinite series is given by $z - z^2 + z^3 - z^4 + \ldots + (-1)^n z^n + \ldots$.

(i) Assuming that the series converges, find an expression for its sum.

(ii) Given that $z = \frac{1}{4}(\cos\theta + \mathrm{i}\sin\theta)$, explain why the above series converges for all values of θ, with $-\pi < \theta \leqslant \pi$.

(b) By using de Moivre's theorem, or otherwise, prove that the sum of the infinite series

$$\frac{\sin\theta}{4} - \frac{\sin 2\theta}{4^2} + \frac{\sin 3\theta}{4^3} - \frac{\sin 4\theta}{4^4} + \ldots + (-1)^n \frac{\sin n\theta}{4^n} + \ldots$$

is $\dfrac{4\sin\theta}{17 + 8\cos\theta}$.

7 You are given that $w = 1 - \mathrm{e}^{\mathrm{i}\theta}\cos\theta$, where $0 < \theta < \frac{1}{2}\pi$.

(a) Express $\mathrm{e}^{\mathrm{i}k\theta}$ and $\mathrm{e}^{-\mathrm{i}k\theta}$ in the form $a + b\mathrm{i}$, and show that $w = -\mathrm{i}\mathrm{e}^{-\mathrm{i}\theta}\sin\theta$.

Series C and S are defined by

$$C = \cos\theta\cos\theta + \cos 2\theta\cos^2\theta + \cos 3\theta\cos^3\theta + \ldots + \cos n\theta\cos^n\theta,$$

$$S = \sin\theta\cos\theta + \sin 2\theta\cos^2\theta + \sin 3\theta\cos^3\theta + \ldots + \sin n\theta\cos^n\theta.$$

(b) Show that $C + \mathrm{i}S$ is a geometric series, and write down the sum of this series.

(c) Using the results in part (a), or otherwise, show that $C = \dfrac{\sin n\theta\cos^{n+1}\theta}{\sin\theta}$, and find a similar expression for S. (MEI, adapted)

8 (a) The set $\{2, 4, 6, 8\}$, together with the operation of multiplication modulo 10, forms a group G.

(i) Construct a combination table for G.

(ii) State the inverse of each element of G.

(b) Transformations I, P, Q, R in the *xy*-plane are represented by the matrices

$$\begin{pmatrix} 1 & 0 \\ 0 & 1 \end{pmatrix}, \begin{pmatrix} -1 & 0 \\ 0 & 1 \end{pmatrix}, \begin{pmatrix} 1 & 0 \\ 0 & -1 \end{pmatrix}, \begin{pmatrix} -1 & 0 \\ 0 & -1 \end{pmatrix}$$

respectively.

Describe briefly the geometric effect of each of the transformations P, Q, R.

The set $\{\mathrm{I}, \mathrm{P}, \mathrm{Q}, \mathrm{R}\}$ forms a group H under the operation of composition of transformations.

(c) State, with a reason, whether or not the two groups G and H are isomorphic. (OCR)

9 (a) Find an approximation to a fourth root of $40+9\mathrm{i}$. Show your working in full, and give your answer in the form $a+b\mathrm{i}$, where a and b are correct to 3 decimal places.

(b) Let $a+b\mathrm{i}=z$. Express the other fourth roots of $40+9\mathrm{i}$ in terms of z. (OCR)

10 Show that the set of all matrices of the form $\begin{pmatrix} 1-n & n \\ -n & 1+n \end{pmatrix}$, where n is an integer (positive, negative, zero), forms a group G under the operation of matrix multiplication. (You may assume that matrix multiplication is associative.)

The subset of G which consists of those elements for which n is an even integer (positive, negative, zero) is denoted by H. Determine whether or not H is a subgroup of G, justifying your answer. (OCR)

11 The set $G=\{e, a, a^2, a^3, b, ab, a^2b, a^3b\}$ is a multiplicative group of order 8 such that $a^4=e,\ a^2=b^2,\ ba=a^3b$.

(a) Show that the order of the element ab is 4.

(b) Show that $ba^2=a^2b$ and that $ba^3=ab$.

(c) Find three subgroups of G of order 4. (OCR)

12 Find the value of c for which the system of equations

$$\begin{aligned} 5x+2y &= 3, \\ 2x+3y-5z &= 1, \\ cx-5y+15z &= c, \end{aligned}$$

does not have a unique solution.

For this value of c,

(a) determine whether or not the equations are consistent,

(b) give a geometrical interpretation of the situation. (OCR)

13 The plane Π has equation $\mathbf{r}=6\mathbf{i}+2\mathbf{j}+\mathbf{k}+\theta(3\mathbf{i}+\mathbf{j})+\phi(\mathbf{j}-2\mathbf{k})$.

The line l_1, which does not lie in Π, has equation $\mathbf{r}=2\mathbf{i}+\mathbf{j}-3\mathbf{k}+\lambda(3\mathbf{i}-\mathbf{j}+4\mathbf{k})$.

The line l_2 has equation $\mathbf{r}=2\mathbf{i}+\mathbf{j}-3\mathbf{k}+\mu(\mathbf{i}+3\mathbf{j}-2\mathbf{k})$.

(a) Show that l_1 is parallel to Π.

(b) Find the position vector of the point in which l_2 meets Π.

(c) Find the perpendicular distance from the point with position vector $4\mathbf{i}-5\mathbf{j}+7\mathbf{k}$ to l_1. (OCR)

Mock examination 1 for P6

Time 1 hour 20 minutes

Answer all the questions.
You are permitted to use a graphic calculator in this paper.

1 Two planes have equations $x+2y-z=3$ and $2x-z=0$.

(i) Find a vector parallel to the line of intersection of these planes. [3]

(ii) Find, in the form $\frac{x-a}{p}=\frac{y-b}{q}=\frac{z-c}{r}$, the equation of this line of intersection. [3]

2 Solve the equation $z^3=\mathrm{i}$. [3]

Hence find the possible values for the argument of a complex number w which is such that $w^3=\mathrm{i}(w^*)^3$. [4]

3 (i) A group has order 12. What are the possible orders of proper subgroups of this group? [1]

(ii) A group C of order 12 has elements {0, 1, 2, 3, 4, 5, 6, 7, 8, 9, 10, 11} and the group operation is addition modulo 12.

(a) For each of the possible orders in your answer to part (i), identify a subgroup of C having that order. [3]

(b) State all the elements of C which have order 12. [3]

4 (i) Prove that $\left(1-\mathrm{e}^{\mathrm{i}\theta}\right)\mathrm{e}^{-\frac{1}{2}\mathrm{i}\theta}=-2\,\mathrm{i}\sin\frac{1}{2}\theta$. [2]

(ii) Write down the sum of the series $1+\mathrm{e}^{\mathrm{i}\theta}+\mathrm{e}^{2\mathrm{i}\theta}+\ldots+\mathrm{e}^{(n-1)\mathrm{i}\theta}$. [1]

(iii) Using the result in part (i), or otherwise, show that this sum may be expressed in the form

$$\frac{\mathrm{i}\left(\mathrm{e}^{-\frac{1}{2}\mathrm{i}\theta}-\mathrm{e}^{\left(n-\frac{1}{2}\right)\mathrm{i}\theta}\right)}{2\sin\frac{1}{2}\theta}.$$ [3]

(iv) Hence show that

$$1+\cos\theta+\cos 2\theta+\ldots+\cos(n-1)\theta=\frac{1}{2}\left(1+\frac{\sin\left(n-\frac{1}{2}\right)\theta}{\sin\frac{1}{2}\theta}\right).$$ [3]

5 G is a multiplicative group with identity element e, and a is a fixed element of G for which $axa = x^{-1}$ for all elements $x \in G$. Prove that

(i) $a = a^{-1}$, [2]

(ii) $ax = (ax)^{-1}$ for all $x \in G$, [2]

(iii) $x = x^{-1}$ for all $x \in G$, [2]

(iv) $xy = yx$ for all $x, y \in G$. [3]

6 The 2×2 matrices **R** and **S** represent the following transformations of the xy-plane.

R: rotation through an angle θ anticlockwise about the origin

S: stretch with scale factor 2 parallel to the x-axis (with the y-axis invariant)

(i) Write down the matrices **R** and **S**. [2]

(ii) Find the matrix $\mathbf{M} = \mathbf{RSR}^{-1}$. [3]

(iii) The point P has position vector $\begin{pmatrix} x \\ y \end{pmatrix}$ and the point Q has position vector $\mathbf{M}\begin{pmatrix} x \\ y \end{pmatrix}$.

Show that $\overrightarrow{PQ}$ makes an angle θ with the x-axis. [3]

(iv) Describe in geometrical terms the transformation represented by **M**. [2]

7 The equations of a plane p and a line l are

$$\mathbf{r} = \begin{pmatrix} 1 \\ 3 \\ 2 \end{pmatrix} + \lambda \begin{pmatrix} a \\ 2 \\ -1 \end{pmatrix} + \mu \begin{pmatrix} 1 \\ 1 \\ 0 \end{pmatrix} \quad \text{and} \quad \mathbf{r} = \begin{pmatrix} 3 \\ a+1 \\ 1 \end{pmatrix} + t \begin{pmatrix} -1 \\ 1 \\ 2 \end{pmatrix}$$

respectively, where a is a constant and λ, μ, t are parameters.

(i) Write down a set of three simultaneous equations satisfied by λ, μ and t if l and p have a point in common. [1]

(ii) By considering an appropriate determinant, or otherwise, show that l and p have a unique point of intersection for all values of a except $a = 3$. [3]

(iii) For the case $a = 0$, verify that l is perpendicular to p, and find the position vector of the point of intersection of l and p. [5]

(iv) For the case $a = 3$, state the geometrical relationship between l and p, justifying your answer. [3]

Mock examination 2 for P6

Time 1 hour 20 minutes

Answer all the questions.
You are permitted to use a graphic calculator in this paper.

1 G is a multiplicative group with identity element e. Given that G is commutative, prove that the set of all elements x for which $x = x^{-1}$ forms a subgroup of G. (You should make clear where in your proof you use the fact that G is commutative.) [6]

2 Use de Moivre's theorem to find expressions for $\cos 5\theta$ and $\sin 5\theta$, each in terms of both $\cos\theta$ and $\sin\theta$. [3]

Hence show that $\tan 5\theta = \dfrac{5\tan\theta - 10\tan^3\theta + \tan^5\theta}{1 - 10\tan^2\theta + 5\tan^4\theta}$. [2]

Deduce that $5\tan^4\left(\frac{1}{10}\pi\right) - 10\tan^2\left(\frac{1}{10}\pi\right) + 1 = 0$. [2]

3 Show that the simultaneous equations

$$\begin{aligned} 3x + 2y - 2z &= 1, \\ x - y + z &= a, \\ 2x + y - z &= 3, \end{aligned}$$

where a is a constant, do not have a unique solution. [3]

Find the value of a for which the equations are consistent, and interpret the situation geometrically in this case. [4]

4 Let $z = e^{i\theta}$. Give expressions involving trigonometrical functions for

$$z^n + \frac{1}{z^n} \quad \text{and} \quad z^n - \frac{1}{z^n},$$

where n is a positive integer. [3]

By considering $\left(z + \dfrac{1}{z}\right)^4 \left(z - \dfrac{1}{z}\right)^2$, show that

$$\cos^4\theta \sin^2\theta = \tfrac{1}{32}(2 + \cos 2\theta - 2\cos 4\theta - \cos 6\theta).$$ [6]

5 The plane p passes through the point with position vector $\mathbf{a}$, and a vector normal to p is $\mathbf{n}$. Explain, with the aid of a sketch, why the equation of p may be expressed as $(\mathbf{r}-\mathbf{a})\cdot\mathbf{n}=0$. [3]

Suppose now that $\mathbf{n}$ is a *unit* vector, directed from the origin O towards p. Show that the perpendicular distance from O to p is $\mathbf{a}\cdot\mathbf{n}$. [3]

The point B has position vector $\mathbf{b}$. Show that the position vector of the foot of the perpendicular from B to the plane p is $\mathbf{b}+((\mathbf{a}-\mathbf{b})\cdot\mathbf{n})\mathbf{n}$. [3]

6 The skew lines l_1 and l_2 have equations as follows.

$$l_1:\ \mathbf{r}=\begin{pmatrix}1\\-1\\-3\end{pmatrix}+\lambda\begin{pmatrix}1\\-1\\2\end{pmatrix},\qquad l_2:\ \mathbf{r}=\begin{pmatrix}6\\2\\2\end{pmatrix}+\mu\begin{pmatrix}2\\0\\-1\end{pmatrix}.$$

Find a vector $\mathbf{n}$ in the direction of the common perpendicular to l_1 and l_2. [2]

The equation $\mathbf{r}=\begin{pmatrix}1+\ \lambda\\-1-\ \lambda\\-3+2\lambda\end{pmatrix}+t\mathbf{n}$ represents a line passing through a general point of l_1 and parallel to the common perpendicular to l_1 and l_2. Find the values of λ, t and μ for which this line intersects l_2. [5]

Hence state the position vectors of the points A on l_1 and B on l_2 such that $\overrightarrow{AB}$ is perpendicular to both l_1 and l_2, and find the distance AB. [3]

7 (i) Matrices $\mathbf{R}$ and $\mathbf{X}$ are given by $\mathbf{R}=\begin{pmatrix}-\frac{1}{2} & -\frac{1}{2}\sqrt{3}\\ \frac{1}{2}\sqrt{3} & -\frac{1}{2}\end{pmatrix}$, $\mathbf{X}=\begin{pmatrix}\frac{1}{2} & \frac{1}{2}\sqrt{3}\\ \frac{1}{2}\sqrt{3} & -\frac{1}{2}\end{pmatrix}$.

Find $\mathbf{RX}$, $\mathbf{XR}$ and $\mathbf{R}^{-1}$. [4]

(ii) Identify the geometrical transformations of the *xy*-plane represented by $\mathbf{R}$ and $\mathbf{X}$. [2]

(iii) The six matrices $\mathbf{I}$, $\mathbf{R}$, $\mathbf{S}$, $\mathbf{X}$, $\mathbf{Y}$, $\mathbf{Z}$, under the operation of matrix multiplication, form a group G. The matrices $\mathbf{R}$ and $\mathbf{X}$ are as in part (i), and

$$\mathbf{I}=\begin{pmatrix}1 & 0\\0 & 1\end{pmatrix},\quad \mathbf{S}=\begin{pmatrix}-\frac{1}{2} & \frac{1}{2}\sqrt{3}\\ -\frac{1}{2}\sqrt{3} & -\frac{1}{2}\end{pmatrix},\quad \mathbf{Y}=\begin{pmatrix}\frac{1}{2} & -\frac{1}{2}\sqrt{3}\\ -\frac{1}{2}\sqrt{3} & -\frac{1}{2}\end{pmatrix},\quad \mathbf{Z}=\begin{pmatrix}-1 & 0\\0 & 1\end{pmatrix}.$$

Draw up the group table for G. [4]

(iv) The group H consists of the six complex numbers $e^{\frac{1}{3}k\pi i}$ for $k=0,1,2,3,4,5$, under the operation of multiplication of complex numbers. State with a reason whether or not G and H are isomorphic. [2]

Answers to P5

1 Roots of polynomial equations

Exercise 1A (page 6)

1 (a) x^2-5x+6 (b) x^2+2x-3
(c) x^2-4 (d) $2x^2-x-1$

2 (a) $2, -1$ (b) $-2, -\frac{3}{2}$ (c) $\frac{1}{3}, \frac{1}{3}$

3 (a) 12 (b) 16 (c) 10
(d) 8 (e) 2 (f) 3

4 (a) $x^2+6x+45=0$ (b) $x^2+4=0$
(c) $x^2+6x+13=0$ (d) $x^2+6x+25=0$
(e) $5x^2+2x+1=0$ (f) $25x^2+6x+1=0$

5 (a) $u^2+12u+63=0$ (b) $u^2+2u+4=0$
(c) $u^2+12u+39=0$ (d) $u^2-2u+49=0$
(e) $7u^2+4u+1=0$ (f) $49u^2-2u+1=0$

Exercise 1B (page 11)

1 (a) $x^3-9x^2+26x-24=0$
(b) $x^3-x^2-2x=0$
(c) $x^3-4x=0$

2 (a) $x^4-10x^3+35x^2-50x+24=0$
(b) $x^4-2x^3-x^2+2x=0$
(c) $x^4-3x^3-4x^2+12x=0$

3 (a) 0 (b) 12 (c) 36 (d) 3

4 (a) 0 (b) 0 (c) $\frac{8}{3}$ (d) -12
(e) 0

5 (a) $u^3+4u^2+12u+32=0$
(b) $u^3-4u^2+7u-2=0$
(c) $u^3+2u^2-7u-16=0$
(d) $4u^3+3u^2+2u+1=0$

6 (a) $u^4-4u^3+8u^2+24u+64=0$
(b) $u^4-10u^3+38u^2-61u+38=0$
(c) $u^4+24u^2+7u+16=0$
(d) $4u^4+3u^3+2u^2-2u+1=0$

7 (a) -3 (b) $\frac{9}{13}$ (c) 0 (d) $-\frac{75}{169}$

8 $2b^3-3bc+d=0$, $\pm\sqrt{\dfrac{b^3-d}{b}}$

9 $b^3d=c^3$, $d^{\frac{1}{3}}r^2+\left(d^{\frac{1}{3}}-b\right)r+d^{\frac{1}{3}}=0$

10 p, q, r can be any permutation of $1, 2, 3$.

11 p, q, r can be any permutation of $-1, 3, 4$.

13 $ex^n+dx^{n-1}+\ldots+bx+a=0$, $e\neq 0$

Miscellaneous exercise 1 (page 12)

1 94, 8818

2 $-1, -1\pm 2\mathrm{i}$

3 $\alpha=1+\mathrm{i}, \beta=1-\mathrm{i}$ or $\alpha=1-\mathrm{i}, \beta=1+\mathrm{i}$

4 p, q, r can be any permutation of $-1, 1, 2$.

5 -4

6 (a) α and β are conjugate complex numbers.
(b) $13u^2+27u+27=0$

7 $16, -36$; $x^2-160x+10\,000=0$

8 $7, 7$; $u^2-11u+19=0$

9 $u^3+4u^2+5u=0$; $3, 1\pm\mathrm{i}$

11 $-\frac{2}{9}$

12 $u^4+5u^3+6u^2+5u+1=0$;
$v^2+5v+4=0$; $-3\pm\sqrt{3}, \frac{1}{2}\left(-3\pm\sqrt{3}\mathrm{i}\right)$

13 $\frac{2}{3}, -\frac{1}{3}, -3$

14 $b^2(1+u)^3+a^3(u+2)=0$

15 $-\frac{1}{3}a$

2 Hyperbolic functions

Exercise 2A (page 19)

1 (a) 3.762... (b) 11.548...
(c) 7.610... (d) $\frac{4}{3}$
(e) -1.935... (f) e
(g) 0.135... (h) $\frac{17}{8}$

2 In parts (a), (d), (f) and (g) replace cos by cosh and sin by sinh.
(b) $2\sinh x\sinh y=\cosh(x+y)-\cosh(x-y)$
(c) $\sinh 3x=3\sinh x+4\sinh^3 x$
(e) $\dfrac{\mathrm{d}}{\mathrm{d}x}(\cosh^2 x)=\sinh 2x$
(h) $\displaystyle\int \sinh^2 u\,\mathrm{d}u=\tfrac{1}{2}(\sinh u\cosh u-u)+k$

3 (a) e^u or e^{-u} (b) $-\mathrm{e}^u$ or e^{-u}
(c) $-\cosh u\pm 1$ (d) $\dfrac{\sinh u}{\cosh u}$ or $-\dfrac{\cosh u}{\sinh u}$

5 (a) $2(\cosh x-\sinh x)$ (b) $2|\sinh x|$
(c) $\dfrac{1}{2\cosh x}$ (d) $\dfrac{\cosh\frac{1}{2}x}{\sinh\frac{1}{2}x}$

6 (a) $2\sinh x\cosh x$ (b) $\dfrac{\sinh x}{2\sqrt{\cosh x}}$
(c) 1 (d) $-\dfrac{\cosh x+2\sinh x}{(\sinh x+2\cosh x)^2}$
(e) $\dfrac{x\cosh x-2\sinh x}{(x+\cosh x)^2}$
(f) $\dfrac{2\cos x\sinh x}{(\cos x+\sinh x)^2}$
(g) e^{2x}

7 (a) $\frac{1}{3}\cosh 3x+k$ (b) $\frac{1}{4}\cosh 2x+k$

(c) $\frac{1}{2}(\sinh x\cosh x+x)+k$

(d) $x\cosh x-\sinh x+k$

(e) $\frac{1}{2}\left(x^2+\frac{1}{2}\right)\sinh 2x-\frac{1}{2}x\cosh 2x+k$

(f) $\frac{1}{4}e^{2x}+\frac{1}{2}x+k$

8 (a) $\dfrac{1}{4-x^2}+\dfrac{2}{x(4-x^2)}$; $\mathbb{R}-\{-2,0,2\}$

(b) $\dfrac{1+x^2}{(1-x^2)^2}+\dfrac{-2x}{(1-x^2)^2}$; $\mathbb{R}-\{-1,1\}$

(c) $\frac{1}{2}+\dfrac{1-e^x}{2(1+e^x)}$; $\mathbb{R}$

(d) $\dfrac{2}{4-\sinh^2 x}+\dfrac{-\sinh x}{4-\sinh^2 x}$; $\mathbb{R}-\{-\sinh^{-1}2,\sinh^{-1}2\}$

(e) $\sec x+(-\tan x)$; $\{x\in\mathbb{R}; x\neq\left(n+\frac{1}{2}\right)\pi\}$

(f) $\dfrac{2(x^2-3)}{(x^2-1)(x^2-4)}+\dfrac{x(x^2-5)}{(x^2-1)(x^2-4)}$; $\mathbb{R}-\{-2,-1,1,2\}$

(g) $\dfrac{-2(x^2+3)}{x^4+3x^2+4}+\dfrac{x(x^2-1)}{x^4+3x^2+4}$; $\mathbb{R}$

(h) Even function

9 (a) $\sinh^{-1}x+k$

(b) $\cosh^{-1}\frac{1}{3}x+k$ for $x\geqslant 3$

(c) $\frac{1}{3}\sinh^{-1}3x+k$

(d) $\frac{1}{2}x\sqrt{4x^2-1}-\frac{1}{4}\cosh^{-1}2x+k$ for $x\geqslant\frac{1}{2}$

(e) $\frac{1}{8}x\sqrt{4x^2+25}-\frac{25}{16}\sinh^{-1}\frac{2}{5}x+k$

(f) $\frac{1}{8}x(2x^2-9)\sqrt{x^2-9}-\frac{81}{8}\cosh^{-1}\frac{1}{3}x+k$ for $x\geqslant 3$

In parts (b), (d), (f) if x is negative, begin by substituting $x=-y$. In the answers, the expressions $\cosh^{-1}cx$ are replaced by $-\cosh^{-1}(-cx)$.

10 $\frac{1}{10}\cosh 5x-\frac{1}{2}\cosh x+k$

11 (a) $1+2x^2+\frac{2}{3}x^4+\frac{4}{45}x^6+\ldots+\dfrac{2^{2r}}{(2r)!}x^{2r}+\ldots$

(b) $x^2+\frac{1}{3}x^4+\frac{2}{45}x^6+\ldots+\dfrac{2^{2r-1}}{(2r)!}x^{2r}+\ldots$

(c) $1+\frac{3}{2}x^2+\frac{7}{8}x^4+\frac{61}{240}x^6+\ldots+\dfrac{(3^{2r}+3)}{4(2r)!}x^{2r}+\ldots$

(d) $x^4+\frac{2}{3}x^6+\ldots+\dfrac{2^{4r-3}-2^{2r-1}}{(2r)!}x^{2r}+\ldots$

Exercise 2B (page 27)

1 (a) $\frac{13}{5}$ $\pm\frac{12}{5}$ $\pm\frac{12}{13}$ $\frac{5}{13}$

(b) 3 $2\sqrt{2}$ $\frac{2}{3}\sqrt{2}$ $\frac{1}{3}$

(c) $\frac{2}{3}\sqrt{3}$ $\frac{1}{3}\sqrt{3}$ $\frac{1}{2}$ $\frac{1}{2}\sqrt{3}$

(d) $\frac{5}{4}$ $\pm\frac{3}{4}$ $\pm\frac{3}{5}$ $\frac{4}{5}$

2 (a) 0.693... (b) 1.443...
(c) −0.255... (d) −0.652...

3 (a) $\frac{4}{5}$ (b) 5 (c) $\frac{3}{5}$ (d) $\frac{4}{3}$

4 (a) $4\sqrt{3}$ (b) $\frac{1}{2}$ (c) $\frac{1}{4}\sqrt{2}$ (d) $\frac{1}{3}\sqrt{3}$

(e) $\frac{1}{2}\left(\sqrt{5}-1\right)$ (f) $\frac{5}{4}$

6 (a) $\operatorname{sech}x\left(\operatorname{sech}^2x-\tanh^2 x\right)$

(b) $\dfrac{1}{2\sqrt{x(1+x)}}$

(c) $\dfrac{\operatorname{sech}x(\operatorname{sech}x-\tanh x)}{2\sqrt{\operatorname{sech}x+\tanh x}}$

(d) $-\dfrac{1}{x\sqrt{1-x^2}}$

(e) $\dfrac{1}{\sqrt{1+x^2}}$ if $x>0$, $-\dfrac{1}{\sqrt{1+x^2}}$ if $x<0$

(f) $-\dfrac{1}{2x}$

7 (a) $\coth x=\dfrac{\cosh x}{\sinh x}$, $\operatorname{cosech}x=\dfrac{1}{\sinh x}$

(b) coth: $\mathbb{R}-\{0\}$, $\{y: y<-1 \text{ or } y>1\}$
cosech: $\mathbb{R}-\{0\}$, $\mathbb{R}-\{0\}$
$\coth^{-1}$: $\{x: x<-1 \text{ or } x>1\}$, $\mathbb{R}-\{0\}$
$\operatorname{cosech}^{-1}$: $\mathbb{R}-\{0\}$, $\mathbb{R}-\{0\}$

(c) $-\operatorname{cosech}^2x$, $-\operatorname{cosech}x\coth x$, $-\dfrac{1}{x^2-1}$, $-\dfrac{1}{|x|\sqrt{x^2+1}}$

(d) $\frac{1}{2}\ln\dfrac{x+1}{x-1}$,

$\ln\dfrac{1+\sqrt{x^2+1}}{x}$ if $x>0$, $\ln\dfrac{1-\sqrt{x^2+1}}{x}$ if $x<0$

8 (a) $\ln\left(1+\sqrt{2}\right)$ (b) $\ln 2$

(c) $\ln\dfrac{3+\sqrt{10}}{1+\sqrt{2}}$ (d) $\ln\left(4-\sqrt{7}\right)$

(e) $\ln\dfrac{2\left(1+\sqrt{2}\right)}{1+\sqrt{5}}$ (f) $\frac{1}{3}\ln\dfrac{7+\sqrt{40}}{4+\sqrt{7}}$

9 (a) $\frac{1}{12}\tan^{-1}\left(\frac{4}{3}e^x\right)+k$

(b) $-\frac{1}{12}\tanh^{-1}\left(\frac{4}{3}e^x\right)+k$

10 (a) $\frac{1}{2}x-\frac{1}{2}(1-x^2)\tanh^{-1}x+k$
(b) $x\tanh^{-1}x+\frac{1}{2}\ln(1-x^2)+k$
(c) $x\sinh^{-1}x-\sqrt{1+x^2}+k$

11 (a) $\ln\cosh x+k$ (b) $x-\tanh x+k$
(c) $\ln\cosh x-\frac{1}{2}\tanh^2 x+k$
(d) $x-\tanh x-\frac{1}{3}\tanh^3 x+k$

12 (a) $-\cosh^{-1}(\sec x)$ (b) $-\cosh^{-1}(\sec x)$

13 (a) $\ln 3$ (b) $0, \ln\frac{7}{5}$
(c) No solution (d) $\ln 2, \ln\frac{2}{7}$

14 (a) $\dfrac{2}{3-e^x}+k$ (b) $\ln\left|\dfrac{5e^x-7}{e^x-1}\right|+k$
(c) $\frac{1}{5}\ln\dfrac{3e^x+13}{e^x+1}+k$ (d) $\frac{1}{12}\ln\left|\dfrac{e^x-2}{7e^x-2}\right|+k$

15 (a) $3\cosh(x-\alpha), \alpha=\ln 3$
(b) $\sqrt{35}\cosh(x-\alpha), \alpha=\frac{1}{2}\ln\frac{7}{5}$
(c) $-\sqrt{39}\cosh(x-\alpha), \alpha=\frac{1}{2}\ln\frac{13}{3}$
(d) $4\sqrt{7}\cosh(x+\alpha), \alpha=\frac{1}{2}\ln\frac{7}{4}$

16 $x-\frac{1}{6}x^3+\frac{3}{40}x^5-\ldots$
$+(-1)^r\dfrac{1\times3\times5\times\ldots\times(2r-1)}{(2r+1)2^r r!}x^{2r+1}+\ldots$

17 $-\cosh^{-1}(-x)+k,\ \ln(2+\sqrt{3})$

18 $-\frac{1}{2}\pi<u<\frac{1}{2}\pi$; $\sec u$, $\sin u$; $\sec u$, $\operatorname{sech} t$;
(a) $\sinh^{-1}(\tan u)+k$
(b) $\tan^{-1}(\sinh t)+k$
$2\tan^{-1}(e^t)=\tan^{-1}(\sinh t)+\frac{1}{2}\pi$

Exercise 2C (page 30)

1 $\cosh z$, $i\sinh z$

3 $\cosh x\cos y+i\sinh x\sin y$; $z=(2n\pm\frac{1}{3})\pi i, n\in\mathbb{Z}$

4 $\sin x\cosh y+i\cos x\sinh y$;
$z=(2n+\frac{1}{2})\pi+\ln(2+\sqrt{3})i, n\in\mathbb{Z}$

Miscellaneous exercise 2 (page 30)

1 $(\pm\ln(1+\sqrt{2}),\frac{1}{2}\sqrt{2})$

2 $\frac{1}{4}\pi-\frac{1}{2}\ln 2$

3 $(\sinh^{-1}\lambda,\sqrt{1+\lambda^2})$

7 $\frac{1}{3}\ln(6+\sqrt{37})$

9 (a) $\dfrac{1}{a}\tanh^{-1}\left(\dfrac{x}{a}\right)+k$ (b) $\dfrac{1}{2a}\ln\dfrac{a+x}{a-x}+k$

10 $y=\operatorname{sech} x$

11 (b) 12 (c) $\ln 2, \ln\frac{2}{9}$
(d) $\frac{1}{6}\tan^{-1}(\frac{3}{2}e^x)+k$

12 If $a>1$, $\dfrac{1}{\sqrt{a^2-1}}\ln\dfrac{e^x\sqrt{a+1}-\sqrt{a-1}}{e^x\sqrt{a+1}+\sqrt{a-1}}+k$
If $a=1$, $-e^{-x}+k$
If $-1<a<1$, $\dfrac{2}{\sqrt{1-a^2}}\tan^{-1}\left(e^x\sqrt{\dfrac{1+a}{1-a}}\right)+k$
If $a=-1$, e^x+k
If $a<-1$, $\dfrac{1}{\sqrt{a^2-1}}\ln\dfrac{\sqrt{1-a}+e^x\sqrt{-1-a}}{\sqrt{1-a}-e^x\sqrt{-1-a}}+k$

13 $1-\frac{1}{6}x^4+\frac{1}{2520}x^8-\ldots+(-1)^r\dfrac{4^r}{(4r)!}x^{4r}+\ldots$

16 $(\cosh t\cos s, \sinh t\sin s)$

17 (a) $1+\dfrac{x}{2!}+\dfrac{x^2}{4!}+\dfrac{x^3}{6!}+\ldots$
(b) $1+\dfrac{x}{2!}+\dfrac{x^2}{4!}+\dfrac{x^3}{6!}+\ldots$; $2\dfrac{dy}{dx}=\sqrt{\dfrac{1-y^2}{-x}}$

3 Arc length and surface area

Exercise 3A (page 36)

1 (a) $2\sqrt{3}=3.464\ldots$, chord $=3$
(b) $2\sinh 2=7.253\ldots$, chord $=4$
(c) $\frac{1}{4}(e^2+1)=2.097\ldots$, chord $=2.038\ldots$
(d) $\ln(2+\sqrt{3})=1.316\ldots$, chord $=1.255\ldots$
(e) $2\sqrt{5}+\ln(2+\sqrt{5})=5.915\ldots$, chord $=5.656\ldots$
(f) $2\sqrt{5}+\ln(2+\sqrt{5})=5.915\ldots$, chord $=5.656\ldots$
(g) $\frac{1}{8}\pi+\frac{1}{2}=0.892\ldots$, chord $=0.878\ldots$
(h) $\frac{1}{2}\ln 3=0.549\ldots$, chord $=0.542\ldots$

2 (a) 4 (b) $2\sqrt{2}\sinh\pi$
(c) $4(2\sqrt{2}-1)$ (d) $\ln\frac{5}{4}$
(e) $\frac{3}{2}$

3 (a) $\frac{8}{3}\left((\pi^2+1)^{\frac{3}{2}}-1\right)$
(b) $\sqrt{1+\pi^2}-\frac{1}{5}\sqrt{1+25\pi^2}+\pi(\sinh^{-1}5\pi-\sinh^{-1}\pi)$
(c) $\frac{5}{3}(e^{\frac{3}{4}\pi}-1)$
(d) $2\sqrt{1+16\pi^2}+\dfrac{1}{2\pi}\sinh^{-1}4\pi$
(e) $\sqrt{2}$

4 1.34 m, 10.0 m

5 (c) $\dfrac{8(n+1)}{n}, \dfrac{8(n+1)}{2\pi n}\to\dfrac{4}{\pi}$

6 (c) $\frac{4}{9}x^2+4y^2=1, \frac{1}{16}x^2+y^2=1$

Exercise 3B (page 41)

1 (a) 3π
(b) $\frac{8}{3}\pi\left(5\sqrt{5}-1\right)$
(c) $\frac{8}{3}\pi\left(5\sqrt{5}-1\right)$
(d) $\pi(4+\sinh 4)$, $2\pi(2\sinh 2-\cosh 2+1)$
(e) 50.67π, $\frac{268}{7}\pi$
(f) $2\pi\left(\sqrt{2}+\ln\left(1+\sqrt{2}\right)\right)$

2 (a) $3\pi(\pi-2)$ (b) $\frac{1}{2}\pi$, $\frac{92}{75}\pi$
(c) $\frac{24}{5}\pi\left(\sqrt{2}+1\right)$ (d) $\pi\left(\frac{75}{2}\sin^{-1}\frac{4}{5}+18\right)$
(e) $2\pi(3\ln 2-1)$, $\pi\left(\frac{15}{4}+4\ln 2\right)$

3 (a) $2\pi a^2$ (b) $\pi^2 a^2$
(c) $\dfrac{2\pi\sqrt{1+k^2}}{1+4k^2}\left(e^{2k\pi}+1\right)$ (d) $\pi a^2\sec\alpha$

4 $4\pi^2 ab$

5 (a) $18\pi^2$ (b) 48π

Exercise 3C (page 44)

1 6000, $\frac{7}{9}$ m

2 0.38

3 $\frac{1}{3}Ah$

4 $500\,000\pi$ m^3

5 $2\frac{26}{27}$ km

6 $\dfrac{2r}{a^2}\delta r$, $\frac{2}{3}a$; $\frac{4}{9}$

7 $\displaystyle\int_0^\infty 4\pi\rho_0(R+h)^2 e^{-kh}\,dh$; 4.4×10^{18} kg

8 $4(9-x^2)$ m^2; 72 m^3

9 $\frac{1}{2}kW$

Miscellaneous exercise 3 (page 45)

3 $\frac{64}{3}\pi a^2$

4 $\frac{1}{2}\pi a^2\left(57\sqrt{10}-3\sqrt{2}-\sinh^{-1}3+\sinh^{-1}1\right)$

5 (a) 3

8 $\frac{2}{15}\pi$

9 Up to about $1\frac{1}{2}$

10 $2\pi a^2(\sin\beta-\sin\alpha)$

4 Reduction formulae

Exercise 4A (page 49)

1 (a) $\ln\cosh x-\frac{1}{2}\tanh^2 x-\frac{1}{4}\tanh^4 x+k$
(b) $x-\tanh x-\frac{1}{3}\tanh^3 x-\frac{1}{5}\tanh^5 x+k$

2 $I_n=\dfrac{1}{n-1}-I_{n-2}$, $n>1$
(a) $\frac{5}{12}-\frac{1}{2}\ln 2$ (b) $\frac{1}{4}\pi-\frac{76}{105}$

3 $9e-24$

4 $I_n=nI_{n-1}-1$, $n>0$; $120e-326$

6 $I_n=0$ for odd n,
$I_n=(n-1)(n-3)\ldots1$ for even n

7 $C_n=-nS_{n-1}$, $n>0$; $S_n=\pi^n+nC_{n-1}$, $n>0$
$\pi\left(\pi^4-20\pi^2+120\right)$

Exercise 4B (page 53)

1 $\frac{388}{2835}$

2 (a) $nI_n=2^{-n}\sqrt{3}+(n-1)I_{n-2}$; $\frac{3}{32}\sqrt{3}+\frac{5}{48}\pi$
(b) $nI_n=\dfrac{3^{n-1}\times5}{4^n}-(n-1)I_{n-2}$; $\frac{3}{8}\ln 2-\frac{225}{1024}$

3 $8(n-1)I_n=3^{-(n-1)}+(2n-3)I_{n-1}$
(a) $\frac{17}{1152}+\frac{3}{512}\ln 3$ (b) $\frac{7}{1080}\sqrt{3}$

4 $n>\frac{1}{2}$
(a) $\dfrac{(2n-3)(2n-5)\ldots1}{(2n-2)(2n-4)\ldots2}\dfrac{\pi}{2}$
(b) $\dfrac{(2n-3)(2n-5)\ldots2}{(2n-2)(2n-4)\ldots3}$

5 $n>1$; $e^{\frac{1}{2}\pi}-1$, $\frac{1}{2}\left(e^{\frac{1}{2}\pi}-1\right)$, $\frac{2}{5}e^{\frac{1}{2}\pi}-\frac{3}{5}$, $\frac{3}{10}e^{\frac{1}{2}\pi}-\frac{2}{5}$

6 $\frac{1942}{35}$

7 $\frac{1}{2}\sec x\tan x+\frac{1}{2}\ln(\sec x+\tan x)+k$,
$\frac{1}{3}\sec^2 x\tan x+\frac{2}{3}\tan x+k$,
$\frac{1}{4}\sec^3 x\tan x+\frac{3}{8}\sec x\tan x+\frac{3}{8}\ln(\sec x+\tan x)+k$

Miscellaneous exercise 4 (page 53)

2 (b) $\frac{3}{4}\pi^2-6$

3 $\frac{3}{16}\pi$, $\frac{8}{15}$

5 0.8814, 0.4142; $n>1$; 0.127, 0.108

6 (b) $\frac{35}{128}\pi$

7 Valid for all n, but no useful special cases are known except for negative integral n.

8 (a) $\frac{128}{109\,395}$ (b) $\frac{128}{230\,945}$ (c) $\frac{35}{131\,072}\pi$

9 $2(n-1)I_{m,n}=(m-1)I_{m-2,n-1}$ for $1<m<2n-1$
(a) $\frac{1}{120}a^{-6}$ (b) $\frac{1}{5}a^{-2}$

10 $I_n=I_{n-1}-\dfrac{x^n}{n!}e^{-x}$

5 Series and integrals

Exercise 5A (page 58)

1 (a) 4.5, 3.5; 4.1, 3.9; exact value 4
(b) 8.15625, 5.90625; 7.455, 6.555; exact value 7
(c) 5.146..., 4.146...; 4.911..., 4.411...; 4.790..., 4.540...; exact value $4\frac{2}{3}$
(d) $\frac{3}{4}\pi, \frac{1}{4}\pi; \frac{2}{3}\pi, \frac{1}{3}\pi$; exact value $\frac{1}{2}\pi$
(e) 14, 6; 11.06, 10.26; exact value $10\frac{2}{3}$

2 (a) $48.08\pi, 28.88\pi; 42.92\pi, 33.32\pi; 40.43\pi, 35.63\pi$; exact value 38π
(b) $1.75\pi, 1.25\pi; 1.6\pi, 1.4\pi; 1.55\pi, 1.45\pi$; exact value 1.5π
(c) $9\pi, 6\pi; 8.25\pi, 6.75\pi; 7.8\pi, 7.2\pi$; exact value 7.5π
(d) $4.38656\pi, 3.18656\pi; 4.04666\pi, 3.44666\pi$; exact value $3\frac{11}{15}\pi$
(e) $0.749\ldots\pi, 0.549\ldots\pi; 0.710\ldots\pi, 0.610\ldots\pi$; exact value $\frac{2}{3}\pi$

3 (a) $2 \pm \frac{1}{n}; \to 2$
(b) $2a^2\left(5 \pm \frac{4}{n}\right); \to 10a^2$
(c) $1 + \frac{1}{3}\left(1 \pm \frac{1}{n}\right)\left(1 \pm \frac{1}{2n}\right); \to 1\frac{1}{3}$
(d) $20 - 4\left(1 \mp \frac{1}{n}\right)^2; \to 16$
(e) $a^3\left(\frac{5}{3} \pm \frac{3}{2n} - \frac{1}{6n^2}\right); \to \frac{5}{3}a^3$
(f) $\frac{1}{4}a^4\left(15 \pm \frac{14}{n} + \frac{3}{n^2}\right); \to \frac{15}{4}a^4$
(g) $16 \times 3^{\frac{2}{n}} \Big/ n\left(3^{\frac{2}{n}} - 1\right), 16 \Big/ n\left(3^{\frac{2}{n}} - 1\right); \to \frac{8}{\ln 3}$
(h) $ba^{\frac{b}{n}}\left(a^b - 1\right) \Big/ n\left(a^{\frac{b}{n}} - 1\right)$,
$b\left(a^b - 1\right) \Big/ n\left(a^{\frac{b}{n}} - 1\right); \to \frac{a^b - 1}{\ln a}$

4 (a) $\frac{1}{2}\pi a^3\left(1 \pm \frac{1}{n}\right); \to \frac{1}{2}\pi a^3$
(b) $\frac{1}{6}\pi a^3\left(14 \pm \frac{9}{n} + \frac{1}{n^2}\right); \to \frac{7}{3}\pi a^3$
(c) $\frac{1}{4}\pi\left(65 \pm \frac{38}{n} + \frac{5}{n^2}\right); \to \frac{65}{4}\pi$
(d) $3\pi 4^{\frac{1}{n}} \Big/ n\left(4^{\frac{1}{n}} - 1\right), 3\pi \Big/ n\left(4^{\frac{1}{n}} - 1\right); \to \frac{3}{\ln 4}$

5 (a) 1.066..., 1.082..., 1.087..., $\to \ln 3$
(b) 0.710..., 0.689..., 0.682..., $\to \frac{2}{3}$
(c) 0.463..., 0.481..., 0.487..., $\to \frac{1}{2}$
(d) 0.683..., 0.671..., 0.667..., $\to 1 \Big/ \left(2^{\frac{4}{3}} - 1\right)$

6 $h\left(y_0 + y_1 + \ldots + y_{n-1}\right), h\left(y_1 + y_1 + \ldots + y_n\right)$; $\frac{(b-a)(\mathrm{f}(b) - \mathrm{f}(a))}{n}$

Exercise 5B (page 63)

1 (a) 13.90, 13.67
(b) 7152, 7146
(c) 30.69, 30.18
(d) 57.29, 56.29
(e) 0.007 854, 0.007 803

2 (a) $\frac{(n+m-1)(n-m+1)}{2(m-1)^2 n^2}, \frac{(n+m+1)(n-m+1)}{2m^2(n+1)^2}$
(b) $\frac{1}{2}\ln\frac{1+n^2}{1+(m-1)^2}, \frac{1}{2}\ln\frac{1+(n+1)^2}{1+m^2}$
(c) $\frac{(n+1)^{n+1}}{(m+1)^{m+1}}\mathrm{e}^{-(n-m)}, \frac{n^n}{m^m}\mathrm{e}^{-(n-m)}$

3 (a) Not convergent
(b) Convergent, $1 < \sum_{r=1}^{\infty} \mathrm{f}(r) < 2$
(c) Not convergent
(d) Convergent,
$2\ln\left(\sqrt{2}+1\right) < \sum_{r=1}^{\infty} \mathrm{f}(r) < 2\ln\left(\sqrt{2}+1\right) + \frac{1}{\sqrt{2}}$

5 $1 - \frac{1}{n+1}, 1, \frac{1}{4} - \frac{1}{2(n+1)(n+2)}; \frac{1}{6} < \ln\frac{4}{3} < \frac{1}{2}$

Miscellaneous exercise 5 (page 64)

2 $4h + 14h^3$; 29; 0.445

3 (b) $\frac{1}{2}\ln 2$

4 (b) $\frac{1}{\mathrm{e}}$
(d) For example, $n = 1666, s = 613$

5 (c) -4
(d) $\int_3^{n+1} x^{-\frac{3}{2}} \ln x \, \mathrm{d}x$

Revision exercise 1 (page 66)

1 0, $-\ln 3$

2 -8α, $-4\lambda^2$; 4, -13; $\pm\frac{1}{2}$, $\pm\frac{1}{2}\left(\pm\sqrt{13} - 1\right)$;
$3y^4 - 2y^3 - 52y^2 + 32y + 64 = 0$

5 (a) $\frac{1}{\sqrt{4-x^2}}$ (b) $-\frac{2}{x\sqrt{4-x^2}}$;
$3\sin^{-1}\left(\frac{x}{2}\right) - \cosh^{-1}\left(\frac{2}{x}\right) + k$

6 (a) $0,\ -\frac{27}{16},\ -16(\alpha+\beta+\gamma)$
(b) $\frac{3}{2}$ (repeated), $-\frac{3}{4}$; -36
(c) $27y^3-81y^2+90y-20=0$

7 $\frac{1}{4}\pi$

8 (a) $1+2x^2+\frac{5}{3}x^4$ (b) $\frac{255}{32}$

9 (a) 9

10 (a) -8 (b) 24 (c) -4 (d) 6;
$y^4-4y^2+4=0$; $\pm\sqrt{2}$ (both repeated);
$\pm\sqrt{2}-2$ (both repeated)

11 $\frac{1}{112}\pi a^3,\ \frac{61}{432}\pi a^2$

13 (b) $\ln 3+\frac{3}{4}x-\frac{45}{128}x^2$

14 $\frac{6}{5}\pi a^2$

15 $x+\frac{1}{6}x^3+\frac{1}{120}x^5$; $\frac{1}{3}\sinh\frac{3}{2}$

17 (a) $\frac{3}{2},\ -6,\ 2$ (b) $\frac{57}{4},\ 30$
(d) $2x^3-15x^2+24x-7=0$

19 $\dfrac{d^{2n}y}{dx^{2n}}=2n\cosh x+x\sinh x$

21 $\frac{4}{3}\pi-2\sqrt{3}$

22 $16\sqrt{3},\ 192\pi$

23 (a) $\displaystyle\int_{m+1}^{n+1}\frac{1}{x^3}\,dx$

24 $\dfrac{13\sqrt{13}-8}{27}\approx 1.440,\ \dfrac{1763\sqrt{41}+2048}{9375}\approx 1.423,$
$\dfrac{714\,425\sqrt{85}-746\,496}{4\,117\,715}\approx 1.418$

25 $(cp-c\tanh p, c\,\text{sech}\, p)$
(a) $c\ln\cosh p$ (c) $2\pi c^2$

26 $\dfrac{10\sqrt{10}-1}{27}\approx 1.134,\ \dfrac{1898\sqrt{26}+2}{9375}\approx 1.033,$
$\dfrac{8\,858\,750\sqrt{2}-8}{12\,353\,145}\approx 1.014$

6 Linear differential equations

Exercise 6A (page 72)

1 (a) First, non-linear
(b) Second, linear
(c) Second, linear
(d) First, linear
(e) Second, non-linear
(f) First, non-linear

2 (a) $x\dfrac{dy}{dx}=2y+(x-2)e^x$
(b) $\dfrac{d^2y}{dx^2}=0$
(c) $\dfrac{d^2x}{dt^2}+4x=0$
(d) $x^2\dfrac{d^2y}{dx^2}+x\dfrac{dy}{dx}-y=0$
(e) $x\left(\dfrac{dy}{dx}\right)^2+(1-x-y)\dfrac{dy}{dx}+y=0$
(f) $\left(\dfrac{d^2y}{dx^2}\right)^2+4\left(\dfrac{dy}{dx}\right)^3=0$

4 (a) $x=\sin t+A$; $\sin t$, A
(b) $y=-\ln x+Ax+B$; $-\ln x$, $Ax+B$
(c) $y\sin x=x+A$; $x\,\text{cosec}\,x$, $A\,\text{cosec}\,x$
(d) $y=-\cos x+A\sin x$; $-\cos x$, $A\sin x$
(e) $y=x+A\ln x+B$; x, $A\ln x+B$
(f) $y=\dfrac{1}{2x^2}+\dfrac{A}{x}+B$; $\dfrac{1}{2x^2}$, $\dfrac{A}{x}+B$

6 (a) Ae^{3x}, $-e^x$; $y=Ae^{3x}-e^x$
(b) $\dfrac{A}{x}$, x^3; $y=\dfrac{A}{x}+x^3$
(c) $Ae^{-x}+B$, e^{-2x}; $y=Ae^{-x}+B+e^{-2x}$
(d) $A\ln x+B$, $\dfrac{3}{x}$; $y=A\ln x+B+\dfrac{3}{x}$

7 $A=-1$, $B=1$

8 $u(x)=x^2$; $y=\frac{1}{12}x^3+\dfrac{A}{x}+B$; $\dfrac{A}{x}+B$, $\frac{1}{12}x^3$

Exercise 6B (page 80)

1 (a) $y=Ae^{3x}+Be^x$
(b) $y=Ae^x+Be^{-4x}$
(c) $x=Ae^{-3t}+Be^{-4t}$
(d) $x=(At+B)e^{-6t}$
(e) $u=A+Be^{-6x}$
(f) $y=(At+B)e^{\frac{1}{2}t}$

2 (a) $y=2e^{-x}-e^{-2x}$
(b) $u=2e^{-6t}$
(c) $x=\sinh 3t$
(d) $z=\dfrac{1}{1-e^2}(e^{2y}-e^2)$
(e) $z=(1-t)e^{-3t}$
(f) $y=\frac{1}{2}(3e^{2x}-e^{4x})$

3 (a) Ae^{-2x}
(b) Ae^{3x}
(c) $Ae^{-x}+Be^{-4x}$
(d) $Ae^{-\frac{1}{3}t}+Be^{-t}$
(e) $A+Be^{-t}$
(f) $(A+Bx)e^{2x}$

4 (a) $2e^{3x}$ (b) -2 (c) $2x-4$
(d) $\frac{1}{5}e^{-2t}$ (e) $-te^{-t}$ (f) $2x+3$

5 (a) $y=Ae^{2x}+Be^{-2x}-3x$
(b) $x=Ae^{-\frac{1}{2}t}+Be^{-t}+e^{t}$
(c) $x=Ae^{-\frac{1}{2}t}+(B-6t)e^{-t}$
(d) $z=2x+A+Be^{-3x}$
(e) $x=Ae^{t}+Be^{-t}-2\cos t$
(f) $y=\left(\frac{1}{2}x^2+Ax+B\right)e^{x}$

6 (a) $y=e^{x}-e^{-3x}+2$
(b) $x=e^{-2t}+2e^{-\frac{1}{2}t}-\cos t$
(c) $y=(2-x)e^{x}$
(d) $y=e^{-3t}-2\sin t-\cos t$
(e) $u=\left(\frac{1}{2}x^2-x+1\right)e^{-x}$
(f) $y=\frac{1}{2}x\sinh x$

7 $y=\dfrac{A}{x}+Bx-1$

8 $k=\frac{1}{2},\ 1;\ y=x^3+A\sqrt{x}+Bx$

Miscellaneous exercise 6 (page 82)

1 $y=3\cos 2x-4\sin 2x-3e^{-x}$

2 (a) $\dfrac{d^2y}{dx^2}+\dfrac{dy}{dx}-2y=3\cos x-9\sin x$
(b) $\dfrac{d^2y}{dx^2}-4\dfrac{dy}{dx}+3y=2-8x+3x^2$
(c) $\dfrac{d^2y}{dx^2}-4y=4e^{2x}$
(d) $\dfrac{d^2y}{dx^2}+\dfrac{dy}{dx}=2$
(e) $\dfrac{d^2y}{dx^2}-2\dfrac{dy}{dx}+y=2e^{x}$
(f) $\dfrac{d^2y}{dx^2}-9y=2\sinh 3x+2\cosh 3x$

3 (a) $y=Ae^{-x}+Be^{-2x}+x-1$
(b) $y=e^{-2x}-e^{-x}+x-1;$
$\ln 4$

4 (a) $y=(2-x)e^{-x}$
(b) $y=\left(x^2-1\right)e^{x}$
(c) $y=(x+1)\cosh x$

5 (a) $x=2e^{t}-3e^{-t}-5t$
(b) $x=2\cosh 2t-2\cos t$
(c) $x=2\sinh 2t+2te^{2t}$

6 (a) $\to 0,\ \dot{x}=0$ when $t=\frac{1}{4}\ln\frac{5}{3}$
(b) $\to -\infty$
(c) $\to -\infty,\ x=0$ when $t=1,\ \dot{x}=0$ when $t=\frac{1}{2}$
(d) $\to -\infty,\ x=0$ when $t=\frac{1}{5}\ln 6$
(e) $\to 0,\ \dot{x}=0$ when $t=\frac{2}{35}$

7 (a) $\to 0$ if $\alpha<0,\ \to\infty$ if $0<\alpha<c$,
$\to -\infty$ if $c<0<\alpha$ or $0<c<\alpha$
(b) If $\alpha>c,\ x=0$ when $t=\dfrac{1}{\alpha-c}$
(c) If $0<c<\alpha,\ \alpha<0<c$ or $c<\alpha<0$,
$\dot{x}=0$ when $t=\dfrac{c}{\alpha(\alpha-c)}$

8 (a) $\to 0$ if $\alpha<0,\ \to 1-\dfrac{c}{\beta}$ if $\alpha=0$,
$\to\infty$ if $\alpha>0$ and $\beta<c$,
$\to -\infty$ if $\alpha>0$ and $\beta>c$;
if $\alpha>0$ and $\beta=c$, $\to\infty$ if $c>0$,
$\to 1$ if $c=0,\ \to 0$ if $c<0$
(b) If $\beta>c,\ x=0$ when $t=\dfrac{1}{\alpha-\beta}\ln\dfrac{\alpha-c}{\beta-c}$
(c) If $\beta>c>0$, or if $\alpha>0$ and $\beta<c<0$, or if $\alpha<0$ and $c>0$, or if $c<\beta<\alpha<0$,
$\dot{x}=0$ when $t=\dfrac{1}{\alpha-\beta}\ln\dfrac{\beta(\alpha-c)}{\alpha(\beta-c)}$

9 $\dfrac{V_0 n}{\sqrt{\left(\frac{1}{C}-Ln^2\right)^2+R^2n^2}}$

10 $y=Ax^3+2x^2+Bx$

7 Calculus with complex numbers

Exercise 7A (page 88)

3 (a) $\frac{1}{5}e^{2x}(2\cos x+\sin x)+k$
(b) $\frac{1}{17}e^{x}(\sin 4x-4\cos 4x)+k$
(c) $\frac{1}{5}e^{-x}(2\sin 2x-\cos 2x)+k$
(d) $-\frac{1}{25}e^{-4x}(4\sin 3x+3\cos 3x)+k$
(e) $\frac{1}{169}e^{2x}\big((26x+5)\cos 3x+(39x-12)\sin 3x\big)+k$
(f) $\frac{1}{2}(x-1)e^{x}\big((x+1)\sin x-(x-1)\cos x\big)+k$
(g) $\frac{1}{10}e^{x}(5-\cos 2x-2\sin 2x)+k$
(h) $\frac{1}{10}e^{-x}(2\sin 2x-\cos 2x)+\frac{1}{34}e^{-x}(\cos 4x-4\sin 4x)+k$
(i) $\frac{1}{2}e^{-x}(\sin 3x-\cos 3x)+k$

4 (a) $2\cos t+\sin t$
(b) $\frac{1}{2}e^{t}\sin 2t$
(c) $-\frac{1}{113}(7\sin 2t+8\cos 2t)$
(d) $\frac{1}{10}(\sin t-3\cos t)$
(e) $-\frac{1}{2}(\cos x+\sin x)$
(f) $-e^{3x}\cos x$
(g) $-\frac{1}{4}t\cos 2t$
(h) $\frac{1}{6}xe^{x}\sin 3x$

5 (a) $y = e^{-2x}(A\sin x + B\cos x)$
(b) $y = e^{3x}(A\sin 4x + B\cos 4x)$
(c) $x = A\sin 3t + B\cos 3t + \frac{2}{5}e^{-t}$
(d) $u = e^{-t}(A\sin t + B\cos t) + \frac{1}{2}(t-1)$
(e) $x = A\sin t + B\cos t - \frac{1}{10}e^{-t}(\sin 3t - 4\cos 3t)$
(f) $y = e^{x}(A\sin 7x + B\cos 7x) + \frac{1}{2405}(49\sin x + 2\cos x)$
(g) $x = Ae^{3t} + Be^{-3t} + \frac{1}{102}(\sin 3t - 4\cos 3t)$
(h) $y = e^{-3t}\left(A\sin t + \left(B - \frac{1}{2}t\right)\cos t\right)$

6 (a) $y = e^{2x}\cos 2x$
(b) $x = e^{-2t}(2\sin 3t + \cos 3t)$
(c) $y = \sin x + 3\cos x - e^{-3x}$
(d) $x = 2e^{-t}\sin^2 t$
(e) $u = (t-1)^2 + e^{-t}(\sin t - \cos t)$
(f) $x = e^{-t}(1 + \sin 3t)$
(g) $y = (1 + e^{-2x})\sin x$
(h) $x = e^{pt}\left(\left(b - \frac{ap}{q} + \frac{t}{2q}\right)\sin qt + a\cos qt\right)$

Exercise 7B (page 94)

1 $2a\sin\frac{1}{2}t$, $\frac{1}{2}(\pi - t)$ for $0 \leqslant t \leqslant \pi$
(a) $4a\left(1 - \cos\frac{1}{2}t\right)$
(b) $\frac{1}{2}(\pi - t)$

2 (b) $8a\left(1 - \cos\frac{1}{2}t\right)$, $\frac{3}{2}t$

3 The tangent makes an angle α with the radius vector.

4 Velocity is $a\Omega$ perpendicular to OP. $-a\Omega^2 e^{\theta i}$; acceleration is $a\Omega^2$ in direction PO.

5 Velocity is $a\dot{\theta}$ perpendicular to OP. $a\ddot{\theta} i e^{\theta i} - a\dot{\theta}^2 e^{\theta i}$; acceleration has components $a\ddot{\theta}$ perpendicular to OP and $a\dot{\theta}^2$ in direction PO.

6 Velocity has components $\dot{r}$ in direction OP and $r\dot{\theta}$ perpendicular to OP. $\left(\ddot{r} - r\dot{\theta}^2\right)e^{\theta i} + \left(2\dot{r}\dot{\theta} + r\ddot{\theta}\right)ie^{\theta i}$; acceleration has components $\ddot{r} - r\dot{\theta}^2$ in direction OP and $2\dot{r}\dot{\theta} + r\ddot{\theta}$ perpendicular to OP.

7 Velocity is $\dot{s}$ in direction of the tangent. $\ddot{s}e^{\psi i} + \dot{s}\dot{\psi}ie^{\psi i}$; acceleration has components $\ddot{s}$ in direction of the tangent and $\dot{s}\dot{\psi}$ in direction of the normal.

8 $\dfrac{(-1)^n n!}{(x^2+1)^{n+1}}\left(x^{n+1} - \binom{n+1}{2}x^{n-1} + \binom{n+1}{4}x^{n-3} + \ldots\right)$

9 $\dfrac{-1-2x}{(1+x+x^2)^2}$, $\dfrac{2(3x+3x^2)}{(1+x+x^2)^3}$, $\dfrac{3!(1-6x^2-4x^3)}{(1+x+x^2)^4}$, $\dfrac{4!(-1-5x+10x^3+5x^4)}{(1+x+x^2)^5}$, $\dfrac{5!(6x+15x^2-15x^4-6x^5)}{(1+x+x^2)^6}$, $\dfrac{6!(1-21x^2-35x^3+21x^5+7x^6)}{(1+x+x^2)^7}$;
$1 - x + x^3 - x^4 + x^6 - \ldots$

Miscellaneous exercise 7 (page 96)

1 (a) $\dfrac{e^{at}}{a^2+b^2}\left(\begin{array}{l}(ap-bq)\cos bt \\ \quad +(aq+bp)\sin bt\end{array}\right) + k$
(b) $\dfrac{t}{b}(p\sin bt - q\cos bt) + \dfrac{1}{b^2}(p\cos bt + q\sin bt) + k$

2 (a) $\dfrac{1}{a^2+1}$
(b) $\dfrac{1}{a^2+1}\coth\frac{1}{2}a\pi$

3 $\dfrac{U}{\sqrt{3}}e^{-t}\sin\left(\sqrt{3}t\right)$; $\dfrac{\pi}{3\sqrt{3}}$

4 $x = \dfrac{V}{k} + e^{-2kt}(A\cos 2kt + B\sin 2kt)$;
$x = \dfrac{V}{k}\left(1 - e^{-2kt}(\cos 2kt + \sin 2kt)\right)$; $\to \dfrac{V}{k}$

5 (a) $I = I_0 e^{-t/RC}$
(b) $I = \dfrac{E_0 C\omega}{1 + R^2C^2\omega^2}(\cos\omega t + RC\omega\sin\omega t - 1)$

6 (a) $5\sin 3t + e^{-t}(\sin t + 2\cos t)$

8 (a) $A\sin 14t + B\cos 14t$
(b) $\dfrac{2}{196-\omega^2}\sin\omega t$,
$x = \dfrac{2}{196-\omega^2}\sin\omega t + A\sin 14t + B\cos 14t$
(c) $x = A\sin 14t + B\cos 14t - \frac{1}{14}t\cos 14t$;
$x = \frac{1}{196}\sin 14t - \frac{1}{14}t\cos 14t$; oscillation whose amplitude increases without limit.

9 (a) $\sqrt{2}(e^t - t - 1)$
(b) $c\ln\cosh t$
(c) $2at - 4a\sin\frac{1}{2}t$

8 Approximations and errors

In this chapter your answers may differ from those given by 1 or 2 in the last decimal place. This will usually depend on whether or not you have rounded intermediate values in the calculations. Don't spend time trying to get an exact match between your answers and those given if they are close enough to indicate that you have used a correct procedure.

Exercise 8A (page 105)

1 (b) F_1, F_3 for smaller root, F_2, F_4 for larger.
(c) F_3 for smaller root, F_2 for larger
(d) 1.58579, 4.41421
(f) About 23, 14, 14, 37

2 (b) F_1 does not converge to either root, F_2 gives the lower, F_3 the higher, F_4 both.
(c) F_4 (with minus sign), F_3
(d) −6.12311, 2.12311
(f) About 14, 14, 14 (lower), over 200 (higher), the last answer is only of theoretical interest.

3 F_3, F_4, F_3; −2.8820, −0.2235, 3.1055

4 F_2, F_3, F_3; −3.7093, −1.1939, 0.9032

5 (a) 4.10724 (b) 3.35530 (c) 0.51493
(d) 0.76501 (e) 0.70329 (f) 1.66080

7 $k \approx 0.5265$; 0.703 290 66

8 (a) 0.714 556 38
(b) 0.876 726 22
(c) 0.111 832 56, 3.577 152 06

9 (a) $1+2x+2x^2+\frac{8}{3}x^3$
(b) $3+\frac{1}{6}x-\frac{1}{216}x^2+\frac{1}{3888}x^3$
(c) $2+2\sqrt{3}x+7x^2+\frac{23}{3}\sqrt{3}x^3$
(d) $\frac{1}{6}\pi+\frac{2}{3}\sqrt{3}x+\frac{2}{9}\sqrt{3}x^2+\frac{8}{27}\sqrt{3}x^3$

10 (a) 0.65292 to 5 significant figures
(b) 0.739 085 to 6 significant figures
(c) 2.302 775 64 to 9 significant figures
(d) 1.146 to 4 significant figures
1.14619 to 6 significant figures

Exercise 8B (page 108)

1 0.347 296 355;
errors -2.7×10^{-3}, -2.9×10^{-6}, 0
1.532 088 886;
errors 3.2×10^{-2}, -1.2×10^{-3}, -1.8×10^{-6}, 0
−1.879 385 241;
errors 2.1×10^{-2}, 3.1×10^{-4}, 7.1×10^{-8}, 0

2 (a) 0.426 302 751; errors 2.6×10^{-2}, -1.1×10^{-3}, -1.9×10^{-6}, 0
(b) 0.739 085 133;
errors -1.1×10^{-2}, -2.6×10^{-5}, 0

3 $x_{r+1}=\frac{1}{3}\left(2x_r+\frac{N}{x_r^2}\right)$; 2.154 434 690

4 $x_{r+1}=\frac{1}{m}\left((m-1)x_r+\frac{N}{x_r^{m-1}}\right)$; 1.974 350 486

Miscellaneous exercise 8 (page 109)

1 $k \approx -0.186$; 0.53139

2 (a) 4, 1, 0.25, 0.0625; $\left(\frac{1}{4}\right)^{r-1}$
(b) 4, −2, 1, −0.5; $\left(-\frac{1}{2}\right)^{r-2}$
(c) x_r diverges; it is negative with a large modulus.
(d) x_r diverges; it is alternately positive and negative with a large modulus.
(e) x_r takes the values 0 and 8 alternately.

3 (a) 4.541 381, −1.541 381
(b) −4.592 253, 0.250 789, 4.341 465
(c) 1.611 793, 3.820 704
(d) −0.815 553, 1.429 612
(e) −1.534 645, 1.612 756, 4.010 988
(f) 2.219 107

4 (c) Not convergent for $k=2$; convergent for $k=-1$.

5 (b) 2.107 086 (c) First iteration

9 The Newton–Raphson method

In this chapter your answers may differ from those given by 1 or 2 in the last decimal place. This will usually depend on whether or not you have rounded intermediate values in the calculations. Don't spend time trying to get an exact match between your answers and those given if they are close enough to indicate that you have used a correct procedure.

Exercise 9A (page 114)

1 (a) 0.8080 (b) 0.5869 (c) 3.7944

2 (a) 2.4973, accurate to 4 decimal places
(b) 2.5051, accurate to 4 decimal places
(c) 0.6417, accurate to 4 decimal places
(d) −1.0920, accurate to only 3 decimal places

3 $n\pi+\frac{(-1)^n}{n\pi}$

4 (a) With $x_0=2.43$, 2.429 7811 to 7 decimal places; 2.429 781 066 to 9 decimal places
(b) With $x_0=1.62$, 1.62135 to 5 decimal places; 1.621 347 946 to 9 decimal places
(c) With $x_0=2.2$, 2.19745 to 5 decimal places; 2.197 451 757 to 9 decimal places

Exercise 9B (page 119)

1 (a) Error $\approx -9.9\times10^{-6}$, 3.1958 to 4 decimal places
(b) Error $\approx 1.7\times10^{-3}$, 2.2 to 1 decimal place
(c) Error $\approx -4.6\times10^{-6}$, 1.503 34 to 5 decimal places
(d) Error $\approx -5.5\times10^{-5}$, 3.7687 to 4 decimal places

2 (a) 0.824 132 312 (b) 1.234 762 161
(c) 0.588 532 744

4 (a) 0.689 139 46 (b) 0.772 882 96
(c) 0.510 973 43 (d) 1.199 678 64

5 2.79 m

6 -3.0×10^{-3}, -2.0×10^{-5}, -1.0×10^{-9}, -2.7×10^{-18}; $\frac{e_{r+1}}{e_r^2}\approx -2.66, -2.60, -2.53$; $\frac{-f''(\alpha)}{2f'(\alpha)}\approx -2.60$

Exercise 9C (page 121)

1 (a) 0.684 124 319, -2.059 142 445
(b) -0.297 632 209, -2.070 275 995
(c) 9.126 123 781
(d) 4.390 977 869, -9.999 997 730
(e) 1.150 584 967
(f) 2.219 107 149

Miscellaneous exercise 9 (page 121)

1 3.686

2 0.739

3 1.986

4 3.327

5 4.026

6 (a) $(0,1), (\pm2.98287, 0.10104)$
(b) $(0,1), (1.10914, 0.44543), (3.69816, -0.84908)$
(c) $(1.43455, 2.95222), (-0.59332, -0.20886)$

7 $(\pm1.19968, \pm0.66274)$

8 (a) $\frac{\pi}{1+a}$ (b) $p=\frac{1}{4n^2\pi^2}$, $q=\frac{1}{(2n+1)^2\pi^2}$

9 (b) $x_{r+1}=x_r-\frac{\tan x_r-2x_r}{\sec^2 x_r-2}$
(c) Converges with $x_0=1.1$
(e) It might diverge, or it might converge to one of the other roots.

10 0.13286

11 $0.3314+0.4721\text{i}$

12 (a) $1.229+0.726\text{i}$ (more accurately $1.228+0.726\text{i}$)
(b) $0.318+1.337\text{i}$ (more accurately $0.318+1.337\text{i}$)

10 Step-by-step approximations

In this chapter your answers may differ from those given by 1 or 2 in the last decimal place. This will usually depend on whether or not you have rounded intermediate values in the calculations. Don't spend time trying to get an exact match between your answers and those given if they are close enough to indicate that you have used a correct procedure.

Exercise 10A (page 125)

1 480 m

2 1450 m

3 Values at selected points are given in
(a) line 4,
(b) line 5 of Table 10.5.

4 (a) (i) $(0.5, 0.5)$, $(1, 0.93879)$
(ii) $(0.5, 0.49223)$, $(1, 0.89821)$
(b) (i) $(2, 2.2)$, $(3, 2.35625)$, $(4, 2.48591)$, $(5, 2.59737)$
(ii) $(2, 2.18772)$, $(3, 2.33725)$, $(4, 2.46260)$, $(5, 2.57105)$
(c) (i) $(1, 3)$, $(2, 5.09993)$
(ii) $(0.5, 2)$, $(1, 3.01037)$, $(1.5, 4.06183)$, $(2, 5.18110)$
(iii) $(0.5, 2.00089)$, $(1, 3.02001)$, $(1.5, 4.08886)$, $(2, 5.23272)$
(d) (i) $(0, 0.92424)$, $(0.5, 1.39645)$, $(1.5, 2.60355)$, $(2, 3.31313)$
(ii) $(0, 0.99054)$, $(0.5, 1.42708)$, $(1.5, 2.63118)$, $(2, 3.36843)$

5 With t-step 4, 97.68; with t-step 2, 95.46

6 (a) 19.7 m, 20.9 m
(b) 22.07 m
Errors 2.4 m, 1.2 m

Exercise 10B (page 129)

3 (a) $y_B=\text{F}(a+h)$, $y_P=\text{F}(a)+h\text{f}(a)$
(b) $y_Q=\text{F}_1(a+h)+h\text{f}(a+h)$

Exercise 10C (page 133)

1 480 m

2 1200 m

4 (a) (i) $(0.5, 0.46940)$, $(1, 0.83482)$
(ii) $(0.5, 0.47733)$, $(1, 0.84990)$
(b) (i) $(2, 2.17812)$, $(3, 2.32197)$, $(4, 2.44352)$, $(5, 2.54923)$
(ii) $(2, 2.17710)$, $(3, 2.32049)$, $(4, 2.44180)$, $(5, 2.54736)$
(c) (i) $(1, 3.04997)$, $(2, 5.31103)$
(ii) $(0.5, 2.00519)$, $(1, 3.03700)$, $(1.5, 4.12616)$, $(2, 5.29661)$
(iii) $(0.5, 2.00356)$, $(1, 3.03407)$, $(1.5, 4.12288)$, $(2, 5.29374)$
(d) (i) $(0, 1.09865)$, $(0.5, 1.46212)$, $(1.5, 2.65656)$, $(2, 3.41965)$
(ii) $(0, 1.07399)$, $(0.5, 1.45836)$, $(1.5, 2.65878)$, $(2, 2.42372)$

5 With t-step 4, 91.67; with t-step 2, 92.87

6 22.24 m, 22.11 m
Errors -0.17 m, -0.04 m

Exercise 10D (page 135)

1 The answers given to this question are based on the answers to Exercise 10A Question 4 and Exercise 10C Question 4, which were rounded to 5 decimal places. This is what was done in Tables 10.14 and 10.15. If you keep more figures in your earlier answers, and round to 5 decimal places after applying the improvement technique, you will sometimes get answers which are 1 more or 1 less in the 5th place than those given. These are indicated by + or – in the answers.
Euler method:
(a) $(0.5, 0.48446)$, $(1, 0.85763^-)$
(b) $(2, 2.17544)$, $(3, 2.31825^-)$, $(4, 2.43929^+)$, $(5, 2.54473)$
(c) With $h = 1$ and 0.5:
$(1, 3.02074)$, $(2, 5.26227^-)$
With $h = 0.5$ and 0.25:
$(0.5, 2.00178^-)$, $(1, 3.02965)$, $(1.5, 4.11589)$, $(2, 5.28434)$
(d) $(0, 1.05684)$, $(0.5, 1.45771^-)$, $(1.5, 2.65881^-)$, $(2, 3.42373)$

Modified Euler method:
(a) $(0.5, 0.47997)$, $(1, 0.85493)$
(b) $(2, 2.17676)$, $(3, 2.32000^-)$, $(4, 2.44123^-)$, $(5, 2.54674^-)$
(c) With $h = 1$ and 0.5:
$(1, 3.03268)$, $(2, 5.29180)$
With $h = 0.5$ and 0.25:
$(0.5, 2.00302)$, $(1, 3.03309)$, $(1.5, 4.12179)$, $(2, 5.29278)$
(d) $(0, 1.06577)$, $(0.5, 1.45711)$, $(1.5, 2.65952^-)$, $(2, 3.42508)$

2 22.17, error -0.10; 22.07, error negligible

3 $(0.2, 0.85111)$, $(0.4, 0.77966)$, $(0.6, 0.76190)$ $(0.8, 0.78328)$; minimum at approximately $(0.58, 0.76)$, no further stationary point

4 (a) (i) 1.85914, 0.42074, 0.75
(ii) 1.75393, 0.45008, 0.70833
(iii) 1.72722, 0.45730, 0.69702
Errors approximately proportional to h^2
1.71832, 0.45971, 0.69325

Miscellaneous exercise 10 (page 136)

1 $(100.0, 0)$, $(199.9, 5.0)$, $(296.9, 29.2)$, $(394.9, 48.9)$, $(494.2, 60.8)$, $(594.2, 64.8)$; $(100.0, 2.5)$, $(198.9, 17.3)$, $(296.4, 39.3)$, $(395.2, 55.1)$, $(494.8, 63.1)$, $(594.8, 65.1)$

2 (b) $y \approx \frac{1}{2}x^2$, 5×10^{-5} with error of order 10^{-8}
(c) 3.4999×10^{-4}
(d) 4.4996×10^{-4}
$y \approx \frac{1}{2}x^2$ gives 4.5×10^{-4}, very close to the modified Euler estimate

3 1.701 302, 1.702 084; 1.70235

4 (a) 1.2 (b) 1.200 909 (c) 1.2022
(d) 1.2033, less accurate than (c)

5 (a) 1.086 857
(b) 0.994 094
(d) -9.34×10^{-4}, -6.51×10^{-3}; 4.1×10^{-5}, 1.09×10^{-3};
errors proportional to h^3, nh^2, nh^3

Revision exercise 2 (page 138)

1 2; $y = Ae^{-x} + (2x + B)e^{4x}$

2 0.53; $f'(0) = 0$, so $\dfrac{f(0)}{f'(0)}$ can't be evaluated

3 (c) $x_{r+1} = 3e^{-\frac{1}{2}x_r}$ converges,
$x_{r+1} = \ln\left(\dfrac{9}{x_r^{\,2}}\right)$ diverges
(d) Converges to 1.4517...

4 $x = \sin 3t + Ae^{-t} + Be^{-4t}$

5 1.7503; 1.6966

6 (b) (i) $(A\cos 2t + B\sin 2t)e^{-t}$
(ii) $0.2t - 0.08 + 0.25e^{-t}$
(iii) $V = 0.2t - 0.08 + 0.25e^{-t} + (A\cos 2t + B\sin 2t)e^{-t}$

7 (a)

5	0.5	(0.4246)	(0.6803)	0.4926
6	0.6	0.4926	0.6427	0.5569
7	0.7	0.5569	0.6101	0.6179
8	0.8	0.6179	(0.5818)	(0.6761)

(b) Because the values of $\frac{dy}{dx}$ are decreasing; no, the curve will either intersect $y^2 = x - 1$ or turn upwards with ever increasing gradient, either way $\frac{d^2y}{dx^2}$ can't remain negative indefinitely.

(c) Less accurate, a larger step length takes less account of the variation in $\frac{dy}{dx}$.

(d) Less, whatever the step length, because Euler's method doesn't allow for the variation in $\frac{dy}{dx}$ over each interval.

8 (a) $(1+x)\frac{d^2y}{dx^2} + x\frac{dy}{dx} - y = 0$

(b) $x^2\frac{d^2y}{dx^2} = 2y - 4x$

(c) $\frac{d^2y}{dx^2} + y = \tan x(1 + 2\sec^2 x)$

9 $0, -\frac{1}{4}$; $\left(A - \frac{1}{4}x\right)\cos 2x + B\sin 2x$; $-\frac{1}{4}n\pi$

10 (b) $f'(x_1) \approx \frac{f(x_0) - f(x_1)}{x_0 - x_1}$ (c) 0.739085

(e) There is no need to find an expression for $f'(x)$; after a few iterations the numerator and denominator both become small, so rounding errors become significant and restrict the accuracy that can be achieved.

11 (a) $I = \frac{1}{20}(5\cos 20t + 3\sin 20t) + Ae^{-20t} + Be^{-5t}$

(b) $I = \frac{1}{20}(5\cos 20t + 3\sin 20t) + \frac{17}{60}e^{-20t} - \frac{8}{15}e^{-5t}$

(c) $\frac{1}{20}(5\cos 20t + 3\sin 20t)$, changing the initial conditions only affects the values of A and B.

(d) $\frac{\sqrt{34}}{20}(\sin 20t + 1.030\ldots)$

12 (a) (i) $y = (2 + A\cos 3x + B\sin 3x)e^{-x}$

(ii) $y = 2(1 - \cos 3x)e^{-x}$; $\frac{2}{3}\pi$, $\frac{4}{3}\pi$

(b) $y = (A\cos 3x + B\sin 3x)e^{-x} + C$

13 (a) About 16

(b) 0.439 743 552, 0.447 441 908
0.441 649 054; 0.441 136 388

(d) 0.444 216 503, 0.444 134 786
[$X = 0.444\,130\,23$ correct to 8 d places]

14 (a) 0.885 057 574, 0.879 745 103
0.877 824 838 (b) 0.876 737 81

(c) (i) About 6, (ii) About 13

(d) 0.877 364 803, 0.876 726 721
0.876 726 215; error estimates
-6.05×10^{-4}, -5.05×10^{-7}, -3.2×10^{-13}

Mock examinations

Mock examination 1 for P5 (page 142)

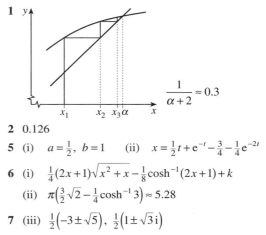

1

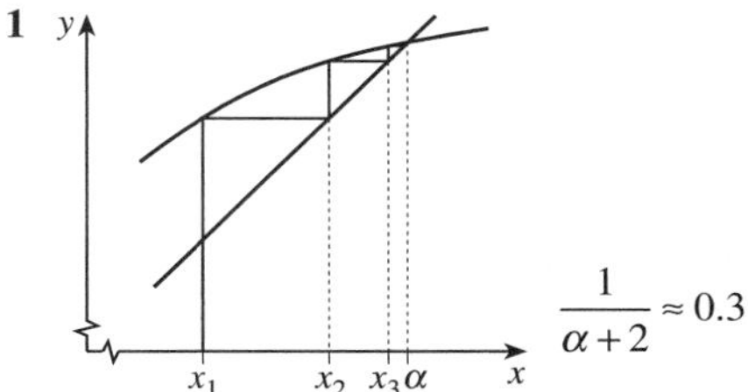

$\frac{1}{\alpha+2} \approx 0.3$

2 0.126

5 (i) $a = \frac{1}{2}$, $b = 1$ (ii) $x = \frac{1}{2}t + e^{-t} - \frac{3}{4} - \frac{1}{4}e^{-2t}$

6 (i) $\frac{1}{4}(2x+1)\sqrt{x^2+x} - \frac{1}{8}\cosh^{-1}(2x+1) + k$

(ii) $\pi\left(\frac{3}{2}\sqrt{2} - \frac{1}{4}\cosh^{-1}3\right) \approx 5.28$

7 (iii) $\frac{1}{2}\left(-3 \pm \sqrt{5}\right)$, $\frac{1}{2}\left(1 \pm \sqrt{3}\,i\right)$

Mock examination 2 for P5 (page 144)

1 $y^3 + 2py^2 + p^2y - q^2 = 0$

2 $y = \frac{1}{4} + \left(\frac{1}{2}x - \frac{1}{4}\right)e^{-2x}$

4 (i), (ii)

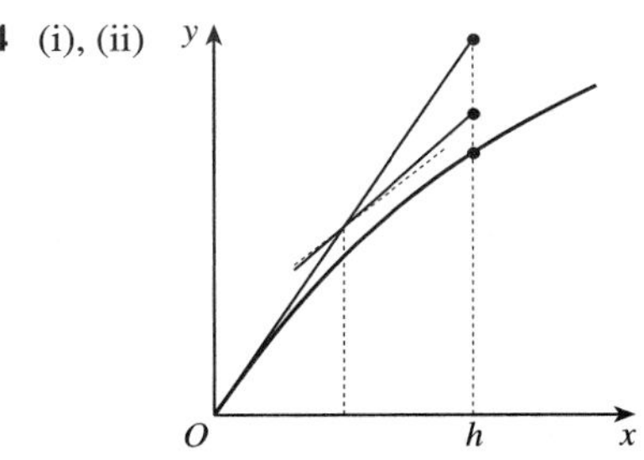

(iii) 0.4, 0.398

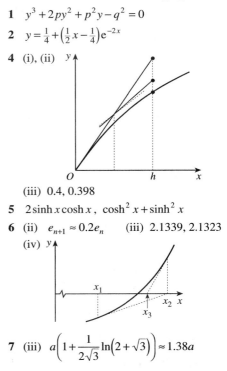

5 $2\sinh x\cosh x$, $\cosh^2 x + \sinh^2 x$

6 (ii) $e_{n+1} \approx 0.2e_n$ (iii) 2.1339, 2.1323

(iv)

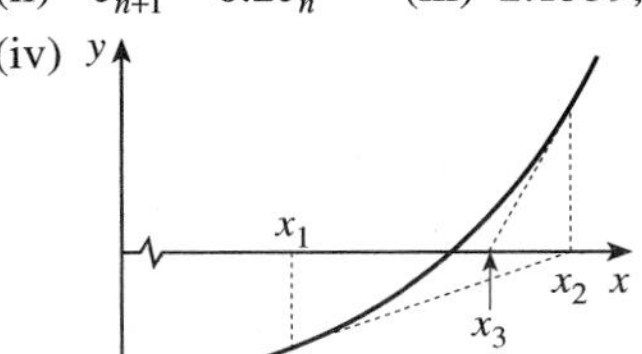

7 (iii) $a\left(1 + \frac{1}{2\sqrt{3}}\ln\left(2+\sqrt{3}\right)\right) \approx 1.38a$

Answers to P6

1 Simultaneous linear equations

Your answers may differ in form from those given. The parmeters s and t are real numbers. The solution $z=t$ means that z can take any real value.

Exercise 1A (page 153)

1 (a) If $a \neq 0$, $x=2a^{-1}$;
if $a=0$, no solution.
(b) If $a \neq 0$, $x=1+a^{-1}$;
if $a=0$, no solution.
(c) If $b \neq 0$, $x=b$;
if $b=0$, $x=t$.
(d) If $a \neq b$; $x=c(a-b)^{-1}$;
if $a=b$ and $c=0$, $x=t$;
if $a=b$ and $c \neq 0$, no solution.
(e) If $a \neq 0$ and $a \neq -1$, $x=1-a^{-1}$;
if $a=0$, no solution;
if $a=-1$, $x=t$.
(f) If $a \neq b$, $x=-(a+b)$; if $a=b$, $x=t$.

2 (a) $x=2+t$, $y=t$ (b) No solution
(c) $x=t$, $y=3t$

3 (a) $\begin{pmatrix}x\\y\end{pmatrix}=\begin{pmatrix}3\\0\end{pmatrix}+t\begin{pmatrix}2\\1\end{pmatrix}$ (b) No solution
(c) $\begin{pmatrix}x\\y\end{pmatrix}=\begin{pmatrix}2\\0\end{pmatrix}+t\begin{pmatrix}3\\5\end{pmatrix}$

4 (a) $\begin{pmatrix}x\\y\end{pmatrix}=\begin{pmatrix}2\\0\end{pmatrix}+t\begin{pmatrix}-2\\1\end{pmatrix}$
(b) $\begin{pmatrix}x\\y\end{pmatrix}=\begin{pmatrix}0\\p\end{pmatrix}+t\begin{pmatrix}-1\\2\end{pmatrix}$
(c) If $a \neq 0$, $\begin{pmatrix}x\\y\end{pmatrix}=\begin{pmatrix}0\\p\end{pmatrix}+t\begin{pmatrix}-1\\a\end{pmatrix}$;
if $a=0$, $\begin{pmatrix}x\\y\end{pmatrix}=\begin{pmatrix}0\\p\end{pmatrix}+t\begin{pmatrix}1\\0\end{pmatrix}$.
(d) $\begin{pmatrix}x\\y\end{pmatrix}=\begin{pmatrix}a\\0\end{pmatrix}+t\begin{pmatrix}-a\\1\end{pmatrix}$
(e) If a, b are not both 0, $\begin{pmatrix}x\\y\end{pmatrix}=\begin{pmatrix}b\\0\end{pmatrix}+t\begin{pmatrix}-b\\a\end{pmatrix}$;
if $a=b=0$, $\begin{pmatrix}x\\y\end{pmatrix}=\begin{pmatrix}s\\t\end{pmatrix}$.
(f) If $a \neq 0$, $\begin{pmatrix}x\\y\end{pmatrix}=\begin{pmatrix}p/a\\0\end{pmatrix}+t\begin{pmatrix}-b\\a\end{pmatrix}$;
if $a=0, b \neq 0$, $\begin{pmatrix}x\\y\end{pmatrix}=\begin{pmatrix}0\\p/b\end{pmatrix}+s\begin{pmatrix}1\\0\end{pmatrix}$;
if $a=b=0$, if $p=0$, $\begin{pmatrix}x\\y\end{pmatrix}=\begin{pmatrix}s\\t\end{pmatrix}$; and if $p \neq 0$, there is no solution.

5 (a) If $a \neq 1$, $x=\left(5-a^2\right)(1-a)^{-1}$;
$y=\left(a^2-2a-3\right)(1-a)^{-1}$;
if $a=1$, no solution
(b) If $a \neq 1$, $x=1+a$, $y=1-a$;
if $a=1$, $x=2-t$, $y=t$.
(c) If $a \neq 1$, $x=2+2a$, $y=-2a$;
if $a=1$, $x=2-t$, $y=t$.

6 (a) $x=2, y=1$
(b) No solution
(c) If $a=-7$, $x=3, y=-1$;
if $a \neq -7$, no solution.

Exercise 1B (page 156)

1 (a) $x=t, y=4t-11, z=3t-8$
(b) $x=2t, y=t-3, z=3t-2$
(c) No solution
(d) $x=s, y=2-2s+3t, z=t$
(e) $x=s$, $y=t$, $z=3-s-t$
(f) $x=2+t, y=1+t, z=t$
(g) $x=4s-5t, y=3s, z=3t$
(h) No solution
(i) $x=t, y=2s-3t+4, z=s$

2 (a) $x=1, y=2, z=-1$
(b) No solution
(c) $x=2-t, y=3-t, z=t$
(d) $x=-1-2t, y=2+t, z=t$
(e) $x=1+t, y=2-t, z=t$
(f) $x=-2, y=-3, z=-4$

3 Any non-zero multiple of $\begin{pmatrix}-5\\-6\\7\end{pmatrix}$.

4 $-3, 2$

5 $k=3, l=29$; $\begin{pmatrix}x\\y\\z\end{pmatrix}=\begin{pmatrix}5+2t\\t\\-2-2t\end{pmatrix}$

6 $k=0, 3$; if $k=0$, no solution;
if $k=3$, $x=t$, $y=3-2t$, $z=t$.

Miscellaneous exercise 1 (page 157)

1 If $ab>0$, $x=\pm\sqrt{\dfrac{b}{a}}$;
if $ab<0$, no solution;
if $a=0$ and $b \neq 0$, no solution;
if $a \neq 0$ and $b=0$, $x=0$;
if $a=0$ and $b=0$, $x=t$.

2 $x=3, y=-1, z=-2$

3 If $k \neq \pm 1$, $x=1, y=1$;
if $k=1$, $x=2-t, y=t$; if $k=-1, x=t, y=t$.

4 $\begin{pmatrix} 2 \\ -9 \\ 5 \end{pmatrix}$

5 $x = 2t, y = t, z = 7t - 8$

6 $k = 1, -\frac{1}{2}$; if $k = 1, x = -s - t, y = s, z = t$;
if $k = -\frac{1}{2}, x = t, y = t, z = t$.

7 If $a^2 \neq b^2$, $x = 1, y = 0$; if $a = b = 0$, $x = s, y = t$;
if $a \neq 0$ and $a^2 = b^2$, $x = 1 - \frac{bt}{a}, y = t$.

8 $k = 0, 1, 2$; if $k = 0, x = t, y = 0, z = 0$;
if $k = 1$, $x = -t, y = t, z = 0$;
if $k = 2, x = 0, y = t, z = t$.

9 (a) If $a \neq 1$ and $b \neq 1$, $x = \frac{a + b - 2}{(a-1)(b-1)}$;
if $a = 1$ and $b \neq 1$, or if $a \neq 1$ and $b = 1$, there is no solution;
if $a = 1$ and $b = 1$, $x = t$.
(b) If $a + b - 2 \neq 0$, $x = \frac{(a-1)(b-1)}{a + b - 2}$;
if $a = 1$ and $b = 1$, $x = t$;
if $a + b - 2 = 0$, and $a \neq 1$, no solution.

10 $a^3 + b^3 + c^3 - 3abc$;
$2(a^2 + b^2 + c^2 - bc - ca - ab)$
$3abc - a^3 - b^3 - c^3 = 0$; $a + b + c = 0$,
$p + q + r = 0$; $a = b = c$, $p = q = r$

11 $x = \frac{ab(c-b)}{(a-b)(a-c)}, y = \frac{a^2}{a-b}, z = \frac{ab}{(c-a)}$
(a) If $a \neq 0$, no solution; if $a = 0, x = -t, y = t, z = 0$.
(b) $x = 0, y = -t, z = t$
(c) $x = a - s - t, y = s, z = t$

2 Lines and planes

Your answers may differ in form from those given.

Exercise 2A (page 163)

1 (a) $\mathbf{r} = \begin{pmatrix} 1 \\ 2 \\ 3 \end{pmatrix} + t\begin{pmatrix} 0 \\ 1 \\ 2 \end{pmatrix}$ (b) $\mathbf{r} = t\begin{pmatrix} 0 \\ 0 \\ 1 \end{pmatrix}$
(c) $\mathbf{r} = \begin{pmatrix} 2 \\ -1 \\ 1 \end{pmatrix} + t\begin{pmatrix} 3 \\ -1 \\ 1 \end{pmatrix}$ (d) $\mathbf{r} = \begin{pmatrix} 3 \\ 0 \\ 2 \end{pmatrix} + t\begin{pmatrix} 4 \\ -2 \\ 3 \end{pmatrix}$

2 (a) $\mathbf{r} = \begin{pmatrix} 2 \\ -1 \\ 2 \end{pmatrix} + t\begin{pmatrix} 1 \\ 0 \\ 2 \end{pmatrix}$ (b) $\mathbf{r} = \begin{pmatrix} 1 \\ 2 \\ 2 \end{pmatrix} + t\begin{pmatrix} 1 \\ -4 \\ 0 \end{pmatrix}$
(c) $\mathbf{r} = \begin{pmatrix} 3 \\ 1 \\ 4 \end{pmatrix} + t\begin{pmatrix} -4 \\ 1 \\ -1 \end{pmatrix}$

3 They all represent the same straight line.

4 The point lies on line (a) only.

5 Set (a) lies on a straight line, but not set (b).

6 (a) $(-3,1,5)$ (b) $(3,-5,4)$

7 (a) $\frac{x-2}{1} = \frac{y+4}{-1} = \frac{z-1}{2}$
(b) $x = 1, \frac{y-5}{1} = \frac{z}{-2}$ (c) $\frac{x}{1} = \frac{y}{3} = \frac{z-1}{2}$

8 (a) $(7,0,3)$ (b) No point of intersection
(c) No point of intersection

9 $\frac{16}{21}$

Exercise 2B (page 173)

1 (a) $\mathbf{r} = s\begin{pmatrix} 1 \\ 0 \\ 0 \end{pmatrix} + t\begin{pmatrix} 0 \\ 1 \\ 0 \end{pmatrix}$
(b) $\mathbf{r} = \begin{pmatrix} 1 \\ -1 \\ 0 \end{pmatrix} + s\begin{pmatrix} -1 \\ 2 \\ -1 \end{pmatrix} + t\begin{pmatrix} -2 \\ 1 \\ 1 \end{pmatrix}$
(c) $\mathbf{r} = \begin{pmatrix} 1 \\ 2 \\ 3 \end{pmatrix} + s\begin{pmatrix} 1 \\ -3 \\ -1 \end{pmatrix} + t\begin{pmatrix} 2 \\ -1 \\ -4 \end{pmatrix}$
(d) $\mathbf{r} = \begin{pmatrix} 4 \\ -1 \\ 2 \end{pmatrix} + s\begin{pmatrix} -4 \\ 1 \\ 1 \end{pmatrix} + t\begin{pmatrix} -5 \\ 3 \\ -2 \end{pmatrix}$

2 (a) $(1,4,-3)$ (b) $(11,-1,2)$ (c) $(8,-2,8)$

3 $(-1,-1,-1)$

4 $5x - 8y + 4z = 1$

5 $2x - y - z = 4$

6 $\mathbf{i} - 4\mathbf{j} - 7\mathbf{k}$, $x - 4y - 7z = 23$

7 $x + y + z = -3$

8 (a) $z = 0$ (b) $x + y + z = 0$
(c) $11x + 2y + 5z = 30$ (d) $5x + 13y + 7z = 21$

9 There are many possibilities. Two are $(2,0,0)$ and $(0,0,1)$.

10 $(0,0,0)$, 7

11 1

13 $5x + y + 7z = 0$

14 $\mathbf{r} = \begin{pmatrix} 4 \\ 2 \\ -1 \end{pmatrix} + t\begin{pmatrix} 3 \\ 4 \\ -1 \end{pmatrix}$

15 53°

Miscellaneous exercise 2 (page 174)

1 $(-4,4,-4)$

2 It does not lie on the line.

3 61.9°

4 $8x + 3y + 4z = -11$

5 (a) $\begin{pmatrix}-6\\5\\13\end{pmatrix}$ (b) $\mathbf{r}=\begin{pmatrix}1\\2\\-3\end{pmatrix}+t\begin{pmatrix}-6\\5\\13\end{pmatrix}$

6 (a) 63.1° (b) $\mathbf{r}=\begin{pmatrix}0\\-2\\8\end{pmatrix}+t\begin{pmatrix}3\\2\\-7\end{pmatrix}$

7 $k=3$, $x=2-2t, y=t, z=1-5t$.
The solution may be written in vector form as $\mathbf{r}=\begin{pmatrix}2\\0\\1\end{pmatrix}+t\begin{pmatrix}-2\\1\\-5\end{pmatrix}$ which represents the line of intersection of the three planes whose cartesian equations are given.

8 (a) $(5,1,-1)$ is a point on the line, so the position vector of $(5,1,-1)$ is suitable for $\mathbf{a}$. The vector $2\mathbf{i}-3\mathbf{j}+\mathbf{k}$ is normal to the plane, and therefore lies along the line, and so is a suitable choice for $\mathbf{b}$.
(b) (i) 69° or 111°

9 (a) $\mathbf{r}=2\mathbf{i}+\mathbf{j}-\mathbf{k}+t(\mathbf{i}-\mathbf{j})$, $\mathbf{r}=5\mathbf{i}-2\mathbf{j}-\mathbf{k}+t(\mathbf{j}+2\mathbf{k})$
(c) 71.6° or 108.4°
(e) $2x+2y-z=7$

10 $\left|\dfrac{ap+bq+cr-d}{\sqrt{a^2+b^2+c^2}}\right|$

11 $a=2$; $\dfrac{x-2}{9}=\dfrac{y-1}{-7}=\dfrac{z-(-2)}{13}$

3 The vector product

Exercise 3A (page 180)

1 (a) $-\mathbf{j}$ (b) $\mathbf{0}$ (c) $\mathbf{k}$
(d) $\mathbf{0}$ (e) $-\mathbf{i}$ (f) $\mathbf{i}$
(g) $\mathbf{0}$ (h) -1 (i) $\mathbf{j}$

2 (a) $\begin{pmatrix}-13\\-4\\7\end{pmatrix}$ (b) $\begin{pmatrix}-5\\-1\\7\end{pmatrix}$ (c) $\begin{pmatrix}-9\\-10\\-2\end{pmatrix}$
(d) $\begin{pmatrix}0\\8\\4\end{pmatrix}$ (e) $\begin{pmatrix}0\\0\\1\end{pmatrix}$ (f) $\begin{pmatrix}-2\\-2\\1\end{pmatrix}$

3 (a) $-2\mathbf{j}+2\mathbf{k}$ (b) $\mathbf{i}+\mathbf{j}+\mathbf{k}$
(c) $12\mathbf{i}-10\mathbf{j}-9\mathbf{k}$ (d) $2\mathbf{i}+2\mathbf{j}+3\mathbf{k}$
(e) $-4\mathbf{j}-5\mathbf{k}$ (f) $3\mathbf{i}-42\mathbf{j}-22\mathbf{k}$

4 $\frac{1}{2}\sqrt{122}$

Exercise 3B (page 182)

1 (a) $4x+y+11z=37$ (b) $x+y+z=0$
(c) $3x-8y+7z=4$ (d) $x-y=-1$

2 They lie in the plane $5x+y=10$.

3 $\dfrac{x+7}{33}=\dfrac{y-3}{-9}=z$

4 $\mathbf{r}=\begin{pmatrix}4\\2\\-3\end{pmatrix}+t\begin{pmatrix}2\\3\\-4\end{pmatrix}$

5 $2x+y-z=0$

6 $5x-y+7z=20$

7 $5x-y+3z=12$

Exercise 3C (page 184)

1 $\mathbf{r}=t(2\mathbf{i}+\mathbf{k})$

2 $\mathbf{r}=\begin{pmatrix}1\\2\\1\end{pmatrix}+t\begin{pmatrix}-1\\2\\-1\end{pmatrix}$

3 3

Miscellaneous exercise 3 (page 184)

1 (a) $\begin{pmatrix}2\\7\\5\end{pmatrix}$ (b) $\begin{pmatrix}14\\-13\\23\end{pmatrix}$ (c) $\begin{pmatrix}0\\-3\\0\end{pmatrix}$

2 (a) $-6\mathbf{j}$ (b) $-10\mathbf{i}+5\mathbf{j}$ (c) $\mathbf{0}$

3 $2x-3y-8z=28$

5 $3x-2y-z=16$

6 $\dfrac{2}{\sqrt{17}}$

7 (a) $\begin{pmatrix}1\\-2\\2\end{pmatrix}, \begin{pmatrix}-2\\-3\\5\end{pmatrix}$ (b) $\frac{1}{2}\sqrt{146}$

8 (a) $\mathbf{r}=\begin{pmatrix}2\\-1\\1\end{pmatrix}+t\begin{pmatrix}-1\\3\\-4\end{pmatrix}$, $\mathbf{r}=\begin{pmatrix}1\\-1\\1\end{pmatrix}+t\begin{pmatrix}0\\-3\\4\end{pmatrix}$
(b) $(1,2,-3)$ (c) $\cos^{-1}\dfrac{5}{\sqrt{26}}$ (d) $\begin{pmatrix}0\\4\\3\end{pmatrix}$

9 (a) $\begin{pmatrix}7\\4\\1\end{pmatrix}$
(b) (i) $\mathbf{r}\cdot\begin{pmatrix}7\\4\\1\end{pmatrix}=14$ (ii) $\frac{1}{2}\sqrt{66}$

10 (a) $\dfrac{1}{\sqrt{6}}\begin{pmatrix}1\\-1\\2\end{pmatrix}$ (b) $\sqrt{6}$

11 (a) 3 (b) $\begin{pmatrix}-17\\-10\\14\end{pmatrix}$ (c) $\dfrac{21}{\sqrt{65}}$

12 (a) $\begin{pmatrix}9\\-11\\-3\end{pmatrix}$ (b) $\mathbf{r}=\begin{pmatrix}8\\-7\\4\end{pmatrix}+t\begin{pmatrix}1\\4\\-1\end{pmatrix}$

(c) $\frac{1}{9}\begin{pmatrix}8\\-1\\4\end{pmatrix}$ (d) $\frac{71}{9}$

13 (a) $\begin{pmatrix}7\\-7\\14\end{pmatrix}$ (b) $(11,6,-2)$

(c) $x-y+2z-1=0$

(d) $11x-5y-8z-107=0$

14 $\left|\dfrac{(\mathbf{a}-\mathbf{c})\cdot(\mathbf{b}\times\mathbf{d})}{|\mathbf{b}\times\mathbf{d}|}\right|$

4 Matrices

Exercise 4A (page 193)

1 (a) $\begin{pmatrix}3&5\\7&3\end{pmatrix}$ (b) $\begin{pmatrix}-1&-1\\-1&5\end{pmatrix}$

(c) $\begin{pmatrix}7&12\\17&10\end{pmatrix}$ (d) $\begin{pmatrix}-2&-1\\0&19\end{pmatrix}$

2 $\mathbf{X}=\frac{3}{2}(\mathbf{A}+\mathbf{B})$; they are all the same size.

4 $\begin{pmatrix}10&1\\22&5\end{pmatrix}$, $\begin{pmatrix}11&16\\1&4\end{pmatrix}$

5 $\begin{pmatrix}21&3&-1\\29&-19&8\\-18&-4&7\end{pmatrix}$, $\begin{pmatrix}15&12&-20\\5&14&4\\-3&-8&-20\end{pmatrix}$

6 $\begin{pmatrix}0&-8\\13&0\end{pmatrix}$, $\begin{pmatrix}-14&10&40\\-5&4&22\\-8&5&10\end{pmatrix}$

7 For example, $\begin{pmatrix}1&-2\\-2&1\end{pmatrix}$ and $\begin{pmatrix}2&-3\\-3&2\end{pmatrix}$.

8 (a) Does not exist. (b) $\begin{pmatrix}-3\\-8\end{pmatrix}$

(c) $\begin{pmatrix}2&3&1\\-2&-3&-1\\2&3&1\end{pmatrix}$ (d) (0)

(e) Does not exist. (f) Does not exist.

(g) Does not exist. (h) Does not exist.

9 $\begin{pmatrix}7&-2\\-3&1\end{pmatrix}$, $\begin{pmatrix}1&0\\0&1\end{pmatrix}$; no such matrix.

11 $\begin{pmatrix}19&-2&-8\\-7&1&3\\-2&0&1\end{pmatrix}$, $\begin{pmatrix}1&0&0\\0&1&0\\0&0&1\end{pmatrix}$

14 $\mathbf{OA}=\mathbf{AO}=\mathbf{O}$

Exercise 4B (page 198)

1 $\begin{pmatrix}2&-3\\-3&5\end{pmatrix}$

2 $\begin{pmatrix}3&-2\\-7&5\end{pmatrix}$

3 (a) $\begin{pmatrix}2&-1\\-\frac{3}{2}&1\end{pmatrix}$ (b) $\begin{pmatrix}7&5\\-3&-2\end{pmatrix}$

(c) $\dfrac{1}{ad-bc}\begin{pmatrix}d&-b\\-c&a\end{pmatrix}$, provided $ad-bc\neq 0$

4 (a) $\begin{pmatrix}-38\\22\end{pmatrix}$ (b) $\begin{pmatrix}-38&-12\\22&8\end{pmatrix}$

6 $\begin{pmatrix}-\frac{5}{2}&\frac{3}{2}\\2&-1\end{pmatrix}$, $x=2, y=-1$

7 $\begin{pmatrix}1&0&0\\-4-2k&3+k&2+k\\0&0&1\end{pmatrix}$, $\begin{pmatrix}1&4&-5\\1&5&-2\\1&3&-7\end{pmatrix}$

Miscellaneous exercise 4 (page 199)

2 It is the 3×3 identity matrix.

3 (b) (i) $\mathbf{M}^2-2\mathbf{M}+17\mathbf{I}=\mathbf{O}$ (ii) $-\frac{1}{17}$, $\frac{2}{17}$

4 $\mathbf{P}=\begin{pmatrix}-1&2\\0&1\end{pmatrix}$, $a=-1, b=2, d=1$; $\mathbf{Q}=\begin{pmatrix}1&0\\-3&1\end{pmatrix}$

5 (a) -1 (b) $\begin{pmatrix}-1&1\\1&3\end{pmatrix}$

6 (b) The result is true for $n=-1$.

7 (a) $\begin{pmatrix}20+3p&0&0\\-28+2p&62&0\\28-2p&0&62\end{pmatrix}$

(b) (i) $p=14$, $k=62$

(ii) $\dfrac{1}{62}\begin{pmatrix}-4&13&7\\12&-8&10\\14&1&-9\end{pmatrix}$

8 No! In part (c) it is not claimed that there are any matrices such that $[\mathbf{A},\mathbf{B}]=\mathbf{I}$. However, if there were such matrices, $[\mathbf{A},\mathbf{B}^m]=m\mathbf{B}^{m-1}$.

5 Matrices and transformations

Exercise 5A (page 204)

1 (a) Reflection in the x-axis.
(b) Reflection in the line $y=x$.
(c) Rotation $\frac{1}{2}\pi$ clockwise about the origin.
(d) Shear parallel to x-axis of angle $\frac{1}{4}\pi$.
(e) Half-turn about the origin.
(f) Stretch in x-direction, scale factor 2.
(g) Enlargement about the origin, scale factor 2, and half-turn about the origin.
(h) Projection onto the line $y=x$, followed by enlargement about the origin with scale factor $\sqrt{2}$.

2 Rotation anticlockwise about the origin through angle of $\cos^{-1}0.8$.

3 Spiral enlargement about the origin, angle $\cos^{-1}0.6$ and scale factor 5.

4 All points are transformed to $(0,0)$.

5 $\frac{1}{2}\pi$

6 120° anticlockwise

Exercise 5B (page 208)

1 (a) $\begin{pmatrix}-1 & 0\\ 0 & 1\end{pmatrix}$ (b) $\begin{pmatrix}0 & -1\\ -1 & 0\end{pmatrix}$ (c) $\begin{pmatrix}1 & 1\\ 0 & 1\end{pmatrix}$

2 (a) $\begin{pmatrix}\frac{1}{2} & -\frac{1}{2}\sqrt{3}\\ \frac{1}{2}\sqrt{3} & \frac{1}{2}\end{pmatrix}$ (b) $\dfrac{1}{\sqrt{a^2+b^2}}\begin{pmatrix}a & -b\\ b & a\end{pmatrix}$

3 $\begin{pmatrix}\frac{25}{169} & \frac{60}{169}\\ \frac{60}{169} & \frac{144}{169}\end{pmatrix}$

4 (a) $(t,2t,2t)$ where $t=\frac{1}{9}(x+2y+2z)$,

$\frac{1}{9}\begin{pmatrix}1 & 2 & 2\\ 2 & 4 & 4\\ 2 & 4 & 4\end{pmatrix}$

(b) $x+2y+2z=9s$
(c) All points (x,y,z) are projected orthogonally onto the plane through the origin with normal vector $\begin{pmatrix}1\\ 2\\ 2\end{pmatrix}$.

Exercise 5C (page 210)

1 $\mathbf{A}=\begin{pmatrix}\frac{1}{2}\sqrt{3} & -\frac{1}{2}\\ \frac{1}{2} & \frac{1}{2}\sqrt{3}\end{pmatrix}$; $\mathbf{B}=\begin{pmatrix}\frac{1}{2} & -\frac{1}{2}\sqrt{3}\\ \frac{1}{2}\sqrt{3} & \frac{1}{2}\end{pmatrix}$. $\mathbf{B}=\mathbf{A}^2$ because a rotation of $\frac{1}{6}\pi$ followed by a rotation of $\frac{1}{6}\pi$ gives a rotation of $\frac{1}{3}\pi$; $\mathbf{AB}=\mathbf{BA}$ because rotations about the origin are commutative.

2 $\mathbf{QP}=\begin{pmatrix}0 & -1\\ -1 & 0\end{pmatrix}$; 6 multiplications by $\mathbf{M}$ will do because $\mathbf{M}^3=\mathbf{P}^2$ is a half-turn about the origin, so $\mathbf{M}^6=\left(\mathbf{M}^3\right)^2=\mathbf{I}$.

3 $\mathbf{N}=\begin{pmatrix}\cos^2\alpha & \sin\alpha\cos\alpha\\ \sin\alpha\cos\alpha & \sin^2\alpha\end{pmatrix}$; $\mathbf{N}$ carries out an orthogonal projection onto the line $y=x\tan\alpha$. The equation $\mathbf{N}^2=\mathbf{N}$ shows that once a point has been projected, it stays where it is.

4 $\mathbf{M}$ carries out a spiral enlargement about the origin with angle $\tan^{-1}\dfrac{b}{a}$ anticlockwise and scale factor $\sqrt{a^2+b^2}$. This is equivalent to multiplying a complex number by $a+b\mathrm{i}$.

Miscellaneous exercise 5 (page 211)

1 $\mathbf{M}=\begin{pmatrix}-\frac{1}{2}\sqrt{3} & -\frac{1}{2}\\ \frac{1}{2} & -\frac{1}{2}\sqrt{3}\end{pmatrix}$, since $\mathbf{M}$ carries out an anticlockwise rotation of $\frac{2}{3}\pi$ about the origin.

2 (a) $\mathbf{A}(\theta)$ is a reflection in the line $y=x\tan\frac{1}{2}\theta$.
(b) $\phi=\alpha-\beta$; a reflection in the line $y=x\tan\frac{1}{2}\beta$ followed by a reflection in the line $y=x\tan\frac{1}{2}\alpha$ is equivalent to a rotation of $\alpha-\beta$.
(c) Successive reflections in lines $y=x\tan\frac{1}{2}\gamma$, then $y=x\tan\frac{1}{2}\beta$, then $y=x\tan\frac{1}{2}\alpha$, are equivalent to successive reflections in $y=x\tan\frac{1}{2}\alpha$, then $y=x\tan\frac{1}{2}\beta$, then $y=x\tan\frac{1}{2}\gamma$.

3 $\mathbf{S}$ carries out a shear parallel to the y-axis, of angle $\tan^{-1}2$. Its image will lie on $y=x$. $\mathbf{R}$ carries out a half-turn about the origin. $\mathbf{X}=\mathbf{S}$ and so represents the same transformation as $\mathbf{S}$.

4 Rotation through $\frac{1}{4}\pi$ about the origin.

(a) $\begin{pmatrix}\sqrt{2} & 0\\ 0 & 1\end{pmatrix}$

(b) Stretch in the x-direction, factor $\sqrt{2}$.

5 $-\frac{3}{10}$, -1

6 (a) $\begin{pmatrix}\frac{1}{2} & -\frac{1}{2}\sqrt{3}\\ \frac{1}{2}\sqrt{3} & \frac{1}{2}\end{pmatrix}$

(b) $\begin{pmatrix}2 & 0\\ 0 & 1\end{pmatrix}$

(c) $\begin{pmatrix}1 & -\sqrt{3}\\ \frac{1}{2}\sqrt{3} & \frac{1}{2}\end{pmatrix}$

7 A reflection in the y-axis, and a stretch, with scale factor 2, parallel to the y-axis.

$\mathbf{A}=\begin{pmatrix}-1 & 0\\ 0 & 1\end{pmatrix}$, $\mathbf{B}=\begin{pmatrix}1 & 0\\ 0 & 2\end{pmatrix}$

8 A shear, parallel to the negative x-axis, of angle $-\frac{1}{4}\pi$.

(a) $\mathbf{B}=\begin{pmatrix}\frac{1}{2} & \frac{1}{2}\sqrt{3}\\ -\frac{1}{2}\sqrt{3} & \frac{1}{2}\end{pmatrix}$

(b) Rotation through $\frac{1}{3}\pi$ clockwise about the origin.

9 It is an orthogonal projection onto the line in the direction of the vector $\begin{pmatrix}l\\ m\\ n\end{pmatrix}$.

6 Determinants and inverses

Exercise 6A (page 221)

1 (a) 0 (b) 1 (c) 1

2 (a) $\cos 2n\theta$ (b) 1 (c) $-\cosh 2\alpha$

3 (a) $\alpha=\pm 1$ (b) $\alpha=\pm(1-k)$
(c) $\alpha=\beta+n\pi,\ n\in\mathbb{Z}$

4 (a) -3 (b) 0 (c) 2

5 (a) 1 (b) -1 (c) abc

6 (a) ± 2 (b) $-1, 4$ (c) 1, 2 ,13

7 (a) $\begin{pmatrix}1 & 0\\ -\dfrac{c}{a} & 1\end{pmatrix}$ (b) $\begin{pmatrix}b\\ d-\dfrac{cb}{a}\end{pmatrix}$

(c) The parallelogram has base a and height $d-\dfrac{cb}{a}$, so its area is $a\left(d-\dfrac{cb}{a}\right)=ad-bc$.

(d) Consider it as a special case; no transformation is needed to find the area.

8 If you enlarge a solid figure with scale factor k, its volume is enlarged by a factor k^3.

Exercise 6B (page 230)

1 (a) $\begin{pmatrix}\frac{1}{2} & \frac{1}{2}\\ -\frac{1}{2} & \frac{1}{2}\end{pmatrix}$ (b) $\begin{pmatrix}7 & -9\\ -3 & 4\end{pmatrix}$ (c) $\begin{pmatrix}7 & 5\\ 4 & 3\end{pmatrix}$

2 (a) $\begin{pmatrix}-3 & 2 & -1\\ 1 & 1 & 1\\ 2 & 0 & 1\end{pmatrix}$ (b) $\begin{pmatrix}1 & -1 & \frac{1}{2}\\ -1 & 1 & -1\\ 1 & 0 & \frac{1}{2}\end{pmatrix}$

(c) $\begin{pmatrix}-\frac{1}{2} & \frac{2}{3} & \frac{1}{6}\\ -\frac{1}{2} & \frac{1}{3} & -\frac{1}{6}\\ -\frac{1}{2} & 0 & \frac{1}{2}\end{pmatrix}$

3 (a) $\begin{pmatrix}\frac{4}{3} & \frac{1}{3}\\ \frac{5}{3} & \frac{2}{3}\end{pmatrix}$ (b) No inverse (c) $\begin{pmatrix}-1 & \frac{3}{5}\\ -2 & 1\end{pmatrix}$

4 (a) $\begin{pmatrix}-\frac{7}{6} & -\frac{1}{6} & \frac{5}{6}\\ -\frac{1}{3} & \frac{2}{3} & -\frac{1}{3}\\ -\frac{1}{2} & -\frac{1}{2} & \frac{1}{2}\end{pmatrix}$ (b) $\begin{pmatrix}\frac{13}{2} & 4 & -\frac{9}{2}\\ \frac{9}{2} & 3 & -\frac{7}{2}\\ -\frac{7}{2} & -2 & \frac{5}{2}\end{pmatrix}$

(c) No inverse

5 (a) $x=4, y=-3$ (b) $x=-3, y=2$
(c) $x=2, y=1$

6 (a) $x=4, y=3, z=1$ (b) $x=2, y=2, z=1$
(c) $x=1, y=1, z=2$

7 $\mathbf{D}=\begin{pmatrix}1 & 1\\ -1 & 1\end{pmatrix}$ (a) $2\mathrm{e}^x(b\cos x-a\sin x)$

(b) $\frac{1}{2}\mathrm{e}^x((a-b)\cos x+(a+b)\sin x)+k$

$$\frac{\mathrm{e}^{px}}{p^2+q^2}\begin{pmatrix}(pa-qb)\cos qx\\ +(pb+qa)\sin qx\end{pmatrix}+k$$

Miscellaneous exercise 6 (page 231)

1 (a) $5, -4$

2 (a) (ii) $\frac{1}{20}\begin{pmatrix}2 & 1 & -3\\ 2 & 3 & 3\\ -4 & 2 & 2\end{pmatrix}$

(b) $x=-2, y=6, z=-3$

3 $k=3$; $x=\frac{8}{5}+\frac{2}{5}t,\ y=\frac{1}{5}-\frac{1}{5}t,\ z=t$
This represents the line of intersection of the three planes.

4 $\mathbf{M}=\begin{pmatrix}-1 & 3 & 1\\ 0 & 4 & 2\\ 1 & -1 & 1\end{pmatrix}$; $\begin{pmatrix}-\frac{5}{2}\\ -\frac{1}{2}\\ 1\end{pmatrix}$

5 (a) $28a-84$

(c) $\dfrac{1}{28a-84}\begin{pmatrix}-34 & 6a-35 & 4a+5\\ -10 & -4a+7 & 2a-1\\ 28 & 14 & -14\end{pmatrix}$,

$\dfrac{1}{28a-84}\begin{pmatrix}-8a-44\\ -4a-8\\ 56\end{pmatrix}$

(d) The equations represent three planes which meet in a line (sheaf), so the solution of the equations is not unique.

6 (a) All real numbers except 2.

(b) $\dfrac{1}{10a-20}\begin{pmatrix}5a-28 & 5 & 4\\ 9a & -5 & -2a\\ -36 & 10 & 8\end{pmatrix}$

(c) $x=\dfrac{a-7}{2a-4},\ y=\dfrac{a+3}{2a-4},\ z=\dfrac{-5}{a-2}$

7 (a) $\mathbf{I}$, $\mathbf{Q}^{-1}\mathbf{P}^{-1}$

(b) $\begin{pmatrix} 2a^2 & 0 & 0 \\ 0 & 2a^2 & 0 \\ 0 & 0 & 2a^2 \end{pmatrix}$, $\dfrac{1}{2a^2}\begin{pmatrix} a & a^2 & a^2 \\ -1 & a & a \\ 0 & 0 & -a \end{pmatrix}$

(c) $\frac{1}{2}\begin{pmatrix} 1 & 1 & 1 \\ -1 & 1 & 1 \\ 0 & 0 & -1 \end{pmatrix}$, $\frac{1}{8}\begin{pmatrix} 2 & -4 & 0 \\ 1 & 2 & 4 \\ 0 & 0 & -4 \end{pmatrix}$,

$\frac{1}{16}\begin{pmatrix} 6 & -2 & -2 \\ -1 & 3 & -1 \\ 0 & 0 & 4 \end{pmatrix}$

8 $\dfrac{1}{6(a-1)}\begin{pmatrix} 3a-1 & a+1 & -4 \\ 1 & 2a-1 & -2 \\ -3 & -3 & 6 \end{pmatrix}$,

$\left(\dfrac{a-11}{6(a-1)}, \dfrac{2a-7}{6(a-1)}, \dfrac{5}{2(a-1)}\right)$

9 (a) $\dfrac{1}{-2a^2+7a-8}\begin{pmatrix} 3a-1 & a-18 & 6-a^2 \\ -1 & 6-2a & a-2 \\ 1-2a & 10 & 2a-6 \end{pmatrix}$

(c) $\left(\frac{19}{5}, \frac{2}{5}, -2\right)$

10 -2, $\frac{1}{2}$; the planes form a triangular prism.

Revision exercise 3 (page 234)

1 $\mathbf{AB} = (a-3)\mathbf{I}$, $\mathbf{A}^{-1} = \dfrac{1}{a-3}\mathbf{B}$;

$x = \dfrac{-1}{a-3}$, $y = \dfrac{3a-4}{a-3}$, $z = -\dfrac{2a-4}{a-3}$;

no solution; the planes represented by the first two equations are parallel, with the third plane intersecting them both.

2 (c) The three planes intersect in a common line.

3 $2x - 2y + z = 3$

(a) 4 (b) 7.76

4 (a) 22 (b) $12\mathbf{i} - 15\mathbf{j} - 9\mathbf{k}$; 2.27

5 (a) $\dfrac{1}{1+a}\begin{pmatrix} 1 & -a & 0 \\ 1 & 1 & 0 \\ -a-5 & a^2-5 & 1+a \end{pmatrix}$

(b) $(-1,1,0)$

6 $3\mathbf{i} + 4\mathbf{j} + \mathbf{k}$, $3x - 2y - 2z = -1$

7 (a) $\begin{pmatrix} 4 & 3 \\ 3 & -4 \end{pmatrix}$ (b) $(-4, 22)$

8 (a) $\mathbf{C} = \begin{pmatrix} \frac{1}{2} & \frac{1}{2}\sqrt{3} \\ \frac{1}{2}\sqrt{3} & -\frac{1}{2} \end{pmatrix}$

(b) Reflection in the line $y = \dfrac{1}{\sqrt{3}}x$.

9 (a) $\begin{pmatrix} 1 & 0 & 0 \\ 1 & -1 & 0 \\ -\frac{1}{a} & 0 & \frac{1}{a} \end{pmatrix}$ (b) $\begin{pmatrix} \frac{1}{a} & 1 & -\frac{1}{a} \\ 1-\frac{1}{2a} & -1 & \frac{1}{2a} \\ -\frac{1}{2a} & 0 & \frac{1}{2a} \end{pmatrix}$

10 (a) $(0,0)$, $(3,0)$, $(2,4)$

(b) 6, 150 (c) 6

7 De Moivre's theorem

Exercise 7A (page 242)

1 (a) 16 (b) $-\frac{1}{512}$ (c) $\dfrac{1+\mathrm{i}}{\sqrt{2}}$

(d) -1 (e) $-\mathrm{i}$

(f) $(8.98 - 4.40\mathrm{i}) \times 10^{29}$ (g) $1.57 - 1.1\mathrm{i}$

(h) $-0.692 - 0.722\mathrm{i}$

2 (a) 2, negative (b) none

(c) 5, positive (d) 3, negative

(e) 6, negative (f) none

(g) 4, negative (h) none

3 (a) ± 1, $\pm\mathrm{i}$, $\dfrac{\pm 1 \pm \mathrm{i}}{\sqrt{2}}$ (the $\pm$ signs are independent of each other)

(b) 1, $0.623 \pm 0.782\mathrm{i}$, $-0.223 \pm 0.975\mathrm{i}$, $-0.901 \pm 0.434\mathrm{i}$

4 (a) $a^2 - ab + b^2$

(b) $a^4 - a^3b + a^2b^2 - ab^3 + b^4$

5 $\beta = \alpha^2$, $\gamma = \alpha^3$, $\delta = \alpha^4$;

(a) 1 (b) -1 (c) 1

(d) 2 (e) -1

6 (a) $\pm\mathrm{i}$ (b) -1, $\exp\left(\pm\frac{1}{3}\pi\mathrm{i}\right)$

(c) $\exp\left(\pm\frac{1}{4}\pi\mathrm{i}\right)$, $\exp\left(\pm\frac{3}{4}\pi\mathrm{i}\right)$

(d) -1, $\exp\left(\pm\frac{1}{5}\pi\mathrm{i}\right)$, $\exp\left(\pm\frac{3}{5}\pi\mathrm{i}\right)$

(e) $\exp\left(\pm\frac{1}{6}\pi\mathrm{i}\right)$, $\pm\mathrm{i}$, $\exp\left(\pm\frac{5}{6}\pi\mathrm{i}\right)$;

$\exp\left(\dfrac{r\pi\mathrm{i}}{n}\right)$ for $r = \pm 1, \pm 3, \ldots, \pm(n-1)$ if n is even,

-1 and $\exp\left(\dfrac{r\pi\mathrm{i}}{n}\right)$ for $r = \pm 1, \pm 3, \ldots, \pm(n-2)$ if n is odd

9 $y = -c\omega^2 - a\omega$, $z = -a\omega^2 - b\omega$;

$a + b\omega^2 + c\omega$, $b + c\omega^2 + a\omega$, $c + a\omega^2 + b\omega$

Exercise 7B (page 246)

1 (a) i, $\pm\frac{1}{2}\sqrt{3} + \frac{1}{2}\mathrm{i}$

(b) $\pm\left(\sqrt{3} - \mathrm{i}\right)$, $\pm\left(1 + \sqrt{3}\mathrm{i}\right)$

(c) $\pm 2\mathrm{i}$, $\pm\sqrt{3} \pm \mathrm{i}$

2 (a) $\pm(0.924-0.383\mathrm{i})$, $\pm(0.383+0.924\mathrm{i})$
(b) $-1-\mathrm{i}$, $1.397+0.221\mathrm{i}$, $0.221+1.397\mathrm{i}$
$-1.260+0.642\mathrm{i}$, $0.642-1.260\mathrm{i}$

3 (a) $(z^2-\sqrt{2}z+1)(z^2+\sqrt{2}z+1)$
(b) $(z-\sqrt{2})(z+\sqrt{2})(z^2+2)$
$\times(z^2-2z+2)(z^2+2z+2)$
(c) $(z^2-z+1)(z^2+z+1)$
(d) $(z^2-2z\cos\frac{1}{9}\pi+1)\times(z^2-2z\cos\frac{5}{9}\pi+1)$
$\times(z^2-2z\cos\frac{7}{9}\pi+1)$

4 Answers are $\exp(k\pi\mathrm{i})$ for the stated values of k.
(a) Both $\pm\frac{1}{3}$, 1
(b) (i) $\frac{1}{2}$ (ii) $\pm\frac{1}{2}$
(c) (i) $-\frac{1}{4},\frac{3}{4}$, (ii) $\pm\frac{1}{4},\pm\frac{3}{4}$
(d) (i) $\frac{3}{8},\frac{5}{8}$
(ii) $\frac{1}{24},\frac{3}{8},\frac{17}{24},-\frac{7}{24},-\frac{5}{8},-\frac{23}{24}$;
$(z^p)^{\frac{1}{q}}$ always has q distinct values; $\left(z^{\frac{1}{q}}\right)^p$ has q distinct values if p and q have no common factors, otherwise it has $\frac{q}{h}$ distinct values where h is the highest common factor of p and q.

7 (a) 2 (b) n

Miscellaneous exercise 7 (page 247)

1 $\sqrt{2}\exp(\frac{1}{4}\pi\mathrm{i}), 2\sqrt{2}\exp(\frac{3}{4}\pi\mathrm{i})$;
$\sqrt{2}\exp(\frac{11}{12}\pi\mathrm{i}), 2\sqrt{2}\exp(-\frac{5}{12}\pi\mathrm{i})$;
$\sqrt{2}\exp(-\frac{11}{12}\pi\mathrm{i}), \sqrt{2}\exp(-\frac{1}{4}\pi\mathrm{i}), \sqrt{2}\exp(\frac{5}{12}\pi\mathrm{i})$

2 $8\mathrm{e}^{\frac{1}{2}\pi\mathrm{i}}$; $-2\mathrm{i}, \pm\sqrt{3}+\mathrm{i}$;
$1-3\sqrt{3}\mathrm{i}, 1-\sqrt{3}\mathrm{i}, -2-2\sqrt{3}\mathrm{i}$

3 $\exp\left(\frac{(2r+1)\pi}{n}\mathrm{i}\right)$

4 $\pm1\pm\mathrm{i}$; $-1\pm2\mathrm{i}, \frac{1}{5}(-1\pm2\mathrm{i})$

5 -2, $2\mathrm{e}^{\pm\frac{1}{5}\pi\mathrm{i}}, 2\mathrm{e}^{\pm\frac{3}{5}\pi\mathrm{i}}$; $\pm\frac{1}{10}\pi, \pm\frac{3}{10}\pi$

8 Further trigonometry

Exercise 8A (page 254)

1 (a) $3s-4s^3$
(b) $16s^5-20s^3+5s$
(c) $32c^6-48c^4+18c^2-1$
(d) $2cs(16s^4-16s^2+3)$
(e) $256c^9-576c^7+432c^5-120c^3+9c$
(f) $256s^9-576s^7+432s^5-120s^3+9s$

2 (a) $\dfrac{4t-4t^3}{1-6t^2+t^4}$
(b) $\dfrac{7t-35t^3+21t^5-t^7}{1-21t^2+35t^4-7t^6}$
(c) $\dfrac{8t-56t^3+56t^5-8t^7}{1-28t^2+70t^4-28t^6+t^8}$

3 $16c^4-16c^2+3=0$; $\frac{1}{2}\sqrt{3}=\cos\frac{1}{6}\pi, \frac{1}{2}=\cos\frac{1}{3}\pi$,
$-\frac{1}{2}=\cos\frac{2}{3}\pi, -\frac{1}{2}\sqrt{3}=\cos\frac{5}{6}\pi$

4 $cs(16s^4-16s^2+3)=0$; $0=\sin 0$,
$\pm\frac{1}{2}=\sin(\pm\frac{1}{6}\pi), \pm\frac{1}{2}\sqrt{3}=\sin(\pm\frac{1}{3}\pi), 0=\cos\frac{1}{2}\pi$

5 $8s^4-8s^2+1=0$; $\frac{1}{2}\sqrt{2-\sqrt{2}}$

6 $\tan\frac{5}{16}\pi, -\tan\frac{3}{16}\pi, -\tan\frac{7}{16}\pi$; $\sqrt{4+2\sqrt{2}}-\sqrt{2}-1$

8 $0, -\frac{3}{4}, \frac{1}{8}$

9 $32s^5-40s^2+10s-1=0$;
$\sin\frac{1}{30}\pi, \sin\frac{1}{6}\pi, \sin\frac{13}{30}\pi, -\sin\frac{7}{30}\pi, -\sin\frac{11}{30}\pi$;
$2s-1$

10 $k=2$, $a=-\frac{1}{2}$, $1.827, 1.338, -0.209, -1, -1.956$

11 $C^n+\binom{n}{2}C^{n-2}S^2+\binom{n}{4}C^{n-4}S^4+\ldots$,
$\binom{n}{1}C^{n-1}S+\binom{n}{3}C^{n-3}S^3+\binom{n}{5}C^{n-5}S^5+\ldots$

12 (a) $4C^3-3C$
(b) $4S^3+3S$
(c) $16C^5-20C^3+5C$
(d) $64S^7+112S^5+56S^3+7S$
(e) $8CS(16S^6+24S^4+10S^2+1)$

13 2.279

14 1.406

15 (a) $2.732, -0.732, -2$
(b) 3.625
(c) 0.760
(d) -4.107
(e) $3.233, 0.423, -3.656\ldots$

Exercise 8B (page 257)

1 (a) $\frac{1}{4}(\cos 3\theta+3\cos\theta)$
(b) $\frac{1}{8}(\cos 4\theta-4\cos 2\theta+3)$
(c) $\frac{1}{32}(\cos 6\theta+6\cos 4\theta+15\cos 2\theta+10)$
(d) $\frac{1}{64}(-\sin 7\theta+7\sin 5\theta-21\sin 3\theta+35\sin\theta)$
(e) $\frac{1}{16}(-\sin 5\theta+\sin 3\theta+2\sin\theta)$
(f) $\frac{1}{64}(\cos 7\theta-\cos 5\theta-3\cos 3\theta+3\cos\theta)$

2 (a) $\frac{1}{4}(\cosh 3u+3\cosh u)$
(b) $\frac{1}{8}(\cosh 4u-4\cosh 2u+3)$
(c) $\frac{1}{32}(\cosh 6u+6\cosh 4u+15\cosh 2u+10)$
(d) $\frac{1}{64}(\sinh 7u-7\sinh 5u+21\sinh 3u-35\sinh u)$
(e) $\frac{1}{16}(\sinh 5u-\sinh 3u-2\sinh u)$
(f) $\frac{1}{64}(\cosh 7u-\cosh 5u-3\cosh 3u+3\cosh u)$

3 (a) $\frac{1}{32}\sin 4\theta+\frac{1}{4}\sin 2\theta+\frac{3}{8}\theta+k$
(b) $-\frac{1}{80}\cos 5\theta+\frac{5}{48}\cos 3\theta-\frac{5}{8}\cos\theta+k$
(c) $\frac{1}{80}\sin 5\theta+\frac{1}{48}\sin 3\theta-\frac{1}{8}\sin\theta+k$

4 (a) $\frac{1}{32}\sinh 4u+\frac{1}{4}\sinh 2u+\frac{3}{8}u+k$
(b) $\frac{1}{80}\cosh 5u-\frac{5}{48}\cosh 3u+\frac{5}{8}\cosh u+k$
(c) $\frac{1}{80}\sinh 5u+\frac{1}{48}\sinh 3u-\frac{1}{8}\sinh u+k$

5 (a) $\frac{2}{3}-\frac{5}{12}\sqrt{2}$ (b) $\frac{35}{256}\pi$ (c) $\frac{1}{16}\pi$

Exercise 8C (page 261)

2 $-\dfrac{\sin 20\theta}{2\cos\theta}, \dfrac{1-\cos 20\theta}{2\cos\theta}$

3 $\dfrac{\cos\left(\alpha+\frac{1}{2}(n-1)\theta\right)\sin\frac{1}{2}n\theta}{\sin\frac{1}{2}\theta}$; terms are the projection on a line of sides of a regular n-gon.

4 (a) $\dfrac{9\sin\theta}{10+6\cos\theta}$
(b) $\cosh(\cos\theta)\cos(\sin\theta)$
(c) $\sin^n\theta\cos n\theta,\ \sin^n\theta\sin n\theta,\ -\sin^n\theta\cos n\theta,$ $-\sin^n\theta\sin n\theta$

5 $\dfrac{9\sinh u}{10+6\cosh u}$, $|u|<\ln 3$

6 $\sinh^n u\cosh nu,\ -\sinh^n u\sinh nu$

7 (a) $-3-4\mathrm{i}$ (b) $3.06+1.29\mathrm{i}$
(c) $34.78+43.76\mathrm{i}$ (d) $5.23+8.72\mathrm{i}$

8 $\dfrac{\beta}{n}\cos\dfrac{(n\mp 1)\beta}{2n}\sin\frac{1}{2}\beta\Big/\sin\dfrac{\beta}{2n}$; $\to\sin\beta$

Miscellaneous exercise 8 (page 262)

6 $(0,1)$, $\left(\pm\sqrt{\dfrac{5+\sqrt{5}}{8}},\dfrac{\sqrt{5}-1}{4}\right)$, $\left(\pm\sqrt{\dfrac{5+\sqrt{5}}{8}},\dfrac{1-\sqrt{5}}{4}\right)$

7 $64s^7-112s^5+56s^3-7s=0$,
$0,\pm\sin\frac{1}{7}\pi,\pm\sin\frac{2}{7}\pi,\pm\sin\frac{3}{7}\pi$;
$64x^3-112x^2+56x-7=0$
(a) $\frac{1}{8}\sqrt{7}$ (b) $-\frac{1}{2}$ (c) 8

8 $64s^7-112s^5+56s^3-7s-1=0$; roots $s=1$ and $s=\sin\frac{3}{14}\pi,-\sin\frac{1}{14}\pi,-\sin\frac{5}{14}\pi$ (all repeated).

9 $8c^3+4c^2-4c-1=0$; 0.623 490, −0.222 521, −0.900 969

10 $\frac{1}{16},-\frac{1}{32},-\frac{1}{16},\frac{1}{32}$

11 $\frac{5}{32}\pi a^2$

12 $\frac{35}{128}\pi^2$

13 $\dfrac{z(1-z^8)}{1-z}$; $-2\mathrm{i}\sin\frac{1}{2}\theta\mathrm{e}^{\frac{1}{2}\theta\mathrm{i}}$; $\dfrac{\sin 4\theta\cos\frac{9}{2}\theta}{\sin\frac{1}{2}\theta}$

14 $\dfrac{2\cos\theta+1}{5+4\cos\theta}, \dfrac{2\sin\theta}{5+4\cos\theta}$

15 $\pm(1\pm\sqrt{3})$; $2\sqrt{2}\cos 15°,\ 2\sqrt{2}\cos 105°,$ $2\sqrt{2}\cos 75°,\ 2\sqrt{2}\cos 165°$; $\dfrac{1+\sqrt{3}}{2\sqrt{2}}$

16 $\frac{1}{3}\left(\exp z+\exp(\omega z)+\exp(\omega^2 z)\right)$;
$\frac{1}{3}\sum_{r=0}^{2}\exp\left(\cos(\theta+\frac{2}{3}r\pi)\right)\cos\left(\sin(\theta+\frac{2}{3}r\pi)\right)$

17 1.041 691 47, 1.008 333 609, 1.001 388 891

18 $-\frac{2}{3}$

9 Groups

Exercise 9A (page 268)

1 (a) Binary operation: not closed; not commutative; not associative
(b) Binary operation: closed; not commutative; associative
(c) Binary operation: closed; not commutative; not associative
(d) Binary operation: closed; commutative; not associative
(e) Binary operation: closed; commutative; associative
(f) Binary operation: closed; commutative; associative
(g) Binary operation: closed; not commutative; associative
(h) Binary operation: closed; not commutative; not associative
(i) Binary operation: closed; commutative; associative

Exercise 9B (page 269)

1 (a) No identity
(b) Identity I; no general inverse
(c) Identity $1+0\mathrm{i}$; no general inverse, e.g. 0
(d) No identity
(e) No identity
(f) Identity $\begin{pmatrix}1&1\\0&0\end{pmatrix}$; inverse $\begin{pmatrix}x^{-1}&x^{-1}\\0&0\end{pmatrix}$
(g) Identity 6; inverses of 2, 4, 6 and 8 are 8, 4, 6 and 2.
(h) No identity
(i) Identity 1; inverses of 1, 3, 7 and 9 are 1, 7, 3 and 9.

Exercise 9C (page 274)

1 (a) Not a group; no identity element.
(c) Not a group; 2 has no inverse.
(e) Not a group; not closed.
(g) Not a group; 5 has no inverse.
(i) Not a group; 0 has no inverse.
All the rest are groups.

2 There is no identity element.

3 $x \mapsto \dfrac{x-1}{x}$, $x \mapsto \dfrac{x}{x-1}$

7 $x \mapsto a^{-1}(x-b)$

8 a^3

Exercise 9D (page 279)

1

	0	1	2	3	4
0	0	1	2	3	4
1	1	2	3	4	0
2	2	3	4	0	1
3	3	4	0	1	2
4	4	0	1	2	3

The inverse of 2 is 3.

2

	1	2	3	4	5	6
1	1	2	3	4	5	6
2	2	4	6	1	3	5
3	3	6	2	5	1	4
4	4	1	5	2	6	3
5	5	3	1	6	4	2
6	6	5	4	3	2	1

3

	1	2	3	4	5
1	1	2	3	4	5
2	2	4		2	4
3	3		3		3
4	4	2		4	2
5	5	4	3	2	1

The operation is not closed, as 2×3 is not in the set. If q is not prime, then $q = mn$ for some $m, n \in (\mathbb{Z}_q - \{0\}, \times)$; $mn = q \notin \mathbb{Z}_q - \{0\}$, so the operation is not closed.

4

	I	X	Y	H
I	I	X	Y	H
X	X	I	H	Y
Y	Y	H	I	X
H	H	Y	X	I

5

D_4	I	R	R^2	R^3	H	L	V	M
I	I	R	R^2	R^3	H	L	V	M
R	R	R^2	R^3	I	M	H	L	V
R^2	R^2	R^3	I	R	V	M	H	L
R^3	R^3	I	R	R^2	L	V	M	H
H	H	L	V	M	I	R	R^2	R^3
L	L	V	M	H	R^3	I	R	R^2
V	V	M	H	L	R^2	R^3	I	R
M	M	H	L	V	R	R^2	R^3	I

6 4, 1; (a) 15 (b) 17 (c) 19 (d) 53

Miscellaneous exercise 9 (page 280)

1

	e	a	b
e	e	a	b
a	a	b	e
b	b	e	a

2 In the table $a^2 \circ b$ is written as a^2b, etc. The second half of the table is below the first half.

	e	a	a^2	a^3
e	e	a	a^2	a^3
a	a	a^2	a^3	e
a^2	a^2	a^3	e	a
a^3	a^3	e	a	a^2
b	b	a^3b	a^2b	ab
ab	ab	b	a^3b	a^2b
a^2b	a^2b	ab	b	a^3b
a^3b	a^3b	a^2b	ab	b

	b	ab	a^2b	a^3b
e	b	ab	a^2b	a^3b
a	ab	a^2b	a^3b	b
a^2	a^2b	a^3b	b	ab
a^3	a^3b	b	ab	a^2b
b	a^2	a	e	a^3
ab	a^3	a^2	a	e
a^2b	e	a^3	a^2	a
a^3b	a	e	a^3	a^2

3 $1, 9, 17, 25, 33, 41, 49, 57$; inverses of 9 etc. are $57, 49, 41, 33, 25, 17, 9$; $9, 57, 25, 41$ are generators.

4

	0	1	2	3	4	5	6
0	0	1	2	3	4	5	6
1	1	1	1	1	1	1	1
2	2	1	0	6	5	4	3
3	3	1	6	4	2	0	5
4	4	1	5	2	6	3	0
5	5	1	4	0	3	6	2
6	6	1	3	5	0	2	4

Delete the element 1.

5 $(bb)b \neq b(bb)$, so the operation is not associative.

7 (a) 0 (b) $-a$
(d) There is a problem with closure when $ab = -1$, so $2 * \left(-\frac{1}{2}\right) \notin S$.

10 Subgroups

Exercise 10A (page 288)

1 The first is not cyclic, since $a^2 = b^2 = c^2 = e$; the second is cyclic, with a and c as generators.

2 1, 2, 3 and 4 are generators of $(\mathbb{Z}_5, +)$; 1 and 5 are generators of $(\mathbb{Z}_6, +)$.

3 $e, 1; a, 2; b, 2; c, 2.$ $e, 1; a, 4; b, 2; c, 4.$

4 (a) $I,1; R,4; R^2,2; R^3,4; H,2; L,2; V,2; M,2.$

(b) $\{I\}$, $\{I,R^2\}$, $\{I,H\}$, $\{I,L\}$, $\{I,V\}$, $\{I,M\}$, $\{I,R,R^2,R^3\}$

(c) $\{I,H,R^2,V\}$, $\{I,L,R^2,M\}$

7 $\{1,-1\}$

8 (a) $(\{0\},+), (\{0,2\},+), (\mathbb{Z}_4,+)$

(b) $(\{0\},+), (\mathbb{Z}_5,+)$

10 (a) $\{I,R,S\}$ (b) $\{I,X\}$

(c) $\left\{\begin{pmatrix} a & b \\ 0 & a \end{pmatrix} : a,b \in \mathbb{R}\right\}$ (d) $\{e,b,q,s\}$

(e) $\{e,x,p\}$

11 $\{e\}$, $\{e,b\}$, $\{e,a,b,c\}$, $\{e,p,b,r\}$, $\{e,q,b,s\}$, Q_4

12 $\{e\}$, $\{e,a\}$, $\{e,b\}$, $\{e,c\}$, $\{e,x,p\}$, $\{e,y,q\}$, $\{e,z,r\}$, $\{e,t,s\}$, $\{e,a,b,c\}$, A_4

Exercise 10B (page 290)

1 1, 2, 3, 4, 6, 8, 12 and 24

Exercise 10C (page 293)

1 $\{I,R,S\}$, $\{X,Y,Z\}$;
$\{I\}$, $\{R\}$, $\{S\}$, $\{X\}$, $\{Y\}$, $\{Z\}$;
D_3

2 $\{0,3\}, \{1,4\}, \{2,5\}$

3 (a) $\{e,a,b,c\}, \{x,y,z,t\}, \{p,q,r,s\}$

(b) $\{e,x,p\}$, $\{a,t,r\}$, $\{b,y,s\}$, $\{c,z,q\}$

4 $\{0,\pm3,\pm6,\ldots\}, \{\ldots,-2,1,4,\ldots\}, \{\ldots,-1,2,5,\ldots\}$

Miscellaneous exercise 10 (page 293)

4 (a) $\{1,12\}$ (b) $\{1,3,9\}$

(c) By Lagrange's theorem, the order of a subgroup divides the order of a group. As 5 does not divide 12, there is no subgroup of order 5.

5 (a) $(b \otimes c)(x) = 1 - \dfrac{1}{1-x} = \dfrac{1-x-1}{1-x} = \dfrac{1}{x-1}$

$\mathrm{d}(x) = \dfrac{x-1}{x}$; $\mathrm{e}(x) = \dfrac{x}{x-1}$

(b)

G	i	a	b	c	d	e
i	i	a	b	c	d	e
a	a	i	c	b	e	d
b	b	d	i	e	a	c
c	c	e	a	d	i	b
d	d	b	e	i	c	a
e	e	c	d	a	b	i

(d) Not commutative as $\mathrm{d} \otimes \mathrm{a} = \mathrm{b}$ and $\mathrm{a} \otimes \mathrm{d} = \mathrm{e}$.

(e) Not cyclic since it is not commutative.

(f) $\{\mathrm{i}\}, \{\mathrm{i,a}\}, \{\mathrm{i,b}\}, \{\mathrm{i,e}\}, \{\mathrm{i,c,d}\}$, G

6 (d) $\begin{pmatrix} \pm1 & b \\ 0 & 1 \end{pmatrix}$

(e) $\left\{\begin{pmatrix} 1 & 0 \\ 0 & 1 \end{pmatrix}, \begin{pmatrix} 0 & -1 \\ 1 & 0 \end{pmatrix}, \begin{pmatrix} -1 & 0 \\ 0 & -1 \end{pmatrix}, \begin{pmatrix} 0 & 1 \\ -1 & 0 \end{pmatrix}\right\}$;
this is the subgroup generated by a rotation of $\frac{1}{2}\pi$ anticlockwise about the origin.

7 (b) $\{2\}, \{2,5\}, \{2,4,0\}, G$

11 Isomorphisms of groups

Exercise 11 (page 299)

3 2 is a generator of $(\mathbb{Z}_{13} - \{0\}, \times(\mathrm{mod}\,13))$. Define a function $\mathrm{f}:\mathbb{Z}_{13} \to \mathbb{Z}_{12}$ by the rule $\mathrm{f}(2^n) = n$ and show that it is an isomorphism.

Miscellaneous exercise 11 (page 303)

1 (a) $9, 17, 25, 33, 41, 49, 57, 1$;
The orders are $1,1$; $9,8$; $17,4$; $25,8$; $33,2$; $41,8$; $49,4$; $57,8$.
The possible generators are $9, 25, 41, 57$.
The subgroups are $\{1\}$, $\{1,33\}$, $\{1,17,33,49\}$, G.

(b) G contains a generator, so it is cyclic. Every element of H apart from the identity has order 2, so H is not cyclic. Therefore G and H are not isomorphic.

2 (a) $p=4$, $q=5$

(b) 1 and 8 are self-inverse; the other inverses occur in pairs, 2, 5 and 4, 7;
$\{1\}$, $\{1,8\}$, $\{1,4,7\}$, G.

(c) The order of the element 2 of G is 6, so G is cyclic. $\omega \in H$ has order 6, so H is cyclic. Therefore G and H are isomorphic.

3 $\{1\}$, $\{1,13\}$

(b) The elements are the rotations of $\frac{2}{3}\pi$, $\frac{4}{3}\pi$ and 0 about the centre of the triangle, together with reflections in the lines of symmetry.

(c) G is a commutative group and H is not, so they are not isomorphic.

$\{1,9,11\}$ is a subgroup of G which is isomorphic to the subgroup of rotations of H.

4 $k=11$. The possible values of n are 1, 2, 4 and 8. $\{1,4,7,13\}$, $\{1,2,4,8\}$ and $\{1,4,11,14\}$. The orders of the elements in these groups are $1,2,4,4$, $1,4,2,4$ and $1,2,2,2$. The first two groups both have generators, and are therefore cyclic and isomorphic. The third group does not have a generator, and is therefore not isomorphic to the other two.

5 The orders of the elements $\{1,-1,\mathrm{i},-\mathrm{i}\}$ are 1, 2, 4, 4. The orders of the elements $\{1,7,18,24\}$ are 1, 4, 4, 2. Both groups have generators, and are therefore both cyclic and isomorphic.

6 (b)

	0	2	3	4	5	6
0	0	2	3	4	5	6
2	2	0	6	5	4	3
3	3	6	4	2	0	5
4	4	5	2	6	3	0
5	5	4	0	3	6	2
6	6	3	5	0	2	4

(d) 3 is a generator for G, so G is a cyclic hexagon has order 6 and is also cyclic. Therefore the groups are isomorphic.

7

G_5	1	2	3	4
1	1	2	3	4
2	2	4	1	3
3	3	1	4	2
4	4	3	2	1

G_8	1	3	5	7
1	1	3	5	7
3	3	1	7	5
5	5	7	1	3
7	7	5	3	1

G_{10}	1	3	7	9
1	1	3	7	9
3	3	9	1	7
7	7	1	9	3
9	9	7	3	1

G_{12}	1	5	7	11
1	1	5	7	11
5	5	1	11	7
7	7	11	1	5
11	11	7	5	1

There are only two groups of order 4, up to isomorphism, the cyclic group $\mathbb{Z}_4$ and the group V. The groups G_5 and G_{10} have generators 2 and 3 respectively, so they are cyclic, and isomorphic. The elements of G_8 and G_{12}, apart from the identity elements, all have order 2, so these groups are not cyclic, and are isomorphic to the four-group V.

Revision exercise 4
(page 305)

1 The binary operation is not associative. For example, $g(gh) = gm = i$, $(gg)h = jh = g$.

2 (b) (i) $\mathbf{B}$ (ii) $\mathbf{I}$ (iii) $\mathbf{A}^2\mathbf{B}$

(c) $\mathbf{I}$ has order 1;
$\mathbf{A}^2$, $\mathbf{B}$, $\mathbf{AB}$, $\mathbf{A}^2\mathbf{B}$, $\mathbf{A}^3\mathbf{B}$ have order 2;
$\mathbf{A}$ and $\mathbf{A}^3$ have order 4.

(e) $\{\mathbf{I}, \mathbf{A}^2, \mathbf{AB}, \mathbf{A}^3\mathbf{B}\}$, $\{\mathbf{I}, \mathbf{A}, \mathbf{A}^2, \mathbf{A}^3\}$

(f) $\{\mathbf{I}, \mathbf{A}, \mathbf{A}^2, \mathbf{A}^3\}$ is cyclic; the others are not.

3 (b)

	e	f	g	h
e	e	f	g	h
f	f	e	h	g
g	g	h	e	f
h	h	g	f	e

(c) In G_1, the order of 2 is 4, so G_1 is cyclic. In G_2, the order of each of the non-identity elements is 2, so G_2 is not cyclic. They are therefore not isomorphic.

4 $-9\,653\,287 + 1\,476\,984\,\mathrm{i}$

5 (b) $\frac{1}{192}(44 + 15\pi)$

6 (a) (i) $\dfrac{z}{1+z}$

(ii) The series is a geometric progression, and the modulus of the common ratio is $\frac{1}{4}$, which is less than 1.

7 (a) $\cos k\theta + \mathrm{i}\sin k\theta$, $\cos k\theta - \mathrm{i}\sin k\theta$

(b) $\dfrac{\mathrm{e}^{\theta\mathrm{i}}\cos\theta\left(1-\mathrm{e}^{n\theta\mathrm{i}}\cos^n\theta\right)}{1-\mathrm{e}^{\theta\mathrm{i}}\cos\theta}$

(c) $\dfrac{\cos\theta\left(1-\cos n\theta\cos^n\theta\right)}{\sin\theta}$

8 (a) (i)

×(mod 10)	2	4	6	8
2	4	8	2	6
4	8	6	4	2
6	2	4	6	8
8	6	2	8	4

(ii) $2^{-1} = 8$, $4^{-1} = 4$, $6^{-1} = 6$, $8^{-1} = 2$

(b) P reflects in the y-axis,
Q reflects in the x-axis,
R rotates through π about the origin.

(c) No; G is cyclic (generator 2), but H is not.

9 (a) One possibility is $2.527 + 0.140\,\mathrm{i}$.

(b) $z\mathrm{i}$, $-z\mathrm{i}$, $-z$

10 Yes, it is a subgroup.

$$M_{2n}M_{2p}=\begin{pmatrix}1-2n & 2n\\ -2n & 1+2n\end{pmatrix}\begin{pmatrix}1-2p & 2p\\ -2p & 1+2p\end{pmatrix}$$
$$=\begin{pmatrix}1-2(n+p) & 2(n+p)\\ -2(n+p) & 1+2(n+p)\end{pmatrix}$$
$$=M_{2n+2p}\in H$$

$M_0 \in H$

$$M_{2n}^{-1}=\begin{pmatrix}1-2n & 2n\\ -2n & 1+2n\end{pmatrix}^{-1}=\begin{pmatrix}1+2n & -2n\\ 2n & 1-2n\end{pmatrix}$$
$$=\begin{pmatrix}1-(-2n) & (-2n)\\ -(-2n) & 1+(-2n)\end{pmatrix}=M_{-2n}\in H$$

Result follows from the theorem in Section 10.4.

11 (c) $\{e, a, a^2, a^3\}$, $\{e, a^2, ab, a^3b\}$,
$\{e, a^2, b, a^2b\}$

12 $c=4$
(a) Not consistent
(b) The planes form a triangular prism.

13 (b) $3\mathbf{i}+4\mathbf{j}-5\mathbf{k}$ (c) 6

Mock examinations

Mock examination 1 for P6 (page 308)

1 (i) $\begin{pmatrix}2\\1\\4\end{pmatrix}$

(ii) $\dfrac{x-1}{2}=\dfrac{y-2}{1}=\dfrac{z-2}{4}$

2 $z=\exp\left(\frac{1}{6}\pi i\right), \exp\left(\frac{5}{6}\pi i\right), \exp\left(-\frac{1}{2}\pi i\right)$;
$\frac{1}{12}\pi, \frac{5}{12}\pi, \frac{3}{4}\pi, -\frac{1}{4}\pi, -\frac{7}{12}\pi, -\frac{11}{12}\pi$

3 (i) 2, 3, 4, 6
(ii) (a) {0, 6}, {0, 4, 8}, {0, 3, 6, 9}, {0, 2, 4, 6, 8, 10}
(b) 1, 5, 7, 11

4 (ii) $\dfrac{1-e^{n\theta i}}{1-e^{\theta i}}$

6 (i) $\begin{pmatrix}\cos\theta & -\sin\theta\\ \sin\theta & \cos\theta\end{pmatrix}$, $\begin{pmatrix}2 & 0\\ 0 & 1\end{pmatrix}$

(ii) $\begin{pmatrix}1+\cos^2\theta & \sin\theta\cos\theta\\ \sin\theta\cos\theta & 1+\sin^2\theta\end{pmatrix}$

(iv) Stretch with scale factor 2 parallel to the line $y=x\tan\theta$.

7 (i) $a\lambda+\mu+t=2$, $2\lambda+\mu-t=a-2$, $\lambda+2t=1$

(iii) $\begin{pmatrix}2\\2\\3\end{pmatrix}$

(iv) l lies in p.

Mock examination 2 for P6 (page 310)

2 $\cos^5\theta-10\cos^3\theta\sin^2\theta+5\cos\theta\sin^4\theta$,
$5\cos^4\theta\sin\theta-10\cos^2\theta\sin^3\theta+\sin^5\theta$

3 12; three planes meeting in a common line

4 $2\cos n\theta$, $2i\sin n\theta$

5

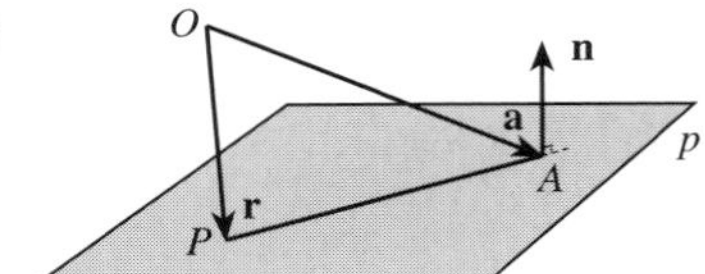

$\overrightarrow{AP}=\mathbf{r}-\mathbf{a}$ lies in p and is thus perpendicular to $\mathbf{n}$.

6 $\begin{pmatrix}1\\5\\2\end{pmatrix}$; $\lambda=2$, $t=1$, $\mu=-1$; $\begin{pmatrix}3\\-3\\1\end{pmatrix}$, $\begin{pmatrix}4\\2\\3\end{pmatrix}$, $\sqrt{30}$

7 (i) $\begin{pmatrix}-1 & 0\\ 0 & 1\end{pmatrix}$, $\begin{pmatrix}\frac{1}{2} & -\frac{1}{2}\sqrt{3}\\ -\frac{1}{2}\sqrt{3} & -\frac{1}{2}\end{pmatrix}$,
$\begin{pmatrix}-\frac{1}{2} & \frac{1}{2}\sqrt{3}\\ -\frac{1}{2}\sqrt{3} & -\frac{1}{2}\end{pmatrix}$

(ii) **R**: rotation through 120° anticlockwise about O,
X: reflection in the line $y=x\tan 30^\circ$

(iii)

	I	**R**	**S**	**X**	**Y**	**Z**
I	**I**	**R**	**S**	**X**	**Y**	**Z**
R	**R**	**S**	**I**	**Z**	**X**	**Y**
S	**S**	**I**	**R**	**Y**	**Z**	**X**
X	**X**	**Y**	**Z**	**I**	**R**	**S**
Y	**Y**	**Z**	**X**	**S**	**I**	**R**
Z	**Z**	**X**	**Y**	**R**	**S**	**I**

(iv) Not isomorphic; for example, H is commutative and G isn't.

Index

The page numbers refer to the first mention of each term, or the shaded box if there is one.